Business and Society

Stakeholders, Ethics, Public Policy

Business and Society

Stakeholders, Ethics, Public Policy   *Twelfth Edition*

Anne T. Lawrence
San Jose State University

James Weber
Duquesne University

Boston   Burr Ridge, IL   Dubuque, IA   Madison, WI   New York   San Francisco   St. Louis
Bangkok   Bogotá   Caracas   Kuala Lumpur   Lisbon   London   Madrid   Mexico City
Milan   Montreal   New Delhi   Santiago   Seoul   Singapore   Sydney   Taipei   Toronto

McGraw-Hill
Irwin

BUSINESS AND SOCIETY: STAKEHOLDERS, ETHICS, PUBLIC POLICY

Published by McGraw-Hill/Irwin, a business unit of The McGraw-Hill Companies, Inc., 1221 Avenue of the Americas, New York, NY, 10020. Copyright © 2008 by The McGraw-Hill Companies, Inc. All rights reserved. No part of this publication may be reproduced or distributed in any form or by any means, or stored in a database or retrieval system, without the prior written consent of The McGraw-Hill Companies, Inc., including, but not limited to, in any network or other electronic storage or transmission, or broadcast for distance learning.

Some ancillaries, including electronic and print components, may not be available to customers outside the United States.

This book is printed on acid-free paper.

2 3 4 5 6 7 8 9 0 WCK/WCK 0 9 8 7

ISBN 978-0-07-353017-8

MHID 0-07-353017-4

Editorial director: *John E. Biernat*
Senior sponsoring editor: *Kelly H. Lowery*
Editorial assistant: *Megan Richter*
Associate marketing manager: *Kelly Odom*
Project manager: *Harvey Yep*
Manager, New book production: *Heather D. Burbridge*
Designer: *Cara David*
Senior media project manager: *Susan Lombardi*
Cover design: *George Kokkonas*
Typeface: *10/12 Times New Roman*
Compositor: *Techbooks*
Printer: *Quebecor World Versailles Inc.*

Library of Congress Cataloging-in-Publication Data

Lawrence, Anne T.
   Business and society: stakeholders, ethics, public policy / Anne T. Lawrence,
James Weber. – 12th ed.
     p. cm.
   Includes index.
   ISBN-13: 978-0-07-353017-8 (alk paper)
   ISBN-10: 0-07-353017-4 (alk. paper)
   1. Social responsibility of business. I. Weber, James, S.J. II. Title.
HD60.F72 2008
658.4′08–dc22

2006102617

www.mhhe.com

About the Authors

Anne T. Lawrence   *San Jose State University*

Anne T. Lawrence is a professor of organization and management at San Jose State University. She holds a Ph.D. from the University of California, Berkeley, and completed two years of postdoctoral work at Stanford University. Her articles, cases, and reviews have appeared in many journals, including the *Academy of Management Review, Administrative Science Quarterly, Journal of Management Education, Case Research Journal, Business and Society Review, Research in Corporate Social Performance and Policy,* and *Journal of Corporate Citizenship.* Her cases in business and society have been reprinted in many textbooks and anthologies. She has served as associate editor of the Case Research Journal and as president of both the North American Case Research Association (NACRA) and of the Western Casewriters Association. She was the recipient of the Outstanding Case of the Year award from NACRA and the Emerson Center Award for Outstanding Case in Business Ethics. At San Jose State University, she was named Outstanding Professor of the Year in 2005.

James Weber   *Duquesne University*

James Weber is a professor of management and business ethics and the director of the Beard Center for Leadership in Ethics at Duquesne University, where he also coordinates the Masters of Science in Leadership and Business Ethics program. He has a Ph.D. from the University of Pittsburgh and has taught at the University of San Francisco, University of Pittsburgh, and Marquette University. His areas of interest and research include managerial and organizational values, cognitive moral reasoning, business ethics, ethics training and education, and corporate social audit and performance. He was recognized by the Social Issues in Management division of the Academy of Management with the Best Paper Award in 1989 and 1994. He has served as division and program chair of the Social Issues in Management division of the Academy of Management. He has also served as president and program chair of the International Association of Business and Society (IABS) and is a member of the Society for Business Ethics.

Brief Contents

Contents

PART THREE
BUSINESS AND THE ETHICAL ENVIRONMENT   87

Chapter 5
Ethics and Ethical Reasoning   88

Chapter 6
Organizational Ethics and the Law   112

PART FOUR
BUSINESS AND GOVERNMENT IN A GLOBAL SOCIETY   137

Chapter 7
The Challenges of Globalization   138

Preface

In a world economy that is becoming increasingly integrated and interdependent, the relationship between business and society is becoming ever more complex. The globalization of business, the emergence of civil society organizations in many nations, and new government regulations and international agreements have significantly altered the job of managers and the nature of strategic decision-making within the firm.

At no time has business faced greater public scrutiny or more urgent demands to act in an ethical and socially responsible manner than the present. Consider the following:

- The corporate scandals of the 2000s—from accounting fraud at Enron and WorldCom, to lapses of governance at Hewlett-Packard, to stock options scams in hundreds of firms across multiple industries—continue to focus a spotlight on issues of business responsibility and ethics. Around the world, people and governments have demanded that executives do a better job of serving shareholders and the public. New laws, like the Sarbanes-Oxley Act in the United States, have raised the standards for corporate governance, but have also raised questions about the proper scope of government oversight. Management educators are placing renewed emphasis on issues of business leadership and accountability.

- A host of new technologies have become part of the everyday lives of billions of the world's people. Advances in the basic sciences are stimulating extraordinary changes in agriculture, telecommunications, and pharmaceuticals. Businesses can now grow medicine in plants, embed nanochips in tennis rackets, and communicate with customers overseas over the Internet and wireless networks. These innovations hold great promise. But they also raise serious ethical issues, such as those associated with genetically modified foods, stem-cell research, or use of the Internet for pornographic purposes or to censor free expression. Businesses must learn to harness new technologies, while avoiding public controversy and remaining sensitive to the concerns of their many stakeholders.

- Businesses in the United States and other nations are transforming the employment relationship, abandoning practices that once provided job security and guaranteed pensions in favor of highly flexible but less secure forms of employment. Many jobs, including those in the service sector, are being outsourced to the emerging economies of China, India, and other nations. As jobs shift abroad, transnational corporations are challenged to address their obligations to workers in far-flung locations with very different cultures—and to respond to initiatives, like the United Nation's Global Compact—that call for voluntary commitment to labor and human rights.

- Ecological and environmental problems have forced businesses and governments to take action. An emerging consensus about the risks of global warming, for example, is leading many companies to adopt new practices, whether or not their governments have endorsed the Kyoto Protocol. Many businesses have cut air pollution, curbed solid waste, and designed products to be more energy-efficient. A better understanding of how human activities affect natural resources is producing a consensus that environmental protection must be achieved with economic growth if development is to be sustainable.

- Many regions of the world are developing at an extraordinary rate. Yet, the prosperity that accompanies economic growth is not shared equally. Personal income, health care, and educational opportunity are unevenly distributed among and within the world's nations. The tragic pandemic of AIDS in sub-Saharan Africa and the threat of an avian flu epidemic have compelled drug makers to rethink their pricing policies and raised troubling questions about the commitment of world trade organizations to patent protection. Many businesses must consider the delicate balance between their intellectual property rights and the urgent demands of public health, particularly in the developing world.

- In many nations, legislators have questioned business's influence on politics. Business has a legitimate role to play in the public policy process, but it has on occasion shaded over into undue influence and even corruption. In the United States, recent reforms of campaign finance and lobbying laws have changed the rules of the game governing how corporations and individuals can contribute to and influence political parties and public officials. Businesses the world over are challenged to determine their legitimate scope of influence and how to voice their interests most effectively in the public policy process.

This new edition of *Business and Society* addresses this complex agenda of issues and their impact on business and its stakeholders. It is designed to be the required textbook in an undergraduate or graduate course in Business and Society; Business, Government and Society; Social Issues in Management; or the Environment of Business. It may also be used, in whole or in part, in courses in Business Ethics and Public Affairs Management. This text is also appropriate for an undergraduate sociology course that focuses on the role of business in society or on contemporary issues in business.

The core argument of this book is that corporations serve a broad public purpose: to create value for society. All companies must make a profit for their owners. Indeed, if they did not, they would not long survive. However, corporations create many other kinds of value as well. They are responsible for professional development for their employees, innovative new products for their customers, and generosity to their communities. They must partner with a wide range of individuals and groups in society to advance collaborative goals. In this book's view, corporations have multiple obligations, and all stakeholders' interests must be taken into account.

A Tradition of Excellence

Since the 1960s, when Professors Keith Davis and Robert Blomstrom wrote the first edition of this book, *Business and Society* has maintained a position of leadership by discussing central issues of corporate social performance in a form that students and faculty have found engaging and stimulating. The leadership of the two founding authors, and later of Professor William C. Frederick and James E. Post, helped *Business and Society* to achieve a consistently high standard of quality and market acceptance. Thanks to these authors' remarkable eye for the emerging issues that shape the organizational, social, and public policy environments in which students will soon live and work, the book has added value to the business education of many thousands of students.

This book has continued through several successive author teams to be the market-leader in its field. The current authors bring a broad background of business and society research, teaching, consulting, and case development to the ongoing evolution of *Business and Society*. The twelfth edition of *Business and Society* builds on its legacy of market leadership by reexamining such central issues as the role of business in society, the nature of corporate responsibility, business ethics practices, and the complex roles of government and business in a global community.

For Instructors

For instructors, this textbook offers a complete set of supplements. An extensive instructor's resource manual—fully revised for this edition—includes lecture outlines, discussion case questions and answers, tips from experienced instructors, and extensive case teaching notes. A computerized test bank and power point slides for every chapter are also provided to adopters. A video supplement, compiled especially for the 12th edition, is comprised of recent segments from the Public Broadcasting Service's news program, The News Hour with Jim Lehrer. These may be used to supplement class lectures and discussions.

Business and Society is designed to be easily modularized. An instructor who wishes to focus on a particular portion of the material may select individual chapters or cases to be packaged in a Primis custom product. Sections of this book can also be packaged with other materials from the extensive Primis database, including articles and cases from the Harvard Business School and *BusinessWeek,* to provide exactly the course pack the instructor needs.

Adopting instructors also have access to PageOut, McGraw-Hill's own Web site creation tool. PageOut enables instructors to easily build a full-featured, professional quality course Web site. PageOut can be used to post a syllabus online, assign McGraw-Hill Online Learning Center or eBook content, add links to off-site resources, and maintain student results in the online grade book. Instructors may also use PageOut to send class announcements, share a course site with colleagues, or upload original files.

For instructors who teach over the Internet and for those who prefer an electronic format, this text may be delivered online, using McGraw-Hill's eBook technology. Ebooks can also be customized with the addition of any of the materials in Primis's extensive collection.

For Students

This textbook has long been popular with students because of its lively writing, up-to-date examples, and clear explanations of theory. *Business and Society* has benefited greatly from feedback over the years from thousands of students who have used the material in the authors' own classrooms. Its strengths are in many ways a testimony to the students who have used earlier generations of this text.

This book is designed to be student-friendly. Each chapter opens with a list of key learning objectives to help focus student reading and study. Numerous figures, exhibits, and blocks of colored text illustrate and elaborate the main points. A glossary at the end of the book provides definitions for bold-faced and other important terms. Internet references and a full section-by-section bibliography guide students who wish to do further research on topics of their choice, and subject and name indices help students locate items in the book.

This latest edition of *Business and Society* comes with several supplements designed specifically for students. McGraw-Hill's Online Learning Center (OLC) is a Web site that follows the text chapter-by-chapter. As students read the book, they can go online to take self-graded quizzes, review material, or review key terms using flashcards. Professors and students can access the OLC directly through the textbook Web site, through PageOut, or within a course management system such as WebCT, Blackboard, TopClass, or eCollege.

Students may also subscribe to *BusinessWeek* at a substantially reduced price in addition to the price of the text, if their instructors choose this option. Students will receive a passcode card shrink-wrapped with their new text. The card directs students to a Web site where they enter the code and then gain access to *BusinessWeek*'s registration page.

New for This Edition

Over the years, the issues addressed by *Business and Society* have changed as the environment of business itself has been transformed. This twelfth edition is no exception, as readers will discover. Some issues have become less compelling and others have taken their place on the business agenda, while others endure through the years.

The 12th edition has been thoroughly revised and updated to reflect the latest theoretical work in the field and statistical data, as well as recent events. Among the new additions to this edition are:

- Theoretical advances in stakeholder theory, corporate citizenship, public affairs management, corporate governance, social performance auditing, social investing, reputation management, business partnerships, and corporate philanthropy.
- New discussion cases on such current topics as business's response to Hurricane Katrina, the shareholder revolt at Disney, Microsoft's antitrust troubles in Europe and Asia, decency standards in online games, the environmental risks of gold mining, Starbucks' political initiatives, the ethics of music downloads, and the sex discrimination lawsuit against Wal-Mart.
- New full-length cases on Merck and Vioxx, environmental initiatives in the hotel industry, and shareholder activism at Johnson & Johnson.

Finally, this is a book with a vision. It is not simply a compendium of information and ideas. This edition of *Business and Society* articulates the view that in a global community, where traditional buffers no longer protect business from external change, managers can create strategies that integrate stakeholder interests, respect personal values, support community development, and are implemented fairly. Most important, businesses can achieve these goals while also being economically successful. Indeed, this may be the *only* way to achieve economic success over the long term.

Anne T. Lawrence

James Weber

Acknowledgments

We are grateful for the assistance of many colleagues at universities in the United States and abroad who over the years have helped shape this book with their excellent suggestions and ideas. We also note the feedback from students in our classes and at other colleges and universities that has helped make this book as user-friendly as possible.

We especially wish to acknowledge the assistance of several esteemed colleagues who provided detailed reviews for this edition. These reviewers were Barbara W. Altman of the University of North Texas, Karen Moustafa of Indiana University-Purdue University Fort Wayne, Deborah Vidaver-Cohen of Florida International University, Lynda Brown of the University of Montana, Kathleen Rehbein of Marquette University, Kathleen A. Getz of American University, Jennifer J. Griffin of George Washington University, Frank Julian of Murray State University, Gordon Rands of Western Illinois University, and Diana Sharpe of Monmouth University. Their thoughtful comments were invaluable to us as we prepared the current edition. We also extend our deep appreciation to Barbara W. Altman of the University of North Texas, who in addition to serving as a reviewer prepared the power point slides to accompany this edition.

In addition, we are grateful to the many colleagues who over the years have generously shared with us their insights into the theory and pedagogy of business and society. In particular, we would like to thank Sandra Waddock of Boston College, Joerg Andriof of Warwick University, Craig Fleisher of the University of New Brunswick-St. John, Margaret J. Naumes of the University of New Hampshire, Michael Johnson-Cramer and Jamie Hendry of Bucknell University, John Mahon and Stephanie Welcomer of the University of Maine, Ann Svendsen of Simon Fraser University, Robert Boutilier of Robert Boutilier & Associates, Kathryn S. Rogers of Pitzer College, Anne Forrestal of the University of Oregon, Kelly Strong of Iowa State University, Daniel Gilbert of Gettysburg College, Gina Vega of Merrimack College, Craig Dunn and Brian Burton of Western Washington University, Lori V. Ryan of San Diego State University, Bryan W. Husted of ITESM/Instituto de Empresa, Sharon Livesey of Fordham University, Barry Mitnick of the University of Pittsburgh, Virginia Gerde and David Wasieleski of Duquesne University, Robbin Derry of Northwestern University, Linda Ginzel of the University of Chicago, Jerry Calton of the University of Hawaii-Hilo, H. Richard Eisenbeis of the University of Southern Colorado, Anthony J. Daboub of the University of Texas at Brownsville, Tara Ceranic of the University of Washington, Bruce Paton of San Francisco State University, Asbjorn Osland of San Jose State University, Linda Klebe Trevino of Pennsylvania State University, Mary Meisenhelter of York College of Pennsylvania, Steven Payne of Georgia College and State University, Amy Hillman and Gerald Keim of Arizona State University, and Jeanne Logsdon of the University of New Mexico. These scholars' dedication to the creative teaching of business and society has been a continuing inspiration to us.

Thanks are also due to Murray Silverman and Tom E. Thomas of San Francisco State University; Brian Burton, Steven Globerman, and James McCafferty of Western Washington University; and Jeanne McNett of Assumption College, who contributed cases to this edition.

A number of research assistants and former students have made contributions throughout this project for which we are appreciative. Among the special contributors to this project were Patricia Morrison of Grossmont College and Micheal MacDonncha of Duquesne University, who provided research assistance. Dana Fortun, formerly of Duquesne University, assisted in preparing the instructor's resource manual and ancillary materials.

We wish to express our continuing appreciation to William C. Frederick, who invited us into this project many years ago and who has continued to provide warm support and sage advice as the book has evolved through numerous editions.

We continue to be grateful to the excellent editorial and production team at McGraw-Hill. We offer special thanks to Kelly H. Lowery, our sponsoring editor, for her skillful leadership of this project. Kelly Odom headed the excellent marketing team. We also wish to recognize the able assistance of Megan Richter, editorial assistant, and Harvey Yep, project manager, whose ability to keep us on track and on time has been critical; Susan Lombardi, supplements coordinator; Peter deLissovoy, copy editor; Cara David, designer; and George Kokkonas, who designed the book cover. Each of these people has provided professional contributions that we deeply value and appreciate.

Finally, we wish to acknowledge the retirement from the author team of James E. Post. Jim was an author of this book from the sixth edition (1988) through the eleventh edition (2005). Over nearly two decades, he made countless contributions to this project, bringing to the author team his wealth of insights into public policy, stakeholder theory, public affairs management, and community relations. His intellectual influence continues to be felt throughout the book. To Jim, we extend our deep appreciation and best wishes as he embarks on new professional challenges.

Anne T. Lawrence

James Weber

Introduction and Overview

The book is divided into parts that are organized around major themes. In this introduction, we explain the overall design of the book. Each chapter contains a number of pedagogical features designed to enhance student learning, including key learning objectives, updated examples, an end-of-chapter summary of key points, a list of key terms, Internet resources, and new or updated discussion cases with questions. Additional materials, among them teaching tips, a complete test bank, student self-study questions, and PowerPoint slides, are included in the Instructor's Resource Manual.

Part One. The Corporation in Society

Chapter 1 introduces the core argument that business and society are part of an interactive system. It provides a model for analyzing the relationships between an organization and its market and nonmarket stakeholders. The chapter also discusses competing theories of the purpose of the modern firm and introduces some of the dynamic forces that are shaping the business and society relationship.

Chapter 2 describes a strategic approach to managing public issues that arise when corporate performance does not match stakeholder expectations. Such an approach requires corporations to work through a range of boundary-spanning departments to engage with stakeholders. An effective public affairs strategy enables an organization to scan its multiple environments, gather and use competitive intelligence, and manage the issue management process to benefit itself and society.

Part Two. Business and the Social Environment

Chapter 3 presents the doctrine of corporate social responsibility and describes its historical evolution. It examines the arguments for and against the proposition that business has an obligation to all of its multiple stakeholders, not only to its shareholders. Striking a balance among its economic, legal, and social responsibilities is a major challenge for today's business firm.

Chapter 4 introduces the concept of global corporate citizenship and presents a multistage model to identify where a firm stands in its corporate citizenship development. The chapter also introduces the practice of social performance auditing and reporting and recognizes leading-edge corporate citizens.

Part Three. Business and the Ethical Environment

Chapter 5 defines ethics. It explains why businesses should act ethically, and shows why sometimes they do not. The chapter also discusses the influence of managerial values and other core elements of ethical character, as well as the various stages of moral reasoning. Finally, the chapter presents an ethical decision-making framework that introduces generally accepted ethics theories.

Chapter 6 focuses on proactive business efforts to promote an ethical environment in the workplace. It provides a method to classify an organization's ethical climate and identifies ethical issues in a variety of business functions, including accounting, finance, marketing, and information technology. The chapter explains the multiple safeguards that make up a comprehensive ethics program. The chapter also contrasts ethics to law and assesses the consequences of illegal behavior.

Part Four. Business and Government in a Global Society

Chapter 7 describes the process of globalization and explores both the benefits and costs of the growing integration of the world economy. It defines the major types of political and economic systems in which companies operate across the world. The chapter also describes emerging codes of conduct and discusses how businesses can work collaboratively with governments and the civil sector to address global social issues.

Chapter 8 defines public policy and introduces the elements of the public policy process. It also describes the major types of government regulation of business and explores the costs and benefits of regulatory oversight in the United States and other nations.

Chapter 9 explores the participation by business and various stakeholder groups in the political process. The chapter presents numerous political action strategies and tactics used by business and by other groups, and examines the issue of campaign finance reform in the United States and in other countries.

Chapter 10 revisits the century-old issue of antitrust in the context of rapid technological change and globalization. It explores the causes of recent corporate mergers and their impacts on competition. As the world economy has become increasingly integrated, policy makers have faced the challenges of harmonizing competition policies across national borders.

Part Five. The Corporation and the Natural Environment

Chapters 11 and 12 address the ecological and natural resource issues that will reshape entire industries as the next century unfolds. Rapid population growth and the explosive development of many of the world's economies have placed new pressures on scarce resources. Water, air, and land pollution have created new constraints for business around the globe. These chapters explore both the challenges and the opportunities presented by the need to move to a more sustainable business model.

Part Six. Business and Technological Change

Business and society will be profoundly affected by a new age of scientific and technological change. Chapter 13 examines technology as a dominant influence in our daily lives and the emergence of technology-oriented businesses in the global economy. It introduces new Internet opportunities—blogs, vlogs, spam and phishing, as well as the challenges they create. As technology explodes as a global economic and social force, this chapter investigates imbalances in people's access to technology, known as the *digital divide*.

The complex relationships between science, technology, business, and society are creating numerous ethical and political issues. Chapter 14 focuses on how managers can address these complicated decisions. The sound management of technological challenges involves protecting privacy and intellectual property and managing scientific breakthroughs responsibly by understanding the impacts and risks technology exerts on business and its stakeholders.

Part Seven. Building Relationships with Stakeholders

In the final part of the book, the concepts developed in earlier chapters are applied to a detailed examination of the relationship between the corporation and each of its market and nonmarket stakeholders.

Chapter 15 explores the rights of stockholders, managers, boards of directors, and other participants in contemporary corporate governance. It takes up the controversial debate over executive compensation and considers the causes of and possible remedies for recent corporate scandals. The chapter also shows how the government protects against stock market abuses, such as fraudulent accounting and insider trading.

Chapter 16 focuses on consumer protection, including such current topics as consumer privacy in the information age and product liability reform. It shows how socially responsible corporations can proactively respond to consumer needs.

The role of the corporation in the community is examined in Chapter 17. This chapter considers new models of corporate community relations and strategic philanthropy.

Chapter 18 focuses on the evolving employee-employer relationship. Governmental influences on this relationship from countries around the world are described in this chapter. Ethical challenges concerning employees' and employers' rights and duties in the workplace are discussed.

Chapter 19 addresses the special issue of diversity in the workplace. What does diversity mean in the modern workplace? What are its benefits, and how is it best achieved? This chapter also describes programs companies have developed to support working parents and eliminate sex discrimination.

Finally, Chapter 20 examines business's relationship with the media. It explains the responsibilities of the public relations manager and to manage a crisis situation effectively. The chapter also explores the ethical implications of advertising by business. The media, as an industry, has its own set of ethical and social responsibilities to the public. The media must be sensitive to maintaining decency, reflecting diversity and equality, and portraying organizations and issues in a fair and balanced way.

Cases

The 12th edition of this book features nine full-length case studies, three of which are new for this edition. The cases are written to provide rich discussion material and present a variety of opportunities for instructors to integrate topics raised in individual chapters.

PART ONE

The Corporation in Society

CHAPTER ONE

The Corporation and Its Stakeholders

Business corporations have complex relationships with many individuals and organizations in society. The term stakeholder refers to all those that affect, or are affected by, the actions of the firm. How corporations manage their interactions with stakeholders powerfully contributes to business success or failure. Building positive and mutually beneficial relationships across organizational boundaries is a growing part of management's role. In a world of fast-paced globalization, shifting public expectations and government policies, growing ecological concerns, and new technologies, managers face the difficult challenge of achieving economic results while simultaneously creating value for all of their diverse stakeholders.

This chapter focuses on these key learning objectives:

- Understanding the relationship between business and society, and the ways in which they are part of an interactive system.
- Considering the purpose of the modern corporation.
- Knowing what is a stakeholder, and who are a corporation's market and nonmarket stakeholders.
- Conducting a stakeholder analysis, and understanding how it can be used to build collaborative relationships.
- Analyzing the forces of change that continually reshape the business and society relationship.

Wal-Mart has been called "a template for 21st century capitalism." In each period of history, a single company seems to best capture the management systems, technology, and social relationships of its era. In 1990, this company was U.S. Steel. In 1950, it was General Motors. Now, in the 2000s, it is Wal-Mart.[1]

In 2006, Wal-Mart was the largest private employer in the world, with 1.3 million employees in the United States alone. The company operated 3,800 facilities and had annual sales of $312 billion. The retailer was enormously popular with customers, drawing them in with its great variety of products under one roof and "always low prices" policy; 175 million customers worldwide shopped there every week. Economists estimated that Wal-Mart had directly through its own actions and indirectly through its impact on its supply chain saved American shoppers $263 billion in 2004, about $895 for every person in the country.[2] Shareholders who invested early were richly rewarded; the share price rose from 5 cents (split adjusted) when the company went public in 1970 to a high of $63 in 2002. Wal-Mart was a major customer for 61,000 suppliers worldwide, ranging from huge multinationals to tiny one-person operations.

Yet, Wal-Mart had become a lightning rod for criticism from many quarters, charged with hurting local communities, discriminating against women, and driving down wages and working conditions. Consider that:

- In 2004, the City Council in Inglewood, California, a predominantly African-American and Hispanic suburb of Los Angeles, voted down a proposed Wal-Mart mega-store on a 60-acre parcel near the Hollywood racetrack. The city expressed concern that the development would adversely impact small businesses, traffic, public safety, and wages. (This case is further discussed in Chapter 2.) This was only one of many communities that mobilized to block Wal-Mart's entry in the mid-2000s.

- The same year, a federal judge ruled that a lawsuit charging Wal-Mart Stores with discrimination against women could go forward as a class action. The case charged that women at Wal-Mart were paid less than men in comparable positions, received fewer promotions into management, and waited longer to move up than men did. (This case is further discussed in Chapter 19.) If the decision ultimately went against Wal-Mart, the cost to the company could be in the hundreds of millions of dollars.

- In 2005, a critical documentary called "Wal-Mart: The High Cost of Low Prices," was released, with a trailer showing the company's yellow smiley-face character as a rapacious plunderer. Thousands of people saw the movie at community screenings and discussed it on the website, *www.walmartmovie.com*. Among the embarrassing allegations made by the filmmakers was that many workers had to apply for public assistance because their wages, which averaged less than $10 an hour, were so low.

Lee Scott, the company's CEO, commented in an interview with *BusinessWeek* in late 2005, "We always believed that if we sat here in Bentonville [the company's headquarters] and took care of our customers and took care of associates that the world itself would leave us alone." That, he acknowledged, was no longer the case. "We have to continue to evolve in how we operate and how we interface with society," he

---

[1] Nelson Lichtenstein, "Wal-Mart: A Template for Twenty-First Century Capitalism," pp. 3–30 in *Wal-Mart: The Face of Twenty-First Century Capitalism*, ed. Nelson Lichtenstein (New York: The New Press, 2006).

[2] Global Insight, "The Economic Impact of Wal-Mart," November 1, 2005, available online at *www.globalinsight.com/walmart*.

said.[3] In an effort to shore up its reputation, the company increased its health insurance for workers, offered grants to small businesses, and donated to wildlife habitat restoration. It also convened a rapid-response public relations team in an office in its Arkansas headquarters, dubbed the "war room" by *The New York Times*, to coordinate its response to critics.[4]

Wal-Mart's experience illustrates, on a particularly large scale, the challenges of managing successfully in a complex global network of stakeholders. The company's actions affected not only itself, but also many other people, groups, and organizations in society. Customers, suppliers, employees, stockholders, creditors, business partners, and local communities all had a stake in Wal-Mart's decisions. Wal-Mart in the mid-2000s was learning, sometimes painfully, just how difficult it could be simultaneously to satisfy multiple stakeholders with diverse and, in some respects, contradictory interests.

Every modern company, whether small or large, is part of a vast global business system. Whether a firm has 50 employees or 50,000—or, like Wal-Mart, more than a million—its links to customers, suppliers, employees, and communities are certain to be numerous, diverse, and vital to its success. This is why the relationship between business and society is important to understand as both a citizen and a manager.

Business and Society

Business today is one of the dominant institutions in society, all around the world. The term *business* refers here to any organization that is engaged in making a product or providing a service for a profit. Consider that in the United States today there are over 5 million businesses, based on the number that file tax returns with the government, and in the world as a whole, there are uncounted millions more. Of course, these businesses vary greatly in size and impact. They range from a woman who helps support her family by selling handmade tortillas by the side of the road in Mexico City for a few pesos, to ExxonMobil, a huge corporation that employs 86,000 workers and earns annual revenues approaching $300 billion in 200 nations worldwide.

Society, in its broadest sense, refers to human beings and to the social structures they collectively create. In a more specific sense, the term is used to refer to segments of humankind, such as members of a particular community, nation, or interest group. As a set of organizations created by humans, business is clearly a part of society. At the same time, it is also a distinct entity, separated from the rest of society by clear boundaries. Business is engaged in ongoing exchanges with its external environment across these dividing lines. For example, businesses recruit workers, buy supplies, and borrow money; they also sell products, donate time, and pay taxes. This book is broadly concerned with the relationship between business and society. A simple diagram of the relationship between the two appears in Figure 1.1.

As the example that opened this chapter illustrates, business and society are highly interdependent. Business activities impact others in society, and actions by various social actors and governments continuously affect business. To manage these interdependencies, managers need an understanding of their company's key relationships, and

---

[3] "Can Wal-Mart Fit into a White Hat?" *BusinessWeek,* October 3, 2005, p. 94; and extended interview with Lee Scott available online at *www.businessweek.com.*

[4] "Wal-Mart Offers Aid to Rivals," *The New York Times,* April 5, 2006, p. C1; "A New Weapon for Wal-Mart: A War Room," *The New York Times,* November 1, 2005, pp. A1, C4.

FIGURE 1.1
Business and Society: An Interactive System

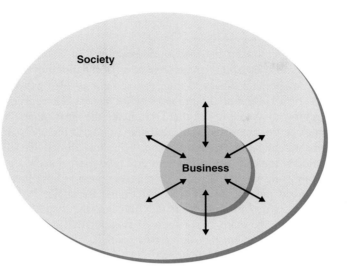

how the social and economic system of which they are a part affects, and is affected by, their decisions.

A Systems Perspective

General systems theory, first introduced in the 1940s, argues that all organisms are open to, and interact with, their external environments. Although most organisms have clear boundaries, they cannot be understood in isolation, but only in relationship to their surroundings. This simple but powerful idea can be applied to many disciplines. For example, in botany, the growth of a plant cannot be explained without reference to soil, light, oxygen, moisture and other characteristics of its environment. As applied to management theory, the systems concept implies that business firms (social organisms) are embedded in a broader social structure (external environment) with which they constantly interact. Corporations have ongoing boundary exchanges with customers, governments, competitors, the media, communities, and many other individuals and groups. Just as good soil, water, and light help a plant grow, positive interactions with society benefit a business firm.

Like biological organisms, moreover, businesses must adapt to changes in the environment. Plants growing in low-moisture environments must develop survival strategies, like the cactus that evolves to store water in its leaves. Similarly, a long-distance telephone company in a newly deregulated market must learn to compete by changing the products and services it offers. The key to business survival is often this ability to adapt effectively to changing conditions. In business, systems theory provides a powerful tool to help managers conceptualize the relationship between their companies and their external environments.

Systems theory helps us understand how business and society, taken together, form an **interactive social system**. Each needs the other, and each influences the other. They are entwined so completely that any action taken by one will surely affect the other. They are both separate and connected. Business is part of society, and society penetrates far and often into business decisions. In a world where global communication is rapidly expanding, the connections are closer than ever before. Throughout this book are examples of organizations and people that are grappling with the challenges of, and helping to shape, business–society relationships.

The Stakeholder Theory of the Firm

What is the purpose of the modern corporation? To whom, or what, should the firm be responsible?[5] No question is more central to the relationship between business and society.

In the ownership theory of the firm (sometimes also called property or finance theory), the firm is seen as the property of its owners. The purpose of the firm is to maximize returns to shareholders; that is, to make the most money it can for the people who own stock in the company. Managers and boards of directors are agents of shareholders and have no obligations to others, other than those directly specified by law. In this view, shareholders' interests are paramount and take precedence over the interests of others.

A contrasting view, called the stakeholder theory of the firm, argues that corporations serve a broad public purpose: to create value for society. All companies must make a profit for their owners; indeed, if they did not, they would not long survive. However, corporations create many other kinds of value as well, such as professional development for their employees and innovative new products for their customers. In this view, corporations have multiple obligations, and all stakeholders' interests must be taken into account. This approach has been expressed well by the pharmaceutical company Novartis, which states in its code of conduct that it "places a premium on dealing fairly with employees, commercial partners, government authorities, and the public. Success in its business ventures depends upon maintaining the trust of these essential stakeholders."[6]

Supporters of the stakeholder theory of the firm make three core arguments for their position: *descriptive, instrumental,* and *normative.*[7]

The *descriptive argument* says that the stakeholder view is simply a more realistic description of how companies really work. Managers have to pay keen attention, of course, to their quarterly and annual financial performance. Keeping Wall Street satisfied by managing for growth—thereby attracting more investors and increasing the stock price—is a core part of any top manager's job. But the job of management is much more complex than this. In order to produce consistent results, managers have to be concerned with producing high quality and innovative products and services for their customers, attracting and retaining talented employees, and complying with a plethora of complex government regulations. As a practical matter, managers direct their energies toward all stakeholders, not just owners.

The *instrumental argument* says that stakeholder management is more effective as a corporate strategy. Companies that take into consideration the rights and concerns of multiple groups perform better, over the long run, than those that do not. For example, a study of 500 large companies found that those that stated their commitment to a code of conduct and to their stakeholders in their annual reports performed better financially than those that did not.[8] This finding makes sense, because good relationships with stakeholders are themselves a source of value for the firm. This issue has been widely studied; some of the other empirical evidence for this proposition is presented in Chapter 3.

---

[5] One summary of contrasting theories of the purpose of the firm appears in Margaret M. Blair, "Whose Interests Should Corporations Serve," Ch. 6 in Margaret M. Blair and Bruce K. MacLaury, *Ownership and Control: Rethinking Corporate Governance for the Twenty-First Century* (Washington, DC: Brookings Institution, 1995), pp. 202–34. More recently, these questions have been taken up in James E. Post, Lee E. Preston, and Sybille Sachs, *Redefining the Corporation: Stakeholder Management and Organizational Wealth* (Palo Alto, CA: Stanford University Press, 2002).

[6] Novartis Corporation Code of Conduct, online at: *www.novartis.com.*

[7] The descriptive, instrumental, and normative arguments are summarized in Thomas Donaldson and Lee E. Preston, "The Stakeholder Theory of the Corporation: Concepts, Evidence and Implications," *Academy of Management Review* 20, no. 1 (1995), pp. 65–71. See also, Post, Preston, and Sachs, *Redefining the Corporation,* Ch. 1.

[8] Curtis C. Verschoor, "A Study of the Link Between a Corporation's Financial Performance and Its Commitment to Ethics," *Journal of Business Ethics* 17 (1998), pp. 1509–16.

The *normative argument* says that stakeholder management is simply the right thing to do. Corporations have great power and control vast resources; these privileges carry with them a duty toward all those affected by a corporation's actions. Moreover, all stakeholders, not just owners, contribute something of value to the corporation. A skilled engineer at Microsoft who applies his or her creativity to solving a difficult programming problem has made a kind of investment in the company, even if it is not a monetary investment. Any individual or group who makes a contribution, or takes a risk, has a moral right to some claim on the corporation's rewards.

A basis for both the ownership and stakeholder theories of the firm exists in law. The legal term *fiduciary* means a person who exercises power on behalf of another; that is, who acts as the other's agent. In U.S. law, managers are considered fiduciaries of the owners of the firm (its stockholders) and have an obligation to run the business in their interest. These legal concepts are clearly consistent with the ownership theory of the firm. However, other laws and court cases have given managers broad latitude in the exercise of their fiduciary duties. In the United States (where corporations are chartered not by the federal government but by the states), most states have passed laws that permit managers to take into consideration a wide range of other stakeholders' interests, including those of employees, customers, creditors, suppliers, and communities. In addition, many federal laws extend specific protections to various groups of stakeholders, such as those that prohibit discrimination against employees or grant consumers the right to sue if harmed by a product.

In other nations, the legal rights of nonowner stakeholders are often more fully developed than in the United States. For example, a number of European countries—including Germany, Holland, Denmark, Finland, and Sweden—require public companies to include employee members on their boards of directors, so that their interests will be explicitly represented. Under the European Union's so-called harmonization statutes, managers are specifically permitted to take into account the interests of customers, employees, creditors, and others.

In short, while the law requires managers to act of behalf of stockholders, it also gives them wide discretion—and in some instances requires them—to manage on behalf of the full range of stakeholder groups. The next section provides a more formal definition and an expanded discussion of the stakeholder concept.

The Stakeholder Concept

The term **stakeholder** refers to persons and groups that affect, or are affected by, an organization's decisions, policies, and operations.[9] The word *stake*, in this context, means an interest in—or claim on—a business enterprise. Those with a stake in the firm's actions include such diverse groups as customers, employees, stockholders, the media, governments, professional and trade associations, social and environmental activists, and nongovernmental organizations. The term *stakeholder* is not the same as *stockholder*, although the words sound similar. Stockholders—individuals or organizations that own shares of a company's stock—are one of several kinds of stakeholders.

Business organizations are embedded in networks involving many participants. Each of these participants has a relationship with the firm, based on ongoing interactions. Each

---

[9] The term *stakeholder* was first introduced in 1963 but was not widely used in the management literature until the publication of R. Edward Freeman's *Strategic Management: A Stakeholder Approach* (Marshfield, MA: Pitman, 1984). For a more recent summary of the stakeholder theory literature, see Thomas Donaldson and Lee E. Preston, "The Stakeholder Theory of the Corporation: Concepts, Evidence, Implications," *Academy of Management Review*, January 1995, pp. 71–83, and Max B. E. Clarkson, ed., *The Corporation and Its Stakeholders: Classic and Contemporary Readings* (Toronto: University of Toronto Press, 1998).

FIGURE 1.2
Market Stakeholders
of Business

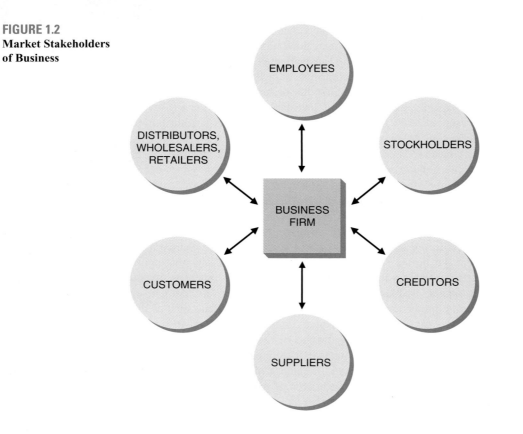

of them shares, to some degree, in both the risks and rewards of the firm's activities. And each has some kind of claim on the firm's resources and attention, based on law, moral right, or both. The number of these stakeholders and the variety of their interests can be large, making a company's decisions very complex, as the opening example illustrates.

Managers make good decisions when they pay attention to the effects of their decisions on stakeholders, as well as stakeholders' effects on the company. On the positive side, strong relationships between a corporation and its stakeholders are an asset that adds value. On the negative side, some companies disregard stakeholders' interests, either out of the belief that the stakeholder is wrong or out of the misguided notion that an unhappy customer, employee, or regulator does not matter. Such attitudes often prove costly to the company involved. Today, for example, companies know that they cannot locate a factory or store in a community that strongly objects. They also know that making a product that is perceived as unsafe invites lawsuits and jeopardizes market share.

Market and Nonmarket Stakeholders

Business interacts with society in a many diverse ways, and a company's relationships differ with various stakeholders. **Market stakeholders** are those that engage in economic transactions with the company as it carries out its primary purpose of providing society with goods and services. (For this reason, market stakeholders are also sometimes called *primary* stakeholders.)

Figure 1.2 shows the market stakeholders of business. Each relationship is based on a unique transaction, or two-way exchange. Stockholders invest in the firm and in return receive the potential for dividends and capital gains. Creditors loan money and collect

Exhibit 1.A   Are Managers Stakeholders?

Are managers, especially top executives, stakeholders? This has been a contentious issue in stakeholder theory.

On one hand, the answer clearly is "yes." Like other stakeholders, managers are impacted by the firm's decisions. As employees of the firm, managers receive compensation—often very generous compensation, as shown in Chapter 15. Their managerial roles confer opportunities for professional advancement, social status, and power over others. Managers benefit from the company's success and are hurt by its failure. For these reasons, they might properly be classified as employees on the perimeter of the stakeholder wheel, as shown in Figure 1.2.

One the other hand, top executives are agents of the firm and are responsible for acting on its behalf. In the stakeholder theory of the firm, their role is to integrate stakeholder interests, rather than to promote their own more narrow, selfish goals. For these reasons, they might properly be classified in the center of the stakeholder wheel, as representatives of the firm.

Management theory has long recognized that these two roles of managers potentially conflict. The main job of executives is to act for the company, but all too often they act primarily for themselves. Consider, for example, the many top executives of Enron, WorldCom, and Tyco, who enriched themselves personally at the expense of shareholders, employees, customers and other stakeholders. The challenge of persuading top managers to act in the firm's best interest is further discussed in Chapter 15.

payments of interest. Employees contribute their skills and knowledge in exchange for wages, benefits, and the opportunity for personal satisfaction and professional development. In return for payment, suppliers provide raw materials, energy, services, and other inputs; and wholesalers, distributors, and retailers engage in market transactions with the firm as they help move the product from plant to sales outlets to customers. All businesses need customers who are willing to buy their products or services. These are the fundamental market interactions every business has with society.

The puzzling question of whether or not managers should be classified as stakeholders along with other employees is discussed in Exhibit 1.A.

Nonmarket stakeholders, by contrast, are people and groups who—although they do not engage in direct economic exchange with the firm—are nonetheless affected by or can affect its actions. Figure 1.3 shows the nonmarket stakeholders of business (also called *secondary* stakeholders by some theorists). Nonmarket stakeholders include the community, various levels of government, activist groups and nongovernmental organizations, the media, business support groups, and the general public. The natural environment is generally not considered a stakeholder, because it is not a social group, but is represented in Figure 1.3 by activists, who include environmentalists.

The classification of government as a nonmarket, or secondary, stakeholder has been controversial in stakeholder theory. Most theorists say that government is a nonmarket stakeholder (as does this book) because it does not normally conduct any direct market exchanges (buying and selling) with business. However, money often flows from business to government in the form of taxes and fees, and sometimes from government to business in the form of subsidies or incentives. Moreover, some businesses—defense contractors for example—*do* sell directly to the government and receive payment for goods and services rendered. For this reason, a few theorists have called government a market stakeholder of business. The unique relationship between government and business is discussed throughout this book.

Both Figures 1.2 and 1.3 should be understood as very simplified ways of understanding the real world. These diagrams show the business firm as, in effect, the center

FIGURE 1.3
Nonmarket
Stakeholders of
Business

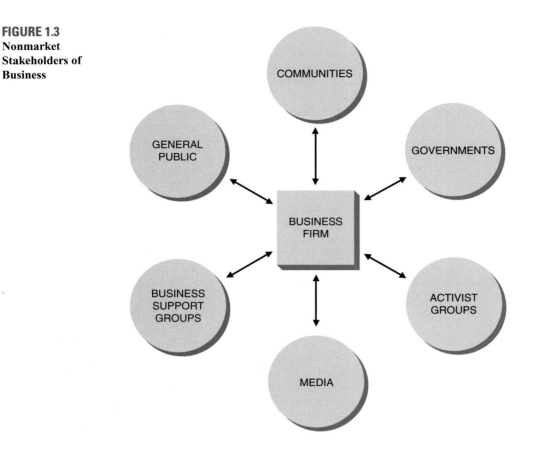

of a system, like the sun with its planets in the solar system. They also illustrate the firm's relationship to each stakeholder, but not stakeholders' relationships with each other. Some theorists have suggested that a more accurate way to visualize the relationship is to show the business firm embedded in a complex network of stakeholders, many of which have independent relationships with each other.[10] This alternative image of the business firm and its stakeholders—as a network with many nodes—is shown in Figure 1.4.

Nonmarket stakeholders are not necessarily less important than others, simply because they do not engage in direct economic exchange with a business. On the contrary, interactions with such groups can be critical to a firm's success or failure. For example, as described in a case study at the end of this book, Shell Oil was forced to shut down part of its operations in Nigeria after widespread community protests there against its environmental and social policies. In this instance, the community was able to block the company's operations, even though it did not have a market relationship with it. Moreover, market and nonmarket areas of involvement are not always sharply distinguished; often, one shades into the other. For example, the environmental effect of an automobile may be of concern both to a customer (a market stakeholder) and to the entire community (a nonmarket stakeholder), which experiences cumulative air pollution emitted from cars.

---

[10] Timothy J. Rowley, "Moving Beyond Dyadic Ties: A Network Theory of Stakeholder Influence," *Academy of Management Review* 22, no. 4 (October 1997).

FIGURE 1.4
A Stakeholder Network

Source: Adapted from Ann C. Svendsen and Myriam Laberge, "Convening Stakeholder Networks: A New Way of Thinking, Being, and Engaging," *Journal of Corporate Citizenship* 19 (Autumn 2005). Used by permission.

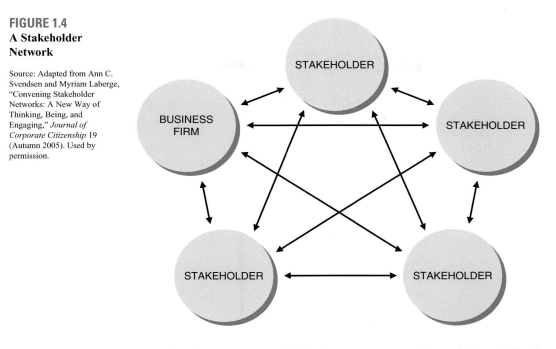

Of further note, some individuals or groups may play multiple stakeholder roles. Some theorists use the term *role sets* to refer to this phenomenon. For example, one person may work at a company, but also live in the surrounding community, own shares of company stock in his or her 401(k) retirement account, and even purchase the company's products from time to time. This person's stakes in a company's actions are several.

Later sections of this book (especially Chapters 15 through 20) will discuss in more detail the relationship between business and its various stakeholders.

Stakeholder Analysis and Engagement

An important part of the modern manager's job is to identify relevant stakeholders and to understand both their interests and the power they may have to assert these interests. This process is called **stakeholder analysis**. It asks four key questions, as follows.

Who are the relevant stakeholders?

The first question requires management to identify and map the relevant stakeholders. Figures 1.2 and 1.3 provide a guide. However, not all stakeholders listed in these figures will be relevant in every management situation. For example, a privately held firm will not have stockholders. Some businesses sell directly to the public, and therefore will not have wholesalers or retailers. In other situations, a firm may have a stakeholder—say, a creditor that has loaned money—but this group is not relevant to a particular decision or action that management must take.

But stakeholder analysis involves more than simply *identifying* stakeholders; it also involves understanding the nature of their interests, power, and links with one another.

Stakeholder Interests and Power

What are the interests of each stakeholder?

Each stakeholder has a unique relationship to the organization, and managers must respond accordingly. **Stakeholder interests** are, essentially, the nature of each group's stake. What are their concerns, and what do they want from their relationship with the firm?[11]

Stockholders, for their part, have an ownership interest in the firm. In exchange for their investment, stockholders expect to receive dividends and, over time, capital appreciation. The economic health of the corporation affects these people financially; their personal wealth—and often, their retirement security—is at stake. They may also seek social objectives through their choice of investments. Customers, for their part, are most interested in gaining fair value and quality in exchange for the purchase price of goods and services. Suppliers, likewise, wish to receive fair compensation for products and services they provide. Employees, in exchange for their time and effort, want to receive fair compensation and an opportunity for professional development. Governments, public interest groups, and local communities have another sort of relationship with the company. In general, their stake is broader than the financial stake of owners, customers, and suppliers. They may wish to protect the environment, assure human rights, or advance other broad social interests. Managers need to understand these complex and often intersecting stakeholder interests.

What is the power of each stakeholder?

Stakeholder power means the ability to use resources to make an event happen or to secure a desired outcome. Experts have recognized four types of stakeholder power: *voting power, economic power, political power,* and *legal power.*

Voting power means that the stakeholder has a legitimate right to cast a vote. Stockholders typically have voting power proportionate to the percentage of the company's stock he or she owns. Stockholders typically have an opportunity to vote on such major decisions as mergers and acquisitions, as well as various social issues that may come before the annual meeting. (Stockholder voting power should be distinguished from the voting power exercised by citizens, which is discussed below.)

In 2002, a group of stockholders at Hewlett Packard (HP) tried to exercise their voting power to block a proposed merger with Compaq Computer. The company's CEO and a majority of its board believed that a merger would benefit both firms by allowing them to bring together their capabilities in printers, peripherals, and computers. But one member of HP's board, Walter Hewlett, a son of the company's founder, opposed the merger on the grounds that it would destroy the egalitarian culture that was a core part of company's legacy. As required by law, the matter was put to a vote of the stockholders. In a series of letters, advertisements, and meetings, Hewlett organized other stockholders to vote against management's proposal. Ultimately, stockholders approved the merger—but by a very narrow margin.

Customers, suppliers, and retailers have *economic power* with the company. Suppliers can withhold supplies or refuse to fill orders if a company fails to meet its contractual responsibilities. Customers may refuse to buy a company's products or services if the company acts improperly. Customers can boycott products if they believe the goods are too expensive, poorly made, or unsafe. Employees, for their part, can refuse to work under certain conditions, a form of economic power known as a strike or slowdown. Economic power often depends on how well organized a stakeholder group is. For example, workers who are organized into unions usually have more economic power than do workers who try to negotiate individually with their employers.

---

[11] A full discussion of the interests of stakeholders may be found in R. Edward Freeman, *Ethical Theory and Business* (Englewood Cliffs, NJ: Prentice Hall, 1994).

Governments exercise *political power* through legislation, regulations, or lawsuits. While government agencies act directly, other stakeholders use their political power indirectly by urging government to use its powers by passing new laws or enacting regulations. Citizens may also vote for candidates that support their views with respect to government laws and regulations affecting business, a different kind of voting power than the one discussed above. Stakeholders may also exercise political power directly, as when social, environmental, or community activists organize to protest a particular corporate action.

Finally, stakeholders have *legal power* when they bring suit against a company for damages, based on harm caused by the firm. These include lawsuits brought by customers for damages caused by defective products, brought by employees for damages caused by workplace injury, or brought by environmentalists for damages caused by pollution or harm to species or habitat. After Enron collapsed, many institutional shareholders, such as state pension funds, joined together to sue to recoup some of their losses.

Some scholars have suggested that managers pay more attention to stakeholders possessing greater salience. (Something is *salient* when it stands out from a background.) Stakeholders stand out to managers when they have power, legitimacy, and urgency. The more of these attributes a stakeholder possesses, the more managers are likely to notice and respond. Stakeholders possessing all three attributes are called *definitive* stakeholders; those possessing two attributes are called *expectant* stakeholders.[12]

Activists often use this insight about salience when they want to change a company's policy. For example, human rights activists wanted to bring pressure on Unocal Corporation to change its practices in Burma, where it had entered into a joint venture with the government to build a gas pipeline. Critics charged that many human rights violations occurred during this project, including forced labor and relocations. In an effort to pressure Unocal to change its behavior, activists organized protests at stockholder meetings (*voting power*), called for boycotts of Unocal products (*economic power*), promoted local ordinances prohibiting cities from buying from Unocal (*political power*), and brought a lawsuit for damages on behalf of Burmese villagers (*legal power)*. These activists became salient because they were able to mobilize many kinds of power and to press their claims with great urgency. This combination of tactics eventually forced Unocal in 2005 to pay compensation to people whose rights had been violated and to fund education and health care projects in the pipeline region.[13]

Exhibit 1.B provides a schematic summary of some of the main interests and powers of both market and nonmarket stakeholders.

Stakeholder Coalitions

An understanding of stakeholder interests and power enables managers to answer the final question of stakeholder analysis: *How are coalitions likely to form?*

Not surprisingly, stakeholder interests often coincide. For example, consumers of fresh fruit and farmworkers who harvest that fruit in the field may have a shared interest in reducing the use of pesticides, because of possible adverse health effects from exposure to chemicals. When their interests are similar, stakeholders may form coalitions, temporary alliances to pursue a common interest. **Stakeholder coalitions** are not static. Groups that are highly involved with a company today may be less involved tomorrow. Issues that are controversial at one time may be uncontroversial later; stakeholders that are

---

[12] Ronald K. Mitchell, Bradley R. Agle, and Donna J. Wood, "Toward a Theory of Stakeholder Identification and Salience: Defining the Principle of Who and What Really Counts," *Academy of Management Review* 22, no. 4 (1997), pp. 853–86.

[13] Further information about the campaign against Unocal is available at: *www.earthrights.org/unocal.*

Exhibit 1.B Stakeholders: Nature of Interest and Power

Stakeholder	Nature of Interest—Stakeholder Wishes To:	Nature of Power—Stakeholder Influences Company By:
Market Stakeholders		
Employees	■ Maintain stable employment in firm ■ Receive fair pay for work ■ Work in safe, comfortable environment	■ Union bargaining power ■ Work actions or strikes ■ Publicity
Stockholders	■ Receive a satisfactory return on investments (dividends) ■ Realize appreciation in stock value over time	■ Exercising voting rights based on share ownership ■ Exercising rights to inspect company books and records
Customers	■ Receive fair exchange: value and quality for money spent ■ Receive safe, reliable products	■ Purchasing goods from competitors ■ Boycotting companies whose products are unsatisfactory or whose policies are unacceptable
Suppliers	■ Receive regular orders for goods ■ Be paid promptly for supplies delivered	■ Refusing to meet orders if conditions of contract are breached ■ Supplying to competitors
Retailers/ Wholesalers	■ Receive quality goods in a timely fashion at reasonable cost ■ Offer reliable products that consumers trust and value	■ Buying from other suppliers if terms of contract are unsatisfactory ■ Boycotting companies whose goods or policies are unsatisfactory
Creditors	■ Receive repayment of loans ■ Collect debts and interest	■ Calling in loans if payments are not made ■ Utilizing legal authorities to repossess or take over property if loan payments are severely delinquent

dependent on an organization at one time may be less so at another. To make matters more complicated, the process of shifting coalitions does not occur uniformly in all parts of a large corporation. Stakeholders involved with one part of a large company often have little or nothing to do with other parts of the organization.

In recent years, coalitions of stakeholders have become increasingly international in scope. Communications technology has enabled like-minded people to come together quickly, even across political boundaries and many miles of separation. Wireless telephones,

Stakeholder	Nature of Interest— Stakeholder Wishes To:	Nature of Power— Stakeholder Influences Company By:
Nonmarket Stakeholders		
Communities	■ Employ local residents in the company ■ Ensure that the local environment is protected ■ Ensure that the local area is developed	■ Refusing to extend additional credit ■ Issuing or restricting operating licenses and permits ■ Lobbying government for regulation of the company's policies or methods of land use and waste disposal
Activist Groups	■ Monitor company actions and policies to ensure that they conform to legal and ethical standards, and that they protect the public's safety	■ Gaining broad public support through publicizing the issue ■ Lobbying government for regulation of the company
Media	■ Keep the public informed on all issues relevant to their health, well-being, and economic status ■ Monitor company actions	■ Publicizing events that affect the public, especially those that have negative effects
Business Support Groups (e.g., trade associations)	■ Provide research and information which will help the company or industry perform in a changing environment	■ Using its staff and resources to assist company in business endeavors and development efforts ■ Providing legal or "group" political support beyond that which an individual company can provide for itself
Governments	■ Promote economic development ■ Encourage social improvements ■ Raise revenues through taxes	■ Adopting regulations and laws ■ Issuing licenses and permits ■ Allowing or disallowing industrial activity
The General Public	■ Protect social values ■ Minimize risks ■ Achieve prosperity for society	■ Supporting activists ■ Pressing government to act ■ Condemning or praising individual companies

the Internet, and fax machines have become powerful tools in the hands of groups that monitor how multinational businesses are operating in different locations around the world.

In the late 1990s, groups came together from all over the world to block development of a salt plant in a remote area on the Pacific coast of Mexico. The proposed plant was a joint venture of Mitsubishi (a multinational corporation based in Japan) and the Mexican government. Together, they wanted to create jobs, taxes, and revenue by mining naturally occurring salt deposits along the Baja California coast. Environmentalists attacked the venture on the grounds that it would hurt the gray whales that migrated every year to a nearby lagoon to give birth to their young. In the past, such objections would probably have attracted little attention. But critics were able to use the Internet and the media to mobilize over 50 organizations worldwide to threaten a boycott of Mitsubishi. One million people sent protest letters to "save the gray whale." Faced with this global outcry, in 2000 the Mexican government cancelled its plans for the salt plant.[14]

This example illustrates how international networks of activists, coupled with the media's interest in such business and society issues, make coalition development and issue activism an increasingly powerful strategic factor for companies. Nongovernmental organizations regularly meet to discuss problems such as global warming, human rights, and environmental issues, just as their business counterparts do. Today, stakeholder coalitions are numerous in every industry and important to every company.

Once managers have answered these four questions, how can they best use this information? Stakeholder analysis is just the first step. It provides a useful tool for managers to help them engage collaboratively with stakeholders to create value, a topic discussed in the next section.

Stakeholder Engagement

Over time, the nature of business's relationship with its stakeholders has changed in important ways. Several experts have observed a shift from an *inactive* to a *reactive* to a *proactive* to an *interactive* relationship.[15]

- *Inactive* companies simply ignore stakeholder concerns. These firms may believe—often incorrectly—that they can make decisions unilaterally, without taking into consideration their impact on others. For example, in the 1970s a company called A. H. Robins manufactured a contraceptive device called the Dalkon Shield, which was inserted into a woman's uterus to prevent pregnancy. The device apparently had not been adequately tested and allowed bacteria to enter the body. When reports began to surface that many women with Dalkon Shields had developed pelvic infections and even infertility, the company's initial response was simply to deny there was a problem.

- Companies that adopt a *reactive* posture generally act only when forced to do so, and then in a defensive manner. For example, in the film *A Civil Action*, based on a true story, W. R. Grace (a company that was later bought by Beatrice Foods) allegedly dumped toxic chemicals that leaked into underground wells used for drinking water, causing illness and death in the community of Woburn, Massachusetts. The company paid no attention to the problem until forced to defend itself in a lawsuit brought by a crusading lawyer on behalf of members of the community.

- *Proactive* companies try to anticipate stakeholder concerns. These firms often have specialized departments, such as public affairs, community relations, consumer affairs, and government relations to identify issues that are, or may become, of concern to key stakeholders. These firms are much less likely to be blind-sided by crises and negative surprises. Stakeholders and their concerns are still, however, considered a problem to be managed, rather than a source of competitive advantage.

---

[14] H. Richard Eisenbeis and Sue Hanks, "When Gray Whales Blush," case presented at the annual meeting of the North American Case Research Association, October 2002.

[15] This typology was first introduced in Lee Preston and James E. Post, *Private Management and Public Policy* (Englewood Cliffs, NJ: Prentice Hall, 1975). For a more recent discussion, see Sandra Waddock, *Leading Corporate Citizens: Visions, Values, and Value Added*, 2nd ed. (McGraw-Hill, 2006), Ch. 1.

- Finally, an *interactive* stance means that companies actively engage with stakeholders in an ongoing relationship of mutual respect, openness, and trust. Firms with this approach recognize that positive stakeholder relationships are a source of value and competitive advantage for the company. They know that these relationships must be nurtured over time. The term **stakeholder engagement** is used to refer to this process of ongoing relationship building between a business and its stakeholders.

The process of engagement can take many forms, but it often involves dialogue with stakeholders. One management theorist has defined dialogue as "the art of thinking together."[16] In **stakeholder dialogue**, a business and its stakeholders come together for face-to-face conversations about issues of common concern. There, they attempt to describe their core interests and concerns, define a common definition of the problem, invent innovative solutions for mutual gain, and establish procedures for implementing solutions. To be successful, the process requires that participants express their own views fully, listen carefully and respectfully to others, and open themselves to creative thinking and new ways of looking at and solving a problem. The promise of dialogue is that together, they can draw on the understandings and concerns of all parties to develop solutions that none of them, acting alone, could have envisioned or implemented.[17]

BC Hydro, the third-largest electric utility in Canada, serves residents in British Columbia and sells power to other provinces and states throughout the Pacific Northwest. Over 90 percent of the company's output comes from hydroelectric dams. In 1995, BC Hydro ran into stiff opposition from locals when it set out to build a new power plant on the Alouette River. Rather than ignore these complaints, the company convened a stakeholder committee, with representation from the local community, First Nations bands (aboriginal peoples), environmentalists, and local regulators. Over many months of dialogue, the committee hammered out a plan for the river that permitted more power generation, but also provided for protection of fish and wildlife, recreational use, and flood control. The group also set up an ongoing governance process, so stakeholders could continue to be consulted in future decisions. Today, BC Hydro has stakeholder dialogues in progress in many locations across the province.[18]

Engaging interactively with stakeholders, whether through dialogue or some other process, carries a number of potential benefits. It can help companies learn about society's expectations, draw on outside expertise, generate creative solutions, and win stakeholder support for implementing them. It can also disarm or neutralize critics and improve a company's reputation for taking constructive action. On the other hand, corporations that do *not* engage effectively with those their actions affect may be hurt. Their reputation may suffer, their sales may drop, and they may be prevented from taking action. The need to respond to stakeholders has only been heightened by the increased globalization of many businesses and by the rise of technologies that facilitate fast communication on a worldwide scale.

The important question of what *organizational* steps businesses need to take to enhance their capacity to respond to and interact with stakeholders in a positive manner is further explored in Chapter 4.

---

[16] William Isaacs, *Dialogue and the Art of Thinking Together* (New York: Doubleday, 1999).

[17] This section draws on the discussion in Anne T. Lawrence and Ann Svendsen, *The Clayoquot Controversy: A Stakeholder Dialogue Simulation* (Vancouver: Centre for Innovation in Management, 2002). The argument for the benefits of stakeholder engagement is fully developed in Ann Svendsen, *The Stakeholder Strategy: Profiting from Collaborative Business Relationships* (San Francisco: Berrett-Koehler, 1998).

[18] We are indebted to Ann Svendsen for this example. More information is available at *www.bchydro.com*.

FIGURE 1.5
Forces That Shape the Business and Society Relationship

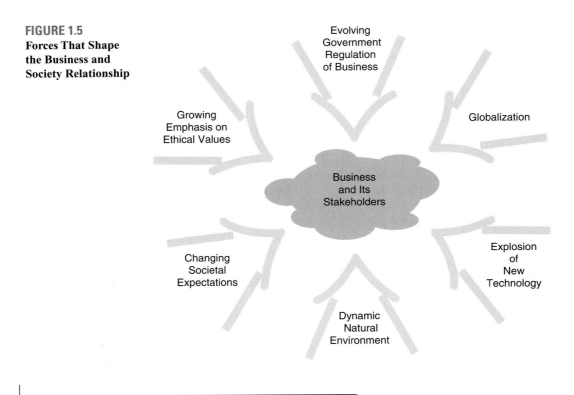

The Dynamic Environment of Business

A core argument of this book is that *the external environment of business is dynamic and ever changing.* Businesses and their stakeholders do not interact in a vacuum. On the contrary, most companies operate in a swirl of social, ethical, global, political, ecological, and technological change that produces both opportunities and threats. Figure 1.5 diagrams the six dynamic forces that powerfully shape the business and society relationship. Each of these forces is introduced briefly below and will be discussed in more detail later in this book.

Changing societal expectations. Everywhere around the world, society's expectations of business are changing. People increasingly expect business to be more responsible, believing companies should pay close attention to social issues and act as good citizens in society. Increasingly, business is faced with the daunting task of balancing its social, legal, and economic obligations, seeking to meet its commitments to multiple stakeholders. Various evaluation standards have been developed to provide business with objective ways to measure how well it has responded to stakeholders. These changes in society's expectations of business, and how managers have responded, are described in Chapters 2, 3, and 4.

Growing emphasis on ethical reasoning and actions. The public also expects business to be ethical and wants corporate managers to apply ethical principles—in other words, guidelines about what is right and wrong, fair and unfair, and morally correct—when they make business decisions. Fair employment practices, concern for consumer safety, contribution to the welfare of the community, and human rights protection around the world have become more prominent and important. Business has created ethics programs to help ensure employees are aware of these issues and act in accordance with ethical standards. The ethical challenges faced by business, both domestically and abroad—and business's response—are further discussed in Chapters 5 and 6.

Globalization. We live in an increasingly integrated world economy, characterized by the unceasing movement of goods, services, and capital across national borders. Today, economic forces truly play out on a global stage. Large transnational corporations do business in scores of countries. Products and services people buy every day in the United States or Germany may have come from Indonesia, Haiti, or Mexico. A currency crisis in Russia, Argentina, or Thailand can affect stock values and interest rates halfway around the world. Globalization is more than just an economic phenomenon, however; it also involves rapid cultural change, the migration of people, and pressures for political reform. Chapter 7 addresses globalization and its impact on the business and society relationship.

Evolving governmental regulation of business. The role of government has changed dramatically in many nations in recent decades. Governments around the world have enacted myriad new policies that have profoundly constrained how business is allowed to operate. Government regulation of business periodically becomes tighter, then looser, much as a pendulum swings back and forth. Because of the dynamic nature of this force, business has developed various strategies to influence elected officials and government regulators at federal, state, and local levels. Government may also restrict business if it believes fair competition has been hindered by monopolistic practices. The changing role of government, its impact, and business's response are explored in Chapters 8, 9, and 10.

Dynamic natural environment. All interactions between business and society occur within a finite natural ecosystem. Humans share a single planet, and many of our resources—oil, coal, and gas, for example—are nonrenewable. Once used, they are gone forever. Other resources, like clean water, timber, and fish, are renewable, but only if humans use them sustainably, not taking more than can be naturally replenished. The relentless demands of human society, in many arenas, have already exceeded the carrying capacity of the earth's ecosystem. Managers are increasingly being challenged to integrate ecological considerations into their decisions. The state of the earth's resources and changing attitudes about the natural environment powerfully impact the business–society relationship. These issues are explored in Chapters 11 and 12.

Explosion of new technology. Technology is one of the most dramatic and powerful forces affecting business and society. New technologies harness the human imagination to create new machines, processes, and software that address the needs, problems, and concerns of modern society. In recent years, the pace of technological change has increased enormously. From genetically modified foods to the Internet, from nanotechnology to wireless communications, change keeps coming. The extent and pace of technological innovation provide massive challenges for business, and sometimes government, as they seek to manage this dynamic force. As discussed in Chapters 13 and 14, new technologies often force managers and organizations to examine seriously the ethical implications of their use.

Creating Value in a Dynamic Environment

These powerful and dynamic forces—fast-paced changes in societal and ethical expectations, the global economy, government policies, the natural environment, and technology—establish the context in which businesses interact with their many stakeholders, as discussed in Chapters 15 through 20. This means that the relationship between business and society is continuously changing in new and often unpredictable ways. Environments, people, and organizations change; inevitably, new issues will arise and challenge managers to develop new solutions. To be effective, corporations must meet the reasonable expectations of stakeholders and society in general. A successful business must meet *both* its economic and social objectives. A core argument of this book is that *the purpose of the firm is not simply to make a profit, but to create value for all its stakeholders.* Ultimately, business success is judged, not simply by a company's financial performance, but by how well it serves broad social interests.

Summary

- Business firms are organizations that are engaged in making a product or providing a service for a profit. Society, in its broadest sense, refers to human beings and to the social structures they collectively create. Business is part of society and engages in ongoing exchanges with its external environment. Together, business and society form an interactive social system in which the actions of each profoundly influence the other.

- According to the stakeholder theory of the firm, the purpose of the modern corporation is to create value for all of its stakeholders. To survive, all companies must make a profit for their owners. However, they also create many other kinds of value as well for their employees, customers, communities, and others. For both practical and ethical reasons, corporations must take all stakeholders' interests into account.

- Every business firm has economic and social relationships with others in society. Some are intended, some unintended; some are positive, others negative. Stakeholders are all those who affect, or are affected by, the actions of the firm. Some have a market relationship with the company, and others have a nonmarket relationship with it.

- Stakeholders can exercise their economic, political, and other powers in ways that benefit or challenge the organization. Stakeholders may also act independently or create coalitions to influence the company. Managers must learn how to engage interactively with stakeholders to create mutually beneficial outcomes. Positive relationships with stakeholders can create value.

- A number of broad forces shape the relationship between business and society. These include changing societal and ethical expectations; redefinition of the role of government; a dynamic global economy; ecological and natural resource concerns; and the transformational role of technology. To deal effectively with these changes, corporate strategy must address the expectations of all of the company's stakeholders.

Key Terms

business, *4*
general systems theory, *5*
interactive social system, *5*
ownership theory of the firm, *6*

society, *4*
stakeholder, *7*
stakeholder analysis, *11*
stakeholder coalitions, *13*
stakeholder dialogue, *17*
stakeholder engagement, *17*

stakeholder interests, *11*
stakeholder (market), *8*
stakeholder (nonmarket), *9*
stakeholder power, *12*
stakeholder theory of the firm, *6*

Discussion Case: *Cisco in the Coyote Valley*

Cisco Systems, based in San Jose, California, is a worldwide leader in high technology business. Founded by a group of scientists in 1984, the company designs and makes hardware for the Internet—the routers, servers, switches, cables, and modems that connect the world's computers. The company employs about 35,000 people globally. Of these, over 40 percent work in or near corporate headquarters in the Silicon Valley, making Cisco the region's largest private-sector employer.

As the Internet took off and demand for its products boomed in the late 1990s, Cisco quickly began to outgrow its urban office space. In 1999, the company proposed a solution: a massive industrial park to be constructed in a semi-rural area called the Coyote Valley, just inside San Jose's southern border. The largely undeveloped 400-acre site was then a mix of orchards and oak-studded grasslands, punctuated by several creeks.

Cisco's plan called for construction of a $1 billion multiple-building campus that would house up to 20,000 employees, with parking spaces for 22,000. The company said it would set aside 270 acres as open space and an additional 90 acres for landscaping and recreation. It also pledged to invest an additional $122 million in public roads, a freeway interchange, and a fire station. The proposed development was so large that locals quickly dubbed it "Cisco City."

Cisco believed that it needed to expand quickly to compete effectively with larger rivals such as Nortel and Lucent. Building in the Coyote Valley would enable it to keep core employees in its home community, as well as to continue to recruit in an area known for its highly skilled workforce. "It's part of our overall strategic plan to really grow where the talent is," said a company vice president.

The company's expansion plan was praised by the San Jose Chamber of Commerce, an organization of local businesses. "Cisco's private investment in public infrastructure is unprecedented in San Jose," said the president of the Chamber. "Cisco's campus will not only pay for itself, it will pay for a lot more." The Coyote Valley development was also supported by trade unions in the construction industry, and by many local politicians who argued that it would bring jobs and tax revenue to the city and county.

The community was divided. In the immediate vicinity, many seemed enthusiastic. "Cisco will add value to our neighborhood and help improve neighborhood services for all San Jose residents," said the president of a local neighborhood association. "South San Jose overwhelmingly supports Cisco."

Outside the city, however, opposition flared. The development plan did not include a provision for housing, and many wondered where the 20,000 or so workers at the Coyote Valley site would live. The towns of Salinas, Watsonville, and Hollister—historically agricultural communities south of San Jose—expressed concern that Cisco employees would move in, driving up housing prices, clogging roads, and putting pressure on already strained local services. "It's a cynical effort to reap the economic benefits of this huge office development for San Jose, but impose the economic burdens . . . on other communities to the south," said an attorney retained by these communities.

Environmentalists also lined up against the project. Chapters of the Sierra Club, the Audubon Society, and a local group called the Committee for Green Foothills charged that the development would pollute the air with automobile emissions, destroy valuable habitat, and contribute to urban sprawl. They pointed out that the site was far from mass transit. "It would be an environmental disaster . . . in terms of air quality, loss of wonderful agricultural land, and traffic," said a spokesperson for the Sierra Club. The environmentalists joined the southern communities and affordable housing activists to bring a lawsuit to block the development.

As the controversy headed for the courts, Cisco managers considered what steps they could take to increase the chances their proposal would succeed. "We are disappointed that these parties have chosen litigation over collaboration," said a company spokesperson. "We have remained willing to work together out of the courts."

Discussion Questions

1. What is Cisco's objective?
2. Who are the relevant market and nonmarket stakeholders in this situation?
3. What are their interests? Please indicate if each stakeholder is in favor of, or opposed to, the Coyote Valley development project, and why.
4. What would be the advantages and disadvantages to the company of working collaboratively with its stakeholders to resolve this dispute?
5. What possible solutions to this dispute do you think might emerge from dialogue between Cisco Systems and its stakeholders?

CHAPTER TWO

Managing Public Issues

Every business organization faces many public issues—matters of common concern to the firm and its stakeholders. The emergence of new public issues presents both a risk and an opportunity for companies. Companies may develop and operate various departments to engage with and learn from stakeholders. Senior executives often proactively manage public issues through these departments or a centralized public affairs office. Public affairs managers have many functions, including environmental scanning and issue management. Because of the importance of public issues, many firms have moved to integrate public affairs activities tightly with strategic management at the highest level of the firm.

This chapter focuses on these key learning objectives:

- Evaluating public issues and their significance to the modern corporation.
- Analyzing the ways business utilizes its boundary-spanning departments to interact with their various stakeholders.
- Knowing the duties of a company's public affairs manager or department both for domestic and international issues.
- Applying available tools or techniques to scan an organization's multiple environments.
- Investigating how competitive intelligence is gathered and used.
- Describing the steps in the issue management process and determining how to make the process most effective.

Every company faces many public issues. Some emerge over a long period of time; others emerge suddenly. Some are predictable; others are completely unexpected. Consider the following examples:

- The release of a report by the U.S. surgeon general in 2001 focused attention on the problem of obesity, which the report called "among the most pressing health challenges we face today."[1] Just as an earlier surgeon general's report had caused many people to give up smoking, the latest call to action led many Americans—60 percent of whom were overweight or obese–to reevaluate their eating and exercise habits. Many food processors and restaurant chains had to scramble to meet the changing preferences of their customers. Those that did so quickly were rewarded for their responsiveness. In the two years after McDonald's introduced premium salads in 2003, the company sold more than 900 million servings of vegetables in the United States. Its "apple dippers" product (sliced apples with a sweet dip), introduced the following year, was popular with both adults and children. "Past customers who have not frequented a McDonald's restaurant in some time are discovering a reason to come back," said a company spokesperson. "The view is that now there is truly something on the menu for them."[2]

- In the mid-2000s, many pharmaceutical companies grappled with the fact that new drugs, developed at great expense, were not as profitable as expected, hurting their bottom lines and share values. A major cause, according to one analysis, was the sudden rise in insurers' use of a technique called outcomes-based assessment, or OBA. Using this methodology, insurers rigorously analyzed the cost-benefit ratio of various medicines. For example, an older generic drug might be more cost effective than a newer, slightly improved—but much more expensive—version. In the early 2000s, many insurers began approving payment only for drugs that had passed strict OBA assessment. Patients could still get nonapproved medicines, but only by paying more out of pocket. The shift generated savings for employers and insurance companies, but at considerable cost to both patients and drug companies. The rapid spread of OBA challenged pharmaceutical companies to apply new criteria for which drugs to develop. Two pharmaceutical industry analysts commented, "Drugmakers caught unaware of or unprepared for OBA are suffering."[3]

- Using newly available technologies, ordinary people can now create short videos in a few hours and post them to the Web; reach strangers all over the world with their blogs; and create, advertise, and sell products online. The result has been the emergence of technology-enabled popular fads, sometimes called *memes,* that spread from one mind to another in an unmanaged creative process. In 2006, a horror film in production starring Samuel Jackson—about snakes that get loose on an airplane—captured the imagination of such a Web-based virtual community. Before long, "snakes on a plane," or "SoaP" for short, had become a catch-phrase meaning, roughly, "stuff happens," and homemade posters, T-shirts, and trailers had sprouted up. Rather than trying to shut down the process, the producers renamed the film "Snakes on a Plane" and let the Internet work. "The producers . . . let go of the creative reins when they saw that the blogosphere had taken it over and was telling the story differently. . . You can't create that in-house," commented the author of a book on viral marketing.[4]

---

[1] A summary of the surgeon general's report is available online at *www.surgeongeneral.gov/topics/obesity/calltoaction.*

[2] "Premium Salads, Apple Dippers Are Good News for Quick Service Giant," *Fresh Cut,* January 2005; and Jim Skinner (McDonald's CEO), "Keynote Address," *Business for Social Responsibility,* November 2005, available online at *www.bsr.org.*

[3] "Drugmakers: A Dose of Reality," *BusinessWeek,* June 19, 2006, p. 98.

[4] "Snakes on a Plane Blog Buzz Forces Hollywood into Overdue Attitude Adjustment," *San Francisco Chronicle,* June 12, 2006, pp. E1, E5.

Businesses today operate in an ever-changing external environment, where effective management requires not just responding to, but anticipating emerging issues. Whether the issue is shifting consumer preferences, new regulatory regimes, or discontinuous technology, managers have to interact across organizational boundaries, learn from external stakeholders, and alter their practices in response. This chapter will introduce the concept of a public issue and explain the stages of the issue management process. It will also describe the corporation's boundary-spanning departments and describe tools that public affairs officers use to anticipate emergent issues that might help or harm an organization, as they develop and implement strategies for responding to stakeholder concerns.

Public Issues

A **public issue** is an issue that is of mutual concern to an organization and one or more of the organization's stakeholders. The emergence of a new public issue often indicates there is a *gap* between what the firm wants to do or is doing and what stakeholders expect. Scholars have called this the **performance–expectations gap.** Stakeholder expectations are a mixture of people's opinions, attitudes, and beliefs about what constitutes reasonable business behavior. Managers and organizations have good reason to identify emergent expectations as early as possible. Failure to understand stakeholder concerns and to respond appropriately will permit the performance–expectations gap to grow: the larger the gap, the greater the risk of stakeholder backlash or of missing a major business opportunity. The performance–expectations gap is pictured in Figure 2.1.

Public issues can be of critical importance to a company. The worldwide managing director of McKinsey, the business consultancy, commented in a recent opinion column in *The Economist:*

> From a defensive point of view, companies that ignore public sentiment make themselves vulnerable to attack. But social pressures can also operate as early indicators of factors core to corporate profitability: for example, the regulations

FIGURE 2.1
The Performance–Expectations Gap

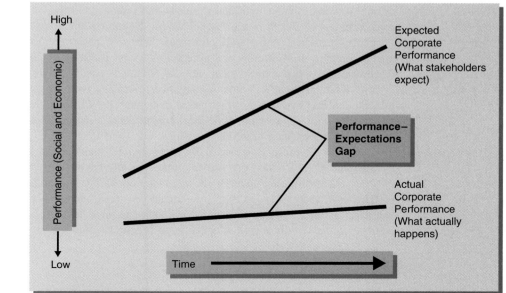

and public policy environment in which companies must operate; the appetite of consumers for certain goods above others; and the motivation (and willingness to be hired in the first place) of employees. Companies that treat social issues as either irritating distractions or simply unjustified vehicles for attack on business are turning a blind eye to impending forces that have the potential fundamentally to alter their strategic future.[5]

Emerging public issues are both a risk and an opportunity. They are a risk because issues that firms do not anticipate and plan for effectively can seriously hurt a company. A classic example of this was Monsanto, which introduced genetically modified corn, soybeans, and other crops in the late 1990s. Although the products were well accepted in the United States, they sparked intense opposition from European consumers, who objected to eating food that had been genetically engineered. Monsanto, which had not anticipated the depth of the opposition it would face, was forced to withdraw its products from the European market. (This situation is further discussed in Chapter 14.)

On the other hand, correctly anticipating the emergence of an issue can confer a competitive advantage. Toyota was one of the first firms to recognize that growing public concern about the environment and related government regulations would spur demand for fuel-efficient and low-emission vehicles. As a result, the company got an early start on developing gas–electric engines and is today the leading producer of such vehicles. Toyota announced in 2006 that they had sold half a million Priuses worldwide since the hybrid car's introduction, exceeding all expectations.

Understanding and responding to changing societal expectations is a business necessity. As Mark Moody-Stuart, former managing director of Royal Dutch/Shell, put it in an interview, "Communication with society . . . is a commercial matter, because society is your customers. It is not a soft and wooly thing, because society is what we depend on for our living. So we had better be in line with its wishes, its desires, its aspirations, its dreams."[6]

The Corporation's Boundary-Spanning Departments

Chapter 1 presented a model of the corporation and its stakeholders. It argued that how corporations interact with stakeholders—and understand their expectations—powerfully contributes to business success or failure. **Boundary-spanning departments** are departments, or offices, within an organization that reach across the dividing line that separates the company from groups and people in society. Building positive and mutually beneficial relationships across organizational boundaries is a growing part of management's role. How do today's companies organize internally to manage relationships with their stakeholders? In a world of fast-paced globalization, shifting public expectations and government policies, growing ecological concerns, and new technologies, doing so successfully has never been more challenging.

Figure 2.2 presents a list of the corporation's market and nonmarket stakeholders, alongside the corporate departments that typically have responsibility for engaging with them. As the figure suggests, the organization of the corporation's boundary-spanning functions is complex. In many organizations, departments of public affairs or government relations interact with public officials and agencies. Departments of investor relations interact with shareholders; human resources with employees; customer relations

---

[5] "The Biggest Contract: Business and Society," *The Economist,* May 28, 2005, p. 87.

[6] Interview conducted for Anne T. Lawrence, "Shell Oil in Nigeria," interactive online case published by *www.i case.com.*

FIGURE 2.2 **The Corporation's Boundary-Spanning Departments**

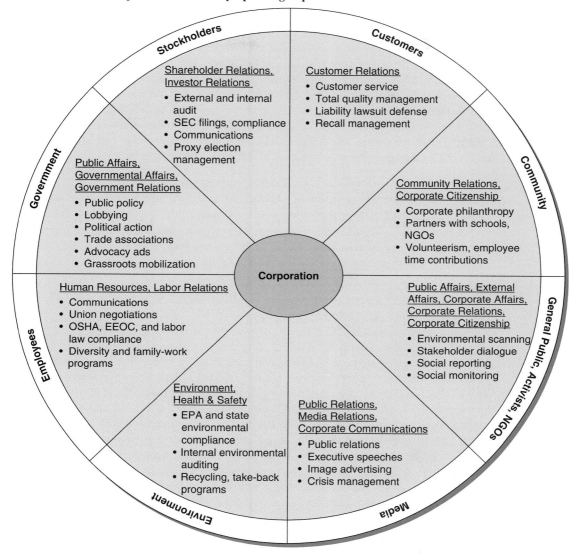

with customers; and community relations with the community. Specialized departments of environment, health, and safety may deal with environmental compliance and worker health and safety, and public relations or corporate communications with the media. Many of these specific departments will be discussed in more detail in later chapters.

The nature of business's external relationship is changing so fast that many corporations are moving to reinvent how they relate with society. In some cases, companies have broadened the job of the public affairs office—once focused mainly on government relations—to include a wider range of tasks, or have created new departments of corporate citizenship or corporate affairs to centralize some of the functions listed in Figure 2.2 under common leadership. This chapter will address the work of the public affairs department; Chapter 4 will discuss in more detail the role of departments of corporate citizenship.

Public Affairs Management

The pressures on business firms that arise from public issues, plus the increasingly complex relationships organizations have with stakeholders, have led many companies to create specialized departments to manage public affairs. The duties of the corporate public affairs function have evolved in recent years, especially as the number of stakeholder issues has grown and issues have become both more complex and more important to business.[7] The creation of public affairs units appears to be a global trend as well, with many companies in Canada, Australia, and Europe developing sophisticated public affairs operations.[8]

The growth of public affairs activities in business organizations has several causes, according to management scholar Craig S. Fleisher. These include:

- *External forces*, such as the loss of public trust in institutions (including government and business), the globalization of world markets, and the rise of the Internet and other technologies that allow stakeholders access to more information than ever before.
- *Internal forces*, such as better communication within organizations, more experience dealing with significant change and complexity, and a growing focus on the interplay between the organization, its environment, and its strategies.[9]

Each of these forces challenges public affairs managers to assess the effectiveness of their current practices and possibly make significant changes in how they interact with their organization's stakeholders.

Public affairs management refers broadly to the active management of a company's external relations, especially its relations with stakeholders such as government and regulatory agencies, customers, investors, and communities. Other names sometimes used to describe the function are corporate affairs, external affairs, and government relations. Exhibit 2.A presents the profile of activities performed by public affairs units as reported by around 150 large and medium-sized companies in 2005. As shown in the exhibit, the main activities of public affairs managers include government relations, issue management, and working with trade associations and stakeholder coalitions.

The activities listed in the exhibit may seem quite different, but all are linked to an organization's need to relate to its many stakeholders. Notice how many of the activities refer to a named stakeholder group (e.g., state and local government relations, community relations, media relations, and employee communications). Others refer to activities that are clearly connected to more than one stakeholder (e.g., coalitions, corporate philanthropy, and grassroots/grasstops communication). ("Grassroots" refers to ordinary citizens; "grasstops" refers to particularly influential people in a community.)

Most companies have a public affairs plan and a senior manager or executive to lead the public affairs department. This manager is often a member of the company's senior management committee, providing expertise about the company's major strategy and policy

---

[7] See James E. Post and Jennifer J. Griffin, "Corporate Reputation and External Affairs Management," *Corporate Reputation Review* 1 (1997), pp. 165–71. The global patterns of public affairs practice are documented in *Journal of Public Affairs*, published by Henry Stewart Publishing beginning in 2001.

[8] For an excellent review of public affairs development around the world see Craig S. Fleisher and Natasha Blair, "Surveying the Field: Status and Trends Affecting Public Affairs across Australia, Canada, EU and the U.S.," in *Assessing, Managing and Maximizing Public Affairs Performance*, Management Handbook series, ed. Craig S. Fleisher (Washington, DC: Public Affairs Council, 1997).

[9] Craig S. Fleisher, "Emerging U.S. Public Affairs Practice: The 2001 PA Model," *Journal of Public Affairs* 1, no. 1 (January 2001), pp. 44–52.

Exhibit 2.A   Corporate Public Affairs Activities

Which of the following activities are currently conducted within your public affairs department?

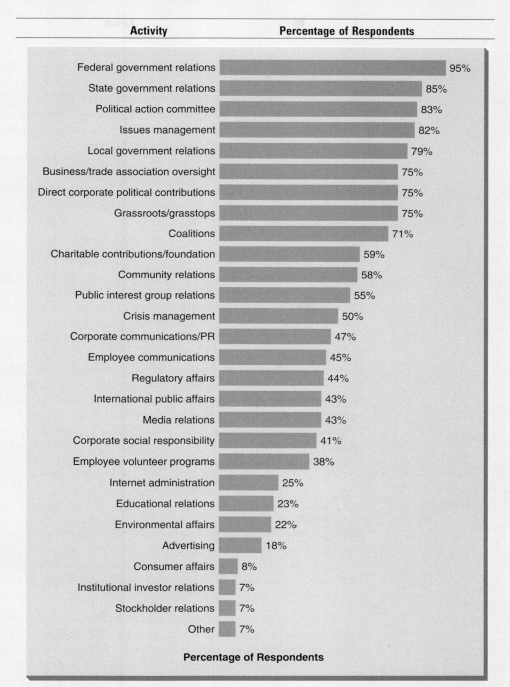

Activity	Percentage of Respondents
Federal government relations	95%
State government relations	85%
Political action committee	83%
Issues management	82%
Local government relations	79%
Business/trade association oversight	75%
Direct corporate political contributions	75%
Grassroots/grasstops	75%
Coalitions	71%
Charitable contributions/foundation	59%
Community relations	58%
Public interest group relations	55%
Crisis management	50%
Corporate communications/PR	47%
Employee communications	45%
Regulatory affairs	44%
International public affairs	43%
Media relations	43%
Corporate social responsibility	41%
Employee volunteer programs	38%
Internet administration	25%
Educational relations	23%
Environmental affairs	22%
Advertising	18%
Consumer affairs	8%
Institutional investor relations	7%
Stockholder relations	7%
Other	7%

Percentage of Respondents

Source: Foundation for Public Affairs, *State of Corporate Public Affairs* (September 2005), p. 9. Based on a survey of 151 companies. Used by permission.

29

decisions. The size of the department and the support staff varies widely among companies. Many companies assign employees from other parts of the business to work on public affairs issues and to help plan, coordinate, and execute public affairs activities. In this way, the formulation and implementation of the policies and programs developed by a company's public affairs unit are closely linked to the primary business activities of the firm.

> Unilever, a transnational corporation based in the Netherlands and the United Kingdom, makes laundry detergent, shampoo, toothpaste, tea, ice cream, frozen foods, and many other consumer products. It provides an example of how one company has organized its public affairs function. The company's chairman and board of directors (called an executive committee in Europe) have overall responsibility for managing external relations at the corporate level. A committee of the board called the External Affairs and Corporate Relations Committee is charged with this specific responsibility. A full-time corporate development director is responsible for working with other managers around the world to handle the public affairs function. For example, in Canada, this role is held by an executive whose title is manager of environmental and corporate affairs. This job is described on the company's Web site as "creating a link between the company and its local communities." Unilever's external relations activities are organized and coordinated at many levels—from the board down to the business unit.[10]

The heads of most public affairs departments are senior vice president or vice president positions; some report directly to the CEO, while others are one level below this in the organizational hierarchy. Most work out of company headquarters; most of the rest—particularly those whose work focuses on government relations—work in Washington, D.C. Thirty percent of major companies have an external relations committee of the board of directors.[11] A 2005 survey of CEOs conducted by McKinsey showed that these executives believed that overall responsibility for managing sociopolitical issues should rest at the top. Fifty-six percent reported that the CEO or chair *did* take the lead in this area, but 74 percent thought the CEO or chair *should* take the lead. This finding suggests their perception of the growing importance of public issues and the need to link the work of the public affairs department closely with strategic oversight at top levels of the corporation.[12] This group's opinion of what tactics used by public affairs managers are most effective is presented in Exhibit 2.B.

International Public Affairs Management

Public affairs management necessarily must be global or international, since public issues know no national boundaries and business practices are increasingly international in scope. Attention to public issues is a common concern in every country. Businesses in other nations have also developed extensive public affairs functions. And many U.S.-based businesses have extended their public affairs activities globally.

> Public affairs managers all over the world were challenged by the explosion of the global issue of outsourcing, where companies would contract for services to be provided by individuals located in a country other than where the company was based. In March 2004, 86 percent of executives polled said they expected to send

---

[10] Information on Unilever's corporate structure is available online at: *www.unilever.com/company/corporatestructure.*

[11] Foundation for Public Affairs, *The State of Corporate Public Affairs,* September 2005 (Washington, DC: FAP, 2005), pp. 4–6.

[12] "The McKinsey Global Survey of Business Executives: Business and Society," *McKinsey Quarterly,* January 2006, Exhibit 3.

Exhibit 2.B
Most Effective Tactics to Manage Sociopolitical Issues

When large companies in your industry try to manage sociopolitical issues, which three tactics do you believe are most effective?

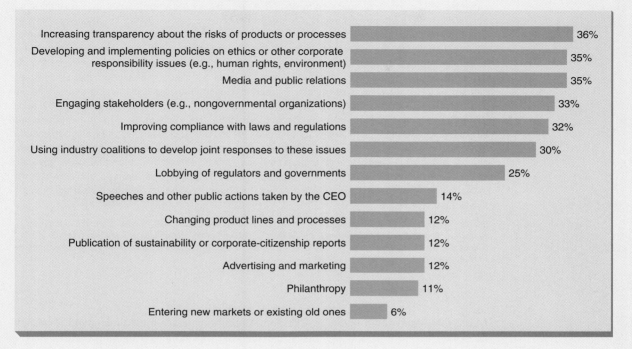

Tactic	Percentage
Increasing transparency about the risks of products or processes	36%
Developing and implementing policies on ethics or other corporate responsibility issues (e.g., human rights, environment)	35%
Media and public relations	35%
Engaging stakeholders (e.g., nongovernmental organizations)	33%
Improving compliance with laws and regulations	32%
Using industry coalitions to develop joint responses to these issues	30%
Lobbying of regulators and governments	25%
Speeches and other public actions taken by the CEO	14%
Changing product lines and processes	12%
Publication of sustainability or corporate-citizenship reports	12%
Advertising and marketing	12%
Philanthropy	11%
Entering new markets or existing old ones	6%

Source: "The McKinsey Global Survey of Business Executives: Business and Society," *McKinsey Quarterly,* January 2006, Exhibit 2. Based on a survey of 4,238 CEOs and top-level executives in 116 countries, conducted in December 2005. Used by permission.

more technical jobs overseas in the next 12 months. Many businesses sought individuals, often in India, the Philippines, Mexico, or China, to provide low-cost communications programming or call-center work to support their operations or services. The Coalition for Economic Growth and American Jobs, composed of 200 U.S. trade groups, began a public relations and political campaign to prevent or slow down the outsourcing of U.S. labor to other countries. However, others argued that more jobs are imported into the United States in the areas of construction, transportation, and education and health services, due to the high technical skills of the American labor force. And, of course, the outsourcing trend provided jobs and helped build a middle class in many developing countries.[13]

Businesses have recently understood the importance of developing public affairs abilities in order to be effective in the international arena. For example, public affairs managers must develop intercultural competencies, understanding cultural disparities as well as similarities. The impact of the organization's policies or practices could have markedly different impacts given the culture, social or political systems, or history of a country

[13] "Business Coalition Battles Outsourcing Backlash," *The Wall Street Journal,* March 1, 2004, pp. A1, A10; "More Work Is Outsourced to U.S., Than Away From It," *The Wall Street Journal,* March 15, 2004, pp. A2, A4; "Offshore Outsourcing Will Increase, Poll Finds," *The Wall Street Journal,* March 26, 2004, p. B3; and "Outsourcing May Create U.S. Jobs," *The Wall Street Journal,* March 30, 2004, p. A2.

Exhibit 2.C   Nike and the Organic Exchange

Corporations often encounter public issues that they cannot effectively address by themselves but only by working collaboratively with other businesses and concerned stakeholders in international networks. One such issue that confronted Nike, Inc., was a growing demand by environmentally aware consumers for apparel and shoes made from organic cotton. Cotton, traditionally cultivated with large quantities of synthetic fertilizers, pesticides, and herbicides, is one of the world's most environmentally destructive crops. In the late 1990s, in response both to consumer pressure and to its own internal commitments, Nike began for the first time to incorporate organic cotton into its sports apparel products. Its intention was to ramp up slowly, achieving 5 percent organic content by 2010. However, Nike quickly encountered many barriers to achieving even these limited objectives. Farmers were reluctant to transition to organic methods without a sure market, processors found it inefficient to shut down production lines to clean them for organic runs, and banks were unwilling to loan money for unproven technologies. The solution, it turned out, involved extensive collaboration with groups throughout the supply chain—farmers, cooperatives, merchants, processors, and financial institutions—as well as other companies that were buyers of cotton, to facilitate the emergence of a global market for organic cotton. The outcome was the formation in 2003 of a new organization called the Organic Exchange, in which Nike continues to play a leading role.

Source: The Web site for the Organic Exchange is *www.organicexchange.org*. Nike's description of its efforts is available online at *www.nike.com/nikebiz*. This case is discussed in Ann C. Svendsen and Myriam Laberge, "Convening Stakeholder Networks: A New Way of Thinking, Being, and Engaging," *Journal of Corporate Citizenship* 19 (Autumn 2005), pp. 91–104.

where the organization operates. The public affairs manager must understand local public policy institutions and processes and the role that nongovernmental entities play in the public policy process. Language skills are critical for a public affairs manager seeking to be effective in an international media environment. The ability to communicate with local media and other stakeholder groups in their native language and avoid embarrassing or misleading communication due to poor translations must be assured. All of these basic public affairs tasks are more complex in an international business environment but must be mastered by an effective public affairs manager.[14]

Nike encountered a complex public issue that needed to be addressed by a well-organized, international public affairs management plan—carried out by a network of companies and stakeholder groups—when it began to introduce organic cotton into its production processes, as described in Exhibit 2.C.

Issue Management

One primary function of the public affairs office, in the United States and in other nations, is to manage public issues as they emerge. **Issue management** is a structured and systematic process to aid organizations in identifying, monitoring, and selecting public issues that warrant organizational action. These are the issues that are perceived to be of greatest importance to the organization. Organizations rarely have full control of a public issue because of the many factors involved. But it is possible for the organization to create a management system that identifies and monitors issues as they emerge and, if they are

[14] For a thorough discussion on these issues see Craig S. Fleisher, "The Development of Competencies in International Public Affairs," *Journal of Public Affairs* 3, no. 3 (March 2003), pp. 76–82.

selected for response, involves managers in action to minimize the negative effects of a public issue or to maximize its positive effects. Some of these issues will have a significant impact on the business's profitability; others might not, or might not for a long time.

Scanning the Environment

To identify those public issues that require attention and action, a firm needs a framework of environmental information. (In this context, *environmental* means *outside the organization*; in Chapters 11 and 12, the term refers to the natural environment.) **Environmental analysis** provides managers with the information about external issues and trends that enables an organization to develop a strategy that minimizes threats and takes advantage of new opportunities.

Environmental intelligence is the acquisition of information gained from analyzing the multiple environments affecting organizations. Acquiring this information may be done informally or as a formal management process. If done well, this environmental intelligence can help an organization avoid crises and spot opportunities.

> Coca-Cola learned their lesson the hard way about how important it is to scan the environment for potential threats when it failed to anticipate the damage to its sales that could be caused by a small group of determined activists halfway around the world. Amit Srivastava ran the India Resource Center, a nonprofit organization that had just one full-time employee: himself. Nonetheless, Srivastava caused significant damage to Coca-Cola's operations in India and the firm's reputation worldwide. During a tour of U.S. college campuses in 2005, Srivastava accused Coca-Cola of stealing water from local residents, poisoning land, and selling drinks laced with dangerous pesticides. In Kerala, India, local officials shut down a $16 million bottling plant after claims made by local residents and Indian activists that Coca-Cola drained and polluted local water supplies. An Indian court issued an order requiring soft-drink makers to list pesticide residues on their labels. Coca-Cola was forced to fight legal and legislative battles across India because of Srivastava's claims, even though some were unsubstantiated.[15]

According to management scholar Karl Albrecht, scanning to acquire environmental intelligence should focus on eight strategic radar screens or environments.[16] The eight environments identified by Albrecht are shown in Figure 2.3 and described next.

- *Customer environment* includes the demographic factors, such as gender, age, marital status, and other factors, of the organization's customers as well as their social values or preferences. For example, the "graying" of the population as members of the baby boom generation age has created opportunities for developers that specialize in building communities for active older adults.

- *Competitor environment* includes information on the number and strength of the organization's competitors, whether they are potential or actual allies, patterns of aggressive growth versus static maintenance of market share, and the potential for customers to become competitors if they "insource" products or services previously purchased from the organization.

- *Economic environment* includes information about costs, prices, international trade, and any other features of the economic environment that affect customers or competitor

---

[15] "How a Global Web of Activists Gives Coke Problems in India," *The Wall Street Journal,* June 7, 2005, *www.wsj.com.*

[16] Adapted from Karl Albrecht, *Corporate Radar: Tracking the Forces That Are Shaping Your Business* (New York: American Management Association, 2000).

FIGURE 2.3
**Eight Strategic
Radar Screens**

Source: Karl Albrecht,
*Corporate Radar: Tracking
Forces That Are Shaping Your
Business* (New York: American
Management Association,
2000).

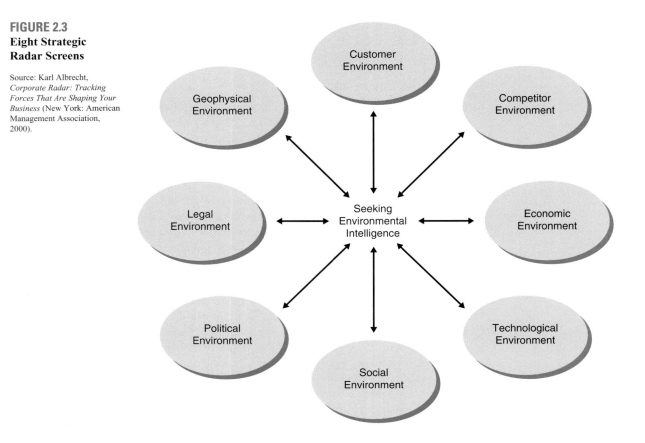

behavior. The example of pressure to reduce drug prices at the beginning of this chapter illustrated a shift in the economic environment of pharmaceutical companies.

- *Technological environment* includes the development of new technologies and their applications affecting the organization, its customers, and other stakeholder groups. The ease with which people could download music from the Internet, and the emergence of software that allowed them to swap files with others, forced the music industry to change its business model fundamentally in the early 2000s.

- *Social environment* includes cultural patterns, values, beliefs, trends, and conflicts among the people in the societies where the organization conducts business or might conduct business. Issues of civil or human rights, family values, and the roles of special interest groups are important elements in acquiring intelligence from the social environment.

- *Political environment* includes the structure, processes, and actions of all levels of government—local, state, national, and international. The stability or instability of a government or the inclination or disinclination to pass laws and regulations are essential environmental intelligence for the organization. The emergence of strict environmental laws in Europe—including requirements to limit waste and provide for recycling at the end of a product's life—have caused firms all over the world that sell to Europeans to rethink how they design and package their products.

- *Legal environment* includes legal considerations of patents, copyrights, trademarks, and intellectual property, as well as antitrust considerations, trade protectionism, and organizational liability.

- *Geophysical environment* includes an awareness of the physical surroundings of the organization's facilities and operations, whether it is the organization's headquarters or its field offices and distribution centers, and the organization's dependency and impact on natural resources such as minerals, water, land, or air. Growing concerns about global warming and climate change, for example, have caused many firms to seek to improve their energy efficiency.

The eight strategic radar screens, as presented in Figure 2.3, represent a system of interrelated segments, each one connected to and influencing the others. The discussion case at the end of this chapter describes how one company, Wal-Mart, was challenged to respond to changes in several aspects of its external environment. It is important that companies attend to potential change in all segments of their external environments.

Companies do not become experts in acquiring environmental intelligence overnight. New attitudes have to be developed, new routines learned, and new policies and action programs designed. Many obstacles must be overcome in developing and implementing the effective scanning of the business environments. Some are structural, such as the reporting relationships between groups of managers; others are cultural, such as changing traditional ways of doing things. In addition, the dynamic nature of the business environments requires the organization to continuously evaluate the effectiveness of its scanning procedures. Building ongoing, positive relationships with stakeholders is one important strategy for learning more on a regular basis about how people outside the organization are thinking, and what issues are important to them.

Competitive Intelligence

Another important environmental scanning function often entrusted to the public affairs manager is collecting competitive intelligence. **Competitive intelligence** is the systematic and continuous process of gathering, analyzing, and managing external information about the organization's competitors that can affect the organization's plans, decisions, and operations. The acquisition of competitive intelligence enhances an organization's marketplace competitiveness through a greater understanding of the competitive environment. Competitive intelligence enables managers in organizations of all sizes to make informed decisions ranging from marketing, research and development, and investing tactics to long-term business strategies. Clearly, numerous ethical issues are raised in the acquisition and use of competitive intelligence. A public affairs officer must be aware of these issues, often clarified in the organization's code of ethics.[17]

A survey of global business leaders indicated the growing importance given to competitive intelligence as a tool for businesses in today's economic environment. "During difficult times, excellent competitive intelligence can be the differentiating factor in the marketplace," explained Paul Meade, vice president at Best Practices.

> Companies that can successfully gather and analyze competitive information, then implement strategic decisions based on that analysis, position themselves to be ahead of the pack.[18]

The importance of ethical considerations when collecting competitive intelligence cannot be overstated. One example where competitive intelligence may have been collected unethically became the focus of an SEC investigation.

---

[17] For information about the professional association serving this public affairs function, particularly the attention to ethical considerations, see the Society of Competitive Intelligence Professionals Web site at *www.scip.org*.

[18] See Best Practices report at *www.benchmarkingreports.com/competitiveintelligence*.

Boeing Company was locked in a fierce battle with Lockheed Martin to be the dominant manufacturer of rockets to launch surveillance, communications, and other satellites for the U.S. government. Kenneth Branch, a well-known space engineer and manager with Lockheed's rocket team, arrived at Boeing's rocket headquarters in California for a scheduled job interview. Before Branch left the interview, he pulled from his briefcase a presentation of Lockheed's rocket project and showed this material to the Boeing executives, according to a sworn statement made by an interview observer. Six months later, Branch was hired to work on Boeing's rocket program. The SEC investigation focused on whether Boeing intentionally obtained or used competitive-sensitive documents belonging to Lockheed as part of a carefully devised plot to win the military rocket contract from the U.S. government. Boeing disciplined six employees involved in this scandal, reportedly to persuade the U.S. government to reinstate the company as its rocket supplier.[19]

As the Boeing–Lockheed Martin story indicates, the importance of acquiring a competitor's intelligence may tempt businesses to use unethical or illegal means. However, the *ethical* acquisition of competitors' intelligence remains one of the most valued benefits emerging from the public affairs function.

The Issue Management Process

Environmental scanning is an ongoing process, designed to turn up public issues that are of concern to the company and its stakeholders. It provides the foundation for the core function of the public affairs officer or office: to act on this knowledge. The **issue management process,** illustrated in Figure 2.4, comprises five steps, or stages.[20] Each of these steps is discussed below, using the example of McDonald's response to emerging stakeholder concerns about the humane treatment of farm animals raised for food. As the largest buyer of beef and the second largest buyer of chicken in the United States, McDonald's was vulnerable to stakeholder pressure on this issue, but also was well positioned to take action and move ahead of its competitors.

Issue Identification

Issue identification involves anticipating emerging concerns, sometimes called "horizon issues" by managers because they seem to be just coming up over the horizon, like the first morning sun—or a potential storm cloud. Sometimes managers become aware of issues by carefully tracking the media, experts' views, and legislative developments to identify issues of concern to the public. Normally, this requires attention to all eight of the environments described in Figure 2.3. Organizations often use techniques of data searching, media analysis, and public surveys to track ideas, themes, and issues that may be relevant to their interests from all over the world. They also rely on ongoing conversations with key stakeholders. Sometimes, awareness of issues is forced on companies by lawsuits or protests by activists who hold strong views about a particular matter.

In 1997, a judge handed down a decision in a legal dispute between McDonald's and several of the company's critics in the United Kingdom, calling the company "culpabl[y] responsible for cruel practices [toward animals]." People for the Ethical Treatment of Animals (PETA), an animal rights organization based in the

---

[19] "U.S. Probes Whether Boeing Misused a Rival's Document," *The Wall Street Journal,* May 5, 2003, pp. A1, A7; and "Boeing Employees Are Disciplined in Espionage Case," *The Wall Street Journal,* September 12, 2003, p. A2.

[20] Other depictions of the development of a public issue can be found in Rogene Buchholz, *Public Issues for Management,* 2nd ed. (Englewood Cliffs, NJ: Prentice Hall, 1992); Robert Heath, *Strategic Issues Management* (Thousand Oaks, CA: Sage, 1997); and Eli Sopow, *The Critical Issues Audit* (Leesburg, VA: Issues Action Publications, 1994).

FIGURE 2.4
The Issue
Management Process

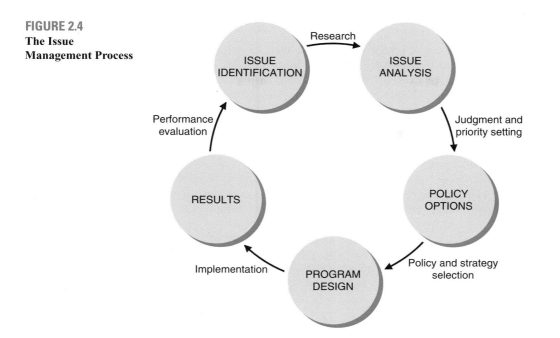

United States, immediately followed up with a campaign against McDonald's and other fast food companies. The group charged, among other things, that chickens used to produce McNuggets were crammed by the tens of thousands into sheds that stunk of ammonia fumes from accumulated waste, suffered broken bones from being bred to be top heavy, and were slaughtered by having their throats slit while still conscious. PETA wrote the McDonald's CEO and campaigned publicly for its goals, including sponsoring shareholder resolutions, placing provocative ads, and mounting public demonstrations to pressure McDonald's and other fast food companies to change their practices.

McDonald's had been aware of the animal welfare issue for some time and had held discussions with organizations such as Animal Rights International. But PETA's challenge elevated the urgency to the company of the issue of humane treatment of animals and put it squarely on the agenda of managers.

Issue Analysis

Once an issue has been identified, its implications must be analyzed. Organizations must understand how the issue is likely to evolve, and how it is likely to affect them. For each company, the ramifications of the issue will be different.

How the animal welfare issue affected McDonald's was complex. On one hand, the company was concerned about public perception, and did not want customers to turn away because of concerns about the mistreatment of cows, pigs, and chickens used for food. On the other hand, it was also concerned about maintaining standards for food quality and keeping down costs. An added complexity was that McDonald's did not raise its own animals for slaughter, but relied on a network of suppliers for its meat, including such major firms as Tyson, ConAgra, and National Beef. In order to influence the treatment of animals, it would need to collaborate closely with companies in its supply chain.

A result of the issue analysis process for McDonald's was an understanding that it would need to work with ranchers, poultry farmers, meat processors, and others to address it stakeholders' concerns.

Option Generation, Evaluation, and Selection

An issue's public profile indicates to managers how significant an issue is for the organization, but it does not tell them what to do. The next step in the issue management process involves generating, evaluating, and selecting among possible options. This requires complex judgments that incorporate ethical considerations, the organization's reputation and good name, and other nonquantifiable factors.

> McDonald's began discussions with Temple Grandin, a renowned academic expert, to consider possible options. Professor Grandin had developed a methodology for objectively measuring animal welfare in slaughterhouses and had created audit protocols based on these measures. McDonald's vice president for corporate responsibility later recalled the "magic moment" in 1997 when Grandin presented her concept of an audit program to company managers. "We saw it as something that had tremendous potential," he commented. The company began experimenting with slaughterhouse audits (inspections) in 1999, to see how the system might work in practice. The company also sought to learn more about animal welfare on the thousands of farms that supplied chickens, cows, and pigs to its meat processing partners. In 2000, McDonald's convened an Animal Welfare Council of experts to continue to advise the company and explore possible options.

Selecting an appropriate response often involves a creative process of considering various alternatives and rigorously testing them to see how they work in practice.

Program Design and Implementation

Once an option has been chosen, the organization must design and implement a program to implement it.

> In 2001, McDonald's issued a set of guiding principles for animal welfare, affirming the company's belief that "animals should be free from abuse and neglect" and that animal welfare is "an integral part of an overall quality assurance program that makes good business sense." The company also formalized its audit program, completing 500 audits worldwide of beef, poultry, and pork processing plants in 2002. In the small number of cases where the results were "not acceptable," the company required the facility to take corrective action. The company also sponsored animal welfare training for its suppliers to bring them on board.

Assessment of Results and Continuous Improvement

Once an organization has implemented the issue management program, it must continue to assess the results and make adjustments if necessary. Many public affairs managers see issue management as a continuous process, rather than one that comes to a clear conclusion.

> McDonald's continued to talk with animal welfare organizations, examine its own practices, and try new approaches. In 2005, the company launched a study of the feasibility of using a more humane way to slaughter chickens, called controlled-atmosphere killing, or CAK. Standard industry practice had been to hang chicken by their feet on a conveyer line and move them through a vat of water charged with electricity. In CAK, by contrast, oxygen in the air was slowly replaced by an inert gas. PETA responded by withdrawing a shareholder proposal that had criticized McDonald's for using a method that was cruel to animals. "McDonald's agreed to do what we asked it to do, and it agreed to do it sooner than we asked," said a PETA spokesperson.[21]

---

[21] "McD Seeks a Less Cruel Way to Kill Chickens," *Nation's Restaurant News,* January 24, 2005, pp. 1–2.

Exhibit 2.D   **Is Issue Management an Art or a Science?**

A recent opinion article published in the *Journal of Public Affairs* by Tony Jacques, issue manager for the Dow Chemical Company in Asia-Pacific and a board member of the issue management council, offered the provocative thesis that issue management often overemphasizes technique and underemphasizes creative problem solving. Jacques pointed out that many of the techniques used to manage issues were highly systematized, involving computerized data scanning, media analysis, and information storing and sharing. The purpose, he suggested, was to "reduce variation and eliminate defects." This approach, Jacques argued, was wrong-headed. In his view, issue management "by definition deals with problems which are often subjective, highly emotive, prone to political whim, demanding judgment and compromise, and where 'perception is reality' and there is seldom a 'right answer.'" Data analysis can be useful in identifying issues, but not in determining out what to do about them. For that, creative problem-solving is required. Jacques concluded, "The reality is that issue management is neither all art nor all science. It has elements of both art and science . . . [T]he desired outcome of getting the balance right is not to deliver the perfect process but to deliver genuine bottom line . . . outcomes."

Source: Tony Jacques, "Issue Management: Process versus Progress," *Journal of Public Affairs* 6, no. 1 (February 2006), pp. 69–74.

This example illustrates the complexity of the issue management process. Figure 2.4 is deliberately drawn in the form of a loop. When working well, the issue management process continuously cycles back to the beginning and repeats, pulling in more information, generating more options, and improving programmatic response. Contemporary issue management is truly an interactive process, as forward-thinking companies continue their dialogue with their stakeholders about issues that matter. In 2006, McDonald's vice president for corporate responsibility began regularly posting to a blog where he talked with interested members of the public about the company's animal welfare policies. As a result, all parties continued to learn from one another.[22] Public affairs managers must not only implement programs, but also continue to reassess their actions to be consistent with both ethical practices and long-term survival. Is the issue management process an art or a science? One practitioner's observations are presented in Exhibit 2.D.

Companies are learning that it is important to take a strategic approach to the management of public issues, both domestically and globally. This requires thinking ahead, understanding what is important to stakeholders, scanning the environment, and formulating action plans that anticipate changes in the external environment. Effective issue management requires involvement by both professional staff and leaders at top levels of the organization. It entails communicating across organizational boundaries, engaging with the public, and working creatively to solve complex problems.

[22] Information on McDonald's animal welfare policies is available online at *www.mcdonalds.com/corp/values/ socialrespons/market/animalwelfare*. Its corporate responsibility blog is available online at: *http://csr.blogs.mcdonalds.com*. Information on PETA's campaign against McDonald's is available online at *www.mccruelty.com*. Dr. Temple Grandin's Web site is *www.grandin.com*.

Summary

- A public issue is an issue that is of mutual concern to an organization and one or more of the organization's stakeholders. Emerging public issues present a risk, but they also present an opportunity, because companies that correctly anticipate and respond to them can often obtain a competitive advantage.

- The organization of the corporation's boundary-spanning functions is complex. Most companies have many departments specifically charged with interacting with stakeholders. One of the most important of these is the department of public affairs.

- An organization's public affairs function or manager is charged with the active management of the organization's external relations. This function encompasses many diverse activities, ranging from government relations to issue management to grassroots communication, and often is international in scope.

- The eight strategic radar screens (the customer, competitor, economic, technological, social, political, legal, and geophysical environments) enable public affairs managers to assess and acquire information regarding their business environments. Managers must learn to look outward to understand key developments and anticipate their impact on the business.

- Competitive intelligence is the systematic and continuous process of gathering, analyzing, and managing information about an organization's competitors; this information is often important, but care must be taken to gather it ethically.

- The issue management process includes identification and analysis of issues, development of policy options, program design, and evaluation of the results of such activities.

Key Terms

boundary-spanning department, *26*	environmental intelligence, *33*	performance–expectations gap, *25*
competitive intelligence, *35*	issue identification, *36*	public affairs management, *28*
environmental analysis, *33*	issue management, *32*	public issue, *25*
	issue management process, *36*	

Internet Resources

www.gpai.org	Global Public Affairs Institute
www.issuemanagement.org	Issue Management Council
www.pac.org	Public Affairs Council
www.scip.org	Society of Competitive Intelligence Professionals
www.wfs.org	World Future Society

Discussion Case: *Wal-Mart and Its Public Opponents*

In the early 2000s, Wal-Mart targeted California for its latest expansion project, announcing plans to build 40 new supercenters—enormous stores that sell groceries alongside many other goods—during the next five years within the state. It soon ran into a broad-based backlash.

In the primarily African-American and Hispanic city of Inglewood, California, Wal-Mart proposed constructing a mega-store and collection of chain stores and restaurants on 60 acres of barren land near the Hollywood Park racetrack. This development promised to generate more than 1,000 permanent new jobs in the neighborhood, add $3 to $5 million annually to the distressed city's tax base, and provide a revenue stream to finance as much as $100 million in new bonds. "We are talking about a new police station, a new community and cultural center, and upgrades for existing parks in the area," said Roosevelt Dorn, Inglewood's mayor, a proponent of the project.

Despite the bright prospects for the city of Inglewood, opponents mobilized to block the retailer. One group that lined up against Wal-Mart was organized labor. The United Food and Commercial Workers (UFCW) at the time was enmeshed in a bruising conflict with the southern California grocery industry. Unionized grocery store chains, anticipating competition from nonunion Wal-Mart, were aggressively fighting the UFCW's wage and benefit demands.

Church groups and community groups also opposed the proposal, citing environmental, traffic, and public safety concerns. They argued that Wal-Mart was requesting exemptions from nearly all city ordinances, which would create a virtual "company town" within the Inglewood city limits where none of the normal zoning or other regulations would apply. While some residents were not opposed to Wal-Mart itself, they were very disturbed by the way the company was attempting to avoid basic commercial rules imposed on all other businesses operating in Inglewood. "The question was whether the wealthiest company in the world could circumvent the law," said a local state assemblyman.

Many small business owners in the area feared that the large retail chain would drive them out of business. Reports circulated around Inglewood from other neighborhoods alleging that Wal-Mart would enter the market with below-cost pricing of key items in order to eliminate the small-business competition. Then, after the competition was gone, the prices would rise to a comfortable profit margin for Wal-Mart. The elected city council, responding to the concerns of its constituents, rejected Wal-Mart's proposed development.

Wal-Mart countered with political advocacy. Using paid signature collectors, Wal-Mart collected more than the 10,000 signatures needed to place their proposal on the ballot. The initiative, if approved by voters, would essentially exempt Wal-Mart from all of the city's planning, zoning and environmental regulations, creating a "city within a city" subject only to its own rules. Wal-Mart hired an advertising and public relations firm to market the initiative and spent more than $1 million to support the measure. Opponents of the initiative accused Wal-Mart of bullying tactics and claimed that if the initiative succeeded in Inglewood, it would be a model for Wal-Mart sovereignty across the nation and around the globe.

In April 2004, Inglewood residents voted 60 to 40 percent against the Wal-Mart initiative. "This means that Wal-Mart has to go through the front door and deal with cities and communities as equals," said Madeline Janis-Aparicio, leader of the Coalition for a Better Inglewood. "They can't trick cities and communities into giving away the store, getting everything they want without any oversight. They're going to have to do business differently if they want to do business in California."

Bob McAdam, vice president of corporate affairs at Wal-Mart explained, "We are disappointed that a small group of Inglewood leaders together with representatives of outside special interests were able to convince a majority of Inglewood voters that they don't deserve the job opportunities and shopping choices that others in the L.A. area enjoy. . . . This is just about one store. . . . It will have no implications beyond that. We're still going to meet our goal of building the stores we predicted we'd build."

Source: "Stymied by Politicians, Wal-Mart Turns to Voters," *The New York Times*, April 5, 2004, *www.nytimes.com;* "Voters in Los Angeles Suburb Say No to a Big Wal-Mart," *The New York Times*, April 8, 2004, *www.nytimes.com;* "Los Angeles to Wal-Mart: Bigger's Not Always Better," *The Washington Post,* February 3, 2004, p. A3.

Discussion Questions

1. Do you think a gap existed between the expectations of the public and Wal-Mart's performance? If so, in what respects did the two differ? In your answer, please refer to the concept of a performance–expectations gap.

2. If Wal-Mart's public affairs managers had scanned the external environment prior to planning its expansion, using the eight strategic radar screens presented in Figure 2.3, what segments would have been of greatest concern to them? Which environments were critical in this case?

3. Referring to the issue management process, shown in Figure 2.4, did Wal-Mart move through all stages of the process in its response to community opposition? If not, which stages are illustrated by this case?

4. Referring to Exhibit 2.A, which public affairs activities did Wal-Mart's managers use to attempt to defuse the opposition to its expansion plans? Do you think Wal-Mart's strategy was appropriate, or not?

5. If you had been a public affairs manager at Wal-Mart, what actions would you have recommended, and why?

PART TWO

Business and the Social Environment

CHAPTER THREE

Corporate Social Responsibility

Corporate social responsibility challenges businesses to attend to and interact with the firm's stakeholders while they pursue traditional economic goals. Both market and nonmarket stakeholders expect businesses to be socially responsible, and many companies have responded by making social goals a part of their overall business operations. What it means to act in socially responsible ways is not always clear, thus producing controversy about what constitutes such behavior, how extensive it should be, and what it costs to be socially responsible.

This chapter focuses on these key learning objectives:

- Understanding the basic meaning of corporate social responsibility.
- Knowing where and when the idea of social responsibility originated.
- Examining the critical arguments for and against corporate social responsibility.
- Assessing how business meets its economic and legal obligations while being socially responsible.
- Investigating how business balances its responsibilities to multiple stakeholders, including its stockholders.

Do managers have a responsibility to their stockholders? Certainly they do, because the owners of the business have invested their capital in the firm. Do managers also have a responsibility, a social responsibility, to their company's other market and nonmarket stakeholders—the people who live where the firm operates, who purchase the firm's product or service, or who work for the firm? While managers may have a clear responsibility to respond to all stakeholders, what happens when these multiple responsibilities seem to clash?

GSK Biologicals, the vaccine subsidiary of GlaxoSmithKline, bet that it could combat a global disease while still making money. In 2004, GSK introduced a new vaccine against rotavirus, a parasite that caused a deadly digestive illness. Typically, pharmaceutical companies roll out new medicines first in wealthy, industrialized countries to recoup their investment in research and development, before taking them to impoverished, developing countries. But, Jean Stephenne, president of GSK Bio, decided to take a bold, new approach, taking the drug first to Latin America, where the company committed $300 million to test the new vaccine—one of the largest and most expensive trials since the Salk vaccine for polio more than 50 years ago. This time, the target population was 60,000 low- and middle-income children living in various Latin American countries. Stephenne believed it was important to concentrate initially where the medical need was the greatest, even if there was little potential for immediate profit. If successful in Latin America, Stephenne planned to roll out the vaccine in Asia, then eventually in Europe, saving the United States, the most lucrative market, for last. "Our business model is to supply vaccines to the world, not just the U.S. and Europe," said Stephenne. The company hoped that its rotavirus vaccine, and others under development, would attract support from charities like the Gates Foundation and government aid to poor countries.[1]

Is GSK Biologicals, under the leadership of Jean Stephenne, acting responsibly toward the firm's stockholders, or are his concerns for helping the poor and sick clouding his business judgment? Should businesses be more concerned about serving customers where the need is greatest, or focus on securing profits? Is it possible that in the long run, Stephenne's strategy will actually make more money for his company than a more conventional strategy might?

This chapter defines corporate social responsibility and discusses the advantages and drawbacks of being socially responsible. Most of all, though, it argues that stakeholders worldwide increasingly demand that corporations practice social responsibility. Whether businesses are large or small, make goods or provide services, operate at home or abroad, willingly try to be socially responsible or fight against it all the way, there is no doubt about what the public expects. Many business leaders also subscribe to the idea of social responsibility. Exhibit 3.A lists some of the organizations that support stakeholders seeking information on or examples of corporate social responsibility.

The Meaning of Corporate Social Responsibility

Corporate social responsibility (CSR) means that a corporation should be held accountable for any of its actions that affect people, their communities, and their environment. It implies that harm to people and society should be acknowledged and corrected if at all

---

[1] "Vaccinating the World's Poor," *BusinessWeek*, April 26, 2004, pp. 65–69.

- Responsible Shopper (*www.responsibleshopper.org*) assists consumers by providing information on businesses' responsible and irresponsible practices, such as their environmental impacts, employee benefit programs, and financial reporting abuses.
- Social Funds (*www.socialfunds.com*) is a Web site run by SRI World Group. This site reports breaking financial news, promotes socially responsible mutual funds, and enables individuals to build an investment portfolio of socially responsible companies. Social Funds provides a free weekly e-mail newsletter, *SRI News Alert,* which includes issues beyond social investing.
- CorpWatch (*www.corpwatch.org*) is called "The Watchdog on the Web." Information on this Web site—often unavailable on other Web sites—focuses on human rights abuses abroad, public policy, and environmental news.
- Business and Social Initiatives Database (*www.ilo.org/public/english/employment/multi/basi.htm*) is sponsored by the International Labor Organization. It compiles Internet sources on employment and labor issues, such as child labor, living wage, safe working conditions, and more.
- Capital Partnership Group (*cog.kent.edu*) is a virtual think tank of individuals who focus on issues of employee ownership. Academics and business leaders contribute to the discussions posted on this Web site, with hundreds of research papers and reports on topics such as labor-sponsored venture capital and employee governance available.
- The Green Business Letter (*www.GreenBiz.com*) emphasizes environmental business activities. Visitors to this Web site can find what companies are doing, pending environmental legislation, job listings for environmental professionals, or access to many other environmentally oriented Web sites.

Source: "Web Watch: Best Resources for Corporate Social Responsibility," *Business Ethics*, Summer 2001, pp. 16–19.

possible. It may require a company to forgo some profits if its social impacts seriously hurt some of its stakeholders or if its funds can be used to have a positive social impact.

The Many Responsibilities of Business

However, being socially responsible does not mean that a company must abandon its other missions. As discussed later in this chapter, a business has many responsibilities: economic, legal, and social. The challenge for management is the blending of these responsibilities into a comprehensive corporate strategy while not losing sight of any of its obligations. At times these responsibilities will clash; at other times they will work together to better the firm. Thus, having multiple and sometimes competing responsibilities does not mean that socially responsible firms cannot be as profitable as others less responsible; some are and some are not.

Social responsibility requires companies to balance the benefits to be gained against the costs of achieving those benefits. Many people believe that both business and society gain when firms actively strive to be socially responsible. Others are doubtful, saying that taking on social tasks weakens business's competitive strength. The arguments on both sides of this debate are presented later in this chapter.

Social Responsibility and Corporate Power

The social responsibilities of business grow directly out of two features of the modern corporation: (1) the essential function it performs for a variety of stakeholders and (2) the immense influence it has on the lives of the stakeholders. We count on corporations for job creation; much of our community well-being; the standard of living we enjoy; the tax base for essential municipal, state, and national services; and our needs for banking and financial services, insurance, transportation, communication, utilities, entertainment, and a growing proportion of health care. These positive achievements suggest that the corporate form of business is capable of performing a great amount of good for society, such as encouraging economic growth, expanding international trade, and creating new technology.

The following well-known quotation, frequently appearing in journals for business executives, challenges the readers to assume a responsible role for business in society:

> Business has become, in the last half century, the most powerful institution on the planet. The dominant institution in any society needs to take responsibility for the whole. . . . Every decision that is made, every action that is taken, must be viewed in light of that kind of responsibility.[2]

Most of the 100 largest economies in the world are global corporations. The world's largest 200 companies account for more than a quarter of the world's economic activity and have twice the economic clout of the poorest four-fifths of humanity. About one-third of world trade is simply transactions among units of the same company.

Many people are concerned about the enormous influence of business. The focused power found in the modern business corporation means that every action it takes could affect the quality of human life—for individuals, for communities, and for the entire globe. This obligation is often referred to as the *iron law of responsibility*. The **iron law of responsibility** says that in the long run, those who do not use power in ways that society considers responsible will tend to lose it.[3] With such technology as global computer networks, instantaneous commercial transactions, and exponentially increasing collection and storage of information drawing the world into a tighter and tighter global village, the entire planet has become a stakeholder of all corporations. All societies are now affected by corporate operations. As a result, social responsibility has become a worldwide expectation.

How Corporate Social Responsibility Began

In the United States, the idea of corporate social responsibility appeared around the start of the 20th century. Corporations at that time came under attack for being too big, too powerful, and guilty of antisocial and anticompetitive practices. Critics tried to curb corporate power through antitrust laws, banking regulations, and consumer-protection laws.

Faced with this social protest, a few farsighted business executives advised corporations to use their power and influence voluntarily for broad social purposes rather than for profits alone. Some of the wealthiest business leaders—steelmaker Andrew Carnegie is a good example—became great philanthropists who gave much of their wealth to educational and charitable institutions. Others, like automaker Henry Ford, developed paternalistic programs to support the recreational and health needs of their employees. (A recent example is Warren Buffet, when in 2006, he gave the bulk of his $44 billion fortune to the Bill and Melinda Gates Foundation and four other philanthropies.) These business leaders believed that business had a responsibility to society that went beyond or worked with their efforts to make profits.[4]

---

[2] David C. Korten, "Limits to the Social Responsibility of Business," *The People-Centered Development Forum*, article 19, release date: June 1, 1996.

[3] This concept first appeared in Keith Davis and Robert Blomstrom, *Business and Its Environment* (New York: McGraw-Hill, 1966).

[4] Harold R. Bowen, *Social Responsibility of the Businessman* (New York: Harper, 1953); and Morrell Heald, *The Social Responsibility of Business: Company and Community, 1900–1960* (Cleveland: Case Western Reserve Press, 1970). For a history of how some of these business philanthropists acquired their wealth, see Matthew Josephson, *The Robber Barons: The Great American Capitalists* (New York: Harcourt Brace, 1934).

FIGURE 3.1
Foundation Principles of Corporate Social Responsibility

	Charity Principle	Stewardship Principle
Definition	• Business should give voluntary aid to society's needy persons and groups	• Business, acting as a public trustee, should consider the interests of all who are affected by business decisions and policies
Type of activity	• Corporate philanthropy • Voluntary actions to promote the social good	• Acknowledging business and society interdependence • Balancing the interests and needs of many diverse groups in society
Examples	• Corporate philanthropic foundations • Private initiatives to solve social problems • Social partnerships with needy groups	• Enlightened self-interest • Meeting legal requirements • Stakeholder approach to corporate strategic planning

As a result of these early ideas about business's expanded role in society, two broad principles emerged; they are described in Figure 3.1 and in the following sections of this chapter. These principles shaped business thinking about social responsibility during the 20th century and are the foundation stones for the modern idea of corporate social responsibility.

The Charity Principle

The **charity principle,** the idea that the wealthiest members of society should be charitable toward those less fortunate, is a very ancient notion. When Andrew Carnegie and other wealthy business leaders endowed public libraries, supported settlement houses for the poor, gave money to educational institutions, and contributed funds to many other community organizations, they were continuing this long tradition of being "my brother's keeper."

> Andrew Carnegie and John D. Rockefeller are usually credited with pioneering the path of the great modern philanthropists. For some years, the world's newspapers kept score on the giving. *The London Times* reported that in 1903 Carnegie had given away $21 million, Rockefeller $10 million. In 1913, *The New York Herald* ran a final box score: Carnegie, $332 million; Rockefeller, $175 million. All this was before the income tax and other tax provisions had generated external incentives to giving. The feeling of duty to the public good arose from inner sources.[5]

This kind of private aid to the needy members of society was especially important in the early decades of the last century. At that time, there was no Social Security, Medicare, unemployment pay, or United Way. There were few organizations capable of counseling troubled families, sheltering women and children who were victims of physical abuse, aiding alcoholics, treating the mentally ill or the disabled, or taking care of the destitute. When wealthy industrialists reached out to help others such as these, they were accepting some measure of responsibility for improving the conditions of life in

---

[5] Michael Novak, *Business as a Calling: Work and the Examined Life* (New York: The Free Press, 1996), p. 197.

their communities. In doing so, their actions helped counteract critics who claimed that business leaders were uncaring and interested only in profits.

Before long, when it was recognized that many community needs outpaced the riches of even the wealthiest persons and families, or beginning in about the 1920s, much of the charitable load was taken on by business firms themselves rather than by the owners alone. Business leaders often gave vigorous support to this form of corporate charity, urging all firms and their employees to unite their efforts to extend aid to the poor and the needy. Businesses built houses, churches, schools, and libraries, provided medical and legal services, and gave to charity.

For some of today's business firms, corporate social responsibility means participating in community affairs by making similar kinds of charitable contributions. The Giving USA Foundation reported that total U.S. charitable contributions (including disaster relief) in 2005 reached $260 billion, an all-time record.[6] Although many corporations today make generous contributions, as will be further discussed in Chapter 17, most observers nowadays believe that corporate social responsibility encompasses much more than just charity.

The Stewardship Principle

Many of today's corporate executives see themselves as stewards, or trustees, who act in the general public's interest. Although their companies are privately owned and they try to make profits for the stockholders, business leaders who follow the **stewardship principle** believe they have an obligation to see that everyone—particularly those in need or at risk—benefits from their firms' actions. According to this view, corporate managers have been placed in a position of public trust. They control vast resources whose use can affect people in fundamental ways. Because they exercise this kind of crucial influence, they incur a responsibility to use those resources in ways that are good not just for the stockholders alone but for society generally. In this way, they have become stewards, or trustees, for society, as well as for the natural environment. As such, they are expected to act with a special degree of responsibility in making business decisions.[7]

This kind of thinking eventually produced the modern theory of stakeholder management, which was described in the opening chapter of this book. According to this theory, corporate managers need to interact skillfully with all groups that have a stake in what the corporation does. If they do not do so, their firms will not be fully accepted by the public as legitimate.

> HP Brazil, a subsidiary of Hewlett-Packard, developed the Digital Garage project where the firm collaborated with local Brazilian foundations and youth clubs to provide young Brazilians from less privileged backgrounds the tools to develop self-esteem, creativity, sociability, entrepreneurship, leadership, citizenship, teamwork, and IT skills. HP Brazil management recognized their stewardship responsibility to serve as volunteer mentors and tutors for the local youths and to empower young people with skills to enable them to participate in the growing technological society.[8]

[6] Giving USA Foundation (formerly AAFRC), *Giving USA 2006* (Indianapolis, IN: 2006), pp. 14, 30.

[7] Two early statements of this stewardship-trustee view are Frank W. Abrams, "Management's Responsibilities in a Complex World," *Harvard Business Review*, May 1951; and Richard Eells, *The Meaning of Modern Business* (New York: Columbia University Press, 1960).

[8] "HP Wins International Corporate Conscience Award," HP press release, *www.hp.com/hpinfo*.

The Corporate Social Responsibility Debate

There are strong arguments on both sides of the debate about business's social responsibilities. When a person is exposed to arguments on both sides of the debate, she or he is in a better position to judge business actions in the social environment and to make more balanced business judgments.

Arguments for Corporate Social Responsibility

Who favors corporate social responsibility? Many business executives believe it is a good idea. A global survey of business executives conducted by McKinsey in 2005 found that 84 percent agreed large corporations should "generate high returns to investors but balance [this] with contributions to the broader public good," as shown in Figure 3.2.

FIGURE 3.2
Business Executives' Opinion of the Role of Business in Society

Which of the following statements best describes the role that large corporations (public and private) should play in society?

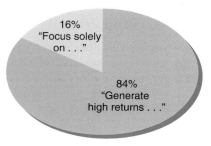

84% "Generate high returns to investors but balance with contributions to the broader public good" and 16% "Focus solely on providing the highest possible returns to investors while obeying all laws and regulations."

Source: "The McKinsey Global Survey of Business Executives: Business and Society," *McKinsey Quarterly,* January 2006. Based on a survey of 4,238 executives (more than a quarter of CEOs or other top executives) in 116 countries, conducted in December 2005. All data weighted by GDP of constituent countries to adjust for differences in response rates from various regions. Used by permission.

Many social groups that seek to preserve the environment, protect consumers, safeguard the safety and health of employees, prevent job discrimination, oppose invasions of privacy through Internet use, and maintain a strong return on their investment stress the importance of social responsibility by businesses. Government officials also ensure corporate compliance with laws and regulations that protect the general public from abusive business practices. In other words, both the supporters and the critics of business have reasons for wanting businesses to act in socially responsible ways. The major arguments used are listed in Figure 3.3.

FIGURE 3.3
The Pros and Cons of Corporate Social Responsibility

Arguments for Corporate Social Responsibility	Arguments against Corporate Social Responsibility
Balances corporate power with responsibility. Discourages government regulation. Promotes long-term profits for business. Improves business value and reputation. Corrects social problems caused by business.	Lowers economic efficiency and profit. Imposes unequal costs among competitors. Imposes hidden costs passed on to stakeholders. Requires skills business may lack. Places responsibility on business rather than individuals.

Balances Corporate Power with Responsibility

Today's business enterprise possesses much power and influence. Most people believe that responsibility must accompany power, whoever holds it. This obligation, presented earlier in this chapter, is called the *iron law of responsibility*. Businesses committed to social responsibility are aware that if they misuse the power they have, they might lose it. The antitrust cases brought against Microsoft by regulators in the United States and Europe, profiled in the discussion case at the end of Chapter 10, are examples of government efforts to reduce a company's abuses of its monopoly power in the marketplace.

Discourages Government Regulation

One of the most appealing arguments for business supporters is that voluntary social acts may head off increased government regulation. Some regulation may reduce freedom for both business and society, and freedom is a desirable public good. In the case of business, regulations tend to add economic costs and restrict flexibility in decision making. From business's point of view, freedom in decision making allows business to maintain initiative in meeting market and social forces. This view also is consistent with political philosophy that wishes to keep power as decentralized as possible in a democratic society. It is said that government is already a massive institution whose centralized power and bureaucracy threaten the balance of power in society. Therefore, if business by its own socially responsible behavior can discourage new government restrictions, it is accomplishing a public good as well as its own private good.

> For example, the natural juice producer Odwalla, described in a case study later in the book, sought to improve the safety of its fresh juice drinks by pasteurizing (heat-treating) them voluntarily. The company hoped that by doing so it would avoid strict and often more costly government regulations of its production processes.

Promotes Long-Term Profits for Business

At times, social initiatives by business produce long-run business profits. A New Jersey judge ruled in *Barlow et al. v. A.P. Smith Manufacturing* that a corporate donation to Princeton University was an *investment* by the firm, thus an allowable business expense. The rationale was that a corporate gift to a school, though costly in the present, might in time provide a flow of talented graduates to work for the company. The court ruled that top executives must take "a long-range view of the matter" and exercise "enlightened leadership and direction" when it comes to using company funds for socially responsible programs.[9]

> A classic example of the long-term benefits of social responsibility was the Johnson & Johnson Tylenol incident. In the 1980s, several people died after they ingested Extra-Strength Tylenol capsules laced with the poison cyanide. To ensure the safety of its customers, Johnson & Johnson immediately recalled the product, an action that cost the firm millions of dollars in the short term. The company's production processes were never found defective. Customers rewarded Johnson & Johnson's responsible actions by continuing to buy its products, and in the long run the company once again became profitable.

In the opening example of this chapter, the CEO of GSK Bio believed that in the long term, its commitment to developing vaccines for underserved populations would

---

[9] *Barlow et al. v. A.P. Smith Manufacturing* (1951, New Jersey Supreme Court), discussed in Clarence C. Walton, *Corporate Social Responsibility* (Belmont, CA: Wadsworth, 1967), pp. 48–52.

strengthen the company's financial performance by attracting new customers, as well as support from governments and public health organizations. An empirical assessment of the question whether corporate social responsibility leads to benefits for companies' stockholders is presented later in this chapter.

Improves Business Value and Reputation

The social reputation of the firm is often viewed as an important element in establishing trust between the firm and its stakeholders. **Reputation** refers to desirable or undesirable qualities associated with an organization or its actors that may influence the organization's relationships with its stakeholders.[10] A firm's reputation is a valuable intangible asset, as it prompts repeat purchases by loyal consumers and helps to attract and retain better employees to spur productivity and enhance profitability. Employees who have the most to offer may be attracted to work for a firm that contributes to the social good of the community, or is more sensitive to the needs and safety of its consumers, or takes better care of its employees. Research has confirmed that a firm's "good deeds" or reputation increases its attractiveness to employees.[11] Thus, a company may benefit from being socially responsible by improving the quality of people it attracts as employees. In this sense, the company's social reputation is one of its intangible assets that add to the organization's wealth.

A concern for company reputation is found at the highest levels of business organizations worldwide. Sixty-five percent of CEOs surveyed in a Korn/Ferry International poll said that it was their personal responsibility to manage their company's reputation. Corporate boards are putting more pressure on CEOs to build corporate reputation. When choosing a successor, the CEOs responding to the survey overwhelmingly agreed (97 percent) that when seeking a new leader of the firm, boards place more weight than ever on a candidate's ability to protect and enhance the company's reputation.[12]

As discussed in Chapter 4, firms are often recognized for their positive reputation by various business magazines or organizations through awards programs. Recently, a "reputation index" was created to measure and hold up as a model those companies with strong social reputations. Rating Research, a British firm, measures the critical intangible assets that constitute corporate reputation and broadly disseminates these ratings to interested parties.[13]

Corrects Social Problems Caused by Business

Many people believe business has a responsibility to compensate society for the harm it has sometimes caused. If consumers are injured due to a product defect, the manufacturer is responsible. If a business does not voluntarily recognize its responsibility, the courts will

---

[10] The definition of *reputation* was adapted from John F. Mahon, "Corporate Reputation: A Research Agenda Using Strategy and Stakeholder Literature," *Business & Society* 41, no. 4 (December 2002), pp. 415–45. Also see Charles Fombrun, *Reputation: Realizing Value from the Corporate Image* (Cambridge, MA: Harvard University Press, 1996) and the December 2002 special issue of *Business & Society.*

[11] Rebecca A. Luce, Alison E. Barber, and Amy J. Hillman, "Good Deeds and Misdeeds: A Mediated Model of the Effect of Corporate Social Performance on Organizational Attractiveness," *Business & Society* 40, no. 4 (2001), pp. 397–415.

[12] "CEOs Taking Greater Responsibility for Corporate Reputations," *Ethics Newsline,* Institute for Global Ethics, October 20, 2003, *www.globalethics.org.*

[13] See Fombrun, *Reputation: Realizing Value from the Corporate Image.* See also *www.reputation.org* and articles in *Corporate Reputation Review* and Rating Research LLC, *www.ratingresearch.com.*

often step in to represent society and its interests. When a business pollutes the environment, the cleanup is the responsibility of that firm, as seen in the following example.

> At the insistence of the Environmental Protection Agency and thousands of concerned citizens, General Electric accepted responsibility for dredging New York's Hudson River to rid the waterway of much of the 1.3 million pounds of toxic PCBs that had been dumped there since the 1940s. Since the mid-1970s, PCBs had been linked to premature birth defects and cancer, particularly to those people who consumed contaminated fish. Although the government had stopped General Electric from continuing to dump PCBs into the river since 1975, the company had assumed no responsibility for cleaning up its mess until 2002, a project that company officials estimated would cost half a billion dollars to complete.[14]

As General Electric learned from its experience in this case, it is often much less expensive to avoid causing problems, such as chemical pollution, than to correct them afterward.

Arguments against Corporate Social Responsibility

Who opposes corporate social responsibility? The economist Milton Friedman famously stated in 1970, "There is only one responsibility of business, namely to use its resources and engage in activities designed to increase its profits."[15] Some people in the business world—such as the 16 percent of CEOs in the survey shown in Figure 3.2 who believe that the appropriate role of business is to provide the highest possible returns to shareholders while obeying all laws and regulations—clearly agree with this view. Some fear that the pursuit of social goals by business will lower firms' economic efficiency, thereby depriving society of important goods and services. Others are skeptical about trusting business with social improvements; they prefer governmental initiatives and programs. According to some of the more radical critics of the private business system, social responsibility is nothing but a clever public relations smokescreen to hide business's true intentions to make as much money as possible. See Figure 3.3 again for some of the arguments against corporate social responsibility, discussed next.

Lowers Economic Efficiency and Profits

According to one argument, any time a business uses some of its resources for social purposes, it risks lowering its efficiency. For example, if a firm decides to keep an unproductive factory open because it wants to avoid the negative social effect that a plant closing would have on the local community and its workers, its overall financial performance may suffer. The firm's costs may be higher than necessary, resulting in lower profits. Stockholders may receive a lower return on their investment, making it more difficult for the firm to acquire additional capital for future growth. In the long run, the firm's efforts to be socially responsible by keeping the factory open may backfire.

Business managers and economists argue that the business of business is business. Businesses are told to concentrate on producing goods and services and selling them at the lowest competitive price. When these economic tasks are done, the most efficient firms survive. Even though corporate social responsibility is well-intended, such social activities lower business's efficiency, thereby depriving society of higher levels of economic production needed to maintain everyone's standard of living.[16]

---

[14] "Healing the Hudson Rover," Natural Resources Defense Council Web site at *www.nrdc.org/water/pollution/hhudson.asp.*

[15] Milton Friedman, "The Social Responsibility of Business Is to Increase Its Profits," *New York Times Magazine,* September 13, 1970.

[16] This argument is most often attributed to Milton Friedman, ibid., pp. 33, 122–26.

Imposes Unequal Costs among Competitors

Another argument against social responsibility is that it imposes greater costs on more responsible companies, putting them at a competitive disadvantage. Consider the following scenario.

> A manufacturer operating in multiple countries wishes to be more socially responsible worldwide and decides to protect its employees by installing more safety equipment at its plants than local law requires. Other manufacturers in competition with this company do not take similar steps, choosing to install only as much safety equipment as required by law. As a result their costs are lower, and their profits higher. In this case, the socially responsible firm penalizes itself and even runs the risk of going out of business, especially in a highly competitive market.

This kind of problem becomes acute when viewed from a global perspective, where laws and regulations differ from one country to the next. If one nation requires higher and more costly pollution control standards, or stricter job safety rules, or more stringent premarket testing of prescription drugs than other nations, it imposes higher costs on business. This cost disadvantage means that competition cannot be equal. Foreign competitors who are the least socially responsible will actually be rewarded because they will be able to capture a bigger share of the market.

Imposes Hidden Costs Passed On to Stakeholders

Many social proposals undertaken by business do not pay their own way in an economic sense; therefore, someone must pay for them. Ultimately, society pays all costs. Some people may believe that social benefits are costless, but socially responsible businesses will try to recover all of their costs in some way. For example, if a company chooses to install expensive pollution-abatement equipment, the air may be cleaner, but ultimately someone will have to pay. Stockholders may receive lower dividends, employees may be paid less, or consumers may be charged higher prices. If the public knew that it would eventually have to pay these costs, and if it knew how high the true costs were, it might not be so insistent that companies act in socially responsible ways. The same might be true of government regulations intended to produce socially desirable business behavior. By driving up business costs, these regulations often increase prices and lower productivity, in addition to making the nation's tax bill higher.

Requires Skills Business May Lack

Businesspeople are not primarily trained to solve social problems. They may know about production, marketing, accounting, finance, information technology, and personnel work, but what do they know about inner-city issues or world poverty or violence in schools? Putting businesspeople in charge of solving social problems may lead to unnecessarily expensive and poorly conceived approaches. In a global survey on social responsibility, it was found that "only 11 percent [of the companies who have developed a CSR strategy] have made significant progress in implementing the strategy in their organization";[17] thus one might question the effectiveness and efficiency of businesspeople seeking to address social responsibility problems. Business analysts might be tempted to believe that methods that succeed in normal business operations will also be applicable to complex social issues, even though different approaches may work better in the social arena.

---

[17] "Corporate Social Responsibility: Unlocking the Value," *www.ey.com/Global.*

A related idea is that public officials who are duly elected by citizens in a democratic society should address societal issues. Business leaders are not elected by the public and therefore do not have a mandate to solve social problems. In short, businesspeople do not have the expertise or the popular support required to address what are essentially issues of public policy.

Places Responsibility on Business Rather than Individuals

The entire idea of *corporate* responsibility is misguided, according to some critics. Only *individual persons* can be responsible for their actions. People make decisions; organizations do not. An entire company cannot be held liable for its actions, only those individuals who are involved in promoting or carrying out a policy. Therefore, it is wrong to talk about the social responsibility of *business* when it is the social responsibility of *individual businesspersons* that is involved. If individual business managers want to contribute their own personal money to a social cause, let them do so; but it is wrong for them to contribute their company's funds in the name of corporate social responsibility.[18]

Together, the above arguments claim that the attempt to exercise corporate social responsibility places added burdens on both business and society without producing the intended effect of social improvement or produces it at excessive cost.

Balancing Economic, Legal, and Social Responsibilities

Any organization or manager must seek to juggle multiple responsibilities. The belief that the business of business is solely to make a profit is no longer widely held, as Figure 3.2 suggests. Rather, many business executives believe the key challenge facing their organizations today is to meet economic and social responsibilities simultaneously.

> Never was the balancing of multiple responsibilities more evident than when Jeffrey Immelt, chairman and CEO at General Electric, announced before 200 corporate officers that it would take four things to keep the company on top: execution, growth, great people, and *virtue*. Immelt appointed the company's first vice president for corporate citizenship, Bob Corcoran, to take his message globally to GE's suppliers, customers, and employees. Within a year after Immelt's announcement, GE had performed more than 3,100 labor, health, environmental and safety audits and opened up discussions with socially responsible investment funds. GE launched a global philanthropic program by providing health care to people in the poorest areas of Ghana.[19]

As shown in Figure 3.4, a business must manage its economic responsibilities to its stockholders, its legal requirements to societal laws and regulations, and its social responsibilities to various stakeholders. Although these obligations may conflict at times, a successful firm is one whose management finds ways to meet each of its critical responsibilities and develops strategies to enable these obligations to help each other.

Economic and Social Responsibilities: Enlightened Self-Interest

Being socially responsible by meeting the public's continually changing expectations requires wise leadership at the top of the corporation. Companies with the ability to

---

[18] This argument, like the "lowers economic efficiency and profits" argument, often is attributed to Friedman, "Social Responsibility of Business."

[19] "Money and Morals at GE," *Fortune*, November 15, 2004, pp. 176–82.

FIGURE 3.4
The Multiple Responsibilities of Business

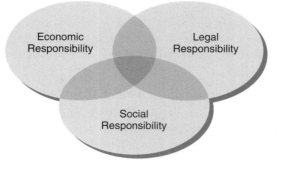

recognize profound social changes and anticipate how they will affect operations have proven to be survivors. They get along better with government regulators, are more open to the needs of the company's stakeholders, and often cooperate with legislators as new laws are developed to cope with social problems.

> What started off as a business envisioning a competitive advantage has turned into a national business alliance of social activity. In 2004, Home Depot CEO Robert Nardelli encouraged his employees to get involved in the community. More than 50,000 of the firm's 325,000 employees responded with more than 2 million hours of donated time. A year later, Nardelli challenged a group of CEOs to get involved at the pace established by the Home Depot employees. Leaders representing Albertson's, BellSouth, Delta Air Lines and SAP America met with Nardelli and agreed to kick off "A Month of Service" in September 2005. The group created Hands-On Network, an alliance of corporate and civic leaders, to develop community service programs that deployed corporate volunteers on 2,000 projects across the country, resulting in 6.4 million volunteer hours over two years. Nardelli explained that at the core of this project was the understanding that "companies are beholden not just to stockholders, but also to suppliers, customers, employees, community members, even social activists. Things have become a lot more interdependent."[20]

The actions taken by Home Depot's CEO Nardelli are an example of a business leader being guided by **enlightened self-interest**. Nardelli recognized the long-term rewards to the company from its civic involvement in enhanced reputation, employee satisfaction, and community support. According to this view, it is in a company's self-interest in the long term to provide true value to its customers, to help its employees to grow, and to behave responsibly as a corporate citizen.[21]

Do socially responsible companies sacrifice profits by working conscientiously to promote the social good? Do they make higher profits, better-than-average profits, or lower profits than corporations that ignore or flout the public's desires for a high and responsible standard of social performance?

Scholars have explored this issue for two decades, with mixed results. In 2003, researchers at the University of Iowa conducted a methodologically rigorous review of

---

[20] "The Debate over Doing Good," *BusinessWeek*, August 15, 2005, pp. 76–78.
[21] Jeff Frooman, "Socially Irresponsible and Illegal Behavior and Shareholder Wealth," *Business & Society*, September 1997, pp. 221–49, argues that the negative effects on shareholder wealth when a firm acts irresponsibly support the enlightened self-interest view: act responsibly to promote shareholders' interests.

all 52 prior studies of the relationship between corporate social responsibility and firm performance. They found that most of the time, more responsible companies also had solid financial results; the statistical association was highly to modestly positive across the range of all prior studies. The authors concluded, "corporate virtue, in the form of social responsibility and, to a lesser extent, environmental responsibility is likely to pay off."[22] In short, most of the time, socially responsibility and financial performance go together, although there may be some conditions under which this is not true.

Any social program—for example, an in-company child care center, a drug education program for employees, or the lending of company executives as advisers to community agencies—will usually impose immediate monetary costs on the participating company. These short-run costs certainly have a potential for reducing the company's profits unless the social activity is designed to make money, which is not usually the purpose of these programs. Therefore, a company may sacrifice short-run profits by undertaking social initiatives, but what is lost in the short run may be gained back over a longer period. For example, if a drug education program prevents or reduces on-the-job drug abuse, then the resulting lower employee turnover, fewer absences from work, healthier workforce, and fewer accidents and injuries may increase the firm's productivity and lower health insurance costs. In that case, the company may actually experience an increase in its long-run profits, although it had to make an expensive outlay to get the program started.

Legal Requirements versus Corporate Social Responsibility

Accompanying a firm's economic responsibility to its stockholders are its **legal obligations**. As a member of society, a firm must abide by the laws and regulations governing the society. How are a firm's legal obligations related to its social responsibilities? Laws and regulations are enacted to ensure socially responsible conduct by businesses. The standards of behavior expected by society are embodied in that society's laws. Can't businesses voluntarily decide to be socially responsible? Of course, but legal rules set minimum standards for businesses to follow. Some firms go beyond the law; others seek to change the law to require competitors to be more socially responsible.

Laws and regulations help create a level playing field for businesses that compete against one another. By requiring all firms to meet the same social standards—for example, the safe disposal of hazardous wastes—government prevents one firm from gaining a competitive advantage over its rivals by acting irresponsibly. If a company dumped its wastes carelessly, it would risk lawsuits, fines, and possible jail terms for some of its managers and employees and unfavorable publicity for its actions.

Businesses that comply with laws and public policies are meeting a minimum level of social responsibility expected by the public. According to one leading scholar of corporate social performance, even legal compliance is barely enough to satisfy the public:

> The traditional economic and legal criteria are necessary but not sufficient conditions of corporate legitimacy. The corporation that flouts them will not survive; even the mere satisfaction of these criteria does not ensure the corporation's continued existence . . .

---

[22] Mark Orlitzky, Frank Schmidt, and Sara Rynes, "Corporate Social and Financial Performance: A Meta-analysis," *Organization Studies*, 2003, pp. 403–41. Other studies investigating this issue include Bernadette M. Ruf et al., "An Empirical Investigation of the Relationship between Change in Corporate Social Performance and Financial Performance: A Stakeholder Theory Perspective," *Journal of Business Ethics*, 2001, pp. 143–56; Marc Orlitzky and John D. Benjamin, "Corporate Social Performance and Firm Risk: A Meta-analytic Review," *Business & Society* 2001, pp. 369–96; and Amy J. Hillman and Gerald D. Keim, "Shareholder Value, Stakeholder Management, and Social Issues: What's the Bottom Line?" *Strategic Management Journal*, 2001, p. 135.

Thus, social responsibility implies bringing corporate behavior up to a level where it is in congruence with currently prevailing social norms, values, and performance expectations. . . . [Social responsibility] is simply a step ahead—before the new societal expectations are codified into legal requirements.[23]

Stockholder Interests versus Other Stakeholder Interests

Top-level managers, along with a corporation's board of directors, are generally expected to produce as much value as possible for the company's owners and investors. This can be done by paying high dividends regularly and by running the company in ways that cause the stock's value to rise. Not only are high profits a positive signal to Wall Street investors that the company is being well-run—thereby increasing the stock's value—but those profits also make possible the payment of high dividends to stockholders. Low profits have the opposite effect and put great pressure on managers to improve the company's financial performance.

However, stockholders are not the only stakeholder group that management must keep in mind. The leaders of some of the world's largest organizations from Europe, Asia, and North America, organized by a group called the Caux Roundtable, recognized that all stakeholders must be considered; none can be ignored. A top manager's job is to interact with the totality of the company's stakeholders, including those groups that advocate high levels of social responsibility by business. Management's central goal is to promote the interests of the entire company, not just any single stakeholder group, and to pursue multiple company goals, not just profit goals.[24]

This broader and far more complex task tends to put more emphasis on the long-run profit picture rather than an exclusive focus on immediate returns. When this happens, dividends paid to stockholders may be less than they desire, and the value of their shares may not rise as rapidly as they would like. These are the kinds of risks faced by corporate managers who have a legal responsibility to produce high value for the company's stockholder-owners but who also must try to promote the overall interests of the entire company. Putting all of the emphasis on short-run maximum profits for stockholders can lead to policies that overlook the interests and needs of other stakeholders. Managers may also downgrade social responsibility programs that increase short-run costs, although it is well known that the general public strongly approves of socially responsible companies.

As a response to the conflict between long- and short-term profit making, an enlightened self-interest point of view may be the most useful and practical approach. That means that incurring reasonable short-run costs to undertake socially responsible activities that benefit both the company and the general public in the long run is acceptable.

The Evolving Notion of Corporate Social Responsibility

William C. Frederick, a leading scholar and a co-author of several earlier editions of this book, described in his recent book how business understanding of corporate social responsibility has evolved over the past half century. During each of the four historical

---

[23] S. Prakash Sethi, "A Conceptual Framework for Environmental Analysis of Social Issues and Evaluation of Business Response Patterns," in S. Prakash Sethi and Cecilia M. Falbe, eds., *Business and Society: Dimensions of Conflict and Cooperation* (Lexington, MA: Lexington Books, 1987), pp. 42–43.

[24] See the Caux Roundtable Web site at *www.cauxroundtable.org*.

FIGURE 3.5

Evolving Phases of Corporate Social Responsibility

	Phases of Corporate Social Responsibility	CSR Drivers	CSR Policy Instruments
CSR$_1$ 1950s–1960s	**Corporate Social Stewardship** Corporate philanthropy—acts of charity Managers as public trustee-stewards Balancing social pressures	Executive conscience Company image/reputation	Philanthropic funding Public relations
CSR$_2$ 1960s–1970s	**Corporate Social Responsiveness** Social-impact analysis Strategic priority for social response Organizational redesign and training for responsiveness Stakeholder mapping and implementation	Social unrest/protest Repeated corporate misbehavior Public policy/government regulation Stakeholder pressures Think-tank policy papers	Stakeholder strategy Regulatory compliance Social audits Public affairs function Governance reform Political lobbying
CSR$_3$ 1980s–1990s	**Corporate/Business Ethics** Foster an ethical corporate culture Establish an ethical organizational climate Recognize common ethical principles	Religious/ethnic beliefs Technology-driven value changes Human rights pressures Code of ethics Ethics committee/officer/audits Ethics training Stakeholder negotiations	Mission/vision/values statements CEO leadership ethics
CSR$_4$ 1990s–2000s	**Corporate/Global Citizenship** Stakeholder partnerships Integrate financial, social, and environmental performance Identify globalization impacts Sustainability of company and environment	Global economic trade/investment High-tech communication networks Geo-political shifts/competition Ecological awareness/concern NGO pressures	Intergovernmental compacts Global audit standards NGO dialogue Sustainability audits/reports

Source: Adapted from William C. Frederick, *Corporation, Be Good! The Story of Corporate Social Responsibility* (Indianapolis, IN: Dog Ear Publishing, 2006). Used with permission.

periods, corporate social responsibility has had a distinct focus, set of drivers, and policy instruments, as shown in Figure 3.5. Frederick explains that the most recent phase of corporate social responsibility is corporate citizenship. The next chapter explores today's corporate citizenship practices.

As the general notion of corporate social responsibility has evolved from a sense of stewardship and charity to others to the more recent understanding of corporate citizenship, business likewise has evolved in how it reacts to and addresses the various challenges made by its stakeholders. The current test of acting as a good global corporate citizen is discussed in the next chapter.

Summary

- Corporate social responsibility means that a corporation should be held accountable for any of its actions that affect people, their communities, and their environment. Businesses must recognize their vast power and wield it to better society.

- The idea of corporate social responsibility in the United States was adopted by business leaders in the early 20th century. The central themes of social responsibility have been charity—which means giving aid to the needy—and stewardship—acting as a public trustee and considering all corporate stakeholders when making business decisions.

- Corporate social responsibility is a highly debatable notion. Some argue that its benefits include discouraging government regulation, promoting long-term profitability for the firm, and enhancing the company's reputation. Others believe that it lowers efficiency, imposes undue costs, and shifts unnecessary obligations to business.

- Socially responsible businesses should attempt to balance economic, legal, and social obligations. Following an enlightened self-interest approach, a firm may be economically rewarded while society benefits from the firm's actions. Abiding by legal requirements can also guide businesses in serving various groups in society.

- Managers should consider all of the company's stakeholders and their interests, not only their shareholders. Management's central goal is to promote the interests of all stakeholders by pursuing multiple company goals. This broader, more complex task emphasizes the long-run objectives and performance of the firm.

Key Terms

charity principle, *48*
corporate social responsibility, *45*
enlightened self-interest, *56*

iron law of responsibility, *47*
legal obligations, *57*
reputation, *52*

stewardship principle, *49*

Internet Resources

www.csracademy.org.uk — CSR Academy

www.csr-monitor.com — CSR Monitor

www.csrwire.com — The Newswire of Corporate Social Responsibility

www.worldbank.org/wbi/corpgov/csr — The World Bank Group, Corporate Governance and Corporate Social Responsibility

Discussion Case: *Hurricane Katrina—Corporate Social Responsibility in Action*

On August 29, 2005, the United States experienced its most destructive and costly natural disaster ever when Hurricane Katrina, a fierce storm with winds of more than 135 miles per hour, battered the central Gulf Coast and caused unparalleled damage to coastal regions of Louisiana, Mississippi, and Alabama. Its storm surge breeched the levee system that protected New Orleans from Lake Pontchartrain and subsequently flooded significant portions of the city. Many communities along the Gulf Coast were battered, damaged and, in some cases, completely destroyed. Two months later, the official death toll stood at 1,163 and the damage was estimated to be more than $200 billion. Over 1 million people were displaced in the aftermath of this disaster.

The outpouring of charity—from cash donations to provisions of water, food and clothing—from individuals across the country and around the world was immediate. Businesses were significantly involved, demonstrating one of the greatest charitable efforts ever seen from the corporate community. While many companies have had long-standing traditions of charitable giving, particularly during economic hard times, the philanthropy provided after Hurricane Katrina emphasized a new level of giving.

Emigrant Savings Bank, a major financial lender in the region, deposited $1,000 into the account of each customer in the areas hardest hit by the storm. The *Chronicle of Philanthropy* in Washington, D.C., estimated that if the contributions continued, it was likely that cash donations by businesses to victims of Hurricane Katrina would surpass those to victims of other recent disasters, such as the September 11, 2001, terrorist attacks on New York City and Washington, D.C., and the recent Asian tsunamis.

In addition to cash, businesses offered consumer products to those in need of these items. Georgia Pacific, a home improvement retailer, sent 65 truckloads of consumer goods—toilet paper, paper towels, paper plates, cutlery—to relief organizations, more than three times the amount it had sent the previous year during hurricane season. Wal-Mart donated $17 million in cash to relief agencies and followed up with shipping more than 100 truckloads of diapers, wipes, toothbrushes, and even beds to the Gulf Coast. Employees of pizza chain Papa John's spent a week in Biloxi, Mississippi, handing out thousands of six-inch pizza pies from a mobile trailer.

In addition to more than a million dollars in cash and equipment, General Electric provided a mobile power plant to restore capacity to a fuel transfer station in Louisiana. Amgen, a biotechnology company, donated $2.5 million worth of medical supplies, focusing on providing assistance to dialysis and cancer patients. Countless thousands of volunteers offered their assistance, including emergency service and utility crews from every state in the nation and dozens of countries.

Business became involved in helping in other ways as well. More than 14,000 casino workers in the region lost their jobs, and many their homes, in the hurricane. Their employers, four Las Vegas–based casino-operating companies—Harrah's Entertainment, MGM Mirage, Boyd Gaming, and Pinnacle Entertainment—told them they would continue to receive paychecks. Harrah's Entertainment pledged to pay workers up to 90 days after the casino was closed from the storm's damage. Although these businesses experienced devastating property damaged from Hurricane Katrina, they committed to paying their employees despite not knowing when the casinos might be in operation again.

Other businesses and their managers assumed new roles in serving their employees affected by the disaster. One day before the storm hit, Standard Company of New Orleans transferred its computer system and call center to a backup location in Boulder, Colorado. By the time New Orleans began flooding, many of the company's employees were in Dallas—a new and unfamiliar location for Standard's employees. Jefferson Gillane, a financial analyst at Standard before the storm hit, became the company's information coordinator. He found office supplies, procedures for filing insurance claims, local doctors, and schools in Dallas that were willing to enroll students from New Orleans. He also found charities that could supply clothing for employees who did not anticipate being away from home for more than a few days and had lost everything back in New Orleans. Gillane even launched a daily newsletter with information about New Orleans' sports teams.

During the nation's greatest disaster, businesses, along with many individuals and charitable organizations, found new ways to demonstrate a concern for others and to offer hope as thousands of people sought to rebuild their lives.

Source: "Hurricane Katrina," *http://en.wikipedia.org/wiki/Hurricane_Katrina*; "Casino Companies Still Paying Displaced Workers' Salaries," *Casino City Times*, September 7, 2005, *www.casinocitytimes.com*; "Challenges Loom for Management in Katrina's Wake," *Pittsburgh Post-Gazette*, September 13, 2005, *www.post-gazette.com*; "Katrina: The Aftermath," *Atlanta Journal-Constitution*, September 13, 2005, *ajc.com*; "When Good Will Is Also Good Business," *The New York Times*, September 14, 2005, *www.nytimes.com/2005/09/14/business*.

Discussion Questions

1. Do the demonstrations of kindness described in this story exemplify the charity principle or the stewardship principle, or both?

2. Which arguments for corporate social responsibility support the actions of the companies profiled here, and which arguments against corporate social responsibility raise questions concerning these actions?

3. Enlightened self-interest occurs when a business recognizes the interrelationship between its company's economic interests and its social obligations. Do you think that the acts of corporate generosity described in this case represent examples of enlightened self-interest? Why or why not?

4. Is it businesses' duty to help those in extreme need, such as victims of Hurricane Katrina, or is this the job of governments and individuals? How far should a company go to assist the community, their employees, and others affected by a natural disaster?

Global Corporate Citizenship

Corporate citizenship means putting a commitment to social and environmental responsibility into practice. It involves building positive relationships with stakeholders, discovering business opportunities in serving society, and transforming a concern for financial performance into a vision of integrated financial *and* social and environmental performance. Establishing effective structures and processes to meet a company's social responsibilities, assess results, and report them to the public is an important part of job of today's managers.

This chapter focuses on these key learning objectives:

- Defining corporate citizenship and global corporate citizenship.
- Contrasting the structures and processes businesses use to manage their social responsibilities.
- Evaluating how the multiple dimensions of corporate citizenship progress through a series of stages.
- Assessing how corporate citizenship differs among various countries and regions of the world.
- Understanding how a business or social groups can audit corporate citizenship activities and report their findings to stakeholders.
- Recognizing the leading-edge corporate citizenship companies and how they carry out their corporate citizenship mission.

Under the headline, "How Barbie Is Making Business a Little Better," *USA Today* reported on how the Mattel toy company, maker of the famous Barbie doll, had undertaken a series of initiatives to improve conditions in its overseas factories. Mattel was one of the world's leading toy companies, with such well-known brands as Hot Wheels, Fisher-Price, and Matchbox. In the late 1990s, Mattel first began monitoring practices at its worldwide manufacturing facilities. The company brought in outside auditors from academia and nonprofit organizations to investigate their operations in Mexico, China, Indonesia, Malaysia, and Thailand. The auditors examined the company's working conditions, on-site medical facilities, worker training, wages, and overtime hours. If a particular supplier did not meet Mattel's standards, it was dropped. For example, the company ended its contract with a sewing factory in Mexico where audits revealed the presence of underage workers, forced overtime, and noxious chemical fumes, after factory owners missed a deadline to fix the problems. "We call it zero tolerance," said Mattel's senior vice president.[1]

Novo Nordisk is a multinational health care company, based in Denmark, dedicated to the treatment of diabetes. It conducts research and markets a range of products, including synthetic insulin and delivery devices—such as a "pen" that diabetics can use to inject medicine more comfortably. Novo Nordisk has publicly committed "to conduct its activities in a financially, environmentally and socially responsible way." The company is publicly owned, and it seeks to produce high returns for investors. But it is equally committed to social and environmental responsibility. Many of the company's citizenship initiatives are linked to its core mission of fighting diabetes. For example, as part of its "Take Action!" project, Novo Nordisk employees visit schools around the world to work with teachers to promote exercise and healthy eating—practices that can cut down the incident of adult-onset diabetes. The company constantly monitors its environmental impacts; for example, a recent initiative was designed to reduce the adverse effects of pharmaceuticals excreted in the urine—potentially a danger to aquatic life when these chemicals enter the sewage system and are eventually discharged into waterways. The company calls its holistic approach the "Novo Nordisk Way of Management."[2]

Cemex, a large Mexican firm that supplies cement to the construction industry in 50 countries, found an innovative way to act as a global citizen. Many Mexican citizens work temporarily in the United States to earn money they hope to use to build a home for the benefit of their families in Mexico. However, these immigrants face a "Catch-22." The problem is that most U.S. banks will not loan money for home construction outside the United States, while most Mexican banks will not loan money to people who are not living in Mexico. Cemex addressed this problem through a program called Construmex, which offered home construction loans of up to $50,000, under flexible terms, to Mexicans in the United States for home construction in their homeland—enough money, in most cases, to build a dwelling comfortable by local standards. In Mexico, the company developed an initiative called *Patrimonio Hoy* which combined grants of construction materials, technical assistance, and small loans to enable the very poor to build homes. "We are granting credit to those who apparently are not creditworthy," said Luis Enrique' Martinez, a Cemex representative. "But

[1] "How Barbie Is Making Business a Little Better," *USA Today,* March 27, 2006, pp. 1B, 2B. Mattel's global manufacturing principles, audits, and corporate social responsibility report are available online at the company's Web site: *www.mattel.com/about_us/Corp_Responsibility.*

[2] More information about Novo Nordisk's Way of Management is available online at: *www.novonordisk.com.*

the most important thing is that we are providing people an opportunity to start building some wealth, to participate in the formal economy and, of course, to help make their dreams a reality."[3]

Chapter 3 presented reasons why more and more businesses today have embraced the idea of corporate social responsibility. This chapter introduces the related concept of corporate citizenship and explains how companies around the world, such as Mattel, Novo Nordisk, and Cemex, have organized themselves to carry out their citizenship responsibilities. It provides examples of what leading-edge companies are doing to put social and environmental responsibility into practice. This chapter also addresses the emerging practice of social auditing, a method for measuring and assessing corporate social performance and reporting results to the public.

Corporate Citizenship

The term **corporate citizenship** came into widespread use in the 1990s. The term broadly refers to putting corporate social responsibility into practice. It entails proactively building stakeholder partnerships, discovering business opportunities in serving society, and transforming a concern for financial performance into a vision of integrated financial *and* social performance.[4] Roberto Civita, chairman and chief executive officer of the Brazilian Abril Group, has defined corporate citizenship as "capitalism with a social conscience." According to many business leaders, corporate citizenship used to be simple and optional. Now, in the mid-2000s, it has become complicated and mandatory. This is because global markets, lightning-quick access to information, and heightened stakeholder expectations have compelled organizations of all sizes to establish an "integrated corporate citizenship strategy" as part of their overall business plan.[5]

What are the core elements of corporate citizenship? One scholar's answer to this question is shown in Exhibit 4.A.

When businesses invest time, money, and effort in citizenship activities, they often reap rewards in the form of enhanced reputation and legitimacy. Recent research by Naomi A. Gardberg and Charles J. Fombrun argues that corporate citizenship programs, particularly those of global firms, should be viewed as "strategic investments comparable to R&D [research and development] and advertising." This is because such programs "create intangible assets for companies that help them overcome nationalistic barriers, facilitate globalization, and build local advantage." (A *tangible* asset is something that can be seen and counted, such as machinery, buildings, or money. An *intangible* asset, by contrast, is something that cannot be seen or counted, but that

---

[3] "CEMEX's Construmex Celebrates Five Years of Service to the Mexican Community in the U.S.," press release, June 6, 2006; "Work in the States, Build a Life in Mexico," *BusinessWeek*, July 18, 2005, p. 64; "Block by Block: How One of Mexico's Largest Companies Builds Loyalty among the Poor," *Stanford Social Innovation Review* 3, no. 2 (Summer 2005), pp. 34–37; and Bryan Husted and David B. Allen, "Creating Competitive Advantage through Corporate Social Strategy," paper presented at the international annual meeting of the Academy of Management, Honolulu, Hawaii, August 2005. We are grateful to Bryan Husted for bringing this example to our attention.

[4] See Barbara W. Altman and Deborah Vidaver-Cohen, "A Framework for Understanding Corporate Citizenship," *Business and Society Review*, Spring 2000, pp. 1–7. An understanding of corporate citizenship as embedded in a "liberal view of citizenship" is presented by Dirk Matten and Andrew Crane in "Corporate Citizenship: Toward an Extended Theoretical Conceptualization," *Academy of Management Review*, 2005, pp. 166–79. The concept of global citizenship grounded in voluntary codes of conduct is developed by Jeanne M. Logsdon and Donna J. Wood in "Global Business Citizenship and Voluntary Codes of Ethical Conduct," *Journal of Business Ethics*, 2005, vol. 59, pp. 55–67.

[5] "Corporate Citizenship on the Rise," New Futures Media, *www.NewFuturesMedia.com*.

Exhibit 4.A   **Principles of Corporate Citizenship**

Good corporate citizens strive to conduct all business dealings in an ethical manner, make a concerned effort to balance the needs of all stakeholders, and work to protect the environment. The principles of corporate citizenship include:

Ethical Business Behavior

1. Engages in fair and honest business practices in its relationship with stakeholders.
2. Sets high standards of behavior for all employees.
3. Exercises ethical oversight of the executive and board levels.

Stakeholder Commitment

4. Strives to manage the company for the benefit of all stakeholders.
5. Initiates and engages in genuine dialogue with stakeholders.
6. Values and implements dialogue.

Community

7. Fosters a reciprocal relationship between the corporation and community.
8. Invests in the communities in which the corporation operates.

Consumers

9. Respects the rights of consumers.
10. Offers quality products and services.
11. Provides information that is truthful and useful.

Employees

12. Provides a family-friendly work environment.
13. Engages in responsible human-resource management.
14. Provides an equitable reward and wage system for employees.
15. Engages in open and flexible communication with employees.
16. Invests in employee development.

Investors

17. Strives for a competitive return on investment.

Suppliers

18. Engages in fair trading practices with suppliers.

Environment Commitment

19. Demonstrates a commitment to the environment.
20. Demonstrates a commitment to sustainable development.

Source: Kimberly Davenport, "Corporate Citizenship: A Stakeholder Approach for Defining Corporate Social Performance and Identifying Measures for Assessment," 1998, doctoral dissertation, Fielding Graduate University, *http://wwww.fielding.edu/library/dissertations/default.asp.*

nevertheless has value—such as a good reputation, trusting relationships, or customer loyalty.) In this respect, corporate citizenship activities can be considered important contributors to "a reinforcing cycle through which global companies create legitimacy, reputation, and competitive advantage." Gardberg and Fombrun suggest this effect is most likely where companies choose a configuration of citizenship activities—they call this a **citizenship profile**—that fits the setting in which the company is working. For

ExxonMobil—"We pledge to be a good corporate citizen in all the places we operate worldwide. We will maintain the highest ethical standards, comply with all applicable laws and regulations, and respect local and national cultures. We are dedicated to running safe and environmentally responsible operations." (*www.exxonmobil.com*)

Ford—"Corporate citizenship has become an integral part of every decision and action we take. We believe corporate citizenship is demonstrated in who we are as a company, how we conduct our business and how we take care of our employees, as well as in how we interact with the world at large." (*www.ford.com*)

Nike—"Our vision is to be an innovative and inspirational global citizen in a world where our company participates. Every day we drive responsible business practices that contribute to profitable and sustainable growth." (*www.nike.com*)

Nokia—"Our goal is to be a good corporate citizen wherever we operate, as a responsible and contributing member of society." (*www.nokia.com*)

Toyota—"With the aim of becoming a corporate citizen respected by international society, Toyota is conducting a wide range of philanthropic activities around the world. Its activities cover five major areas: education, the environment, culture and the arts, international exchange and local communities." (*www.toyota.co.jp*)

Source: These quotations first appeared in Dirk Matten and Andrew Crane, "Corporate Citizenship: Toward an Extended Theoretical Conceptualization," *Academy of Management Review*, 2005, Table 1, p. 167.

example, the public's expectations of corporate philanthropy, management of environmental risk, and worker rights vary across nations and regions. Companies whose citizenship profile best matches public expectations are most likely to benefit from strategic investments in corporate citizenship.[6]

Clearly, the public expects corporations to act responsibly. In a 2004 survey of 2,770 Americans, more than two-thirds of respondents (69 percent) said that corporate citizenship was "important to their trust in business." And 52 percent were "inclined to start or increase their business due to corporate citizenship." This was a nine-point increase over the previous year's survey results, showing that corporate citizenship was gaining importance as a way to build brand value, create competitive differentiation, and cement stakeholder loyalty.[7]

Examples of corporate commitment to citizenship, central to the organization's mission and strategic plan, are shown in Exhibit 4.B.

Global Corporate Citizenship

As companies expand their sphere of commercial activity around the world, expectations grow that they will behave in ways that enhance the benefits and minimize the risk to all stakeholders, wherever they are. This is the essence of legitimacy in a global economy. A company must earn—and maintain—its "license to operate" in every country in which it does business through its efforts to meet stakeholder expectations. (This concept is further explained in Chapter 17.)

[6] Naomi A. Gardberg and Charles Fombrun, "Corporate Citizenship: Creating Intangible Assets across Institutional Environments," *Academy of Management Review* 3, no. 2 (2006), pp. 329–46.

[7] "Americans' Corporate Citizenship Expectations Continue to Rise," *Ethics News*, Institute for Global Ethics, October 11, 2004, *www.globalethics.org*.

When a company is doing business in more than one country, the idea of citizenship must be translated into the concept of **global corporate citizenship**. A research report from a leading academic center defines the concept in these terms:

> Global corporate citizenship is the process of identifying, analyzing, and responding to the company's social, political, and economic responsibilities as defined through law and public policy, stakeholder expectations, and voluntary acts flowing from corporate values and business strategies. Corporate citizenship involves actual results (what corporations do) and the processes through which they are achieved (how they do it).[8]

This definition of global corporate citizenship is consistent with several major themes discussed throughout this book:

- Managers and companies have responsibilities to all of their stakeholders.
- Corporate citizenship involves more than just meeting legal requirements.
- Corporate citizenship requires that a company focus on, and respond to, stakeholder expectations and undertake those voluntary acts that are consistent with its values and business mission.
- Corporate citizenship involves both what the corporation does and the processes and structures through which it engages stakeholders and makes decisions, a subject to which this chapter next turns.

Management Systems for Corporate Citizenship

Global corporate citizenship is more than espoused values; it requires action. In order to become leading citizens of the world, companies such as those profiled in Exhibit 4.B must establish management processes and structures to carry out their citizenship commitments. This section describes some of the ways forward-thinking companies are changing to improve their ability to act in a socially responsible way.

In 2004, Business for Social Responsibility surveyed how companies had organized to carry out their citizenship functions. They observed great variation in what they termed CSR (corporate social responsibility) management systems:

> The goal of a CSR management system is to integrate corporate responsibility concerns into a company's values, culture, operations, and business decisions at all levels of the organization. Many companies have taken steps to create such a system by assigning responsibility to a committee of the board, an executive level committee, or a single executive or group of executives who can identify key CSR issues and evaluate and develop a structure for long-term integration of social values throughout the organization. One important observation is that there is no single universally accepted method for designing a CSR management structure. This is definitely not a "one-size-fits-all" exercise.[9]

---

[8] James E. Post, "Meeting the Challenge of Global Corporate Citizenship," *Center Research Report* (Chestnut Hill, MA: Boston College Center for Corporate Community Relations, 2000), p. 8. The document is available through the center Web site: *http://www.bc.edu/cccr.*

[9] Business for Social Responsibility, Issue Brief: "Overview of Corporate Social Responsibility," available online at: *www.bsr.org.* See also: *Designing a CSR Structure: A Step-by-Step Guide Including Leadership Examples and Decision-Making Tools* (San Francisco: Business for Social Responsibility, 2002).

Corporate citizenship, as this study recognized, is a rapidly evolving area of managerial practice in many organizations. As discussed in Chapter 2, in some cases companies have broadened the job of the public affairs office to include a wider range of tasks. Others have created a **department of corporate citizenship** to centralize under common leadership wide-ranging corporate citizenship functions.

For example, in 2001 Hewlett-Packard (HP) consolidated many of its corporate social responsibility citizenship initiatives in a single office. The company named Debra Dunn to a new position as senior vice president of corporate affairs and global citizenship. She was given a broad portfolio, including social and environmental responsibility, government and public affairs, corporate philanthropy, and "e-inclusion" (bringing technology to underserved markets). The company published its first corporate social and environmental responsibility report the following year. It also undertook a series of initiatives, including developing a supply chain code of conduct, establishing a privacy policy, recycling electronic products, and launching "digital village" projects in many communities. In 2005, Dunn commented in HP's global citizenship report, "What we have learned over time is that the work we are doing around the world to advance social and economic development and environmental sustainability is not separate from our long-term business goals, but fundamental to them."[10]

An emerging trend is the creation of separate departments of corporate citizenship, like the one at HP, which may encompass community relations, philanthropy, stakeholder engagement, social auditing and reporting, and other functions. The heads of many of these departments are senior vice presidents or vice presidents. Some report directly to the CEO, while others are one level below this in the organizational hierarchy. A number of companies support the work of these officers by appointing a committee of board members and a steering committee of top managers to direct and monitor the firms' citizenship efforts.

As businesses have become more committed to citizenship, specialized consultancies and professional associations for managers with responsibility in this area have emerged. Three of these organizations—including Business for Social Responsibility, whose study was cited above—are profiled in Exhibit 4.C.

Stages of Corporate Citizenship

Companies do not become good corporate citizens overnight. The process takes time. New attitudes have to be developed, new routines learned, new policies and action programs designed, and new relationships formed. Many obstacles must be overcome. What process do companies go through as they proceed down this path? What factors push and pull them along?

In 2006, Philip H. Mirvis and Bradley K. Googins of the Center for Global Citizenship at Boston College proposed a five-stage model of corporate citizenship, based on their work with hundreds of practitioners in a wide range of companies.[11] In their view, firms typically pass through a sequence of five stages as they develop as corporate citizens.

---

[10] HP's Global Citizenship Reports are available online at: *www.hp.com/go/report.*

[11] Philip Mirvis and Bradley Googins, "Stages of Corporate Citizenship," *California Management Review,* vol. 48, no. 2, Winter 2006, pp. 104–26. For a contrasting stage model, based on the experience of Nike, see Simon Zadek, "The Path to Corporate Responsibility," *Harvard Business Review,* December 2004, pp. 125–32.

As the practice of corporate citizenship has spread, so have professional associations and consultancies serving managers active in this arena. Among the leading organizations are these:

- In the United States, Business for Social Responsibility, based in San Francisco, functions as a membership organization for companies and provides consulting services to its members and others. The organization, which was founded in 1992, describes itself as a "global resource for companies seeking to sustain their commercial success in ways that demonstrate respect for ethical values, people, communities, and the environment." The organization provides hands-on guidance in setting up social programs, as well as providing useful research and best-practices examples for its member organizations.

- Corporate Social Responsibility Europe's mission is to promote the integration of corporate social responsibility into the mainstream of European business. Based in Brussels, Belgium, the organization's Web site provides a database of best practices in the areas of human rights, cause-related marketing, ethical principles, and community involvement. CSR Europe was founded in 1996 by former European Commission president Jacques Delors.

- Asian Forum on Corporate Social Responsibility, based in the Philippines, sponsors conferences to provide CSR practitioners in Asia an opportunity to learn, collaborate, and share insights. The organization also gives awards for excellence in environmental management, education, poverty alleviation, workplace practices, and health care.

Source: More information about these organizations is available online at *www.bsr.org, www.csreurope.org,* and *www.asianforumcsr.com.*

Each stage is characterized by a distinctive pattern of concepts, strategic intent, leadership, structure, issues management, stakeholder relationships, and transparency, as illustrated in Figure 4.1.

Elementary Stage. At this stage, citizenship is undeveloped. Managers are uninterested and uninvolved in social issues. Although companies at this stage obey the law, they do not move beyond compliance. Companies tend to be defensive; they react only when threatened. Communication with stakeholders is one-way: from the company to the stakeholder. In the mid-1990s, Nike, Inc., discussed in a case study at the end of this book, was at this first stage.

Engaged Stage. At this second stage, companies typically become aware of changing public expectations and see the need to maintain their license to operate. Engaged companies may adopt formal policies, for example governing labor standards or human rights. They begin to interact with and listen to stakeholders, although engagement occurs mainly through established departments. Top managers become involved. Often, a company at this stage will step up its philanthropic giving or commit to specific environmental objectives. When Home Depot announced that after 2002 it would sell only environmentally certified wood products, this was an example of a company at the engaged stage of corporate citizenship.

Innovative Stage. At this third stage, organizations may become aware that they lack the capacity to carry out new commitments, prompting a wave of structural innovation. Departments begin to coordinate, new programs are launched, and many companies begin reporting their efforts to stakeholders. (Social auditing and reporting are further discussed later in this chapter.) External groups become more influential. Companies begin to understand more fully the business reasons for engaging in citizenship. Various actions

FIGURE 4.1 **Stages of Corporate Citizenship**

	Stage 1. Elementary	Stage 2. Engaged	Stage 3. Innovative	Stage 4. Integrated	Stage 5. Transforming
Citizenship Concept	Jobs, Profits, and Taxes	Philanthropy, Environmental Protection	Stakeholder Management	Sustainability or Triple Bottom Line	Change the Game
Strategic Intent	Legal Compliance	License to Operate	Business Case	Value Proposition	Market Creation or Social Change
Leadership	Lip Service, Out of Touch	Supporter, in the Loop	Steward, On Top of It	Champion, in Front of It	Visionary, Ahead of the Pack
Structure	Marginal: Staff Driven	Functional Ownership	Cross-Functional Coordination	Organizational Alignment	Mainstream: Business Driven
Issues Management	Defensive	Reactive, Policies	Responsive, Programs	Pro-Active, Systems	Defining
Stakeholder Relationships	Unilateral	Interactitve	Mutual Influence	Partnership	Multi-Organization Alliances
Transparency	Flank Protection	Public Relations	Public Reporting	Assurance	Full Disclosure

Source: Philip Mirvis and Bradley Googins, "Stages of Corporate Citizenship," *California Management Review,* vol. 48, no. 2, Winter 2006, pp. 104–26. Adapted from Figure 1, p. 108. Copyright © 2006, The Regents of the University of California. Reprinted from *California Management Review.* vol. 48, no. 2. By permission of the Regents.

taken by Shell during the late 1990s, described in the case "The Transformation of Shell" at the end of this book, illustrate a company at this stage.

Integrated Stage. As they move into the fourth stage, companies see the need to build more coherent initiatives. Mirvis and Googins cite the example of Asea Brown Boveri (ABB), a Switzerland-based multinational producer of power plants and automation systems, which carefully coordinates its many sustainability programs from the CEO level down to line officers in more than 50 countries where the company has a presence. Integrated companies may adopt triple-bottom line measures (explained later in this chapter), turn to external audits (as Mattel has done, as explained in the opening example of this chapter), and enter into ongoing partnerships with stakeholders.

Transforming Stage. This is the fifth and highest stage in the model. Companies at this stage have visionary leaders and are motivated by a higher sense of corporate purpose. They partner extensively with other organizations and individuals across business, industry, and national borders to address broad social problems and reach underserved markets. Hewlett-Packard's "e-inclusion" initiative, mentioned earlier in this chapter, is an example of a company that is working hard to spread the benefits of technology, both to help alleviate poverty and to build future markets.

HP has partnered with other organizations around the world to make computers available to people who would not otherwise have access to them. Slavutych, Ukraine, is a town populated almost entirely by people working to decommission the Chernobyl nuclear power plant, site of the worst nuclear accident in history, and their families. Working with a nearby university, HP established a 3-room computer center in the town library and furnished it with computers, printers, and other equipment. Vocational training offered at the center helps prepare the young people of Slavutych, including disabled children and orphans, for a better future after the reactor is fully decommissioned. This project is part of a global effort by HP to build "digital communities."[12]

The model's authors emphasize that individual companies can be at more than one stage at once, if their development progresses faster in some areas than in others. For example, a company might audit their activities and disclose the findings to the public in social reports (transparency, stage 5), but still be interacting with stakeholders in a pattern of mutual influence (stakeholder relationships, stage 3). This is normal, the authors point out, because each organization evolves in a way that reflects the particular challenges it faces. Nevertheless, because the dimensions of corporate citizenship are linked, they tend to become more closely aligned over time.

As corporate citizenship commitments have become more widespread in the global business community, they have attracted critics as well as admirers. Citizenship initiatives have been challenged on the grounds either that they represent superficial attempts to enhance reputation, without real substance, or that they are inherently limited by the corporation's profit-maximizing imperative, or both. Excerpts from several recent commentaries on the limits of corporate citizenship are presented in Exhibit 4.D.

Corporate Citizenship in Comparative Perspective

Businesses in many different countries now practice active citizenship. Corporate citizenship programs and partnerships have spread to every corner of the world map. At the same time, however, how businesses interpret and act on their citizenship commitments varies in important ways among and within regions. Consider the following recent research findings:

- A 2004 survey of companies in 15 countries in Europe, North America, and Asia found significant variations among regions, reflecting differences in laws, public expectation, and local practices. Companies in North America and Europe were more likely than ones in Asia to have written policies on most aspects of corporate citizenship (including human rights, freedom of association, and equal opportunity). However, Asian companies were more likely to have written policies on ethics (bribery and corruption), inspection of suppliers, and labor standards than were countries in the other two regions surveyed. This may reflect the fact that these were issues that many Asian companies experience directly and therefore identify as problems that need to be addressed.[13]
- However, corporate citizenship varied considerably among Asian countries as a 2005 study found. For example, Indian firms were 3 times more likely to engage in and report their social programs than firms in Indonesia, 72 to 24 percent. Rather than attributing numerous variations to economic development factors, the researchers found that national factors, such as government public policies supporting corporate social action or public assistance replacing the need for private, corporate programs, account for the variations across Asia.[14]

---

[12] More information about HP's e-inclusion initiative is available online at: *www.hp.com/e-inclusion/en.*

[13] Richard Welford, "Corporate Social Responsibility in Europe, North America, and Asia: 2004 Survey Results," *Journal of Corporate* Citizenship 17 (Spring 2005), pp. 33–42.

[14] Wendy Chapple and Jeremy Moon, "Corporate Social Responsibility (CSR) in Asia," *Business & Society* 44, no. 4 (December 2005), pp. 415–41.

Exhibit 4.D The Limits of Corporate Citizenship

"For most companies, CSR [corporate social responsibility] does not go very deep. There are many interesting exceptions—companies that have modeled themselves in ways different from the norm; often, particular practices that work well enough in business terms to be genuinely embraced; charitable endeavors that happen to be doing real good, and on a meaningful scale. But for most conventionally organized public companies—which means almost all of the big ones—CSR is little more than a cosmetic treatment. The human face that CSR applies to capitalism goes on each morning, gets increasingly smeared by day and washes off at night."

Source: "The Good Company: A Survey of Corporate Social Responsibility," *The Economist,* January 22, 2005, p. 4. Used by permission.

"CSR . . . is now a big, growing industry, seen as a vital tool in promoting and improving the public image of some of the world's largest corporations. In simple terms, companies make loud, public commitments to principles of ethical behavior and undertake 'good works' in the communities in which they operate. . . . The problem is that companies frequently use such initiatives to defend operations or ways of working which come in for public criticism . . . CSR, in other words, can become merely a branch of PR [public relations]. . . . Christian Aid is saying that CSR is a completely inadequate response to the sometimes devastating impact that multinational companies can have in an ever-more globalized world—and that is actually used to mask that impact."

Source: "Behind the Mask: The Real Face of Corporate Social Responsibility," *Christian Aid,* www.christian-aid.org.uk (released January 2004). Used by permission.

"Business leaders today say their companies care about more than profit and loss, that they feel responsible to society as a whole, not just to their shareholders. Corporate social responsibility is their new creed, a self-conscious corrective to earlier greed-inspired visions of the corporation. Despite this shift, the corporation itself has not changed. . . . Corporate social responsibility . . . holds out promises of help, reassures people, and sometimes works. We should not, however, expect very much from it. A corporation can do good only to help itself do well, a profound limit on just how much good it can do."

Source: Joel Bakan, *The Corporation: The Pathological Pursuit of Profit and Power* (New York: The Free Press, 2004), pp. 28, 50. Used by permission.

"[P]recisely because CSR is voluntary and market-driven, companies will engage in CSR only to the extent that it makes business sense for them to do so. . . . Unlike government regulation, it cannot force companies to make unprofitable but socially beneficial decisions. In most cases, CSR only makes business sense if the costs of more virtuous behavior remain modest. This imposes important constraints on the resources that companies can spend on CSR, and limits the improvements in corporate social and environmental performance that voluntary regulation can produce."

Source: David J. Vogel, *The Market for Virtue: The Potential and Limits of Corporate Social Responsibility* (Washington, DC: The Brookings Institution, 2005), p. 4. Used by permission.

- A comparative study of corporate citizenship in Latin America and the Caribbean found what the author called "a huge gap" between the practices of companies in Canada and the United States and those elsewhere in the Americas. The study found four levels of CSR activity, which it characterized as "running" (Canada and the United States), "catching up" (most developed Latin American countries, including Chile, Argentina, and Mexico), "walking" (the rest of South America), and "stalled" (Central America and the Caribbean). A standout in South America was Brazil, where companies such as Petrobras, the state-run oil company, had exemplary citizenship practices.[15]

[15] Paul Alexander Haslam, *The CSR System in Latin America and the Caribbean* (Ottawa: Canadian Foundation for the Americas, March 2004).

- Overall, corporate citizenship initiatives are more advanced in northern than in southern Europe. The idea of CSR has been slow to gain a foothold in the former communist nations of eastern and central Europe, where it is often associated with the paternalistic practices of discredited state-owned enterprises. In Hungary, for example, most major companies report regularly to shareholders but rarely provide public information about human rights, codes of conduct, social responsibilities, or compliance.[16]
- A comparison of company behavior in the United States and Europe found that governments in Europe played a much more important role in promoting CSR than in the United States, where citizenship activities were mostly voluntary (that is, not mandated by law). The European Commission, the executive body of the European Union, has strongly encouraged businesses to adopt CSR (although it has rejected mandatory rules). Shareholder activism was more pronounced in the United States; consumer activism was more pronounced in Europe.[17]

These studies suggest that corporate citizenship, while worldwide, varies across nations and regions. These differences are driven by variations in regulatory requirements, governmental involvement, stakeholder activism, and cultural traditions.

Social Performance Auditing

As companies around the world expand their commitment to corporate citizenship, they have also improved their capacity to measure performance and assess results. A **social performance audit** is a systematic evaluation of an organization's social, ethical, and environmental performance. Typically, it examines the impact of a business against two benchmarks: a company's own mission statement or policies and the behavior of other organizations and social norms often taking the form of global standards.[18]

Over the past decade, the demand for social auditing has gained momentum in Europe as well as in the United States. In Europe, auditing is in some cases required by law. In The Netherlands, for example, about 250 companies considered to have serious environmental impacts have been required since 1999 to conduct public environmental studies. In 2002, the French Parliament passed the "new economic regulations" law, which mandated that all French companies assess the sustainability of their social and environmental performance. The law divides social auditing into three categories: human resources (including employment indicators, remuneration, equity, and diversity); community (including the impact on and engagement with local populations and stakeholders); and labor standards (including respect for and promotion of International Labour Organization conventions). Social and environmental accounting has been required of businesses in the United Kingdom since 2005 under new regulations passed in response to corporate scandals in the United States.[19]

---

[16] East-West Management Institute, *Report on a Survey of Corporate Social Responsibility of the Largest Listed Companies in Hungary* (Budapest, Hungary, March 2004).

[17] David J. Vogel, "Corporate Social Responsibility: A European Perspective," presentation to the Business and Organizational Ethics Partnership, Santa Clara University, July 22, 2003.

[18] The concept of a social audit was first introduced in Howard R. Bowen, *Social Responsibilities of the Businessman* (New York: Harper, 1953).

[19] "New French Law Mandates Corporate Social and Environmental Reporting," SocialFunds.com, *www.socialfunds.com/news*; "Environmental, Social Policies Pierce Companies," *The Wall Street Journal*, August 28, 2002, p. A5; and "Mandated Risk Reporting Begins in UK," Business Ethics magazine, Spring 2005, p. 13.

In the United States, attention to social auditing lags behind Europe, but the gap may diminish soon. Although not legally mandated to do so, many U.S.-based companies now carry out social and environmental audits. According to 89 percent of the executives surveyed by PricewaterhouseCoopers in 2002, socially acceptable behavior, environmentally sensitive policies, and sound economic performance were likely to become important measures of corporate performance in the next five years. About 73 percent surveyed said they planned to begin issuing reports that measured corporate citizenship in the next five years, up from the 32 percent of the firms that already did so.

In response to the emerging interest shown by corporate executives, researchers have developed various ideal corporate citizenship scales against which a firm's citizenship activities can be compared. (One such list of principles appears in Exhibit 4.A, presented earlier in this chapter.) Social performance audits look not only at what an organization does, but also at the results of these actions. For example, if a company supports a tutorial program at a local school, the performance audit might not only look at the number of hours of employee volunteerism, but also assess change in student test scores as an indicator of the program's social impact. One company that has raised the bar for social auditing is Freeport-McMoran Copper and Gold, one of the world's largest metal mining companies.

In Indonesia, Freeport-McMoran operates the largest gold mine and the third-largest copper mine in the world. The company's mines there have long been criticized by human rights, shareholder, and environmental activists for abuses ranging from cooperation with the repressive military government to dumping toxic mining waste into rivers. In the early 2000s, the company responded by developing social and human rights policies and hiring an independent organization, the International Center for Corporate Accountability (ICCA), to carry out an audit of its Indonesian operations. ICCA's report, issued in late 2005, revealed many problems—including some that surprised the company, such as the fact their security personnel were serving as drivers for the Indonesian military. What shocked many observers then was that the company—instead of hiding the auditor's report—posted it to the Web for all to see. Commented *BusinessWeek,* "The company's willingness to open up so wide is a major development in the corporate responsibility movement. Certainly, no other global mining or oil company has come close to such transparency, long a key demand by human-rights groups."[20]

Freeport's auditing efforts suffered a setback in 2006, however, when protests broke out after people living nearby were prevented from panning for gold in rivers carrying the mine's waste. Company officials put the audit on hold until order could be restored. This incident served as a reminder that the ultimate purpose of audits is to change company behavior toward stakeholders, not just measure and report it.[21]

Some companies' social audits have met with harsh criticism from critics who have charged them with being deceptive efforts to enhance a company's reputation, without real substance. For example, activists attacked a social report produced by British American Tobacco (BAT) as hypocritical. Clive Bates, director of Action on Smoking and Health (ASH), accused the company of smuggling, unethical marketing practices, and

---

[20] "Freeport's Hard Look at Itself: The Mining Giant's Gutsy Human-Rights Audit May Set a Standard for Multinationals," *BusinessWeek,* October 24, 2005, pp. 108 ff. The audit report may be found at ICCA's Web site at *www.icca-corporateaccountability.org.*

[21] "So Much Gold, So Much Risk," *BusinessWeek,* May 29, 2006, pp. 52 ff.

document shredding.[22] Other public health activists criticized BAT for its promotion of teenage smoking and contributing to the harmful effects of smoking upon the general public. Paul Adams, managing director at BAT, acknowledged this criticism:

> I have readily accepted the role of championing CSR and social reporting throughout the Group. I see it as an opportunity, like our aspiration to launch potentially reduced exposure products, or our move to marketing with less mass media and more one-to-one relationships with adult smokers, that will help us further in taking accounting of society's concerns. . . . We recognised that some stakeholders would be unwilling to engage with us at all. We understand that trust can be fragile and difficult to build. . . . However, I feel that we . . . [need] to build more mutual understanding and that some stakeholders may even have been surprised by positive actions our companies are already taking.[23]

In another example, The Body Shop, a beauty products retailer, commissioned a social audit to provide an independent assessment of the company's social and ethical achievements, in response to concerns raised by some stakeholders. In the report, high marks were given to The Body Shop in areas such as the quality of its mission statement, corporate philanthropy, and environmental and animal welfare. But according to Kirk Hanson, who conducted the audit, the company was resistant to outside criticism and had a poor relationship with the public and the media.

Global Social Audit Standards

Standards to judge corporate performance have been developed by a number of organizations. These include the International Organisation for Standards (ISO 14001, 14063, and 26000), the Global Reporting Initiative, Social Accountability 8000, and the Institute of Social and Ethical Accountability's (ISEA)Accountability, or AA 1000, and the more general guidelines promulgated in the United Nations Global Compact (discussed in Chapter 7). The major characteristics of these global audit standards are summarized in Figure 4.2.

The acceptance and use of all of these audit standards by companies have grown since their inception. Each standard recognizes and concentrates on a combination of internally focused economic benefits for the firm, as well as externally focused social benefits for the environment and key stakeholders. The standards utilize a multiple stakeholder governance structure so that the firm interacts with many of the stakeholders it seeks to serve through its multiple performance targets. Many companies committed to socially responsive practices have used these and other standards and have made their reports available online for their stakeholders and the general public. While most of the standards are voluntary, some businesses have incorporated the standards into their strategic plans and more stakeholders are expecting firms to adhere to these global standards. A discussion case of an innovative corporate social audit is provided at the end of this chapter, featuring Gap Inc.

Social and Environmental Reporting

In addition to conducting extensive social performance measurement, some organizations have undertaken the additional action of reporting their efforts through corporate **social and environmental reports**. These reports are on the rise, as reported in an international survey on corporate responsibility in 2005. The survey report states corporate responsibility

---

[22] "Ethical Performance—Company Focus: British American Tobacco," *Ethical Performance, www.ethicalperformance.com.*

[23] "Social Report 2001/2002," British American Tobacco Web site, *www.bat.com/socialreport.*

FIGURE 4.2 **Summary of Global Social Audit Standards**

	ISO 14001	Global Reporting Initiative	SA 8000
Origin	1996	1997	1997
Scope	Environmental management standards	Economic, environmental, and social performance	Improved labor conditions for verification and public reporting
Governance	ISO council, technical management board, technical committees	Multistakeholder board of directors, technical advisors, stakeholder councils	SAI multistakeholder advisory board—experts from business, NGOs, government, and trade unions
Participants	ISO member countries, environmental NGOs, technical experts	Businesses; United Nations; human rights, environmental, labor groups; industry associations; governments	Businesses and their suppliers, trade associations, unions, auditing firms, NGOs, government
Funding	ISO member dues, document sales, volunteer efforts	Foundations, companies, Dutch government	Foundations, government grants, income from services and programs

	ISEA AA 1000	United Nations Global Compact	ISO 14063	ISO 26000
Origin	1999	1999	2001	Implementation target: 2008
Scope	Social/ethical accounting, auditing, and reporting	Business operating principles: human rights, labor, environment	Guidance on environmental communication	Social responsibility standards
Governance	ISEA; business members; nonprofits, academic, and consultancy organizations	UN Secretary General, Global Issues Network, ILO, stakeholder groups	ISO technical committee, working group	ISO technical management board, working group
Participants	Multistakeholder membership	Businesses, labor organizations, NGOs	ISO member countries experts: business, NGOs, standards organizations, consultants	ISO member countries, public and private sectors
Funding	Membership income, commissioned research, foundations	Voluntary government and foundation contributions	ISO member dues, document sales, volunteer efforts	ISO member dues, document sales, volunteer efforts

Sources: International Organisation for Standards, ISO 14001, *http://www.iso.org*; Global Reporting Initiative, *www.globalreporting.org*; Social Accountability International, SA 8000, *www.sa-intl.org*; Accountability, AA 1000, *www.accounability.org.uk*; United Nations Global Compact, *www.unglobalcompact.org*; International Organisation for Standards, ISO 14063, *www.iso14000.org*; International Organisation for Standards, ISO 26000, *isotc.iso.org*.

FIGURE 4.3

Trend in Corporate Social Reporting, 1993–Present

Source: KPMG's International Survey of Corporate Responsibility Reporting 2005 at *www.kpmg.com*.

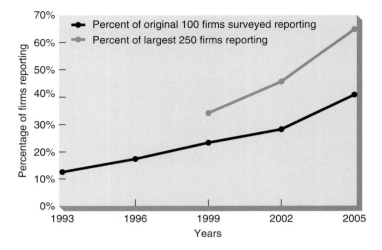

reporting has been steadily rising since 1993 and it has increased substantially in the past three years since 2002, as shown in Figure 4.3.

In another study undertaken by the Social Investment Research Analysts Network (SIRAN) in 2006, 79 companies from the Standard and Poor's (S&P) 100 Index had special sections of their Web sites dedicated to sharing information about their social and environmental policies and performance. Over one-third reported that their reports were based on the Global Reporting Initiative Sustainability Reporting guidelines. Forty-three companies in the S&P Index issued corporate social responsibility reports, up from 39 percent in 2005.[24]

According to the firms with social responsibility reports, economic drivers (74 percent) and ethical drivers (53 percent) were primary motivators for publishing the reports. Stakeholder dialogue was mentioned in almost 40 percent of the reports. Firms focused on various social issues, such as labor standards, working conditions, community involvement, and philanthropy, as well as economic issues. One of the most pressing issues of 2005—climate change—was discussed in about 85 percent of the reports.

When analyzed by geographic region, the survey found that social responsibility reporting was growing in many areas of the world. Companies in Japan (80 percent) and the United Kingdom (71 percent) have taken the lead in social reporting, with the highest percentage of stand-alone social reports. The largest increases in social reporting since 2002 have been in Italy, Spain, Canada, and France. In South Africa, the number of social reports rose from only 1 in 2002 to 18 reports issued in 2005.[25]

However, progress has been slower in some regions.

In Mexico, only 10 out of 75 companies studied by a research team in the early 2000s engaged in significant public reporting on their CSR practices. They were mostly situated in industries—such as petroleum, mining, tobacco, and cement—that were particularly vulnerable to criticism for their social and environmental impacts. Interestingly, multinational corporations that were themselves doing a good job of reporting were often not doing a good job of communicating their expectations in this regard to their Mexican business partners and subsidiaries.[26]

[24] "Socially Responsible Investment Analysts Find More Large U.S. Companies Reporting on Social and Environmental Issues," Social Investment Research Analysts Network report, *www.kld.com*.

[25] Data found in KPMG's International Survey of Corporate Responsibility Reporting 2005 at *www.kpmg.com*.

[26] Karen Paul et al., "Corporate Social Reporting in Mexico," *Journal of Corporate Citizenship* 22 (2006), pp. 67–80.

Balanced Scorecard

In addition to formal social responsibility reports, organizations have turned to other social reporting methods to communicate with their stakeholders. The **balanced score-card** system emerged on the scene in 1992. Introduced by two professors, Robert Kaplan and David Norton, the balanced scorecard is a focused set of key financial and nonfinancial indicators, with four quadrants or perspectives—people and knowledge, internal, customer, and financial. Balanced, in this case, does not necessarily mean equal; rather, it is a tool to encourage managers to develop and use performance metrics that cover all aspects of performance.

According to Kaplan and Norton, traditional financial measures are necessary, but no longer sufficient. Financial measures tell the story of past events, an adequate story for industrial-age companies for which investments in long-term capabilities and customer relations were not critical for success. These measures are inadequate, however, for guiding and evaluating the journey that information-age companies must take to create future value through investment in customers, suppliers, employees, processes, technology, and innovation.[27]

Organizations report several motivations for adopting a balanced scorecard approach. These include economic considerations, ethical considerations, innovation and learning, employee motivation, risk management or risk reduction, access to capital or increased shareholder value, reputation or brand, market position or share, strengthened supplier relationships, and cost savings. In a survey of nearly 200 firms that use the balanced scorecard system, four primary reasons were cited for adopting this system: the need to track progress toward achieving organizational goals, the need to align employee behavior with an organization's strategic objectives, the need to communicate strategy to everyone in a clear and simple manner, and the need to measure performance at different levels in an organization's strategies.[28]

Triple Bottom Line

Another approach to reporting corporate social performance is captured by the term **triple bottom line**.[29] Bottom line refers, of course, to the figure at the end of a company's financial statement that summarizes its earnings, after expenses. Triple bottom line reporting is when companies report to stakeholders not just their financial results—as in the traditional annual report to shareholders—but also their environmental and social impacts. Financial, social, and environmental results, taken together as an integrated whole, constitute a company's *triple* bottom line. Novo Nordisk, described in an opening example in this chapter, is one company that has adopted this approach.

As in the trend toward social reporting, firms in Europe have more quickly accepted triple bottom line than have those in the United States. European executives have seized on this notion as both a proactive way to provide stakeholders with increased transparency and a broader framework for decision making. A few American executives have also begun to see the appeal of the idea. "Triple bottom line reporting as it currently

---

[27] Adapted from the Balanced Scorecard Institute Web site at *www.balancedscorecard.org*.

[28] Raef Lawson, William Stratton, and Toby Hatch, "Scorecard Goes Global," *Strategic Finance*, March 2006, pp. 34–41.

[29] One of the more popular books on this topic is John Elkington, *Cannibals with Forks: The Triple Bottom Line of 21st Century Business—Conscientious Commerce* (Gabriola Island, British Columbia: New Society Publishers, 1998). For a critique of triple bottom line accounting, see Wayne Norman and Chris MacDonald, "Getting to the Bottom of 'Triple Bottom Line,'" *Business Ethics Quarterly*, 2004, pp. 243–62.

"We believe the real success of a business enterprise is measured by a 'triple bottom line': its impact on people, profits, and the planet," according to Rolltronics' annual triple bottom line report. Rolltronics, a Silicon Valley technology company, uses many innovative approaches to produce profits while protecting the environment. For example, an innovative manufacturing process enabled the firm to produce more electronic devices with less expensive equipment, while simultaneously saving on materials, energy, and labor costs.

"Our people create our success. Accordingly, all who work in our company share in our success," the company reported. Rolltronics includes those who live in the local communities and the global community in their quest to serve "their people." The concern for "the plant" is demonstrated in the firm's focus on sustainability, referring to the firm's ability to meet the needs of the current generation without compromising the ability of future generations to meet their needs. "Rolltronics will be one of the leaders in the transition to more sustainable industry. We believe that this is both good citizenship and good business practice."

Traveling halfway around the globe, we discover Sanford Limited, a large and long-established fishing company devoted to the harvesting, farming, processing, storage, and marketing of quality New Zealand seafood. Although Sanford Limited may be miles away from Rolltronics, it shares in the same triple bottom line considerations and reporting practices.

Sanford's first triple bottom line report made the following commitments: "to ensure that our operations are sustainable, to maximize positive social outcomes from both the employee and general community perspectives, and to maximize the economic growth and prosperity of the company for the benefits of shareholders, staff, customers, suppliers, and the general community." To further elaborate, Sanford provides an extensive performance scorecard emphasizing its commitments to areas of corporate governance, shareholder value, stakeholder satisfaction, employee orientation, and environmental performance. Sanford has "adopted a wider meaning to the term sustainability—achieving economic growth in an environmentally and socially responsible manner."

Both Rolltronics and Sanford Limited acknowledge and practice the interconnection between a concern for people, a pursuit of profitability, and sensitivity to the natural environment and report on their performance in the quest to balance these three business objectives.

Source: All quotations and other information were taken from the firms' respective Web sites at *www.rolltronics.com* and *www.sanford.co.nz.*

---

stands has its limitations but it's a great way for companies to disclose meaningful non-financial information that impacts their financial results," said Sunny Misser, global and U.S. leader of PricewaterhouseCoopers' sustainability practice. "This is the time for companies, especially in the U.S., to seize the opportunity."[30] Exhibit 4.E presents examples of U.S. and New Zealand-based businesses that have adopted a triple bottom line approach.

Businesses have recognized, either through adherence to their values and mission or from externally imposed pressures, that stakeholders demand greater **transparency**, that is, clear public reporting of an organization's performance to various stakeholders, and full reporting of not only financial but also social and environmental data. As firms accept the importance of stakeholders in their quest for financial viability, companies have discovered and welcomed new approaches for disclosure of information such as social auditing, use of the balanced scorecard, and triple bottom line reporting.

[30] "Europe Leads International Trend in 'Triple Bottom Line' Reporting," *Ethics Newsline*, Institute for Global Ethics, October 7, 2002, *www.globalethics.org.*

Exhibit 4.F — The Best Corporate Citizenship For the Past Seven Years

These organizations have made *Business Ethics'* The 100 Best Corporate Citizens list since the list began in 2000.

Brady Corporation	Hewlett-Packard	Southwest Airlines
Cisco Systems	Intel	Starbucks
Cummins Engine	Modine Manufacturing	Timberland
Ecolab	Pitney Bowes	Whirlpool
Graco	Procter & Gamble	
Herman Miller	St. Paul Travelers Cos.	

Source: "100 Best Corporate Citizens 2006," *Business Ethics*, Spring 2006, p. 26.

Awards for Corporate Citizenship

Recognition of corporate citizenship by business has increased dramatically. Since 2000, academic scholars have teamed with KLD Research and Analytics to assess and score businesses' stakeholder relations to create a list of the "100 Best Corporate Citizens." In 2006, the highest scores were achieved by Green Mountain Coffee, Hewlett-Packard, Advanced Micro Devices, Motorola, and Agilent Technologies.[31] Some firms have demonstrated sustained citizenship performance since the *Business Ethics* rankings began; these companies are shown in Exhibit 4.F.

Company reputation was the basis for the rankings developed through an online Harris Interactive and Reputation Institute–sponsored survey. The assessment focused on how people perceive the reputation of companies. For the seventh year in a row, Johnson & Johnson was rated number one by the public, maintaining its "caring company" image. People cited Johnson & Johnson's strong financial performance coupled with its customer service, vision and leadership, positive workplace environment, and social responsibility as contributing to its lasting reputation. Other firms among the leaders were Coca-Cola and Google (which made the list for the first time). Technology companies had the strongest reputation of any industry, with Sony, Microsoft, Intel, IBM, and Apple Computer contributing to this ranking along with Google. Perhaps reflecting the effects of the corporate scandals of the early 2000s (further discussed in Chapter 15), the overall reputation of American businesses continued to slip, despite the growing commitment of many companies to ethics and social responsibility. In 2005, 71 percent of the respondents rated American businesses' reputation as "not good" or "terrible," compared with 68 percent in 2004.[32]

In addition to the rankings calculated by academics and reported from public opinion polls, business managers conducted their own assessment of corporate reputation and citizenship performance. *Fortune* magazine's America's Most Admired list annually identifies companies that are admired by their peers for social responsibility.

[31] For a complete list of the 100 best corporate citizens and an explanation of the methodology used to develop the list, see *Business Ethics*, Spring 2006, pp. 20–28.

[32] "Ranking Corporate Reputations," *The Wall Street Journal*, December 6, 2005, *www.wsj.com*.

UPS topped the list in 2005 for the third consecutive year. The company was recognized for its sustainability and philanthropy. UPS strives to increase fuel efficiency and decrease emissions of its massive transportation fleet, utilizing alternative fuel vehicles. In addition, the company donated $43 million in 2005 to charities focusing on hunger and literacy. Publix Super Markets was also recognized on *Fortune*'s list. The company's founder, George W. Jenkins, believed in customer service, charitable giving, and sharing the wealth of his business with his workers, known as associates, from 1930 until his death in 1996. These values are still the mainstay of company practices of corporate citizenship. Starbucks was acknowledged by business executives as a pioneer in corporate responsibility by offering healthcare benefits and stock, called bean stock, even to its part-time employees. The company also forged partnerships with coffee growers around the world designed to provide growers with a fair price for their beans, often higher than the fair market price. Herman Miller, a manufacturer of stylish furniture based in Zeeland, Michigan, another admired company, has a tradition of social and environmental responsibility that dates back to the 1920s. The company has received prizes for the environmental design of its products and buildings.[33]

These companies exemplify some of the best of corporate citizenship practice in an era when firms are increasingly being called upon to move beyond rhetoric and put their commitment to social and environmental responsibility into action.

Summary

- Corporate citizenship refers to putting social responsibility into practice by building stakeholder partnerships, discovering business opportunities in serving society, and transforming a concern for financial performance into a vision of integrated financial *and* social performance. When a company does business in more than one country in this way, it is practicing global corporate citizenship. Corporate citizenship programs can be considered a strategic investment by the firm.

- Leading-edge companies have developed a variety of structures and processes to manage their citizenship responsibilities, including creating departments of corporate citizenship.

- Companies progress through five distinct stages as they develop as corporate citizens; these are termed the elementary, engaged, innovative, integrated, and transforming stages. A particular company may be at more than one stage at once, as it may progress more quickly on some dimensions than on others.

- Corporate citizenship differs among various countries and regions of the world, according to variations in regulatory requirements, stakeholder expectations, and historical and cultural patterns of behavior.

- Many companies have experimented with systemic audits of their social, ethical, and environmental performance, measured against company policies as well as auditing standards developed by global standard-setting organizations. An emerging trend is the practice of communicating social, environmental, and financial results to stakeholders through a balanced scorecard system or in an integrated, triple bottom line report.

- Recent awards for corporate citizenship illustrate best practices against which other firms may benchmark their own programs.

[33] "How UPS, Starbucks, Disney Do Good," *Fortune*, February 25, 2006, *www.money.cnn.com.*

Key Terms	balanced scorecard, *79*	global corporate	social performance
	citizenship profile, *66*	citizenship, *68*	audit, *74*
	corporate citizenship, *65*	social and environmental	transparency, *80*
	department of corporate	reports, *76*	triple bottom line, *79*
	citizenship, *69*		

Internet Resources

www.accountability.org.uk	AccountAbility: Institute for Social and Ethical Accountability
www.bsr.org	Businesses for Social Responsibility
www.globalreporting.org	Global Reporting Initiative
www.iso14000.org	International Organization for Standardization
www.sa-intl.org	Social Accountability International

Discussion Case: *The Gap Inc.'s Social Responsibility Report*

In 2004, Gap Inc. issued a Social Responsibility Report that was widely seen as unprecedented in the annals of social auditing. "This report is historic," said Nikki Bas, executive director of Sweatshop Watch, an activist organization. "It really raises the bar," commented David Schilling of the Interfaith Center on Corporate Responsibility. "It's in the category of pioneer work."

Gap Inc., based in San Francisco, was one of the world's largest specialty retailers of clothing, accessories, and personal care products. Under the brands The Gap, Banana Republic, Old Navy, and Forth & Towne, the company operated more than 3,000 stores in the United States, the United Kingdom, Canada, France, and Japan, earning $16 billion in revenue in 2004.

In the 1990s and early 2000s, the company became the target of repeated protests by human rights groups, charging that Gap products were often made in sweatshops—factories where underage, underpaid workers performed 16-hour or longer days in abhorrent, unsafe conditions. Activist investors filed a shareholder resolution demanding greater transparency. United Students Against Sweatshops organized rallies at colleges and universities, claiming that Gap was more concerned about profits than the well-being of workers.

Rather than deny these allegations, Gap Inc. stepped up by developing one of the most comprehensive factory-monitoring programs in the apparel industry. The company pledged to undertake a thorough assessment of its operations around the world. Gap Inc. turned to Social Accountability International (SAI), discussed earlier in this chapter, to help it develop a Code of Vendor Conduct. The company pledged to do business only with vendors (contractors) that agreed to a high set of standards, including the following:

- No discrimination in employment.
- Support for internationally recognized human rights.
- Protection of freedom of association and the right to collective bargaining.
- No child labor.
- No forced or compulsory labor.
- No corruption, including extortion and bribery.

To make sure that contractors were abiding by the code, the company hired more than 90 vendor compliance officers, or VCOs. These individuals came from the communities where they worked, so they would be able to communicate well and understand the culture of the contractors they audited. In preparing the 2004 social responsibility report, these VCOs made 8,500 visits to more than 3,000 factories in 50 countries.

What was extraordinary about the resulting report, which the company released publicly, was that it did not pull its punches. The audit acknowledged that forced labor, child labor, pay below the minimum wage, physical punishment, and coercion of workers had occurred at factories where contractors produced Gap products. The most common issues flagged were health and safety problems, breaches of local laws, faulty age documentation, excessive hours, and unclear wage statements. Problems were particularly serious in China, the report noted.

Gap recognized that it was taking a risk by releasing its findings—negative as well as positive. "For us to be transparent, we had to be willing to live with bad reactions to the report," said Anne Gust, Gap's chief compliance officer. "We knew it was not going to be strictly, 'Gap is good.' It's more complicated than that."

In a departure from usual apparel industry practice, the company acted on its findings by actually terminating its contracts with 70 factories that did not meet its standards. In a letter to shareholders, Paul Pressler, Gap's president and CEO, declared his intention to correct these problems. "I'm optimistic," he said, "[that] progress in our industry over the next decade will be more profound than anything we've seen, including improved labor standards, factory conditions and business practices—because ethical sourcing represents a better way of doing business in a global economy."

In another unusual move, Gap invited Social Accountability International to audit its auditing effort, and brought in another nongovernmental organization, Verité, to help provide additional training for its vendor compliance officers.

Going forward, the company set out to forge partnerships with local governments, civil society groups, trade unions, and businesses to address the underlying causes of poor working conditions. The idea was to work collaboratively with external stakeholders to address systemic issues that had made poor working conditions common in the garment industry. For example, the company participated in a Vendor Summit to forge better relationships with its suppliers, and held "outreach" sessions with stakeholders in the United States, the United Kingdom, and Central America. It worked with the International Labour Organization to improve working conditions in Cambodia.

The company also committed to improving its ability to record, analyze and report compliance data in meaningful ways. More complete data would help it work with contractors to better their performance and to track improvements over time, it said.

Claiming that Gap Inc. has completely turned the corner, and that activists should look elsewhere for targets for their concerns, may be premature. But there certainly appears to be a new way of doing business at Gap Inc. Said CEO Pressler, "We've learned the power of collective engagement, and of open, honest discussion about the issues that we and many other companies face."

Source: The Gap Inc. 2004 Social Responsibility Report may be found at *www.gapinc.com/public/documents /CSR_Report_04.pdf*. All quotations are from this document, except as noted. Other information is drawn from Fighting Against Gap Sweatshops, *www.service.emory.edu/~mpovari/fightingagainst.htm*; Fresno GAP Anti-sweatshop Campaign, *www.fresnoalliance.com/home/gap%20article.htm*; and "Gap's New Look: See-Through," *Fast Company,* September 2004.

Discussion Questions

1. Do you think Gap Inc. has demonstrated global corporate citizenship, as defined in this chapter? Why or why not?

2. In its response to problems in its contractor factories, do you think Gap Inc. moved through the stages of corporate citizenship presented in this chapter? Why or why not?

3. Compare Gap Inc.'s social audit and reporting practices with those of other companies described in this chapter. In what ways is Gap's effort different, and in what ways is it similar? Do you think Gap's social auditing and reporting is better or worse than those of other companies, and why?

4. What are the costs and benefits to Gap Inc. of its approach?

PART THREE

Business and the Ethical Environment

CHAPTER FIVE

Ethics and Ethical Reasoning

People who work in business frequently encounter and must deal with on-the-job ethical issues. Being ethical is important to the individual, the organization, and the global marketplace, all the more so in today's business climate post-Enron. Managers and employees alike must learn how to recognize ethical dilemmas and know why they occur. In addition, they need to be aware of the role their own ethical character plays in their decision-making process, as well as the influence exerted by the ethical character of others. Finally, managers and employees must be able to analyze the ethical problems they encounter at work to determine an ethical resolution to these dilemmas.

This chapter focuses on these key learning objectives:

- Defining ethics and business ethics.
- Evaluating why businesses should be ethical.
- Knowing why ethical problems occur in business.
- Identifying managerial values as influencing ethical decision making.
- Recognizing the core elements of ethical character.
- Understanding stages of moral reasoning.
- Analyzing ethical problems using generally accepted ethics theories.

Most people are familiar with recent corporate scandals and the high-profile executives sentenced and fined for their actions—Bernard Ebbers (WorldCom), Dennis Kozlowski (Tyco), John and Timothy Rigas (Adelphia), and Kenneth Lay and Jeffrey Skilling (Enron). But how many know the names Betty Vinson, Troy Normand, David Myers, Deryck C. Maughan, Thomas W. Jones, Peter Scaturro, or Hannibal Crumpler?

Betty Vinson, a former manager in WorldCom's accounting department, was sentenced to five months in jail and five months of house arrest. Troy Normand, also a WorldCom accounting manager, received three years probation. David Myers, former WorldCom controller, pleaded guilty to fraud, conspiracy, and filing false documents. He was sentenced to one year and one day in prison. All three of these managers played a role in the largest accounting fraud in U.S. history.

Citigroup's bank operations were shut down in Japan after regulators found a lack of internal controls that had enabled employees to engage in fraudulent activities. Three executives were forced to resign in the wake of the scandal: Deryck C. Maughan, chairman of Citigroup's extensive international operations; Thomas W. Jones, head of the bank's asset management division; and Peter Scaturro, chief executive of private banking.

Hannibal Crumpler, former vice president and division controller, was the only Health-South manager convicted by jurors in the $2.7 billion accounting fraud. Crumpler was sentenced to 8 years in federal prison. Other HealthSouth executives pleaded guilty and the chief executive, Richard Scrushy, was acquitted on all charges.[1]

Not only have CEOs and CFOs been the targets of criminal investigations and held liable for their actions in recent ethics scandals, so too have lower-level managers involved in the operations or accounting departments of their firms. The Justice Department, the Securities and Exchange Commission, and federal and state prosecutors have aggressively pursued all employees involved in unethical or illegal activity, not just top executives.

How does a person know what behavior is right or wrong in the business world? What might lead an individual to act unethically? Does the root cause lie in a person's character or direction given by top management? Were these mid-level executives simply following orders? If so, should they be sent to jail or forced to resign for doing what their bosses told them to do? How can an employee refuse to follow orders, even when their boss is the CEO or CFO of the firm? These questions will be discussed later in this chapter.

With examples of the largest business frauds in the history of the United States as a backdrop, this chapter explores the meaning of ethics, explains why businesses should be ethical, identifies the different types of ethical problems that occur in business, and focuses on an ethical decision-making framework influenced by the core elements of an individual's ethical character. Chapter 6 then explains how ethical performance in business can be improved by strengthening the organization's culture and climate and by providing organizational safeguards, such as policies, training, and reporting procedures.

---

[1] "Former Executive at WorldCom Gets 5-Month Jail Term," *The Wall Street Journal*, August 8, 2005, *online.wsj.com*; "WorldCom Ex-Controller Myers Gets Year-and-a-Day Jail Term," *The Wall Street Journal*, August 11, 2005, *online.wsj.com*; "Citigroup Forces Resignations of 3 Senior Executives," *The New York Times*, October 20, 2004, *www.nytimes.com*; and "HealthSouth Executive Sentenced to Eight Years," *The New York Times*, June 16, 2006, *www.nytimes.com*.

The Meaning of Ethics

Ethics is the conception of right and wrong conduct that tells us whether our behavior is moral or immoral, good or bad. Ethics deals with fundamental human relationships—how we think and behave toward others and how we want them to think and behave toward us. **Ethical principles** are guides to moral behavior. For example, in most societies lying to, stealing from, deceiving, and harming others are considered unethical and immoral. Honesty, keeping promises, helping others, and respecting the rights of others are considered ethically and morally desirable behavior. Such basic rules of behavior are essential for the preservation and continuation of organized life everywhere.

These notions of right and wrong come from many sources. Religious beliefs are a major source of ethical guidance for many. The family institution—whether two parents, a single parent, or a large family with brothers and sisters, grandparents, aunts, cousins, and other kin—imparts a sense of right and wrong to children as they grow up. Schools and schoolteachers, neighbors and neighborhoods, friends, admired role models, ethnic groups, and the ever-present electronic media and the Internet influence what we believe to be right and wrong in life. The totality of these learning experiences creates in each person a concept of ethics, morality, and socially acceptable behavior. This core of ethical beliefs then acts as a moral compass that helps to guide a person when ethical puzzles arise.

Ethical ideas are present in all societies, organizations, and individual persons, although they may vary greatly from one to another. Your ethics may not be the same as your neighbor's; one particular religion's notion of morality may not be identical to another's; and what is considered ethical in one society may be forbidden in another society. These differences raise the important and controversial issue of **ethical relativism**, which holds that ethical principles should be defined in the context of various periods in history, a society's traditions, the special circumstances of the moment, or personal opinion. In this view, the meaning given to ethics would be relative to time, place, circumstance, and the person involved. In that case, there would be no universal ethical standards on which people around the globe could agree. But for companies conducting business in several societies at one time, whether or not (and which) ethics are relevant can be vitally important; we discuss those issues in more detail in Chapter 6.

For the moment, we can say that despite the diverse systems of ethics that exist within our own society and throughout the world, all people everywhere do depend on ethical systems to tell them whether their actions are right or wrong, moral or immoral, approved or disapproved. Ethics, in this sense, is a universal human trait, found everywhere.

What Is Business Ethics?

Business ethics is the application of general ethical ideas to business behavior. Business ethics is not a special set of ethical ideas different from ethics in general and applicable only to business. If dishonesty is considered to be unethical and immoral, then anyone in business who is dishonest with stakeholders—employees, customers, stockholders, or competitors—is acting unethically and immorally. If protecting others from harm is considered to be ethical, then a company that recalls a dangerously defective product is acting in an ethical way. To be considered ethical, business must draw its ideas about what is proper behavior from the same sources as everyone else. Business should not try to make up its own definitions of what is right and wrong. Employees and managers may

FIGURE 5.1

Observations of Unethical Behavior at Work

Source: *2005 National Business Ethics Survey*, Ethics Resource Center, Washington, D.C.

Fifty-two percent of employees observed at least one type of misconduct in the workplace in the past year. Types of misconduct include (in order of frequency observed):

- Abusive or intimidating behavior toward employees
- Lying to employees, customers, vendors, or the public
- A situation that places employee interests over organizational interests
- Violations of safety regulations
- Misreporting of actual time worked
- Discrimination on the basis of race, color, gender, age or similar categories
- Stealing or theft
- Sexual harassment

FIGURE 5.2

Why Should Business Be Ethical?

To meet demands of business stakeholders.
To enhance business performance.
To comply with legal requirements.
To prevent or minimize harm.
To promote personal morality.

believe at times that they are permitted or even encouraged to apply special or weaker ethical rules to business situations, but society does not condone or permit such an exception. Evidence of unethical behavior at work is shown in Figure 5.1.

Why Should Business Be Ethical?

Why should business be ethical? What prevents a business firm from piling up as much profit as it can, in any way it can, regardless of ethical considerations? Figure 5.2 lists the major reasons why business firms should promote a high level of ethical behavior.

Meet Demands of Business Stakeholders

We mentioned one reason businesses should be ethical when discussing social responsibility in Chapter 3. Organizational stakeholders demand business to exhibit high levels of ethical performance and social responsibility. In a 10-country poll of public opinion, people in 9 of the 10 countries (Australia, Canada, Great Britain, Mexico, Japan, Germany, South Africa, Russia, and the United States, with only the Chinese people disagreeing) preferred setting higher ethical standards and improving society over the more traditional corporate goals of making a profit, paying taxes, creating jobs, and obeying the law.[2]

Some businesses know that meeting stakeholders' expectations is good business. When a company upholds ethical standards, consumers may conduct more business with the firm and the stockholders may benefit as well, as illustrated in the story of the Co-operative Bank, a retail bank based in Manchester, United Kingdom, whose slogan is "Customer led, ethically guided."

[2] Juliet Altham, "Business Ethics versus Corporate Social Responsibility: Competing or Complementary Approaches," *International Business Ethics Review*, Spring 2001, pp. 10–12.

The Co-operative Bank revealed that it had turned away $12 million in business annually from firms whose policies violated the bank's ethical standards, saying the loss was more than made up by income from consumers who supported the bank's strong ethical stand. The bank's policies precluded it from lending funds to firms that were involved in animal testing, nuclear power, unfair labor practices, or weapons.[3]

Enhance Business Performance

Some people argue that another reason for businesses to be ethical is that it enhances the firm's performance, or simply: *ethics pays.*

A study conducted by a DePaul University accounting professor found a statistically significant linkage between management commitment to strong controls that emphasize ethically responsible behavior on the one hand and favorable corporate financial performance on the other. Further support for the relationship between being ethical and being profitable was found in a study conducted by the Institute for Business Ethics in the United Kingdom. Three of the four measures used in the study—economic value added, market value added, and price/earnings ratio—were stronger for companies that had a code of ethics than for those that did not. The study data also indicated that firms with an explicit commitment to doing business ethically had produced profit/turnover ratios 18 percent higher than those without a similar commitment.[4]

Being ethical imparts a sense of trust, which promotes positive alliances among business partners. If this trust is broken, the unethical party may be shunned and ignored. This situation occurred when Malaysian government officials gave the cold shoulder to executives of a French company. When asked why they were being unfriendly, a Malaysian dignitary replied, "Your chairman is in jail!" The nurturing of an ethical environment and the development of ethical safeguards, discussed in the next chapter, can be critical influences in positively affecting a firm's financial performance.

Comply with Legal Requirements

Doing business ethically is also often a legal requirement. Two recent laws, in particular, provide direction for companies interested in being more ethical in their business operations. Although they apply only to U.S.-based firms, these legal requirements also provide a model for firms that operate outside the United States.

The first is the **U.S. Corporate Sentencing Guidelines**, which provides a strong incentive for businesses to promote ethics at work.[5] The sentencing guidelines come into play when an employee of a firm has been found guilty of criminal wrongdoing and the firm is facing sentencing for the criminal act, since the firm is responsible for actions taken by its employees. To determine the sentencing, the judge computes a

---

[3] "U.K. Bank Foregoes Business—But Not Profits—Due to Ethical Stance," Institute for Global Ethics, *Ethics Newsline,* May 10, 2004, *www.globalethics.org/newsline.*

[4] Curtis C. Verschoor, "A Study of the Link between a Corporation's Financial Performance and Its Commitment to Ethics," *Journal of Business Ethics* 17 (1998), pp. 1509–16; and Simon Webley and Elise More, *Does Business Ethics Pay? Ethics and Financial Performance,* Institute of Business Ethics, 2003.

[5] For a thorough discussion of the U.S. Corporate Sentencing Guidelines, see Dan R. Dalton, Michael B. Metzger, and John W. Hill, "The 'New' U.S. Sentencing Commission Guidelines: A Wake-Up Call for Corporate America," *Academy of Management Executive* 8 (1994), pp. 7–13; and Dove Izraeli and Mark S. Schwartz, "What Can We Learn from the U.S. Federal Sentencing Guidelines for Organizational Ethics?" *Journal of Business Ethics,* 1998, pp. 1045–55.

culpability (degree of blame) score using the guidelines, based on whether or not the company has:

1. Established standards and procedures to reduce criminal conduct.
2. Assigned high-level officer(s) responsibility for compliance.
3. Not assigned discretionary authority to "risky" individuals.
4. Effectively communicated standards and procedures through training.
5. Taken reasonable steps to ensure compliance—monitor and audit systems, maintain and publicize reporting system.
6. Enforced standards and procedures through disciplinary mechanisms.
7. Following detection of offense, responded appropriately and prevented reoccurrence.

Companies that have taken these steps, or most of them, receive lesser sentences, such as lower fines.

> The impact of the sentencing guidelines was felt by Hoffman-LaRoche. The multinational pharmaceutical company pleaded guilty to a price-fixing conspiracy in the vitamins market that spanned nine years and was fined $500 million. Although this was a significant financial blow to the firm, the government noted that the sentencing guidelines permitted a fine as high as $1.3 billion against Hoffman-LaRoche. The sentence was reduced because Hoffman-LaRoche had met many of the sentencing guidelines directives.

In 2005 the U.S. Supreme Court weakened this legal requirement when the court ruled that federal judges were not required to follow the federal sentencing guidelines but could rely upon them in an advisory role.[6] However, many firms have developed and maintain ethics and compliance programs based on the Sentencing Commission's "seven steps."

Another legal requirement imposed upon U.S. businesses is the **Sarbanes-Oxley Act** of 2002.[7] Born from the ethics scandals at Enron, WorldCom, Tyco, and others, this law sought to ensure that firms maintained high ethical standards in how they conducted and monitored business operations. Specifically, the Act addresses the following issues:

- The firm's audit committee is entrusted with auditor oversight with all independent directors on the committee.
- Certain nonaudit services by auditors to clients are banned, nonaudit services must be preapproved by the audit committee, the lead auditor must be rotated every five years, and auditors report to the audit committee.
- The CEO and CFO must sign off on financial statements as accurate and fair and must repay bonuses if a restatement of financials is undertaken.
- A Public Company Accounting Oversight Board is established.
- Firms are not permitted to offer loans to their executive officers or board of directors.
- SEC rules will create guidelines for internal controls and financial reporting procedures; require the adoption of, or waiver for, a code of ethics for the board; mandate that a financial expert serve on the board; and compel the firm to state its financial condition in plain English on a rapid or current basis.

---

[6] "High Court Ruling Casts Doubt on Federal Sentencing Guidelines," *The Wall Street Journal,* January 12, 2005, *online.wsj.com.*

[7] See Howard Rockness and Joanne Rockness, "Legislated Ethics: From Enron to Sarbanes-Oxley, the Impact on Corporate America," *Journal of Business Ethics,* 2005, pp. 31–54.

Exhibit 5.A   Nonprofit Voluntarily Seeks Sarbanes-Oxley Compliance

University of Pittsburgh Medical Center (UPMC) voluntarily accepted this regulatory standard established by Sarbanes-Oxley, despite the fact that, as a private firm, it was not governed by the Act. In a reported push to improve its corporate governance and the transparency of its operations to the public, UPMC's Chairman G. Nicholas Beckwith III said the organization was "on schedule to become one of the first academic medical centers in the country to comply with the most rigorous provisions of Sarbanes-Oxley." UMPC recognized that voluntary compliance might yield unexpected benefits through improved efficiency and set a standard for transparency for nonprofit organizations.

The public trust appeared to be the cornerstone theme for Beckwith and his management of UPMC. "Who owns us? The entire Western Pennsylvania region owns us. That's the people we are accountable to," explained Robert Cindrich, who chaired the UPMC audit committee. "Nick [Beckwith] really defined us as an asset belonging to the region."

The benefits to the UPMC system of Sarbanes-Oxley compliance were several. For example, billing shops at three different health care facilities were standardized and consolidated in one place. Forecasting and accounting information was available faster, and supply chain management improved. Best of all for UPMC, the cost of compliance was much less than anticipated. UPMC budgeted $6 million for Sarbanes-Oxley compliance efforts, but CFO Rob DeMichiei stated that out-of-pocket expenses would likely be less than $1 million. The anticipated savings easily exceeded the cost of compliance, and the endeavor brought peace of mind to the organization's leaders. "I can't tell you how much better we feel about our internal controls," said DeMichiei.

Source: Kris B. Mamula, "UPMC Seeks Nonprofit First: Experts Hail Sarbanes-Oxley Compliance Effort," *Pittsburgh Business Times,* October 28, 2005, *www.bizjournals.com/pittsburgh;* and Christopher Snowbeck, "UPMC Draws Line at Children's in New Effort at Corporate Compliance," *Pittsburgh Post-Gazette,* January 14, 2006, p. A9.

After passage of the Sarbanes-Oxley Act, many business leaders grumbled over the significant costs incurred to comply with the Act's various requirements. Experts estimated that compliance costs were likely to total $7 billion annually for firms governed by the legislation. Even European financial officers were critical of the Act, as well as its European counterpart, the International Financial Reporting Standards. Seven out of eight of 236 European CFOs questioned believed that these regulations offered no positive benefits. Forty percent believed them to be an outright hindrance, increasing time and cost commitments for no positive results.[8]

However, a columnist for the *Financial Times,* Morgen Witzel, argued that "there are many benefits to be gained from a positive approach to regulation." He mentioned better investor and customer relations, enhanced internal processes, greater efficiencies, and the opportunity for proactive organizations to shape the regulatory agenda. These benefits from compliance are shown in Exhibit 5.A.[9] The Sarbanes-Oxley Act is discussed further in Chapter 15.

Prevent or Minimize Harm

Another reason businesses and their employees should act ethically is to prevent harm to the general public and the corporation's many stakeholders. One of the strongest ethical principles is stated very simply: *Do no harm.* A company that is careless in disposing

[8] "The Virtues of Compliance over Complaint," *Financial Times,* January 15, 2006, *www.ft.com;* "Here It Comes: The Sarbanes-Oxley Backlash," *The New York Times,* April 17, 2005, *www.nytimes.com;* and "Learning to Love Sarbanes-Oxley," *BusinessWeek,* November 21, 2005, pp. 126–28.

[9] "The Virtues of Compliance over Complaint"; and "UPMC Seeks Nonprofit First: Experts Hail Sarbanes-Oxley Compliance Efforts," *Pittsburgh Business Times,* October 28, 2005, *www.bizjournals.com.*

of toxic chemical wastes that cause disease and death is breaking this ethical injunction. Many ethical rules operate to protect society against various types of harm, and businesses are expected to observe these commonsense ethical principles.

Preventing harm also relates to protecting business firms from abuse by unethical employees and unethical competitors. Employee theft and fraud have reached epidemic proportions for businesses throughout the world. The European Retail Theft Barometer, a Europewide study of crime in the retail sector, reported that retail crime cost European businesses 29.6 billion pounds annually. A 2004 report by the Association of Certified Fraud Examiners (ACFE) indicated that the situation in the United States might be even worse.

> The ACFE report uncovered 508 cases of occupational fraud totaling more than $761 million in losses to American businesses. The typical business lost about 6 percent of its annual revenues to fraud each year, according to the report. In total ACFE estimated that U.S. businesses lost about $660 billion annually due to employee fraud. In addition, losses due to theft by low-level employees were a critical problem. Companies with fewer than 100 employees suffered average losses of $98,000 annually due to employee theft.[10]

Promote Personal Morality

A final reason for promoting ethics in business is a personal one. Most people want to act in ways that are consistent with their own sense of right and wrong. Being pressured to contradict their personal values creates emotional stress for people. Knowing that one works in a supportive ethical climate contributes to one's sense of psychological security. According to a LRN study, a California-based legal and ethics training company, 94 percent of employees said it was critical or important that the company they work for is ethical. An Ethics Resource Center report noted that when employees "perceive that others are held accountable for their actions," the overall employee satisfaction at work is 32 percent higher.[11]

Why Ethical Problems Occur in Business

If businesses have so many reasons to be ethical, why do ethical problems occur? Although not necessarily common or universal, ethical problems occur frequently in business. Finding out what causes them is one step toward minimizing their impact on business operations and on the people affected. Some of the main reasons are summarized in Figure 5.3 and are discussed next.

Personal Gain and Selfish Interest

Desire for personal gain, or even greed, causes some ethics problems. Businesses sometimes employ people whose personal values are less than desirable. They will put their own welfare ahead of all others, regardless of the harm done to other employees, the company, or society.

A manager or employee who puts his or her own self-interest above all other considerations is called an **ethical egoist**. Self-promotion, a focus on self-interest to the point

---

[10] *2004 Report to the Nation on Occupational Fraud and Abuse*, Association of Certified Fraud Examiners, *www.acfe.com*.

[11] "Workers Value Ethical Managers," Institute for Global Ethics, *Ethics Newsline*, August 7, 2006, *www.globalethics.org*, and *2005 National Business Ethics Survey: How Employees View Ethics in Their Organizations, 1994–2005* (Washington, DC: Ethics Resource Center, 2005).

FIGURE 5.3
**Why Ethical
Problems Occur in
Business**

Reason	Nature of Ethical Problem	Typical Approach	Attitude
Personal gain and selfish interest	Selfish interest versus others' interests	Egotistical mentality	"I want it!"
Competitive pressures on profits	Firm's interest versus others' interests	Bottom-line mentality	"We have to beat the others at all costs!"
Conflicts of interest	Multiple obligations or loyalties	Favoritism mentality	"Help yourself and those closest to you!"
Cross-cultural contradictions	Company's interests versus diverse cultural traditions and values	Ethnocentric mentality	"Foreigners have a funny notion of what's right and wrong."

of selfishness, and greed are traits commonly observed in an ethical egoist. The ethical egoist tends to ignore ethical principles accepted by others, believing that ethical rules are made for others. *Altruism*—acting for the benefit of others when self-interest is sacrificed—is seen to be sentimental or even irrational. "Looking out for number one" is the ethical egoist's motto, as the following stories show.[12]

One of the most egregious ethical egoists in recent history was Dennis Kozlowski, former CEO of Tyco. New York prosecutors charged Kozlowski with stealing more than $170 million from the company. Kozlowski also was accused of borrowing $270 million from a company loan program intended to help him pay taxes, but he improperly used 90 percent of this money for personal expenses, such as yachts, jewelry, fine art, and real estate. Kozlowski was sentenced to up to 25 years in a New York state prison in 2005.[13]

Competitive Pressures on Profits

When companies are squeezed by tough competition, they sometimes engage in unethical activities to protect their profits. This may be especially true in companies whose financial performance is already substandard. Research has shown that poor financial performers and companies with financial uncertainty are more prone to commit illegal acts.

Senior executives at Samsung of South Korea, the world's largest memory-chip maker by revenue, pleaded guilty to a U.S. price-fixing charge and were ordered to pay $300 million in fines for its role in a global cartel designed to drive up prices for electronic memory. The U.S. Justice Department uncovered evidence that Samsung and other firms under investigation repeatedly met to discuss prices on dynamic random-access memory chips, agreed on the prices to be quoted to customers, and exchanged information about sales volume in order to

---

[12] For a compact discussion of ethical egoism, see Tom L. Beauchamp and Norman E. Bowie, *Ethical Theory and Business,* 7th ed. (Upper Saddle River, NJ: Prentice Hall, 2004), pp. 12–16.

[13] "Kozlowski, Swartz Sentenced to Up to 25 Years in Prison," *The Wall Street Journal,* September 19, 2005, *online.wsj.com.*

stabilize, control and bolster the industry, which had experienced sharp swings in pricing and production in the past few years.[14]

However, a precarious financial position or intense competition in the global market-place are not the only reasons for illegal and unethical business behavior, because profitable companies and their executives can also act contrary to ethical principles. In fact, it may be simply a single-minded drive for profits, regardless of the company or individual's financial condition, that creates a climate for unethical activity.

Thomas Coughlin, former vice chairman of Wal-Mart, pleaded guilty to five counts of wire fraud and one count of filing a false tax return and was sentenced to 27 months of home confinement. His sentence was substantially reduced due to his fragile health. Coughlin was a protégé of Wal-Mart founder Sam Walton and earned more than $1 million in base salary and more than $3 million in bonuses in his final year as the company's vice chairman of the board of directors. He admitted that he embezzled $500,000 from the company to purchase snakeskin boots, hunting trips, care for his hunting dogs, upgrades for his pickup truck, and liquor.[15]

Conflicts of Interest

Another reason ethical problems occur in business is because of conflicts of interest. A **conflict of interest** occurs when an individual's self-interest conflicts with acting in the best interest of another, when the individual has an obligation to do so.[16] For example, if a purchasing agent directed her company's orders to a firm from which she had received a valuable gift, even if this firm did not offer the best quality or value, she would be guilty of a conflict of interest. In this situation, she would have acted to benefit herself, rather than in the best interests of her employer. Conflicts of interest are normally considered unethical, because a failure to disclose a conflict of interest represents deception and may hurt the person or organization on whose behalf judgment has been exercised. Many ethicists believe that even the *appearance* of a conflict of interest should be avoided, because it undermines trust.

Both individuals and organizations can find themselves or place themselves in a conflict of interest. In recent years, much attention has been focused on organizational conflicts of interest in the accounting profession. When an accounting firm audits the books of a public company, it has an obligation to shareholders to provide an honest account of the company's financial health. Sometimes, though, accounting firms may be tempted to overlook irregularities to increase their chances of attracting lucrative consulting work from the same company. This type of conflict is now significantly curtailed by provisions in the Sarbanes-Oxley Act, which limit the right of accounting firms to provide both audit and consulting services to the same client

Many of the recent cases of financial fraud are illustrations of conflicts of interest, in which self-enrichment by senior managers was in conflict with the long-term viability of

---

[14] "Samsung to Pay Fine for Price Fixing," *The Wall Street Journal,* October 14, 2005, *online.wsj.com.* Pressuring subordinates may also result in unethical behavior as reported in Barrie E. Litzky, Kimberly A. Eddleston, and Deborah L. Kidder, "The Good, the Bad, and the Misguided: How Managers Inadvertently Encourage Deviant Behavior," *The Academy of Management Perspective,* February 2006, pp. 91–103.

[15] "Ex-Wal-Mart Vice Chairman Pleads Guilty in Fraud Case," *The Wall Street Journal,* January 31, 2006, *online.wsj.com;* and "Wal-Mart Legend to Serve Sentence Confined to Home," *The Wall Street Journal,* August 12, 2006, *online.wsj.com.*

[16] Based on John R. Boatright, *Ethics and the Conduct of Business,* 4th ed. (Upper Saddle River, NJ: Prentice Hall, 2003), p. 140.

the firm and the best interests of employees, customers, suppliers, and stockholders. Most organizations seek to guard against conflicts of interest by including prohibitions of this practice in their code of ethics, as discussed in Chapter 6.

Cross-Cultural Contradictions

Some of the knottiest ethical problems occur as corporations do business in other societies where ethical standards differ from those at home. Today, the policy makers and strategic planners in all multinational corporations, regardless of the nation where they are headquartered, face this kind of ethical dilemma. Consider the following situation:

> The pesticide methyl parathion is officially banned or restricted in many countries including the United States, China, Malaysia, Indonesia, and Cambodia. The World Health Organization classified methyl parathion as "extremely hazardous." The chemical can be fatal for humans if swallowed, inhaled, or absorbed through the skin. Yet, methyl parathion and nearly 50 other dangerous pesticides are being sold in Thailand and Vietnam and, from there, being illegally exported to Cambodia. Cambodian farmers argue that they need the pesticides to increase agricultural production, despite the lack of protective safety equipment or procedures for properly disposing of used containers. Multinational companies that manufacture the chemicals say that they are not responsible because they do not directly market to Cambodia.[17]

This episode raises the issue of ethical relativism, alluded to earlier in this chapter. *Although the foreign sales of methyl parathion to Thailand and Vietnam were legal, were they ethical? Is dumping unsafe products ethical if it is not forbidden by the receiving nation, especially if the companies know that the products are exported to another country where farmers there mishandle the product and use it without safety precautions? Are multinational companies ethically responsible for what happens to their products, even though they are being sold legally? What or whose ethical standards should be the guide?*

As business becomes increasingly global, with more and more corporations penetrating overseas markets where cultures and ethical traditions vary, these questions will occur more frequently.

The Core Elements of Ethical Character

The ethical analysis and resolution of ethical dilemmas in the workplace depend on the values, virtues, personal character, and spirituality of managers and other employees. Good ethical practices not only are possible, but also become normal with the right combination of these components.

Managers' Values

Managers are one of the keys to whether a company and its employees will act ethically or unethically. As major decision makers, they have more opportunities than others to create an ethical tone for their company. The values held by managers, especially top-level managers, serve as models for others who work in any organization.

The ethical scandals that rocked corporate America and were felt throughout the global marketplace have led to a widespread crisis of confidence in business leadership.

[17] "Bayer Pesticides Cause Poisoning in Cambodia," CBGnetwork, September 25, 2001, *www.pmac.net/bayer_cambodia.html.*

In a survey of 22,000 people in 21 countries, only politicians ranked as less trustworthy than managers of large companies, who finished behind lawyers and journalists. Of the 15 social organizations listed in a Gallup poll, people's confidence in big business was ranked next to last, just ahead of HMOs. The public reportedly had more confidence in churches, the Supreme Court, television news and newspapers, Congress, and organized labor than in business.

In a Gallup poll conducted every 10 years, perception of business executives' ethics has steadily fallen. This distrust has spread to specific industries; for example, 74 percent of those polled believed that manipulation by the oil industry caused increases in gas prices. Joining oil and gas as industries at the bottom of the list were the federal government and the sports industry. And this distrust spread to Europe where nearly 80 percent of British people believe that corporate executives cannot be trusted.[18]

Differences in ethical values were found among European employees. Researchers found that workers in the U.K. are among the most honest in Europe, avoiding ethical breaches that are more common in France, Germany, and Spain. Only 14 percent of U.K. workers approve of taking office supplies home for personal use—the lowest of workers from all 12 countries surveyed—and only 21 percent approve of using office software at home—second lowest in the survey.[19]

However, across the Atlantic, studies generally show that most U.S. managers focus on themselves and are primarily concerned about being competent. They place importance on values such as having a comfortable and exciting life and being capable, intellectual, and responsible. Researchers also found that new CEOs tend to be more self-interested and short-term focused, possibly in an effort to immediately drive up company profits, rather than valuing long-term investments in research and development or capital expenditures. However, some managers show a strong concern for values that include others, living in a world at peace, or seeking equality among people. One out of four managers emphasizes this latter set of values—moral values. These managers place greater importance on the value of forgiving others, being helpful, and acting honestly.[20]

But what about future managers? In a poll conducted by Duke University every three years, MBA students across the country consistently rank ethics (having strong moral principles) as their third most important goal, behind marriage and health. Another survey of over 2,100 graduate business students found that 79 percent believed that a company must weigh its impact on society. This impact could be seen in the company's environmental responsibility, practices of equal opportunity, treatment of workers' families, and other ethical issues. A survey of senior-level college students across the United States found that they want to have fun on the job but also seek employers that contribute to society and make ethics a priority.[21]

---

[18] "Few Trust Corporate Managers, Survey Finds," *The Wall Street Journal*, November 25, 2003, p. A16; B. Stevens, "The Ethics of the U.S. Business Executive: A Study of Perceptions," *Journal of Business Ethics*, 2004, pp. 163–71; and "Restaurants Highest-Rated Industry; Oil and Gas Lowest," Institute for Global Ethics, *Ethics Newsline*, August 22, 2005, *www.globalethics.org*.

[19] "U.K. Workers Give High Marks for Employees' Ethics: Survey," Institute for Global Ethics, *Ethics Newsline*, September 12, 2005, *www.globalethics.org*.

[20] See James Weber, "Managerial Value Orientations: A Typology and Assessment," *International Journal of Value-Based Management*, 1990, pp. 37–54; and Jeffrey S. Harrison and James O. Fiet, "New CEOs Pursue Their Own Self-Interests by Sacrificing Stakeholder Value," *Journal of Business Ethics* 19 (1999), pp. 301–8.

[21] "A National Survey: MBA 2003," Duke University, The Fuqua School of Business, *www.fuqua.duke.edu/admin/extaff/news;* "Bleeding Hearts at B-School?" *BusinessWeek*, April 7, 1997, p. 8; and "What New Grads Want from Their Bosses and Jobs," *Pittsburgh Post-Gazette*, June 12, 2006, pp. A8–A9.

Virtue Ethics

Some philosophers believe that the ancient Greeks, specifically Aristotle, developed the first ethical theory, which was based on values and personal character. Commonly referred to as **virtue ethics**, it focuses on character traits that a good person should possess, theorizing that these values will direct the person toward good behavior. Virtue ethics is based on a way of being and on valuable characteristics rather than on rules for correct behavior. Moral virtues are habits that enable a person to live according to reason, and this reason helps the person avoid extremes. Aristotle argued, "Moral virtue is a mean between two vices, one of excess and the other of deficiency, and it aims at hitting the mean in feelings, desires, and action."[22]

Moral values acknowledged by Aristotle include courage, temperance, justice, and prudence. St. Thomas Aquinas added the Christian values of faith, hope, and charity to the list of morally desirable virtues. Aquinas believed that these additional values were essential for a person to achieve a union with God, which was a significant purpose in Aquinas's notion of virtue ethics. Additional virtues include honesty, compassion, generosity, fidelity, integrity, and self-control.

Personal Character, Spirituality, and Moral Development

Clarence Walton, a seasoned observer of managerial behavior, noted that personal character is one of the keys to higher ethical standards in business. People of integrity produce organizations with integrity. When they do, they become moral managers—those special people who make organizations and societies better. Others speculate that there is a close connection between ethical leadership and a person's belief system or values.

Personal Spirituality

Personal spirituality, that is, a personal belief in a supreme being, religious organization, or the power of nature or some other external, life-guiding force, has always been a part of the human makeup. In 1953 *Fortune* published an article titled "Businessmen on Their Knees" and claimed that American businessmen (women generally were excluded from the executive suite in those days) were taking more notice of God. In the past 10 years, cover stories in *Fortune, BusinessWeek,* and other business publications have documented a resurgence of spirituality or religion at work.

Forty-eight percent of Americans polled said that they have had an occasion to talk about their religious faith in the workplace on a daily basis. And 78 percent admitted that they felt a need in their life for spiritual growth, up from only 20 percent five years later. Recently, efforts appear to be on the rise to integrate people's work with their spirituality.[23] Most companies use chaplains on an outsourced basis from secular employee-assistance programs or from chaplaincy providers such as Marketplace Ministries, a nonprofit concern that provides about 1,000 Protestant chaplains to more than 240 companies nationwide.

Across the country, thousands of top executives begin their day at a breakfast prayer meeting. In Minneapolis, hundreds of business executives gather for lunch and listen to

---

[22] For discussions of virtue ethics see Manuel G. Velasquez, *Business Ethics: Concepts and Cases,* 6th ed. (Upper Saddle River, NJ: Prentice Hall, 2006), pp. 108–14; Rogene A. Buchholz and Sandra B. Rosenthal, *Business Ethics: The Pragmatic Path beyond Principles to Process* (Upper Saddle River, NJ: Prentice Hall, 1998), pp. 38–42; and Robert C. Solomon, *A Better Way to Think about Business* (New York: Oxford University Press, 1999).

[23] "When Religion Is Part of the Business Plan," *American Banker,* January 25, 2005, p. 1.

consultants draw business solutions from the Bible. There are over 10,000 Bible and prayer groups that regularly meet in the workplace, according to the Fellowship for Companies for Christ International.[24]

Research conducted by the McKinsey&Company's Australia office reported that when companies engaged in spiritual techniques for their employees, productivity improved and turnover was reduced. Employees who worked for organizations they considered to be spiritual were less fearful on the job, less likely to compromise their values and act unethically, and more able to become committed to their work. At Elf Atochem, a subsidiary of the French oil company Elf-Aquitane, teaching people how to be spiritual improved productivity, employee relations, and customer service. The firm reported that it saved as much as $2 million in operating costs by showing its employees how to be more inspired about their work.[25]

However, others disagree with the trend toward a stronger presence of religion in the workplace. They hold the traditional belief that business is a secular, that is, nonspiritual, institution. They believe that business is business, and spirituality is best left to churches, synagogues, mosques, and meditation rooms, not corporate boardrooms or shop floors. This, of course, reflects the traditional separation of church and state in the United States and many other countries.

Others note that ethical misconduct or greed is often cloaked in the robes of religion. Scandals involving religious leaders, such as sexual abuse by Catholic priests or fraud committed by self-interested television evangelists, have caused many people to be wary of religion whether at work or elsewhere.

Beyond the philosophical opposition to bringing spirituality into the business environment, procedural challenges arise. *Whose spirituality should be promoted? The CEO's? With greater workplace diversity comes greater spiritual diversity, so which organized religion's prayers should be recited or ceremonies enacted? How should businesses handle employees who are agnostics (who do not follow any religion)?* Opponents of spirituality at work point to the myriad of implementation issues as grounds for keeping spirituality out of the workplace. Nonetheless, many believe that religion is making inroads into the workplace. Employees are becoming more accustomed to seeing a Bible on a work desk or hearing someone at work respond to a casual "How's it going?" with an earnest "I'm blessed."

Just as personal values and character strongly influence employee decision making and behavior in the workplace, so does personal spirituality, from all points on the religious spectrum, impact how businesses operate.

Managers' Moral Development

Taken together, personal values, character, and spirituality exert a powerful influence on the way ethical work issues are treated. Since people have different personal histories and have developed their values, character, and spirituality in different ways, they are going to think differently about ethical problems. This is as true of corporate managers as it is of other people. In other words, the managers in a company are likely to be at various **stages of moral development**. Some will reason at a high level, others at a lower level.

[24] "More Chaplains Take Ministering into Workplace," *The Wall Street Journal,* November 27, 2001, pp. B1, B10; and "Religion in the Workplace: The Growing Presence of Spirituality in Corporate America," *BusinessWeek,* November 1, 1999, pp. 151–58.

[25] See Ian Mitroff and Elizabeth A. Denton, *A Spiritual Audit of Corporate America* (San Francisco: Jossey-Bass, 1999).

FIGURE 5.4
Stages of Moral Development and Ethical Reasoning

Source: Adapted from Lawrence Kohlberg, *The Philosophy of Moral Development* (New York: Harper & Row, 1981).

Age Group	Development Stage and Major Ethics Referent	Basis of Ethics Reasoning
Mature adulthood	**Stage 6** Universal principles: justice, fairness, universal human rights	Principle-centered reasoning
Mature adulthood	**Stage 5** Moral beliefs above and beyond specific social custom: human rights, social contract, broad constitutional principles	Principle-centered reasoning
Adulthood	**Stage 4** Society at large: customs, traditions, laws	Society- and law-centered reasoning
Early adulthood, adolescence	**Stage 3** Social groups: friends, school, co-workers, family	Group-centered reasoning
Adolescence, youth	**Stage 2** Reward seeking: self-interest, own needs, reciprocity	Ego-centered reasoning
Childhood	**Stage 1** Punishment avoidance: avoid harm, obedience to power	Ego-centered reasoning

A summary of the way people grow and develop morally is diagrammed in Figure 5.4. From childhood to mature adulthood, most people move steadily upward in their moral reasoning capabilities from stage 1. Over time, they become more developed and are capable of more advanced moral reasoning, although some people never use the most advanced stages of reasoning in their decision processes.

At first, individuals are limited to an ego-centered focus (stage 1), fixed on avoiding punishment and obediently following the directions of those in authority. (The word *ego* means "self.") Slowly and sometimes painfully, the child learns that what is considered to be right and wrong is pretty much a matter of reciprocity: "I'll let you play with my toy, if I can play with yours" (stage 2). At both stages 1 and 2, however, the individual is mainly concerned with his or her own pleasure. The self-dealing of Dennis Kozlowski, described earlier in this chapter, exemplifies ego-centered reasoning. By taking money from his company for his personal use, this executive acted to benefit himself and his immediate family, without apparent concern for others.

In adolescence the individual enters a wider world, learning the give-and-take of group life among small circles of friends, schoolmates, and similar close-knit groups (stage 3). Studies have reported that interaction within groups can provide an environment that improves the level of moral reasoning. This process continues into early adulthood. At this point, pleasing others and being admired by them are important cues to proper behavior. Most people are now capable of focusing on other-directed rather than self-directed perspectives. When a manager "goes along" with what others are doing or what the boss expects, this would represent stage 3 behavior. On reaching full adulthood—the late teens to early 20s in most modern, industrialized nations—most people are able to focus their reasoning according to society's customs, traditions, and laws as the proper way to define what is right and wrong (stage 4). At this stage, a manager would seek to follow the law; for example, he or she might choose to curtail a chemical pollutant because of government regulations mandating this.

Stages 5 and 6 lead to a special kind of moral reasoning. At these highest stages, people move above and beyond the specific rules, customs, and laws of their own societies. They are capable of basing their ethical reasoning on broad principles and relationships, such as human rights and constitutional guarantees of human dignity, equal treatment, and freedom of expression. In the highest stage of moral development, the meaning of right and wrong is defined by universal principles of justice, fairness, and the common rights of all humanity. For example, at this stage, an executive might decide to pay wages above the minimum required by law, because this was the morally just thing to do.[26]

Recently, researchers have found that most managers typically rely on criteria associated with reasoning at stages 3 and 4, although some scholars argue that these results may be slightly inflated.[27] Although they may be capable of more advanced moral reasoning that adheres to or goes beyond society's customs or law, managers' ethical horizons most often are influenced by their immediate work group, family relationships, or compliance with the law. The development of a manager's moral character can be crucial to a company. Some ethics issues require managers to move beyond selfish interest (stages 1 and 2), beyond company interest (stage 3 reasoning), and even beyond sole reliance on society's customs and laws (stage 4 reasoning). What is needed is a manager whose personal character is built on a caring attitude toward all affected, recognizing others' rights and their essential humanity (a combination of stage 5 and 6 reasoning). The moral reasoning of upper-level managers, whose decisions affect companywide policies, can have a powerful and far-reaching impact both inside and outside the company.

Analyzing Ethical Problems in Business

Underlying an ethical decision framework is a set of universal ethical values or principles, notions that most people anywhere in the world would hold as important. While this list of ethical principles may not be exhaustive, five values seem to be generally accepted and are helpful in most ethical dilemmas: do no harm, be fair and just, be honest, respect others' rights, and do your duty/act responsibly. In applying these principles, business managers and employees need a set of decision guidelines that will shape their thinking when on-the-job ethics issues occur. The guidelines should help them (1) identify and analyze the nature of an ethical problem and (2) decide which course of action is likely to produce an ethical result. The following three methods of *ethical reasoning* can be used for these analytical purposes, as summarized in Figure 5.5.

Utility: Comparing Benefits and Costs

One approach to ethics emphasizes *utility,* the overall amount of good that can be produced by an action or a decision. This ethical approach is called **utilitarian reasoning**. It is often referred to as cost-benefit analysis because it compares the costs and benefits of a decision, a policy, or an action. These costs and benefits can be economic (expressed in dollar amounts), social (the effect on society at large), or human (usually a psychological or emotional impact). After business managers add up all the costs and benefits

---

[26] For details and research findings, see Lawrence Kohlberg, *The Philosophy of Moral Development* (San Francisco: Harper & Row, 1981); and Anne Colby and Lawrence Kohlberg, *The Measurement of Moral Judgment, Volume I: Theoretical Foundations and Research Validations* (Cambridge, MA: Cambridge University Press, 1987).

[27] James Weber and Janet Gillespie, "Differences in Ethical Beliefs, Intentions, and Behaviors," *Business & Society,* 1998, pp. 447–67; and James Weber and David Wasieleski, "Investigating Influences on Managers' Moral Reasoning," *Business & Society,* 2001, pp. 79–111.

FIGURE 5.5
Three Methods of
Ethical Reasoning

Method	Critical Determining Factor	An Action Is Ethical When . . .	Limitations
Utilitarian	Comparing benefits and costs	Net benefits exceed net costs	Difficult to measure some human and social costs; majority may disregard rights of the minority
Rights	Respecting entitlements	Basic human rights are respected	Difficult to balance conflicting rights
Justice	Distributing fair shares	Benefits and costs are fairly distributed	Difficult to measure benefits and costs; lack of agreement on fair shares

and compare them with one another, the net cost or the net benefit should be apparent. If the benefits outweigh the costs, then the action is ethical because it produces the greatest good for the greatest number of people in society. If the net costs are larger than the net benefits, then it is probably unethical because more harm than good is produced.

The main drawback to utilitarian reasoning is the difficulty of accurately measuring both costs and benefits. Some things can be measured in monetary terms—goods produced, sales, payrolls, and profits—but other items are trickier, such as employee morale, psychological satisfactions, and the worth of a human life. Human and social costs are particularly difficult to measure with precision. But unless they can be measured, the cost-benefit calculations will be incomplete, and it will be difficult to know whether the overall result is good or bad, ethical or unethical. Another limitation of utilitarian reasoning is that the majority may override the rights of those in the minority. Since utilitarian reasoning is primarily concerned with the end results of an action, managers using this reasoning process often fail to consider the means taken to reach the end.

Despite these drawbacks, cost-benefit analysis is widely used in business. Because this method works well when used to measure economic and financial outcomes, business managers sometimes are tempted to rely on it to decide important ethical questions without being fully aware of its limitations or the availability of still other methods that may improve the ethical quality of their decisions.

Is it ethical to close a plant? Using utilitarian reasoning, the decision maker must consider all the benefits (improving the company bottom line, higher return on investment to the investors, etc.) versus the costs (employee layoffs, reduced economic activity to the local community, etc.).

Rights: Determining and Protecting Entitlements

Human rights are another basis for making ethical judgments. A right means that a person or group is entitled to something or is entitled to be treated in a certain way. The most basic human rights are the right to life, safety, free speech, freedom, to be informed, due process, property, and others. Denying those rights or failing to protect them for other persons and groups is normally considered to be unethical. Respecting others, even those with whom we disagree or dislike, is the essence of human rights, provided that others do the same for us. This approach to ethical reasoning holds that individuals are to be treated as valuable ends in themselves just because they are human beings. Using others for your own purposes is unethical if, at the same time, you deny them their goals and purposes.

The main limitation of using rights as a basis of ethical reasoning is the difficulty of balancing conflicting rights. For example, an employee's right to privacy may be at odds with an employer's right to protect the firm's assets by testing the employee's honesty. Rights also clash when U.S. multinational corporations move production to a foreign nation, causing job losses at home but creating new jobs abroad. In such cases, whose job rights should be respected?[28]

Despite this kind of problem, the protection and promotion of human rights is an important ethical benchmark for judging the behavior of individuals and organizations. Surely most people would agree that it is unethical to deny a person's fundamental right to life, freedom, privacy, growth, and human dignity. By defining the human condition and pointing the way to a realization of human potentialities, such rights become a kind of common denominator of ethical reasoning, setting forth the essential conditions for ethical actions and decisions.

For example, is it ethical to close a plant? Using human rights reasoning, the decision maker must consider the rights of all affected (the right to a livelihood for the displaced workers or business owners in the local community versus the right of the employees to be informed of the layoffs and plant closing versus the right of the managers to the freedom to make decisions they believe are within their duty to the company, etc.).

Justice: Is It Fair?

A third method of ethical reasoning concerns **justice**. A common question in human affairs is, Is it fair or just? Employees want to know if pay scales are fair. Consumers are interested in fair prices when they shop. When new tax laws are proposed, there is much debate about their fairness—where will the burden fall, and who will escape paying their fair share?

Justice, or fairness, exists when benefits and burdens are distributed equitably and according to some accepted rule. For society as a whole, social justice means that a society's income and wealth are distributed among the people in fair proportions. A fair distribution does not necessarily mean an equal distribution. Most societies try to consider people's needs, abilities, efforts, and the contributions they make to society's welfare. Since these factors are seldom equal, fair shares will vary from person to person and group to group. Justice reasoning is not the same as utilitarian reasoning. A person using utilitarian reasoning adds up costs and benefits to see if one is greater than the other; if benefits exceed costs, then the action would probably be considered ethical. A person using justice reasoning considers who pays the costs and who gets the benefits; if the shares seem fair (according to society's rules), then the action is probably just.

For example, is it ethical to close a plant? Using justice reasoning, a decision maker must consider the distribution of the benefits (to the firm, its investors, etc.) versus the costs (to the displaced employees, local community, etc.). To be just, the firm closing the plant might decide to accept additional costs for job retraining and outplacement services for the benefit of the displaced workers. The firm might also decide to make contributions to the local community over some period of time to benefit the local economy, in effect to balance the scales of justice in this situation.

Applying Ethical Reasoning to Business Activities

Anyone in the business world can use these three methods of ethical reasoning to gain a better understanding of ethical issues that arise at work. Usually, all three can be applied

---

[28] For a discussion of ethical rights, see John R. Boatright, *Ethics and the Conduct of Business,* 5th ed. (Upper Saddle River, NJ: Prentice Hall, 2007), pp. 37–40; and Manuel G. Velasquez, *Business Ethics: Concepts and Cases,* 6th ed. (Upper Saddle River, NJ: Prentice Hall, 2006), pp. 71–84.

FIGURE 5.6
**An Analytical
Approach to Ethical
Problems**

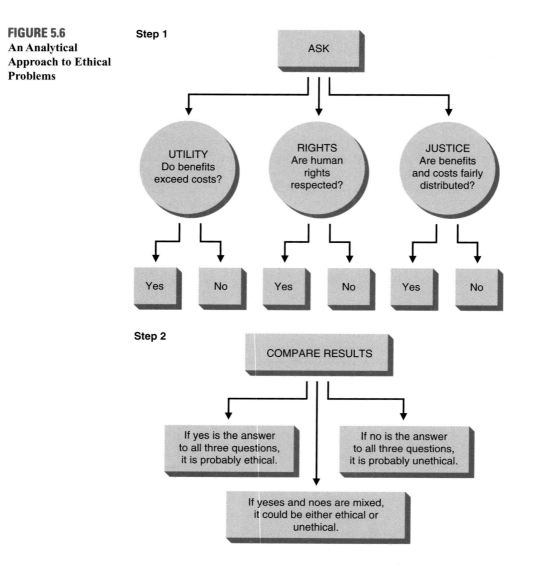

at the same time. Using only one of the three methods is risky and may lead to an incomplete understanding of all the ethical complexities that may be present. It also may produce a lopsided ethical result that will be unacceptable to others. Figure 5.6 diagrams the kind of analytical procedure that is useful to employ when one is confronted with an ethical problem or issue.

Once the ethical analysis is complete, the decision maker should ask the question: Do all three ethics approaches lead to the same decision? If so, then the decision or policy or activity is probably ethical. If answers to all three are no, then you probably are looking at an unethical decision, policy, or activity. The reason you cannot be absolutely certain is that different people and groups (1) may honestly and genuinely use different sources of information, (2) may measure costs and benefits differently, (3) may not share the same meaning of justice, or (4) may rank various rights in different ways. Nevertheless, any time an analyst obtains unanimous answers to these three questions, it indicates that a strong case can be made for either an ethical or an unethical conclusion.

What happens when the three ethical approaches do not lead to the same conclusion? A corporate manager or employee then has to assign priorities to the three methods of ethical reasoning. What is most important to the manager, to the employee, or to the organization—utility, rights, or justice? What ranking should they be given? A judgment must be made, and priorities must be determined. These judgments and priorities will be strongly influenced by a company's culture and ethical climate. The type of ethical reasoning chosen also depends heavily on managers' values, especially those held by top management, and on the personal character of all decision makers in the company. Some will be sensitive to people's needs and rights; others will put themselves or their company ahead of all other considerations.

Whistle-Blowing

Sometimes when employees work through an ethical decision process, they believe that their organization or industry is acting unethically. Many organizations developed mechanisms for employees to use to "blow the whistle" internally and enable the organization or industry group to investigate and possibly address the unethical situation. When these opportunities are not available or fail to respond to the issue, an employee may decide to become an external **whistle-blower**, that is, speak with the media or appropriate government agency. Whistle-blowing can be quite challenging and potentially hazardous to one's career.

The Consequences of Whistle-Blowing

Media attention to the recent business ethical scandals brought the role of the whistle-blower to the attention of the public. *Time* honored as its "2002 Person of the Year" three whistle-blowers: Enron's Sherron Watkins, WorldCom's Cynthia Cooper, and the FBI's Coleen Rowley. Each employee tried to work within the organization to expose wrongdoing—financial mismanagement at Enron and WorldCom and a culture of no response at the Federal Bureau of Investigation. Each employee acted out of a commitment to the organization, not setting out to destroy the company or to cause negative consequences. Other whistle-blowers appeared during this recent period of ethical scandals.[29]

> But the life of a whistle-blower is a potentially tragic one. Consider the story of Christine Casey. Casey believed that her employer, Mattel, was misleading its shareholders about its likely future sales performance. She decided to contact the SEC, assuming the matter would be investigated, the truth would become known, and she would feel better about her role as a whistle-blower. Three years later, Casey had lost her job and found it impossible to find another one since many firms check with the applicant's previous employers during the pre-employment screening process. Casey also lost the lawsuit she brought against Mattel for wrongful dismissal, and Mattel sought to make Casey pay the company's legal costs.

Following the 2003 Columbia space shuttle disaster, NASA commissioned a study to investigate the whistle-blowing climate in the organization. Disappointingly, they found a "high level of fear" regarding whistle-blowing activity. While employees were committed to safety, they pointed to a culture where delivering bad news was unacceptable.[30]

---

[29] "Year of the Whistle-Blower," *BusinessWeek,* December 16, 2002, pp. 107–10.

[30] "Christine Casey: Whistle-Blower," *The Economist,* January 18, 2003, p. 66; and "NASA Survey Finds Employees Still Afraid to Speak Up," Institute for Global Ethics, *Ethics Newsline,* April 19, 2004, *www.globalethics.org.*

Exhibit 5.B   Whistle-Blowing Protection around the World

Here is a summary of some legislative efforts to protect whistle-blowers in various countries.

- European Union—The EU published a charter for whistle-blower protection, identifying the terms under which commission staff may blow the whistle, imposing a duty upon officials to report suspected wrongdoing, and outlining the channels for reporting malpractice.
- Ghana—A whistle-blower protection act has been proposed to offer rewards and protection to people who volunteer information leading to the prosecution of white-collar criminals.
- Israel—This country adopted whistle-blowing protection legislation that protects corporate and government workers.
- South Africa—The Protected Disclosures Act 26 prohibits employers from subjecting an employee to an occupational detriment (e.g., disciplinary action, suspension, dismissal, demotion, harassment) for raising concerns about unlawful or irregular conduct.
- South Korea—The Anti-Corruption Act established the Korea Independent Commission Against Corruption, whose mission includes the encouragement, protection, and compensation of whistle-blowers.
- United Kingdom—The U.K. Public Interest Disclosure Act protects most workers from retaliation by their employers, including dismissal, disciplinary action, or transfer.

Source: Lori Tansey Martens and Amber Crowell, "Whistle-Blowing: A Global Perspective (Part I)," *Ethikos*, May–June 2002, pp. 6–8.

Government Action and the Whistle-Blower

Governmental efforts recently have focused on the role of the whistle-blower. The SEC requires lawyers to blow the whistle on their clients if they suspect ethical misbehavior, or at least requires them to make a **noisy withdrawal**, meaning that when a lawyer sees evidence of a client company's committing a material securities law violation and is unable to get the company's board to stop it, the lawyer must quit and inform the SEC that the resignation is for professional considerations. The SEC most likely would investigate this case based upon the lawyer's actions.

Employee whistle-blowing has gained the attention of government bodies around the world, as shown in Exhibit 5.B. The effectiveness of these legal protection regulations varies greatly from country to country.

There are many stigmas or reasons employees may choose not to become whistle-blowers.

- Divided loyalties—For example, in some Asian countries, members of the company are treated as family members and it is considered wrong to report on family members.
- History—The country may have a tragic history of reporting on others, such as the Gestapo tactics in Germany during World War II. Thus, whistle-blowing may not be considered as a realistic option.
- Logistics—Employees of global companies may be faced with numerous time zones and language differences that could prevent whistle-blowing or make it more difficult.
- Fear of retribution—Despite government laws to protect whistle-blowers, many employees of global businesses fear retaliation and their fears may be warranted. A spokesperson for the Trade Union Advisory Committee noted that the organization had received reports of employees being murdered for exposing corruption.[31]

[31] Lori Tansey Martens and Amber Crowell, "Whistle-Blowing: A Global Perspective (Part I)," *Ethikos*, May–June 2002, pp. 6–8.

The importance of being attentive to ethical issues at work and the ability to reason to an ethical resolution of these knotty dilemmas are essential given the increasing ethical scrutiny and consequences for unethical behavior in the workplace. But employees do not work in a vacuum. The organization where they work and the culture that exists within any organization exert significant influence on the individual as an ethical decision maker. Businesses are making significant efforts to improve the ethical work climates in their organizations and providing safeguards to encourage ethical behavior by their employees, as the next chapter discusses.

Summary

- Ethics is a conception of right and wrong behavior, defining for us when our actions are moral and when they are immoral. Business ethics is the application of general ethical ideas to business behavior.

- Ethical business behavior is demanded by business stakeholders, enhances business performance, complies with legal requirements, prevents or minimizes harm, and promotes personal morality.

- Ethics problems occur in business for many reasons, including the selfishness of a few, competitive pressures on profits, the clash of personal values and business goals, and cross-cultural contradictions in global business operations.

- Managers' on-the-job values tend to be company-oriented, assigning high priority to company goals. Managers often value being competent and place importance on having a comfortable or exciting life, among other values, although values in America may be changing in the post–2001 terrorist attacks and post–Enron and WorldCom era.

- Personal character and spirituality can greatly assist managers when coping with ethical dilemmas. Personal spirituality has emerged as a more common topic for discussion at work and has influenced company-sponsored activities during work hours and after work.

- Individuals reason at various stages of moral development, with most managers focusing on personal rewards, recognition from others, or compliance with company's rules as guides for their reasoning.

- People in business can analyze ethics dilemmas by using three major types of ethical reasoning: utilitarian reasoning, rights reasoning, and justice reasoning.

Key Terms

business ethics, *90*
conflict of interest, *97*
ethical egoist, *95*
ethical principles, *90*
ethical relativism, *90*
ethics, *90*
human rights, *104*

justice, *105*
noisy withdrawal, *108*
personal spirituality, *100*
Sarbanes-Oxley Act, *93*
stages of moral development, *101*

U.S. Corporate Sentencing Guidelines, *92*
utilitarian reasoning, *103*
virtue ethics, *100*
whistle-blower, *107*

Internet Resources

www.ibe.org.uk — Institute for Business Ethics
www.usoge.gov — United States Office of Government Ethics
www.sarbanes-oxley.com — Sarbanes-Oxley Act
www.ussc.gov — United States Sentencing Commission
www.charactercounts.org — Josephson Institute, Character Counts
www.workplacespirituality.info — Workplace Spirituality

Discussion Case: *The Warhead Cable Test Dilemma*

It was Monday morning at Bryson Corporation's cable division assembly plant. Stanton Wong, the quality supervisor, had been worrying all weekend about a directive he had received from his boss before leaving work on Friday. Harry Jackson, the plant manager and a vice president of operations, had told Stanton unambiguously to disregard defects in a batch of laminated cable they had produced for a major customer, a military contractor. Now, Stanton was wondering what if anything he should say or do.

Bryson Corporation was large conglomerate headed by an aggressive CEO who had established a track record of buying and turning around low-performing manufacturing firms. Harry Jackson had been sent to the cable plant shortly after it had been acquired, and he was making headway rescuing what had been a marginal operation. The word in the plant was that corporate was pleased with his progress.

Harry ran the plant like a dictator, with nearly absolute control, and made sure everyone inside and outside the organization knew it. Harry would intimidate his direct reports, yelling at them and insulting them at the least provocation. He harassed many of the young women in the office and was having an affair with one of the sales account managers.

Stanton's two-year anniversary on the job had just passed. He was happy with his progress. He felt respected by the factory workers, by management colleagues, and often even by Harry. His pay was good enough that he and his wife felt confident to buy a house and start a family. He wanted to get a reputation as a loyal employee. He had decided early on that he was not about to challenge Harry. At least, that was Stanton's approach until the warhead cable came along.

The warhead cable was part of a fuse system used in missiles. In the production process, a round cable was formed into a flat, ribbon-like shape by feeding it through a lamination machine and applying specific heat, speed, and pressure. The flattened cable was then cut into specific lengths and shapes and shipped to the customer, a defense contractor.

As part of his quality control duties, Stanton used a standard procedure called an elevated heat seal test to ensure the integrity of the product. The cable was bent at a 90-degree angle and placed in an oven at 105 degrees C for seven hours. If the seal did not de-laminate (pop open at the corners), then the product passed the test. This procedure was usually performed on cable from early runs while the lamination machine operator was still producing a batch. That way, if there was a problem, it could be spotted early and corrected.

When a batch of cable was ready for shipment, Stanton was responsible for preparing a detailed report of all test results. The customer's source inspector, Jane Conway, then came to the plant and performed additional sample testing there. On inspection days, Jane tended to arrive around 9:00 a.m. and spend the morning reviewing Stanton's test data. Typically, she would pull samples from each lot and inspect them. She rarely conducted her own elevated heat seal test, however, relying instead on Bryson's test data. Stanton and Jane often had lunch together at a nearby restaurant and then finished up the paperwork in the afternoon.

The prior week, during a very busy time, a large order for the warhead cable came in with a short turnaround period. Stanton tested a sample taken from an early lot and had good results. But his testing on Friday revealed problems. Of 10 samples, two failed. That afternoon, Stanton went to Harry's office with the failed samples to show him the de-lamination. Before Stanton could say a word, Harry called in the production manager and cursed him out. He then turned to Stanton and said, "Let's wait and see if the source inspector catches this problem." Stanton reminded him that typically the source inspector didn't perform this particular test. Harry responded, "Well, most of the samples passed." Stanton replied, "Yes, but some failed. That shows inconsistency in the lot. The protocol requires a test failure be reported for such results."

Harry had already made up his mind. "Don't tell me what I can and cannot do! The decision is mine to make, and what I have decided is that we will see if the source inspector finds the failure!"

All weekend, Stanton worried about Harry's directive. Bryson cables were used to manufacture fuses in missiles. Stanton thought about several people he knew from high school who were now on active duty in a war zone overseas. He thought about possible harm to innocent civilians or even to U.S. service members if a missile misfired. He wondered if anyone in the parent corporation could help, but did not know anyone there to call.

Source: Case written by Jeanne McNett, Assumption College. The event described in this case is real, but the names of the individuals and the company have been disguised. An earlier version of this case was presented at the 2005 annual meeting of the North American Case Research Association. Used by permission. © 2006 Jeanne McNett and the North American Case Research Association.

Discussion Questions

1. What stage of moral development do you think Stanton Wong is at? What about Harry Jackson? Why do you think so?

2. What do you think Stanton should do now, and why? Use one or more of the methods of ethical reasoning presented in the chapter to support your view.

3. Should Stanton blow the whistle on his company? Why or why not?

4. What steps could the company take to prevent a situation like this from occurring in the future?

CHAPTER SIX

Organizational Ethics and the Law

Faced with increasing pressure to create an ethical and law-abiding environment at work, businesses can take tangible steps to improve their ethical performance. The organization's culture and ethical work climate play a central role in promoting ethics at work. Ethical situations arise in all areas or functions of business, and often professional associations seek to guide managers in addressing these challenges. Corporations can also implement ethical safeguards such as ethics policies, ethics and compliance officers or ombudspersons, and employee ethics training. In addition to developing a comprehensive ethics program, corporations must of course follow the laws of the nation. This can become a complex challenge when facing different customs and regulations around the world. Although ethics and the law are not exactly the same, both are important emphases for businesses, especially when operating in the global marketplace.

This chapter focuses on these key learning objectives:

- Classifying an organization's culture and ethical climate.
- Recognizing ethics challenges across the multiple functions of business.
- Developing effective ethics policies, ethics training programs, ethics assist lines, and similar safeguards.
- Assessing the strengths and weaknesses of a comprehensive ethics program.
- Understanding how to conduct business ethically in the global marketplace.
- Knowing the differences between ethics and the law.

Nortel Networks, a Canadian telecommunications equipment maker, fired 10 financial managers over accounting irregularities following a review by Nortel's audit committee. A former tax-planning executive at Dynegy, Jamie Olis, was sentenced to more than 24 years in prison for his role in a secretive project to disguise a $300 million loan as cash flow for the U.S. oil and gas company. Calisto Tanzi, founder and former chairman of Parmalat, along with 15 other executives from the firm, were accused of market rigging, providing false accounting information, and misleading an Italian stock market regulator in an $18 billion scandal called the "European Enron." The accounting firm KPMG and the law firm of Brown & Wood agreed to pay $195 million to 280 investors who bought four different types of tax shelters, in addition to paying $30 million in plaintiff's lawyer fees. McKesson, the largest U.S. drug distributor, agreed to pay nearly $1 billion to settle a class-action suit that accused the firm of defrauding investors. At the time, this was the nation's third largest settlement of a class-action suit, trailing settlements of $3.2 billion by Cendant and more than $2.6 billion by WorldCom.[1]

In addition to the cases described above, dozens and dozens of other companies have been charged with accounting fraud, mishandling investors' funds, market improprieties, and many other illegal activities. *Why are businesses repeatedly being caught conducting illegal activities? How does this pattern of unethical behavior become common among businesses and their executives? And, most important, what can businesses, and possibly government regulators and the courts, do about stemming illegal and unethical activity?*

Corporate Culture and Ethical Climates

Personal values and moral character play key roles in improving a company's ethical performance, as discussed in Chapter 5. However, they do not stand alone, because personal values and character can be affected by a company's culture.

Corporate culture is a blend of ideas, customs, traditional practices, company values, and shared meanings that help define normal behavior for everyone who works in a company. Culture is "the way we do things around here." Two experts testify to its overwhelming influence:

> Every business—in fact every organization—has a culture . . . [and it] has a powerful influence throughout an organization; it affects practically everything—from who gets promoted and what decisions are made, to how employees dress and what sports they play. . . . When [new employees] choose a company, they often choose a way of life. The culture shapes their responses in a strong, but subtle way.[2]

The emphasis on ethics and value-based leadership is at the core of the Holt Company's culture, a four-generation, family-owned Caterpillar equipment dealership in San Antonio, Texas. How did the Holt Company adopt this ethical culture? The company's executives point to a day in the late 1980s when Peter Holt, the company's CEO, changed his mind.

---

[1] "7 More Managers Fired over Nortel Accounting," *The New York Times*, August 20, 2004, www.nytimes.com; "Ex-Executive of Dynegy Is Sentenced to 24 Years," *The New York Times*, March 26, 2004, www.nytimes.com; "Parmalat Fraud Trial Opens in Milan," *The New York Times*, September 28, 2005, www.nytimes.com; "Law Firm and KPMG Settle Suit by Tax Clients," *The New York Times*, September 20, 2005, www.nytimes.com; and, "McKesson Agrees to Pay $960 Million in Fraud Suit," *The New York Times*, January 13, 2005, www.nytimes.com.

[2] Terrence E. Deal and Allan A. Kennedy, *Corporate Cultures: The Rites and Rituals of Corporate Life* (Reading, MA: Addison-Wesley, 1982), pp. 4, 16.

FIGURE 6.1   **The Components of Ethical Climates**

Source: Adapted from Bart Victor and John B. Cullen, "The Organizational Bases of Ethical Work Climates," *Administrative Science Quarterly* 33 (1988), p. 104.

Ethical Criteria	Focus of Individual Person	Organization	Society
Egoism (self-centered approach)	Self-interest	Company interest	Economic efficiency
Benevolence (concern-for-others approach)	Friendship	Team interest	Social responsibility
Principle (integrity approach)	Personal morality	Company rules and procedures	Laws and professional codes

Holt was prepared to confront his senior managers and let them know he was not happy with things at the firm. The company's sales had slowed and the firm had serious financial concerns. Instead, Holt surprised his management team by asking: "What am I doing wrong?" The focus on personal responsibility and not blaming others marked the beginning of instituting a new culture at the firm. Leadership at the Holt Company developed five core values, in descending order of importance: ethical, success, excellence, commitment, and dynamic. Ethical was defined as "being honest, showing integrity, being consistent, and showing fair treatment." As a Holt manager noted, "Profits are conspicuously absent in our core values." The company stressed things like making sure that decisions were balanced and took into account all stakeholders: employees, customers, and shareholders.[3]

Ethical Climates

In most companies, a moral atmosphere can be detected. People can feel the way the ethical winds are blowing. They pick up subtle hints and clues that tell them what behavior is approved and what is forbidden.

The unspoken understanding among employees of what is and is not acceptable behavior is called an **ethical climate**. It is the part of corporate culture that sets the ethical tone in a company. One way to view ethical climates is diagrammed in Figure 6.1. Three different types of ethical yardsticks are egoism (self-centeredness), benevolence (concern for others), and principle (respect for one's own integrity, for group norms, and for society's laws). These ethical yardsticks can be applied to dilemmas concerning individuals, a company, or society at large.

For example, if a manager approaches ethics issues with benevolence in mind, he or she would emphasize friendly relations with an employee, emphasize the importance of team play and cooperation for the company's benefit, and recommend socially responsible courses of action. However, a manager using egoism to think about ethical problems would be more likely to think first of promoting the company's profit and striving for efficient operations at all costs.

The ethical work climate at Computer Associates International, the world's fourth largest software maker, was discovered by federal securities investigators through e-mail messages sent within the company. These messages indicated that senior executives ordered employees to backdate or modify dates on sales orders at the

---

[3] "How Holt Company Introduced Its 'Managing by Values' Process," *Ethikos*, March–April 1997, pp. 4–6, 11.

end of the fiscal quarter to enable the firm to meet revenue and sales targets. Prosecutors described the climate at Computer Associates as a business with a "35-day month" because company accountants were instructed to keep the financial records open for days beyond the calendar month.[4]

Researchers have found that multiple climates, or subclimates, may exist within one organization. For example, if employees interacted with the public or government regulators, a society focus coupled with a principle or integrity approach (law and professional code climate) might be found. However, if employees were isolated from these influences and their work was geared toward routine process tasks with a concern toward higher personal pay or company profits, the climate may be self-interest or company interest.[5]

Corporate cultures can also signal to employees that ethical transgressions are acceptable. By signaling what is considered to be right and wrong, corporate cultures and ethical climates can pressure people to channel their actions in certain directions desired by the company. This kind of pressure can work both for or against good ethical practices.

Business Ethics across Organizational Functions

Not all ethics issues in business are the same. Because business operations are highly specialized, ethics issues can appear in any of the major functional areas of a business firm. Accounting, finance, marketing, information technology, and other areas of business all have their own particular brands of ethical dilemmas. In many cases, professional associations in these functional areas have attempted to define a common set of ethical standards, as discussed next.

Accounting Ethics

The accounting function is a critically important component of every business firm. By law, the financial records of publicly held companies are required to be audited by a certified professional accounting firm. Company managers, external investors, government regulators, tax collectors, and labor unions rely on such public audits to make key decisions. Honesty, integrity, and accuracy are absolute requirements of the accounting function. Thus, the scandals that rocked the accounting industry and led to the demise of Arthur Andersen hit the integrity of this professional group hard.

Accountants often are faced with conflicts of interest, introduced in Chapter 5, where loyalty or obligation to the company (the client) is divided or in conflict with self-interest (of the accounting firm) and the interest of others (shareholders and the public). For example, while conducting an audit of a company, should the auditor look for opportunities to recommend to the client consulting services that the auditor's firm can provide? Sometimes, accounting firms may be tempted to soften their audit of a company's financial statements if the accounting firm wants to attract the company's nonaudit business. For this reason, the Sarbanes-Oxley Act severely limits the offering of nonaudit consulting services by the auditing firm.

[4] "Ex-Chief of Computer Associates Kumar Pleads Not Guilty," *The New York Times*, September 23, 2004, *www.nytimes.com*; and "In CA Probe: Recovered E-Mails, Surprise Cache of Documents," *The Wall Street Journal*, September 24, 2004, pp. A1, A6.

[5] James Weber, "Influences upon Organizational Ethical Subclimates: A Multi-departmental Analysis of a Single Firm," *Organization Science* 6 (1995), pp. 509–23.

The issue of conflicts of interest was at the core of the decision made by management at PricewaterhouseCoopers (PWC), one of the largest accounting firms in the United States and Canada, when it decided to withdraw as the auditor for the Royal Bank of Canada. PWC leadership cited a concern over a possible conflict of interest since it was worried that it may have violated auditor independence rules when it performed nonaudit work for a subsidiary of the Royal Bank, even though the work accounted for less than $150,000 in services. Peter Currie, CFO for PWC, said that the firm made a "bad judgment" when it assured Royal Bank executives that its independent audit status would not be jeopardized by its consulting work for the Royal Bank subsidiary.[6]

Other ethical issues appear in the accounting industry, with accounting fraud being one of the most visible and involving the largest amount of money. While many examples of accounting fraud appeared in the United States during the past few years, lapses in accounting ethics can be found elsewhere.

Kanebo Limited, a Japanese household goods company, reported that it had inflated its profits by $1.37 billion over four years. These errors were found during an internal investigation that uncovered a lengthy period of bogus bookkeeping, sparking an investigation by the Tokyo Stock Exchange. Kanebo's accounting fraud was the largest in Japan involving a nonfinancial firm.[7]

Government regulators have responded strongly to the accounting scandals of the past few years by tightening their grip over auditors in their countries to prevent what happened in the United States from occurring there. Britain's Department of Trade and Industry shook up the current accounting industry's self-regulatory system by passing new rules that required greater disclosure of accounting firms' revenue and how they handle conflicts of interest. Although the new rules did not ban an auditing firm from providing some nonaudit services, as the U.S. Sarbanes-Oxley Act does, they did impose greater and more aggressive oversight by the government. The European Union followed with the creation of the International Accounting Standards (IAS). These standards are seen as essential by the European regulators for the integration of European Union capital markets and for the global convergence of accounting standards.[8]

In the United States, professional accounting organizations, such as the American Institute of Certified Public Accountants and the Financial Accounting Standards Board, have developed generally accepted accounting principles whose purpose is to establish uniform standards for reporting accounting and auditing data. In 1993, the American Institute for Certified Public Accountants (AICPA) dramatically changed its professional code by requiring CPAs to act as whistle-blowers when detecting "materially misstated" financial statements or face losing their license to practice accounting. In 2003, on the heels of the Sarbanes-Oxley Act, the AICPA sought input from its members as it revised its Rule 101—Independence guideline.

[6] "PricewaterhouseCoopers Withdraws from Audit Role, Citing Conflict of Interest," Institute for Global Ethics, *Ethics Newsline*, September 29, 2003, *www.globalethics.org.*

[7] "Japanese Firm Admits $1.37 Billion Accounting Fraud," Institute for Global Ethics, *Ethics Newsline*, April 18, 2005, *www.globalethics.org.*

[8] *International Accounting Standards*, The European Commission, *europa.eu.int.*

Examples of this profession's efforts toward promoting ethics are shown in Exhibit 6.A. Spurred by the increasing threat of liability suits filed against accounting firms and the desire to reaffirm professional integrity, these standards go far toward ensuring a high level of honest and ethical accounting behavior.[9]

Financial Ethics

In the field of finance, business practices involving securities trading, investments strategies, banking practices and the like have produced some of the most spectacular ethics scandals of recent times. Wall Street financiers have been found guilty of insider trading, illegal stock transactions, and various other financial abuses. Examples of ethical abuses within the financial community were seen in the late 1990s, when the Securities and Exchange Commission launched investigations into the practices of two of the three largest stock exchanges in the United States, and these lapses of ethical conduct continue today.

> Richard S. Strong, founder of Strong Capital Management, a firm that helped fuel the extraordinary growth of mutual funds for over three decades, agreed to pay $60 million in fines and was banned from the financial industry for life as a settlement of accusations involving illegal trades at the expense of investors in his funds. New York attorney general Eliot Spitzer said, "The magnitude of his breach of duty is greater than what we have seen in other cases. When you're the CEO, your duty could not be more clear."[10]

Lapses in ethical conduct are evident despite efforts by the finance professions to foster an ethical environment, as shown in Exhibit 6.A, that emphasizes self-regulation as the best path for ethical compliance. In 2006, the National Association of Securities Dealers and the New York Stock Exchange asked Wall Street finance companies to self-regulate what constitutes excessive client entertainment. After a number of regulatory investigations, the general belief among regulators was that the industry was best equipped to determine what was excessive when it came to gifts offered to clients. There are, however, skeptics that do not believe the industry can self-regulate when it comes to monitoring gifts, entertainment, and other incentive perks.[11]

In addition, the government took action to minimize unethical behavior in the finance industry after the September 11, 2001, attack on the United States. The U.S. Treasury Department now requires firms to implement comprehensive money-laundering compliance programs, similar to the standards established by the U.S. Sentencing Guidelines. Firms must designate a special money-laundering compliance officer, provide training for employees to detect money laundering, conduct independent audits, and establish policies and procedures to identify risks and minimize opportunities for abuse.[12]

Marketing Ethics

Relations with customers tend to generate many ethical problems. Pricing, promotions, advertising, product information, relations between advertising agencies and their clients, marketing research—all of these are potential problem areas.

---

[9] For several excellent examples of ethical dilemmas in accounting, see Leonard J. Brooks, *Business & Professional Ethics for Accountants*, 3rd ed. (Cincinnati: South-Western College Publishing, 2004); and Ronald Duska and Brenda Duska, *Accounting Ethics* (Malden, MA: Blackwell, 2003).

[10] "Fund Executive, Fined $60 Million, Accepts Life Ban," *The New York Times*, May 21, 2004, *www.nytimes.com*.

[11] "Party Tab: Wall Street to Set Limits on Gifts," *The Wall Street Journal*, January 24, 2006, *www.wsj.com*. For several good examples of other financial ethics issues, see Larry Alan Bear and Rita Maldonado-Bear, *Free Markets, Finance, Ethics, and Law* (Englewood Cliffs, NJ: Prentice Hall, 1994); and John R. Boatright, ed., *Ethics in Finance* (Malden, MA: Blackwell, 1999).

[12] "New Money-Laundering Rules to Cut Broad Swath in Finance," *The Wall Street Journal*, April 23, 2002, pp. A1, A11.

Exhibit 6.A — Professional Codes of Conduct in Accounting and Finance

AMERICAN INSTITUTE OF CERTIFIED PUBLIC ACCOUNTANTS (AICPA)

Code of Professional Conduct

These Principles of the Code of Professional Conduct of the American Institute of Certified Public Accountants express the profession's recognition of its responsibilities to the public, to clients, and to colleagues. They guide members in the performance of their professional responsibilities and express the basic tenets of ethical and professional conduct. The Principles call for an unswerving commitment to honorable behavior, even at the sacrifice of personal advantage.

- Responsibilities—In carrying out their responsibilities as professionals, members should exercise sensitive professional and moral judgments in all their activities. . . .
- The Public Interest—Members should accept the obligation to act in a way that will serve the public interest, honor the public interest, and demonstrate commitment to professionalism. . . .
- Integrity—To maintain and broaden public confidence, members should perform all professional responsibilities with the highest sense of integrity. . . .
- Objectivity and Independence—A member should maintain objectivity and be free of conflicts of interest in discharging professional responsibilities. A member in public practice should be independent in fact and appearance when providing auditing and other attestation services. . . .
- Due Care—A member should observe the profession's technical and ethical standards, strive continually to improve competence and the quality of services, and discharge professional responsibility to the best of the member's ability. . . .
- Scope and Nature of Services—A member in public practice should observe the Principles of the Code of Professional Conduct in determining the scope and nature of services to be provided.*

CHARTERED FINANCIAL ANALYST (CFA)®

Summary from CFA Institute Code of Ethics and Standards of Professional Conduct

Members of CFA Institute (including Chartered Financial Analyst® (CFA®) charterholders) and candidates for the CFA designation ("Members and Candidates") must:

- Act with integrity, competence, diligence, respect, and in an ethical manner with the public, clients, prospective clients, employers, employees, colleagues in the investment profession, and other participants in the global capital markets.

Two of Britain's best-known toy stores, Argos and Littlewoods, were hit with a record $35.5 million fine for colluding to keep prices of Hasbro products artificially high. According to the U.K. Office of Fair Trading (OFT), the companies agreed to block discounts on a range of Hasbro products, including board games Cluedo, Monopoly, Scrabble, and Trivial Pursuit, as well as Harry Potter merchandise. Argos denounced the OFT investigation as a one-sided affair since Hasbro was given a reprieve for its help and spared a $24.5 million fine, even though Hasbro has a history of collusion and was fined $7.8 million in 2002 for entering into a price-fixing agreement with 10 distributors.

Some marketing ethics issues affect the public through an organization's advertising practices, which are discussed in Chapter 20. To improve the marketing profession, the American Marketing Association (AMA) adopted a code of ethics for its members, as shown in Exhibit 6.B. The AMA code advocates professional conduct guided by ethics, adherence to applicable laws, and honesty and fairness in all marketing activities. The code

- Place the interests of clients, the interests of their employer, and the integrity of the investment profession above their own personal interests.
- Use reasonable care and exercise independent professional judgment when conducting investment analysis, making investment recommendations, taking investment actions, and engaging in other professional activities.
- Practice and encourage others to practice in a professional and ethical manner that will reflect credit on themselves and the profession.
- Promote the integrity of, and uphold the rules governing, global capital markets.
- Maintain and improve their professional competence and strive to maintain and improve the competence of other investment professionals.

The Standards of Professional Conduct include:

- Professionalism, which discusses knowledge of the law, independence and objectivity, misrepresentation, and misconduct.
- Integrity of capital markets, which discusses material nonpublic information and market manipulation.
- Duties to clients, which discusses loyalty, prudence and care, fair dealing, suitability, performance presentation, and preservation of confidentiality.
- Duties to employers, which discusses loyalty, additional compensation arrangements, and responsibilities of supervisors.
- Investment analysis, recommendations, and action, which discusses diligence and reasonable basis, communication with clients and prospective clients, and record retention.
- Conflicts of interest, which discusses disclosure of conflicts, priority of transactions, and referral fees.
- Responsibilities as a CFA Institute member or CFA candidate, which discusses conduct as members and candidates in the CFA program and reference to CFA Institute, the CFA designation, and the CFA program.[†]

* Reprinted with permission from the AICPA Code of Professional Conduct, copyright © 2006 by the American Institute of Certified Public Accountants, Inc. For a full text of the professional code for American Certified Public Accountants see *www.aicpa.org*.
† Copyright 2005, CFA Institute. Reproduced with permission from CFA Institute. All Rights Reserved. For full text see *http://www.cfainstitute.org/cfacentre/pdf/English2006CodeandStandards.pdf*.

also recognizes the ethical responsibility of marketing professionals to the consuming public and specifically opposes such unethical practices as misleading product information, false and misleading advertising claims, high-pressure sales tactics, bribery and kickbacks, and unfair and predatory pricing. These code provisions have the potential for helping marketing professionals translate general ethical principles into specific working rules.[13]

Information Technology Ethics

One of the fastest-growing areas of business ethics is in the field of information technology. Ethical challenges involving invasions of privacy; the collection, storage, and access of

[13] The AMA Code for Market Researchers and a discussion of numerous marketing ethics issues can be found in David D'Alessandro and Michele Owens, *Ethics in Marketing* (New York: McGraw-Hill/Irwin, 1996); Bodo B. Schlegelmilch, *Marketing Ethics: An International Perspective* (London: International Thomson Business Press, 1998); and Patrick E. Murphy et al., *Ethical Marketing* (Upper Saddle River, NJ: Prentice Hall, 2005).

AMERICAN MARKETING ASSOCIATION (AMA)

Code of Ethics

Members of the American Marketing Association (AMA) are committed to ethical professional conduct. They have joined together in subscribing to this Code of Ethics embracing the following topics:

- Responsibilities . . . —Marketers must accept responsibility for the consequences of their activities and make every effort to ensure that their decisions, recommendations, and actions function to identify, serve, and satisfy all relevant publics: customers, organizations, and society.

- Honesty and Fairness—Marketers shall uphold and advance the integrity, honor, and dignity of the marketing profession.

- Rights and Duties of Parties . . . —Participants in the marketing exchange process should be able to expect that: (1) products and services offered are safe and fit for their intended uses; (2) communications about offered products and services are not deceptive; (3) all parties intend to discharge their obligations, financial and otherwise, in good faith; and (4) appropriate internal methods exist for equitable adjustment and/or redress of grievances concerning purchases.

- Organizational Relationships—Marketers should be aware of how their behavior may influence or impact the behavior of others in organizational relationships. They should not demand, encourage, or apply coercion to obtain unethical behavior in their relationships with others.

Any AMA members found to be in violation of any provision of this Code of Ethics may have his or her Association membership suspended or revoked.*

ASSOCIATION FOR COMPUTING MACHINERY (ACM)

Code of Ethics and Professional Conduct

Preamble. Commitment to ethical professional conduct is expected of every member (voting members, associate members, and student members) of the Association for Computing Machinery (ACM).

This code, consisting of 24 imperatives formulated as statements of personal responsibility, identifies the elements of such a commitment. It contains many, but not all, issues professionals are likely to face. . . . The code and its supplemental guidelines are intended to serve as a basis for ethical decision making in the conduct of professional work. Secondarily, they may serve as a basis for judging the merit of a formal complaint pertaining to violation of professional ethical standards.

The general imperatives for ACM members include contribute to society and human well-being, avoid harm to others, be honest and trustworthy, be fair and take action not to discriminate, honor property rights including copyrights and patents, give proper credit for intellectual property, respect the privacy of others, and honor confidentiality.

Adherence of professionals to a code of ethics is largely a voluntary matter. However, if a member does not follow this code by engaging in gross misconduct, membership in ACM may be terminated.†

* Adapted with permission from the American Marketing Association's Code of Ethics, published by the American Marketing Association. For a full text of the professional marketing code see *www.ama.org*.

† Copyright © 1997, Association for Computing Machinery, Inc. A full text of the ACM code of ethics can be found at *www.acm.org/constitution/code*.

personal and business information, especially through e-commerce transactions; confidentiality of electronic-mail communication; copyright protection regarding software, music, and intellectual property; and numerous other related issues exploded in the 1990s and early 2000s.

Jason Smathers, an engineer at America Online (AOL) was arrested and charged with stealing 92 million e-mail addresses of AOL customers and selling them to spammers that were marketing penis enlargement pills and online gambling sites. Sean Dunaway, accused of brokering the e-mail lists, was also arrested. Under the U.S. "spam law," passed on January 1, 2004, Smathers and Dunaway each faced a maximum sentence of five years in prison and a fine of $250,000 or twice the gross gain from their activities.[14]

As discussed in later chapters of this book, the explosion of information technology has raised serious questions of trust between individuals and businesses. In response to calls by businesspeople and academics for an increase in ethical responsibility in the information technology field, professional organizations have developed or revised professional codes of ethics, as shown in Exhibit 6.B.[15]

Other Functional Areas

Production and operations functions, which may seem to be remote from ethics considerations, have also been at the center of some ethics storms. Flawed manufacturing and lack of inspection of aircraft fuse pins, which hold the engines to the wing on Boeing 747 airplanes, were suspected in some accidents, endangering the lives of passengers as well as innocent bystanders.

> After a series of mine disasters killed 16 miners in one month, the governor of West Virginia ordered a "time-out" and suspended production in all 544 mines in the state, the nation's second leading coal-producing state. Those concerned with the miners' safety pointed to the lack of safety precautions, education, and equipment that may have contributed to many of these accidents and the resulting fatalities. The governor ordered extensive safety inspections of the operations of the mines and more than 6,000 miners were provided with updated safety training.[16]

Ethics issues also arise in purchasing and supply management departments. The Institute for Supply Management (ISM) revised its professional code of ethics in 2005. Its code advocates "loyalty to your organization, justice to those with whom you deal, and faith in your profession." The professional code denotes 12 principles and standards "to encourage adherence to an uncompromising level of integrity."[17]

Efforts by professional associations to guide their members toward effective resolution of ethical challenges make one point crystal clear: All areas of business, all people in business, and all levels of authority in business encounter ethics dilemmas from time to time. Ethics issues are a common thread running through the business world. Specific steps that businesses can take to make ethics work are discussed next.

Making Ethics Work in Corporations

Any business firm that wishes to do so can improve the quality of its ethical performance. Doing so requires a company to build ethical safeguards into its everyday routines. This is sometimes called *institutionalizing* ethics. How often organizations adopt these safeguards is shown in Figure 6.2.

---

[14] "AOL Worker Is Accused of Selling 93 Million E-Mail Names," *The New York Times,* June 24, 2004, *www.nytimes.com.*

[15] For further discussion of ethics in information technology see Richard Spinello, *Cyber Ethics: Morality and Law in Cyberspace,* 3rd ed. (Sudbury, MA: Jones and Bartlett, 2006); Paul A. Alcorn, *Practical Ethics for a Technology World* (Upper Saddle River, NJ: Prentice Hall, 2001); and the ISWorld Net Professional Ethics Web page at *www.cityu.edu.hk/is/ethics.*

[16] "West Virginia Mines Take Safety Timeout," CNN.com, February 2, 2006, *www.cnn.com.*

[17] All quotations are from the Institute for Supply Management's Principles and Standards of Ethical Supply Management Conduct, available to members of the association at *www.ism.ws.*

FIGURE 6.2

Organizations' Ethics Safeguards at Work*

Ethics Safeguard	Fortune 1000 (1992)	Southwest Pennsylvania Organizations (1996)	NBES (2005)
Promoted ethics at work	93%	71%	
Developed code of ethics	93	57	86%
Created ethics office/advice		17	65
Established ethics hotline		9	73
Offered ethics training	25	20	69
Conducted audit/evaluation		11	67

* The 1992 Fortune 1000 survey looked at the 500 largest industrial and 500 largest service companies according to the *Fortune* listing. The southwestern Pennsylvania organizations survey looked at organizations in that region of all sizes (30 percent of the sampled organizations had less than 50 employees, and 22 percent had more than 1,000 employees) and at multiple industry groups (health care, finance, manufacturing, etc.). The National Business Ethics Survey contacted employees working for companies of all sizes (48% from large firms and 69% from for-profit organizations).

Source: 1992 Fortune 1000 from Center for Business Ethics, "Instilling Ethical Values in Large Corporations," *Journal of Business Ethics* 11 (1992), pp. 863–67; 1996 Pennsylvania organizations from Beard Center for Leadership in Ethics, *Ethics Initiatives in Southwestern Pennsylvania: A Benchmarking Report* (Pittsburgh: Duquesne University, 1999); and the *National Business Ethics Survey: How Employees View Ethics in Their Organizations* (Washington, DC: Ethics Resource Center, 2005).

Building Ethical Safeguards into the Company

Managers and employees need guidance on how to handle day-to-day ethical situations; their own personal ethical compass may be working well, but they need to receive directional signals from the company. Several organizational steps can be taken to provide this kind of ethical awareness and direction.

> Lynn Sharp Paine, a Harvard Business School professor, has described two distinct approaches to ethics programs: a compliance-based approach and an integrity-based approach. A compliance-based program seeks to avoid legal sanctions. This approach emphasizes the threat of detection and punishment in order to channel employee behavior in a lawful direction. Paine also described an integrity-based approach to ethics programs. Integrity-based ethics programs combine a concern for the law with an emphasis on employee responsibility for ethical conduct. Employees are told to act with integrity and conduct their business dealings in an environment of honesty and fairness. From these values a company will nurture and maintain business relationships and will be profitable.[18]

Researchers found that both approaches lowered unethical conduct, although in somewhat different ways. Compliance-based ethics programs increased employees' willingness to seek ethical advice and their awareness of ethical issues at work. Integrity-based programs, for their part, also increased employees' sense of integrity, commitment to the organization, willingness to deliver bad news to supervisors, and their perception that better decisions were made.[19]

Top Management Commitment and Involvement

Research has consistently shown that the "tone at the top"—the example set by top executives—is critical to fostering ethical behavior. When senior-level managers signal employees, through their own behavior, that they believe ethics should receive high

---

[18] Lynn Sharp Paine, "Managing for Organizational Integrity," *Harvard Business Review*, March–April 1994, pp. 106–17.

[19] Gary R. Weaver and Linda Klebe Trevino, "Compliance and Values Oriented Ethics Programs: Influences on Employees' Attitudes and Behavior," *Business Ethics Quarterly* 9 (1999), pp. 315–35.

priority in all business decisions, they have taken a giant step toward improving ethical performance throughout the company. One prominent group recognized this in their response to the multiple ethics scandals that shook the confidence of the American public toward business.

> The Business Roundtable, a coalition of top executives, created an Institute for Corporate Ethics to develop and conduct training programs for senior managers. "This Institute is a bold investment that will bring together the best educators in the field of ethics, active business leaders, and business school students to forge a new and lasting link between ethical behavior and business practices," pledged Business Roundtable co-chairman Franklin Raines, chairman and CEO of Fannie Mae.[20]

Whether the issue is sexual harassment, honest dealing with suppliers, or the reporting of expenses, the commitments (or lack thereof) by senior management and the employees' immediate supervisor and their involvement in ethics as a daily influence on employee behavior are the most essential safeguards for creating an ethical workplace.

Ethics Policies or Codes

As shown in Figure 6.2, nearly all large U.S. corporations and most businesses of any size have **ethics policies or codes**. Their purpose is to provide guidance to managers and employees when they encounter an ethical dilemma. The rationales underlying the ethics policies differ from country to country. In the United States and Latin America, it was found that policies were primarily *instrumental*, that is, provided rules and procedures for employees to follow in order to adhere to company policies or societal laws. In Japan, most policies were found to be a mixture of *legal compliance* and *statements of the company's values and mission*. The *values and mission* policies also were popular with European and Canadian companies.[21]

Typically, ethics policies cover issues such as developing guidelines for accepting or refusing gifts from suppliers, avoiding conflicts of interest, maintaining the security of proprietary information, and avoiding discriminatory personnel practices. Researchers have found that writing ethics policies alone was insufficient in promoting ethics at work. Ethics policies must be frequently and widely distributed among employees and to external stakeholder groups (customers, suppliers, competitors, etc.). The creation of an ethics policy must be followed up with employee ethics training to further the influence of the policy's provisions on day-to-day company activities.[22]

Ethics Officers, Compliance Officers, and Ombudspersons

Ethical lapses in large corporations throughout the 1980s prompted many firms to create a new position: the **ethics officer, compliance officer,** or **ombudsperson.** A second surge of attention to ethics and the creation of ethics offices came in response to the 1991

---

[20] "Nation's Top CEOs Announce Plans for Center on Corporate Ethics," Institute for Global Ethics, *Ethics Newsline,* January 20, 2004, *www.globalethics.com.*

[21] Ronald C. Berenbeim, *Global Corporate Ethics Practices: A Developing Consensus* (New York: Conference Board, 1999).

[22] Betsy Stevens, "Communicating Ethical Values: A Study of Employee Perceptions," *Journal of Business Ethics* 20 (1999), pp. 113–20. For examples of codes, see Ivanka Mamic, *Implementing Codes of Conduct* (Sheffield, UK: Greenleaf Publishing, 2004); and Oliver F. Williams, C.S.C., ed., *Global Codes of Conduct: An Idea Whose Time Has Come* (Notre Dame, IN: University of Notre Dame Press, 2000).

U.S. Corporate Sentencing Guidelines, discussed in Chapter 5. Finally, the recent wave of corporate ethics scandals and the passage of the Sarbanes-Oxley Act have again turned businesses' attention toward entrusting ethical compliance and the development and implementation of ethics programs to an ethics or compliance officer or ombudsperson. From 2000 to 2004, the number of members in the professional association, the Ethics Officers Association, doubled from 632 to more than 1,200 members. To reflect the growing number of compliance officers heading companies' ethics programs, this association recently changed its name to the Ethics and Compliance Officers Association.

> According to a survey of its members, ethics and compliance officers and corporate ombudspersons have been entrusted with reducing the risks to the company of employee misconduct (79 percent), ensuring commitment to corporate values (75 percent), and establishing a better corporate culture (68 percent).[23]

Similar to an ethics or compliance officer, an ombudsperson is an impartial, confidential, and informal resource for resolving conflicts within an organization. These conflicts range from compensation and performance appraisal issues to discrimination, harassment and safety matters. Coca-Cola Enterprises, the largest producer, marketer and distributor of Coca-Cola products, created an ombuds office in 2001. Thomas Zgambo, Coca-Cola Enterprises' ombudsperson, reported that the company averaged 2,500 contacts annually.

Ethics Assist Lines or Helplines

In some companies, when employees are troubled about some ethical issue but may be reluctant to raise it with their immediate supervisor, they can place a call on the company's **ethics assist line or helpline** (the new preferred term to hotline or crisis line). Daniel Kile, former director of ethics at Bell Helicopter Textron, noted that assist lines typically have three uses: (1) to provide interpretations of proper ethical behavior involving conflicts of interest and the appropriateness of gift giving, (2) to create an avenue to make known to the proper authorities allegations of unethical conduct, and (3) to give employees and other corporate stakeholders a way to discover general information about a wide range of work-related topics.[24] An ethics assist line may work with other ethics safeguards, such as at Raytheon where the assist line served as an early warning system for the need to develop a new ethics training program for the firm's supervisors.

This approach has become more common, found in more than 83 percent of all organizations with 500 or more employees, according to the National Business Ethics Survey conducted by the Ethics Resource Center in 2005. The growth of help or assist lines is partly due to Section 301 of the Sarbanes-Oxley Act, which since 2002 has required companies to provide employees with a mechanism to report potentially criminal misconduct to top managers and the board. Companies are learning how to make these mechanisms more effective, as illustrated by the following example.

> Shell Oil Company, based in Houston, Texas, implemented a hotline in 1993. Employees calling the number could leave voice messages from 8 a.m. to 5 p.m., Monday through Fridays. The response was decidedly cool—a total of only 32 calls from 1993 to 2000, while the company employed 30,000 workers. In 2000,

[23] "EOA Survey: Companies Seeking to Integrate Ethics through the Whole Organization," *Ethikos*, July–August 2001, pp. 1–3, 16.

[24] "Operating an Ethics Hotline: Some Practical Advice," *Ethikos*, March–April 1996, pp. 11–13.

Exhibit 6.C   Not So Fast—Ethics Hotlines in Europe, Maybe Not

The U.S. Sarbanes-Oxley Act, passed in 2002, requires companies to take several steps to assure accurate financial reporting, including setting up a confidential whistle-blowing mechanism. As U.S.-based multinationals have sought to meet the requirements of this law in their European operations, they have run into some unexpected obstacles. The core of the problem is the hotlines' anonymity.

For example, the French Data Protection Authority told McDonald's and Exide Technologies that they could not use ethics hotlines to gather information on possible corporate problems. The French regulators asserted that hotlines violated French privacy laws, because callers to the hotlines could remain anonymous. The French maintained that anyone named by a whistle-blower should be told of the complaint, so they could have a chance to prove their innocence. The French have a long-standing unease with anonymity, dating back at least to Nazi Germany's occupation of France during World War II, when individuals were forced to inform on others.

The European Union's Data Protection laws give individuals the right to know what data are being processed about them. It also assures that data are processed fairly and lawfully, are kept secure, and are not transferred to a country that fails to protect privacy rights, such as the United States, in the opinion of EU regulators.

One consultant recommended that U.S. multinationals operating in Europe develop a tri-level program in response to the Sarbanes-Oxley requirement: (1) a fully developed program for its U.S. operations, (2) another program posted on the parent company's global Web site and addressed to the world (employees and the general public), and (3) a "Europeanized" version of the program for its EU subsidiaries to adapt and ratify, consistent with local laws and procedures in Europe.

Source: "U.S. Helplines Raise EU Privacy Concerns," *Ethikos*, September–October 2005, pp. 1–4, 18–20; and "Blow the Whistle—No Wait: Ethics Hotlines May Be Illegal in Europe," *Business Ethics*, Fall 2005, p. 10.

they changed the name to a "helpline" and it was staffed by Global Compliance Services on a full-time, seven-day, 24-hour basis. By 2004, Shell's helpline was averaging 117 calls annually. Why the increase? "We advertised the helpline," recalled Danna Walton, Shell's senior counsel. The company distributed helpline brochures to employees. Company ethics and compliance officers posted signs around the workplace. The helpline number was printed on every other page of the company's code of conduct. It was promoted on the company's Web site. The company assured employees that allegations would be investigated and acted upon if something was found to be amiss. "You've got to make people understand that you're going to do something about it" when they make a report, said Walton. If not, they will stop using the mechanism.[25]

Some of the challenges of introducing the use of ethics helplines worldwide are profiled in Exhibit 6.C.

Ethics Training Programs

Another step companies can take to build in ethical safeguards is to offer employee training. The number of companies offering employee ethics training ranges from less than 40 percent for firms with 25 or fewer employees to more than 75 percent for organizations with 500 or more employees. Training generally is offered annually and held for less than two hours on average. Ethics training is offered to managers, rather than the rank and file, and usually involves lectures offered by a company trainer or general group discussions. Topics covered in ethics training range from compliance with governmental

---

[25] "Developing Effective Helplines: Shell Oil and Lubrizol," *Ethikos*, September–October 2005, pp. 5–7, 17.

regulations, such as antitrust, to adherence to the company's sexual harassment or conflicts of interest policies.[26]

Ethics training has been found to be an effective method for promoting ethical behavior in the workplace. In a sample of 313 business professionals, researchers reported "significant statistical support for the notion that businesspersons employed in organizations that have formalized ethics training programs have more perceptions of their companies' ethical context than do individuals employed in organizations that do not [have ethics training]."[27]

> Coors Brewing Company encountered serious resistance from its employees when it tried to initiate its ethics program. The ethics policy was printed on a large, single piece of cardboard with a tear-off card to be signed by each employee attesting that she or he had read and understood the rules. About 30 percent of the workforce refused to sign the card, but the company learned an important lesson. The employees wanted and needed to experience the ethics training program first, and then would agree to the company's request for the sign-off to the ethics policy.

Ethics Audits

Some firms have attempted to assess the effectiveness of their ethical safeguards by documenting evidence of increased ethical employee behavior. One technique used was an **ethics audit**. Typically, the auditor was required to note any deviations from the company's ethics standards and bring them to the attention of the audit supervisor. Often the managers of each operating entity were required to file a report with the auditor on the corrective action they took to deal with any deviations from the standards that emerged in the prior year's audit. Managers also reported on the written procedures they established for informing new employees of the standards and for providing ongoing reviews of the standards with other employees.

> Macroinnovation Associates announced in 2003 its Openness Audit™, an independent advisory service aimed at supporting the needs of ethics officers and other executives concerned with corporate accountability, transparency, and governance. According to the company, the audit is a management tool that profiles the policies, programs, and practices behind information and knowledge processing in a firm.

Although United Technologies objected to the term *ethics audit*, the company did embrace the value of assessing the effectiveness of its ethics compliance program. "There is no such thing as an ethics audit," according to United Technologies' vice president of business practices. "What we do are system audits." The system audit at UT examined the controls in place at its business units for preventing compliance and ethics irregularities. These often included a *desk audit* where auditors went into a sales manager's actual office to see if they could find any so-called red flags. The UT auditors also looked into the manager's file cabinets, correspondence, and e-mail.[28]

Comprehensive Ethics Programs

The critical component in creating an effective ethics design is the integration of various appropriate ethics safeguards into a comprehensive program. In an Ethics Resource Center

---

[26] Beard Center for Leadership in Ethics, *Ethics Initiatives in Southwestern Pennsylvania: A Benchmarking Report* (Pittsburgh: Duquesne University, 1996); and Ethics Resource Center, *National Business Ethics Survey: How Employees View Ethics in Their Organizations* (Washington, DC, 2005).

[27] Sean Valentine and Gary Fleischman, "Ethics Training and Businesspersons' Perceptions of Organizational Ethics," *Journal of Business Ethics* 52 (2004), pp. 381–90.

[28] "Audits Reduce Compliance Risk at United Technologies," *Ethikos*, March–April 2001, pp. 12–13.

survey of U.S. employees, only 26 percent of the employees reported that their employer had developed a comprehensive, six-element ethics program, that is, a program integrating written standards, training, advice resources, hotline for anonymous reporting, ethics discipline and evaluation systems. The startling discovery, however, was the dramatic impact a comprehensive ethics program, along with a strong ethical culture, had in creating an ethical work environment for employees. People working at a firm with a comprehensive ethics program were more likely to report ethical misconduct in the workplace to the appropriate company authority and be satisfied with the company's investigation of and response to charges of ethical misconduct. In contrast, firms with only an ethics policy or code were often perceived as less ethically responsible and less able to address ethical misconduct in the workplace than firms without any ethical safeguards.[29] An example of a comprehensive ethics program is described in the discussion case at the end of this chapter.

Corporate Ethics Awards

Firms have been honored for their efforts to create an ethical climate and improve ethical performance. Business Ethics Awards, sponsored by *Business Ethics* magazine, have been awarded since 1989. In 2002 *Business Ethics* magazine created a new Living Economy Award, based on the work of theorist David Korten, author of *The Post-Corporate World*. He emphasized the need to build a living economy based on firms that focused on fair profits rather than maximum profits and were locally based, stakeholder-owned, democratically accountable, life-serving, and operated on a human scale.

> The first Living Economy Award went to the White Dog Café, a $5 million café in Philadelphia that paid living wages to all employees, including dishwashers, and purchased humanely raised meat from local family farmers. A year later the Living Economy Award was presented to Organic Valley, a $156 million, 633 farmer-owned cooperative located in LaFarge, Wisconsin. Chroma Technology Corporation, a global high-technology manufacturer of optic filters, received the Living Economy Award in 2004. No employee at Chroma is paid more than $75,000 or less than $37,500, there are no designated managers, and employees hold seats on the board of directors. In 2005, Weaver Street Cooperative, a North Carolina firm, was honored with the Living Economy Award for its sustainable products, community focus, and democratic governance.[30]

These and other award-winning firms provide the foundation for a collection of corporate ethics role models. Their commitment to ethical values and efforts to establish effective ethics programs demonstrate that firms can be financially successful and ethically focused.

Ethics in a Global Economy

Doing business in a global context raises a host of complex ethical challenges. Examples of unethical conduct by business employees are reported from nearly every country. One example of unethical activity is **bribery**, a questionable or unjust payment often to a government official to ensure or facilitate a business transaction. Bribery is found in nearly every sector of the global marketplace.

---

[29] See Joshua Joseph, *2000 National Business Ethics Survey, Volume I: How Employees Perceive Ethics at Work* (Washington, DC: Ethics Resource Center, 2000).

[30] "14th Annual Business Ethics Awards," *Business Ethics*, Fall 2002, pp. 10–12; "15th Annual Business Ethics Awards," *Business Ethics*, Winter 2003, pp. 8–16; "16th Annual Business Ethics Awards," *Business Ethics*, Fall 2004, pp. 8–17; and, "17th Annual Business Ethics Awards," *Business Ethics*, Fall 2005, pp. 15–20.

A Berlin-based watchdog agency, Transparency International, annually publishes a survey that ranks corruption by country according to perceptions of executives and the public. Countries where having to pay a bribe is least likely included Iceland, Finland, New Zealand, Denmark, Singapore, Sweden, and Switzerland. At the other end of the index—countries most likely to demand or accept bribes—were Chad, Bangladesh, Turkmenistan, Myanmar, Haiti, Nigeria, Equatorial Guinea, and Cote d'Ivoire. The United States ranked 17th on the list of 159 countries, with United Kingdom 11th, Canada 14th, Germany 16th, France 18th, Japan 21st, Italy 40th, India 88th, and Russia 126th.[31]

An analysis of Transparency International's Corruption Perceptions Index (CPI) by a business scholar revealed that bribe-taking was more likely in countries with low per capita income, low salaries for government officials, and less variation in income distribution. The report also argued that "a legalistic approach, by itself, is unlikely to be effective in curbing bribery," since the culture of the society plays an important role in the occurrence of bribery. What may be effective in combating bribery is an integrative approach of economic advancement policies, social investment in education, and friendly business policies to foster economic growth, in addition to anticorruption laws and punishments to combat bribery while seeking to enhance economic development and gradual cultural adjustments.[32]

Examples of bribery and corruption in business have been frequently reported. Companies in central and eastern Europe, for example, reported that 30 to 60 percent of all business transactions in the region involved paying bribes, and these firms paid from 2 to 8 percent of annual revenues in bribes. The average cost of bribery in the former Soviet Union was reported to range from 4 to more than 8 percent of company revenue. Globally, bribery occurred most often in public works contracts and construction, arms and defense industry exchanges, and business dealings in the petroleum and energy industries, according to a Transparency International report.[33]

Efforts to Curtail Unethical Practices

Numerous efforts are under way to curb unethical business practices throughout the world. The most common control is through government intervention and regulation. Efforts to address unethical business behavior often begin with national governments, which can enact stiff legislative controls, but recently include efforts by international organizations.

One of the most widespread and potentially powerful efforts to combat bribery was initiated by the Organization for Economic Cooperation and Development (OECD). The OECD treaty called on member countries to take steps to deter, prevent, and combat the bribery of public officials in foreign countries. As of 2006, 36 countries had ratified the treaty, meaning that bribery is a crime in the country and punishable by the courts.

Other examples of multinational and national anticorruption efforts include the Southern Africa Forum Against Corruption, an annual meeting since 2000, which is dedicated to lobby member countries to ratify the Southern African Development Community Protocol Against Corruption. Eight countries already have approved the protocol—Botswana, Mauritius, South Africa, Malawi, Tanzania, Zambia, Lesotho and Namibia. Other efforts

---

[31] Transparency International Corruption Perceptions Index 2005, *www.transparency.org/cpi/2005.*

[32] Rajib Sanyal, "Determinants of Bribery in International Business: The Cultural and Economic Factors," *Journal of Business Ethics* 59 (2005), pp. 139–45.

[33] "Bribery, Corruption Are Rampant in Eastern Europe, Survey Finds," *The Wall Street Journal*, November 9, 1999, p. A21; "Corruption Stunts Growth in Ex-Soviet States," *The Wall Street Journal,* July 5, 2000, p. A17; and "Chronikos," *Ethikos*, March–April 2000, p. 10.

Exhibit 6.D   Anticorruption and Bribery Efforts in Russia

Russian President Vladimir Putin was serious about his pledge to clean up Russia, since he realized that the entrepreneurial sector of his country's economy could never achieve its full potential without a full-scale battle against corruption. "The authorities are speaking out about corruption, and I think it is going to have a positive impact on this problem," said Pavel Chickov, head of Public Verdict, a group that monitors governmental agencies. Putin sought closer ties with the West, prompting his cooperation with Western-initiated anticorruption efforts.

A number of actions underscored Putin's commitment to end bribery and corruption:

- A probe of high-level bureaucrats led to charges against many officials including Railways Minister Nikolai Aksyonenko for illegally spending ministry funds.
- Judges' salaries were increased fivefold in an effort to cut down on courtroom bribery.
- A new law banned the intervention of state prosecutors in private litigation between contending business parties, eliminating another potential bribery situation.
- Other regulations sharply restricted discounts that railroad regulators could give to shippers.
- The number of business activities that required a license was drastically reduced from 2,000 to 100—fewer licenses meant fewer chances for a bureaucrat to be in line for a bribe.

Source: "Cleanup Time: The Kremlin Is Launching a Major Attack on Corruption," *BusinessWeek*, January 14, 2002, pp. 46–47; and "Russia Gets Tougher on Corruption," *Pittsburgh Post-Gazette*, September 24, 2004, p. A6.

begun in the 1990s continue today, such as the Council of Europe's Criminal Law Convention on Corruption and the Global Forum on Fighting Corruption and Safeguarding Integrity among Justice and Security Officials.

In past years, various international organizations, such as the International Labour Organization and the United Nations, have attempted to develop an international code of conduct for multinational corporations. These efforts have emphasized the need for companies to adhere to universal ethical guidelines when conducting business throughout the world. These codes and their ethical focus are discussed further in Chapter 7.

At the country level, Morocco marked January 6 as a national day to fight corruption. The Chilean government, intent on maintaining its reputation as "the cleanest country in Latin America," passed 50 anticorruption laws in 2003. At a conference of the Association of National Accountants of Nigeria, its director encouraged accountability and transparency when granting loans and technical aids as a way of reducing corruption. An independent corruption body was established in Indonesia as part of the president's vow to end corruption in that country. The government of Slovakia made combating corruption a top priority. The Swiss government nullified the tax advantages of paying commissions to consultants in foreign countries, a practice that had long been illegal in other countries. The interim president of Peru pledged to take a tough stance against corruption and established measures to prevent corruption suspects from fleeing the country without standing trial. Russian President Vladimir Putin pledged to reduce corruption in his country, as described in Exhibit 6.D.

Executives representing U.S.-based companies are prohibited by the **U.S. Foreign Corrupt Practices Act** (FCPA) from paying bribes to foreign government officials, political parties, or political candidates. To achieve this goal, the FCPA requires U.S. companies with foreign operations to adopt accounting practices that ensure full disclosure of the company's transactions. While the number of cases filed under the Foreign Corrupt Practices Act doubled from 2002 to 2004, the actual number of cases is still relatively small—18 reported investigations in 2004, compared to 7 in 2002—yet the impact is noticeable.

Titan Corporation, a San Diego–based security-technology firm, was accused of paying a $3.5 million bribe to secure a lucrative military contract to an agent in Benin, although the specific details were sealed by court order. In 2005, Titan agreed to pay a fine under the FCPA that was eight times the amount of the bribe—$28.5 million. As a result of this settlement, many law firms advised their corporate clients that aggressive and continuous enforcement of the FCPA should be expected.[34]

Some people question the effectiveness of governmental legislation or corporate policies. Rather than establishing rules, some businesses, including Motorola and Reebok, are trying to educate and motivate their employees worldwide to both respect the customs of other nations and adhere to basic ethical principles of fairness, honesty, and respect for human rights.[35] Some who study international business ethics say that such higher standards of ethics already exist. Thomas Donaldson, a leading ethics scholar, has outlined a set of fundamental human rights—including the rights to security, freedom of movement, and subsistence income—that should be respected by all multinational corporations. These standards and other ethical values are at the core of the development of transnational codes of conduct promoted by the United Nations and other international organizations.[36]

Ethics, Law, and Illegal Corporate Behavior

It is important when discussing specific ways to improve business's ethical performance to consider the relationship of laws and ethics. Some people have argued that the best way to assure ethical business conduct is to insist that business firms obey society's laws. However, this approach is not as simple as it seems.

Laws and ethics are not quite the same. Laws are similar to ethics because both define proper and improper behavior. In general, laws are a society's attempt to formalize—that is, to reduce to written rules—the general public's ideas about what constitutes right and wrong conduct in various spheres of life. Ethical concepts—like the people who believe in them—are more complex than written rules of law. Ethics deal with human dilemmas that frequently go beyond the formal language of law and the meanings given to legal rules. Sometimes businesses or industries preempt legislation and voluntarily adopt ethically based practices.

Such was the case when the Interactive Digital Software Association, which represents video game makers, established a five-category system that was voluntarily adopted by the industry to inform consumers of the intended target audience. The video game industry also agreed to provide content warnings, such as mild profanity, and to use warning symbols.

This example suggests that following laws cannot always define proper action, that is, what is ethical or unethical. Although laws attempt to codify a society's notions of right and wrong, they are not always able to do so completely. Obeying laws is usually

---

[34] "Ethics Alert: Foreign Corrupt Practices Prosecutions Doubled," *Business-Ethics.com,* Winter 2005, p. 9; and "Titan Comments on Government Investigation Settlements," Titan Corporation press release, *www.titan.com.*

[35] For a description of Motorola's global ethics program see R. S. Moorthy, Richard T. DeGeorge, Thomas Donaldson, William J. Ellos, Robert C. Solomon, and Robert B. Textor, *Uncompromising Integrity: Motorola's Global Challenge* (Schaumberg, IL: Motorola University Press, 1998); and Reebok's company policies on human rights at *www.reebok.com/about_reebok/human_rights.*

[36] For a complete list of fundamental human rights, see Thomas Donaldson, *The Ethics of International Business* (New York: Oxford University Press, 1989).

one way of acting ethically, and the public generally expects business to be law-abiding. But at times, the public expects business to recognize that ethical principles are broader than laws. Because of the imperfect match between laws and ethics, business managers who try to improve their company's ethical performance need to do more than comply with laws.

Corporate Lawbreaking and Its Costs

Although estimates vary, lawbreaking in business may cause serious financial losses to the firms, often inflicted by the company's own employees.

"Over a third of companies were victims of fraud, suffering an average loss of over $2 million," according to the PricewaterhouseCoopers Global Economic Crime Survey. Two law professors estimated that corporate crimes in the form of faulty goods, monopolistic practices, and other law violations annually cost American consumers between $174 billion and $231 billion. Ten percent of the $1 trillion spent on U.S. health care is believed lost due to fraud every year.[37]

The United States is not the only nation suffering losses from illegal acts. German officials believe that more than 50 billion marks ($29.07 billion) a year is lost from the German economy as a result of inflated accounting, tax evasion, and illegal kickbacks. In a survey commissioned by the U.K. Fraud Advisory Panel, researchers found that **white-collar crime** cost U.K. businesses about $73 billion each year. Crimes involving embezzlement, money laundering, and check fraud were found to be widespread, with nearly half of the firm admitting that they conceal such crimes from external auditors.[38]

Beyond these monetary costs of illegal behavior are the physical and social costs. It is estimated that each year 200,000 to 500,000 workers are exposed to toxic agents such as radioactive materials and poisonous chemicals because of corporate failure to obey safety laws. Occupational diseases, many resulting from violations of health and safety laws, cause more than 100,000 deaths each year in the United States, and more than 6,000 workers die from on-the-job injuries. This amounts to an average of nearly 17 workplace deaths each day. Tragically, many of these deaths might have been avoided if employers and workers were informed about the risks and complied with established safety and health regulations.

In response to the economic costs of criminal activity and spurred by the passage of the Sarbanes-Oxley Act, the U.S. Justice Department announced new sentencing guidelines for criminals who harm more than 250 victims, who substantially jeopardize the health of a financial institution or publicly traded company, or who break securities laws while serving as a director or officer of a public firm. "Crimes in the suites will be treated the same [as] or more seriously than crimes in the streets," warned U.S. district judge Ruben Castillo.

The Justice Department also warned that fewer executives convicted of white-collar crimes would be allowed to serve their time in halfway houses and similar low-security facilities in the future. About 125 federal inmates serving their sentences in such facilities in January 2003 were transferred to federal penitentiaries. "The prospect of prison,

---

[37] For more information on the costs of corporate crime see "More than One-Third of Global Companies Hit by Economic Crime," Institute for Global Ethics, *Ethics Newsline*, July 14, 2003, *www.globalethics.org*.

[38] "Economic Crime Costs U.K. Billions: Survey," Institute for Global Ethics, *Ethics Newsline*, October 25, 2004, *www.globalethics.com*.

more than any other sanction, is feared by white-collar criminals and has a powerful deterrent effect," said Deputy Attorney General Larry Thompson.[39]

But there is still an unanswered question: "Does crime pay?" Although Dennis Kozlowski of Tyco and Bernie Ebbers of WorldCom received stiff penalties for their deeds, consider the fates for these executives who committed illegal acts:

- Michael Milken, guru of the junk-bond scandals in the 1980s, left prison in 1992 after serving less than two years and with his fortune of $500 million intact.
- Global Crossing founder Gary Winnick pocketed millions from allegedly fraudulent stock sales and faced no criminal or civil charges at all.
- Investment banker Frank Quattrone had his conviction and 18-month prison sentence overturned on appeal and will keep most of his $200 million made through allegedly questionable initial public offerings.
- Mark H. Swartz, Tyco's former CFO, received a $44 million cash severance, deferred compensation and supplemental pension package from the company. (Swartz voluntarily returned an additional $91 million in severance to the company.)
- Andrew Wiederhorn, CEO of Fog Cutter Capital Group, was sentenced to 18 months in prison after pleading guilty to two felony counts involving a $160 million loan by his company which resulted in its financial collapse. The firm's board of directors voted to keep Wiederhorn on the company's payroll, so while in jail he will receive $2.5 million in compensation.[40]

In a Conference Board–supported survey, 62 percent of the executives responding said that executives who leave their firm because of major violations of ethics and compliance codes "get a financial package and go." So, while the risks are great, some evidence supports the adage "crime does pay," although governmental and business efforts may seek to change this situation in the future.

Yet, the more likely lesson to be learned from the outcomes for many of the recent business ethics scandals is that "crime does *not* pay." There are serious consequences for acting unethically and illegally, as the "perp walks" portrayed in the media of business executives going off to jail in handcuffs would indicate. Therefore, businesses have taken significant measures to foster an ethical environment in the workplace and to provide mechanisms to ensure their employees know what is the "right thing to do" and consistently act in an ethical manner.

Summary

- A company's culture and ethical climate tend to shape the attitudes and actions of all who work there, sometimes resulting in high levels of ethical behavior and at other times contributing to less desirable ethical performance.
- Not all ethical issues in business are the same, but ethical challenges occur in all major functional areas of business. Professional associations for each functional area often attempt to provide a standard of conduct to guide practice.
- Companies can improve their ethical performance by creating a value-based ethics program that relies on top management leadership and organizational safeguards, such

---

[39] "U.S. Stiffens Sentences for White-Collar Criminals," Institute for Global Ethics, *Ethics Newsline*, January 13, 2003, *www.globalethics.org/newsline*.

[40] "White-Collar Crime: Who Does Time?" *BusinessWeek*, February 6, 2006, pp. 60–61; "Windfalls Are Common in Ousters over Alleged Ethics Violations," *The Wall Street Journal*, November 25, 2003, p. B8; and "Convicted CEO Will Get $2.5 Million Salary Plus a Bonus While Serving Prison Time," *SFGate.com*, August 2, 2004, *www.sfgate.com*.

as ethics policies or codes, ethics or compliance officers or ombudspersons, ethics training programs, and ethics audits.

- Companies that have a comprehensive, or multifaceted, ethics program often are better able to promote ethical behavior at work and avoid unethical action by employees.

- Ethical issues, such as bribery, are evident throughout the world, and many international agencies and national governments are actively attempting to minimize such unethical behavior through economic sanctions and international codes.

- Although laws and ethics are closely related, they are not the same; ethical principles tend to be broader than legal principles. Illegal behavior by businesses and employees imposes great costs on business generally and the general public.

Key Terms

bribery, *127*
compliance officer, *123*
corporate culture, *113*
ethical climate, *114*
ethics assist line or helpline, *124*

ethics audit, *126*
ethics officer, *123*
ethics policies or codes, *123*
laws, *130*

ombudsperson, *123*
U.S. Foreign Corrupt Practices Act, *129*
white-collar crime, *131*

Internet Resources

www.TheCRO.com
www.theecoa.org
www.integrity-interactive.com
www.dii.org

www.ethicscan.on.ca
www.globalethics.org

CRO Magazine
Ethics & Compliance Officers Association
Integrity Interactive Company
Defense Industry Initiative on Business Ethics and Conduct
EthicScan, Toronto-based ethics clearinghouse
Institute for Global Ethics

Discussion Case: *PPG's Corporate Ethics Program*

Founded in 1883, PPG Industries is a major global supplier of coatings, glass, fiberglass, and chemicals. In 2005, this Pittsburgh-based multinational operated more than 110 manufacturing facilities and equity affiliates in over 20 countries and had global sales of $10.2 billion.

In keeping with its reputation as an honest, fair, and capable firm, PPG Industries had developed a multifaceted ethics program. At its core was the PPG Industries Blueprint, describing the company's values, statement of mission, and objectives. This document identified the company's critical values as dedication to the customer; respect for the dignity, rights, and contributions of employees; recognition of the concerns and needs of society; commitment to integrity and high ethical standards; supplier relationships focusing on continuous improvement and shared responsibility; and responsibility to shareholders.

To put these values into practice through policies and programs, PPG management implemented a number of ethical safeguards and called on its employees to implement them through their personal conduct. Over a period of several years, PPG began issuing its Business Conduct Policies, which defined possible ethical issues encountered by PPG employees, as well as guidelines for handling their ethical challenges. The policies concluded by stating, "It is the policy of PPG and its subsidiaries, its agents and employees, to make every effort to operate as good, responsible, and ethical corporate citizens and to comply with all applicable laws of the jurisdiction in which they are present or operating."

Although the Business Conduct Policies clearly set the ethical tone for PPG's operations, PPG management felt a need to include an explicit global focus since the firm had acquired several overseas businesses with cultures and histories that differed from PPG's. The Global Ethics Committee was created, with members drawn from PPG operations in Europe, Asia, and South and North America. It was charged with advising top management on ethical issues, making recommendations concerning company policies and codes of conduct, developing an ethics training program, and providing a forum for the review of ethical issues. In addition, it assumed the role of the compliance committee after the passage of the U.S. Federal Sentencing Guidelines in 1991.

One of the most significant actions taken by the Global Ethics Committee was drafting PPG's initial Global Code of Ethics (GCOE) in 1989. In 2004, the Committee combined PPG's compliance-based Business Conduct Policies with the GCOE, creating a single unambiguous document that reaffirmed the importance of the company's ethical standards, introduced new and prospective employees to the company's ethical tradition and the high standards to which PPG holds its people, and served as a primary reference document by drawing together main elements of PPG's ethical convictions. The global code covered PPG's relationships with customers, suppliers, and competitors (issues such as gifts, inappropriate entertainment, and product safety) and responsibility to PPG people (such as health and safety and diversity issues). It also discussed protecting corporate assets (such as security of information and intellectual property) and company responsibilities to the public and public officials (ranging from corporate lobbying to environmental responsibility). Finally, the global code addressed differences in local laws and customs and reporting violations or workplace misconduct.

For example, the revised GCOE began with a letter of commitment from PPG Industries' chairman and chief executive officer: "Our reputation rests not only on our ability to be a provider of quality goods and services but also on our integrity and high ethical standards. Our continuing business success rests, in large part, on the work of every PPG employee to preserve and enhance our reputation with customers, suppliers, government officials and the public in general. . . ." The GCOE defined possible ethical issues encountered by PPG employees, as well as guidelines for handling their ethical challenges. The Code concluded by stating, "Your personal commitment to the principles and values outlined in this document is the single most important tool we have in ensuring PPG's continued reputation as a valued business partner."

To ensure that any instances of ethical misconduct were reported, PPG instituted the PPG ethics hotline in 1999, a toll-free telephone number maintained by an independent company located in another state, which assured callers it would protect their anonymity. Calls from PPG employees ranged from questions about employee relations to reports of fraud, discrimination, conflict of interest, or the release of proprietary information. On the basis of communications through the ethics hotline, PPG Industries improved communication channels within the firm, changed policies, and prosecuted violators as necessary.

Most recently PPG has ramped up the ethics and compliance training for employees, adding timely online modules in critical areas including Records Management, Foreign Corrupt Practices Act, Antitrust, Workplace Harassment and Discrimination, and an annual course and certification on Ethics. These courses have reached thousands of PPG employees worldwide. To ensure that the ethics message reaches even those without computer access, PPG sends paper copies of the relevant information to overseas employees and developed a phone-in ethics training and certification process for U.S. and Canada employees.

PPG's multifaceted corporate ethics program is one example of a business seeking to maintain an ethical culture while honoring its economic responsibilities. The firm was recognized for its exemplary ethics program as the recipient of the Pittsburgh Chapter's American Business Ethics Award for large companies in 2003. As PPG's chairman and CEO explained, "Let . . . us all work together toward our mutual goals: to furnish goods and services that meet our customers' and society's needs; to provide all employees with a safe, healthy, and fulfilling work environment; to afford our shareholders a superior return on their investment; and to contribute as a good corporate citizen to each nation and each community in which we operate."

Source: Quotations are from PPG's Global Code of Ethics. Additional information taken from the PPG Industries Blueprint and interviews with PPG's global director, security and compliance, Regis Becker.

Discussion Questions

1. From the ethics climates defined in this chapter, which climate best describes PPG Industries? Do you think this climate type is the best for promoting ethics in the workplace?

2. How many of the ethical safeguards described in this chapter has PPG Industries adopted in its corporate ethics program?

3. Do you see any deficiencies or weaknesses in PPG Industries' ethics program? What further steps, if any, would you recommend to the company?

PART FOUR

Business and Government in a Global Society

CHAPTER SEVEN

The Challenges of Globalization

The world economy is becoming increasingly integrated, and many businesses have extended their reach beyond national borders. Yet the process of globalization is controversial, and the involvement of corporations in other nations is not always welcome. Doing business in diverse political and economic systems poses difficult challenges. When a transnational corporation buys resources, manufactures products, or sells goods and services in multiple countries, it is inevitably drawn into a web of global social and ethical issues. Understanding what these issues are and how to manage them through collaborative action with governments and civil society organizations is a vital skill for today's managers.

This chapter focuses on these key learning objectives:

- Defining globalization, and classifying the major ways in which companies enter the global marketplace.
- Recognizing the major drivers of the globalization process and the international financial and trade institutions that have shaped this process in recent decades.
- Analyzing the benefits and costs of the globalization of business.
- Identifying the major types of political and economic systems in which companies operate across the world and the special challenges posed by doing business in diverse settings.
- Examining the major codes of conduct governing the social and ethical behavior of transnational corporations.
- Assessing how businesses can work collaboratively with governments and the civil sector to address global social issues.

In 2000, a bitter dispute erupted in Bolivia over control of a very basic commodity— water. As part of a program of privatization promoted by the World Bank, the government of Bolivia had auctioned off the water utility of Cochabamba, the nation's third-largest city. The buyer was a consortium controlled by the U.S. construction and engineering firm Bechtel. Under the terms of the deal, Bechtel agreed to improve the badly dilapidated water system. In exchange, the company received exclusive rights to all the water in the city, including the underground aquifer, and was guaranteed a minimum 15 percent annual return on its investment. The company moved in, began the upgrades, and promptly hiked water rates—stunning local households and small businesses who were then expected to pay up to a quarter of their income for basic water service. A broad coalition quickly formed, and people took to the streets by the thousands. The army moved in and declared a state of siege. Faced with a popular insurrection, the Bolivian government informed Bechtel that it had revoked the contract. The company retaliated by filing a complaint with the World Bank, demanding $25 million in compensation. This was an amount that Bolivia, a land-locked nation high in the Andes and the poorest country in South America, could hardly afford. In 2005, Bechtel finally dropped its claim in the face of intense public pressure in Bolivia and around the world.[1]

This extraordinary episode captures much of the turmoil and controversy that surrounds the globalization of business and its far-reaching social impacts. We live in a world that seems increasingly small, more connected, and highly interdependent. It is a world in which transnational companies such as Bechtel often bring much-needed technical know-how, capital, and managerial experience to poorer nations deeply in need of these resources. Yet corporate involvement abroad often involves challenging social and ethical issues. In this case, Bechtel had to proceed in the context of World Bank mandates over which it had, at best, indirect control. It faced contradictory stakeholder expectations, confusing norms about subsidies for basic services, and a surprise military intervention. Moreover, it failed almost completely to anticipate any of this or to resolve the problem effectively when it arose. How companies can best negotiate the difficult challenges of doing business in a global world is the subject of this chapter.

The Process of Globalization

Globalization refers to the increasing movement of goods, services, and capital across national borders. Globalization is a *process*, that is, an ongoing series of interrelated events. International trade and financial flows integrate the world economy, leading to the spread of technology, culture, and politics. Thomas Friedman, a columnist for *The New York Times* and a well-known commentator, has described globalization as a *system* with its own internal logic:

> (G)lobalization is not simply a trend or a fad but is, rather, an international system. It is the system that has now replaced the old Cold War system, and, like that Cold War system, globalization has its own rules and logic that today directly or indirectly influence the politics, environment, geopolitics, and economics of virtually every country in the world.[2]

---

[1] William Finnegan, "Leasing the Rain," *The New Yorker,* April 8, 2002, pp. 43–53. Updates may be found at the Web site of the Democracy Center, *www.democracyctr.org.*

[2] Thomas L. Friedman, *The Lexus and the Olive Tree* (New York: Anchor Books, 2000), p. ix.

Firms can enter and compete in the global marketplace in several ways. Many companies first build a successful business in their home country, then export their products or services to buyers in other countries. In other words, they develop *global market channels* for their products. Nokia, for example, began in Finland, but now sells its cellular phones and other products all over the world. Other firms begin in their home country, but realize that they can cut costs by locating some or all of their *global operations* in another country. This decision leads to establishing manufacturing plants or service operations abroad. Sometimes, companies own their own factories and offices overseas; sometimes, they subcontract this work to others. For example, in the apparel and shoe industries, companies such as Nike, Gap, and Guess have extensive networks of subcontractors outside the United States who make products of their design. Finally, a third strategy involves purchasing raw materials, components, or other supplies from sellers in other countries. In other words, these companies develop *global supply chains*. Although they do not make entire products overseas, they source supplies that are then assembled in the home country.

These three strategies of globalization can be summarized in three words: *sell, make,* and *buy.* Today, many companies have all three elements of global business—market channels, manufacturing operations, and supply chains.

Major Transnational Corporations

According to United Nations estimates, there are about 70,000 **transnational corporations (TNCs)** operating in the modern global economy (defined by the United Nations as firms that control assets abroad). These corporations, in turn, have almost 700,000 affiliates, meaning suppliers, subcontractors, retailers, and other entities with which they have some business relationship.[3] Although many firms conduct business across national boundaries, most global commerce is carried out by a small number of powerful firms. Just the top 100 transnational corporations, for example, are responsible for fully 14 percent of the sales of all TNCs.

Who are these leading transnational corporations? Figure 7.1 lists the top 10 nonfinancial transnational corporations, ranked in order of the value of the foreign assets they control. Leading the list is General Electric, the American electrical equipment and electronics conglomerate. Rounding out the group are several of the world's leading oil companies, automakers, and telecommunications firms. The world's major financial corporations also extend across the globe; Citigroup, the largest of these, has 320 foreign affiliates in 77 host counties.

Figure 7.1 lists the companies with the most foreign assets, but these are not necessarily the most truly transnational companies. The United Nations computes a *transnationality index,* a measure that captures the proportion of a firm's assets, sales, and employment that is located in foreign countries—in other words, how much of a firm's business is conducted outside its home nation. Not surprisingly, some of the most truly global firms are based in home countries with relatively small markets, workforces, or supplies of raw materials. Firms with very high transnationality indices include Thomson (a media company based in Canada), CRH PLC. (building materials; Ireland), News Corporation (media; Australia); Roche Group (pharmaceuticals; Switzerland); and Cadbury Schweppes (food and beverages; United Kingdom).[4] These companies extend their reach far beyond the borders of their home nations.

The Acceleration of Globalization

Global commerce has taken place for hundreds of years, dating back to the exploration and colonization of Africa, Asia, and the Americas by Europeans beginning in

---

[3] United Nations, *World Investment Report 2005: Transnational Corporations and the Internationalization of R&D* (New York: United Nations, 2005).

[4] *World Investment Report 2005,* Annex Table A.I.9, p. 269.

FIGURE 7.1

The World's Top 10 Nonfinancial Transnational Corporations, Ranked by Foreign Assets

Source: United Nations, *World Investment Report 2005*, Annex Table A.I.9, p. 267. All data are for the year 2003.

Corporation	Home Economy	Industry	Foreign Assets (in $ millions)
General Electric	United States	Electrical Equipment	$258,900
Vodafone	United Kingdom	Telecommunications	243,839
Ford Motor Company	United States	Motor Vehicles	173,882
General Motors	United States	Motor Vehicles	154,466
BP	United Kingdom	Petroleum	141,551
ExxonMobil	United States	Petroleum	116,853
Royal Dutch/Shell	UK/Netherlands	Petroleum	112,587
Toyota Motor	Japan	Motor Vehicles	94,164
Total	France	Petroleum	87,840
France Telecom	France	Telecommunications	81,370

FIGURE 7.2

Exports of Services, in Millions of U.S. $, 1990 and 2004, World and Selected Countries and Regions

Source: World Bank, *World Development Indicators 2006*, Table 4.6, "Structure of Service Exports." Services include all commercial service exports, minus exports of government services. Such services include transportation; travel; insurance and financial services; and computer, information, and communications services, among others.

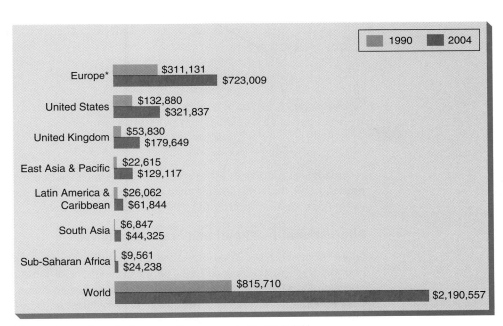

*Europe refers to nations using the common European currency, the euro, in 2004.

the 15th century. But it is during the past 60 years or so, since the end of World War II, that global commerce has truly transformed the world's economy. According to the World Bank, about one-fourth of all goods and services produced worldwide are sold to other nations, rather than domestically; this is almost double the percentage in 1960. In other words, the world's economy is becoming increasingly integrated, as an ever-higher share of output is being exported across national borders.[5] In earlier years, most exports were of goods; an important recent trend is the globalization of services, as shown in Figure 7.2, which chronicles growth in this sector over the most recent decade and a half.

[5] Current data on exports of goods and services as a percentage of gross domestic product are available at *www.devdata.worldbank.org*.

The acceleration of globalization has been driven by several factors:

- *Technological innovation:* Sophisticated software, Internet, fiber optics, wireless, and satellite technologies, among others, have made it easier and faster for companies to communicate with employees, partners, and suppliers all over the globe in real time. In the words of Thomas Friedman, the world has become increasingly "flat," as technology has leveled the playing field and allowed all to participate on an equal footing in global commerce.[6]

- *Transportation systems:* Improvements in transportation—from air freight, to high-speed rail, to new generations of ocean-going vessels—enable the fast and cheap movement of goods and services from one place to another.

- *The rise of major transnational corporations:* Big, well-capitalized firms are better equipped to conduct business across national borders than smaller, local companies.

- *Social and political reforms:* Critical changes, including the rise of dynamic growth economics on the Pacific Rim and the collapse of the former communist states of central and eastern Europe, have opened new regions to world trade.

In recent years, Volkswagen, Renault, Audi, and other European car companies have shifted much of their production across the former Iron Curtain that divided communist and noncommunist Europe, drawn by the availability of cheap skilled labor, from assemblers to engineers. The VW Touareg and Porsche Cayenne are now made in Slovakia, the Renault Logan in Romania, and the Audi TT roadster in Hungary. The Asian companies Toyota, Kia, and Suzuki have followed suit, either operating or planning to build plants in Slovakia, Hungary, and the Czech Republic. The concentration of auto factories in Central and Eastern Europe has gone so far that some have begun to call the region "Detroit East."[7]

Finally, the process of globalization has also been spurred by the rise of international financial and trade institutions that stabilize currencies and promote free trade. These institutions are discussed in the next section.

International Financial and Trade Institutions

Global commerce is carried out in the context of a set of important **international financial and trade institutions (IFTIs)**. The most important of these are the World Bank, the International Monetary Fund, and the World Trade Organization. By setting the rules by which international commerce is transacted, these institutions increasingly determine who wins and who loses in the global economy.

The **World Bank (WB)** was set up in 1944, near the end of World War II, to provide economic development loans to its member nations. Its main motivation at that time was to help rebuild the war-torn economies of Europe. Today, the World Bank is one of the world's largest sources of economic development assistance, providing almost $22 billion in loans in 2005 for roads, dams, power plants, and other infrastructure projects, as well as for education, health, and social services. The bank gets its funds from dues paid by its member countries and from money it borrows in the international capital markets. Representation on the bank's governing board is based on economic power; that is, countries have voting power based on the size of their economies. Not surprisingly, the United States and other rich nations dominate the bank.

---

[6] Thomas Friedman, *The World Is Flat: A Brief History of the Twenty-First Century* (New York: Farrar, Straus and Giroux, 2005).

[7] "Detroit East: Eastern Europe Is Becoming the World's New Car Capital," *BusinessWeek,* August 1, 2005, pp. 47–53.

The World Bank often imposes strict conditions on countries that receive its loans, to make sure the debtor countries can pay back what they owe. These conditions, called *structural adjustment plans*, may include demands that governments cut spending, devalue their currencies, increase exports, liberalize financial markets, reduce wages, and remove agricultural price subsidies. These conditions often lead to hardship, particularly for the poor. Critics charge that developing countries are unfairly burdened by these conditions. They also say that poor countries are often hard pressed to pay back principal and interest on World Bank loans.

The World Bank's sister organization is the **International Monetary Fund (IMF)**. Founded at the same time as the bank (and today residing across the street from it in Washington, D.C.), the IMF has a somewhat narrower purpose: to make currency exchange easier for member countries so that they can participate in global trade. It does this by lending foreign exchange to member countries. Like the World Bank, the IMF imposes strict conditions on governments that receive its loans. Some observers think that over the years, the IMF has become even harsher than the World Bank in the conditions it imposes.

One country that has been particularly hard hit by IMF conditions is Jamaica, a developing island nation in the Caribbean. In exchange for IMF loans, Jamaica agreed to a number of conditions, including opening up its borders to free trade with other nations. The problem was that Jamaican dairy, poultry, vegetable, and fruit farmers were unable to compete with the United States, whose meat and produce were produced more efficiently by large agribusiness companies. The result was that many Jamaican farms failed, and the country became increasingly reliant on imports to feed its people. Jamaica fell into an increasing spiral of debt, its citizens became poorer, and the country found it increasingly difficult to repay its IMF loans.[8]

Recently, major lending organizations, including the IMF, have begun to extend **debt relief** to some poor nations, a subject that is explored in Exhibit 7.A.

The final member of the triumvirate of IFTIs is the **World Trade Organization (WTO)**. The WTO, founded in 1995 as a successor to the General Agreement on Tariffs and Trade (GATT), is an international body that establishes the ground rules for trade among nations. Its major objective is to promote free trade, that is, to eliminate barriers to trade among nations, such as quotas, duties, and tariffs. The WTO conducts negotiations, called *rounds*, on various topics, rotating its meetings among different cities. Most of the world's nations are members of the WTO, which is based in Switzerland. Unlike the WB and the IMF, the WTO does not lend money or foreign exchange; it simply sets the rules for international trade.

Under the WTO's most favored nation rule, member countries may not discriminate against foreign products for any reason. All import restrictions are illegal unless proven scientifically, for example, on the basis that a product is unsafe. If countries disagree about the interpretation of this or any other WTO rule, they can bring a complaint before the WTO's Dispute Settlement Body (DSB), a panel of appointed experts, which meets behind closed doors. Rulings are binding; the only way a decision can be overruled is if every member country opposes it. One contentious issue that recently came before the WTO, involving agricultural subsidies, is profiled in Exhibit 7.B. Another area of controversy has involved the WTO's position on intellectual property rights, particularly as they relate

---

[8] *Life and Debt,* a film by Stephanie Black. For more information, see *www.lifeanddebt.org.*

Exhibit 7.A   Debt Relief

Many developing countries now owe huge debts to the World Bank, the IMF, and other lenders. The total amount of money owed is almost $3 trillion.

One of the unintended consequences of past loans has been persistent poverty, because a large share of many nations' earnings goes to pay off debt rather than to develop the economy or improve the lives of citizens. (Imagine an individual who accumulates a large credit card debt, and then has to use most of his income just to make payments, rather than saving money or buying things he needs now.) One of the troubling aspects about developing nations' debt is that in some cases the original loans never even helped the people of these countries. Some funds were used to buy arms, bolster oppressive regimes, or personally enrich dictators such as Marcos of the Philippines and Suharto of Indonesia.

Some people feel that developing nations ought to pay off their debts, just as individuals have to pay off their credit cards. But others believe that accumulated debt imposes such a huge burden on poor nations that if something is not done they will never be able to develop. Since the 1990s, several initiatives have advocated debt forgiveness. In this approach, international financial institutions would permit debtor nations to "declare bankruptcy" and start over. One of the best known of these initiatives was called Jubilee. It took its name from a passage in the Old Testament that called for the forgiveness of debt every 50 years, on the occasion of a celebration called a *jubilee* at which the community celebrated its unity.

Recently the international community has made significant progress in implementing debt relief. In 2005, the G-8 (the eight industrialized nations France, Germany, Italy, Japan, the United Kingdom, the United States, Canada, and Russia, as well as the European Union) called for the cancelation of the debt owed by 18 heavily indebted poor countries to the World Bank, IMF, and African Development Fund. The amount to be forgiven was about $41 billion. The IMF later agreed to most aspects of this proposal. Advocates of debt cancelation praised this move, saying that "After decades of paying back often illegitimate debts contracted under dictatorships for dubious projects, and siphoning away critical funds from social spending and development, these [poor] countries now have the opportunity to invest . . . much-needed resources into their societies."

Sources: The quotation is from Sameer Dossani of the 50 Years Is Enough Network, a debt relief organization, in "IMF Debt Relief Is Welcomed as First Step," *Inter News Service,* December 21, 2005. For more information on recent debt reduction initiatives and on the Jubilee Debt Reduction Campaign, see *www.worldbank.org, www.imf.org,* and *www.jubileeusa.org.*

to the protection of patents for pharmaceutical drugs. This issue is explored in the case study, "GlaxoSmithKline and AIDS Drugs for Africa," at the end of this book.

These three international financial and trade institutions are important because no business can operate across national boundaries without complying with the rules set by the WTO, and many businesses in the developing world are dependent on World Bank and IMF loans for their very lifeblood. The policies these institutions adopt, therefore, have much to do with whether or not globalization is perceived as a positive or negative force, a subject to which we turn next.

The Benefits and Costs of Globalization

Globalization is highly controversial. One need only look at television coverage of angry protests at recent meetings of the World Trade Organization, World Bank, and International Monetary Fund to see that not all people and organizations believe that globalization—at least as currently practiced—is a positive force. Yet, many others feel that globalization holds tremendous potential for pulling nations out of poverty, spreading technological innovation, and allowing people everywhere to enjoy the bounty generated by modern

Exhibit 7.B Free Trade and Farm Subsidies

Is trade among nations really free when governments aid their own producers? This issue has been at the heart of an ongoing dispute within the World Trade Organization over farm subsidies.

The European Union, the United States, and Japan all provide generous agricultural subsidies. In the mid-2000s, for example, the U.S. government paid farmers around $16 billion a year to support production of a range of commodities, including cotton, wheat, rice, and peanuts. The farm lobby strongly backed these subsidies, which it said were necessary to protect the rural way of life. Critics, however, said that subsidies allowed farmers to "dump" their products on world markets at artificially reduced prices, competing unfairly with agricultural products from poor countries that could not afford similar support payments.

In the cotton industry, for example, every acre under cultivation in the United States received an annual government payment of $230. Elimination of these payments, according to one economic analysis, would raise the world price of cotton by 26 percent. Particularly hurt by U.S. cotton subsidies were poor farmers in west and central Africa, where more than 10 million people depended on this crop for their livelihoods. In a painful irony, the U.S. government provided more dollars to its own cotton farmers than to all of Africa in the form of development aid.

In 2005, ruling in a complaint brought by Brazil with support from several African nations, the WTO declared the United States and other countries would have to end their cotton subsidies. "These rulings are a triumph for developing countries and a warning bell for rich countries who consistently flout the rules at the WTO and whose unfair systems are creating misery and poverty for millions," said a representative of Oxfam International. The ruling did not put an end to the broader controversy over farm subsidies, however, which continued to be a major point of contention at the WTO meetings a few months later in Hong Kong.

Sources: "The Cotton Debate: A Global Industry Argues over Government Subsidies," *The National Peace Corps Association Worldview,* Fall 2005; "Busted: World Trade Watchdog Declares EU and U.S. Farm Subsidies Illegal," Oxfam International, September 9, 2004; "Cultivating Poverty: The Impact of U.S. Cotton Subsidies on Africa," Oxfam International, 2002, available online at *www.oxfam.org;* "Brazil Triumphs over U.S. in WTO Subsidies Dispute," *Inter Press Service,* March 3, 2005; "WTO Agreement on Agriculture: A Decade of Dumping," Institute for Agriculture and Trade Policy, 2005, available online at *www.globalpolicy.org.*

business. Clearly, some benefit from globalization, while others do not. In this section, we present some of the arguments advanced by both sides in the debate over this important issue.

Benefits of Globalization

Proponents of globalization point to its many benefits. One of the most important of these is that globalization tends to increase economic productivity. That means, simply, that more is produced with the same effort.

Why should that be? As the economist David Ricardo first pointed out, productivity rises more quickly when countries produce goods and services for which they have a natural talent. He called this the *theory of comparative advantage.* Suppose, for example, that one country had a climate and terrain ideally suited for raising sheep, giving it an advantage in the production of wool and woolen goods. A second country had a favorable combination of iron, coal, and water power that allowed it to produce high-grade steel. The first country would benefit from trading its woolen goods for the second country's steel, and vice versa; and the world's economy overall would be more productive than if both countries had tried to make everything they needed for themselves. In other words, in the context of free trade, specialization (everyone does what they are best at) makes the world economy as a whole more efficient, so living standards rise.

Many countries today have developed a specialization in one or another skill or industry. India, with its excellent system of technical education, has become a world powerhouse in the production of software engineers. France and Italy, with their strong networks of skilled craftspeople and designers, are acknowledged leaders in the world's high fashion and footwear design industries. The United States, with its concentration of actors, directors, special effects experts, and screenwriters, is the global headquarters for the movie industry.

Comparative advantage can come from a number of possible sources, including natural resources; the skills, education, or experience of a critical mass of people; or an existing production infrastructure.

Globalization also tends to reduce prices for consumers. If a shopper in the United States goes into Wal-Mart to buy a shirt, he or she is likely to find one at a very reasonable price. Wal-Mart sources its apparel from all over the world, enabling it to push down production costs. Globalization also benefits consumers by giving them access to a wide range of diverse goods and the latest "big thing." Teenagers in Malaysia can enjoy the latest Tom Cruise or Will Smith movie, while American children can play with new Nintendo or Sega games from Japan.

For the developing world, globalization also brings benefits. It helps entrepreneurs the world over by giving all countries access to foreign investment funds to support economic development. Globalization also transfers technology. In a competitive world marketplace, the best ideas and newest innovations spread quickly. Multinational corporations train their employees and partners how to make the fastest computer chips, the most productive food crops, and the most efficient lightbulbs. In many nations of the developing world, globalization has meant more manufacturing jobs in export sectors and training for workers eager to enhance their skills.

The futurist Allen Hammond identifies two additional benefits of globalization. First, he says that world trade has the potential of supporting the spread of democracy and freedom.

The very nature of economic activity in free markets . . . requires broad access to information, the spread of competence, and the exercise of individual decision-making throughout the workforce—conditions that are more compatible with free societies and democratic forms of government than with authoritarian regimes.[9]

Second, according to Hammond, global commerce can reduce military conflict by acting as a force that binds disparate peoples together on the common ground of business interaction. "Nations that once competed for territorial dominance," he writes, "will now compete for market share, with money that once supported military forces invested in new ports, telecommunications, and other infrastructure." In this view, global business can become both a stabilizing force and a conduit for Western ideas about democracy and freedom.

Costs of Globalization

If globalization has all these benefits, why are so many individuals and organizations so critical of it? The answer is complex. Just as some gain from globalization, others are hurt by it. From the perspective of its victims, globalization does not look nearly so attractive.

---

[9] Allen Hammond, *Which World? Scenarios for the 21st Century* (Washington DC: Island Press, 1998), p. 30.

One of the costs of globalization is job insecurity. As businesses move manufacturing across national borders in search of cheaper labor, workers at home are laid off. Jobs in the domestic economy are lost as imports replace homemade goods and services.

In the American South, tens of thousands of jobs in the textile industry have been lost over the past several decades, as jobs have shifted to low-labor cost areas of the world, leaving whole communities devastated. In 2003, Pillowtex, the last remaining major textile company operating in the region, declared bankruptcy and shut down 16 plants, citing intense foreign competition. Pillowtex (formerly Fieldcrest Cannon) had at one time been the world's largest producer of household textiles like towels, sheets, and blankets.

In the past, mainly manufacturing was affected by the shift of jobs abroad; today, clerical, white-collar and professional jobs are, too. Many customer service calls originating in the United States are now answered by operators in the Philippines and India. The back office operations of many banks—sorting and recording check transactions, for example—are done in India and China. Aircraft manufacturers are using aeronautical specialists in Russia to design parts for new planes. By one estimate, as many as 3.3 million white-collar jobs will be outsourced from the United States to lower wage countries by 2015.[10] Even when jobs are not actually relocated, wages may be driven down because companies facing foreign competition try to keep their costs in check. Much of the opposition to globalization in affluent nations comes from people who feel their own jobs, pay, and livelihoods threatened by workers abroad who can do their work more cheaply.

Not only workers in rich countries are affected by globalization. When workers in Indonesia began organizing for higher wages, Nike Corporation moved much of its production to Vietnam and China. Many Indonesian workers lost their jobs. Some call this feature of global capitalism the "race to the bottom."

Another cost of globalization is that environmental and labor standards may be weakened as companies seek manufacturing sites where regulations are most lax. Just as companies may desire locations offering the cheapest labor, they may also search for locations with few environmental protections; weak regulation of occupational health and safety, hours of work, and discrimination; and few rights for unions. For example, the so-called gold coast of southeastern China has become a world manufacturing center for many products, especially electronics. One journalist offered the following description of a young worker there:

Pan Qing Mei hoists a soldering gun and briskly fastens chips and wires to motherboards streaming past on a conveyor belt. Fumes from the lead solder rise past her face toward a ventilating fan high above the floor of the spotless factory. Pan, a 23-year-old migrant worker, said the fumes made her light-headed when she first arrived from a distant farm village three years ago. Now she's used to them—just as she's used to the marathon shifts, sometimes 18 hours a day.[11]

Weak health and safety and environmental regulations—and lax enforcement of the laws that do exist—are a major draw for the companies that manufacture in factories in China's industrial zones.

A related concern is that the World Trade Organization's most favored nation rules make it difficult for individual nations to adopt policies promoting environmental or

[10] "Is Your Job Next?" *BusinessWeek*, February 3, 2003, pp. 50–60.
[11] "Cheap Products' Human Cost," *San Jose Mercury News*, November 24, 2002.

social objectives, if these have the effect of discriminating against products from another country.

> One incident that provoked considerable controversy involved protection for endangered sea turtles. In response to concerns voiced by consumers and environmentalists, the United States passed a law that required shrimp trawlers to use nets equipped with special devices that allowed turtles to escape. It also banned the import of wild shrimp from nations that did not require such devices. Shortly thereafter, Thailand, Pakistan, Malaysia, and India brought a complaint before the WTO, saying that the U.S. law violated trade rules by discriminating against their shrimp (which were caught without protection for sea turtles). The WTO ruled against the United States and ordered it to either change its law or pay compensation to the other nations for lost trade.

Critics of globalization say that incidents such as this one show that free trade rules are being used to restrict the right of sovereign nations to make their own laws setting environmental or social standards for imported products.

Another cost of globalization is that it erodes regional and national cultures and undermines cultural, linguistic, and religious diversity. In other words, global commerce makes us all very much the same. Is a world in which everyone is drinking Coke, watching Hollywood movies, talking on Motorola cell phones, and wearing Gap jeans a world we want, or not? Some have argued that the deep **anti-Americanism** present in many parts of the world reflects resentment at the penetration of the values of dominant U.S.-based transnational corporations into every corner of the world.

With respect to the point that globalization promotes democracy, critics charge that market capitalism is just as compatible with despotism as it is with freedom. Indeed, transnational corporations are often drawn to nations that are governed by antidemocratic or military regimes, because they are so effective at controlling labor and blocking efforts to protect the environment. For example, Unocal's joint-venture collaboration to build a gas pipeline with the military government of Myanmar (Burma), a notorious abuser of human rights, may have brought significant financial benefits to the petroleum company.

Figure 7.3 summarizes the major points in the discussion about the costs and benefits of globalization.

FIGURE 7.3
Benefits and Costs of Globalization

Benefits of Globalization	Costs of Globalization
Increases economic productivity.	Causes job insecurity.
Reduces prices for consumers.	Weakens environmental and labor standards.
Gives developing countries access to foreign investment funds to support economic development.	Prevents individual nations from adopting policies promoting environmental or social objectives, if these discriminate against products from another country.
Transfers technology.	Erodes regional and national cultures and undermines cultural, linguistic, and religious diversity.
Spreads democracy and freedom, and reduces military conflict.	Is compatible with despotism.

What is public opinion on these issues? A survey of 20,000 people in 20 countries around the world in 2005 found that in all countries except one (France), most people thought that the free market economic system was best. But solid majorities in all countries also favored more regulation of big companies to protect the environment and the rights of workers, consumers, and shareholders. The director of the study concluded, "There is now an extraordinary level of consensus about the best economic system. But . . . there is also near-unanimous rejection of unbridled capitalism."[12]

This discussion raises the very real possibility that globalization may benefit the world economy as a whole, while simultaneously hurting many individuals and localities. An ongoing challenge to business, government, and society is to find ways to extend the benefits of globalization to all, while mitigating its adverse effects.

Doing Business in a Diverse World

Doing business in other nations is much more than a step across a geographical boundary; it is a step into different social, political, cultural, and economic realities. As shown in Chapter 1, even businesses operating in one community or one nation cannot function successfully without considering a wide variety of stakeholder needs and interests. When companies operate globally, the number of stakeholders to be considered in decision making, and the diversity of their interests, increases dramatically.

Comparative Political and Economic Systems

The many nations of the world differ greatly in their political, social, and economic systems. One important dimension of this diversity is how power is exercised, that is, the degree to which a nation's people may freely exercise their democratic rights. **Democracy** refers broadly to the presence of political freedom. Arthur Lewis, a Nobel laureate in economics, described it this way: "The primary meaning of democracy is that all who are affected by a decision should have the right to participate in making that decision, either directly or through chosen representatives." According to the United Nations, democracy has four defining features:[13]

- Fair elections, in which citizens may freely choose their leaders from among candidates representing more than one political party.
- An independent media, in which journalists and citizens may express their political views without fear of censorship or punishment.
- Separation of powers among the executive, legislative, and judicial branches of government.
- An open society where citizens have the right to form their own independent organizations to pursue social, religious, and cultural goals.

One of the truly remarkable facts about the past century has been the spread of democratic rights for the first time to many nations around the world. Consider, for example, that at the beginning of the 20th century *no* country in the world had universal suffrage (all citizens could vote); today, the majority of countries do. One hundred and forty

[12] The full survey results are available at *www.worldpublicopinion.org.*

[13] United Nations Development Programme, *Human Development Report 2000* (New York: Oxford University Press, 2000), Ch. 3, "Inclusive Democracy Secures Rights," pp. 56–71. The quotation from Arthur Lewis appears on p. 56.

of the world's nearly 200 countries now hold multiparty elections, the highest number ever. The collapse of communist party rule in the former Soviet Union and its satellites in eastern and central Europe in the early 1990s was followed by the first open elections ever in these countries. These changes have led some observers to call the end of the 20th century the "third wave of democracy."

On the other hand, many countries still lack basic democratic rights. Single-party rule by communist parties remains a reality in China, Vietnam, Cuba, and the People's Democratic Republic of Korea (North Korea). **Military dictatorships**, that is, repressive regimes ruled by dictators who exercise total power through control of the armed forces, are in place in, among others, Myanmar, Equatorial Guinea, Turkmenistan, and Belarus.[14] Some countries, such as Pakistan, for example, have reverted to authoritarian rule after a period of democracy. The rights of citizens to organize in support of cultural and religious goals are restricted in a number of Arab states, including Iran, Syria, and Saudi Arabia. According to United Nations estimates, 106 countries still limit important civil and political freedoms.

Even in some countries that are formally democratic, people perceive that they have little influence on policy. A survey of citizens in 60 countries conducted by Gallup International showed that less than a third said their country was "governed by the will of the people," even though most of these countries held open elections.[15]

The degree to which human rights are protected also varies widely across nations. As explained in Chapter 5, *human rights* refers broadly to the rights and privileges accorded to all people, simply by virtue of being human, for example, the rights to a decent standard of living, free speech, religious freedom, and due process of law, among others. Fundamental human rights have been codified in a number of international agreements, the most important of which is the Universal Declaration of Human Rights of 1948.[16] The second half of the 20th century was a period of great advances in human rights in many regions, and over half of the world's nations have now ratified *all* of the United Nations' human right covenants. Nonetheless, many human rights problems remain. Consider the following examples:

- More than 10 million children die each year before their fifth birthday. Most of these deaths are preventable.[17]

- Gross violations of human rights have not been eliminated. *Genocide*, mass murder of innocent civilians, has occurred all too recently in Rwanda, Iraq, Bosnia and Herzegovina, the Congo, and Sudan.

- Over a million girls and young women under the age of 18 are forced into prostitution every year.

- Minority groups and indigenous peoples in many nations still lack basic political and social rights. In Nepal, the life expectancy of "untouchables," the lowest caste, is fully 15 years less than that of Brahmins, the highest caste.

The absence of key human rights in many nations remains a significant issue for companies transacting business there.

---

[14] For profiles of the dictators of these nations, see David Wallechinsky, "*Parade*'s Annual List of the World's 10 Worst Dictators," *Parade,* January 22, 2006.

[15] United Nations Development Programme, *Human Development Report 2002* (New York: Oxford University Press, 2002), "Deepening Democracy in a Fragmented World," pp. 1–11.

[16] For more information on the Universal Declaration of Human Rights and other United Nations agreements on human rights, see the Web site of the U.N. High Commissioner for Human Rights at *www.unhchr.ch.*

Another dimension of difference among nations today is how economic assets are controlled, that is, the degree of economic freedom. On one end of the continuum are societies in which assets are privately owned and exchanged in a free and open market. Such **free enterprise systems** are based on the principle of voluntary association and exchange. In such a system, people with goods and services to sell take them voluntarily to the marketplace, seeking to exchange them for money or other goods or services. Political and economic freedoms are, of course, related: as people gain more control over government decisions they often press for greater economic opportunity; open markets may give people the resources to participate effectively in politics.

At the other end of the continuum are systems of **central state control**, in which economic power is concentrated in the hands of government officials and political authorities. The central government owns the property that is used to produce goods and services. Private ownership may be forbidden or greatly restricted, and most private markets are illegal. Very few societies today operate on the basis of strict central state control of the economy. More common is a system of mixed free enterprise and central state control in which some industries are state controlled, and others are privately owned. For example, in Nigeria, the oil industry is controlled by a government-owned enterprise that operates in partnership with foreign companies such as Shell and Chevron, but many other industries are privately controlled. In the social democracies of Scandinavia, such as Norway, the government operates some industries but not others.

The Heritage Foundation, a conservative think tank, has scored the nations of the world according to an *index of economic freedom* defined as "the absence of government coercion or constraint on the production, distribution, or consumption of goods and services beyond the extent necessary for citizens to protect and maintain liberty itself." Among the freest nations in 2006, by this measure, were Hong Kong, Singapore, and Ireland; among the most repressed were Burma, Iran, and—the least free in the world—North Korea.[18]

Nations also differ greatly in their overall levels of economic and social development. Ours is a world of great inequalities. To cite just one simple measure, the richest 1 percent of people in the world receive as much income annually as the poorest 57 percent. The lives of a software engineer in Canada, say, and a subsistence farmer in Mali (in central Africa) could not be more different. The engineer would have a life expectancy of 80 years, access to excellent medical care, and a comfortable home in an affluent suburb. His children would likely be healthy, and they could look forward to a college education. The farmer, by contrast, could expect to live only to age 48, probably could not read or write, and would earn an annual income of less than $1,000 (U.S.)—in good years when his crops did not fail. He would likely not have access to clean drinking water, and his children would be poorly nourished and unprotected by vaccination against common childhood illnesses. Several of his children would die before reaching adulthood.[19] Even as the world has become freer politically and economically, inequality has grown; the gaps between the richest and poorest nations are rising, as are gaps between the richest and poorest people in many nations.

---

[17] United Nations Development Programme, *Human Development Report 2005* (New York: Oxford University Press, 2005), Ch. 1, p. 24.

[18] Available at *www.heritage.org*.

[19] Profiles derived from human development statistics published annually by the United Nations Development Programme.

Meeting the Challenges of Global Diversity

As the preceding discussion suggests, transnational corporations today do business in a world of staggering diversity and complexity. Not surprisingly, the wide range of political, social, and economic environments in which business operates poses complex and challenging questions for managers, such as the following, for example:

- If a company does business in a nation that does not grant women equal rights such as Saudi Arabia, for example, should that company hire and promote women at work, even if this violates local laws or customs?

- Should a company enter into a business joint venture with a government-owned enterprise if that government has a reputation for violating the human rights of its own citizens? For example, Unocal, mentioned earlier in this chapter, was criticized and later successfully sued for entering into a joint venture with the repressive military government of Myanmar.

- Does a company have a duty to offer its products or services—say, life-saving medication—at a lower price in poor countries like Mali, or to customers who desperately need them?

- If a government fails to provide basic services to its citizens, such as primary education, decent housing, and sanitation services, is it the duty of a company to provide these things for its own employees or for members of the community in which it is located? This question is particularly likely to arise for companies in extractive industries, such as oil, natural gas, and metal mining, where production may be located far from established communities.

Many people believe that when transnational corporations operate according to strong moral principles, they can become a force for positive change in other nations where they operate. This is known as **constructive engagement**. Under some situations, however, constructive engagement may not be possible. At what point do violations of political, human, and economic rights become so extreme that companies simply cannot morally justify doing business in a country any more?

The experience of Shell Oil in Nigeria, further explored in a case study at the end of this book, illustrates this dilemma. Shell entered into a joint venture with the Nigerian government, then ruled by a military dictator, to produce and export oil. Citizens of the oil-producing regions organized to protest Shell's behavior, charging that the company had despoiled the environment, failed to provide services to the community adequately, and not hired enough indigenous people from the local area. In response, the Nigerian government imposed martial law and arrested the leaders of the protest. Civilians were killed, and several leaders of the protest were executed after military tribunals where they were not given the right to defend themselves. Should Shell have intervened? Was Shell responsible for what the government did? Should Shell have provided basic services in the oil-producing regions that the government had not? Should Shell leave Nigeria, or try to work with the government and communities there to improve conditions in the oil-producing regions?

In this situation, Shell decided not to take a public stance against the government's actions, on the grounds that it should "stay out of politics." The company was strenuously criticized for this and later had to rethink its position on political action (a subject that is explored in the companion case study at the end of this book, "The Transformation of Shell"). Eventually, Shell announced that it had changed its view and was prepared to make known to governments its position on political matters, such as this one, that affected the company or its stakeholders. It also took action to better protect the environment and to train its managers in human rights principles.

Like Shell, many companies face ongoing dilemmas deciding how to respond to conditions in repressive nations.

Global Codes of Corporate Conduct

In recent years, a number of important efforts have been made to address the challenges facing transnational companies as they confront a bewildering diversity of laws, norms, cultures, and stakeholder expectations. Most companies take for granted that they should, unless the circumstances are truly exceptional, follow the laws of the nations where they do business. But beyond merely obeying the law, what other standards should transnational corporations follow? Do universal standards, applicable to all companies in all global circumstances, exist? What guidelines would help a company in a situation like the one that confronted Shell in Nigeria?

These difficult questions have been addressed by international organizations such as the United Nations, by corporations and business advisory groups, and by scholars and ethicists. Recent years have seen a proliferation of **global codes of conduct** that seek to define acceptable and unacceptable behavior for today's transnational corporations.

Of the codes that have been developed by groups representing multiple nations, two of the most important are those developed by the United Nations and by the Organization for Economic Cooperation and Development (OECD), a group representing 30 advanced industrial countries, mostly in Europe.

- The *United Nations Global Compact* was initiated in 2000 by Kofi Annan, the secretary-general of the United Nations. In consultation with corporations and nonprofit organizations, the secretary-general proposed core basic principles covering labor, human rights, and environmental standards and invited corporations to voluntarily endorse them. The United Nations described the Compact as "a values-based platform designed to promote institutional learning." As of 2006, over 2,000 businesses had endorsed the principles, and many had participated in a series of dialogues on corporate responsibility designed to share best practices.[20] The experience of one company that has endorsed the United Nations Global Compact, Novartis, is profiled in Exhibit 7.C.

- The *OECD Guidelines for Multinational Enterprises* is a code of conduct for corporations developed by member nations of the OECD. The guidelines, which like the UN Global Compact are voluntary, address employment relations, information disclosure, environmental stewardship, consumer interests, and the management of technology.

Codes have also been developed by businesses themselves or by groups or individuals that advise businesses. Among these are the following:

- The *Global Sullivan Principles* were proposed by the late Reverend Leon Sullivan in 1999. Reverend Sullivan, who for many years had served on the boards of General Motors and other corporations, had earlier sponsored a code for companies doing business in South Africa before the end of apartheid in that country. The objectives of the Global Sullivan Principles were to support economic, social, and political justice by

---

[20] More information is available at *www.unglobalcompact.org*.

Exhibit 7.C — Implementing the Global Compact at Novartis

An early endorser of the United Nations Global Compact was Novartis, a major pharmaceutical firm based in Switzerland.

In 2000, CEO Daniel Vasella publicly signed the Global Compact, saying, "Novartis would like to see [it] become a catalyst for concrete action of enterprises and nations . . . furthering worldwide acceptance of fundamental human rights, labor and environmental standards." The company reworked its own code of conduct to include the Compact's principles. It established a steering committee made up of representatives from its major operating divisions and functional areas. A senior member of the executive committee (board of directors) was put in charge, and the process was named the Novartis Corporate Citizenship Initiative.

One major challenge faced by the committee was to apply the Compact's very general prescriptions to specific business circumstances. For example, Principle 1 calls on companies to "support and respect the protection of international human rights." The committee quickly concluded that some human rights principles, such as protecting people from such acts as murder, arbitrary imprisonment, and torture, had nothing to do with corporate reality and could be dismissed as irrelevant.

Applying other human rights principles, however, proved more complex. The Universal Declaration of Human Rights states that each person has "the right to a standard of living adequate for the health and well-being of himself and of his family." What did this mean for Novartis? Did it mean the company had to provide health insurance to all employees? Did the right to medical care mean that the company had a duty to provide its pharmaceutical drugs to the needy? If so, at what price? Clearly, the Compact itself provided no specific guidance on these questions.

The committee took its job seriously, consulting widely within the company, writing briefs on various topics, and engaging in dialogue with stakeholders. As a result of this process, the committee announced that Novartis would undertake several health care initiatives. Among other things the company agreed to provide antimalarial drugs at cost for use in poor countries, to subsidize research on diseases of poverty such as dengue fever, and to donate thousands of treatments for tuberculosis. It also said it would provide prevention, diagnosis, treatment, and counseling services for its employees and their immediate family members for HIV/AIDS, TB, and malaria in developing countries. Similar efforts were undertaken in other areas covered by the Compact, leading to a series of actions on labor and the environment, as well as human rights.

One researcher who examined the process at Novartis concluded: "[Making] the general commitment is probably the easiest part of the Global Compact adventure for a company. The real challenge is to translate the top management's signature into an organizational commitment for concrete action and into the sustained motivation of employees that it is the right thing to do."

Sources: Klaus M. Leisinger, "Opportunities and Risks of the United Nations Global Compact: The Novartis Case Study," *Journal of Corporate Citizenship* 11 (Autumn 2003), pp. 113–31; and Klaus M. Leisinger, "Towards Globalization with a Human Face: Implementation of the UN Global Compact Initiative at Novartis," *Parallax: The Journal of Ethics and Globalization,* January–February 2003, *www.novartisfoundation.com/en/articles/csr /novartis_un_global_compact_globalization_print.htm*. For a full description of Novartis's corporate citizenship initiatives, see *www.novartis.com/corporate_citizenship*.

companies where they do business. It also called on companies to support human rights and to encourage equal opportunity at all levels of employment, including racial and gender diversity on decision-making committees and boards.

- The *Caux Principles*, developed by a consortium of European, Asian, and North American business leaders called the Caux Roundtable, emphasizes *kyosei* (that is, working for the common good) and a respect for human rights.

It should be noted that the issues of bribery and improper payments, conflicts of interest, and receiving gifts are addressed in nearly all global codes of conduct. These issues were discussed in Chapters 5 and 6.

Although they differ in emphasis and particulars, all these codes converge on a few key elements. All emphasize the responsibility of transnational corporations to protect human rights, respect the rights and dignity of their employees and other stakeholders, and act as stewards for the natural environment.

Collaborative Partnerships for Global Problem Solving

As the preceding section suggested, doing business in a diverse world is exceptionally challenging for businesses. Multiple codes of conduct have been developed to guide the actions of transnational corporations, yet most of them are too general to provide a road map for many of the specific problems that confront today's large corporations doing business abroad.

Since the questions facing transnational corporations are so challenging, one solution is to approach them collectively, through a collaborative process. An emerging trend is the development of collaborative, multisector partnerships focused on particular social issues or problems in the global economy. This final section of Chapter 7 describes this approach.

A Three-Sector World

The term *sector* refers to broad divisions of a whole. In this context, it refers to major parts or spheres of society, such as business (the private sector), government (the public sector), and civil society. **Civil society** comprises nonprofit, educational, religious, community, family, and interest-group organizations, that is, social organizations that do not have a commercial or governmental purpose.

The process of globalization has spurred development of civil society. In recent decades, the world has witnessed the creation and growth of large numbers of **nongovernmental organizations (NGOs)** concerned with such issues as environmental risk, labor practices, worker rights, community development, and human rights. The number of NGOs accredited by the United Nations has soared in recent years, rising from 1,000 in 1996 to more than 3,000 in 2006. This figure counts just major organizations. In the United States, the number of NGOs large and small is estimated to be more than 2 million, 70 percent of which are less than 30 years old. A similar pattern exists in Europe, where half of all NGOs were founded in the last decade.[21]

Experts attribute the growth of NGOs to several factors, including the new architecture of global economic and political relationships. As the Cold War has ended, with democratic governments replacing dictatorships, greater openness has emerged in many societies. More people, with more views, are free to express their pleasure or displeasure with government, business, or one another. NGOs form around specific issues or broad concerns (environment, human rights) and become voices that must be considered in the public policy debates that ensue.

Recent research has recognized that each of the three major sectors—business, government, and civil society—has distinctive resources and competencies, as well as weaknesses. For example, businesses have access to capital, specialized technical knowledge, networks of commercial relationships, and the management skills to get projects completed on time and on budget. On the other hand, businesses tend to disregard the impacts of their actions on others, especially in the long term. For their part, government agencies

---

[21] Data are from *www.un.org/esa* and *www.globalpolicy.org/ngos*; and Curtis Runyan, "Action on the Front Lines," *WorldWatch*, November–December 1999, pp. 12–22.

FIGURE 7.4

Distinctive Attributes of the Three Major Sectors

Source: Adapted from Steven Waddell, "Core Competences: A Key Force in Business-Government-Civil Society Collaborations," *Journal of Corporate Citizenship,* Autumn 2002, pp. 43–56, Tables 1 and 2. Used by permission.

	Business	Government	Civil Society
Organizational form	For-profit	Governmental	Nonprofit
Goods produced	Private	Public	Group
Primary control agent	Owners	Voters/rulers	Communities
Primary power form	Money	Laws, police, fines	Traditions, values
Primary goals	Wealth creation	Societal order	Expression of values
Assessment frame	Profitability	Legality	Justice
Resources	Capital assets, technical knowledge, production skills	Tax revenue, policy knowledge, regulatory and enforcement power	Community knowledge, inspirational leadership
Weaknesses	Short-term focus, lack of concern for external impacts	Bureaucratic, slow-moving, poorly coordinated internally	Amateurish, lack of financial resources, parochial perspective

have knowledge of public policy, an ability to enforce rules, and revenue from taxation, but are often inflexible, slow to mobilize, and poorly coordinated. Finally, NGOs often enjoy strong community knowledge, volunteer assets, and inspirational leaders, but may lack financial resources and technical skill and may suffer from a narrow, parochial focus.[22] One model highlighting various of the attributes of actors in the business, government, and civil society sectors is presented in Figure 7.4.

Many businesses have realized that these differences across sectors can be a resource to be exploited. In this view, alliances among organizations from the three sectors, **collaborative partnerships**, can draw on the unique capabilities of each and overcome particular weaknesses that each has.

The opening example of this chapter illustrated a failed effort by a transnational corporation to modernize the water utility in a developing country. Contrast that example with the following more successful one, in which a company used a collaborative partnership strategy:

> A collaborative partnership formed to bring water and sanitation services to some of the poorest regions of South Africa. Ondeo (formerly, Suez-Lyonnaise), a French transnational corporation, brought its expertise in designing and managing large-scale water works. Group 5, a local construction company, brought construction know-how. The government agency in charge of water services provided public funding and staff for regulation and monitoring. A local NGO called the Mvula Trust, headed by a former antiapartheid crusader who had turned his attention to economic development after the overthrow of the racist

---

[22] This paragraph draws heavily on Steven Waddell, "Core Competences: A Key Force in Business-Government-Civil Society Collaborations," *Journal of Corporate Citizenship,* Autumn 2002, pp. 43–56. See also Steve Waddell, "Societal Learning: Creating Big Systems Change," *The Systems Thinker* 12, no. 10 (December 2001/January 2002), pp. 1–5; Jonathan Cohen, "State of the Union: NGO-Business Partnership Stakeholders," in *Unfolding Stakeholder Thinking II,* ed. Joerg Andriof et al. (Sheffield, UK: Greenleaf Publishing, 2003), pp. 106–27; and Dennis A. Rondinelli and Ted London, "How Corporations and Environmental Groups Cooperate: Assessing Cross-Sector Alliances and Collaborations," *Academy of Management Executive* 17, no. 1 (2003), pp. 61–76.

regime, mobilized the community to define what services were needed and later to help maintain the system. All three groups worked together, drawing on the special talents of each in service of a single goal. This successful collaboration has brought running water and sanitation to many rural communities.[23]

Collaborative partnerships, like this one, carry a number of important advantages for transnational companies. They can enlist the special skills of governments and communities, educate the company about stakeholder expectations, and ensure that a particular project is consistent with local norms and values. Other applications of the principle of cross-sector collaborations are explored in Chapters 12 and 17.

The process of globalization presents today's business leaders with both great promise and great challenge. Despite the ever-present threat of war and terrorism, the world's economy continues to grow more integrated and interdependent. Transnational corporations, with their financial assets and technical and managerial skills, have a great contribution to make to human betterment. Yet, they must operate in a world of great diversity, and in which their presence is often distrusted or feared. Often, they must confront situations in which political and economic freedoms are lacking and human rights are routinely violated. The challenge facing forward-looking companies today is how to work collaboratively with stakeholders to promote social and economic justice, while still achieving strong bottom-line results.

Summary

- Globalization refers to the increasing movement of goods, services, and capital across national borders. Firms can enter and compete in the global marketplace by exporting products and services; locating operations in another country; or buying raw materials, components, or supplies from sellers abroad.

- The process of globalization is driven by technological innovation, improvements in transportation, the rise of major multinational corporations, and social and political reforms.

- Globalization brings both benefits and costs. On one hand, it has the potential to pull nations out of poverty, spread innovation, and reduce prices for consumers. On the other hand, it may also produce job loss, reduce environmental and labor standards, and erode national cultures. An ongoing challenge is to extend the benefits of globalization to all, while mitigating its adverse effects.

- Multinational corporations operate in nations that vary greatly in their political, social, and economic systems. They face the challenge of deciding how to do business in other nations, while remaining true to their values.

- Several important global codes of conduct have established standards for companies doing business across national borders. These include the UN Global Compact, the OECD Guidelines for Multinational Enterprises, the Global Sullivan Principles, and the Caux Principles.

- Businesses can work with governments and civil society organizations around the world in collaborative partnerships that draw on the unique capabilities of each to address common problems.

---

[23] Business Partnerships for Development, "Flexibility by Design: Lessons from Multi-Sector Partnerships in Water and Sanitation Projects," available at *www.bpd-waterandsanitation.org.*

Key Terms

anti-Americanism, *148*
central state
control, *151*
civil society, *155*
collaborative
partnership, *156*
constructive
engagement, *152*
debt relief, *143*
democracy, *149*

free enterprise
system, *151*
global codes of
conduct, *153*
globalization, *139*
international financial
and trade institution
(IFTI), *142*
International Monetary
Fund (IMF), *143*

military dictatorship,
150
nongovernmental
organizations
(NGOs), *155*
transnational corporation
(TNC), *140*
World Bank, *142*
World Trade Organization
(WTO), *143*

Internet Resources

www.wto.org   World Trade Organization
www.imf.org   International Monetary Fund
www.worldbank.org   World Bank
www.ifg.org   International Forum on Globalization
www.globalpolicy.org Global Policy Forum

Discussion Case: *Conflict Diamonds*

In the 2000s, a common concern emerged among members of an oddly matched group: the diamond industry, the United Nations, several governments, and human rights campaigners. All wished to end the trade in *conflict diamonds*—gemstones that are mined or stolen by rebels fighting internationally recognized governments.

The $6 billion a year diamond industry has long been dominated by the De Beers Corporation. Founded in South Africa by Cecil Rhodes in the 1880s, De Beers' strategy has been to own as many diamond mines as possible and to sell its rough (uncut) stones exclusively to a small group of preferred dealers at prices set by the company. To maintain its control over supply, De Beers operates buying offices all over the world, "sweeping up" diamonds produced in mines operated by others. The result, for many years, has been a virtual monopoly.

De Beers has also been a shrewd marketer, pouring millions of dollars over the years into advertising. Using the slogan "a diamond is forever," the company cultivated an association between diamonds and romance. The company first promoted solitaire engagement rings; later, it shifted its marketing focus to the so-called eternity ring, a band of multiple smaller stones aimed at older married couples.

In the 1990s, events in several diamond-rich African nations converged to tarnish the gem's carefully cultivated image of love and purity.

During the Cold War, many partisans in civil conflicts in Africa received funding from either the United States or the Soviet Union, both anxious to maintain alliances in the nonaligned developing world. After the collapse of the Soviet Union in 1991, this source of funding largely dried up. Accordingly, some combatants began to seize control of valuable mineral resources to finance their operations.

The situation was particularly gruesome in Sierra Leone, a small nation in West Africa, which was devastated by civil war for much of the 1990s. A journalist who covered the war there described the methods of the Revolutionary United Front (RUF), the rebel force:

> The RUF's whole mode of operation was just to roll into a village that had a diamond mining operation. . . . What made the RUF stand out as a brutal organization was their campaign of amputation. That served no strategic purpose but to terrorize the population. Little children, women, men had their hands and arms chopped off as if they were wood.

By some estimates, the RUF mutilated as many as 20,000 people in Sierra Leone in this manner. Needless to say, the rebels quickly secured control of the mines, and they began selling rough diamonds in exchange for weapons, food, and other supplies.

Similar stories emerged from Angola and the Democratic Republic of the Congo, other African nations with active civil wars and considerable diamond wealth. In Angola alone, the UNITA rebels were reported to have built up a war chest of almost $4 billion during the 1990s from the sale of diamonds, which they used to fund a sophisticated military operation. By some estimates, as many as 6 million civilians were forced from their homes and 3.7 million died in these African conflicts.

By the mid-1990s, several human rights organizations had begun to spread the word about these atrocities. In 1998, Global Witness, a British NGO, issued a report called *A Rough Trade* estimating that up to 8 percent of the world's diamonds were coming from conflict areas. It joined with other NGOs, including Amnesty International and Oxfam, in a campaign to alert the public to the issue of conflict diamonds.

The United Nations also acted; its Security Council passed a resolution in 2000 prohibiting the import of diamonds from Sierra Leone until a process could be set up to certify they did not come from the RUF. The governments of several countries with legitimate diamond industries, including Botswana, South Africa, Namibia, Canada, and Australia, also expressed concern that their economies would be hurt.

Countries with large retail operations were worried about the possible impact of lost sales. The United Kingdom's foreign minister, for example, told the press: "We want to ensure that if somebody goes to buy a diamond from a jeweler's shop, they know that when they put it on the finger of their loved one, they are not pledging a diamond that has cut off the finger of a child in Sierra Leone or Angola."

De Beers reacted swiftly and decisively to these events. In 1999 the company suspended all buying operations in West and Central Africa and, shortly thereafter, stopped buying diamonds from any mines outside its own direct control. In 2000, a De Beers representative appeared before a U.S. Congressional hearing and readily acknowledged that conflict diamonds were a problem: "Having spent hundreds of millions of dollars on advertising its product, De Beers is deeply concerned about anything that could damage the image of diamonds as a symbol of love, beauty, and purity."

Shortly thereafter, the industry association, the World Diamond Congress, passed a resolution banning conflict diamonds. It also took the unusual step of establishing a new organization, called the World Diamond Council, to bring together diamond companies, government representatives, and other interested parties. In 2002, their joint efforts led to the development of what became known as the Kimberley Process Certification Scheme, a system for tracking diamonds all the way from the mine to the jewelry shop, so that consumers could be assured that their gem was "conflict-free."

By 2006, 45 diamond-producing countries, accounting for virtually all of the world's rough diamond production, had endorsed the Kimberley Process. Although human rights activists praised the progress that had been made, some also called for independent monitoring to eliminate abuses. "Despite repeated commitments by the diamond industry to combat conflict diamonds, some of its members still evade Kimberley Process controls while the rest turn a blind eye," said a representative of Global Witness.

Sources: Greg Campbell, *Blood Diamonds: Tracing the Deadly Path of the World's Most Precious Stones* (Boulder, CO: Westview Press, 2002); also, articles appearing online at *www.cnn.com, www.salon.com, www.fpa.org, www.worlddiamondcouncil.com, www.un.org/peace/africa,* and *www.globalwitness.org.*

Discussion Questions

1. What are *conflict diamonds*? What groups benefited from the trade in conflict diamonds? What groups were hurt by it?
2. What three *sectors* were concerned with the problem of conflict diamonds? What was the interest of each, and in what ways did their interests converge?
3. Do you believe that any of these three sectors could have addressed the problem of conflict diamonds unilaterally? Why or why not?
4. Do you believe the Kimberley Process will be successful in achieving its objective? Why or why not?

CHAPTER EIGHT

Business–Government Relations

Governments establish the rules under which business operates in society. Therefore, a government's influence on business through public policy and regulation is a vital concern for managers. Government's relationship with business can be either cooperative or adversarial. Various economic or social assistance policies significantly affect society, in which businesses must operate. Many government regulations also impact business directly. Managers must understand the objectives and effects of government policy and regulation, both at home and abroad, in order to conduct business in an ethical and legal manner.

This chapter focuses on these key learning objectives:

- Understanding why governments sometimes seek to cooperate with business and other times work against business.
- Defining public policy and the elements of the public policy process.
- Knowing the major types of government regulation of business.
- Explaining the reasons for regulation.
- Comparing the costs and benefits of regulation for business and society.
- Examining how regulation affects business in a global context.

William Clay Ford is the fourth generation of Fords to hold the top leadership position at the Ford Motor Company, founded in the early 1900s. He became chairman of the board in 1999 and served as chief executive officer of the family's business from 2001 to 2006. Like each of his predecessors, he faces great challenges as he tries to improve Ford's position as a world-class automobile company. Not the least of those challenges involves dealing with the changing role of government.

In 1903, when Henry Ford organized the Ford Motor Company, his relationship with government was relatively simple. There was only one antitrust law on the books, and his business was too small to be bothered by it. There was no federal income tax. Ford faced no serious foreign competition. No unions were permitted in Ford plants, and government regulations about wages, hours, working conditions, and safety and health were unheard of. The government exacted no payments for employee retirement and pension plans because none existed. The company faced no issues of pollution, energy shortages, or consumer complaints about auto safety, all of which in later years would bring the wrath of government down on Ford and the auto industry. Mr. Ford's main worry in those days was a patent infringement suit brought against him by competitors. (He eventually won the lawsuit in the courts.)

When Henry Ford II, the founder's grandson, became chief executive officer in the 1970s, it was a very different world. Government closely observed how Mr. Ford and his peers at other auto companies behaved. That single antitrust law known to his grandfather had grown into a tangle of laws and court rulings regulating competition, product pricing, mergers, and acquisitions. Labor laws legalized unions and controlled wages, hours, working conditions, safety and health, and employee discrimination. Federal, state, local, and foreign governments levied taxes on company income, plants and equipment, capital gains, auto and truck sales, and salaries.

Over the course of 100 years, the leaders of Ford Motor Company have seen government's role in their business become much more extensive and complex. As chairman of the company, William Ford knows that Ford Motor Company faces new challenges in the 21st century. Foreign competition has increased in the United States, and the company competes in dozens of countries around the world. In many countries, national governments are partners with Ford's competitors and jointly plan how to compete against it; European and Asian competitors loom large. The company's customers and global workforce include people of many races and nationalities. Technological change is transforming many aspects of the business. Today's Ford Motor Company is designing automobiles powered by cleaner fuel sources; built of new, safer materials; and controlled by computers with navigation systems that help drivers avoid traffic congestion. Government-set fuel economy, safety, and emissions standards are important factors affecting automobile design. In all of this, government policy—public policy—plays an increasingly important role in the success and operation of the company.[1]

Why are governments involved in such decisions? How do the government's actions affect businesses and what they are permitted to do? What happens when government experts and industry experts disagree about the best way to achieve the public interest?

Governments create the conditions that make it possible for businesses to compete in the modern economy. Their role is to create and enforce the laws that *balance* the relationship between business and society. Governments become involved when unintended costs of manufacturing a product are imposed on others and government is needed to

---

[1] William Clay Ford's leadership of the Ford Motor Company has drawn many commentaries. See, for example, Danny Hakim, "William Clay Ford, Jr.: Just Another Short-Sighted Auto Executive," *The New York Times,* March 18, 2002, *www.nytimes.com;* and "Ford Did Indeed Have a Better Idea," Mackinac Center for Public Policy, July 7, 2003, *www.secure.mackinac.org.*

control or redirect these costs. Governments also hold the power to grant or refuse permission for many types of business activity. Even the largest multinational companies, such as Ford, which operate in dozens of countries, must obey the laws and public policies of national governments.

This chapter considers the ways in which government actions impact business through the powerful twin mechanisms of public policy and regulation. The next chapter addresses the related question of actions business may take to influence the political process.

How Business and Government Relate

The relationship between business and government is dynamic and complex. The stability of a government can be shaky or solid. Even within a stable government, different individuals or groups can acquire or lose power through elections, the natural death of a public official, or other means. Understanding the government's authority and its relationship with business is essential for managers in developing their strategies and achieving their organization's goals.

Government Cooperates with Business

In some situations, government may work closely with business to build a cooperative relationship and seek mutually beneficial goals. The basis for this cooperation may be at the core of the nation's societal values and customs. In some Asian countries, society is viewed as a collective family that includes both government and business. Thus, working together as a family leads these two powers to seek results that benefit both society and business.

In Europe, the relationship between government and business often has been cooperative. European culture includes a sense of teamwork and mutual aid. Unions, for example, are often included on administrative boards with managers to lead the organization toward mutual goals through interactive strategies.

> When faced with the migration of the European pharmaceutical industry to the United States, the European Commission (EC), a governing body of the European Union, adopted a more flexible pricing proposal. Many European countries had previously banned the sale of drugs until the government fixed a price, often much lower than the price found in the United States. The EC proposal permitted companies to market their drugs at whatever price they chose. This created a "framework of action that we believe can help the Europe-based pharmaceutical industry regain its competitive edge," said European Enterprise Commissioner Erkki Liikanen.[2]

Cooperation between business and government, as shown in this example, often occurs when both groups encounter a common problem or enemy requiring a joining of forces. Even traditional adversaries can find grounds for collaboration and support when the need presents itself.

Government Conflicts with Business

In other situations, government's goals and business's objectives are at odds, and these conflicts result in an adversarial relationship. Following the Enron and other business

---

[2] "EU Body Moves to Ease Curbs on Drug Pricing to Aid Sector," *The Wall Street Journal,* July 2, 2003, p. B3.

scandals, in which the auditing industry had failed to police itself adequately, the U.S. Securities and Exchange Commission passed new rules, and Congress passed the Sarbanes-Oxley Act of 2003. This law limited the ability of accounting firms to offer both consulting and auditing services to their clients. (The Sarbanes-Oxley Act is also discussed in Chapters 5 and 15.)

> In 2003, with dramatic power shifts occurring in the Middle East and growing uncertainty over the world oil market, business leaders in Russia pleaded with government officials to loosen their grip on Russian oil production. Private industry was ready to invest billions of dollars in new pipelines and ports, but the government was unwilling to relinquish its control over the export infrastructure. Russian officials pointed to concerns over whether there would be sufficient oil supplies for the Russian people and businesses and wanted to retain control over this vital Russian industry.[3]

Governments also may act in an adversarial role against business when negative externalities arise. **Negative externalities**, or spillover effects, result when the manufacture or distribution of a product gives rise to unplanned or unintended costs (economic, physical or psychological) borne by consumers, competitors, neighboring communities, or other business stakeholders. To control or reverse these costs, government may step in to regulate business action.

> As further described in a case study at the end of the book, patients taking Vioxx, a prescription pain medication made by Merck, became deeply concerned when evidence emerged of cardiovascular risk. The Drug Safety Oversight Board was established in 2005 to monitor Food and Drug Administration–approved medicines once they were on the market and to update physicians and patients with pertinent and emerging information on possible risks and benefits.[4]

In short, the relationship between government and business can range from one of cooperation to one of conflict, with various stages in between. Moreover, this relationship is constantly changing. A cooperative relationship on one issue does not guarantee cooperation on another issue. The stability of a particular form of government in some countries may be quite shaky, while in other countries the form of government is static but those in power can change unexpectedly or government rulers can change on a regular basis. The business–government relationship is one that requires managers to keep a careful eye trained toward significant forces that might alter this relationship or to promote forces that may encourage a positive business–government relationship.[5]

Legitimacy Issues

When dealing with a global economy, business may encounter governments whose authority or right to be in power is questioned. Political leaders may illegally assume lawmaking or legislative power, which can become economic power over business. Elections can be rigged, or military force can be used to acquire governmental control.

Business managers may be challenged with the dilemma of doing business in such a country where their business dealings would support this illegitimate power. Sometimes,

---

[3] "In Russia, Politics vs. Pipelines," *The Wall Street Journal,* January 30, 2003, p. A22.

[4] "FDA to Establish New Drug Oversight Board," *SFGate,* February 15, 2005, *www.sfgate.com.*

[5] See George Lodge, *Comparative Business–Government Relations* (Englewood Cliffs, NJ: Prentice Hall, 1990).

they may choose to become politically active, or refuse to do business in this country until a legitimate government is installed. The military dictatorship in Myanmar (Burma) is one example of an illegitimate government, as discussed in Chapter 7.

The ability of a government leader or group of leaders to maintain political power can be influenced by businesses' actions. Businesses may boycott economic relations with a country or decide to withdraw operations from that country, as many U.S. firms did in South Africa to protest the practice of apartheid in the 1970s. Some businesses have been ordered by their country to not conduct business with another country due to war or in protest of an illegitimate government, such as the U.S. boycott of Iraq in the 1990s. The United States has imposed economic sanctions on nearly 30 countries due to political and human rights concerns.

Government's Public Policy Role

Government performs a vital and important role in modern society. Although vigorous debates occur about the proper size of programs government should undertake, most people agree that a society cannot function properly without some government activities. Citizens look to government to meet important basic needs. Foremost among these are safety and protection provided by homeland security, police, and fire departments. These are collective or public goods, which are most efficiently provided by government for everyone in a community. In today's world, governments are also expected to provide economic security and essential social services, and to deal with the most pressing social problems that require collective action, or public policy.

Public policy is a plan of action undertaken by government officials to achieve some broad purpose affecting a substantial segment of a nation's citizens. Or as the late U.S. Senator Patrick Moynihan said, "Public policy is what a government chooses to do or not to do." In general, these ideas are consistent. Public policy, while differing in each nation, is the basic set of goals, plans, and actions that each national government follows in achieving its purposes. Governments generally do not choose to act unless a substantial segment of the public is affected and some public purpose is to be achieved. This is the essence of the concept of governments acting in the public interest.

The basic power to make public policy comes from a nation's political system. In democratic societies, citizens elect political leaders who can appoint others to fulfill defined public functions ranging from municipal services (e.g., water supplies, fire protection) to national services, such as public education or homeland security. Democratic nations typically spell out the powers of government in the country's constitution.

Another source of authority is *common law*, or past decisions of the courts, the original basis of the U.S. legal system. In nondemocratic societies, the power of government may derive from a monarchy (e.g., Saudi Arabia), a military dictatorship (e.g., Iraq before the fall of Saddam Hussein), or religious authority (e.g., the mullahs in Iran). These sources of power may interact, creating a mixture of civilian and military authority. The political systems in Russia, South Africa, and other nations have undergone profound changes in recent times. And democratic nations can also face the pressures of regions that seek to become independent nations exercising the powers of a sovereign state, as does Canada with Quebec.

Elements of Public Policy

The actions of government in any nation can be understood in terms of several basic elements of public policy. These are inputs, goals, tools, and effects.

Public policy inputs are external pressures that shape a government's policy decisions and strategies to address problems. Economic and foreign policy concerns, domestic political pressure from constituents and interest groups, technical information, and media attention all play a role in shaping national political decisions. For example, many state and local governments have been asked to ban or regulate the use of cell phones by drivers.

Robert Shelton, executive director of the National Highway Traffic Safety Administration, told Congress that 54 percent of drivers have cell phones in their vehicles or carry cell phones when they drive; 80 percent of those drivers leave their cell phones turned on while driving; and 73 percent talk on the phone while driving. Opponents of the use of cell phones while driving noted that wireless communication and entertainment devices, such as navigation systems, televisions, DVD players and computers, are becoming more common.[6]

Government bodies—legislatures, town councils, regulatory agencies—need to consider all relevant inputs in deciding whether or not to take action, and if so, what kind of action.

Public policy goals can be broad (e.g., full employment) and high-minded (equal opportunity for all) or narrow and self-serving. National values, such as freedom, democracy, and a fair chance for all citizens to share in economic prosperity, have led to the adoption of civil rights laws and economic assistance programs for those in need. Narrow goals that serve special interests are more apparent when nations decide how tax legislation will allocate the burden of taxes among various interests and income groups, or when public resources, such as oil exploration rights or timber cutting privileges, are given to one group or another. Whether the goals are broad or narrow, for the benefit of some or the benefit of all, most governments should ask, "What public goals are being served by this action?" For example, the rationale for a government policy to regulate cell-phone usage has to be based on some definition of public interest, such as preventing harm to others, including innocent drivers, passengers, and pedestrians.

In a study published in the *British Medical Journal,* researchers estimated that motorists are four times more likely to be involved in a crash requiring hospital admittance when they are using cell phones. A report by the Harvard Center for Risk Analysis suggested that drivers talking on their cell phones are responsible for about 6 percent of U.S. auto accidents each year, killing an estimated 2,600 people and injuring 330,000 others. A California Highway Patrol study concluded that cell phones were cited as a factor in 11 percent of inattention-related crashes, more than any other single factor. "Simply put, this legislation is about saving lives. Just a few seconds of distraction while talking on a cell phone can mean the difference between safety and peril, between life and death. We must make our roads safer," explained Senator Jon Corzine of New Jersey.[7]

Thus, the goals of saving lives, reducing injuries, and eliminating health care costs might justify some form of cell-phone regulation. The policy decision would depend, in part, on whether the benefits of the regulation are greater or less than the costs that would be imposed on the public.

---

[6] "NY Passes Law: Hands off Cell Phones While Driving," *WirelessNewsFactor,* June 26, 2001, *www.wirelessnewsfactor.com;* and *Cell Phones and Highway Safety: 2005 State Legislative Update,* National Conference of State Legislatures, *www.ncsl.org.*

[7] "Cell Phone Road Hazard Target of U.S. Lawmakers," *WirelessNewsFactor,* May 23, 2001, *www.wirelessnewsfactor.com/perl/story/9956.html;* and 2005 National Conference of State Legislatures report, *www.ncsl.org.*

Governments use different *public policy tools* to achieve policy goals. The tools of public policy involve combinations of incentives and penalties that government uses to prompt citizens, including businesses, to act in ways that achieve policy goals. Governmental regulatory powers are broad and constitute one of the most formidable instruments for accomplishing public purposes.

> After congressional action limiting cell-phone use stalled, the public looked to state and local governments to ban the use of cell phones by drivers while operating their vehicles. By 2005, 22 states and the District of Columbia had laws governing cell-phone use in the car. Legislators in 39 states, including some states that had adopted weaker forms of legislation, proposed 129 bills related to driver distraction in 2005. The Cleveland suburb of Brooklyn, Ohio, became the first jurisdiction in the United States to ban using a cell phone while driving. By 2005, 26 municipalities had passed cell-phone restriction laws. And this is not just a public policy issue for Americans. As many as 40 nations, including Australia, Israel, Great Britain, Russia and Japan, ban calling while driving.[8]

Public policy effects are the outcomes arising from government regulation. Some are intended; others are unintended. Because public policies affect many people, organizations, and other interests, it is almost inevitable that such actions will please some and displease others. Regulations may cause businesses to improve the way toxic substances are used in the workplace, thus reducing health risks to employees. Yet other goals may be obstructed as an unintended effect of compliance with such regulations. For example, when health risks to pregnant women were associated with exposure to lead in the workplace, some companies removed women from those jobs. This action was seen as a form of discrimination against women that conflicted with the goal of equal employment opportunity. The unintended effect (discrimination) of one policy action (protecting employees) conflicted head-on with the public policy goal of equal opportunity.

> The debate over cell-phone legislation was filled with conflicting predicted effects. The proponents obviously argued that the ban on cell-phone use reduced accidents and saved lives. Opponents of such legislation pointed to numerous other distractions that were not banned, such as drivers reading the newspaper, eating, putting on makeup or shaving. Cell-phone owners cited benefits such as security and peace of mind, increased productivity, privacy, and quicker crime and accident reporting to justify the use of cell phones. A study funded by AT&T found that the cost of lives saved by banning cell phones while driving was estimated to be about $2 billion, compared with about $25 billion in benefits lost, meaning a cell-phone ban would cost society about $23 billion.[9]

As the cell-phone safety examples illustrate, managers must try to be aware of the public policy inputs, goals, tools, and effects relevant to regulation affecting their business.

Types of Public Policy

Public policies created by governments are of two major types: economic and social.

---

[8] 2005 National Conference of State Legislatures report, *www.ncsl.org.*

[9] "Hello? Cell Phones Cause Crashes," *Wired News,* December 2, 2002, *www.wired.com/news/wireless.*

Economic Policies

One important kind of public policy directly concerns the economy. The term **fiscal policy** refers to patterns of government taxing and spending that are intended to stimulate or support the economy. Governments spend money on many different activities. Local governments employ teachers, trash collectors, police, and firefighters. State governments typically spend large amounts of money on roads, social services, and park lands. National governments spend large sums on military defense, international relationships, and hundreds of public works projects. During the Great Depression of the 1930s, public works projects employed large numbers of people, put money in their hands, and stimulated consumption of goods and services. Today, fiscal policy remains a basic tool to achieve prosperity. Public works projects (e.g., roads, airports) remain among the most popular means of creating employment while achieving other public goals.

By contrast, the term **monetary policy** refers to policies that affect the supply, demand, and value of a nation's currency. The worth, or worthlessness, of a nation's currency has serious effects on business and society. It affects the buying power of money, the stability and value of savings, and the confidence of citizens and investors about the nation's future. This, in turn, affects the country's ability to borrow money from other nations and to attract private capital. In the United States, the Federal Reserve Bank—known as the Fed—plays the role of other nations' central banks. By raising and lowering the interest rates at which private banks borrow money from the government, the Fed influences the size of the nation's money supply and the value of the dollar.

Other forms of economic policy include *taxation policy* (raising or lowering taxes on business or individuals), *industrial policy* (directing economic resources toward the development of specific industries), and *trade policy* (encouraging or discouraging trade with other countries).

Social Assistance Policies

The last century produced many advances in the well-being of people across the globe. The advanced industrial nations have developed elaborate systems of social services for their citizens. Developing economies have improved key areas of social assistance (such as health care and education) and will continue to do so as their economies grow. International standards and best practices have supported these trends. Many of the **social assistance policies** that affect particular stakeholders are discussed in subsequent chapters of this book.

One particularly important social assistance policy—health care—has been the focus for concern on the international front, as profiled in Exhibit 8.A, and for national and state lawmakers.

> Wal-Mart found itself in the middle of a health care coverage controversy in 2005, when a social watchdog group named WakeUpWalMart reported that 57 percent of the company's 1.39 million workers and their families had no company-paid health insurance. The group estimated that the cost to the U.S. taxpayers to provide health care to Wal-Mart employees and their families, through Medicare and various state public assistance programs, was $1.37 billion annually and would rise to $9.1 billion over the next five years.[10]

Clearly, governments' ability to provide social assistance, for example in the area of health care, is a costly and complex challenge.

---

[10] "Stop the Wal-Mart Health Care Crisis," *www.wakeupwalmart.com.*

Exhibit 8.A   **Health Care Crisis Response Plan: A Global Imperative**

Health care is the most essential of social services, in part because public health problems affect every person in every nation. Two recent health crises point to the need for a global, not just national, response to health care.

The first crisis involved the outbreak of SARS (Severe Acute Respiratory Syndrome) in 2003, in which nearly 3,000 cases were reported and more than 100 people died. This was a dramatic example of how important it is for countries around the world to take care of their citizens' health. The United States, Canada, Germany, Japan, and United Kingdom all invest heavily in providing health care to their populations. Many nations emphasize meeting basic health care needs through local clinics, community education, and reliance on locally available medicines. Investment in such primary health care tends to produce significant improvement in indicators such as infant mortality, illness rates of small children, and vaccination of the population against disease.

The second crisis was known as the Avian (or Bird) Flu Pandemic. Researchers have determined that all strains of influenza virus can be traced back to their origins with birds. Typically these viruses mutate each year, requiring the development of new strains of vaccine to protect humans. The avian flu virus was first detected in southeast Asia in 2005 and spread along the migratory flyways of birds to China and Russia before moving westward to Europe. By February 2006, the avian flu had infected 170 people in southeast Asia and Turkey, killing 90 people.

President George W. Bush, fearing that the avian flu was heading toward the United States, announced in October 2005 a commitment to "keep the American people safe" from this spreading virus by pledging to "detect outbreaks when they occur . . . and be ready to respond at the federal, state and local levels in the event that a pandemic reaches our shores." Yet, a national response to a global problem was quickly seen as insufficient. President Bush also promised $334 million to support a global campaign against the avian flu virus. This amount represented the largest single nation contribution and was used to improve surveillance and response systems, train local rapid-response health teams and medical personnel, and support public awareness campaigns to minimize the spread of the avian flu virus.

Other responses by various nations gave rise to the "International Partnership" to combat avian influenza and to deal with the threat of a possible human pandemic. Over 90 nations and international organizations banded together to elevate the political and financial profile of the avian flu pandemic crisis. Robert Egge, project director for the Center for Health Transformation said, we need "to emphasize 21st century strategies such as building electronic health record and biosurveillance networks, capitalizing on genomics and other breakthroughs to create new diagnostics, vaccines, and therapies" in order to meet and defeat global health crises such as the avian flu pandemic.

Source: Quotations are from "Safeguarding America against Pandemic Influenza Fact Sheet," *www.whitehouse.gov/news/releases/2006/01/20060118-6.html*; and "Avian Flu Virus Requires Calm, Educated Concern," Health Care News, *www.pacificresearch.org*. Additional information from "Update 83—One Hundred Days into the Outbreak," World Health Organization, June 18, 2003, *www.who.int/csr/don/2003_06_18/en*; and "UK to Buy Bird Flu Vaccine Stock," BBC News, news.bbc.co.uk.

Government Regulation of Business

Societies rely on government to establish rules of conduct for citizens and organizations called *regulations*. **Regulation** is a primary way of accomplishing public policy, as described in the previous section. Because government operates at so many levels (federal, state, local), modern businesses face complex webs of regulations. Companies often require lawyers, public affairs specialists, and experts to monitor and manage the interaction with government, as described in Chapter 2. Why do societies turn to more regulation as a way to solve problems? Why not just let the free market allocate resources, set prices, and constrain socially irresponsible behavior by companies? There are a variety of reasons.

Market Failure

One reason is what economists call **market failure**—that is, the marketplace fails to adjust prices for the true costs of a firm's behavior. For example, a company normally has no incentive to spend money on pollution control equipment if customers do not demand it. The market fails to incorporate the cost of environmental harm into the business's economic equation, because the costs are borne by someone else. In this situation, government can use regulation to force all competitors in the industry to adopt a minimum antipollution standard. The companies will then incorporate the extra cost of compliance into the product price. Companies that want to act responsibly often welcome carefully crafted regulations, because they force competitors to bear the same costs.

Natural Monopolies

In some industries, **natural monopolies** occur. The electric utility industry provides an example. Once one company has built a system of poles and wires or laid miles of underground cable to supply local customers with electricity, it would be inefficient for a second company to build another system alongside the first. But once the first company has established its natural monopoly, it can then raise prices as much as it wishes, because there is no competition. In such a situation, government often comes in and regulates prices and access. Other industries that sometimes develop natural monopolies include cable TV, broadband Internet service, software, and railroads.

Ethical Arguments

There is often an ethical rationale for regulation as well. As discussed in Chapter 5, for example, there is a utilitarian ethical argument in support of safe working conditions: It is costly to train and educate employees only to lose their services because of preventable accidents. There are also fairness and justice arguments for government to set standards and develop regulations to protect employees, consumers, and other stakeholders. In debates about regulation, advocates for and against regulatory proposals often use both economic and ethical arguments to support their views. Sometimes firms will agree to self-regulate their actions to head off more costly government-imposed regulatory reform as shown in the following example.

> As Internet technology and applications have become more sophisticated, privacy concerns have been raised. It is unethical, in the view of critics, for companies to sell private information without customer approval. Faced with mounting government and public pressure, companies such as Cisco Systems, Dell, Intel, Microsoft, and Sun Microsystems, working through the Information Technology Industry Council (a trade association), agreed to a set of principles intended to give consumers confidence and trust that privacy rights will be respected when they engage in electronic commerce.[11]

Types of Regulation

Government regulations come in different forms. Some are directly imposed; others are more indirect. Some are aimed at a specific industry (e.g., banking); others, such as those

---

[11] For a complete description of the Information Technology Industry Council's mission, activities, members and press releases, see *www.itic.org*.

The Federal Communications Commission (FCC) announced in 2000 that it would auction off 422 licenses in 195 geographic markets across the United States. The auction would enable private parties (organizations, businesses) to use portions of the electromagnetic spectrum that had been kept out of commercial public use. The decision to license the right to use more of the spectrum, which has been called "the most precious natural resource of the information age," was made by the FCC after extensive debates about whether the public interest would be served by making more frequencies available.

The FCC is responsible for regulating and promoting the communications industries. Companies engaged in wireless communications need electromagnetic frequencies on which they can transmit messages. Many of the bidders for the new licenses were major players in the communications business such as AT&T Wireless, Sprint PCS, and Verizon Wireless. They needed to fill in holes in their networks, enter new cities, increase overall capacity, and gain the national "footprint" that has eluded them. Other bidders included second-tier firms such as Nextel Communications, VoiceStream Wireless, and Cingular, a joint venture of SBC Communications and BellSouth, all of which were looking to expand.

In setting the rules for the auction, the FCC commissioners decided that the public interest required that some of the licenses be reserved for small businesses, minority enterprises, and rural companies. These licenses would enable small niche players to develop services for particular cities or regions. The auction rules therefore set aside some of the licenses for companies with assets less than $500 million and gross revenues of less than $125 million in each of the last two years.

Among the interesting bids received were those from three Alaskan companies owned by 38,000 natives. These companies were working with AT&T Wireless Group. The Native American companies, created by a special act of Congress in 1970, negotiated a deal with AT&T Wireless wherein cash from the no. 3 wireless-service provider would help them win valuable airwaves in the auction. In return, AT&T has a chance to gain access to some restricted frequencies and for less money.

After 101 rounds of bidding and the sale of all 422 licenses, the FCC announced that it had taken in nearly $17 billion. Verizon Wireless spent nearly $9 billion for 113 licenses. AT&T Wireless paid close to $2.9 billion for licenses through Alaska Native Wireless, including one of the three prized New York licenses. Some firms, such as Nextel and Sprint PCS, dropped out of the bidding early.

Source: "Wireless Licenses Expected to Raise $15 Billion for U.S.," *The New York Times,* December 8, 2000, pp. C1, C4; "AT&T, 3 Native Alaska Companies Seek U.S. Airwaves," *Bloomberg News,* December 8, 2000; and "U.S. Auction Ends, Raising $16.85 Billion," *Mobileinfo,* January 5, 2001, *www.mobileinfo.com/news_2001/Issue05/US_Auction.htm.*

dealing with job discrimination or pollution, apply to all industries. Some have been in existence for a long time—for example, the Food and Drug Administration was formed in 1906—whereas others, such as those governing state lotteries and other forms of legalized gambling, are of recent vintage in many states. As shown in Exhibit 8.B, regulatory agencies have the challenge of setting rules that are fair and effective in achieving public policy goals.

Just as public policy can be classified as either economic or social, so too can regulations be classified.

Economic Regulations

The oldest form of regulation is primarily economic in nature. **Economic regulations** aim to modify the normal operation of the free market and the forces of supply and demand. Such modification may come about because the free market is distorted by the size or monopoly power of companies, or because the consequences of actions in the marketplace are thought to be undesirable. Economic regulations include those that control prices or wages, allocate public resources, establish service territories, set the number of participants, and ration resources. The decisions of the Federal Communications Commission (FCC) about how to allocate portions of the electromagnetic spectrum, described in Exhibit 8.B, illustrated one kind of economic regulation. Consider the following additional examples:

- Local telephone companies are allowed to offer long-distance service, but only if they open their networks to other service providers. The purpose of this FCC regulation is to promote open competition for long-distance service, giving customers more choices and lower prices.

- The Federal Energy Regulatory Commission, in some situations, controls prices for electricity. For example, the agency capped (placed an upper limit on) wholesale energy prices in California, after prices had spiked upward and blackouts had occurred.

- Regulators at both the state and federal levels set strict rules for when and where commercial fishing boats can operate, as well as rules about what kinds of fish can be caught. One reason for such rules is to divide a common resource (wild fish) among numerous businesses in a fair way.

Certain operations or functions of business have been singled out for special attention by government regulators. Many labor practices, for example, are no longer left to the operation of free market forces. Government agencies set minimum wages, regulate overtime pay, establish the rules for labor union campaigns, and mediate serious and troublesome labor–management disputes, including, in recent years, strikes by airline pilots, flight attendants, schoolteachers, and even professional baseball players. Competition is another business function strongly affected by regulation. Antitrust laws attempt to prevent monopolies, preserve competitive pricing, and protect consumers against unfair practices; they are further described in Chapter 10.

Economic regulations, like social regulations, sometimes cut across industry lines and apply generally to all enterprises, as they do in the case of antitrust and labor practices. Or they may, as in the case of regulations governing stock exchanges and the issuance of corporate securities, be confined to specific institutions such as the stock markets or the companies whose stocks are listed on those exchanges.

Social Regulations

Social regulations are aimed at such important social goals as protecting consumers and the environment and providing workers with safe and healthy working conditions. Equal employment opportunity, protection of pension benefits, and health care for employees are other important areas of social regulation. Unlike the economic regulations mentioned above, social regulations are not limited to one type of business or industry. Laws concerning pollution, safety and health, and job discrimination apply to all businesses; consumer protection laws apply to all relevant businesses producing and selling consumer goods.

Consider the following examples of social regulations:

- The Consumer Product Safety Commission sets strict rules for children's toys. The reason is to prevent the sale of playthings that could harm youngsters, such as toys with small parts that could come loose and pose a choking hazard.

- The Environmental Protection Agency sets limits on the amounts of sulfur dioxide that can be emitted into the air from the smokestacks of power plants. The government wants to reduce the amount of acid rain that falls on forests, lakes, farms, and cities—and that sometimes travels across international boundaries and causes friction with neighboring countries.

- The National Highway Traffic Safety Administration requires new cars to be equipped with air bags, seatbelts, and other protective gear and to meet strict fuel-efficiency standards.

- Many social regulations are discussed in later chapters of this book that take up the relationship between business and specific stakeholders.

Who regulates? Normally, for both economic and social regulation, specific rules are set by agencies of government and by the executive branch, and may be further interpreted by the courts. Many kinds of business behavior are also regulated at the state level. Government regulators and the courts have the challenging job of applying the broad mandates of public policy.

Figure 8.1 depicts these two types of regulation—economic and social—along with the major regulatory agencies responsible for enforcing the rules at the federal level in the United States. Only the most prominent federal agencies are included in the chart. Individual states, some cities, and other national governments have their own array of agencies to implement regulatory policy.

There is a legitimate need for government regulation in modern economies, but regulation also has problems. Businesses feel these problems firsthand, often because the regulations directly affect the cost of products and the freedom of managers to design their business operations. In the modern economy, the costs and effectiveness of regulation, as well as its unintended consequences, are serious issues that cannot be overlooked. Each is discussed below.

The Effects of Regulation

Regulation affects many societal stakeholders, including business. Sometimes the consequences are known and intended, but at other times unintended or accidental consequences emerge from regulatory actions. In general, government hopes that the benefits arising from regulation outweigh the costs.

Costs of Regulation

The call for regulation may seem irresistible to government leaders and officials, but there are always costs to regulation. An old economic adage says, "There is no free lunch." Eventually, someone has to pay for the benefits created.

An industrial society such as that of the United States can afford almost anything, including social regulations, if it is willing to pay the price. Sometimes the benefits are worth the costs; sometimes the costs exceed the benefits. The test of **cost-benefit analysis** helps the public understand what is at stake when new regulation is sought. For example, when the U.S. Congress debated the Clinton administration's national health care proposals in the 1990s, opposition increased when it was shown that the plan would impose large regulatory costs. Congress realized that the American public did not want the benefits of a national health care plan at any cost; they wanted them at little or no cost. On the other hand, when it became known that the National Highway Traffic Safety Administration (NHTSA) had received information about defective Firestone tires more than one year before their recall, the public was outraged that NHTSA's budget was not large enough to enable it to analyze the data and protect lives.

FIGURE 8.1   **Types of Regulation and Regulatory Agencies**

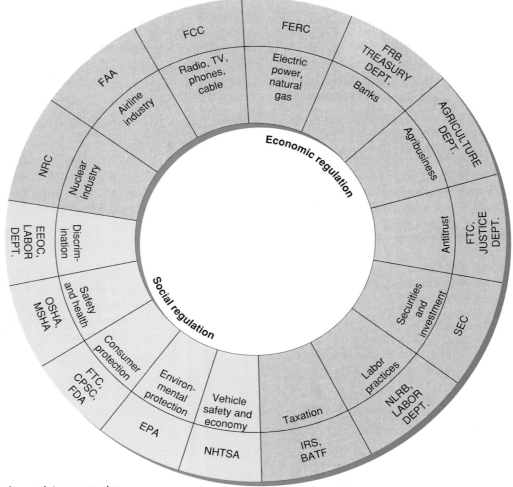

Economic regulatory agencies

NRC	Nuclear Regulatory Commission
FAA	Federal Aviation Administration
FCC	Federal Communications Commission
FERC	Federal Energy Regulatory Commission
FRB	Federal Reserve Board

FTC	Federal Trade Commission
SEC	Securities and Exchange Commission
NLRB	National Labor Relations Board
IRS	Internal Revenue Service
BATF	Bureau of Alcohol, Tobacco, and Firearms

Social regulatory agencies

EEOC	Equal Employment Opportunity Commission
OSHA	Occupational Safety and Health Administration
MSHA	Mine Safety and Health Administration
FTC	Federal Trade Commission

CPSC	Consumer Product Safety Commission
FDA	Food and Drug Administration
EPA	Environmental Protection Agency
NHTSA	National Highway Traffic Safety Administration

FIGURE 8.2
Spending on U.S. Regulatory Activities

Source: Susan Dudley and Melinda Warren, "Moderating Regulatory Growth: An Analysis of the U.S. Budget for Fiscal Years 2006 and 2007," *Regulatory Budget Report 28*, Mercatus Center, *www.mercatus.org*.

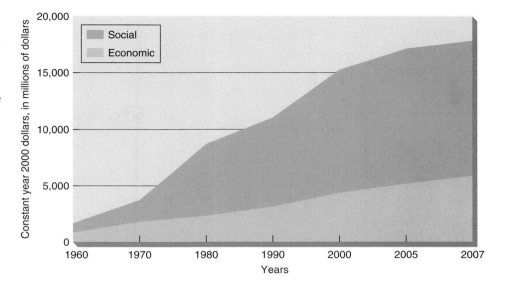

Figure 8.2 illustrates the increase in costs of federal regulation in the United States since the 1960s. Economic regulation has existed for many decades, and its cost has grown more slowly than social regulation. Social regulation spending reflects growth in such areas as environmental health, occupational safety, and consumer protection. The rapid growth of social regulation spending that occurred from 1970 until the late 1990s has slowed considerably during the George W. Bush era of the 2000s.

To help reduce national deficits, the Bush administration proposed shifting the cost burden to those businesses regulated by government agencies, calling the plan a user-fee strategy. Some of the corporate targets were drug and medical-device makers seeking FDA approval, telemarketers affected by the Federal Trade Commission's do-not-call registry, and pesticide makers regulated by the Environment Protection Agency. Under Bush's plan, these businesses would help fund the very agencies that were regulating them. The user-fee strategy has been used in the United States by other agencies, such as the Federal Communications Commission, but on a much smaller scale. The Bush administration hoped to add $2.1 billion to the more than $170 billion needed for regulatory activities. This governmental proposal met significant resistance as the costs of user fees were passed along to the consumers, particularly devastating to limited-income subscribers of prescription drugs.[12]

The growth in regulatory programs is not a new phenomenon. As scholars at the Center for the Study of American Business have documented, staffing regulatory activities in the United States took off during the 1960s and 1970s, as shown in Figure 8.3. In 1960, fewer than 40,000 federal employees monitored and enforced government regulations. Two decades later, in 1980, nearly 100,000 federal regulatory employees did so. In the early 1980s, President Reagan led a campaign to cut government regulation. This campaign continued during both of the Bush presidencies and the number of full-time federal employees dedicated to regulatory activities has modestly increased since the 1990s.[13]

---

[12] "Paying for Regulation," *The Wall Street Journal*, February 4, 2003, p. A4.

[13] See Susan Dudley and Melinda Warren, "Regulatory Response: An Analysis of the U.S. Budget for Fiscal Years 2005 and 2006," *Regulatory Budget Report 27*, Mercatus Center, *www.mercatus.org/pdf/materials/1246.pdf*.

FIGURE 8.3
**Staffing of U.S.
Regulatory Activities**

Source: Susan Dudley and
Melinda Warren, "Moderating
Regulatory Growth: An
Analysis of the U.S. Budget for
Fiscal Years 2006 and 2007,"
Regulatory Budget Report 28,
Mercatus Center,
www.mercatus.org.

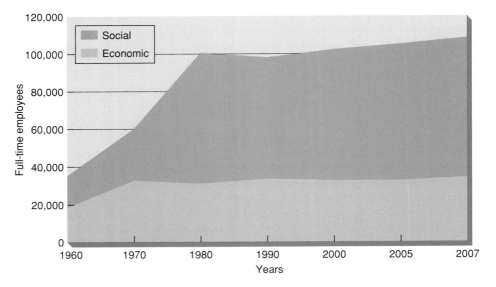

Although the costs of regulation continue to climb, some argue that the benefits outweigh these costs. In the United States, regulatory agencies seek to protect employees from discrimination, sexual harassment, and unnecessary workplace hazards. Consumer interests are likewise the concern of regulatory agencies. Protection of the natural environment may require increasing staff and other associated costs, but many claim that preserving our air, land, and water is worth the expenditures. Small-business owners are able to compete in the marketplace and are protected from economic abuses by other firms due to regulatory oversight. Many of these benefits cannot be measured by dollars and cents, but the need for regulation must be balanced against both its costs and assessments of whether it will accomplish its intended purpose.

The United States has experimented with different forms of government regulation for more than 200 years, and experts have learned that not all government programs are effective in meeting their intended goals. Thus, government is called on from time to time to regulate certain types of business behavior and, at other times, to deregulate that behavior if it is believed that the industry no longer needs that regulation or that other, better means exist to exercise control (e.g., market pressures from competitors).

Continuous Regulatory Reform

The amount of regulatory activity often is cyclical—historically rising during some periods and declining during others. Businesses in the United States have experienced a lessening of regulation—*deregulation*—only to observe the return of regulatory activity—*reregulation.*

Deregulation is the removal or scaling down of regulatory authority and regulatory activities of government. Deregulation is often a politically popular idea. President Ronald Reagan strongly advocated deregulation in the early 1980s, when he campaigned on the promise to "get government off the back of the people." Major deregulatory laws were enacted beginning in 1975 when Gerald Ford was president and continued through the administrations of Jimmy Carter, Ronald Reagan, and (the first) George Bush. Deregulation has occurred in the following industries, among others:

• *Commercial airlines:* removed government-set rates and allowed domestic airlines to compete and more easily make mergers and acquisitions.

- *Interstate trucking companies:* permitted to charge lower prices and provide services over a wider area.
- *Railroads:* given the freedom to set rates in some parts of their business and to compete in new ways.
- *Financial institutions:* allowed to be more flexible in setting interest rates on loans and to compete across state lines.

Deregulation has also occurred in Europe, especially in the arena of social regulation. In the United Kingdom, for example, the Approved Code of Practice (ACoP) governing various employee safety and health issues was downgraded to a "Guidance," a weaker form of regulatory control. In the Netherlands, the Ministry of Social Affairs proposed the deregulation of the Work Environment Act.[14]

Proponents of deregulation often challenge the public's desire to see government solve problems. This generates situations in which government is trying to deregulate in some areas while at the same time creating new regulation in others. **Reregulation** is the increase or expansion of government regulation, especially in areas where the regulatory activities had previously been reduced. The scandals that rocked corporate America in the early 2000s brought cries from many stakeholder groups for reregulation in the area of securities law. Clearly, businesses had not effectively regulated themselves, and the market had not deterred business misdeeds. A flood of regulatory reforms were proposed, to an extent unseen in America for decades, leading some to call this a "New Reform Era." The target was clear: the overhaul of the financial reporting practices in America. Government and society must constantly strive to achieve the right balance between market freedoms and government oversight of business behavior.

Regulation in a Global Context

International commerce unites people and businesses in new and complicated ways, as described in Chapter 7. U.S. consumers routinely buy food, automobiles, and clothing from companies located in Europe, Canada, Latin America, Australia, Africa, and Asia. Citizens of other nations do the same. As these patterns of international commerce grow more complicated, governments recognize the need to establish rules that protect the interests of their own citizens. No nation wants to accept dangerous products manufactured elsewhere that will injure its citizens, and no government wants to see its economy damaged by unfair competition from foreign competitors. These concerns provide the rationale for international regulatory agreements and cooperation.

Regulation of Imported Products

Every nation has the power to set standards for products to be sold in the country. For example, toys made abroad but sold in the United States must meet U.S. safety standards, so long as domestic manufacturers must also meet them. However, governments are often under pressure from other interests, including local companies, labor organizations, and communities, to close local markets to foreign sellers. These stakeholders may feel threatened by foreign competitors and seek to block the importation of their products. An example of such a situation is presented in the discussion case about imported steel at the end of this chapter. In other examples, businesses have tried to block imports, if they would undercut their own pricing policies.

---

[14] From the Sixth European Work Hazards Conference, the Netherlands, *www.geocities.com/rainforest/8803/dereg1.html.*

Responding to pressure from U.S. insurance companies, the Food and Drug Administration issued a warning to third parties, such as the UnitedHealth Group, Inc., that they might be violating the law by making it possible for Americans to buy drugs from Canadian firms. The price of some prescription drugs had risen dramatically, a burden on many senior citizens in the United States who did not have adequate insurance to cover their prescription drugs. Senior citizens were crossing the U.S.–Canadian border in the thousands to purchase cheaper but equivalent drugs in Canada, or ordering the drugs online from Canadian Internet companies, causing a flood of pharmaceutical imports into the United States.[15]

In this case, drug companies lobbied for laws that would make importation of cheaper Canadian drugs illegal or more costly. The economic loss to the U.S. insurance and pharmaceutical industries, and the focus of American regulatory policy, was pitted against U.S. consumers seeking to purchase needed prescription drugs on the international market.

Regulation of Exported Products

Governments have an interest in knowing what products their businesses are exporting to the rest of the world. The federal government is understandably concerned that products that say "Made in America" are of good quality. U.S. companies have sometimes exported products to other nations that were banned from sale at home because of safety concerns. Although such practices may not be illegal, they are almost always unethical. The government is also concerned that U.S. companies not sell military technology to unfriendly nations. In recent years, a number of cases arose in which U.S. businesses illegally sold sophisticated technology with potential military applications to Libya, Iran, and Iraq. These transactions violated U.S. laws that restrict the sale of classified military technology to only those customers approved by the Defense Department.

In 2003, the U.S. Treasury Department fined nearly 60 firms, including Amazon.com, Bank of New York, Caterpillar, Citibank, ExxonMobil, the New York Yankees, and Wal-Mart, a collective $1.1 million for exporting goods and providing services to nations in violation of federal trade sanctions. The fines ranged from a slap-on-the-wrist $9,000 fine to Chevron Texaco to a $244,250 fine assessed against GRE Insurance Group and Albany Insurance Company, which insured seven cargo shipments from Iraq to Libya between 1991 and 1995.[16]

Regulation of International Business Behavior

Nations have sought to standardize trade practices through various international organizations. As described in Chapter 7, the world's nations have formed specialized institutions, such as the World Trade Organization, to define the rules under which international trade is conducted. These rules can be considered multinational regulations. To cite another example, the World Health Organization, an agency of the United Nations, has

---

[15] "The FDA Begins Cracking Down on Cheaper Drugs from Canada," *The Wall Street Journal,* March 12, 2003, pp. A1, A2; "FDA Bid to Halt Drugs from Canada Stirs Uproar," *The Wall Street Journal,* March 13, 2003, pp. A3, A7; and "FDA Defends Tougher Stance on Drug Imports," *The Wall Street Journal,* April 4, 2003, p. A6.

[16] "U.S. Firms Fined for Trading with Sanctioned Nations," Institute for Global Ethics, *Ethics Newsline,* April 21, 2003, *www.globalethics.org/newsline.*

FIGURE 8.4
Forms of International Regulation

Unilateral Regulation

| Country A National Government | regulates | • All companies doing business in Country A.
• Country A companies doing business in any other nation. |
| Country B National Government | regulates | • All companies doing business in Country B.
• Country B companies doing business in any other nation. |

Bilateral Regulation

| Country A and Country B | Agree to mutually accepted rules of doing business in both nations (e.g., no government subsidies for certain agricultural products). |

Multilateral Regulation

| Country A
Country B
Country C | Agree to common rules governing use of common resources (e.g., oceans, Earth's atmosphere) or to impose sanctions on Country D, which fails to comply with international standards (e.g., boycotts, human rights violations). |

worked with the pharmaceutical industry to create databases on the side effects of drug products, establish quality standards, and resolve conflicting manufacturing and marketing practices that might harm the public. As shown in Figure 8.4, the creation of bilateral or multilateral regulation causes elaborate consultation between leaders of business, governmental, and nongovernmental organizations (e.g., consumer groups). This interaction is required because of the vast number of stakeholders involved. The World Health Organization's international marketing code for infant formula products, for example, required nearly three years of meetings and consultations before a suitable code was ready for adoption by national governments.

Nations also cooperate to establish standards for the use of global resources not owned by any nation. Multilateral international agreements govern ocean fishing, protection of sea mammals such as dolphins and whales, chemical emissions affecting the earth's ozone layer, and dumping of hazardous chemical waste in oceans. In each case, governments acknowledge the problem cannot be solved through one nation's actions. The result is a framework of international agreements, standards, and understandings that attempts to harmonize business activity and the public interest.

Summary

- Government's relationship with business ranges from cooperative to adversarial. This relationship often is tenuous, and managers must be vigilant to anticipate any change that may affect business and its operations.

- A public policy is an action undertaken by government to achieve a broad public purpose. The public policy process involves inputs, goals, tools or instruments, and effects.

- Regulation can take the form of laws affecting an organization's economic operations (e.g., trade and labor practices, allocation of scarce resources, price controls) or focus on social good (e.g., consumer protection, employee health and safety, environmental protection).

- Regulation is needed to correct for market failure, overcome natural monopoly, and protect stakeholders who might otherwise be hurt by the unrestricted actions of business.

- Although regulations are often very costly, many believe that these costs are worth the benefits they bring. The ongoing debate over the need for and effectiveness of regulation leads to alternating periods of deregulation and reregulation.

- Regulation in a global context affects business because nations recognize their need to cooperate in controlling business activities that cross national borders. International regulations focus on imports, exports, and business practices.

Key Terms

cost-benefit analysis, *173*
deregulation, *176*
economic regulation, *171*
fiscal policy, *168*
market failure, *170*

monetary policy, *168*
natural monopoly, *170*
negative externalities, *164*
public policy, *165*
regulation, *169*

reregulation, *177*
social assistance
policies, *168*
social regulation, *172*

Internet Resources

www.federalreserve.gov
www.cato.org
www.ncpa.org
www.mercatus.org/regradar

www.regulations.gov

Board of Governors of the Federal Reserve System
Cato Institute
National Center for Policy Analysis
RegRadar.org, Mercatus Center,
George Mason University
Regulations.gov

Discussion Case: *Protecting the U.S. Steel Industry*

Between 1997 and 2002, America's steel industry was under attack. Foreign companies had allegedly dumped large amounts of cheap steel into the American market, sending 35 companies into bankruptcy and costing 54,000 industry employees their jobs. Dumping is the practice where a product is exported to another country at a low price, sometimes below the cost of production.

Recognizing that the domestic steel industry faced a crisis that threatened its very existence, President Bush asked the U.S. International Trade Commission (ITC), an independent, bipartisan government agency, to investigate whether the U.S. steel industry had been injured by the unprecedented surge of foreign imports. After a seven-month analysis, the ITC made a unanimous determination that the industry had suffered serious injury as a result of the surge of imports and strongly encouraged President Bush to take significant steps to remedy this situation.

In 2002, President Bush proposed a 30 percent tariff, an import tax, on most steel sold in the United States by foreign companies for three years. The outcry in reaction to Bush's plan was immediate. From Beijing to London, governments threatened a serious international trade fight and retaliatory action. The European Union said the tariffs would cost European steelmakers as much as $2 billion a year in lost trade. Russia computed its losses at $500 million annually. Officials in South Korea and Brazil also expressed their dismay at the proposed tariffs, but made it clear that they had little desire to pick a fight with the United States over this issue.

The European Union accounted for approximately 37 percent of all steel affected by the tariffs, and thus the EU response was viewed as the most critical in determining if Bush's plan would succeed. Other significant steel exporters to the United States included South Korea, Russia, and Japan. Bush did not have to wait long for a response from the international community. Less than two months after Bush's tariff proclamation, the EU threatened retaliatory actions against $300 million of U.S. goods within two months as a political counterattack to impose additional costs on U.S. exports to the EU if Bush did not withdraw or seriously modify his tariff plan. The next day Japan joined the EU by announcing its intentions of slapping tariffs on some imports of U.S. steel. The Japanese action would be imposed the same day that the EU tariffs on U.S. products took effect.

A few weeks later, President Bush began to back down from his aggressive plan. He excluded about 136,000 tons of annual steel imports from the tariffs, representing about 1 percent of the steel that would have been affected. Two months later the administration excluded an additional 178 products from the tariff proposal. The last exclusion was mainly aimed at reducing barriers to steel exports from the EU and Japan.

By the end of 2002, Bush's tariff proposal had been significantly watered down. Once the key to his 2000 presidential campaign, the tariff plan was designed to bring an end to international steel wars, provide time for U.S. steel manufacturers to modernize their plants, and give hope to thousands of unemployed steelworkers. Things did not turn out the way Bush had planned. By the end of the year, steel prices had risen more sharply than Bush and his advisors had anticipated. Lured by higher prices, steel mills around the world began to produce more than they had two years ago, worsening the global glut of steel. Brazil produced 36 percent more steel in July 2002 than a year earlier. Production in Russia, the EU, and Japan rose about 3 percent over this period.

Nonetheless, Bush's supporters maintained that the steel tariff plan, even the modest effort that was finally implemented, was necessary. "We live in a world that isn't always about living on a free-trade basis. It's about moving the process in the right direction. And I truly believe that this action [Bush's tariff proposal] has done that," said Grant Aldonas, undersecretary for international trade at the U.S. Commerce Department.

Bush's saga with the tariff proposal was not over. In early 2003, the World Trade Organization (WTO) determined that the United States had acted illegally when it raised tariffs on imported steel in 2002. The WTO said the U.S. decision to raise tariffs had been based on bogus information (that unfair prices were undercutting U.S. businesses and imperiling the nation's steel industry). Rather than being flooded by cheap foreign steel, on the contrary, the United States had actually witnessed declining steel imports. Therefore, the consequent tariffs were illegal. The WTO authorized the European Union, Canada and five other countries to impose nearly $150 million in trade sanctions on the U.S. in retaliation from Bush's steel tariffs.

Eventually, President Bush lifted all tariff restrictions on steel imports well before the protections were to expire, bowing to economic and political pressure from within and outside the United States. Critics of Bush's tariff plan argued that the critical blow occurred when the WTO fought back and confronted Bush by authorizing European and Asian nations to impose retaliatory tariffs against the United States, just 11 months before a presidential election. The Europeans went so far as pulling out an electoral map and proudly announced they would single out products made in states Bush most needed to win a second presidential term. Industry analysts claimed that the tariffs had hurt the

U.S. manufacturing sector and cost more jobs than they saved. One of Bush's senior aides said, "Defiance had real costs. It was going to cost us exports and export jobs. It was going to cost us credibility around the world."

Source: Information for this case was drawn from "U.S. Steel Industry Progress Report: The President's Steel Program," American Iron and Steel Institute, March 2003; "Europe Parries U.S. on Tariffs," *The Wall Street Journal,* June 11, 2002, p. A10; "Backing Down on Steel Tariffs, U.S. Strengthens Trade Group," *The New York Times,* December 5, 2003, *www.nytimes.com;* "Bush Set to Lift Tariffs on Steel," *The New York Times,* December 4, 2003, *www.nytimes.com;* and "WTO Authorizes Trade Sanctions against the United States," *The New York Times,* November 27, 2004, *www.nytimes.com.* Quotations are from "So Far, Steel Tariffs Do Little of What President Envisioned," *The Wall Street Journal,* September 13, 2002, pp. A1, A12; and "Bush Abandons Steel Tariff Plan," *The Wall Street Journal,* December 5, 2003, pp. A3, A6.

Discussion Questions

1. Which relationships (between the WTO, national governments, and business industries) would you characterize as cooperative and which were adversarial, and why?

2. What public policy inputs, goals, tools, and effects can be found in this discussion case?

3. Why wasn't Bush's tariff proposal more effective? Did it achieve any of the effects he intended?

4. Should there be some sort of international regulation of steel imports and exports? If so, who should administer and enforce such international regulation?

CHAPTER NINE

Influencing the Political Environment

Businesses face complicated issues in managing their relationships with politicians and government regulators. Managers must understand the political environment and be active and effective participants in the public policy process. They need to ensure that their company is seen as a relevant stakeholder when government officials make public policy decisions and must be familiar with the many ways that business can influence these decisions. The opportunities afforded businesses to participate in the public policy process differ from nation to nation. Sound business strategies depend on an understanding of these differences, enabling businesses to manage worldwide business–government relations effectively.

This chapter focuses on these key learning objectives:

- Understanding the arguments for and against business participation in the political process.
- Knowing the types of corporate political strategies and the influences on an organization's development of a particular strategy.
- Assessing the tactics businesses can use to be involved in the political process.
- Analyzing how the problem of money and campaign financing in the American political system affects business.
- Recognizing the challenges business faces in managing business–government relations in different countries.

Dean Kamen was a 50-year-old entrepreneur who combined a boyish enthusiasm for science with an unswerving drive to achieve business success. Kamen had marketed a cardiac stint (a device that reduces artery blockages in heart patients), a portable insulin pump for diabetes sufferers, and the iBot wheelchair that could climb stairs. He was confident that his latest invention—the Segway transporter—would also be widely successful. Kamen's confidence began to wane, however, as he began his difficult and frustrating journey into the political process.

Kamen predicted that the Segway transporter would "revolutionize transportation by curbing car use and relieving urban congestion." The Segway is a single-person, motorized apparatus whereon the operator stands on a small platform and grips the handlebar. As the rider leans forward or backward, the device moves in the corresponding direction. The Segway is about four feet tall, has no brake or accelerator (it stops when the operator stands straight up), moves up to 12.5 miles per hour, and weighs 65 pounds. The Segway was introduced with great fanfare when it rolled across the stage of "Good Morning America" and was taken for a spin by Jay Leno and Russell Crowe on "The Tonight Show."

In 2001, the Segway received approval from the Consumer Product Safety Commission (CPSC). All that stood between the Segway and the market were thousands of municipal ordinances that banned the operation of motorized vehicles on city sidewalks. Kamen believed that users would not want to drive the Segway on city streets, out of fear of being hit by faster-moving automobiles, but government officials feared that pedestrians would be at risk if the Segway were operated on sidewalks.

Although the Segway was engineered to gently stop and roll backward if it ran into something, Kamen had not performed any crash testing to support his claim that a pedestrian encounter with the Segway would be no worse than if two people collided at a comparable speed. Others were not so sure. "If a Segway hits a pedestrian, there will be serious damage," said Charles Trainor, chief traffic engineer in Philadelphia. "I would not be in favor of changing the law."

The challenge before Kamen was clear: Get states and cities to change their laws to permit the Segway on the sidewalks. And thus began months of relentless lobbying of state legislatures and city council members. Opponents of the Segway argued that pedestrians were already afraid of being injured through a collision with a skateboard, permitted on most public sidewalks. Others cited that scooter-related injuries treated in emergency rooms had more than tripled to 4,390 in the past year.

Kamen provided trial runs for police and government officials, who genuinely seemed to enjoy the ride but were hesitant to support a change in the law. The CPSC approval was used as evidence of government support for the product. Finally, after years of lobbying, Kamen successfully convinced 41 states to allow sidewalk usage of the Segway, although about one-third of their laws included language giving ultimate discretion to local governments.

The state of New York, one of the states without supportive legislation, agreed to evaluate a small fleet of Segways to be used by the New York City police. The Chicago Police Department purchased 28 units on a trial basis to patrol the city airports. Walt Disney Company purchased 100 Segways for its workers but prohibited visitors at the parks from using them. Yet, Kamen's prediction of 50,000 to 100,000 in annual Segway sales remained a distant goal as of 2006. New woes plagued Kaman as the company announced in September 2006 a voluntary recall of all units due to a software glitch that could cause rider injury. His dream of providing American consumers with a single-rider, upright, motorized vehicle continued to be a challenge.[1]

---

[1] "Lobbying Campaign Could Determine Fate of a Hyped Scooter," *The Wall Street Journal*, March 1, 2002, pp. A1, A6; and "The Segway: Bright Idea, Wobbly Business," *The Wall Street Journal*, February 12, 2004, pp. B1, B6.

What strategies should businesspeople like Kamen use to influence state and local government officials to change laws enabling new innovations to be sold? Should governments rigorously protect citizens, or should the marketplace decide what products or services should be sold? Would Kamen have been more successful if he had developed "friendships" with key politicians or legislators, providing them with various gifts? Would these actions be ethical?

This chapter focuses on managing business–government relations and political issues. Businesses do not have an absolute right to exist and pursue profits. The right to conduct commerce depends on compliance with appropriate laws and public policy. As discussed in Chapter 8, public policies and government regulations are shaped by many actors, including business, special interest groups, and government officials. The emergence of public issues often encourages companies to monitor public concerns, respond to government proposals, and participate in the political process. This chapter discusses how managers can ethically and practically meet the challenge of managing the business–government relationship.

Participants in the Political Environment

In many countries the political environment features numerous participants. These participants may have differing objectives and goals, varying access to political tools, and disparate levels of power or influence. The outcomes sought by businesses may be consistent, or at odds, with the results desired by interest groups. Participants may argue that their needs are greater than the needs of other political actors, or that one group or another group does not have the right to be involved in the public policy process. To better understand the dynamic nature of the political environment, it is important to explore who participates in the political process and their claims of legitimacy.

Business as a Political Participant

There is a serious debate between those who favor and those who oppose business involvement in governmental affairs. This debate involves the question of whether, and to what extent, business should legitimately participate in the political process. As shown in Figure 9.1, some people believe business should stay out of politics, while others argue that business has a right to be involved.

Proponents of business involvement in the political process often argue that since other affected groups (such as special interest groups) are permitted to be involved, it is only fair that business should be, too. This justice and fairness argument becomes even stronger when one considers the significant financial consequences that government actions may have on business.

FIGURE 9.1
The Arguments for and against Political Involvement by Business

Why Business Should Be Involved	Why Business Should Not Be Involved
A pluralistic system invites many participants.	Managers are not qualified to engage in political debate.
Economic stakes are high for firms.	Business is too big, too powerful—an elephant dancing among chickens.
Business counterbalances other social interests.	Business is too selfish to care about the common good.
Business is a vital stakeholder of government.	Business risks its credibility by engaging in partisan politics.

As high-speed Internet became widely available, growing numbers of people were accessing unauthorized digital copies of movies and other entertainment, circumventing the payment of royalties to the companies and artists who held copyrights to these creative works. In response, technology firms banded together to form a powerful lobbying group, the Alliance for Digital Progress, to get the government's attention. This group was backed by Microsoft, Dell Computer, Motorola, and other businesses, as well as consumer rights advocates. The Alliance vowed to eliminate free online swapping and advocated strict penalties for people who violated its member companies' intellectual property rights.[2]

Businesses see themselves as countervailing forces in the political arena and believe that their progress, if not very survival, depends on participating actively in politics. But others are not as confident that the presence of business enhances the political process. In this view, business has disproportionate influence, based on its great power and financial resources.

In a 2005 Harris poll, a large majority of those polled believed that big companies had too much political power (90 percent), up from 80 percent two years earlier. Political action committees, a favorite political instrument for businesses, were seen as too powerful by 85 percent of the public, as were political lobbyists (by 74 percent). In general, the public feared the economic power and influence wielded by businesses, whereas only 16 percent of those polled believed that public opinion had too much power in the political environment. In 2006, in the wake of the lobbying scandal involving Jack Abramoff and key elected officials, the American public felt that their worse fears were simply confirmed—81 percent believed that lobbyists bribing lawmakers was common behavior in Congress.[3]

Although the debate over whether businesses should be involved in the political environment rages on, the facts are that in many countries businesses are permitted to engage in political discussions, influence political races, and introduce or contribute to the drafting of laws and regulations. But businesses do not act alone in these activities. Other stakeholders also are active participants in the political environment.

Interest Groups in Politics

Interest groups, representing many varied concerns and populations, have a voice in politics and the public policy process. These groups often use the same tactics as businesses to influence government officials, elections, and regulation.

One example of an interest group is the Fraternal Order of Police (FOP). Founded in Pittsburgh, Pennsylvania, in 1915, the FOP's membership had grown to more than 324,000 by 2006. Its power increased when it aligned with other law enforcement groups, such as the National Association of Police Organizations and the International Association of Police Chiefs. In the 2000 and 2004 presidential elections, the FOP overrode the recommendation of its five-member presidential-endorsement panel and supported George W. Bush. That move paid off significantly when Bush won the election. FOP members were appointed to

---

[2] "Tech Firms Rally to Fight Hollywood's Antipiracy Demands," *The Wall Street Journal*, January 23, 2003, pp. B1, B8.

[3] "Large Majority of U.S. Adults Continue to Think that Big Business, PACs, and Lobbyists Have Too Much Power and Influence in Washington," *HarrisInteractive*, December 1, 2005, *www.harrisinteractive.com*; and "U.S. Public Unfazed by Washington Scandals: Poll," Institute for Global Ethics, *Ethics Newsline*, January 16, 2006, *www.globalethics.org/newsline*.

serve on five federal advisory panels, and its leading officials were invited to dinners at the White House and private conferences with the head of the Office of Homeland Security.[4]

Labor unions, such as the FOP, have been involved in U.S. politics for decades. The AFL-CIO approved a 4-cent-per-member monthly dues increase to support political activity, bringing the total amount to 10.5 cents per member per month. This increase provided an additional $7 million annually as the labor federation geared up for the 2004 presidential election.[5] The increase was controversial because the labor movement was not politically unified. Traditionally, the AFL-CIO had supported Democratic candidates in elections. But some unions had begun to change their views. The Teamsters, for example, had drawn closer to the Bush administration, and members of the International Association of Machinists were skeptical of Democrats' support of unions on trade and employment issues.

Coalition Political Activity

Business organizations and interest groups do not always act alone in the political process; often two or more participants join together to act in concert. Such **ad hoc coalitions** bring diverse groups together to organize for or against particular legislation or regulation. Politics can create unusual alliances and curious conflicts, as the following example illustrates.

Daylight saving time involves setting clocks forward in specific areas of the country to increase the amount of daylight that falls later in the day. At various times, different industries have lobbied for or against extending these adjustments. For example, the barbecue industry has argued that an extra few weeks of daylight saving would boost the sale of grills, charcoal, and utensils, which are usually used in the evening. The candy industry said that if daylight saving was not extended past Halloween, candy sales would decline as fewer children went out to trick or treat. The Air Transport Association, representing major U.S. airlines, argued that daylight saving time placed U.S. international flight schedules out of sync with European schedules. The National Parent Teacher Association also was opposed, claiming children would be going to school in the dark morning hours, increasing the potential for more accidents and abductions. In 2006, President Bush signed into law a National Energy Plan that, among other energy initiatives, extended daylight saving time four weeks. The major reason was to conserve electricity, by having most work activity fall within daylight hours.[6]

Influencing the Business–Government Relationship

Most scholars and businesspeople agree: Business must participate in politics. Why? Quite simply, the stakes are too high for business not to be involved. Government must and will act upon many issues, and these issues affect the basic operations of business and its pursuit of economic stability and growth. Therefore, businesses must develop a corporate political strategy.

---

[4] "Police Union Has Friends in White House," *The Wall Street Journal*, August 1, 2002, p. A4.

[5] "AFL-CIO to Raise More Political Funds," *The Wall Street Journal*, May 23, 2002, p. A6.

[6] "Daylight Savings Extension Draws Heat over Safety, Cost; PTA, Airlines Fight 4-Week Proposal," *USA Today*, July 22, 2005, p. A1; and "President Bush Signs Into Law a National Energy Plan," White House Press Release, August 8, 2005, *www.whitehouse.gov*.

Corporate Political Strategy

A **corporate political strategy** involves the "activities taken by organizations to acquire, develop, and use power to obtain an advantage." This advantage may involve, for example, changing or not changing a particular allocation of resources, such as government support for a project supported by business. These strategies might seek to continue the firms' economic survival or growth, to hinder their competitors' progress and ability to compete, or to exercise their right to a voice in government affairs.[7]

Organizations differ in how actively they are involved in politics on an ongoing basis. Some companies essentially wait for a public policy issue to emerge before building a strategy to address that issue. This is likely when they believe the threat posed by unexpected public issues is relatively small. An example of the hesitancy of one firm, Starbucks, to engage in political action is described in the discussion case at the end of this chapter.

On the other hand, other companies develop an ongoing political strategy, so that they are ready when various public issues arise. Firms are most likely to have a long-term political strategy if they believe the risks of harm from unexpected public issues are great, or when the firm is a frequent target of public attention. For example, firms in the chemical industry, which must contend with frequently changing environmental regulations and the risk of dangerous accidents, usually have a sophisticated political strategy. The same may be true for firms in the entertainment industry, which must often contend with policy issues such as intellectual property rights, public standards of decency, and licensing rights to new technologies.

Political actions by businesses often take the form of one of the following three strategic types, also shown in Figure 9.2:

- *Information strategy* (where businesses seek to provide government policy makers with information to influence their actions, such as lobbying).
- *Financial-incentives strategy* (where businesses provide incentives to influence government policy makers to act in a certain way, such as making a contribution to a political action committee that supports the policymaker).
- *Constituency-building strategy* (where businesses seek to gain support from other affected organizations to better influence government policy makers to act in a way that helps them).[8]

The various tactics used by businesses when adopting each of these political strategies are discussed next in this chapter.

Most companies understand the importance of having a corporate political strategy. Whether a firm has the substantial resources to employ permanent lobbyists in the nation's capital or simply tries to meet local politicians at community gatherings, all companies need to have a clear purpose, message, and plan for engaging in the political environment. Yet, sometimes even the best strategy can fail.

Global Crossing's founder Gary Winnick set out in the 1990s to sell high-speed fiber networks. Central to his plan was a high-powered political strategy. He placed a top Democratic fund-raiser and a former Republican senator on Global

---

[7] The quotation is from John F. Mahon and Richard McGowan, *Industry as a Player in the Political and Social Arena* (Westport, CT: Quorum Press, 1996), p. 29. Also see Jean-Philippe Bonardi, Amy J. Hillman, and Gerald D. Keim, "The Attractiveness of Political Markets: Implications for Firm Strategy," *Academy of Management Review* 30 (2005), pp. 397–413, for a thorough discussion of this concept.

[8] Amy J. Hillman and Michael A. Hitt, "Corporate Political Strategy Formulation: A Model of Approach, Participation, and Strategy Decisions," *Academy of Management Review* 24 (1999), pp. 825–42.

FIGURE 9.2
Business Strategies for Influencing Government

Source: Adapted from Amy J. Hillman and Michael A. Hitt, "Corporate Political Strategy Formulation: A Model of Approach, Participation, and Strategy Decisions," *Academy of Management Review* 24 (1999), Table 1, p. 835. Used by permission.

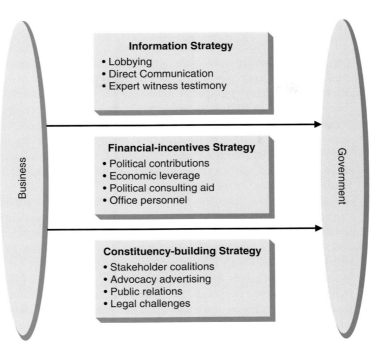

Crossing's board of directors. He hired lobbyists to target both the executive and legislative branches of government. The company and its employees flooded Washington with donations, surpassing even Enron Corporation in the amount of contributions to election campaigns. Yet Global Crossing repeatedly failed to persuade members of the Federal Communications Commission, the Pentagon, and Congress. Winnick discovered that writing big checks gained access to some individuals, but it also brought about greater scrutiny from others. A well-funded political strategy could not mask the weakness of Global Crossing's business plan and could not rescue the firm when its business began to fail.[9]

Political Action Tactics

The tactics or tools used by business to influence the public policy process are often similar to those available to other political participants. Sometimes business may have an advantage since it might have greater financial resources, but often it is how tactics are used—not the amount of money spent—that determines their effectiveness. This section will discuss tactics used by business in the three strategic areas of information, financial incentives, and constituency building.

Promoting an Information Strategy

As shown in Figure 9.2, some firms pursue a political strategy that tries to provide government policy makers with information to influence their actions. Lobbying is the political action tool most often used by businesses when pursuing this type of political strategy, but some firms also use various forms of direct communication with policy makers. These various information-strategy approaches are discussed next.

[9] "Global Crossing Gave Politicians Big Money, but Got Little Return," *The Wall Street Journal*, March 4, 2002, pp. A1, A10.

Lobbying

An important tool of business involvement in politics is **lobbying**. Many companies hire full-time representatives in Washington, D.C., state capitals, or local cities (or the national capital in other countries where they operate) to keep abreast of developments that may affect the company and, when necessary, to communicate with government officials. These individuals are called lobbyists. Their job is to represent the business before the people and agencies involved in determining legislative and regulatory outcomes. Lobbying involves direct contact with a government official to influence the thinking or actions of that person on an issue or public policy. Lobbyists communicate with and try to persuade others to support an organization's interest or stake as they consider a particular law, policy, or regulation.

Under U.S. law, lobbying activities must be disclosed publicly. Lobbying firms and organizations employing in-house lobbyists must register with the government. They must also file regular reports on their earnings (lobbyists) or expenses (organizations), and indicate the issues and legislation that were the focus of their efforts. Lobbyists provide politicians with various perks and gifts. The Center for Public Integrity reported in 2006 that members of Congress and their aides took 23,000 trips financed by lobbyists representing corporations, trade associations, and other private groups, costing more than $50 million from January 2000 through June 2005. Such gifts from lobbyists to legislators are legal only if they do not exceed a value of $100 a year from any one source. However, many exceptions exist, including for payments to legislators to attend training or other events related to their public duties. In 2006, after several embarrassing scandals involving lobbyists, Congress debated but did not pass legislation to tighten these rules.[10]

> In 2006, well-known lobbyist Jack Abramoff received the minimum sentence of less than six years in prison after he pleaded guilty to charges of fraud, conspiracy, and tax evasion. The light sentence was attributed to Abramoff's cooperation with investigations of bribery and political corruption involving numerous members of Congress. Federal records showed that 220 members of Congress received more than $1.7 million in political contributions from Abramoff and his associates and clients, as well as enjoying the benefits of lavish trips, free meals, and entertainment.[11]

A significant amount of lobbying by businesses is conducted through industry trade groups or industry representatives. Figure 9.3 shows the top 20 business industry groups with the highest expenditures for lobbyists during the 2005–2006 election cycle.

Businesses sometimes hire former government officials as lobbyists and political advisors. These individuals bring with them their personal connections and detailed knowledge of the public policy process. This circulation of individuals between business and government is often referred to as the **revolving door**. For example, 43 percent of former Congressional representatives who left office between 1998 and June 2004 and were eligible to lobby Congress or other governmental agencies have become lobbyists. The report from the Project on Government Oversight states, "The revolving door

---

[10] "Congress, Staff Took 23,000 Trips Worth $50 Million from Lobbyists," *Pittsburgh Post-Gazette*, June 6, 2006, p. A5. A summary of the Lobbying Disclosure Act may be found at the Web site of the U.S. Senate at *www.senate.gov*; further information about rules governing gifts to legislators is available at *www.lobbyinginfo.org*.

[11] "Guilty Plea by Lobbyist Raises Prospect of Wider Investigation," *The Wall Street Journal Online*, January 4, 2006, *online.wsj.com*; "Abramoff Pleads Guilty, Agrees to Cooperate in Sprawling Probe," Institute for Global Ethics, *Ethics Newsline*, January 9, 2006, *www.globalethics.com*; and "Jack Abramoff Gets Nearly Six Years for Fraud in Miami Scam," Institute for Global Ethics, *Ethics Newsline*, April 3, 2006, *www.globalethics.com*.

FIGURE 9.3

Top 20 Industry Group Lobbyist Expenditures for 2005–2006 Election Cycle

Source: Compiled from *www.opensecrets.org/industries.*

Rank	Industry	Lobbying Total
1	Lawyers/Law Firms	$27,322,728
2	Retired (e.g., AARP)	16,432,651
3	Real Estate	14,852,052
4	Health Professionals	13,142,745
5	Securities/Investments	11,605,456
6	Leadership PACs	9,973,175
7	Insurance	9,139,578
8	Lobbyists	8,375,845
9	Commercial Banks	7,683,426
10	Misc. Finance	6,399,510
11	Electric Utilities	5,806,149
12	Pharmaceuticals/Health Products	5,733,715
13	TV/Movies/Music	5,655,062
14	Business Services	5,365,130
15	Public Sector Unions	5,195,468
16	Transport Unions	5,147,831
17	Building Trade Unions	4,818,900
18	Computers/Internet	4,636,522
19	Oil & Gas	4,199,383
20	Air Transportation	4,152,085

has become such an accepted part of federal contracting in recent years that it is frequently difficult to determine where the government stops and the private sector begins."[12] Lockheed Martin, the world's largest defense contractor, has seen the greatest revolving door activity with 57 government officials on the company's payroll as lobbyists and consultants. Other firms, all major U.S. defense contractors, have followed Lockheed Martin's pattern: Boeing (33 former government officials on the company's payroll), Raytheon (23), Northrop Grumman (20), and General Dynamics (19), according to the Project on Government Oversight.

The revolving door is present in other countries in addition to the United States. Shuhei Kishimoto left a prestigious government position to work for Toyota Motor Corporation, but then returned to government work as a special advisor to Japan's Minister of Economic and Fiscal Policy. According to Kishimoto, "I hope more people will move back and forth between the public and private sectors in Japan. I want to be a pioneer for the 'revolving door' life."[13]

Sometimes, businesspeople leave the private sector to take employment in government, serving for a time before returning to the corporate world. These individuals can become an important conduit for information between business and government. Before William Donaldson became the chairman of the Securities and Exchange Commission in 2003, he founded the investment banking firm of Donaldson Lufkin and Jenrette. Marianne Lamont Horinko, before being named the acting administrator of the Environmental Protection Agency in 2003, was the president of Clay Associates, a national environmental policy consulting firm.

[12] "Members of Congress Increasingly Use Revolving Door to Launch Lucrative Lobbying Careers," *www.citizen.org/pressroom*; quotation is from "New Report Highlights Concerns about 'Revolving Door,'" Institute for Global Ethics, *Ethics Newsline*, July 6, 2004, *www.globalethics.com.*

[13] "Japan Economic Adviser Believes In 'Revolving Door' Career Path," *The Wall Street Journal*, October 13, 2004, p. B2B.

While it is perfectly legal for government officials to seek employment in industry, and vice versa, the revolving door carries potential for abuse. Although it may be praised as an act of public service when a business executive leaves a corporate position to work for a regulatory agency, that executive may be inclined to act favorably toward his or her former employer. Such favoritism would not be fair to other firms also regulated by the agency. Businesses can also seek to influence public policy by offering jobs to regulators in exchange for favors, a practice that is considered highly unethical, as shown in the following example.

> In the final days before leaving their government offices, two administrators quietly reversed the findings of the Interior Department staff historians, resulting in the recognition of three groups as Indian tribes. This recognition gave the three groups the right to open gaming casinos, which could provide the groups with the opportunity to make millions of dollars. According to a *Boston Globe* article, the two officials, Bureau of Indian Affairs head Kevin Gover and his deputy Michael J. Anderson, immediately left government service and became executives representing the now-recognized Indian tribes.[14]

In general, lobbying—as well as hiring former government officials for positions in the corporate world—is normally legal, but great care must be exercised to act ethically.

Direct Communications

Businesses can also promote an information strategy through direct communication with policy makers.

Democracy requires citizen access and communication with political leaders. Businesses often invite government officials to visit local plant facilities, give speeches to employees, attend awards ceremonies, and participate in activities that will improve the officials' understanding of management and employee concerns. These activities help to humanize the distant relationship that can otherwise develop between government officials and the public.

Although such contacts are legal, strict rules govern payments to public officials. For example, under congressional ethics rules, members of the House of Representatives and Senate may accept no honoraria (payments) for speeches given to businesses or other groups (although they may request that a charitable donation of up to $2,000 per speech be made on their behalf). They also may not accept gifts worth more than $50. They may, however, accept reimbursement for food, transportation, and lodging expenses incurred during travel to a speaking engagement, fact-finding visit, or similar activity. These rules were established to prevent a business organization, or other interested group, from seeking to influence policy by offering generous speaking fees and other favors to legislators.

One of the most effective organizations promoting direct communications between business and policy makers is **The Business Roundtable**. Founded in 1972, the Roundtable is an organization of chief executive officers (CEOs) of leading corporations. The organization studies various public policy issues and advocates for laws that it believes "foster vigorous economic growth and a dynamic global economy." Some issues the Roundtable has taken a position on in recent years include corporate governance, education, health care, and civil justice reform. One of the most distinctive aspects of the Roundtable's work is that CEOs are directly involved. Once the Roundtable has formulated a position on a

---

[14] "Aides OK Casinos, Get Jobs," *Boston Globe*, March 25, 2001, p. A11.

Exhibit 9.A   **The Business of Internet Politics**

American politics has been transformed by the business of the Internet. More than ever before, politicians are becoming aware of the opportunities through electronic mail, interactive Web sites, candidate and party blogs, and text messaging to raise money and support. Internet companies and telecommunications experts offer politicians a far more efficient and less costly method of campaigning than the traditional tools of knocking on doors and calling people via the telephone. Technology companies coordinate "podcasts" for political candidates, in which daily messages are downloaded from campaign headquarters, and so-called viral attach videos, designed to trigger peer-to-peer distribution through e-mail chains without being directed by or attributed to any candidate or political party. Campaign staffs mimic popular Internet social networks, such as Friendstar and Facebook, as ways to reach groups of potential supporters with similar political views or interests.

Business entrepreneurs are finding the world of politics to be an exciting challenge. Chris Lilik, a Duquesne University law student in Pittsburgh, Pennsylvania, assembled his own high-speed computer and created a grassroots campaign for Senate hopeful Patrick Toomey in an effort to unseat long-time Pennsylvania Senator Arlen Specter. While unsuccessful in the pro-Toomey campaign, Lilik regularly blasted e-mails to more than 500 conservative allies on his mailing lists and was personally responsible for more than 800 people signing up online for the latest in political get-togethers, called Meetups.

The American public has embraced the business of Internet politics. The percentage of Americans who went online to view network or cable Web sites for election news jumped from 13 percent in the 2002 election cycle to 29 percent by 2004. With more than 50 million Americans visiting the Internet for news (as of April 2006), candidates and their staffers are aware of the potential avenue for the dissemination of political information. Mark Warner, the former governor of Virginia, hired Jerome Armstrong, a blogging pioneer, as part of his presidential campaign run for 2008, indicating the new trend in political information broadcasting.

Sources: "Click the Vote," *BusinessWeek*, March 29, 2004, pp. 102–6; and "Internet Injects Sweeping Change into U.S. Politics," *New York Times Online*, April 2, 2006, *www.nytimes.com*.

matter of public policy, CEOs go to Washington, D.C., to talk personally with lawmakers. The organization has found that this direct approach works very well.[15]

Expert Witness Testimony

A common method of providing information to legislators is for CEOs and other executives to give testimony in various public forums. Businesses may want to provide facts, anecdotes, or data to educate and influence government leaders. One way that government officials collect information in the United States is through public congressional hearings, where business leaders may be invited to speak. These hearings may influence whether legislation is introduced in Congress, or change the language or funding of a proposed piece of legislation, or shape how regulation is implemented.

How businesses become involved in and help support political campaigning and elections has faced a major upheaval with the advent of the Internet. As discussed in Exhibit 9.A, new ways have emerged for businesses and individuals to influence elections via high technology.

Promoting a Financial-Incentive Strategy

Businesses may wish to influence government policy makers by providing financial incentives in the hope that the legislator will be persuaded to act in a certain way or cast

[15] More information about The Business Roundtable is available at *www.brtable.org.*

a vote favorable to the business's interests. Political action committees and economic leverage are the two most common political action tools when pursuing this strategy.

Political Action Committees

One of the most common political action tools used by business is to form and contribute to a political action committee. By law, corporations are not permitted to make direct contributions to political candidates for national and most state offices. That is, companies cannot simply write a check from their own corporate treasuries to support a candidate, say, for president. Since the mid-1970s, however, companies have been permitted to spend company funds to organize and administer **political action committees (PACs)**. PACs are independently incorporated organizations that can solicit contributions and then channel those funds to candidates seeking political office. Companies that have organized PACs are not permitted to donate corporate funds to the PAC or to any political candidate; all donations to company-organized PACs must come from individuals, such as business executives, company employees or stockholders, or other interested individuals.

In 2002, the limits for campaign contributions changed for individuals but not for political action committees. Under the old law, an individual could directly contribute up to $1,000 to any candidate per election. That increased to $2,000 with the new law. Individuals can also now give up to $25,000 per political party and $10,000 to each state or local party committee; both limits increased by $5,000 under the new rules. The old law set an aggregate total of $25,000 per year for individuals. Now individuals can contribute up to $95,000 per two-year election cycle: $37,500 per cycle to candidates and $57,500 per cycle to party committees and PACs. However, the contribution limits for PACs remained the same under the new law: $5,000 per candidate per election, $15,000 to any national committee per year, and $5,000 to any state or local party per year. PACs have no aggregate total limit. As a result of these changes, individuals can now give more to PACs, but the PACs themselves cannot give more to each individual candidate.

Federal PACs raised $629.3 million from January 2003 through June 2004, according to a Federal Election Commission summary. This represented a 27 percent increase compared to 2002. Overall, PAC contributions to House candidates increased by 21 percent over 2002 levels. Contributions to Republican House candidates increased by 40.2 percent compared to a 4 percent increase for Democratic House candidates. PAC contributions to U.S. Senate candidates during the first 18 months of the 2004 election year increased 20 percent, with Democratic candidates receiving 55 percent more funds, with Republican candidates virtually unchanged.[16]

Despite the laws limiting political action contributions, businesses have found PAC contributions to be one of the most effective political action tools. When an industry becomes a target of a hot political issue, such as the effort to regulate or tax the U.S. tobacco industry, firms within that industry often increase their political spending. In only 18 months, from January 2003 to June 2004, the top 10 corporate PACs contributed nearly $19 million, with the United Parcel Service PAC ($3.245 million), Federal Express PAC ($2.221 million), Wal-Mart PAC ($1.862 million), and Pfizer PAC ($1.671 million) leading the way.[17]

---

[16] "PAC Activity Increases at 18 Month Point in 2004," Federal Election Commission news release, *www.fewc.gov /press/press2004/20040830pacstat/20040831pacstat.html.*

[17] "Top 50 Corporate PACs by Receipts," Federal Election Commission news release, *http://www.fec.gov/press /press2004/20040830pacstat/top_50_corp_receipts.pdf.*

FIGURE 9.4
Political Action
Committee Activity

Source: "FEC Issues Semi-annual Federal PAC Count," Federal Election Commission News Releases, February 23, 2006, *www.fec.gov/press/20060223pac_count.html.*

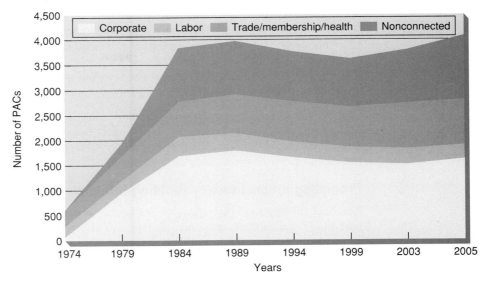

As Figure 9.4 shows, the number of PACs reached a peak in 1989 and then, after a small decline, rebounded in 2005 to more than 4,000 registered federal PACs. PACs have been very popular with business as well as with other groups. Corporate PACs are the most numerous, accounting for nearly 40 percent of the active PACs in 2005. But trade, membership, and health organization PACs (e.g., National Rifle Association, American Medical Association), labor unions, and nonconnected organizations (e.g., National Association of Realtors) also played important roles in the political environment through their PACs.

Although most efforts to use financial incentives to influence politics are legal, at times businesspeople circumvent campaign finance laws and regulations.

Vernon L. Jackson, chairman of iGate Inc., based in Kentucky, pleaded guilty to charges of bribing a Congressional representative, later identified as Louisiana Democrat William J. Jefferson. Jackson admitted to paying $367,500 over four years to Jefferson to promote iGate's technology products to federal agencies, as well as to African governments and companies. In addition, it was reported that Jefferson sought jobs for Jackson's children and other favors in exchange for official acts on behalf of iGate to set up Internet and cable television services in Nigeria.[18]

Economic Leverage

Another political action tool often used by businesses when pursuing a financial incentive strategy is to use their economic leverage to influence public policy makers. **Economic leverage** occurs when a business uses its economic power to threaten to leave a city, state, or country unless a desired political action is taken. Economic leverage also can be used to persuade a government body to act in a certain way that would favor the business, as seen in the following story.

In 2003, the state of Pennsylvania was considering legalizing slot machines at racetracks. At the same time, the owners of a National Hockey League team located in the state, the Pittsburgh Penguins, were lobbying for a new ice hockey arena to be built with public funds. Government leaders were hesitant to use

---

[18] "Businessman Pleads Guilty to Bribing a Representative," *The New York Times,* May 4, 2006, *www.nytimes.com;* and "F.B.I. Contends Lawmaker Hid Bribe in Freezer," *The New York Times,* May 22, 2006, *www.nytimes.com.*

public funds for a new arena unless substantial private funds were also available. Ted Arneault, owner of the Mountaineer Racetrack and Gaming Resort and part owner of the Pittsburgh Penguins, offered a deal. He said his company would contribute $60 million to build the new ice hockey arena if the state would approve the use of slot machines at Pennsylvania racetracks, including his proposed racetrack facility near Pittsburgh. Legislators agreed.[19]

In this example, the business owner successfully used economic leverage. By committing his own private money to help support the construction of a new ice hockey arena, he was able to persuade politicians to vote in favor of legislation to approve the use of slot machines at racetracks in the state.

Promoting a Constituency-Building Strategy

The final strategy used by business to influence the political environment is to seek support from organizations or people who are also affected by the public policy or who are sympathetic to business's political position. This approach is sometimes called a *grassroots strategy*, because its objective is to shape policy by mobilizing the public in support of a business organization's position. Firms use several methods to build support among constituents. These include advocacy advertising, public relations, and building coalitions with other affected stakeholders.

Stakeholder Coalitions

Businesses may try to influence politics by mobilizing various organizational stakeholders—employees, stockholders, customers, and the local community—to support their political agenda. If a political issue can negatively affect a business, it is likely that it also will negatively affect that business's stakeholders. If pending regulation will impose substantial costs on the business, these costs may result in employee layoffs, or a drop in the firm's stock value, or higher prices for the firm's customers. Often, businesses organize programs to get organizational stakeholders, acting as lobbyists or voters, to influence government officials to vote or act in a favorable way. For example, some companies have asked their shareholders to participate in grassroots efforts to persuade their congressional representatives to reduce capital gains taxes and thereby make stock purchases and other investments more lucrative. These programs send strong messages to elected officials that voters support the desired action.

Advocacy Advertising

A common method of influencing constituents is **advocacy advertising**. Advocacy ads focus not on a particular product or service, like most ads, but rather on a company's views on controversial political issues. Advocacy ads, also called issue advertisements, can appear in newspapers, on television, or in other media outlets. They have been legal in the United States since 1978. Mobil (now ExxonMobil) pioneered the use of advocacy advertising, focusing on issues such as gasoline price controls and environmental regulations at a time when such advertising was largely unknown. Supporters of advocacy advertisements believe that they identify a company as an interested and active stakeholder and can help mold public opinion on a particular policy issue. One example of an industry's use of an advocacy ad campaign—along with other methods of political influence—is shown in Exhibit 9.B. In 2002, campaign finance reform legislation (discussed later in this chapter) placed some limits on the use of advocacy advertising.

---

[19] "Penguins, Arneault Make $107 Million Private Funding Proposal for New Arena Project," *Pittsburgh Post-Gazette,* June 24, 2003, p. A1.

For more than a decade the U.S. Congress wrestled with an important public policy decision: Should drug benefits be extended to Medicare recipients? During this debate the Pharmaceutical Research and Manufacturers Association (PhRMA) developed a multifaceted political strategy that, in 2003, appeared to yield payback. At the core of the strategy was an advocacy advertising campaign designed to make clear to the public and government leaders that the pharmaceutical industry strongly supported the extension of drug benefits to Medicare patients.

Other important political efforts supported the advertising campaign. In addition to making $57.9 million in political campaign contributions from 1991 through 2002, PhRMA spent more than $435 million to lobby Congress, the White House, and federal regulators. But many political experts pointed to the effectiveness of the advertising campaign as the final step necessary to ensure success.

From 1993 to 2000, PhRMA spent well over $65 million on advertising to fight various legislative proposals that the industry disliked. The organization also engaged in political coalition-building. During the 2002 election cycle, PhRMA donated an undisclosed amount to the United Seniors Association to run an advertisement campaign that supported the pharmaceutical industry's legislative agenda. It was one of the largest advocacy advertising campaigns of 2002, costing an estimated $17 million.

The result was positive for the industry: the passage of legislation creating a $400 billion program to extend prescription drug benefits to Medicare patients. Moreover, the drugmakers succeeded in defeating a provision that would have allowed the government to use the mass purchasing power of Medicare recipients as a lever to negotiate lower drug prices for all Medicare beneficiaries. The industry did not want this, because it would have the effect of driving down drug prices. According to one industry lobbyist, "Now was the time to lock in the best deal it (the pharmaceutical industry) could get." The industry believed this measure would take the pressure off Congress to impose stringent drug price controls.

This political victory came at a time when the pharmaceutical industry was thriving. In 2002, the pharmaceutical industry was America's most profitable industry, according to *Fortune* magazine, with the top 10 companies posting revenues of more than $217 billion and profits of almost $37 billion, a 17 percent return on revenues compared to the Fortune 500 median of 3.1 percent.

Source: "Follow the Dollar PhRMA Report: Spending More Than a Half Billion on Political Contributions, Lobbying and Ad Campaigns, PhRMA Wins Big on Medicare," Common Cause: *Campaign Finance Reform*, July 1, 2003, *www.commoncause.org/news*.

Public Relations and Trade Associations

Businesses also make effective use of their public relations and public affairs staffs to communicate with the public about political issues. Their efforts may be something as simple as including a politically charged comment in a speech given by a senior company executive or as elaborate as a well-funded, long-running public relations campaign targeting a proposed legislation or regulation. Many businesses work through **trade associations**—coalitions of companies in the same or related industries—to coordinate their grassroots mobilization campaigns. Examples of trade associations include the National Realtors Association (real estate brokers), National Federation of Independent Businesses (small businesses), the National Association of Manufacturers (manufacturers only), or the U.S. Chamber of Commerce (broad, diverse membership).[20]

The U.S. Chamber of Commerce has a membership of more than 200,000 companies. The chamber has a multimillion-dollar budget, publishes a widely circulated magazine, and operates a satellite television network to broadcast its political messages. The Chamber of

[20] The classic discussion of corporate political action can be found in Edwin Epstein, *The Corporation in American Politics* (Englewood Cliffs, NJ: Prentice Hall, 1969). An up-to-date discussion of current trends in American political and civic life is in Robert D. Putnam, *Bowling Alone* (New York: Simon and Schuster, 2000), especially Ch. 4.

Commerce takes positions on a wide range of political, economic, and regulatory questions and actively works to promote its members' views of what conditions are necessary for them to effectively compete in a free marketplace.

Activities of trade associations may include letters, faxes, telegrams, telephone calls, and Internet communications to register approval or disapproval of a government official's position on an important issue.

Legal Challenges

A political tactic available to businesses (and other political participants) is the use of legal challenges. In this approach, business seeks to overturn a law after it has been passed or threatens to challenge the legal legitimacy of the new regulation in the courts. Such an approach is shown in the following example.

> The state of California took an aggressive stance against the proliferation of spam (unsolicited electronic commercials) when it passed the nation's strictest anti-spam law in January 2004, despite an aggressive series of legal challenges by opponents of the new law, mostly e-marketers and civil liberties groups, who argued that the law was unconstitutional. They challenged the legitimacy of the law in state court as a violation of the First Amendment, claiming the law was a limitation of free speech. Although in this case ultimately unsuccessful in repealing the California law, the legal challenge political strategy often receives the attention of lawmakers and can inject business values into the political process.[21]

Levels of Political Involvement

Business executives must decide on the appropriate level of political involvement for their company. As shown in Figure 9.5, there are multiple levels of involvement and many ways to participate. To be successful, a business must think strategically about objectives and how specific political issues and opportunities relate to those objectives.

FIGURE 9.5
Levels of Business Political Involvement

Level 3 Aggressive Organizational Involvement—direct and personal

- Executive participation
- Involvement with industry working groups and task forces
- Public policy development

Level 2 Moderate Organizational Involvement—indirect yet personal

- Organizational lobbyist
- Employee grassroots involvement
- Stockholders and customers encouraged to become involved

Level 1 Limited Organizational Involvement—indirect and impersonal

- Contribution to political action committee
- Support of a trade association or industry activities

[21] "Spam Law Is Sure to Face Legal Test," *The Wall Street Journal*, September 25, 2003, p. B13; and "California Adopts New Curbs on ID Theft," *Crime Control Digest* 39, no. 39 (September 30, 2005), p. 2.

Organizations often begin at the lowest level of political participation, *limited organizational involvement.* Here managers of the organization are not ready or willing to become politically involved by giving their own time or getting their stakeholders involved, but they want to do something to influence the political environment. Organizations at this level may show their political interest, for example, by writing out a check to a trade association to support an industry-backed political action, such as hiring a lobbyist on a specific issue.

When the organization is ready for *moderate political involvement,* managers might directly employ a lobbyist to represent the company's political strategy in Washington or the state capital to push the firm's political agenda. This is a more active form of political involvement since the lobbyist is an employee of the organization. Getting the organization's stakeholders involved is another way a firm can increase its political involvement. Employees can write letters to their congressperson or become involved in a political campaign. Senior executives might communicate with stockholders or customers on particular issues that might affect the firm and its stakeholders and encourage them to write letters or otherwise voice their concerns. Some firms have sent letters to their stockholders soliciting their political contributions for a particular candidate or group of candidates but have asked that the contributions be sent to the company. Then the company takes all of the contributions to the candidate or candidates, clearly indicating that the contributions are from the firm's stockholders. This technique is called bundling.

The most direct and personal involvement in the political environment is achieved at the third level—*aggressive organizational involvement*—where managers become personally involved in developing public policy. Some executives are asked to sit on important task forces charged with writing legislation that will affect the firm or the firm's industry. When state legislatures were writing laws limiting the opportunities for corporate raiders to acquire unwilling companies in their states, the legislators turned to corporate general counsels, the company attorneys, to help draft the law. Another example of aggressive organizational involvement is provided by The Business Roundtable, described earlier in this chapter.

Campaign Finance Reform: A Special Issue

During the 1990s, it became clear to Americans that the cost of running for political office was rising at an unbelievable rate and was only getting worse. The total amount spent on the 2000 congressional and presidential elections was nearly $3 billion, up from $2.2 billion in 1996 and $1.8 billion in 1992.[22] Critics feared that the growing amount of money pouring into elections would become a corrupting influence on politics. Politicians would become more and more beholden to the interest groups, individuals, and businesses that had supported their expensive campaigns.

In response to the public outcry for change, Republican Senator John McCain of Arizona and Democratic Senator Russell Feingold of Wisconsin proposed new campaign finance reform legislation, called the Bipartisan Campaign Reform Act. At the crux of their proposal was a ban on soft money—unlimited contributions to the national political parties by individuals or organizations for party-building activities. Federal Election Commission records showed that the two major U.S. national parties raised a record-breaking $470.6 million in soft money in the 2001–2002 election cycle, more than double the amount the parties collected during the 1998 nonpresidential

---

[22] "Campaign Finance Reform: What Is the Issue?" *Opensecrets.org,* February 6, 2002, *www.opensecrets.org /news/campaignfinance.*

FIGURE 9.6   **Top Soft Money Overall Donors, 2001–2002**

Source: Opensecrets.org, *www.opensecrets.org/news/campaignfinancing.*

Donor	Total Contribution	Given to Democrats	Given to Republicans
Haim Saban, chair, Saban Entertainment	$9,252,936	$9,252,936	$ 0
American Federation of State, County and Municipal Employees	7,484,000	7,483,500	500
Fred Eychaner, president, Newsweb Co.; owner, WPWR	7,387,936	7,387,936	0
Stephen L. Bing, producer, Shangri-La Entertainment	7,075,936	7,075,936	0
Service Employees International Union (SEIU)	4,914,240	4,872,618	41,622
Communications Workers of America	4,028,150	4,028,150	0
United Brotherhood of Carpenters and Joiners	3,946,209	3,926,209	20,000
American Financial Group	3,503,108	125,000	3,378,108
American Federation of Teachers	3,422,150	3,412,150	10,000
Pharmaceutical Research and Manufacturers Association	3,392,087	143,000	3,249,087

election cycle.[23] In the 20 days before the McCain-Feingold proposal was about to become law in November 2002, the national party committees furiously raised an average of $3.5 million a day. Figure 9.6 shows some of the largest soft money contributors during the final year of unrestricted soft money contributions.

What was anticipated as a revolutionary change in American campaign financing quickly turned into a legal nightmare. On the day after the McCain-Feingold proposal became law, an extraordinary cross section of American politics formed an unexpected coalition. The National Rifle Association, the American Civil Liberties Union, antiabortion groups, the U.S. Chamber of Commerce and the Republican and Democratic National Committees joined together in filing a lawsuit arguing that the law was unconstitutional. Some of these groups were concerned about possible violations of free speech; others were simply concerned that their rights to donate money and influence policy would be restricted.

In December 2003, the U.S. Supreme Court upheld key provisions of the law stating that while the law may step lightly on the toes of free-speech rights, it more importantly restricts a large source of likely government corruption: soft money.

The immediate reactions to the new campaign reforms were mixed. Some companies were relieved to be free of pressure to contribute large amounts of money indirectly to campaigns. Verizon, International Paper, and several other companies that had poured unprecedented amounts of cash into the political system in the 1990s reported that they were largely dropping out of the political money race. "It was an opportunity to draw the line in the sand and say no," said Kristin Krouse, FedEx Corporation spokesperson.[24]

Yet other firms learned how to manage the new rules. One way they did so was to use so-called **527 organizations**, groups organized under section 527 of the Internal Revenue Service tax code for the sole purpose of influencing elections. The Democratic Party, which was often unable to raise as much money as the Republicans through the remaining legal, "hard money" channels, recruited 527 organizations sympathetic to

[23] "Last Days of Soft Money Yield Record-Breaking Totals," Common Cause, January 6, 2003, *www.commoncause.org/news.*
[24] "In New Law's Wave, Companies Slash Their Political Donations," *The Wall Street Journal,* September 3, 2004, pp. A1, A4.

their political agenda or opposed to the Republican views or candidates. Groups such as Americans Coming Together, The Media Fund, America Votes, Voices for Working America, and The Partnership for America's Families reported budgets of more than $200 million in 2003 to mobilize voters and run advertisements against Republicans. The Republican Party leadership challenged this wave of pro-Democrat support through the courts. In 2004, the Federal Election Commission ruled that 527 advocacy groups that were organized to circumvent the new fund-raising campaign restrictions were legal and could continue to spend unlimited contributions for television commercials and other communications.[25]

Business Political Action: A Global Challenge

Most of the discussion so far in the chapter has focused on business political activity in the United States. As more companies conduct business abroad, it is critical that managers be aware of the opportunities for and restrictions on business involvement in the political processes in other countries. Other societies and governments also struggle with issues of participation in the political environment, campaign financing, and maintaining a fair ethical climate throughout the public policy process. One example is Japan.

In Japan, a pluralistic political environment characterizes the public policy process. The major actors are members of big business, agriculture, and labor. These special interest groups are quite powerful and influential. Some of the largest interest groups support more than a few hundred candidates in each important election and provide them with large financial contributions. The *Kiedanren,* or federation of economic organizations, is mostly concerned with Japanese big business, but other interest groups promote the concerns of small and medium-sized businesses, such as barbers, cosmeticians, dry cleaners, innkeepers, and theater owners. Some political influence is in the hands of smaller groups such as the teachers union (*Nikkyoso*), Japan Medical Association, employers association (*Nikkeiren*), and a labor union (*Rengo*).[26]

A different political system is in place in China, which is governed by a one-party communist state. This has important implications for political strategies used by businesses there. Direct political participation by businesses in China occurs in one of three ways. First, a firm's leader can be elected as a congressman to the National People's Congress in China. Second, the firm's leader can be elected as a member of the National Political Consultation Conference, an organization somewhat like the U.S. Congress but that offers advice rather than formulates laws. Third, the firm can become a member of groups organized to prepare industrial policy or standards for government (similar to the third level of political involvement described earlier in the chapter). Businesses in China also may become involved through information strategy tactics, such as lobbying or mobilizing support for legislative issues. But before lobbying can occur, the firm must build *guanxi*, a relationship, with government officials first. Financial strategies also occur in the Chinese political system even though there is no political campaigning. Businesses use gift-giving, charity and education contributions, honoraria for speaking

---

[25] "A Hard Sell on 'Soft Money,'" *The Wall Street Journal*, December 2, 2003, p. A4; and "Advocacy Groups Allowed to Raise Unlimited Funds," *The New York Times*, February 19, 2004, *www.nytimes.com*.

[26] Ryan Beaupre and Patricia Malone, "Interest Groups and Politics in Japan," *alpha.fdu.edu/~woolley/JAPANpolitics /Beaupre.htm*.

engagements, and other personal services as ways to financially influence the political system.[27]

Controlling Corruption in Politics

Despite their efforts to maintain an ethical political environment, political corruption is common in many countries around the world. If a videotape released after the death of a political aide to French President Chirac is authentic, his party paid for his successful 1995 campaign with illegal kickbacks from companies that won public works contracts. The German people have seen multiple political scandals, including the resignation of Helmut Kohl in 2000 as the honorary chairman of his party following the revelation of illegal donations to his party during his chancellorship of Germany. The discovery in 1993 of secret ties between leading politicians, Mafia bosses, and businessmen brought down the Italian political system, destroying the Christian Democratic Party that had ruled Italy since the 1940s.[28]

> According to a report developed by Transparency International, a German-based international organization that studies bribery and corruption, Mohammed Suharto, Ferdinand Marcos, and Mobutu Sese Seko, the leaders of Indonesia, the Philippines, and Zaire, respectively, combined to personally take more than $50 billion from their impoverished nations and people. According to Transparency International's chairman, Peter Eigen, "The abuse of political power for private gain deprives the most needy of vital public services, creating a level of despair that breed conflicts and violence."[29]

More than any other cause, political scandals have given rise to efforts to develop fairer and less corrupt political processes for electing government officials around the world.

Campaign Financing Reform Abroad

Recent efforts to regulate electoral spending in Canada are described in Exhibit 9.C. In general, efforts to reform campaign financing in countries have focused on the following themes:

- Limits on expenditures—for example, ceilings on permitted spending by each candidate or political party.
- Contribution limits—restricting the amount an individual or organization is permitted to donate.
- Disclosure regulations—mandating the reporting of the names of campaign contributors and the amount contributed.
- Bans against certain types of contributions—for example, the prohibition or restriction of payments by businesses, unions, or foreign organizations and foreign citizens.
- Bans against certain types of expenditures—for example, bans on bribes to individual electors, on entertainment, or on the purchasing of advertising time.
- Measures designed to encourage donations—providing tax relief or tax credits for political donations.

[27] Yongquiang Gao and Zhilong Tian, "A Comparative Study on Corporate Political Action in China," *Journal of American Academy of Business* 8 (2006), pp. 67–72.

[28] Uwe Johannen, "Countering Corruption through Controlling Party and Campaign Finances—The European Experience: A Comparative Analysis," *www.accessdemocracy.org/NDI/library.*

[29] "Suharto, Marcos, and Mobutu Head Corruption Table with $50 Billion Scams," *Political Corruption: A Collection of Links on Politics and Political Corruption in Relation to Financial Scandals*, March 26, 2004, *www.ex.ac.uk/~RDavies /arian/scnadals/political.html.*

Exhibit 9.C   Campaign Finance Reform or Just Politics as Usual in Canada?

In 2003 the Liberal Party in Canada introduced a sweeping political campaign finance reform bill, called C-24, aimed at "making the electoral system more transparent and fair by reforming significantly the rules on financing of political participants." The legislation included a controversial proposal to ban corporate and trade union donations to political parties or leadership contests. Many viewed the new bill simply as an effort by the ruling party to thwart the opposition party's leadership and goals.

Supporters of C-24 argued that the old law, the 1974 Election Expenses Act, was outdated given new campaign financing practices. The old law tried to curtail runaway spending during election campaigns by providing some public financing to candidates and requiring public disclosure. Yet it appeared to many that the old law had failed in its goals. In 2001, 95 of the top 100 donors to the Liberal Party were businesses. The same figure held true for two other major parties, the Canadian Alliance Party and the New Democratic Party. Bombardier, a Canadian firm, donated more than $140,000 to the Liberal Party and received more than $100 million in government contracts. People were increasingly concerned that business and other powerful groups simply had too much influence in politics.

The new law effectively banned political donations from corporations and unions and limited contributions by individuals. To compensate for the loss of corporate and labor donations, C-24 significantly increased the amount of public financing available to political parties. At the time, individuals were eligible for a 75 percent tax credit for donations up to $200. The new law doubled this amount to $400.

The proposal met with strong skepticism and concerns from Canadian politicians and political analysts. Progressive Conservative leader Joe Clark said, "We strongly support the principle of campaign finance reform and will study carefully the details of this proposal, the details being where the government usually hides the devil." Democracy Watch, an independent, nonprofit advocate for democratic reforms, believed that the new bill made a good start toward limiting the political influence of corporations and wealthy individuals. However, it argued that the bill did not go far enough and contained too many loopholes to be truly effective. Others were clearly opposed to this effort toward campaign finance reform. Canadian Alliance leader Stephen Harper commented, "The central idea proposed is that we replace corporate and union contributions as the basis for financing political parties with forced funding from taxpayers. Our view is that this solution is worse than the problem."

Despite the objections raised by the opposition, C-24 was passed and came into force on January 1, 2004.

Source: Information for this exhibit and all quotations are from "Party and Campaign Financing in Canada," Mapleleafweb, *www.mapleleafweb.com/features/parliment/party_financing*; and LEGISinfo, Library of Parliament, *www.parl.gc.ca/LEGISINFO.*

- Subsidies in kind—where candidates are provided with free postage for election literature or free television airtime.
- Public subsidies—providing financial payments to political parties or candidates from public funds.[30]

Underlying these themes are attempts to minimize political corruption, promote fairness in the electoral process, control the rapid rise in the costs of campaigning, enhance the role of political parties in elections, and encourage grassroots participation by various societal groups.

Political action by business—whether to influence government policy or the outcome of an election—is natural in a democratic, pluralistic society. In the United States, business

---

[30] "Party and Campaign Financing," ACE Web site, *www.aceproject.org/main/english/pc.*

has a legitimate right to participate in the political process, just as consumers, labor unions, environmentalists, and others do. One danger arising from corporate political activity is that corporations may wield too much power. As businesses operate in different communities and countries, it is important that ethical norms and standards guide managers as they deal with political issues. If corporate power tips the scales against other interests in society, both business and society may lose. Whether it is in the media-rich arena of electoral politics or the corridors of Congress where more traditional lobbying prevails, business leaders must address the issues of how to manage relationships with government and special interests in society in ethically sound ways. Ultimately, business has an important long-term stake in a healthy, honest political system.

Summary

- Some believe that businesses should be involved in politics because their economic stake in government decisions is great and they have a right to participate, just as do others in a pluralistic political system. But others believe that businesses are too big, powerful, and selfish, and that they wield too much influence in the political arena.

- There are three political strategies: information, financial incentives, and constituency-building. Some firms implement strategies as needed, on an issue-by-issue basis, while other firms have a long-term, ongoing political strategy approach.

- Some of the political action tactics available for business include lobbying, direct communications, expert witness testimony, political action committee contributions, economic leverage, advocacy advertising, public relations and trade association involvement, legal challenges, and encouraging the involvement of other stakeholders.

- Businesses are a major contributor to campaigns, although the U.S. government and other countries have limited the kinds and amounts of contributions.

- The differing national rules and practices governing political activity make business's political involvement complex in the global environment. Many governments, like the United States, are trying to restrict political contributions or make campaign financing more transparent.

Key Terms

ad hoc coalitions, *187*	economic leverage, *195*	revolving door, *190*
advocacy advertising, *196*	527 organizations, *200*	soft money, *199*
bundling, *199*	lobbying, *190*	The Business
campaign finance	political action	Roundtable, *192*
reform, *199*	committees (PACs), *194*	trade associations, *197*
corporate political		
strategy, *188*		

Internet Resources

www.commoncause.org	Common Cause
www.ncpa.org	National Center for Policy Analysis
www.nfib.com	National Federation of Independent Businesses
www.opensecrets.org	Opensecrets.org
www.pdc.wa.gov	Public Disclosure Commission
www.fec.gov	U.S. Federal Election Commission

Discussion Case: *The New Business Political Activist: Behind the Scenes, Less Visible*

Founded in 1971 and headquartered in Seattle, Washington, by 2006 Starbucks Corporation had grown to more than 1,200 coffeehouses located in 37 countries. Despite its size and rapid growth, Starbucks had traditionally been a cautious participant in the political scene, reflecting a corporate culture that focused internally on serving its customers, taking care of its employees (called partners), and maintaining profits. The company acknowledged, however, that some political activity might be necessary to influence public policy in areas directly relevant to its operations. As it noted on its Web site, "[a]s a growing and increasingly more complex global business, Starbucks participates in the public policy arena, which includes direct and indirect lobbying at the local, state and federal levels in the U.S."

Starbucks' historic reluctance to engage in political action began to change in the mid-2000s, when the firm recognized the importance of U.S. government trade policies to Starbucks' plans for future expansion. In particular, the company wanted the federal government to lower barriers to trade with countries in Central America and Southeast Asia that were major sources of coffee beans. Starbucks was also facing rising health care costs, particularly important to a company whose signature employee benefit program extended even to part-time workers. Starbucks believed it was essential for its CEO and chairman Howard Schultz and other company executives to "engage U.S. national policymakers in an effort to raise awareness and begin discussions about policy that will make America's health care system more efficient, reliable, transparent and affordable while also improving quality." Starbucks management realized that it could not remain in the political shadows any longer, since the firm's financial success was increasingly dependent on its political achievements.

Poised to become a reluctant but engaged political participant, Starbucks' new commitment to activism met its first big test in 2004. Congress drafted a measure to create a new lower tax rate for manufacturing to replace an export tax break. Under this new measure, Starbucks could continue to deduct a portion of the cost of roasting and packaging green coffee beans. This provision was worth millions to the company. However, the Council of Economic Advisors, in reviewing the new proposed bill, suggested that this new provision was too arbitrary. A subsequent draft addressed this issue by specifically eliminating Starbucks from the exemption.

Starbucks responded to this challenge by hiring a lobbying firm, Preston Gates Ellis & Roulelas Meeds. The lobbyists went to work, contacting many key members of Congress—an uncharacteristic move for the company. Schultz met personally with a number of political leaders, even though he appeared quite uncomfortable in this environment. These lobbying efforts were successful, and in the final draft of the tax bill the exemption covered Starbucks. But in an apparent effort to make a point, the Senate staff nicknamed the provision "The Starbucks Footnote," ensuring that it would be noticed. This enraged Schultz, who had been uneasy with the direction of the company's political strategy and new political visibility.

But Starbucks was now a political player and a successful one. The new tax bill continued to provide Starbucks with needed financial benefits. Other issues on the political horizon would suggest that continued political efforts by Starbucks and its chief political officer, Kris Engskov, would be necessary. When a reporter reminded Schultz that many companies have political action committees, an effective form of financial influence by business, he asked about Starbucks' plans to form a PAC. Schultz replied, "I don't think we're forming a PAC in the near term," but then glanced at Engskov for confirmation. Engskov added diplomatically, "I think we will employ that as a tool at some point." Schultz visibly slumped and said, "I think that will be up to Kris."

Since Starbucks' initial plunge into the political waters, the company has pursued a very limited, behind-the-scenes political action strategy. The company retains a skeletal staff of political advisers; avoids making political contributions at the local, state, or federal levels; and supports a low-key, ad hoc (acting only when a specific issue arises) approach to political activity.

Starbucks unwittingly found itself embroiled in politics in 2006 when a group of Democratic Party activists met at a Starbucks coffeehouse in Newport, Kentucky. The group was told they would have to leave, since the coffeehouse could not host a political gathering. Starbucks later apologized for the incident, which had angered the local activists, but remained firm in the company's policy prohibiting its coffeehouses from being used for political meetings.

By 2006, Schultz and Starbucks management were painfully aware that many public policies directly affected their company requiring their involvement, despite their efforts to avoid politics when possible. Starbucks was involved in the messy political action arena whether it wanted to be or not.

Source: Quotations and supportive material are from "Legislative Grind: Cautiously, Starbucks Puts Lobbying on Corporate Menu," *The Wall Street Journal*, April 12, 2005, p. A1; Starbucks company Web site at *www.starbucks.com*; the company's 2005 *Corporate Social Responsibility* report at *www.starbucks.com/aboutus/FY05_CSR_Total.pdf*; and "Starbucks Boots College Dems," *Music for America*, July 14, 2006, *www.musiforamerica.org/node/106225*.

Discussion Questions

1. Is Schultz's desire to keep Starbucks out of the U.S. political arena a realistic goal in today's business–government environment?

2. What political strategies would you recommend that Engskov pursue to enhance Starbucks' likelihood of success in politics? In your answer, please refer to Figure 9.2.

3. What level of involvement should Engskov recommend for Starbucks as it becomes more involved in the political arena? In your answer, please refer to Figure 9.5.

4. Should Engskov avoid or delay developing certain strategies, given Schultz's reluctance to involve Starbucks in political action? What would be the costs and benefits of doing so?

CHAPTER TEN

Antitrust, Mergers, and Competition Policy

All societies face the problem of deciding how much power should be held by leading enterprises. In the United States and in many other nations, antitrust laws have long been used to foster competition and protect consumers. A particular aim of such laws and competition policies is to assure that mergers and acquisitions do not reduce choice in the marketplace. Advancing technology and globalization have raised new issues concerning business competitiveness. These trends have presented public policy makers with the challenge of protecting consumers and promoting fair competition in an era of great corporate power.

This chapter focuses on these key learning objectives:

- Understanding the dilemmas corporate power presents in a democratic society.
- Knowing the objectives of antitrust and competition laws.
- Recognizing the key issues in contemporary antitrust policy.
- Analyzing the reasons for mergers and acquisitions and how they affect the relationship between business and its stakeholders.
- Assessing how competition policies compare around the world and what impact globalization has had on antitrust enforcement.

In 2005, the two leading providers of online courseware, Blackboard and WebCT, announced plans to merge. Together, the companies served almost 4,000 higher education, K-12, corporate, and government customers, comprising 80 to 90 percent of the market. The CEO of Blackboard hailed the merger as an opportunity to "improve the access, quality, and efficiency of education on a global scale." But some observers expressed concern. "You're talking about the No. 1 and No. 2 companies worldwide in course management software," said the associate vice president of information technology at Purdue University. "This is a big shift in the market, . . . and there are justifiable concerns in terms of costs and software issues."[1] U.S. antitrust regulators approved the merger the following year after the Justice Department completed a review of its competitive impacts.

Coach, the U.S. maker of luxury goods, filed a complaint in 2005 with the Japanese Fair Trade Commission, that country's antitrust agency. Coach said it had been the victim of anticompetitive practices by the French firm LVMH, the producer of rival Louis Vuitton handbags. That brand was extremely popular in Japan, where 92 percent of people in their 20s in Tokyo were estimated to own at least one Louis Vuitton accessory or article of clothing. Coach complained that when it tried to sell its goods in department stores where LVMH was already established, Vuitton had threatened to pull out. After a several-month investigation, Japanese authorities declined to bring action. For its part, Vuitton dismissed Coach's complaint, calling it "a desperate effort . . . to compensate for the inability of their products, manufactured in regions with cheap labor, to compete with true luxury brands manufactured in Europe."[2]

In Europe, antitrust regulators raided the offices of the four leading manufacturers of elevators and escalators, seizing documents and records. The European Competition Commission charged that the companies (ThyssenKrupp of Germany; Schindler of Switzerland; Kone of Finland; and Otis, a unit of U.S.-based United Technologies), which together accounted for two-thirds of the world market, had conspired to divide up the market for service contracts in several European countries. Much of the revenue from elevators and escalators comes not from the cost of the units themselves, but from ongoing maintenance and repair. By agreeing not to compete for service contracts, the companies had artificially propped up prices, regulators said. If convicted, the companies could face huge fines. Price fixing like this was the "worst kind" of antitrust abuse, the commissioner said.[3]

These examples of conflicts involving private businesses, customers, and government regulators around the world illustrate how anticompetitive practices or the perception of them can arise in the free market system and what can be done about them. This chapter looks at how the United States and other countries and regions have traditionally sought to preserve and enhance competition through antitrust and related policies. As business becomes increasingly global, and as deregulation and technological change reshape many industries, antitrust and other competition policies are being reexamined.

---

[1] "Blackboard and WebCT Announce Plans to Merge," press release, October 12, 2005, *www.blackboard.com;* "Courseware Providers Merge," *Library Journal,* November 15, 2005, p. 19; and "Blackboard's WebCT Deal Spurs Antitrust Questioning," *The Washington Post,* November 26, 2005, p. D1.

[2] "Coach Files Complaint against LVMH Japan," *Financial Times* (London), March 11, 2005, p. 26; "LVMH Escapes Censure in Japan," *Financial Times* (London), September 5, 2005, p. 24.

[3] "Lift Groups Charged with Price-Fixing Support Services," *Financial Times* (London), October 12, 2005, p. 29.

The Dilemma of Corporate Power

At the heart of antitrust policy everywhere is the dilemma of corporate power—and if and to what extent government should constrain it. **Corporate power** refers to the capability of corporations to influence government, the economy, and society, based on their organizational resources.

Power is often a function of size, and by almost any measure used, the world's largest business enterprises are impressively big, as shown in Figure 10.1. As measured by revenue, the "big five" in 2005–2006 were ExxonMobil, Wal-Mart, Royal Dutch/Shell, BP, and General Motors. The most profitable companies in the top 10—during a period of rapidly rising oil prices—were all in the petroleum industry: ExxonMobil, Royal Dutch/Shell, BP, Chevron, and ConocoPhillips.

One way to sense the economic power of the world's largest companies is to compare them with nations. Figure 10.2 shows some of leading companies alongside countries whose total gross domestic product is about the same as these companies' revenue. The revenues of automaker Toyota, for example, are about equal to the entire economic output of Portugal. Wal-Mart's are about the size of the economy of Austria; and BP's are about the size of the economy of Indonesia.

FIGURE 10.1

The 10 Largest Global Corporations, 2005–2006

Source: "Fortune Global 500," *Fortune*, July 24, 2006. Data rounded to the nearest million. © 2006 Time Inc. All rights reserved. Used by permission.

Rank (by revenue)	Company	Revenues (U.S. $ millions)	Profits (U.S. $ millions)
1	ExxonMobil	$339,938	$ 36,130
2	Wal-Mart Stores	315,654	11,231
3	Royal Dutch/Shell	306,731	25,331
4	BP	267,600	22,341
5	General Motors	192,604	−10,567
6	Chevron	189,481	14,099
7	DaimlerChrysler	186,106	3,536
8	Toyota Motor	185,806	12,120
9	Ford Motor	177,210	2,024
10	ConocoPhillips	166,683	13,529

FIGURE 10.2

Comparison of Annual Sales Revenue and the Gross Domestic Product for Selected Transnational Corporations and Nations, 2004, in $ Billions

Sources: "Special Report; Forbes Global 2000," *www.forbes.com*, March 31, 2005; and World Bank data, *www.worldbank.org*.

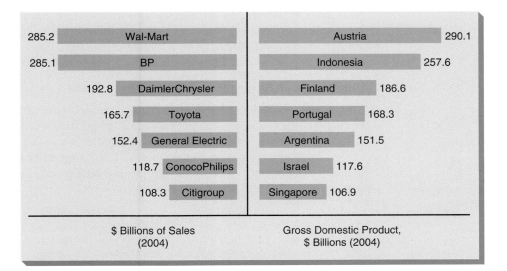

$ Billions of Sales (2004)	Gross Domestic Product, $ Billions (2004)
285.2 Wal-Mart	Austria 290.1
285.1 BP	Indonesia 257.6
192.8 DaimlerChrysler	Finland 186.6
165.7 Toyota	Portugal 168.3
152.4 General Electric	Argentina 151.5
118.7 ConocoPhilips	Israel 117.6
108.3 Citigroup	Singapore 106.9

The size and global reach of major transnational corporations such as Wal-Mart and the others listed in Figure 10.2 give them tremendous power. Through their ever-present marketing, they influence what people want and how they act around the world. McDonald's, Disney, Microsoft, and Sony products and images are known almost everywhere. These corporations have the resources to make substantial contributions to political campaigns, as discussed in Chapter 9, thus influencing the policies of governments. They dominate not only the traditional domains of product manufacture and service delivery, but also increasingly reach into such traditionally public-sector activities as education, law enforcement, and the provision of social services.

The tremendous power of the world's leading corporations has both positive and negative effects. A big company may have definite advantages over a small one. It can command more resources, produce at a lower cost, plan further into the future, and weather business fluctuations somewhat better. Big companies make tougher competitors against foreign firms. Globalization of markets can bring new products, technologies, and economic opportunities to developing societies. And yet, the concentration of corporate power can also harm society. Huge businesses can disproportionately influence politics, shape tastes, and dominate public discourse. They can move production from one site to another, weakening unions and communities. These companies can also use their economic influence to collude to fix prices, divide markets, and quash competition—the direct focus of antitrust policy.

The dilemma of corporate power concerns how business uses its influence, not whether it should have power in the first place. Most people want to know if business power is being used to affirm broad public-purpose goals, values, and principles. If so, then corporate power is considered to be legitimate, and the public accepts large size as just another normal characteristic of modern business. On the other hand, when corporate power is misused—for example, to gain an unfair advantage over competitors, as Microsoft was accused of doing—then public policy may be required to check abuses.[4]

At the start of the 21st century, new realities of global competition and technological change are forcing a reexamination of how power and social control are best balanced. We examine those issues after outlining the goals of antitrust regulation and major U.S. antitrust federal laws.

Antitrust Laws

Trust is an old-fashioned term for groups of companies that joined together to divide up markets and limit competition. Thus, **antitrust laws** are laws that prohibit unfair, anticompetitive practices by business. Today, trusts are more commonly called *cartels*. The term *antitrust law* is used in the United States; most other countries use the term *competition law*.

Objectives of Antitrust and Competition Laws

Antitrust and competition laws serve multiple goals. Some of these goals, such as preserving competition or protecting consumers against deceptive advertising, are primarily economic in character. Others, though, are more concerned with social and ethical matters, such as a desire to curb the power of large corporations or even a nostalgic wish to return to a society of small-scale farmers and businesses. The result is multiple, overlapping, changing, and sometimes contradictory goals.

[4]For two classic analyses of corporate power, see Alfred C. Neal, *Business Power and Public Policy* (New York: Praeger, 1981); and Edwin M. Epstein and Dow Votaw, eds., *Rationality, Legitimacy, Responsibility: Search for New Directions in Business and Society* (Santa Monica, CA: Goodyear, 1978). More recent treatments may be found in David C. Korten, *When Corporations Rule the World* (San Francisco: Berrett-Koehler, 1996); Carl Boggs, *The End of Politics: Corporate Power and the Decline of the Public Sphere* (New York: Guilford Press, 2000); and Alastair McIntosh, *Soil and Soul: People versus Corporate Power* (London: Aurum Press, 2004).

The most important economic objectives of antitrust laws are the following:

The protection and preservation of competition is the central objective. Antitrust laws do this by outlawing monopolization, prohibiting unfair competition, and eliminating price discrimination and collusion. They also protect competition by blocking mergers that would allow a single company to dominate a market. For example, U.S. antitrust regulators blocked a proposed merger of Nestlé and Dreyer's, because the combined firm would control 60 percent of the market for super-premium ice cream.[5] The reasoning is that customers will be best and most economically served if business firms compete vigorously for the consumer's money. Prices should fluctuate according to supply and demand, with no collusion between competitors, whether out in the open or behind the scenes.

A second objective of antitrust policy is *to protect the consumer's welfare by prohibiting deceptive and unfair business practices.* The original antitrust laws were aimed primarily at preserving competition, assuming that consumers would be safeguarded as long as competition was strong. Later, though, policy makers realized that some business methods could be used to mislead consumers, regardless of the amount of competition. For this reason, antitrust laws also prohibit deceptive advertising, as illustrated by the following example.

> One of the hottest areas of advertising today is called "buzz marketing." Is this practice deceptive, and therefore a violation of antitrust law? A consumer advocacy group called Commercial Alert filed a complaint with U.S. regulators, claiming that Procter & Gamble's buzz marketing unit, Tremor, had crossed the legal line. P&G had recruited 250,000 teenagers, mostly girls, to talk with their friends about new products, such as hair coloring. The teens were paid in product samples, not cash. The company defended the practice, saying, "To be a member [of Tremor] is empowering for a teen. You have a voice that will be heard, and you get cool information before your friends receive it." But Commercial Alert said the company was "perpetuating large-scale deception upon consumers," who were often unaware that a company was behind the "buzz."[6]

A third objective of antitrust regulation is *to protect small, independent business firms from the economic pressures exerted by big business competition.* Antitrust laws prohibit **predatory pricing**, the practice of selling below a producer's cost to drive rivals out of business, as shown in the following example.

> Air Canada was investigated in 2003 by the Canadian Competition Tribunal, that nation's antitrust regulatory agency. The tribunal was concerned that the airline might have slashed fares to below cost on some routes in the Atlantic provinces in order to drive smaller competitors out of business. Air Canada, which had filed for protection under its country's bankruptcy laws, said it had lowered prices to stay competitive and had not violated the Canadian Competition Act.[7]

In this instance, although price-cutting by Air Canada helped consumers in the short run, it could hurt them in the long run if it allowed the airline to regain a near-monopoly. In other cases, large businesses may undersell small ones because manufacturers are willing to give price discounts to large-volume buyers. For example, a tire maker wanted to sell automobile and truck tires to a large retail chain at a lower price than it offered

---

[5] "FTC Moves to Stop $2.8 Billion Ice Cream Deal," *The New York Times,* March 5, 2003, p. C6.

[6] "P&G 'Buzz Marketing' Unit Hit with Complaint," *USA Today,* Octobr 19, 2005, p. B1; and "I Sold It Through the Grapevine," *BusinessWeek,* May 29, 2006, pp. 32–34.

[7] "Carrier's Prices Are Below Cost on Atlantic Routes: Tribunal," *Ottawa Citizen,* July 23, 2003, p. D1.

Exhibit 10.A   Retailers versus Credit Card Fees

The owner of Traditions Classic Home Furnishings, a small business with two retail stores, took on a big adversary when it brought an antitrust case against Visa USA and MasterCard International. The owner was frustrated with the fees he had to pay each time a customer bought a sofa or chair using a credit card. "The percentage we have had to pay to credit card companies has been climbing over the past few years," he complained.

Normally, when a person uses a credit card—say, at a convenience store or gas station—the merchant has to pay fees both to its own bank and to the bank that issued the card. These two fees combined usually amount to about 1.75% of the purchase price. In 2005, the credit card industry took in nearly $30 billion in such fees. In the case of small businesses, these fees can be significant. For example, in 2004 the average convenience store paid $31,000 in credit card fees, not much less than its pretax profit of $36,000.

The store owner's attorney contacted other retailers, and eventually four trade associations representing drug stores, pharmacies, convenience stores, and cooperative grocers joined the suit. The group charged that the credit card companies had colluded to keep fees high, despite the fact their costs had declined because of technology and economies of scale.

For their part, Visa and MasterCard defended the fees, saying they were necessary to cover the cost of the transactions and to insure against nonpayment by the customer. Moreover, both retailers and consumers benefited by not having to keep a lot of cash on hand. The retail groups disagreed. "The credit card [fee] system serves as a hidden tax, both on merchants and consumers," said the chief executive of the National Association of Convenience Stores.

Sources: "Credit Where It's Due," *The Wall Street Journal,* January 12, 2006, p. A12; "Suit Charges Credit-Card Firms with Anticompetitive Practices," *The Wall Street Journal,* September 27, 2005, p. A8; and "Taking on Credit Card Fees, with Allies," *The New York Times,* October 5, 2005, p. C5.

to a small gasoline station. Antitrust laws prohibit giving such discounts exclusively to large buyers unless there is a genuine economic saving in dealing with the larger firm. A situation in which a small business used antitrust laws to contest possible collusion by larger firms is profiled in Exhibit 10.A.

A fourth objective of antitrust policy is *to preserve the values and customs of small-town life.* A strong populist philosophy has long been part of the antitrust movement. Late-19th century populists favored small-town life, neighborly relations among people, a democratic political system, family-operated farms, and small-business firms. They believed that concentrated wealth posed a threat to democracy, that big business would drive small local companies out of business, and that hometown merchants and neighboring farmers might be replaced by large impersonal corporations headquartered in distant cities. Antitrust restrictions on big business, populists believed, might further these social and political goals. One hundred years after the first antitrust laws were enacted, however, these populist goals often conflict with business views of what is required in a world of global competition.[8]

The Major U.S. Antitrust Laws

This section describes the major antitrust laws in the United States. Competitions laws in the European Union and elsewhere in the world are described in a later section of this chapter. Figure 10.3 summarizes the purpose of the four main federal antitrust statutes and the major components of the enforcement process. States also have antitrust laws with similar purposes.

---

[8] A lucid historical account may be found in Louis Galambos and Joseph Pratt, *The Rise of the Corporate Commonwealth: Business and Public Policy in the Twentieth Century* (New York: Basic Books, 1988).

FIGURE 10.3
Antitrust Laws and Enforcement at the Federal Level

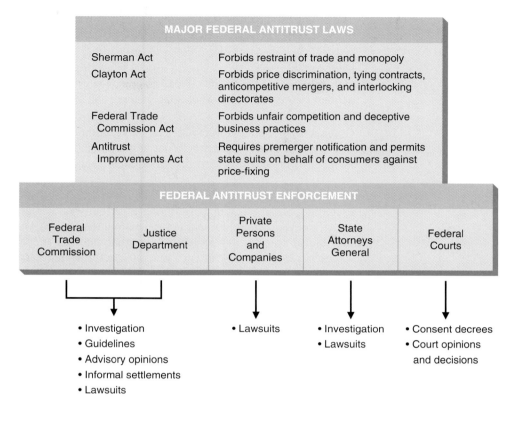

The Sherman Act

The Sherman Act of 1890 is considered to be the foundation of antitrust regulation in the United States. The Sherman Act:

- Prohibits contracts, combinations, or conspiracies that restrain trade and commerce. For example, if music companies colluded with retailers to set minimum prices for CDs, this would be against the law.
- Prohibits all attempts to monopolize trade and commerce. (A **monopoly** exists when one company dominates the market for a particular product or service.) Using predatory pricing, as illustrated in the example about Air Canada, is one method of monopolization. Monopolies are further discussed later in this chapter.
- Provides for enforcement by the Justice Department, and authorizes penalties, including fines and jail terms, for violations.

The Clayton Act

Originally passed in 1914 to clarify some of the ambiguities and uncertainties of the Sherman Act, the Clayton Act, as amended, now:

- Prohibits price discrimination by sellers, if it would injure competition.
- Forbids requiring someone to buy an unwanted product or service in order to get another one they want. For example, it would be illegal for a computer company to force the purchaser of a new laptop to accept a service contract as a condition of the sale.

The customer should be free to buy the laptop without a service contract, or to buy one from another vendor. In antitrust law, this practice is called **tying**.

- Prohibits companies from merging if competition is lessened or a monopoly is created. For example, several years ago U.S. antitrust regulators blocked a proposed merger between Staples and Office Depot, on the grounds that it would eliminate competition between the two office supply stores and lead to higher prices for consumers in some markets.
- Outlaws interlocking directorates in large competing corporations. For example, Chevron and ExxonMobil would not be permitted to have a single person serve as a member of the board of directors of both companies at the same time.

The Federal Trade Commission Act

This act, too, became law in 1914 during a period when populist sentiment against big business was very strong. In addition to creating the Federal Trade Commission to help enforce the antitrust laws, it prohibited all unfair methods of competition (without defining them in specific terms). In later years, the act was amended to give more protection to consumers by forbidding unfair business practices, such as deceptive advertising, bait-and-switch merchandising, and other consumer abuses.

The Antitrust Improvements Act

All of the important additions made to the antitrust laws during the 1930s and 1950s were incorporated into the three major laws as summarized above. But in 1976, Congress put a new and separate law on the books. The Antitrust Improvements Act strengthens government's hand in enforcing the other three laws. This law:

- Requires large corporations to notify the Justice Department and the Federal Trade Commission about impending mergers and acquisitions so that regulators can study any possible violations of the law that may be caused by the merger and order any divestitures necessary to preserve competition.
- Expands the Justice Department's antitrust investigatory powers.
- Authorizes the attorneys general of all 50 states to bring suits against companies that fix prices and to recover damages for consumers.

Exemptions

Not all organizations are subject to these four antitrust laws. Major League Baseball, for example, has been exempt from antitrust regulation since 1922 (although a 1998 law revoked this exemption for labor relations only). This exemption has been criticized for permitting baseball owners to collude to restrict the number of teams, drive up ticket prices, and force concessions from cities eager to attract or keep a major league team. Also not covered by U.S. antitrust laws are labor unions, agricultural cooperatives, insurance companies (which are regulated by state, not federal, laws), and some business transactions related to national defense. The exemption of cooperative research and development efforts is discussed later in this chapter.

Enforcing U.S. Antitrust Laws

The two main antitrust enforcement agencies shown in Figure 10.3 are the Antitrust Division of the U.S. Department of Justice and the Federal Trade Commission. Both agencies may bring suits against companies they believe to be guilty of violating antitrust laws. They also may investigate possible violations, issue guidelines and advisory opinions for firms planning mergers or acquisitions, identify specific practices considered to be illegal, and negotiate informal settlements out of court. Antitrust regulators have been active in prosecuting price fixing, blocking anticompetitive mergers, and dealing with foreign companies that have violated U.S. laws on fair competition. At the same time, regulators have tried to be sensitive to the impact of antitrust policy on the competitiveness of U.S. firms internationally, as described in a later section in this chapter.

Antitrust suits also can be initiated by private persons or companies who believe themselves to have been damaged by the anticompetitive actions of a business firm and who seek compensation for their losses. Nearly 95 percent of all antitrust enforcement actions in the United States are initiated by private parties, not government officials.

Attorneys general of the various states also may take action against antitrust violators, not only to protect consumers from price fixing (under the Antitrust Improvements Act) but also to enforce the antitrust laws of their own states. The National Association of Attorneys General has a special section on antitrust laws, and state officials often cooperate in the investigation and prosecution of cases. For example, 19 state attorneys general joined the Justice Department in its suit against Microsoft Corporation.

Finally, the courts usually have the last word in enforcement, and the outcome is never certain. Cases may be tried before a jury, a panel of judges, or a single judge. The Supreme Court is the court of final appeal, and its opinions carry great weight. Antitrust regulators and businesses alike often appeal their cases to this final forum because the stakes are so high and the judicial precedents created by the high court are so important in the long-run development of antitrust regulation.

If a company is found guilty of antitrust violations, what are the penalties? The government may levy a fine—sometimes a large one, such as the $100 million penalty paid by Archer Daniels Midland for fixing the price of lysine and citric acid. In the case of private lawsuits, companies may also be required to pay damages to firms or individuals they have harmed. In addition, regulators may impose other, nonmonetary remedies. A *structural remedy* may require the breakup of a monopolistic firm; this occurred when AT&T was broken up by government order in 1984. A *conduct remedy,* more commonly used, involves an agreement that the offending firm will change its conduct, often under government supervision. For example, a company might agree to stop certain anticompetitive practices. Finally, an *intellectual property remedy* is used in some kinds of high-technology businesses; it involves disclosure of information to competitors. All these are part of the regulator's arsenal.

Key Antitrust Issues

The business community, government policy makers, and the general public have to seek answers to several key issues if antitrust laws and regulations are to serve both business and society well. Some of the most important ones are briefly discussed.

Monopoly

The key question here is: Is monopoly always bad? In other words, does domination of an industry or a market by one or a few large corporations necessarily violate the antitrust laws? Should the biggest firms in each industry be broken up? In general, the courts have found that monopoly per se is not illegal. If a company dominates the market because it offers a superior product or service, has invented something unique, or even because it is just lucky, that is not against the law. If, however, a firm uses its market dominance to restrain commerce, compete unfairly, or hurt consumers, then it may be found guilty of violating antitrust laws. For example, in the U.S. government's suit against Microsoft, the government's argument was not that Microsoft *had* a monopoly in the market for computer operating systems, but that it *used* its monopoly to hurt its rivals unfairly.

Innovation

Another current focus of attention in antitrust policy is innovation. In the early years of antitrust, regulators promoted competition in order to provide consumer choice and keep prices down. This was an appropriate strategy for markets in which technologies were relatively stable. But in today's fast-paced economy, regulators have increasingly promoted competition in order to foster technological innovation. In other words, the rationale for bringing antitrust actions is changing.

For example, in 2000 the Justice Department brought suit against Visa and MasterCard. The government's argument was not that these two credit card giants were artificially propping up prices, but rather that they had colluded to restrain the adoption of innovations like smart cards—ones with embedded chips that could make health and other data available—that might pose a competitive threat. In 2003, a court ruled that Visa and MasterCard could not prevent its affiliated banks from distributing American Express and Discover cards, potentially opening the way for more competition—and hence more innovation.[9]

The chairman of the Federal Trade Commission commented, "Innovation is more and more the central arena in which competition plays out. [It] is the hot issue for the foreseeable future."[10]

High-Technology Businesses

A related issue is how competition policy should be applied to high-technology businesses. Most antitrust laws were crafted in the late 19th and early 20th century, an era when the economy was dominated by extractive, transportation, and manufacturing industries. The economy has now been fundamentally transformed by the rise of the information age; the primary currency now is intellectual property.

Some people argue that the basic principles of antitrust law apply poorly to today's economy. One reason is that monopolies in many high-tech businesses are inherently unstable, because barriers to entry are low, and dynamic technological change constantly changes the basis of competition. For example, Microsoft argued that the rise of information appliances, such as smartphones, undermined its dominance of desktop computing software. The counterargument is that the principles of antitrust law apply perfectly well; in fact, certain characteristics of high-tech industry tend to favor monopoly formation. For example, consumers tend to gravitate toward a standard computer operating system because most software is written for it, creating a kind of natural monopoly. New information technologies also enable some kinds of collaboration that might not have been possible before. For example, some companies have established joint-venture Internet sites, sometimes called e-exchanges, to sell either to each other or directly to customers.[11] Do these purchasing exchanges violate antitrust laws, or not? One such e-exchange is discussed in Exhibit 10.B.

The courts are struggling to define in what ways high-technology industries are similar to, and in what ways they are different from, other businesses to which antitrust laws have been applied over the years.

One other important issue in antitrust policy, the impact of globalization, is discussed at the end of this chapter.

[9] "Credit Card Ruling Upheld," *The New York Times,* September 18, 2003, p. C2; and "Visa and MasterCard Ordered to Allow Rival Cards at Banks," *The New York Times,* October 10, 2001, p. C17.

[10] "Antitrust for the Digital Age," *BusinessWeek,* May 15, 2000, pp. 46–48; and "The Next Big Antitrust Case," *The New York Times,* June 15, 2000, p. A26.

[11] "E-Exchanges May Keep Trustbusters Busy," *BusinessWeek,* May 1, 2000, p. 52.

Exhibit 10.B   Covisint: Collusion among Buyers?

The rise of the Internet has enabled the emergence of purchasing exchanges where businesses can buy and sell with other companies online. One of most important of these was Covisint, a centralized electronic marketplace for the automotive industry scheduled to open in 2001. Supported by General Motors, Ford, DaimlerChrysler, Renault, and Nissan, among others, Covisint promised to be a place where big automakers could interact with tens of thousands of parts suppliers to efficiently transact the many deals necessary to equip new cars and trucks. The business-to-business site held out the potential of cutting costs and streamlining purchasing in a very complex industry. But the initiative raised antitrust concerns. Could a small number of powerful buyers (the automakers), acting in concert, dictate prices and other terms to a large number of weaker suppliers? Usually, in antitrust violations, *sellers* are accused of fixing prices; in this case, it was feared that *buyers* would do so. In late 2000, Covisint was reviewed by antitrust regulators in the United States and in Germany, and given a green light to proceed. But a report from regulators in the United Kingdom warned, "Internet technology might seem to offer the ideal micro-climate for collusion."

Sources: Richard Meares, "Inside Track: Watchdogs Eye Online Exchanges," *Reuters News Service,* November 2, 2000; "Electronic Commerce: Covisint's Up and Running, but Are Roadblocks Ahead?" *Investor's Business Daily,* November 27, 2000, p. A8; "Don't Cheat, Children," *BusinessWeek E.Biz,* December 11, 2000, p. 116.

Corporate Mergers

A **corporate merger** is a combination of one company with another. Because mergers sometimes lead to monopoly and lessen competition, antitrust regulators are deeply involved in deciding which mergers are acceptable and which are not.

Students of corporate mergers usually distinguish between three different types of business combinations, as shown in Figure 10.4. **Vertical mergers** occur when the combining companies are at different stages of production in the same general line of business. For example, a rubber tire manufacturer may combine with a company owning

FIGURE 10.4 Three Different Types of Corporate Mergers

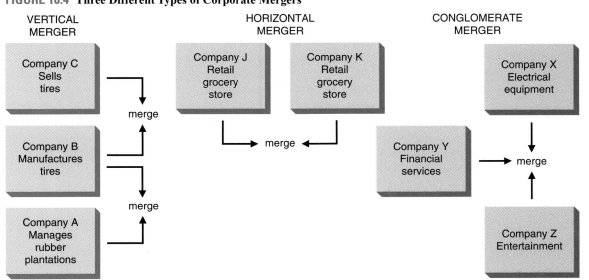

rubber plantations and with a chain of auto parts dealers that sells the tires. Production from the ground up is then brought under a single management, so it is referred to as a vertical combination. **Horizontal mergers** occur when the combining companies are at the same stage or level of production or sales. For example, if two retail grocery chains in an urban market tried to combine, antitrust regulators probably would not permit the merger if the combined firms' resultant market share appeared to lessen competition in that area. Finally, a **conglomerate merger** occurs when firms that are in totally unrelated lines of business are combined. One of the best-known conglomerates, General Electric, combines under a single corporate umbrella an extraordinary diversity of businesses. These include units that make aircraft engines, plastics, buses and trains, appliances, and medical imaging devices; that provide loans, leases, and financing programs to consumers and other companies; that sell insurance; and that entertain with NBC, CNCB, Telemundo, and Bravo.

Mergers may be wanted or unwanted. In some cases, the target firm welcomes the acquisition, seeing an opportunity to benefit its shareholders, reach new customers, or provide its employees with greater professional development. In other cases, however, the target firm does not wish to be taken over. In such **hostile takeovers**, the bidder generally makes an offer to buy outstanding shares of the company for more than the current market price. If enough stockholders come forward to sell their shares, the bidder can gain a majority of votes and take control of the company. (The process of corporate governance is further described in Chapter 15.) Managers trying to thwart a hostile takeover use a number of tactics, including trying to convince shareholders that the merger is not in their long-term interest. For example, Oracle's 2004 merger with PeopleSoft was considered hostile because PeopleSoft and its board of directors vigorously resisted the acquisition, preferring to remain independent. The merger went through, however, after Oracle made an offer high enough to attract many shareholders.

Corporate mergers seem to occur in waves at different periods of history, each wave with its own distinctive characteristics. The 1950s and 1960s saw many mergers that produced conglomerates. This wave may have been motivated in part by strict antitrust enforcement that made vertical and horizontal mergers more difficult at that time. Most observers seem to agree that one factor stimulating a surge in the 1980s, by contrast, was the government's general philosophy of deregulation and a more relaxed attitude toward enforcement of the nation's antitrust laws. In this general climate of greater permissiveness, the number of both horizontal and vertical corporate mergers ballooned. Many of the 1980s mergers were hostile takeovers in which conglomerates were acquired, often with high interest rate financing, and the various parts sold off.[12]

The late 1990s and early 2000s witnessed yet another major wave of corporate mergers, sometimes called the era of the *mega-mergers*. As Figure 10.5 shows, merger and acquisition activity, after dipping in the early 1990s, was up sharply in the mid-1990s, peaking in 2000 with deals valued at $1.8 *trillion*. The pace fell in the early 2000s, as the stock market declined and the U.S. economy slipped into recession, and hit a trough in 2003. Since then, the pace has once again picked up, nearly reaching the trillion dollar mark again in 2005.

The mergers of the 1990s and 2000s were driven by several forces.

Technological change: AT&T's $67 billion acquisition of BellSouth in 2006 was just one of several blockbuster mergers in telecommunications, as major companies

---

[12] This classification of eras of merger activity draws on Patrick A. Gaughan, *Mergers, Acquisitions, and Corporate Restructurings* (New York: John Wiley & Sons, 1996).

FIGURE 10.5 Value of Mergers and Acquisitions, 1990–2005

Sources: Martin Sikora, "The Era of Good Dealmaking," *Mergers and Acquisitions*, February 2006, pp. 24–27; and "M&A Profile," published annually by *Mergers and Acquisitions*. Where applicable, the most recently corrected data have been used. Data for 2005 are preliminary. Used by permission of *Mergers and Acquisitions*.

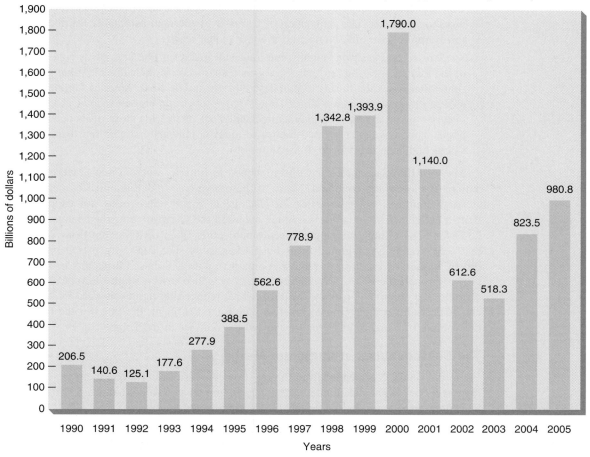

jockeyed for a favorable position as rapidly evolving technologies enabled the integration of telephone, wireless, Internet, and television services.[13] The need to keep ahead of advances in biotechnology have driven many recent mergers in the pharmaceutical and chemical industries.

Changes in the regulatory environment: Telecommunications deregulation led to a wave of mergers among long-distance phone companies, regional carriers, and cable operators. Several big combinations in health care were spurred by anticipated regulatory changes in the delivery of health care. In financial services, a cluster of mergers, including one that produced the behemoth Citigroup, followed repeal of a federal law that had prohibited commercial banks, brokerage houses, and insurance companies from operating under the same corporate umbrella.

[13] "Wedding Bells: A Reborn AT&T to Buy BellSouth; $67 Billion Deal Sets Field for a Race with Cable over Phones and TV," *The Wall Street Journal,* March 6, 2006, p. A1.

Globalization: Other deals were prompted by a rapidly globalizing economy where many companies have found they had to be big to compete effectively on the world stage. "We are moving toward a period of the mega-corporate state in which there will be a few global firms within particular economic sectors," commented one investment banker. The acquisition of Chrysler by German automaker Daimler-Benz, for example, gave both companies a wider global reach.

Stock price appreciation: Finally, the long bull market of the late 1990s contributed to the merger wave during those years, as a sharp rise in their market value gave some companies the means to purchase other firms. In 2000, America Online was able to purchase the much-larger Time Warner—then the biggest merger in U.S. history—by swapping its highly appreciated stock shares for those of its acquisition target. This move later seemed foolish to many commentators, who felt that AOL shares had been overvalued at the time.

Many of the same forces have been echoed in Europe, where a new wave of combinations has swept the continent. Many of these mergers crossed national borders to create new, multinational companies. In just one of many transactions, for example, the British cellular firm Vodafone AirTouch acquired the German company Mannesmann in 2000 for $183 billion, creating a telecommunications giant that vaulted from 70 to 6 in that year's rankings of global firms by market value. The European merger wave was driven, in part, by an effort to remain competitive with U.S.-based firms that had recently grown through their own acquisitions. But it was also driven by the European Union's creation of a common currency, the euro, which reduced foreign exchange risk and made cross-border investments more attractive within the continent. In 2001, for the first time, the volume of mergers in Europe exceeded the number in the United States.[14]

The Consequences of Corporate Mergers

When the smoke has cleared from the most recent wave of corporate mergers, what will the results be? What stakeholders were helped, and what stakeholders were hurt? No one knows the final story, but some results are already observable.

Mergers often bring great benefits to both firms, including economies of scale and access to new technologies and markets. When Disney purchased Pixar in 2006, it was seen as a way for the company to stay current with the latest developments in animation and special effects. The merger of Chase Manhattan and J. P. Morgan enabled the combined company to extend its market reach and offer its customers a broader array of products and services.

Sometimes, however, mergers may undermine corporate responsibility to various stakeholders. Employees often lose their jobs when companies merge, as duplicate positions are eliminated, and local communities suffer when a large company moves out or shifts its activities to other regions. Following the acquisition of Gillette by Procter & Gamble, for example, 6,000 Gillette workers lost their jobs including 40 percent of the company's top managers.[15] Some worried that Ben & Jerry's, known for its charitable contributions, would cut back in the wake of its takeover by the Dutch conglomerate Unilever.

The results of mergers are mixed for stockholders. Share values often rise when a merger or acquisition is announced if shareholders perceive benefits from synergies (complementary strengths) between the two firms. But shareholders can also be hurt, particularly where an acquisition is overpriced or not well thought out. A study by *BusinessWeek* of major mergers in the United States between 1995 and 2001 found that

---

[14] "Europe's Lead Over U.S. Widens in Merger and Acquisition Deals," *The Wall Street Journal*, March 28, 2003, p. C5.

[15] "Gillette Losing 40% of Its Top Managers," *Boston Globe*, December 7, 2005, p. D1.

61 percent of the time, shareholders did worse than if the merger had never occurred. (The study measured this by comparing the stock performance of the merged firm, after the merger, with that of others in its industry.) Overall, the average return for all buyers (companies that had acquired others during this period) was 9 percent below that of overall market indices. The study concluded that many companies had simply gotten carried away and paid too much for their acquisitions.[16]

Mergers and acquisitions can serve as a dynamic stimulus, producing gains for shareholders and the entire economy from improved efficiency and market pressure. When carried to excess, however, experience has shown that such business combinations can be costly in economic and social terms for some stakeholders. Social control, expressed through antitrust policy, will continue to seek the best balance between competition and other social goals.

Comparative Competition Policies

Other nations have their own versions of antitrust laws, often referred to as **competition policies**. By 2000, 80 nations, accounting for 80 percent of world trade, had adopted some form of antitrust or competition policy. Many of these countries modeled their policies after those of the United States.[17]

Europe has historically lagged the United States in antitrust regulation, but it has been rapidly catching up.[18] As late as the 1960s, only one country in Europe, Germany, had an antitrust enforcement agency. Today, the European Union (EU) has a complete set of competition policies, covering many of the same issues as U.S. antitrust law. Because of Europe's unique historical experience, the enforcement emphasis there has differed somewhat from that of the United States, however. Regulators have given special attention to market domination by formerly state-run enterprises in eastern and central European nations, for example. They have also been concerned about price discrimination across national borders within Europe. For instance, regulators fined VW for prohibiting their dealers in Italy from filling orders for German and Austrian customers attracted by lower prices of cars in Italy. EU regulators have also shown a strong inclination to protect small businesses from big business dominance.[19]

EU member states also have their own policies, and they enforce them vigorously within their own national borders.

In 2005, France's Competition Council imposed the largest antitrust fine in the country's history, $625 million. The country's three leading providers of cell-phone service, regulators found, had met regularly to divide the market. A crucial piece of evidence was a document seized in a raid of one of the companies that discussed a "market-share Yalta," an apparent reference to the meeting at the end of World War II where Roosevelt, Churchill, and Stalin divided Europe. The government investigation had been prompted by a consumer group concerned about high prices for cellular service, as more and more French people were using mobile phones.[20]

[16] "Mergers: Why Most Big Deals Don't Pay Off," *BusinessWeek*, October 14, 2002, pp. 58–70.

[17] "The New Trustbusters," *Foreign Affairs*, January/February 2002.

[18] Antitrust in a Transatlantic Context," address by R. Hewitt Pate, Assistant Attorney General, Antitrust Division, U.S. Department of Justice, Brussels, Belgium, June 7, 2004.

[19] European Commission, "EU Competition Policy and the Consumer," available online at *www.europa.eu.int/comm /competition/publications/competition_policy_and_the_citizen/*.

[20] "A Crackdown on Cartels by European Regulators," *The New York Times*, December 27, 2005, p. C3; "Consumers Suffered after Market-Share Yalta," *Financial Times*, December 2, 2005, p. 26.

Exhibit 10.C   How Sweet a Deal?

Brazil's antitrust regulators faced a difficult decision in 2003 when they were called on to review a proposed acquisition of Garoto, a Brazilian chocolate company.

Brazilians love chocolate: they eat $1.1 billion worth of the sweet confection every year. In 2002, Nestlé, the Swiss-based transnational, offered $230 million for Garoto in a bid to overtake its rival Kraft, which had a strong position in the Brazilian market with its popular Lacta brand. Nestlé's purchase, if it went through, would give the company a 56 percent market share. It would also create a monopoly of some parts of the industry, such as liquid confectioner's chocolate.

Brazil was relatively new to antitrust policy. Regulators there had only achieved real power in 1994, when new legislation strengthened their agency. The decision they faced was politically tricky. On one hand, consumers and small chocolate companies were worried about the merger and urged them to block it. An executive of an independent candy company that bought its supplies from Garoto said that the merger would create "hyperconcentration in the supply chain. . . . We are going to be completely dependent on them." Said an industry analyst, "The consumer will definitely suffer, because there will be less competition and, as a result, serious price hikes."

But others expected strong political pressures on the fledgling agency to approve the deal. Nestlé, with almost a billion dollars invested in Brazil's developing economy, was a powerful player. "Brazil is under a lot of pressure to be seen to be receptive to foreign investment," said one analyst.

Source: "Brazil Ponders Nestlé's Acquisition of Competitor," *The New York Times,* July 3, 2003, p. W1.

Developing nations around the world have also moved to adopt competition policies, as they have increasingly entered the global economy. U.S. antitrust regulators have worked with officials in Zimbabwe and Kazakhstan, for example, to help them develop their own antitrust laws. Competition policies have even been proposed in countries that long shunned them, as shown in the following example.

In 2003, China—long considered a laggard in promoting fair competition—took the unprecedented step of adopting a comprehensive antitrust policy. Responding to pressure from the World Trade Organization, a Chinese government commission proposed rules that for the first time would ban price-fixing, monopolies, and predatory pricing. Observers noted, however, great resistance within China to these rules. "There are significant political sensitivities," said one business executive with an international firm, who was based in Beijing. The Chinese government still faced the challenge of enforcing the new policy effectively.[21]

Some of the particular challenges faced by developing nations that, like China, are trying to create and enforce competition policies are profiled in Exhibit 10.C.

Globalization and Competition Policy

The first antitrust laws were created in the late 19th century, when most commerce was regional or national in scope. This is no longer the case. Today, business has greatly expanded its global reach. An increasing proportion of products and services purchased by consumers are made in other nations. As shown in Chapter 7, trade barriers are falling, and new regions of the world are rapidly entering the world marketplace.

[21] "China Unveils Competition Rules," *South China Morning Post,* July 2, 2003, Business Section, p. 1.

The rapid globalization of business has created many new challenges for antitrust enforcement in all nations. Regulators, policy makers, and the courts must now address difficult and complex questions, often not anticipated by the framers of antitrust law, such as the following:

- Should a government permit mergers, joint ventures, or other cooperative arrangements among companies, even if they reduce competition within a country's borders, if they enhance the ability of domestic businesses to compete internationally?
- Should a government move to break up monopolies within a country, if the global marketplace for the products or services offered by these companies is highly competitive?
- Should regulators and the courts try to enforce antitrust laws against foreign companies if these companies operate subsidiaries—or sell their products or services—within their borders?
- What steps can governments take to create a level playing field, so that corporations operate under a common set of antitrust rules and regulations wherever they do business?

Government officials in many countries today face the challenge of maintaining conditions necessary for fair competition in an increasingly global economy. This section will discuss how government, business, and society have tried to answer the above questions in recent years.

Antitrust Enforcement and National Competitiveness

Both in the United States and elsewhere, regulators have become increasingly sensitive to the impact of enforcement on the ability of domestic firms to compete effectively in the global economy. They have been reluctant to block mergers, break up monopolies, or prevent joint research efforts where these would strengthen **national competitiveness**. This sometimes creates dilemmas for regulators, when the goal of a free, competitive market nationally conflicts with the goal of a strong economy, relative to other countries.

In the United States, since the mid-1980s, the government has generally permitted cooperative activities among firms where appropriate to enhance their competitiveness in the global economy. The National Cooperative Research Act (NCRA), passed in 1984, clarified the application of U.S. antitrust laws to joint research and development (R&D) activities. This law sought to balance the positive effects of cooperative R&D with the preservation of competition by instructing the courts to use a "rule of reason" in assessing individual cases. European regulators have similarly permitted some joint R&D aimed at improving the competitiveness of their industries, such as a recent consortium formed to develop integrated circuits with nanometric (microscopically small) dimensions.

Regulators have also loosened the rules governing joint production agreements to permit important economies of scale. Joint manufacturing and marketing deals between U.S. and foreign firms are becoming more frequent, often without serious antitrust objections being raised by government. Hewlett Packard, for example, has formed strategic alliances with Samsung (Korea), Northern Telecom (Canada), and Japanese firms including Sony, Hitachi, Canon, and Yokogawa.

Enforcing Antitrust Laws against Foreign Firms

In recent years, regulators have been increasingly willing to address possible violations of antitrust law by foreign companies.

In some instances, regulators have moved to prosecute international companies that have set up operations or bought a subsidiary in their countries. In others, authorities have gone even further, going after foreign companies that violate antitrust law within their own borders. When Swiss drugmakers Sandoz and Ciba-Geigy merged, for example, the FTC required the companies to divest some product lines to avoid a monopoly, even though neither company was based in the United States. In some cases, the U.S. Justice Department has prosecuted foreign firms for price-fixing if they sell their products or services in the United States, even though they are based overseas. For example, it levied fines against firms in France, Germany, and Japan for anticompetitive practices in the food additive business.[22]

For their part, European regulators have also become more active in bringing enforcement actions against U.S. firms. For example, in 2005 a European court upheld the EU's veto of General Electric's plans to acquire Honeywell—both American firms—because the merger would make it harder for other firms to compete.[23] U.S. regulators had earlier approved the merger. The Europeans claimed jurisdiction because both firms were active on the continent.

Antitrust actions taken by the EU and South Korea against Microsoft, an American firm, are described in the discussion case at the end of this chapter.

Harmonization

As more and more countries have adopted competition policies, efforts have been made to coordinate laws and enforcement efforts among nations, in a process called **harmonization**. Several bilateral (two-country) treaties are in place, and the Organization for Economic Cooperation and Development (OECD), a 28-nation group, has worked to coordinate antitrust enforcement. Its goal is to create a level playing field among their members' competing national economies. The European Union and the United States now jointly review global mergers that fall under both their jurisdictions to avoid conflicting decisions on the same case. The EU is also now coordinating much more closely with the Japan Fair Trade Commission, the Japanese antitrust authority.[24]

In one case, antitrust regulators in the United States, Europe, and Canada joined forces to investigate possible price-fixing in the copper industry. Government officials noted that copper prices had risen 25 percent between 2001 and 2003, and suspected that companies might be fixing prices. The problem was that the firms involved were based in many nations, cutting across regulatory jurisdictions. As cartels become global, so must international cooperation among regulators, noted the European Commission.[25]

Issues of antitrust and competition policy have also been taken up in international trade negotiations, such as those conducted under the auspices of the World Trade Organization. But the explosion of international commerce has far outstripped the pace of international negotiations, and global business still lacks a common, enforceable set of competition policies. The lack of common standards poses a problem for businesses engaged in cross-border mergers; they must often face conflicting regulatory hurdles in multiple countries. A report by the Brookings Institution recommended a broad multicountry effort to harmonize competition policies. Among other ideas, the

---

[22] "An Industry under Constant Scrutiny," *The New York Times,* April 17, 2003, p. W1.

[23] "European Court Upholds Veto of G.E.-Honeywell Deal," *The New York Times,* December 15, 2005, p. C7.

[24] "Global Trade: Cooperation Agreement," *The New York Times,* July 11, 2003, p. W1.

[25] "U.S., Europe and Canada Investigate Copper Pricing," *The New York Times,* May 15, 2003, p. W1.

study recommended the establishment of regional antitrust authorities in Latin America and Asia and teamwork among regulators of different nations.[26]

Antitrust policy makers are wrestling with the new realities of global business competition. The days of self-contained national economies are gone. Virtually all businesses are touched, directly or indirectly, by the world marketplace. Cooperation among companies of diverse national origins often makes economic sense. But the need for some form of social control on the excesses of anticompetitive business behavior has not disappeared, either in the United States or in other nations. The optimal fit between antitrust protection and the global marketplace is not easily achieved.

Summary

- The world's largest corporations are capable of wielding much influence because of the central functions they perform in their respective societies and throughout the world. Corporate power is legitimate when used to affirm broad public purposes, but may also be abused.

- The objectives of antitrust and competition laws in all countries are to protect consumers, small businesses, and others from unfair, anticompetitive practices.

- Courts and regulators have generally maintained that monopoly does not in itself constitute a violation of antitrust laws; what is important is whether a company has competed unfairly. Other key issues include how to use antitrust policy to foster innovation and national competitiveness.

- The key causes of mergers and acquisitions in recent years were technological change, globalization, shifts in the regulatory environment, and increases in stock valuations. Some believed that mergers were good for stockholders and other stakeholders, while others expressed concern about the long-run effects such mergers would have on stakeholders.

- Many countries have adopted or are adopting competition policies, and efforts are under way to better harmonize these policies across national borders.

Key Terms

antitrust laws, *210*
competition policy, *221*
conglomerate mergers, *218*
corporate mergers, *217*
corporate power, *209*

harmonization, *224*
horizontal mergers, *218*
hostile takeover, *218*
monopoly, *213*

national competitiveness, *223*
predatory pricing, *211*
tying, *214*
vertical mergers, *217*

Internet Resources

www.usdoj.gov
www.ftc.gov
www.abanet.org/antitrust
www.yahoo.com/Government/Law/Cases
http://europa.eu.int/comm/competition

U.S. Department of Justice
U.S. Federal Trade Commission
American Bar Association, Antitrust Section
Information on current antitrust cases
European Commission, Director-General for Competition

[26] Simon J. Evenett et al., *Antitrust Goes Global: What the Future Holds for Transatlantic Cooperation* (Washington, DC: Brookings Institution Press, 2000).

Discussion Case: *Microsoft's Antitrust Troubles in Europe and Asia*

When the United States and several state governments finally settled their long-running antitrust suit against Microsoft in 2002 the company's troubles were not yet over. Regulators in Europe and Asia were already engaged in their own investigations of possible anticompetitive practices by the world's most powerful maker of computer operating systems.

Microsoft is one of the great business success stories of the information age. Founded in 1975 by Bill Gates, the company first made its mark by developing an operating system for early personal computers (PCs). Microsoft later developed a new generation of operating systems, sold under the brand name Windows. By the late 1990s, Microsoft controlled over 90 percent of the market for all PC operating systems. The company had also branched out into applications software, developing word processing, spreadsheet, and other desktop programs, as well as a Web browser, Internet Explorer (IE).

In the U.S. case, the Justice Department and several states had argued that Microsoft had used its market dominance in operating systems to leverage the competitive success of IE. One way Microsoft had done so was by integrating IE into Windows, making it difficult for users to uninstall and posing a barrier to their adoption of competing browsers. In the final settlement of the long-running dispute, Microsoft agreed not to retaliate against any computer makers that installed non-Microsoft software, such as a competing browser or media player. It also agreed to ongoing monitoring to ensure compliance with the terms of the settlement.

The European case focused on a similar issue, but with a twist. There, regulators were mainly concerned that Microsoft had used its dominant position in operating systems to thwart the developers of independent software—including open source software popular in Europe—so that customers would be forced to choose Microsoft's own applications. After a five-year investigation, the European Commission ordered Microsoft to disclose publicly the interfaces that enabled applications software to "talk" with Windows. The company was fined $613 million, the largest antitrust fine ever leveled by the European Commission. In 2006, the Commission fined the company again—this time, for $357 million—saying that Microsoft had not yet supplied the necessary technical information to its rivals.

The EU action was criticized by U.S. assistant attorney general Hewitt Pate, who called the penalties imposed on Microsoft "unfortunate." "Sound antitrust policy must avoid chilling innovation and competition even by dominant companies. A contrary approach," he added, "risks protecting competitors, not competition, in ways that may ultimately harm innovation and the consumers that benefit from it."

Meanwhile, South Korea's Fair Trade Commission (FTC) was also investigating possible illegal action by the company. In 2005, it found that Microsoft had been guilty of bundling Windows with Media Player and Instant Messenger, both Microsoft programs. Microsoft's practices had "constitute[d] abuse of a market dominant position and unfair trade practices," said South Korea's top antitrust regulator. One reason his agency had taken up the case was that a Korean company, Daum Communications, had complained that its messaging software was being unfairly shut out by Windows.

Korean regulators fined Microsoft $32 million and ordered the company to offer two new versions of Windows for sale there, one with Media Player and Instant Messenger removed and the other with links to competitors' Web sites. They also ordered the company to send existing customers a CD allowing them to replace the bundled software. Microsoft was given six months to comply.

Microsoft said it was disappointed and would appeal the Korean decision. "In essence, the FTC is asking us to create two new versions of Windows that are not sold anywhere else in the world," said a company spokesperson. "That is bad for the consumer and bad for the Korean IT industry." Some analysts speculated that Microsoft might withdraw from Korea altogether, if it determined that revenue from sales would not be enough to make up the costs of developing a special product.

Sources: "DOJ Critiques EU's Microsoft Ruling," IDG News Service, March 25, 2004, *www.infoworld.com*; "Microsoft Fined US $32M by South Korea," *TechWorld*, December 7, 2005, *www.techworld.com*; "Regulators Penalize Microsoft in Europe," *The New York Times,* July 13, 2006, p. C1.

Discussion Questions

1. What differences do you observe in how regulators in the United States, Europe, and Asia dealt with anticompetitive practices by Microsoft? What do you think explains these differences?

2. Antitrust and competition policies are designed to protect both consumers and other businesses from unfair competition. In this case, do you think regulators were more concerned about consumers, other businesses, or both?

3. If you were an executive of Microsoft faced with multiple antitrust actions in different regions of the world, how would you respond?

4. What do you think is the best remedy for Microsoft's market dominance: structural, conduct, intellectual property, or something else? Why do you think so?

PART FIVE

The Corporation and the Natural Environment

CHAPTER ELEVEN

Ecology and Sustainable Development in Global Business

The world community faces unprecedented ecological challenges in the 21st century. Many political and business leaders have embraced the idea of sustainable development, calling for economic growth without destroying the natural environment or depleting the resources on which future generations depend. Yet the concept has remained controversial, and implementation has been difficult. The task for government policy makers and corporate leaders will be to find ways to meet both economic and environmental goals in the coming decades, without sacrificing either.

This chapter focuses on these key learning objectives:

- Defining sustainable development.
- Understanding the obstacles to developing the world's economy to meet the needs of the present without hurting future generations.
- Assessing the major threats to the Earth's ecosystem.
- Recognizing the ways in which population growth, inequality, and industrialization have accelerated the world's ecological crisis.
- Examining common environmental issues that are shared by all nations.
- Analyzing the steps the global business community can take to reduce ecological damage and promote sustainable development.

In 1992, representatives of the world's nations gathered in Rio de Janeiro, Brazil, for a groundbreaking event, the first World Summit on Sustainable Development. In a series of contentious sessions, delegates considered, on one hand, the growing dangers of environmental degradation and, on the other hand, the urgent need for economic development in poorer nations. Would it be possible, they asked, to foster economic growth sufficient to lift the majority of the world's people out of poverty without compromising the ability of future generations to meet their own needs?

Now, a decade and a half later, progress toward achieving these goals had been in many respects disappointing. Consider that at the 1992 gathering:

- Delegates had pledged to attack the problem of global warming, increases in the Earth's temperature caused in part by carbon dioxide emissions from the world's factories, utilities, and vehicles. The conference had called on developed countries to cut back to 1990 levels by the year 2000. But only half the developed countries had met this target, and annual emissions of carbon dioxide had reached new highs, threatening disruption of the world's climate. The United States, the world's largest emitter of greenhouse gases, had not signed an international treaty to curb carbon emissions.[1]

- Delegates had committed to a framework Convention on Biological Diversity, dedicated to conserving the earth's biological resources, particularly in species-rich tropical forests. But many plants and animals remained endangered. Vast stretches of rain forest had been cut down. In Indonesia, for example, home to large numbers of endangered birds, mammals, and reptiles, tropical forest was being logged for timber and burned to clear land at an astonishing rate, destroying habitat and, not incidentally, causing serious air pollution throughout Southeast Asia.[2]

- Many developed nations had pledged to increase foreign aid to 0.7 percent of their gross national income (GNI) to help poorer countries develop their economies in an environmentally sustainable way. But during the intervening years, aid had actually fallen to just 0.26 percent of GNI, lower than it was in 1992.[3] Now the question was just as urgent as it had been before: Who would pay for the costs of clean development in the poorer countries?

However, important progress had been made. Although the world population was still growing, the rate of growth had dropped somewhat. The World Bank, an important lender to developing countries, had instituted a strict environmental review process, refusing to fund ecologically destructive projects. Important gains had been made in efforts to restore the health of the ozone layer. Many nations, notably in Europe, had made progress on energy conservation. And possibly most promisingly, many segments of the global business community had become increasingly active in promoting environmentally sound management practices. Could the world's governments, businesses, nongovernmental organizations, and individuals, working together, meet the ecological challenges of the 21st century and put the global economy on a more sustainable course?[4]

---

[1] The Web site for the United Nations Framework Convention on Climate Change is available at *http://unfccc.int.*

[2] The Web site for the Convention on Biological Diversity is available at *www.biodiv.org.*

[3] Data on percent of GNI devoted to development assistance by industrialized nations are available at the Web site of the Organization for Economic Cooperation and Development, Development Assistance Committee, at *www.oecd.org/dac.*

[4] For current data, including the biannual report *Global Environmental Outlook,* see the Web site of the United Nations Environment Programme at *www.unep.org.*

Ecological Challenges

Humankind is now altering the face of the planet, rivaling the forces of nature herself—glaciers, volcanoes, asteroids, and earthquakes—in impact. Human beings have literally rerouted rivers, moved mountains, and burned forests. By the last decade of the 20th century, human society had transformed about half of the earth's ice-free surface and made a major impact on most of the rest. In many areas, as much land was used by transportation systems as by agriculture. Although significant natural resources—fossil fuels, fresh water, fertile land, and forest—remained, exploding populations and rapid industrialization had reached the point where, by some measures, the demands of human society had already exceeded the carrying capacity of the earth's ecosystem.

Ecology is the study of how living things—plants and animals—interact with one another in such a unified natural system, or ecosystem. Damage to the ecosystem in one part of the world often affects people in other locations. Depletion of the ozone layer, destruction of the rain forests, and species extinctions have an impact on all of society, not just particular regions or nations.

The Global Commons

Throughout history, communities of people have created *commons*. A **commons** is a shared resource, such as land, air, or water, that a group of people use collectively. The paradox of the commons is that if all individuals attempt to maximize their own private advantage in the short term, the commons may be destroyed, and all users, present and future, lose. The only solution is restraint, either voluntary or through mutual agreement.[5] The tragedy of the commons—that freedom in a commons brings ruin to all—is illustrated by the following parable.

> There was once a village on the shore of a great ocean. Its people made a good living from the rich fishing grounds that lay offshore, the bounty of which seemed inexhaustible. Some of the cleverest fishermen began to experiment with new ways to catch more fish, borrowing money to buy bigger and better equipped boats. Since it was hard to argue with success, others copied their new techniques. Soon fish began to be harder to find, and their average size began to decline. Eventually, the fishery collapsed, bringing economic calamity to the village. A wise elder commented, "You see, the fish were not free after all. It was our folly to act as if they were."[6]

In a sense, we live today in a global commons, in which many natural resources, like the fishing grounds in this parable, are used collectively. The image of the earth as seen from space, a blue-and-green globe, girdled by white clouds, floating in blackness, dramatically shows us that we share a single, unified ecosystem. Preserving our common ecosystem and assuring its continued use is a new imperative for governments, business, and society. As we move into the 21st century, to quote Maurice Strong, secretary general of the 1992 World Summit, "We now face the ultimate management challenge, that of managing our own future as a species."

[5] Garrett Hardin, "Tragedy of the Commons," *Science* 162 (December 1968), pp. 1243–48.

[6] Abridgment of "The Story of a Fishing Village," from *1994 Information Please Environmental Almanac.* copyright © 1993 by World Resources Institute. Reprinted by permission of Houghton Mifflin Co. All rights reserved.

Sustainable Development

The need for balance between economic and environmental considerations is captured in the concept of **sustainable development.** This term refers to development that "meets the needs of the present without compromising the ability of future generations to meet their own needs."[7] The concept includes two core ideas:

- Protecting the environment will require economic development. Poverty is an underlying cause of environmental degradation. People who lack food, shelter, and basic amenities misuse resources just to survive. For this reason, environmental protection will require providing a decent standard of living for all the world's citizens.

- But economic development must be accomplished sustainably, that is, in a way that conserves the earth's resources for future generations. Growth cannot occur at the expense of degrading the forests, farmland, water, and air that must continue to support life on this planet. We must leave the earth in as good shape—or better shape—than we found it.

In short, the idea of sustainable development encompasses a kind of puzzle. It challenges government and business leaders to eradicate poverty and develop the world economy but to do so in a way that does not degrade the environment or plunder natural resources.

Sustainable development is an appealing idea but also a controversial one. For sustainable development to work, rich nations such as the United States and Japan would have to consume fewer resources and dramatically cut pollution, without simply exporting environmental stresses to other countries. Developing nations, such as Brazil or Pakistan, for their part, would have to use less destructive agricultural practices, cut birthrates, and industrialize more cleanly. This would be possible only with the aid of money, technology, and skills from the developed nations.

What would the idea of sustainable development mean for business? One attempt to apply this concept to business operations has been made by an initiative in Sweden called The Natural Step, described in Exhibit 11.A. Other voluntary efforts by the global business community to operate with less harm to the environment are addressed in the last section of this chapter and in Chapter 12.

Threats to the Earth's Ecosystem

Sustainable development requires that human society use natural resources at a rate that can be continued over an indefinite period. Human activity affects three major forms of natural resources: water, air, and land. Biologists distinguish between *renewable* resources, such as fresh water or forests, that can be naturally replenished and *nonrenewable* resources, such as fossil fuels (oil, gas, and coal), that once used are gone forever. Many natural resources, renewable and nonrenewable, are now being depleted or polluted at well above sustainable rates. Consider the following examples.

Water Resources

Only 3 percent of the water on the Earth is fresh, and most of this is underground or locked up in ice and snow. Only about one-tenth of 1 percent of the Earth's water is in

[7]World Commission on Environment and Development, *Our Common Future* (Oxford: Oxford University Press, 1987), p. 8

Exhibit 11.A   The Natural Step

The Natural Step (TNS) was founded in 1989 by a prominent Swedish physician, Karl-Henrik Robert. Dr. Robert joined other leading scientists in Sweden to develop a consensus document on how businesses, governments, and individuals could act in a way that was consistent with the principle of sustainable development. Their report was endorsed by the King of Sweden, and a summary was distributed to all households in the country.

The Natural Step encouraged businesses to act voluntarily to cut back on the use of synthetics and nonrenewable resources, minimize their consumption of energy, and preserve natural diversity and ecosystems. Within a decade, more than 300 companies and half the cities in Sweden had adopted TNS principles, and the movement was spreading to other countries, including the United States, the Netherlands, and Australia. An example of a company that has followed The Natural Step is IKEA, the Swedish-based global home-furnishings retailer. IKEA signed on, committing itself to the use of materials, technologies, and transportation methods that had the least possible damaging effect on the environment. For example, the company switched from truck to rail shipping where possible to conserve fuel and introduced a new line of furnishings, called the Eco-Line, that used only recycled materials or wood and fibers that had been sustainably harvested. The company said the initiative not only had enabled it to protect the environment and attract "green" customers, it had also actually helped the bottom line by avoiding waste and saving on energy and materials.

Sources: Hilary Bradbury and Judith A. Clair, "Promoting Sustainable Organizations with Sweden's Natural Step," *Academy of Management Executive* 13, no. 4 (November 1999), pp. 63–74; Andrea Larson and Joel E. Reichart, "IKEA and The Natural Step," Darden School of Management, University of Virginia, 1996. IKEA's corporate Web site, including material on the company's environmental policies, is available at *www.ikea-group.ikea.com.* The Web site of The Natural Step in the United States is at *www.naturalstep.org.*

lakes, rivers, and accessible underground supplies, and thus available for human use. Water is, of course, renewable: Moisture evaporates from the oceans and returns to earth as freshwater precipitation, replenishing used stocks. But in many areas, humans are using up or polluting water faster than it can be replaced or naturally purified, threatening people and businesses that depend on it.

> The Ganges River supports more than 400 million Indians, providing water for drinking, irrigation, fishing, transportation, and trade along its 1,500 mile course from high in the Himalayan mountains to the coastal city of Kolkata (Calcutta). Hindus believe the river to be holy, and it is the site of many religious observances. But the Ganges is increasingly polluted, choked with raw sewage, industrial waste, animal carcasses, and even human remains. "Our forefathers worshipped this river; today, it is killing us," said one Indian.[8]

By one estimate, if society were able to eliminate all pollution, capture all available fresh water, and distribute it equitably—all of which are unlikely—demand would exceed the supply within a hundred years. In the mid-2000s, water shortages had already caused the decline of local economies and in some cases had contributed to regional conflicts. In Africa, for example, water disputes had flared among Egypt, Ethiopia, and Sudan, the three countries traversed by the world's longest river, the Nile. In the Middle East, disagreement over access to water from the River Jordan had exacerbated conflict between

[8]"India's Holiest River, The Ganges, Brings Disease and Pollution," Associated Press, May 7, 2002; "New Delhi: A Sewer Runs Through It," *The Toronto Star*, November 6, 1999.

Israel and Palestine.[9] According to a United Nations study, one-third of the world's population lives in countries experiencing moderate to high water stress.[10]

Fossil Fuels

Fossil fuels, unlike water, are nonrenewable. Human society used 60 times as much energy in the late 20th century as it did in 1860, when industrialization was in its early stages. Most of this came from the burning of fossil fuels; 80 percent of all commercial energy comes from the combustion of coal, oil, and natural gas. The amount of fossil fuel burned by the world economy in one year took about a million years to form, and only one barrel is discovered for every three or four consumed. No one knows how much longer it will be possible to produce oil economically. However, some recent estimates suggest that oil production will peak sometime between 2010 and 2020.[11] Coal reserves are plentiful and could last three to four more centuries, although coal is more polluting than either oil or natural gas. Eventually, however, many fossil fuel reserves will be depleted, and the world economy will need to become much more energy efficient and switch to renewable energy sources, such as those based on water, wind, and sunshine.

Arable Land

Arable (fertile) land is necessary to grow crops to feed the world's people. Land, if properly cared for, is a renewable resource. Although the productivity of land increased through much of the 20th century, by the mid-2000s much of the world's arable land was threatened with decline. About half of irrigated farmland in developing countries required reclamation because of salinization (excess salt) or poor drainage. In many areas, overly intensive farming practices had caused previously arable land to turn into desert. In 2001, a massive dust storm caused by overgrazed grasslands in China blew all the way across the Pacific, darkening skies over North America.[12] The United Nations has estimated that 10 million hectares of arable land are lost every year to desertification (one hectare equals about two and a half acres).[13]

Forces of Change

Pressure on the earth's resource base is becoming increasingly severe. Three critical factors have combined to accelerate the ecological crisis facing the world community and to make sustainable development more difficult. These are population growth, world income inequality, and the rapid industrialization of many developing nations.

The Population Explosion

A major driver of environmental degradation is the exponential growth of the world's population. A population that doubled every 50 years, for example, would be said to be growing exponentially. Many more people would be added during the second 50 years

---

[9] "Water Wars: Climate Change May Spark Conflict," *The Independent,* February 28, 2006.

[10] A report on world water resources may be found at *www.wri.org/wri/trends/water.html.* For a projection of water stress levels in 2025, see the United Nations Environmental Program *Global Environmental Outlook* at *www.unep.org/geo2000/english/i42a.htm.*

[11] "Peak Oil Forum," *World Watch,* January/February 2006, available online at *www.worldwatch.org.* The Web site of the Association for the Study of Peak Oil and Gas may be found at *www.peakoil.net.*

[12] This dust storm was tracked by NASA; see *http://science.nasa.gov.*

[13] "Implementation of Desertification Convention Seen as Key to Promoting Sustainable Development, Fighting Poverty in Drylands," available online at *www.johannesburgsummit.org/html/whats_new/otherstories_desertification.htm.*

FIGURE 11.1
World Population Growth

Source: United Nations Population Division, "Long-Range World Population Projections," November 23, 2005. These figures represent the medium-range scenario. Other estimates are higher and lower. All estimates are available at *www.un.org/esa /population.*

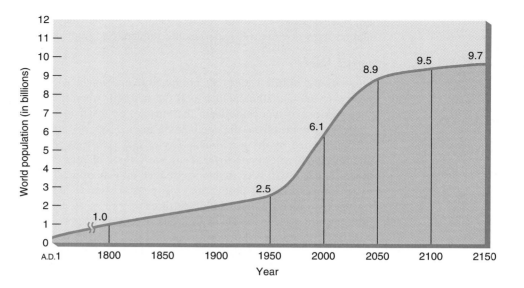

than during the first, even though the rate of growth would stay the same. Just 10,000 years ago, the earth was home to no more than 10 million humans, scattered in small settlements. For many thousands of years, population growth was gradual. Around 1950, as shown in Figure 11.1, the world population reached 2.5 billion. World population crossed the 6 billion mark in 1999. The United Nations estimates that the population will eventually level out at just under 10 billion around 2150. To gain some perspective on these figures, consider that someone born in 1950 who lives to be 75 years old will have seen the world's population increase by more than 5 billion people.

This growth will not be distributed equally. In the industrialized countries, especially in Europe, population growth has already slowed. About 95 percent of the world's population growth over the next 30 years is predicted to be in less developed countries, especially in Africa, Latin America, and Asia.

The world's burgeoning population will put increasing strain on the earth's resources. Each additional person uses raw materials and adds pollutants to the land, air, and water. The world's total industrial production would have to quintuple over the next 40 years just to maintain the same standard of living that people have now. Protecting the environment in the face of rapid population growth is very difficult. For example, in some parts of western Africa, population growth has put great pressure on available farmland, which is not allowed to lie fallow. Because much of the available firewood has already been cut, people use livestock dung for fuel instead of fertilizer. The result has been a deepening cycle of poverty, as more and more people try to live off less and less productive land.

World Income Inequality

A second important cause of environmental degradation is the inequality between rich and poor. Although economic development has raised living standards for many, large numbers of the world's people continue to live in severe poverty. According to the most recent estimates, around 2.5 billion people (about 40 percent of the world's population) had incomes below the international poverty line of $2 a day. These people, most of them in sub-Saharan Africa, South Asia, East Asia, and the Pacific, lived very near the margin

FIGURE 11.2
World Income Distributed by Deciles (Tenths) of the Population, 2000

Source: Yuri Dikhanov, "Trends in Global Income Distribution, 1970–2000, and Scenarios for 2015," United Nations Development Programme, Human Development Report Office Occasional Paper, 2005, p. 12.

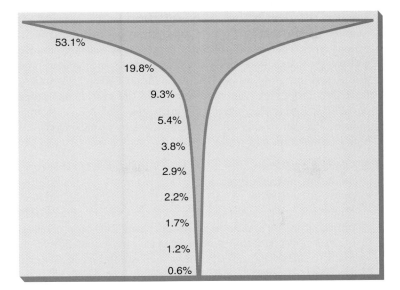

53.1%
19.8%
9.3%
5.4%
3.8%
2.9%
2.2%
1.7%
1.2%
0.6%

of subsistence. They had only a tiny fraction of the goods and services enjoyed by those in the industrialized nations.[14]

> Some of the most extreme poverty is found on the outskirts of rapidly growing cities in developing countries. In many parts of the world, people have moved to urban areas in search of work. Often, they must live in slums, in makeshift dwellings without sanitation or running water. In Bangkok, Thailand, a sprawling city of 9 million, 20 percent of the population live in such areas. In Manila in the Philippines, where a quarter of the 10 million inhabitants live in squatter settlements, hundreds died when a garbage dump nearby shifted, burying scores of people.

The world's income is not distributed equally. The United Nations' 2005 *Human Development Report* found that the gap between the richest and poorest countries was large and getting larger. The income of the average American, for example, was 61 times the income of the average Tanzanian. The richest 20 percent of the world's people held 73 percent of the income; the poorest 20 percent held just 2 percent.[15] Figure 11.2 shows how just how inequitably the world's income is distributed.

Inequality is an environmental problem because countries (and people) at either extreme of income tend to behave in more environmentally destructive ways than those in the middle. People in the richest countries consume far more fossil fuels, wood, and meat, for example. People in the poorest countries, for their part, often misuse natural resources just to survive, for example, cutting down trees for fuel to cook food and keep warm.

Parts of the Third World are industrializing at a rapid pace. This is positive because it holds out the promise of reducing poverty and slowing population growth. But

[14] United Nations Development Programme, *Human Development Report 2005* (New York: Oxford University Press, 2005); and Yuri Dikhanov, "Trends in Global Income Distribution, 1970–2000, and Scenarios for 2015," United Nations Development Programme, 2005.

[15] *Human Development Report 2005*, pp. 36–37.

economic development has also contributed to the growing ecological crisis. Industry requires energy, much of which comes from burning fossil fuels, releasing pollutants of various types. The complex chemical processes of industry produce undesirable by-products and wastes that pollute land, water, and air. Its mechanical processes often create dust, grime, and unsightly refuse. The agricultural "green" revolution, although it has greatly increased crop yields in many parts of the world, has caused contamination from pesticides, herbicides, chemical fertilizers, and refuse from cattle-feeding factories. Industrialization is also often accompanied by rising incomes, bringing higher rates of both consumption and waste.

> China dramatically illustrates the tight connection between industrial develop-
> ment and environmental risk. China is one of the fastest-growing economies in
> the world, expanding at a rate approaching 10 percent annually. The evidence of
> industrialization is everywhere, from skyscrapers under construction, to cars
> crowding the streets, to factories operating 24/7 to produce goods for export. Yet
> a major consequence has been increased pollution. Fifty-eight percent of China's
> main rivers are too dirty for human consumption. In Beijing, residents can rarely
> see nearby mountains because of bad air. The country has some of the world's
> worst acid rain, and 30 percent of its agricultural land is acidified, according to
> the Worldwatch Institute. China and other fast-growing developing nations chal-
> lenge business and society to "leapfrog" stages and move directly to cleaner
> technologies and methods of production.[16]

The Limits to Growth

Some observers believe that the earth's rapid population growth, people's rising expectations, and the industrialization of less developed countries are on a collision course with a fixed barrier: the limited **carrying capacity** of the earth's ecosystem. In this view, the world's resource base, the air, water, soil, minerals, and so forth, is essentially finite, or bounded. If human societies use up resources faster than they can be replenished, and create waste faster than it can be dispersed, environmental devastation will be the inevitable result.[17] According to *Beyond the Limits* by Donella Meadows and her colleagues, human society is already overshooting the carrying capacity of the Earth's ecosystem. Just as it is possible to eat or drink too much before your body sends you a signal to stop, so too are people and businesses using up resources and emitting pollution at an unsustainable rate. But because of delays in feedback, society will not understand the consequences of its actions until the damage has been done. One method of measuring the Earth's carrying capacity, and how far human society has exceeded it, is called the **ecological footprint**. This approach is described in Exhibit 11.B.

If human society does not change its practices, a collapse may occur, possibly within the lifetimes of many who are alive today. What kind of collapse? Meadows and her colleagues developed several computer models to predict what would happen under different scenarios. If the world continued on its present course, with no major technical or policy changes, they predicted that by the year 2015, food production would begin to

---

[16] Worldwatch Institute, *State of the World 2006: Special Focus—China and India* (New York: W.W. Norton, 2006).

[17] Herman E. Daly, *Beyond Growth: The Economics of Sustainable Development* (Boston: Beacon Press, 1996); Paul Hawken, Amory Lovins, and L. Hunter Lovins, *Natural Capitalism: Creating the Next Industrial Revolution* (Boston: Little, Brown, 1999); Kenneth Arrow et al., "Economic Growth, Carrying Capacity, and the Environment," *Science* 28 (April 1995).

Exhibit 11.B   The Ecological Footprint

The term *ecological footprint* has been defined as the amount of land and water a human population needs to produce the resources it consumes and to absorb its wastes, given prevailing technology.

In 2005, for each living human being, the earth contained 4.4 acres of biologically productive area—farmland, forest, fresh water, and so forth. That year, each person had, on average, an ecological footprint of 5.4 acres. What that means is that human society was using resources at a rate well above what the earth's ecosystem could sustainably support. (Overshooting the earth's carrying capacity is possible in the short run because people can consume resources without allowing them to regenerate.) Historical data show that human resource use first exceeded world ecological capacity in the late 1980s, and the gap between the two has been widening steadily since then.

Not surprisingly, some nations and individuals have bigger ecological footprints than others. For example, in the United States the average citizen has an ecological footprint of 24 acres, more than 5 times their share of the world's resources. By comparison, in Panama the average citizen's ecological footprint is 4.2 acres, and in Tanzania it is just 1.7 acres. In part, a nation's footprint size is a function of affluence: rich societies tend to use more resources per person. But footprint size also reflects national policy and individual choices. The Netherlands, for example, is a relatively affluent nation, but has a footprint of 10.9 acres per person, less than half that of the United States, because of a strong public commitment to sustainability.

Source: Global Footprint Network, at *www.footprintnetwork.org.* Individuals can estimate their own ecological footprint by taking a quiz available at *www.myfootprint.org.*

fall, as pollution degraded the fertility of the land. Around 2020, nonrenewable resources such as oil would begin to run out, and more and more resources would be needed to find, extract, and refine what remained. By midcentury, industrial production would begin to collapse, pulling down with it the service and agricultural sectors. Life expectancy and population would fall soon after, as death rates were driven up by lack of food and health care.[18]

Critics of the **limits to growth hypothesis** suggest that these doomsday predictions are unnecessarily bleak. In their view, the hypothesis fails to consider the effect of market forces. For example, as natural resources such as oil and gas become scarcer, their prices will rise, and people and businesses may be motivated to use natural resources more efficiently or to find substitutes, such as solar power. In addition, technological advances may slow environmental degradation. For example, the U.S. Energy Department is developing a design for an innovative coal-burning power plant that would extract nonpolluting hydrogen to power fuel-cells and pump carbon-dioxide deep into the earth where it would not cause atmospheric warming.[19] Substitutes can be developed for nonrenewable resources. For example, in photography, digitalization makes the use of silver unnecessary; in telecommunications fiber optics are replacing copper wire. Defenders of *Beyond the Limits* acknowledge these points but stick to their conclusion that if human society does not adopt sustainable development, economic and social catastrophe are just a matter of time.[20]

[18] Donella H. Meadows, Dennis L. Meadows, and Jorgen Randers, *Beyond the Limits: Confronting Global Collapse, Envisioning a Sustainable Future* (Boston: Chelsea Green, 1992).

[19] "U.S. Seeking Cleaner Model of Coal Plant," *The New York Times,* February 28, 2003.

[20] For a critique of the limits to growth hypothesis, see Bjorn Lomborg and Olivier Rubin, "Limits to Growth," *Foreign Policy,* November/December 2002, online at *www.foreignpolicy.com.* Lomborg's views are fully elaborated in his book *The Skeptical Environmentalist* (Cambridge: Cambridge University Press, 2001). A defense of the limits to growth view by Keith Suter on Australian television, titled "Fair Warning," may be found online at *www.abc.net.au/science /slab/rome/default.htm.* Allen Hammond, in *Which World? Scenarios for the 21st Century* (Washington, DC: Island Press, 1998), contrasts three possible future environmental scenarios that might arise under differing conditions.

Global Environmental Issues

Some environmental problems are inherently global in scope and require international cooperation. Typically these are issues pertaining to the global commons, that is, resources shared by all nations. Four global problems that will have major consequences for business and society are ozone depletion, global warming, decline of biodiversity, and threats to the world's oceans.

Ozone Depletion

Ozone is a bluish gas, composed of three bonded oxygen atoms, that floats in a thin layer in the stratosphere between 8 and 25 miles above the planet. Although poisonous to humans in the lower atmosphere, ozone in the stratosphere is critical to life on earth by absorbing dangerous ultraviolet light from the sun. Too much ultraviolet light can cause skin cancer and damage the eyes and immune systems of humans and other species.

In 1974, scientists first hypothesized that chlorofluorocarbons (CFCs), manufactured chemicals widely used as refrigerants, insulation, solvents, and propellants in spray cans, could react with and destroy ozone. Little evidence existed of actual ozone depletion, however, until 1985, when scientists discovered a thin spot, or hole, in the ozone layer over Antarctica. Studies showed that in the upper atmosphere, intense solar rays had split CFC molecules, releasing chlorine atoms that had reacted with and destroyed ozone. Scientists later found evidence of ozone depletion in the northern latitudes over Europe and North America during the summer, when the sun's ultraviolet rays are the strongest and pose the greatest danger.

World political leaders moved quickly in response to scientific evidence that CFCs posed a threat to the earth's protective ozone shield. In 1987, a group of nations negotiated the **Montreal Protocol,** agreeing to cut CFC production; the agreement was later amended to ban CFCs, along with several other ozone-depleting chemicals. Developing countries were given until 2010 to phase out CFCs completely. As of 2006, 189 countries, all but a tiny handful, had signed the protocol.[21]

By the turn of the century, most businesses in the developed world had completed the transition to CFC substitutes, and many had made money by doing so. Du Pont, Allied Signal, Elf-Altochem, and several other chemical companies had developed profitable substitutes for banned ozone-depleting chemicals. All the major appliance manufacturers, such as Electrolux in Sweden and Whirlpool in the United States, had brought out successful new lines of CFC-free refrigerators and freezers, and carmakers had developed air-conditioners that operated without the dangerous coolant.

Have the Montreal Protocol and business efforts to respond to it been successful? One scientific study found that the concentration of ozone-depleting chemicals in the atmosphere peaked in 1994, and then began a slow decline. The authors predicted that, because of a lag effect, the highest levels of ozone depletion would occur in the early 2000s. The protective layer would then recover gradually, provided that regulations continued to be

---

[21] The text of the Montreal Protocol and its various amendments and a list of signatories may be found at *http://ozone.unep.org.*

FIGURE 11.3
Global Warming

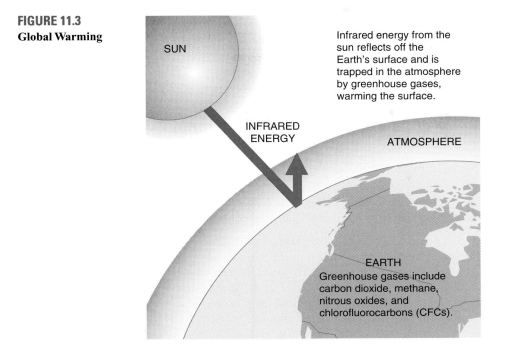

effective.[22] The world community still faces the challenge of restricting the manufacture of other ozone-depleting substances not yet fully regulated by treaty. But overall, this is an example of world governments working together effectively to address a global environmental threat.

Global Warming

Another difficult problem facing the world community is the gradual warming of the Earth's atmosphere. Although uncertainty remains about the rate and causes of **global warming,** business and governments have begun to respond to the issue.

The Earth's atmosphere contains carbon dioxide and other trace gases that, like the glass panels in a greenhouse, prevent some of the heat reflected from the Earth's surface from escaping into space, as illustrated in Figure 11.3. Without this so-called greenhouse effect, the Earth would be too cold to support life. Since the Industrial Revolution, which began in the late 1700s, the amount of greenhouse gases in the atmosphere has increased by as much as 25 percent, largely due to the burning of fossil fuels such as oil and natural gas. According to the Intergovernmental Panel on Climate Change (IPCC), a group of the world's leading atmospheric scientists, the earth has already warmed by between 0.3 and 0.6 degrees Celsius over the past century. (One degree Celsius equals 1.8 degrees Fahrenheit, the unit commonly used in the United States.) If societal emissions of greenhouse gases continue to grow unchecked, the IPCC predicted, the Earth could warm by as much as 6 degrees Celsius more by 2100, and possibly even more.[23]

[22] World Meteorological Organization, National Oceanic and Atmospheric Administration, National Aeronautics and Space Administration, European Commission, and United Nations Environment Program, "Scientific Assessment of Ozone Depletion: 1998." An executive summary may be found at *www.al.noaa.gov/wwwhd/pubdocs/Assessment98/executive-summary.html #A.*

[23] A complete set of materials may be found at IPCC's Web site at *www.ipcc.ch.*

The possible causes of global warming are numerous. The burning of fossil fuels, which releases carbon dioxide, is the leading contributor. But consider the following additional causes.[24]

- *Deforestation*. Trees and other plants absorb carbon dioxide, removing it from the atmosphere. Deforestation—cutting down and not replacing trees—thus contributes to global warming. Burning forests to clear land for grazing or agriculture also releases carbon directly into the atmosphere as a component of smoke. Large-scale deforestation thus contributes in two ways to global warming.
- *Beef production*. Methane, a potent greenhouse gas, is produced as a by-product of the digestion of some animals, including cows. Large-scale cattle ranching releases significant amounts of methane.
- *CFCs*. In addition to destroying the ozone, these are also greenhouse gases. The Montreal Protocol will have the unintended beneficial consequence of slowing global warming.

If global warming continues, the world may experience extreme heat waves, air pollution crises, violent storms, damaging wildfires, and even epidemics of tropical diseases in the 21st century. The polar ice caps may partially melt, raising sea levels and causing flooding in low-lying coastal areas such as Florida, Bangladesh, and the Netherlands. It may become as difficult to grow wheat in Iowa as it is now in arid Utah. Such climate change could devastate many of the world's economies and destroy the habitats of many species.[25]

In 1997, many of the world's nations gathered in Kyoto, Japan, to consider amendments to the Convention on Climate Change, an international treaty on global warming. In difficult negotiations, the parties hammered out an agreement called the **Kyoto Protocol** that would require industrial countries to reduce greenhouse gas emissions more than 5 percent below 1990 levels, over a period of several years. The Kyoto Protocol went into effect in 2005, after countries representing 55 percent of the world's carbon emissions had ratified it. The European Union took an immediate lead, restricting the amount of carbon that could be emitted by power, steel, paper, cement, and glass plants. An official there commented that although compliance with Kyoto would cost money in the short run, energy conservation would cause European firms to become "leaner and more efficient, and that could turn into a long-term business advantage."[26] By 2006, 161 nations, representing 62 percent of the world's carbon emissions, had ratified; the United States, the world's largest producer of carbon emissions, was a notable exception.[27] (The United States declined to ratify the treaty on the grounds it would harm the U.S. economy.)

Addressing the challenge of climate change will require action not only by governments, but also by the world corporate community. The efforts of several business organizations to reduce their carbon emissions are profiled in Exhibit 11.C.

Decline of Biodiversity

Biodiversity refers to the number and variety of species and the range of their genetic makeup. To date, approximately 1.7 million species of plants and animals have been named

---

[24] For a collection of diverse views on global warming, see Andrew J. Hoffman, ed., *Global Climate Change: A Senior Level Debate at the Intersection of Economics, Strategy, Technology, Science, Politics, and International Negotiations* (San Francisco: New Lexington Press, 1997).

[25] Photographs of observable evidence of global warming appear in "Signs from Earth: Heating Up, Melting Down," *National Geographic*, September 2004.

[26] "New Limits on Pollution Herald Change in Europe," *The New York Times*, January 1, 2005.

[27] The Web site of the U.N. Framework Convention on Climate Change is at *http://unfccc.int*.

Exhibit 11.C   Trading Carbon

In 2003, the Chicago Climate Exchange (CCX) opened for business. Unlike other trading exchanges operating out of the Windy City, the CCX did not trade pork bellies or soybean futures but something even more exotic—carbon emissions credits. A group of large American companies, including Ford, DuPont, International Paper, and BP America, had come together to launch the project. The participating companies agreed to reduce their overall carbon emissions—a major cause of global warming—by 2 percent from their 1999 levels in the first year, and then another 1 percent a year thereafter. Companies that did not meet these goals would have to buy credits from other companies that had earned them by exceeding their goals. Participants could also earn credits by supporting projects that removed carbon from the atmosphere, such as reforestation or energy efficiency. By 2005, the exchange had more than 100 members, including companies, municipalities, and even some universities. What was remarkable about the whole experiment was that it was entirely voluntary, since the United States had not ratified the Kyoto Protocol, and no U.S. law required companies to cut their carbon emissions.

Sources: "Voluntary Scheme Proves Its Point," *Financial Times* (London), July 6, 2005, p. 32; "Trading Hot Air: A New Approach to Global Warming," *The Economist,* October 17, 2002; "Firms Start Trading Program for Greenhouse Gas Emissions," *The Washington Post,* January 17, 2003, p. A14; and "New Market Shows Industry Moving on Global Warming," *The Wall Street Journal,* January 16, 2003, pp. A1, A8.

and described. Many scientists believe these are but a fraction of the total. The earth contains at least 10 million species and possibly more than 100 million. Scientists estimate that species extinction is now occurring at 100 to 1,000 times the normal, background rate, mainly because of pollution and the destruction of habitat by human society. Biological diversity is now at its lowest level since the disappearance of the dinosaurs some 65 million years ago. The eminent biologist Edward O. Wilson has eloquently stated the costs of this loss:

> Every species extinction diminishes humanity. Every microorganism, animal, and plant contains on the order of from one million to 10 billion bits of information in its genetic code, hammered into existence by an astronomical number of mutations and episodes of natural selection over the course of thousands or even millions of years of evolution. . . . Species diversity—the world's available gene pool—is one of our planet's most important and irreplaceable resources. . . . As species are exterminated, largely as the result of habitat destruction, the capacity for natural genetic regeneration is greatly reduced. In Norman Myers' phrase, we are causing the death of birth.[28]

Genetic diversity is vital to each species' ability to adapt and survive and has many benefits for human society as well. By destroying this biological diversity, we are actually undermining our survivability as a species.

A major reason for the decline in the earth's biodiversity is the destruction of rain forests, particularly in the tropics. Rain forests are woodlands that receive at least 100 inches of rain a year. They are the planet's richest areas in terms of biological diversity. Rain forests cover only about 7 percent of the earth's surface but account for somewhere between 50 and 90 percent of the earth's species. Only about half of the original tropical rain forests still stand, and at the rate they are currently being cut, all will be gone or severely depleted within 30 years. The reasons for destruction of rain forests include

[28] Edward O. Wilson, "Threats to Biodiversity," in *Managing Planet Earth: Readings from Scientific American Magazine* (New York: W. H. Freeman, 1990), pp. 57–58. This article originally appeared in *Scientific American,* September 1989. Used by permission.

commercial logging, cattle ranching, and conversion of forest to plantations to produce cash crops for export. Overpopulation also plays a part, as landless people clear forest to grow crops and cut trees for firewood.

The destruction is ironic because rain forests may have more economic value standing than cut. Rain forests are the source of many valuable products, including foods, medicines, and fibers. The pharmaceutical industry, for example, each year develops new medicines based on newly discovered plants from tropical areas. The U.S. National Cancer Institute has identified 1,400 tropical forest plants with cancer-fighting properties. As rain forests are destroyed, so too is this potential for new medicines. The Convention on Biological Diversity, an international treaty first negotiated in 1992, addresses many of these issues. By 2006 it had been ratified by 188 countries. (The United States was not among them; it declined to ratify, citing concerns with provisions on intellectual property rights and financial assistance to developing countries.) The treaty commits these countries to draw up national strategies for conservation, to protect ecosystems and individual species, and to take steps to restore degraded areas. It also allows countries to share in the profits from sales of products derived from their biological resources.

Threats to Marine Ecosystems

A final issue of concern is threats to the world's **marine ecosystems.** This term refers broadly to oceans and the salt marshes, lagoons, and tidal zones that border them, as well as the diverse communities of life that they support. Salt water covers 70 percent of the earth's surface and is home to a great variety of species, from tiny plankton to the giant blue whale, from kelp beds to mangrove forests. Marine ecosystems are important to human society in many ways. Fish, marine mammals, and sea plants provide food and other useful products such as fertilizer, animal feed, cooking and heating oil, medicines, clothing, and jewelry. Healthy coastal zones protect coastlines from erosion and filter run-off from the land. Many communities have survived for centuries off the bounty of the sea.

Today, the health of these ecosystems is increasingly threatened. Some of the key issues include the following:

Fish populations. Oceans provide 90 percent of the world's fish catch. The United Nations has estimated that of the world's commercial fish species, almost one-fourth are overexploited or depleted, and some fisheries—such as those for cod off the Grand Banks (eastern United States and Canada) and for anchovies off Peru—have probably been permanently destroyed by overfishing. Active management, such as limiting the number of fishing boats, establishing fish quotas, or banning fishing for periods of time, has allowed fish to regenerate in some areas.

Coral reefs. Coral reefs are limestone structures that develop from the skeletons of aquatic life and are host to great biological diversity. Today, however, they are in decline from pollution, oceanic warming, damage from ships, and cyanide and dynamite fishing. The Nature Conservancy estimates that at their current rate of decline, 70 percent of coral reefs will be gone within 50 years.

Coastal development. Much of the world's population growth is now concentrated in coastal areas, often in ecologically fragile areas. In the United States, for example, 50 percent of the population lives in counties bordering the ocean—which comprise just 17 percent of the land. Inappropriate development can put pressure on ecologically fragile areas.[29]

[29] Pew Charitable Trusts, "Coastal Sprawl: The Effects of Urban Development on Aquatic Ecosystems in the United States," available at *www.pewtrusts.org.*

One group of businesses whose actions directly affect the health of the oceans is the cruise ship industry.

> In 2006, more than 200 cruise ships, many carrying 5,000 or more passengers and crew members, plied the world's seas. By 2010, 14 million people a year are expected to take a cruise vacation. Cruise ships are literally floating cities, producing on average 30,000 gallons of human waste and seven tons of garbage and solid waste a day. Under international agreements, beyond 12 miles from shore, cruise ships are permitted to discharge untreated sewage, gray water (from kitchens, baths, and laundries), and garbage (except plastic) directly into the ocean. Cruise ships also produce large amounts of oily bilge water, toxic chemicals, and diesel pollution, and carry invasive species in their ballast water. These impacts are especially worrisome because 70 percent of cruise ship destinations are considered biodiversity "hot spots."[30]

In a voluntary effort to address these issues, the International Council of Cruise Lines, a trade association, entered into a partnership with Conservation International in 2003 to promote responsible practices. Individual cruise operators also took action. Celebrity Cruises, for example, began outfitting its ships with smokeless gas engines. Carnival Cruises began an onboard recycling program, and Royal Caribbean decided not to discharge any waste water while cruising near Australia's Great Barrier Reef.[31]

Response of the International Business Community

Since so many ecological challenges cross national boundaries, the international business community has a critical role to play in addressing them. This section describes some of the important initiatives undertaken by companies around the world to put the principle of sustainable development into practice.

World Business Council for Sustainable Development

One of the leaders in the global effort to promote sustainable business practices is the World Business Council for Sustainable Development (WBCSD). In 2006, the council was made up of about 180 companies drawn from more than 30 countries and 20 industries, among them such major transnational corporations as IBM, Nokia, Deutsche Bank, Honda, Samsung, and Cemex. The WBCSD's goals were to encourage high standards of environmental management and to promote closer cooperation among businesses, governments, and other organizations concerned with sustainable development.[32]

The WBCSD called for businesses to manufacture and distribute products more efficiently, to consider their lifelong impact, and to recycle components. In a series of publications, the group set forth the view that the most eco-efficient companies—those that added the most value with the least use of resources and pollution—were more competitive and more environmentally sound.

Eco-efficiency was only possible, the council concluded, in the presence of open, competitive markets in which prices reflected the true cost of environmental and other resources. In the past, environmental costs have not been fully accounted, for example,

---

[30] The Ocean Conservancy, "Cruise Control: A Report on How Cruise Ships Affect the Marine Environment," available at *www.oceanconservancy.org;* and "Protect Our Oceans: Stop Cruise Ship Pollution," *www.northamerica.oceana.org.*

[31] Center for Environmental Leadership in Business, "A Shifting Tide: Environmental Challenges and Cruise Industry Responses," *www.celb.org.*

[32] The WBCSD's agenda is described in Charles O. Holliday, Jr., Stephan Schmidheiny, and Philip Watts, *Walking the Talk: The Business Case for Sustainable Development* (San Francisco: Berrett-Koehler, 2002).

Exhibit 11.D   International Codes of Environmental Conduct

A number of national and international organizations have developed codes of environmental conduct. Among the most important ones are the following.

INTERNATIONAL CHAMBER OF COMMERCE (ICC)

The ICC developed the Business Charter for Sustainable Development, 16 principles that identify key elements of environmental leadership and call on companies to recognize environmental management as among their highest corporate priorities.

GLOBAL ENVIRONMENTAL MANAGEMENT INITIATIVE (GEMI)

A group of over 40 companies dedicated to fostering environmental excellence, GEMI developed several environmental self-assessment programs, including one that helps firms assess their progress in meeting the goals of the Business Charter for Sustainable Development.

CERES PRINCIPLES

These are 10 voluntary principles developed by the Coalition for Environmentally Responsible Economies that commit signatory firms to protection of the biosphere, sustainable use of natural resources, energy conservation, risk reduction, and other environmental goals.

INTERNATIONAL ORGANIZATION FOR STANDARDIZATION (ISO)

ISO 14000 is a series of voluntary standards introduced in 1996 by the ISO, an international group based in Geneva, Switzerland, that permit companies to be certified as meeting global environmental performance standards.

Sources: For further information on these organizations and their codes, see *www.iccwbo.org/policy/environment* (International Chamber of Commerce); *www.gemi.org* (Global Environmental Management Initiative); *www.ceres.org* (Coalition for Environmentally Responsible Economies); and *www.iso.org* (International Organization for Standardization).

in calculating measures of production such as the gross domestic product. The WBCSD recommended revising systems of national accounting to include the costs of environmental damage, and pricing products to reflect their full environmental costs.[33]

Several other groups, in addition to the WBCSD, have given serious attention to the idea of sustainable development and its implications for business. Exhibit 11.D profiles the efforts of several important organizations to develop codes of environmental conduct, including the 14000 certification program of the International Organization for Standardization (ISO).

Many individual businesses and industry groups have also undertaken voluntary initiatives to improve their environmental performance. These are the subject of the next section.

Voluntary Business Initiatives

Many firms around the world have tried to determine how sustainable development translates into actual business practice. Some of the more important voluntary initiatives undertaken by businesses include the following.

Life-cycle analysis involves collecting information on the lifelong environmental impact of a product, all the way from extraction of raw material to manufacturing to its distribution, use, and ultimate disposal. The aim of life-cycle analysis is to minimize the adverse impact of a particular product at all stages. For example, Dell Computer has redesigned one of its lines of personal computers with a recyclable chassis and offers

[33] Stephan Schmidheiny and Federico J. L. Zorraquin, *Financing Change: The Financial Community, Eco-Efficiency, and Sustainable Development* (Cambridge, MA: MIT Press, 1997). A full list of the WBCSD's publications is available online at *www.wbcsd.ch*.

incentives to its customers to return their old computers to be taken apart and rebuilt with new internal parts. The redesign greatly reduced waste from discarded PCs.[34]

Industrial ecology refers to designing factories and distribution systems as if they were self-contained ecosystems. For example, businesses can save materials through closed-loop recycling, use wastes from one process as raw material for others, and make use of energy generated as a by-product of production.

> An example of industrial ecology may be found in the town of Kalundborg, Denmark, where several companies have formed a cooperative relationship that produces both economic and environmental benefits. The local utility company sells excess process steam, which had previously been released into a local fjord (waterway), to a local pharmaceutical plant and oil refinery. Excess fly ash (fine particles produced when fuel is burned) is sold to nearby businesses for use in cement making and road building. Meanwhile, the oil refinery removes sulfur in the natural gas it produces, to make it cleaner burning, and sells the sulfur to a sulfuric acid plant. Calcium sulfate, produced as a residue of a process to cut smoke emissions, is sold to a gypsum manufacturer for making wallboard. The entire cycle both saves money and reduces pollution.[35]

Design for disassembly means that products are designed so that at the end of their useful life they can be disassembled and recycled. At Volkswagen, the German carmaker, engineers design cars for eventual disassembly and reuse. At the company's specialized auto recycling plant in Leer, old cars can be taken apart in just three minutes. Plastics, steel, precious metals, oil, acid, and glass are separated and processed. Many materials are used again in new Volkswagens.

Sustainable development will require technology cooperation through long-term partnerships between companies in developed and developing countries to transfer environmental technologies, as shown in the following example.

> In South Africa, Shell entered a partnership with Eskom, a local utility company, to provide electricity to 50,000 homes in isolated rural communities not served by the national power grid. The two firms cooperated to set up technologically advanced solar panels and metering units measuring power flow to individual homes. People could pay for the amount of electricity they actually used, without any up-front investment. The cost to customers, averaging about $8 a month, was comparable to the amount they had been spending on candles, paraffin, and other less efficient fuels.[36]

The idea of sustainable development is increasingly accepted in the business community. A survey of business leaders in 50 countries, for example, reported that 9 in 10 executives said sustainable development was accepted as a desirable goal in their companies. Six in 10 said that the benefits of working toward this goal outweighed the costs, and 7 in 10 regularly reported on their environmental performance to stakeholders.[37]

---

[34] Matthew B. Arnold and Robert M. Day, *The Next Bottom Line: Making Sustainable Development Tangible* (Washington, DC: World Resources Institute, 1998), p. 31.

[35] Stephen W. Peck, "Industrial Ecology: From Theory to Practice," *www.newcity.ca*.

[36] *Building A Better Future: Industry, Technology, and Sustainable Development: A Progress Report* (World Business Council on Sustainable Development, June 2000), p. 19.

[37] "GlobalScan Survey of Business Leaders on Sustainable Development," *www.environicsinternational.com /specialreport/GlobeScan_Biz/survey.pdf*.

Protecting the environment and the well-being of future generations is, as a founder of the WBCSD put it, "fast becoming a business necessity and even an opportunity."[38] Environmental regulations are getting tougher, consumers want cleaner products, and employees want to work for environmentally conscious companies. Finding ways to reduce or recycle waste saves money. Many executives are championing the importance of corporations' moral obligations to future generations. The most successful global businesses in coming years may be those, like the ones profiled in this chapter, that recognize the imperative for sustainable development as an opportunity both for competitive advantage and ethical action.

Summary

- Many world leaders have supported the idea of sustainable development—economic growth without depleting the resources on which future generations will depend. But achieving sustainable development remains a challenge, and the community of nations has not yet worked out who will pay.

- Major threats to the earth's ecosystem include depletion of nonrenewable resources such as oil and coal, air and water pollution, and the degradation of arable land.

- Population growth, income inequality, and rapid industrialization in many parts of the world have contributed to these ecological problems. The limits to growth hypothesis maintains that if human society continues to exceed the carrying capacity of the earth's ecosystem, dire consequences will follow.

- Four environmental issues—ozone depletion, global warming, declining biodiversity, and threats to the marine ecosystem—are shared by all nations. International agreements are addressing these issues, although more remains to be done.

- Global businesses have begun to put the principles of sustainable development into action through such innovative actions as life-cycle analysis, industrial ecology, design for disassembly, and technology cooperation.

Key Terms

biodiversity, *242*
carrying capacity, *238*
commons, *232*
eco-efficiency, *245*
ecological footprint, *238*
ecology, *232*

global warming, *241*
industrial ecology, *247*
Kyoto Protocol, *242*
life-cycle analysis, *246*
limits to growth
hypothesis, *239*

marine ecosystems, *244*
Montreal Protocol, *240*
ozone, *240*
sustainable
development, *233*

Internet Resources

www.ipcc.ch — Intergovernmental Panel on Climate Change
www.epa.gov/docs/ozone — Environmental Protection Agency ozone site
www.unep.org — United Nations Environmental Program
unfccc.int — United Nations Framework Convention on Climate Change
www.wbcsd.ch — World Business Council on Sustainable Development

---

[38] Stephan Schmidheiny, "The Business Logic of Sustainable Development," *Columbia Journal of World Business* 27, nos. 3–4 (1992), pp. 19–23.

Discussion Case: *Damming the Yangtze River*

In 2003, after years of construction, workers finally closed the gates of the massive Three Gorges Dam across the Yangtze River in central China. Water began to fill up the reservoir behind the one-and-a-half-mile-long hydroelectric dam, the largest such project in the world. Within months, the dam had begun to produce its first electricity, and the first ships had passed through its locks. The Yangtze quickly became the second most heavily navigated river in the world, after the Mississippi.

When fully completed in 2009, the Three Gorges Dam was expected to have the capacity to generate 18,200 megawatts of electricity, 18 times as much as a standard nuclear power plant. This energy would be crucial to the fast-developing Chinese economy, where demand for electricity was projected to double every 15 years. "The dam will make life better for our children," said one construction worker. "They'll have electric lights, TV, be able to study their lessons. With luck they'll go to the university."

The 400-mile-long reservoir and locks that would be created behind the dam would be deep enough to bring oceangoing ships 1,500 miles inland to the city of Chongquing, opening markets in the vast interior of China. The government also hoped that the dam would end the disastrous floods that had inundated the region every five or so years throughout history. In the 20th century alone, 300,000 lives had been lost and millions of homes destroyed. In 1998, a flood on the river had killed 3,656 people and cost the nation $38 billion. The construction effort itself employed 40,000 people and pumped billions of dollars into the local economy.

But the project had its share of critics, both inside and outside China. To make way for the water, 1.9 million Chinese, mostly in rural towns and villages along the river, would have to be resettled to higher ground by the time the project was completed. Homes and jobs would need to be found for them. A quarter-million acres of fertile farmland would be flooded, as would many unexcavated archaeological sites.

The project would inundate the Three Gorges, thought by many to be among the most starkly beautiful scenery in the world. At this point in its course, the Yangtze passes through a narrow passage, with dramatic limestone walls towering as high as 3,000 feet above the river. In addition to destroying this landscape, the dam would radically transform the ecology of the river. Environmentalists pointed out that fish migrations would be blocked and plants and animals adapted to the river habitat would die out.

Moreover, no provisions had been made to treat the billions of tons of industrial and municipal sewage expected to flow into the reservoir. In the past, the fast-moving river had carried untreated waste to the sea. No provisions had been made, either, to relocate existing landfills and dumps, many containing toxic waste, that lay in the area that would be flooded.

But other environmentalists thought the project had merit. Hydroelectric power, of the sort to be generated by the Three Gorges Dam, was nonpolluting. The main practical alternative to the dam was to build more coal-fired power plants, which in the late-1990s supplied over three-fourths of China's energy. Coal combustion produces sulfur dioxide, a cause of acid rain, and carbon dioxide, a major contributor to global warming. China was already the second-biggest emitter of carbon in the world (after the United States); it was responsible for 13 percent of the world's emissions, even though its economy accounted for only 2 percent of the world's GDP. The air in much of China is fouled by coal dust and smoke, and one-fourth of all deaths are caused by lung disease.

Sources: "Yangtze Highway," *Newsweek,* July 25/August 1, 2005; "As Dam on Yangtze Closes, Chinese Tally Gain and Loss," *The New York Times,* June 9, 2003; and Kari Huus, "The Yangtze's Collision Course," November 22, 1999, *www.msnbc.com/news.* Dramatic photographs may be found in Arthur Zich, "China's Three Gorges: Before the Flood," *National Geographic* 92, no. 3 (September 1997), pp. 2–33.

Discussion Questions

1. What stakeholders will be helped by the Three Gorges Dam? What stakeholders will be hurt by it?

2. How does construction of a dam on the Yangtze River relate to the issues of global warming, biodiversity, and water pollution discussed in this chapter?

3. Do you agree with the decision of the Chinese government to construct the Three Gorges Dam? Why or why not?

4. What strategies do you believe would best promote economic development in China without destroying the environmental resources on which future generations depend?

CHAPTER TWELVE

Managing Environmental Issues

Growing public interest in protecting the environment has prompted political and corporate leaders to become increasingly responsive to environmental issues. In the United States and other nations, government policy makers have moved toward greater reliance on market-based mechanisms, rather than command and control regulations, to achieve environmental goals. At the same time, many businesses have become increasingly proactive and have pioneered new approaches to effective environmental management, often conferring a competitive advantage.

This chapter focuses on these key learning objectives:

- Knowing the main features of environmental laws in the United States and other nations.
- Understanding the advantages and disadvantages of different regulatory approaches.
- Assessing the costs and benefits of environmental regulation.
- Defining an ecologically sustainable organization and the stages through which firms progress as they become more sustainable.
- Understanding how businesses can best manage environmental issues.
- Analyzing how effective environmental management makes firms more competitive.

Hewlett-Packard, a manufacturer of computers and printers, has long been an innovator in its environmental practices. In the 1990s, the company decided to move beyond merely preventing pollution to embrace a strategy of providing products and services that were environmentally sound throughout their life cycles. It appointed product stewards, each of whom was responsible for ensuring that a particular product minimized the use of hazardous materials, was safe to use, and enabled recycling or reuse. For example, the company initiated a program to take back and recycle used laser printer cartridges. In the early 2000s, Hewlett-Packard made a further commitment to "invent tomorrow's sustainable businesses." The company began an internal discussion of some radical questions. Did it want to be in the business of selling disposable printers, or in the business of selling printing services? Could printing services be delivered in an entirely sustainable way?[1]

In 2005, the European Union (EU) launched an innovative environmental policy—a system of tradable permits for carbon dioxide emissions. In an effort to curb global warming, the Europeans opted for a flexible, market-based approach. Under the new system, the European Commission (the EU's governing body) allocated permits, or quotas, for carbon dioxide emissions to various member governments. They, in turn, distributed them to 12,000 plants across the 25 member states, including power generators, chemical factories, and pulp and paper mills. Companies that were able to cut their emissions of the greenhouse gases could sell their permits to others that had exceeded their quota, providing an incentive for them to reduce their pollution. Over time, the European Commission planned to reduce the number of permits in circulation, driving down overall carbon dioxide emissions. "Europe will be an example to the world," said the chief executive of a trading exchange for the permits. "It's the first time that you [will be] rewarded for being an environmentally friendly manager."[2]

Environmental Defense, a leading environmental advocacy organization, believed that its old strategy of suing companies and lobbying legislators was not working well enough. Instead, the group tried a cooperative approach, working directly with companies, including McDonald's, Dell Computer, Citigroup, and Starbucks, to improve their environmental performance. Environmental Defense also entered an innovative partnership with FedEx, the world's largest express transportation company, to develop a more environmentally friendly delivery truck. Environmental Defense scientists worked with FedEx and with Eaton, a truck manufacturer, to design a new hybrid vehicle, powered by both a conventional combustion engine and an electric motor, that burned 50 percent less fuel and decreased emissions by more than 75 percent. FedEx rolled out its first hybrid truck in 2004 and said it planned to replace its entire 30,000 truck fleet with the new model.[3]

In the early years of the 21st century, many businesses, governments, and environmental advocacy organizations became increasingly concerned that old strategies for promoting environmental protection were failing and new approaches were necessary. Government policy makers moved toward greater reliance on market-based mechanisms to achieve environmental goals. Environmentalists engaged in greater dialogue and cooperation with industry leaders. Many businesses pioneered new approaches to effective environmental management, such as product stewardship programs.

---

[1] Lynelle Preston, "Sustainability at Hewlett-Packard: From Theory to Practice," *California Management Review* 43, no. 3 (Spring 2001), pp. 26–37. Hewlett-Packard's annual Global Citizenship Report, including information on its environmental initiatives, is available at *www.hp.com/hpinfo/globalcitizenship/environment*.

[2] "New Limits on Pollution Herald Change in Europe," *International Herald Tribune*, January 1, 2005. Information about the EU Emissions Trading Scheme is available at *www.euractiv.com*.

[3] "FedEx, Environmental Defense Delivering Clean Air," *www.environmentaldefense.org*.

The challenge facing government, industry, and environmental advocates alike, as they tried out new approaches and improved on old ones, was how to further economic growth in an increasingly competitive and integrated world economy while promoting sustainable and ecologically sound business practices.

Role of Government

In many nations, government is actively involved in regulating business activities in order to protect the environment. Business firms have few incentives to minimize pollution if their competitors do not. A single firm acting by itself to reduce discharges into a river, for example, would incur extra costs. If its competitors did not do the same, the firm might not be able to compete effectively and could go out of business. Government, by setting a common standard for all firms, can take the cost of pollution control out of competition. It also can provide economic incentives to encourage businesses, communities, and regions to reduce pollution, and it can offer legal and administrative systems for resolving disputes.

In the United States, government has been involved in environmental regulation at least since the late 19th century, when the first federal laws were passed protecting navigable waterways. The government's role began to increase dramatically, however, around 1970. Figure 12.1 summarizes the major federal environmental laws enacted by the U.S. Congress in the modern environmental era. The nation's main pollution control agency is the **Environmental Protection Agency (EPA)**. It was created in 1970 to coordinate most of the government's efforts to protect the environment. Other government agencies involved in enforcing the nation's environmental laws include the Nuclear Regulatory Commission (NRC), the Occupational Safety and Health Administration (OSHA), and various regional, state, and local agencies.

Major Areas of Environmental Regulation

In the United States, the federal government regulates in three major areas of environmental protection: air pollution, water pollution, and land pollution (solid and hazardous waste). This section will review the major ecological issues and the U.S. laws pertaining to each, with comparative references to similar initiatives in other nations.

Air Pollution

Air pollution occurs when more pollutants are emitted into the atmosphere than can be safely absorbed and diluted by natural processes. Some pollution occurs naturally, such as smoke and ash from volcanoes and forest fires. But most air pollution today results from human activity, especially industrial processes and motor vehicle emissions. Air pollution degrades buildings, reduces crop yields, mars the beauty of natural landscapes, and harms people's health.

The American Lung Association (ALA) estimated in 2005 that 152 million Americans, more than half the population, were breathing unsafe air for at least part of each year. This number had risen more than 10 percent in the prior two years. Of particular concern to the ALA was diesel exhaust from trucks, farm and construction equipment, marine vessels, and electric generators. Fully 70 percent of the cancer risk from air pollution, it reported, was due to diesel exhaust.[4]

---

[4] American Lung Association, "State of the Air: 2005," *www.lungusa.org/reports/sota05*; and "Closing the Diesel Divide: Protecting Public Health from Diesel Air Pollution," Environmental Defense Fund and the American Lung Association, 2003, *www.environmentaldefense.org*.

FIGURE 12.1
Leading U.S. Environmental Protection Laws

1969	National Environmental Policy Act	Created Council on Environmental Quality to oversee quality of the nation's environment.
1970	Clean Air Act	Established national air quality standards and timetables.
1972	Water Pollution Control Act	Established national goals and timetables for clean waterways.
1972	Pesticide Control Act	Required registration of and restrictions on pesticide use.
1973	Endangered Species Act	Conserved species of animals and plants whose survival was threatened or endangered.
1974 & 1996	Safe Drinking Water Act	Authorized national standards for drinking water.
1974	Hazardous Materials Transport Act	Regulated shipment of hazardous materials.
1976	Resource Conservation and Recovery Act	Regulated hazardous materials from production to disposal.
1976	Toxic Substances Control Act	Established national policy to regulate, restrict, and, if necessary, ban toxic chemicals.
1977	Clean Air Act amendments	Revised air standards.
1980	Comprehensive Environmental Response Compensation and Liability Act (Superfund)	Established Superfund and procedures to clean up hazardous waste sites.
1986	Superfund Amendments and Reauthorization Act (SARA)	Established toxics release inventory.
1987	Clean Water Act amendments	Authorized funds for sewage treatment plants and waterways cleanup.
1990	Clean Air Act amendments	Required cuts in urban smog, acid rain, greenhouse gas emissions; promoted alternative fuels.
1990	Pollution Prevention Act	Provided guidelines, training, and incentives to prevent or reduce pollution at the source.
1990	Oil Pollution Act	Strengthened EPA's ability to prevent and respond to catastrophic oil spills.
1999	Chemical Safety Information, Site Security, and Fuels Regulatory Relief Act	Set standards for the storage of flammable chemicals and fuels.

The EPA has identified six criteria pollutants, relatively common harmful substances that serve as indicators of overall levels of air pollution. These are lead, carbon monoxide, particulate matter, sulfur dioxide, nitrogen dioxide, and ozone. (Ozone at ground level is a particularly unhealthy component of smog.) In addition, the agency also has identified a list of toxic air pollutants that are considered hazardous even in relatively

Exhibit 12.A   **Moving Mountains to Fight Acid Rain**

As part of its efforts to control acid rain, the U.S. government in 1990 initiated stricter new restrictions on the emission of sulfur dioxide by utilities. Many electric companies complied with the law by switching from high-sulfur coal, which produces more sulfur dioxide when burned, to low-sulfur coal, which produces less. This action had the beneficial effect of reducing acid rain.

But the law had some environmentally destructive results that had been unintended by regulators. Much of the highest-quality low-sulfur coal in the United States lies in horizontal layers near the tops of rugged mountains in Appalachia, including parts of West Virginia, Kentucky, Tennessee, and Virginia. Some coal companies discovered that the cheapest way to extract this coal was through what came to be known as mountaintop removal. Explosives were used to blast away up to 500 feet of mountaintop. Massive machines called draglines, 20 stories tall and costing $100 million each, were then used to remove the debris to get at buried seams of coal. By the mid-2000s, 400,000 acres had been ravaged in this manner by surface mining.

Although coal operators were required to reclaim the land afterward—by filling in adjacent valleys with debris and planting grass and shrubs—many environmentalists believed the damage caused by mountaintop removal was severe. Many rivers and creeks were contaminated and habitat destroyed. Aquifers dried up, and the entire region became vulnerable to devastating floods. Many felt it was deeply ironic that a law that had benefited the environment in one way had indirectly harmed it in another.

Source: "The High Cost of Cheap Coal: When Mountains Move," *National Geographic,* March 2006, pp. 105–23.

small concentrations. These include asbestos, benzene, chloroform, dioxin, vinyl chloride, and radioactive materials. Emissions of toxic pollutants are strictly controlled.

Failure to comply with clean air laws can be very expensive for business. In 2005, DaimlerChrysler spent $94 million to settle government charges that it had broken environmental law by installing defective catalytic converters on nearly 1.5 million Jeep and Dodge vehicles over a 5-year period. Catalytic converters are designed to cut pollution in car and truck exhaust. The EPA ordered the company to recall and repair the faulty units, extend warranties, and set up better reporting procedures. The company was also required to pay a $1 million fine.[5]

A special problem of air pollution is **acid rain**. Acid rain is formed when emissions of sulfur dioxide and nitrogen oxides, by-products of the burning of fossil fuels by utilities, manufacturers, and motor vehicles, combine with natural water vapor in the air and fall to earth as rain or snow that is more acidic than normal. Acid rain can damage the ecosystems of lakes and rivers, reduce crop yields, and degrade forests. Structures, such as buildings and monuments, are also harmed. Within North America, acid rain is most prevalent in New England and eastern Canada, regions that are downwind of coal-burning utilities in the Midwestern states.[6] Acid rain is especially difficult to regulate because adverse consequences often occur far—often, hundreds of miles—from the source of the pollution, sometimes across international borders. The major law governing air pollution is the Clean Air Act, passed in 1970 and most recently amended in 1990. The 1990 Clean Air Act toughened standards in a number of areas, including stricter restrictions on emissions of acid rain-causing chemicals.

The efforts of the U.S. government to reduce acid rain illustrate some of the difficult trade-offs involved in environmental policy. These are described in Exhibit 12.A.

[5] "U.S. Announces $94 Million Clean Air Settlement with Chrysler over Emission Control Defects on 1.5 Million Jeep and Dodge Vehicles," U.S. Environmental Protection Agency Press Release, December 21, 2005.

[6] More information about acid rain may be found at *www.epa.gov/airmarkets/acidrain.*

Water Pollution

Water pollution, like air pollution, occurs when more wastes are dumped into waterways than can be naturally diluted and carried away. Water can be polluted by organic wastes (untreated sewage or manure), by the chemical by-products of industrial processes, and by the disposal of nonbiodegradable products (which do not naturally decay). Heavy metals and toxic chemicals, including some used as pesticides and herbicides, can be particularly persistent. Like poor air, poor water quality can decrease crop yields, threaten human health, and degrade the quality of life.

In 2000, more than 2,000 people in Walkerton, Ontario, a small farming community, became ill with severe diarrhea. About 1 in 10 had to be hospitalized, and 7 people died. The mass outbreak had been caused by *E. coli* bacteria in the municipal water supply. Investigators found that manure contaminated by the dangerous bacterium had washed into a public well during a heavy rainstorm, and the water company had failed to disinfect the water as required by law. One of its managers was later convicted and served a prison term in connection with the incident.[7]

In the United States, regulations address both the pollution of rivers, lakes, and other surface bodies of water and the quality of the drinking water. The main U.S. law governing water pollution is the Water Pollution Control Act, also known as the Clean Water Act. This law aims to restore or maintain the integrity of all surface water in the United States. It requires permits for most *point* sources of pollution, such as industrial emissions, and mandates that local and state governments develop plans for *nonpoint* sources, such as agricultural runoff or urban storm water. The Pesticide Control Act specifically restricts the use of dangerous pesticides, which can pollute groundwater.

The quality of drinking water is regulated by another law, the Safe Drinking Water Act of 1974, most recently amended in 1996. This law sets minimum standards for various contaminants in both public water systems and aquifers that supply drinking wells.

Land Pollution

The third major focus of environmental regulation is the contamination of land by both solid and hazardous waste. The United States produces an astonishing amount of solid waste, adding up to about five pounds per person per day. Of this, 44 percent is recycled, composted, or incinerated, and the rest ends up in municipal landfills.[8] Many businesses and communities have tried to reduce the solid-waste stream by establishing recycling programs. The special case of recycling electronic products is described in Exhibit 12.B.

Of all the world's nations, Germany has made probably the greatest progress in reducing its solid-waste stream. In the early 1990s, faced with overflowing landfills and not enough space for new ones, the German government passed a series of strict recycling laws. Manufacturers and retailers were required to take back almost all packaging waste, from aluminum cans, to plastic CD wrappers, to cardboard shipping boxes. Packaging material was labeled with a green dot, indicating that it could be disposed of in special garbage bins, from which it would

---

[7] "Waterworks Manager Jailed," *Montreal Gazette,* December 21, 2004, p. A12; and "Few Left Untouched after Deadly E. Coli Flows through an Ontario Town's Water," *The New York Times,* July 10, 2000, p. A8.

[8] Environmental Protection Agency, "Municipal Solid Waste," available at *www.epa.gov/garbage.*

Exhibit 12.B **Electronic Waste: What Is the Solution?**

What happens to old personal computers (PCs), cell phones, televisions, and other electronic equipment when they are no longer wanted? The dimensions of the problem are huge. In the United States alone, around 100 million PCs, monitors, and televisions become obsolete every year, and this number is growing. Discarded electronic equipment, sometimes called e-waste, now makes up 5 percent of the trash dumped in municipal landfills, according to EPA. This is a problem because e-waste is not only bulky, but is also loaded with toxic metals like lead, zinc, mercury, and cadmium. Is recycling the answer? Potentially, yes. Unfortunately, as much as 80 percent of recycled e-waste from the United States is shipped overseas to China, India, Pakistan, and the Philippines. There, workers who disassemble it to recover valuable metals are exposed to a veritable "witch's brew of chemicals," according to a journalistic investigation. In response, some forward-looking companies are taking action. Dell and IBM both take back used equipment for a small fee. Sony, Panasonic, and Toshiba now offer lead-free monitors. After an internal investigation showed that "a lot of the leftover guts" of its machines were being sent to China, Hewlett-Packard opened its own facilities in California and Tennessee where it works to safely recycle obsolete equipment. "We don't hurt the environment or the people in any place our products are made, used, or disposed of," said the company's product recycling manager. "It's not good for the bottom line, and it's not good for HP's image."

Sources: Government Accounting Office, "Electronic Waste: Strengthening the Role of the Federal Government in Encouraging Recycling and Reuse," November 2005; Silicon Valley Toxics Coalition and Basel Action Network, "Exporting Harm: The High-Tech Trashing of Asia," February 25, 2002, www.svtc.org; and San Jose Mercury News, "Where Computers Go to Die" (three part series), November 24, 25, and 26, 2002. Comparative international statistics are available at www.e-waste.ch/facts_and_figures/economics/quantities. Information on HP's program is available at www.hp.com/recycle.

be whisked to processing centers for recycling and reuse, at the manufacturer's expense. By the mid 2000s, Germany was recycling an extraordinary 70 percent of its plastic packaging waste and had become a model for the rest of Europe.[9]

The safe disposal of hazardous waste is a special concern. Several U.S. laws address the problem of land contamination by hazardous waste. The Toxic Substances Control Act of 1976 requires EPA to inventory the thousands of chemicals in commercial use, identify which are most dangerous, and, if necessary, ban them or restrict their use. For example, polychlorinated biphenyls (PCBs), dangerous chemicals formerly used in electrical transformers, were banned under this law. The Resource Conservation and Recovery Act of 1976 (amended in 1984) regulates hazardous materials from "cradle to grave." Toxic-waste generators must have permits, transporters must maintain careful records, and disposal facilities must conform to detailed regulations. All hazardous waste must be treated before disposal in landfills.

Some studies have suggested that hazardous-waste sites are most often located near economically disadvantaged African-American and Hispanic communities. Since 1994, EPA has investigated whether state permits for hazardous waste sites violate civil rights laws and has blocked permits that appear to discriminate against minorities. The effort to prevent inequitable exposure to risk, such as from hazardous waste, is sometimes referred to as the movement for **environmental justice**.[10]

[9] "EU Implements Tough New Laws That Will Increase Recycling by 100%," August 18, 2005, Environmental News Service, www.ens-newswire.com.

[10] Robert D. Bullard, "Environmental Justice in the 21st Century," Environmental Justice Resource Center, available at www.ejrc.cau.edu/ejinthe21century.htm; Christopher H. Foreman, Jr., The Promise and Perils of Environmental Justice (Washington, DC: Brookings Institution, 2000); and Bunyan Bryant, ed., Environmental Justice: Issues, Policies, and Solutions (Washington, DC: Island Press, 1995).

A promising regulatory approach to waste management, sometimes called **source reduction**, was taken in the Pollution Prevention Act of 1990. This law aims to reduce pollution at the source, rather than treat and dispose of waste at the end of the pipe. Pollution can be prevented, for example, by using less chemically intensive manufacturing processes, recycling, and better housekeeping and maintenance. Source reduction often saves money, protects worker health, and requires less abatement and disposal technology. The law provides guidelines, training, and incentives for companies to reduce waste.

The major U.S. law governing the cleanup of existing hazardous-waste sites is the Comprehensive Environmental Response, Compensation, and Liability Act, or **CERCLA**, popularly known as **Superfund**, passed in 1980. This law established a fund, supported primarily by a tax on petroleum and chemical companies that were presumed to have created a disproportionate share of toxic wastes. EPA was charged with establishing a National Priority List of the most dangerous toxic sites. Where the original polluters could be identified, they would be required to pay for the cleanup; where they could not be identified or had gone out of business, the Superfund would pay.

An example of a hazardous waste site on EPA's list is the Brio Superfund site, two former waste disposal plants located near the Southbend subdivision outside Houston, Texas. Local wells have been polluted by dangerous chemicals such as xylene, and a black tarlike substance has bubbled into driveways and garages. Air pollution is suspected as a possible cause of a rash of birth defects, and children have contracted leukemia and other serious illnesses. The once-thriving community of 2,800 is largely boarded up, and although progress has been made, the cleanup has still not been completed.[11]

Remarkably, one in four U.S. residents now lives within four miles of a Superfund site. The 1,200 or so sites originally placed on the National Priority List may be just the tip of the iceberg. Congressional researchers have said that as many as 10,000 other sites may need to be cleaned up.

Although Superfund's goals were laudable, it has been widely regarded as a public policy failure. Although cleanup was well under way at almost all sites by 2006, just 309 sites—about a fifth of the total—had been removed from the list, indicating that no further actions were required to protect human health or the environment. Some analysts estimated that the entire cleanup could cost as much as $1 trillion and take half a century to complete.

Alternative Policy Approaches

Governments can use a variety of policy approaches to control air, water, and land pollution. The most widely used method of regulation historically has been to impose environmental standards. Increasingly, however, government policy makers have relied more on market-based and voluntary approaches, rather than command and control regulations, to achieve environmental goals.

Environmental Standards

The traditional method of pollution control is through **environmental standards**. Standard allowable levels of various pollutants are established by legislation or regulatory action and applied by administrative agencies and courts. This approach is also called **command and control regulation**, because the government commands business firms to comply with certain standards and often directly controls their choice of technology.

---

[11] Data on the current status of the cleanup of this and other Superfund sites may be found at *www.epa.gov/superfund*.

One type of standard is an *environmental-quality standard*. In this approach a given geographical area is permitted to have no more than a certain amount or proportion of a pollutant, such as sulfur dioxide, in the air. Polluters are required to control their emissions to maintain the area's standard of air quality. A second type is an *emission standard*. For example, the law might specify that manufacturers could release into the air no more than 1 percent of the ash (a pollutant) they generated. Emission standards, with some exceptions, are usually set by state and local regulators who are familiar with local industry and special problems caused by local topography and weather conditions. Sometimes, EPA mandates that companies use the *best available technology*, meaning a particular process that the agency determines is the best economically achievable way to reduce negative impacts on the environment.

> In recent years, EPA has given companies more flexibility in how they meet government standards, so long as they achieve certain overall goals. For example, under an initiative called Project XL, EPA negotiated an agreement with Intel covering the company's huge semiconductor chip-making factory in Chandler, Arizona. Intel agreed to cap overall air pollution at a level below existing EPA limits and to recycle much of the water used and nonhazardous waste generated at the plant. It also agreed to monitor its own emissions on an ongoing basis and to report complete and current information on the Internet as well as with the government. In exchange, EPA gave the company a facilitywide permit and wide latitude on the technologies and processes it used to meet these goals.[12]

Market-Based Mechanisms

In recent years, regulators have begun to move away from command and control regulation, favoring increased use of **market-based mechanisms**. This approach is based on the idea that the market is a better control than extensive standards that specify precisely what companies must do.

One approach that has become more widely used is to allow businesses to buy and sell the right to pollute. The European Union's *tradable permit* program for carbon emissions, described in one of the opening examples of this chapter, illustrates this approach. The U.S. Clean Air Act of 1990 also incorporated the concept of tradable permits as part of its approach to pollution reduction. The law established emission levels and permitted companies that achieved emissions below the standard to sell their rights to the remaining permissible amount to firms that faced penalties because their emissions were above the standard. Over time, the government would reduce permissible emission levels. The system would therefore gradually reduce overall emissions, even though individual companies might continue to pollute above the standard. Companies could choose whether to reduce their emissions—for example, by installing pollution abatement equipment—or to buy allowances from others. One study showed that the tradable permit program for acid rain may have saved companies as much as $3 billion per year, by allowing them the flexibility to choose the most cost-effective methods of complying with the law.[13]

---

[12] Further information about Project XL and the Intel agreement are available at EPA's Web site at *www.epa.gov/project*. A comparative analysis of several Project XL experiments may be found in Alfred A. Marcus, Donald A. Geffen, and Ken Sexton, *Reinventing Governmental Regulation: Lessons from Project XL* (Washington, DC: Resources for the Future, 2002).

[13] See *www.epa.gov/airmarkets/acidrain*.

Another market-based type of pollution control is establishment of *emissions charges* or *fees*. Each business is charged for the undesirable waste that it emits, with the fee varying according to the amount of waste released. The result is, "The more you pollute, the more you pay." In this approach, polluting is not illegal, but it is expensive, creating an incentive for companies to clean up. In recent years, both federal and state governments have experimented with a variety of so-called *green taxes* or *eco-taxes* that levy a fee on various kinds of environmentally destructive behavior. In addition to taxing bad behavior, the government may also offer various types of positive incentives to firms that improve their environmental performance. For example, the government may decide to purchase only from those firms that meet a certain pollution standard, or it may offer aid to those that install pollution control equipment. Tax incentives, such as faster depreciation for pollution control equipment, also may be used.

> In the United Kingdom, environmental activists proposed an eco-tax on airfares. Under the plan, passengers would pay a special tax, based on the number of miles they flew; the proceeds would go to programs to undo the environmental damage caused by airplanes. The main purpose of the tax was to discourage people from flying, particularly on short routes, and to take less polluting trains instead. Predictably, the aviation and tourism industries opposed the proposal. But in a poll of readers conducted by a British newspaper, three-quarters said they would be willing to pay such an eco-tax. Said one reader, "I think air travel is very damaging to the environment, and growth must be restricted."[14]

In short, in the 2000s the trend was to use more flexible, market-oriented approaches—tradable allowances, pollution fees and taxes, and incentives—to achieve environmental objectives where possible.

Information Disclosure

Another approach to reducing pollution is popularly known as *regulation by publicity*, or *regulation by embarrassment*. The government encourages companies to pollute less by publishing information about the amount of pollutants individual companies emit each year. In many cases, companies voluntarily reduce their emissions to avoid public embarrassment.

The major experiment in regulation by publicity has occurred in the area of toxic emissions to the air and water. The 1986 amendments to the Superfund law, called SARA, included a provision called the Community Right-to-Know Law, which required manufacturing firms to report, for about 300 toxic chemicals, the amount on site, the number of pounds released, and how (if at all) these chemicals were treated or disposed of. EPA makes this information available to the public in the *Toxics Release Inventory*, or *TRI*, published annually and posted on the Internet.

From 1988 to 2002, reporting manufacturers in the United States cut their releases of these chemicals to the air by 42 percent and into water by 32 percent, according to TRI data (releases to land increased during this period).[15] Some of the biggest cuts were made by the worst polluters. These dramatic results were especially surprising to regulators, because many of the hazardous chemicals were not covered under clean air and water regulations at the time. The improvements, in many instances, had been completely

---

[14] "Turbulent Future for Eco-Tax," *The Times* (London), June 4, 2003, p. 4; and "No More Airports, Please," *The Daily Telegraph* (London), June 28, 2003, p. 5.

[15] Data available at *www.scorecard.org*.

FIGURE 12.2

Advantages and Disadvantages of Alternative Policy Approaches to Reducing Pollution

Policy Approach	Advantages	Disadvantages
Environmental standards	• Enforceable in the courts • Compliance mandatory	• Across-the-board standards not equally relevant to all businesses • Requires large regulatory apparatus • Older, less efficient plants may be forced to close • Can retard innovation • Fines may be cheaper than compliance • Does not improve compliance once compliance is achieved
Market-based mechanisms		
Tradable allowances	• Gives businesses more flexibility • Achieves goals at lower overall cost • Saves jobs by allowing some less efficient plants to stay open • Permits the government and private organizations to buy allowances to take them off the market • Encourages continued improvement	• Gives business a license to pollute • Allowances are hard to set • May cause regional imbalances in pollution levels • Enforcement is difficult
Emissions fees and taxes	• Taxes bad behavior (pollution) rather than good behavior (profits)	• Fees are hard to set • Taxes may be too low to curb pollution
Government incentives	• Rewards environmentally responsible behavior • Encourages companies to exceed minimum standards	• Incentives may not be strong enough to curb pollution
Information disclosure	• Government spends little on enforcement • Companies able to reduce pollution in the most cost-effective way	• Does not motivate all companies
Civil and criminal enforcement	• May deter wrongdoing by firms and individuals	• May not deter wrongdoing if penalties and enforcement efforts are perceived as weak

voluntary. Apparently, fear of negative publicity had compelled many companies to act. "We knew the numbers were high, and we knew the public wasn't going to like it," one chemical industry executive explained. In 2005, EPA proposed to change reporting requirements for companies from every year to every other year and to allow companies to emit 5,000 pounds of a particular chemical (up from 500 pounds) before they were required to file a report.[16]

The advantages and disadvantages of alternative policy approaches to reducing pollution are summarized in Figure 12.2.

[16] Further information is available at *www.rtk.net.*

Civil and Criminal Enforcement

Companies that violate environmental laws are subject to stiff civil penalties and fines, and their managers can face prison if they knowingly or negligently endanger people or the environment. Proponents of this approach argue that the threat of fines and even imprisonment can be an effective deterrent to corporate outlaws who would otherwise degrade the air, water, or land. Since 1989, about 100 individuals and companies have been found guilty of environmental crimes each year.

> For example, in 2005 Motiva Enterprises paid $24 million to settle charges stemming from a massive explosion at its Delaware City refinery that had killed one worker, injured several others, and sent a massive plume of sulfuric acid into the surrounding community. Investigators found that workers had complained about the corroded tank for years, but the company had delayed taking it out of service. The Delaware attorney general also filed charges of negligent homicide against the company.[17]

European regulators and prosecutors have also actively pursued corporate environmental criminals. For example, the EU recently standardized its laws against marine pollution and raised maximum penalties to $1.8 million after a series of oil tanker wrecks fouled the coasts of France, Spain, and Portugal.[18]

The U.S. Sentencing Commission, a government agency responsible for setting uniform penalties for violations of federal law, has established guidelines for sentencing environmental wrongdoers. Under these rules, penalties would reflect not only the severity of the offense but also a company's demonstrated environmental commitment. Businesses that have an active compliance program, cooperate with government investigators, and promptly assist any victims would receive lighter sentences than others with no environmental programs or that knowingly violate the law. These guidelines provide an incentive for businesses to develop active compliance programs to protect themselves and their officers from high fines or even prison if a violation should occur.[19]

Costs and Benefits of Environmental Regulation

One central issue of environmental protection is how costs are balanced by benefits. In the quarter century or so since the modern environmental era began, the nation has spent a great deal to clean up the environment and keep it clean. Some have questioned the value choices underlying these expenditures, suggesting that the costs—lost jobs, reduced capital investment, and lowered productivity—exceeded the benefits. Others, in contrast, point to significant gains in the quality of life and to the economic payoff of a cleaner environment.

As a nation, the United States has invested heavily in environmental cleanup. According to the EPA, by 1990 environmental spending exceeded $100 billion a year, about 2 percent of the nation's gross national product, and reached around $160 billion annually

---

[17] "Motiva Enterprises Settles Federal–State Lawsuit Resulting from Explosion at Delaware City Refinery," EPA press release, September 20, 2005.

[18] "Europe Unites against Marine Polluters," *Environmental News Service*, June 11, 2005, *www.ens-newswire.com.*

[19] For a discussion of criminal liability in environmental law, and how to avoid it, see Frank B. Friedman, *Practical Guide to Environmental Management,* 9th ed. (Washington, DC: Environmental Law Institute, 2003).

by 2000. Business spending to comply with environmental regulation has diverted funds that might otherwise have been invested in new plants and equipment or in research and development. Sometimes, strict rules have led to plant shutdowns and loss of jobs. Some regions and industries, in particular, have been hard hit by environmental regulation, especially those with high abatement costs, such as paper and wood products, chemicals, petroleum and coal, and primary metals. Economists often find it difficult, however, to sort out what proportion of job loss in an industry is attributable to environmental regulation and what proportion is attributable to other causes.

In many areas, the United States has made great progress in cleaning up the environment. The benefits of this progress have often been greater than the costs, as these figures show:

- Although problems remain, as noted earlier in this chapter, overall emissions of nearly all major air pollutants in the United States have dropped substantially since 1990, the date of the Clean Air Act amendments. During the decade after the law passed, for example, levels of volatile organic compounds dropped by 27 percent, nitrous oxides by 26 percent, and sulfur dioxide by 25 percent. A study done for the EPA showed that by the year 2010, the Clean Air Act amendments will have prevented 23,000 premature deaths from air pollution, averted almost 2 million asthma attacks, and prevented 4 million lost workdays, among other gains. The cost of compliance was estimated at $27 billion, about one-fourth of the economic value of the act's benefits.[20]

- Water quality has also improved. Since the Water Pollution Control Act went into effect in 1972, many lakes and waterways have been restored to ecological health. The Cuyahoga River in Ohio, for example, which at one time was so badly polluted by industrial waste that it actually caught on fire, has been restored to the point where residents can fish and even swim in the river. By one estimate, 33,000 more miles of rivers and steams were swimmable in 2000 than would have been the case without the Clean Water Act.[21] The cumulative cost to industry and the public of compliance with the act was estimated at $14 billion in 1997; this was much less than the estimated benefits of clean water of $11 billion *a year*.[22]

Environmental regulations also stimulate some sectors of the economy. The environmental services and products industry, for example, has grown dramatically. While jobs are being lost in industries such as forest products and high-sulfur coal mining, others are being created in areas like recycling and reuse, environmental consulting, instrument manufacturing, waste management equipment, and air pollution control.[23] Other jobs are saved or created in industries such as fishing and tourism when natural areas are protected or restored. Moreover, environmental regulations can stimulate the economy by compelling businesses to become more efficient by conserving energy, and less money is spent on treating health problems caused by pollution.

---

[20] "The Benefits and Costs of the Clean Air Act 1990 to 2010: EPA Report to Congress," prepared for the U.S. Environmental Protection Agency, November 1999.

[21] "A Benefits Assessment of Water Pollution Control Programs Since 1972," prepared for the U.S. Environmental Protection Agency, January 2000.

[22] "A Retrospective Assessment of the Costs of the Clean Water Act: 1972 to 1997," prepared for the U.S. Environmental Protection Agency, October 2000; and "A Benefits Assessment of Water Pollution Control Programs Since 1972," prepared for the U.S. Environmental Protection Agency, January 2000.

[23] For a study of the economic impact of the recycling and reuse industries, see National Recycling Coalition, Inc., *U.S. Recycling Economic Information Study*, prepared by R.W. Beck, Inc., July 2001.

FIGURE 12.3
Costs and Benefits of Environmental Regulations

Costs	Benefits
• $160 billion a year spent by business and individuals in the United States by 2000.	• Emissions of nearly all pollutants have dropped since 1970.
• Job loss in some particularly polluting industries.	• Air and water quality improved, some toxic-waste sites cleaned; improved health; natural beauty preserved or enhanced.
• Competitiveness of some capital-intensive, "dirty" industries impaired.	• Growth of other industries, such as environmental products and services, tourism, and fishing.

Because of the complexity of these issues, economists differ on the net costs and benefits of environmental regulation. In some respects, government controls hurt the economy, and in other ways they help, as summarized in Figure 12.3. An analysis of data from several studies found that, on balance, U.S. environmental regulations did not have a large overall effect on economic competitiveness because losses in one area tended to balance gains in another.[24] What is clear is that choices in the area of environmental regulation reflect underlying values, expressed in a democratic society through an open political process. Just how much a society is prepared to pay and how "clean" it wants to be are political choices, reflecting the give and take of diverse interests in a pluralistic society.

The Greening of Management

Environmental regulations, such as the laws governing clean air, water, and land described in this chapter, establish minimum legal standards that businesses must meet. Most companies try to comply with these regulations, if only to avoid litigation, fines, and, in the most extreme cases, criminal penalties. But many firms are now voluntarily moving beyond compliance to improve their environmental performance in all areas of their operations. Researchers have sometimes referred to the process of moving toward more proactive environmental management as the **greening of management**. This section describes the stages of the greening process and discusses what organizational approaches companies have used to manage environmental issues effectively. The following section explains why green management can improve a company's strategic competitiveness.

Stages of Corporate Environmental Responsibility

Although environmental issues are forcing all businesses to manage in new ways, not all companies are equally green, meaning proactive in their response to environmental issues. One widely used model identifies three main stages of corporate environmental responsibility.

---

[24] Adam B. Jaffe, Steven R. Peterson, Paul R. Portney, and Robert N. Stavins, "Environmental Regulations and the Competitiveness of U.S. Industry," prepared for the U.S. Department of Commerce, July 1993. For another summary of the evidence that comes to a similar conclusion, see Steven Peterson, Barry Galef, and Kenneth Grant, "Do Environmental Regulations Impair Competitiveness?" prepared for the U.S. EPA, September 1995.

According to this model, companies pass through three distinct stages in the development of green management practices.[25] The first stage is *pollution prevention,* which focuses on "minimizing or eliminating waste before it is created." For example, Dow Chemical Corporation has adopted a wide-ranging program called Waste Reduction Always Pays, WRAP for short. Realizing that it would be more efficient and less expensive to prevent pollution in the first place than to treat and dispose of pollutants at the "end of the pipe," the company has radically cut the use of hazardous chemicals in its manufacturing processes, saving over $20 million a year.[26] The second stage is *product stewardship.* In this stage, managers focus on "all environmental impacts associated with the full life cycle of a product," from the design of a product to its eventual use and disposal. Hewlett-Packard, mentioned earlier in this chapter, is an example of a company at this stage. Finally, the third and most advanced stage is *clean technology,* in which businesses develop innovative, new technologies that support sustainability.

> General Electric, a company long associated with pollution, from building coal-fired power plants to dumping toxic chemicals in the Hudson River, took a dramatic turn in 2005. Jeffrey Immelt, the company's new CEO, announced a new strategy he dubbed "ecomagination." He pledged to double GE's investment by 2010 (from $700 million to $1.5 billion) in developing renewable energy, fuel cells, efficient lighting, water filtration systems, and cleaner jet engines. Immelt's reason was that clean technologies represented a huge commercial opportunity. "Increasingly for business," he said, "green is green."[27]

Where are most companies on this continuum of environmental responsibility? A survey of 140 large U.S. firms conducted by the accounting firm PricewaterhouseCoopers found that 75 percent had adopted at least some environmental initiatives. Most of these, however, were efforts to prevent pollution. Almost 9 out of 10, though, thought that corporate commitment to sustainability would grow over the next five years.[28] In short, most big companies are still in the pollution prevention stage, but many are in a transition to higher stages in the developmental sequence.

Researchers have discovered that several factors push companies along the continuum from lower to higher levels of corporate environmental responsiveness. One study of firms in the United Kingdom and Japan found three main motivations for "going green": the chance to gain a *competitive advantage,* a desire to gain *legitimacy* (approval of the public or regulators), and a moral commitment to *ecological responsibility.*[29] Other research has cited a desire to avoid the risks associated with environmental harm.

[25] Stuart Hart, "Beyond Greening: Strategies for a Sustainable World," *Harvard Business Review,* January–February 1997. All quotes in this paragraph are taken from this article. An alternative stage model may be found in Dexter Dunphy, Suzanne Benn, and Andrew Griffiths, *Organisational Change for Corporate Sustainability* (New York: Routledge, 2003).

[26] Information on Dow Chemical Corporation's environmental, health, and safety programs is available at *www.dow.com/environment.*

[27] "A Clean, Lean Electric Machine," *The Economist,* December 10, 2005, pp. 77–79; and "GE Turns Green," *Forbes.com,* August 15, 2005.

[28] "U.S. Firms Are Getting 'Greener' But They Fail to Codify Practices," *The Wall Street Journal,* August 19, 2002, p. B2; and Andrew W. Savitz, "Sustainable Business Practices: Managing Risk and Opportunity," *Re: Business,* March 2003, available at *www.pwcglobal.com.*

[29] Pratima Bansal and Kendall Roth, "Why Companies Go Green: A Model of Ecological Responsiveness," *Academy of Management Journal,* August 2000, pp. 717–36.

The Ecologically Sustainable Organization

An **ecologically sustainable organization (ESO)** is a business that operates in a way that is consistent with the principle of sustainable development, as presented in Chapter 11. In other words, an ESO could continue its activities indefinitely, without altering the carrying capacity of the earth's ecosystem. Such businesses would not use up natural resources any faster than they could be replenished or substitutes found. They would make and transport products efficiently, with minimal use of energy. They would design products that would last a long time and that, when worn out, could be disassembled and recycled. They would not produce waste any faster than natural systems could absorb and disperse it. They would work with other businesses, governments, and organizations to meet these goals.[30]

Of course, no existing business completely fits the definition of an ecologically sustainable organization. The concept is what social scientists call an ideal type, that is, a kind of absolute standard against which real organizations can be measured. A few visionary businesses, however, have embraced the concept and begun to try to live up to this ideal.

> One such business is Interface, a $1 billion company based in Atlanta, Georgia, that makes 40 percent of the world's commercial carpet tiles. In 1994, CEO Ray C. Anderson announced, to many people's surprise, that Interface would seek to become "the first sustainable corporation in the world." Anderson and his managers undertook hundreds of initiatives. For example, the company started a program by which customers could *lease*, rather than *purchase*, carpet tile. When tile wore out in high-traffic areas, Interface technicians would replace just the worn units, reducing waste. Old tiles would be recycled, creating a closed loop. In 2004, Interface reported that in 10 years it had saved $262 million by cutting waste, and revenues and profits had soared. But Anderson said it was "just a start. It's daunting, trying to climb a mountain taller than Everest."[31]

No companies, including Interface, have yet become truly sustainable businesses, and it will probably be impossible for any single firm to become an ESO in the absence of supportive government policies and a widespread movement among many businesses and other social institutions.

Environmental Partnerships

Many businesses that are seeking to become more sustainable have formed voluntary, collaborative partnerships with environmental organizations and regulators to achieve specific objectives, as illustrated by the FedEx example at the beginning of this chapter. These collaborations, called **environmental partnerships**, draw on the unique strengths of the different partners to improve environmental quality or conserve resources.[32]

---

[30] Mark Starik and Gordon P. Rands, "Weaving an ntegrated Web: Multilevel and Multisystem Perspectives of Ecologically Sustainable Organizations," *Academy of Management Review,* October 1995, pp. 908–35.

[31] Ray C. Anderson, *Mid-Course Correction: Toward a Sustainable Enterprise—The Interface Model* (Atlanta, GA: The Peregrinzilla Press, 1998). Interface's sustainability initiatives are described at *www.interfacesustainability.com.*

[32] Dennis A. Rondinelli and Ted London, "How Corporations and Environmental Groups Cooperate," *Academy of Management Executive* 17, no. 1 (2003), pp. 61–76; and Frederick J. Long and Matthew B. Arnold, *The Power of Environmental Partnerships* (Fort Worth, TX: Dryden Press, 1995).

Unilever, the Anglo-Dutch consumer goods company, is the largest buyer of seafood in the world. Concerned about the rapidly declining stocks of many species of fish used in its frozen food products, Unilever entered into a partnership with the World Wildlife Fund, a conservation organization. Together, they formed the nonprofit Marine Stewardship Council to set standards for sustainable fisheries, educate suppliers, and certify harvested catch. In 2005, Unilever began marketing frozen fish sticks sourced from the newly certified Alaskan pollock fishery. "This certification is very good news for the protection of fish stocks in general, and good news for the ever-increasing number of discerning consumers who want to choose sustainable fish for their families," said one of the company's managers.[33]

Environmental Management in Practice

Companies that have begun to move toward environmental sustainability have learned that new structures, processes, and incentives are often needed. Some of the organizational elements that many proactive green companies share are the following.[34]

Top management with a commitment to sustainability. The most environmentally proactive companies almost all have top leaders with a strong espoused commitment to sustainability. Most also give their environmental managers greater authority and access to top levels of the corporation. Many leading firms now have a vice president for environmental affairs with a direct reporting relationship with the CEO. These individuals often supervise extensive staffs of specialists and coordinate the work of managers in many areas, including research and development, marketing, and operations.

Line manager involvement. Environmental staff experts and specialized departments are most effective when they work closely with the people who carry out the company's daily operations. For this reason, many green companies involve line managers and workers directly in the process of change. At the Park Plaza Hotel in Boston, green teams of employees make suggestions ranging from energy-efficient windows to refillable bottles of soap and shampoo.

Codes of environmental conduct. Environmentally proactive companies put their commitment in writing, often in the form of a code of conduct or charter that spells out the firm's environmental goals. A recent study of a group of European companies found, perhaps not surprisingly, that employees at firms with a well-communicated environmental policy were much more likely to come up with creative proposals for helping the environment.[35]

Cross-functional teams. Another organizational element is the use of ad hoc, cross-functional teams to solve environmental problems, including individuals from different departments. These teams pull together key players with the skills and resources to get the job done, wherever they are located in the corporate structure. At Lockheed Missiles and Space Corporation's facility in Sunnyvale, California, a Pollution

[33] "Fishing for the Future: Unilever's Sustainable Fisheries Initiative." Information about Unilever's environmental initiatives is available at *www.unilever.com/ourvalues/environmentandsociety*.

[34] Anne T. Lawrence and David Morell, "Leading-Edge Environmental Management: Motivation, Opportunity, Resources, and Processes," *Research in Corporate Social Performance and Policy*, supp. 1 (1995), pp. 99–127; and James Maxwell, Sandra Rothenberg, Forrest Briscoe, and Alfred Marcus, "Green Schemes: Corporate Environmental Strategies and Their Implementation," *California Management Review* 39, no. 3 (March 22, 1997), pp. 118 ff.

[35] Catherine A. Ramus and Ulrich Steger, "The Roles of Supervisory Support Behaviors and Environmental Policy in Employee Ecoinitiatives at Leading European Companies," *Academy of Management Review*, August, 2000, pp. 605–26.

Prevention Committee includes representatives from each of the five major business areas within the company. Each year, the committee selects about a dozen projects from among many proposed from each area. Interdivisional, cross-functional teams are set up to work on approved projects, such as one to recycle wastewater.

Rewards and incentives. Businesspeople are most likely to consider the environmental impacts of their actions when their organizations acknowledge and reward this behavior. The greenest organizations tie the compensation of their managers, including line managers, to environmental achievement and take steps to recognize these achievements publicly.

Environmental Audits

Green companies not only organize themselves to achieve environmental goals; they also closely track their progress toward meeting them. Chapter 4 introduced the concept of social performance auditing and presented recent evidence on what proportion of companies report results to their stakeholders. In the 1990s, in a parallel development, many companies began to audit their environmental performance. In the mid-2000s, in a significant change in practice, many firms moved to integrate their social, environmental, and economic reporting into a single **sustainability report.** In 2005, 68 percent of the world's top 250 companies issued such an integrated report, up from just 14 percent in 2002.

> An example of a company that made such a shift is Toyota, which issued its first environmental report in 1998; since 2003, the company has moved to integrated sustainability reporting. Its reports present detailed data on the company's progress in meeting stated past and future goals. "In the future, Toyota plans to continue enhancing disclosure of information [on] both the environmental and social aspects of its activities," said the company's executive vice president.[36]

As discussed earlier in Chapter 4, the movement to audit and report on social and environmental performance has gained momentum in recent years in many regions of the world.

Environmental Management as a Competitive Advantage

Some researchers believe that by moving toward ecological sustainability, business firms gain a competitive advantage. That is, relative to other firms in the same industry, companies that proactively manage environmental issues will tend to be more successful than those that do not.[37] One top business executive who has embraced this view is William Clay Ford, chairman of the Ford Motor Company. Under his leadership, the company undertook development of efficient hybrid gasoline-electric vehicles, set out to remodel its venerable Rouge factory complex as a state-of-the-art environmental facility, and joined a partnership to develop hydrogen fuel cells—a new kind of engine based on a totally renewable energy source. Said Ford, "We can't expand in potentially huge markets such as India and China, and provide a better life for the world's poorest people, unless we can do it in a sustainable way. . . . We look at [sustainability] not just as a requirement, but as an incredible opportunity."[38]

---

[36] *KPMG International Survey of Corporate Responsibility Reporting 2005,* www.kpmg.com. Toyota's social and environmental reports are available at *www.toyota.co.jp.*

[37] For a full elaboration of this argument, see Forest L. Reinhardt, "Bringing the Environment Down to Earth," *Harvard Business Review,* July–August 1999.

[38] Speech by Bill Ford, April 14, 2000, available at *www.ceres.org/eventsandnews/news/Fordspeech.html*

Effective environmental management confers a competitive advantage in four different ways, as follows.

Cost Savings

Companies that reduce pollution and hazardous waste, reuse or recycle materials, and operate with greater energy efficiency can reap significant cost savings. An example is Herman Miller, the office furniture company.

Herman Miller goes to great lengths to avoid wasting materials. The company sells fabric scraps to the auto industry for use as car linings; leather trim to luggage makers for attaché cases; and vinyl to the supplier to be re-extruded into new edging. Burnable solid waste is used as fuel for a specialized boiler that generates all the heating and cooling for the company's main complex in Zeeland, Michigan. The result is that the company actually makes money from materials that, in the past, it would have had to pay to have hauled away and dumped.[39]

Product Differentiation

Companies that develop a reputation for environmental excellence and that produce and deliver products and services with concern for their sustainability can attract environmentally aware customers. For example, when Home Depot announced it would sell only sustainably harvested wood products, it attracted new customers impressed with its environmental commitment. This approach is sometimes called **green marketing**. The size of the green market is difficult to estimate. Some surveys show, for example, that 40 percent of consumers say that they are willing to buy "green" products, but only 4 percent actually do.[40] Environmental excellence may also attract business customers, a trend that has emerged in the gold mining industry, as illustrated in the discussion case at the end of this chapter.

Technological Innovation

Environmentally proactive companies are often technological leaders, as they seek imaginative new methods for reducing pollution and increasing efficiency. In many cases, they produce innovations that can win new customers, penetrate new markets, or even be marketed to other firms as new regulations spur their adoption.

Nikon, a Japanese firm that makes cameras and other optical products, became concerned about use of environmentally harmful materials in the production of optical glass. The company invested several years of effort and millions of yen to develop a new product, dubbed "eco-glass," that equaled the performance of other optical glass but was made entirely without lead or arsenic. By 2005, Nikon had switched to eco-glass in all the consumer products it shipped. The company's innovation attracted customers such as environmentally aware birdwatchers who were impressed with eco-glass binoculars.[41]

In Europe, new rules that went into effect in 2006 banned all electronics products that included six toxic substances, including lead, cadmium, and mercury. Companies that had learned how to make their products free of these substances suddenly had a big advantage in winning European accounts.[42]

[39] Herman Miller's sustainability initiatives are described at *www.hermanmiller.com.*

[40] Joel Makower, "Green Marketing and the '4/40 Gap,'" *www.makower.typepad.com.*

[41] "Environmental Report 2005," *www.nikon.co.jp.*

[42] "Europe Says: Let's Get the Lead Out," *BusinessWeek,* February 7, 2005, p. 12.

Strategic Planning

Companies that cultivate a vision of sustainability must adopt sophisticated strategic planning techniques to allow their top managers to assess the full range of the firm's effects on the environment. The complex auditing and forecasting techniques used by these firms help them anticipate a wide range of external influences on the firm, not just ecological influences. Wide-angle planning helps these companies foresee new markets, materials, technologies, and products.

> Since 2005, the Global 100 Most Sustainable Corporations in the World have been announced annually at the World Economic Forum in Davos, Switzerland. The winners are selected based on their "ability to manage strategic opportunities in new environmental and social markets." On the list in both 2005 and 2006 was BP, formerly British Petroleum. As one of the world's leading producers of oil and gas, BP clearly contributes to global warming and other environmental ills. Nonetheless, the company was cited for investing in solar, fuel cell, and wind power technologies; introducing low-emissions fuels at its retail outlets; and entering cross-industry sustainability partnerships. In 2006, the company announced the formation of a new business unit, BP Alternative Energy, and said it anticipated sales of $6 billion annually within a decade. BP's environmental initiatives were consistent with long-range strategic planning that anticipated an eventual decline in the world's supply of fossil fuels, a rising threat of climate change, and a tighter regulatory environment.[43]

In short, proactive environmental management may help businesses not only promote sustainability but also become more competitive in the global marketplace by reducing costs, attracting environmentally aware customers, spurring innovation, and encouraging long-range strategic planning that anticipates external change.[44]

Summary

- Government environmental regulations focus on protecting the ecological health of the air, water, and land. Environmental laws are designed to limit the amount of pollution that companies may emit.

- Environmental laws have traditionally been of the command and control type, specifying standards and results. New laws, in both the United States and Europe, have added market incentives to induce environmentally sound behavior and have encouraged companies to reduce pollution at the source.

- Environmental laws have brought many benefits. Air, water, and land pollution levels are in many cases lower than in 1970. But some improvements have come at a high cost. A continuing challenge is to find ways to promote a clean environment and sustainable business practices without impairing the competitiveness of the U.S. economy.

[43] "BP Forms Alternative Energy Unit," press release, November 28, 2005. More information about BP's sustainability initiatives is available at *www.bp.com*. A list of the Global 100 most sustainable corporations is available at *www.global100.org*.

[44] For a recent collection of articles by leading scholars, see Sanjay Sharma and J. Alberto Aragon-Correa, eds., *Corporate Environmental Strategy and Competitive Advantage* (Northampton, MA: Edgar Elgar Academic Publishing, 2005). For a general statement of the argument that environmental management confers a competitive advantage, see Michael E. Porter and Claas van der Linde, "Green and Competitive: Beyond the Stalemate," *Harvard Business Review*, September–October 1995, pp. 120 ff; Stuart L. Hart, "Beyond Greening: Strategies for a Sustainable World," *Harvard Business Review*, January–February 1997, pp. 66–76; and Renato J. Orsato, "Competitive Environmental Strategies: When Does It Pay to Be Green?" *California Management Review* 48, no. 2 (Winter 2006), pp. 127–43.

- Companies pass through three distinct stages in the development of green management practices. Many businesses are now moving from lower to higher stages. An ecologically sustainable organization is one that operates in a way that is consistent with the principle of sustainable development.

- Effective environmental management requires an integrated approach that involves all parts of the business organization, including top leadership, line managers, and production teams, as well as strong partnerships with stakeholders and effective auditing.

- Many companies have found that proactive environmental management can confer a competitive advantage by saving money, attracting green customers, promoting innovation, and developing skills in strategic planning.

Key Terms

acid rain, *255*
command and control regulation, *258*
ecologically sustainable organization (ESO), *266*
environmental justice, *257*
environmental partnerships, *266*

Environmental Protection Agency (EPA), *253*
environmental standards, *258*
greening of management, *264*
green marketing, *269*

market-based mechanisms, *259*
source reduction, *258*
Superfund (CERCLA), *258*
sustainability report , *268*

Internet Resources

www.epa.gov
www.envirolink.org
www.GreenBiz.com
www.sustainablebusiness.com

Environmental Protection Agency
Environmental organizations and news
Green Business Network
Network of sustainable small businesses

Discussion Case: *Digging Gold*

Gold mining is one of the most environmentally destructive industries in the world. Most gold today is extracted using a technique called cyanide heap-leaching. Workers dig and blast the earth in open-pit mines so massive that astronauts can see them from space. Using huge earth-moving machines, they pile the gold-bearing ore into mounds the size of pyramids, then spray them with a solution of cyanide to leach out the gold. In a series of steps, gold is then removed from the drainage at the bottom of the heap and is further refined in smelters into pure bars of the precious metal.

Heap-leaching enables the economic extraction of gold from low-grade ores; some modern mines use as much as 30 tons of rock to produce a single ounce of precious metal. But this process can be highly damaging to the environment. Cyanide is one of the most potent poisons known; a pellet the size of a grain of rice can kill a person. Most spent cyanide solution is stored in reservoirs, where it gradually breaks down. But these reservoirs are prone to accidents. In 2000, at a gold mine in Romania operated by the Australian firm Esmeralda Exploration, 100,000 tons of wastewater laced with cyanide spilled into a tributary of the Danube River. The toxic plume washed all the way to the Black Sea, causing a massive kill of fish and birds and contaminating the drinking water of 2.5 million people.

After this incident, a Romanian citizen's group called Alburnus Maior organized to block construction of a new gold mine by the Canadian firm Gabriel Resources at Rosia Montana. "We have to decide whether we want [these] mountains to become a no man's land," said Eugen David, a local farmer and activist.

Transportation of materials to and from mines, which are often located in remote areas, poses additional risks. A truck carrying containers of mercury (a by-product of gold extraction) from the Yanacocha Mine in Peru, owned by U.S.-based Newmont Mining, spilled its load on a rural road. Villagers from the area, not understanding the danger, collected the hazardous liquid metal. More than 1,000 people became ill, some permanently, a lawsuit later filed on their behalf charged.

In most developed nations, environmental laws prohibit the discharge of mining waste directly into waterways. But elsewhere in the world, laws are often weaker and regulations poorly enforced. In Indonesia, U.S.-based Freeport McMoran's Grasberg operation, the largest gold mine in the world, dumps its waste directly into local rivers, badly damaging downstream rain forests and wetlands. An official of the Environment Ministry said that the agency's regulatory tools were so weak that it was like "painting on clouds" to get the company even to follow the law.

Gold mining also pollutes the air. The entire process of metal extraction—from diesel-powered earth-moving equipment to oil- and coal-burning smelters—consumes large quantities of fuel, contributing to global warming. Smelters produce oxides of nitrogen and sulfur, components of acid rain, as well as traces of toxic metals such as lead, arsenic, and cadmium.

Another environmental hazard of gold extraction is acid mine drainage. Often, the rock that harbors gold also contains sulfide minerals. When this rock is crushed and exposed to air and water, these minerals form sulfuric acid. As this acid drains from mine debris, it picks up other metals, such as arsenic, mercury, and lead, creating a toxic brew that can drain into groundwater and waterways. This process can go on for decades, long after a mine has shut down.

In the United States, although mining companies have to follow environmental laws, no law specifically ensures that a mine will not create acid runoff. Sixty-three Superfund sites are abandoned mines; the EPA has estimated their cleanup cost at $7.8 billion. In a study for Congress in 2005, the General Accounting Office called for new rules to require mining companies to post adequate surety bonds (a kind of insurance) to cover the costs of remediation if they went out of business.

Pegasus Gold, a Canadian company, declared bankruptcy in 1998 and abruptly shut down its Zortman-Landusky mine in Montana, once the largest gold mine in the United States, sticking the state's taxpayers with a $33 million bill for ongoing water treatment and cleanup. The citizens of Montana subsequently voted to ban cyanide heap-leach mining completely anywhere in the state. After an effort to overturn this initiative failed, Canyon Resources, a company that held the rights to a valuable Montana deposit, said it was looking into other ways to extract gold, including an innovative new technology that used bacteria instead of cyanide.

In 2004, Earthworks, an environmental NGO based in the United States, launched a campaign called "No Dirty Gold," picketing stores on Fifth Avenue in Manhattan and calling on consumers to boycott gold jewelry. At least one retailer was listening. Michael Kowalski, chairman of the jewelry retailer Tiffany & Co., announced that his company would fund an independent study to define environmentally sound mining practices.

Tiffany had already committed to sourcing its gold from Bingham Canyon, a mine in Utah operated by Kennecott, a company that had made a public commitment to sustainability. "For Tiffany, responsible mining is absolutely a part of our brand contract," Kowalski said.

Sources: "Dirty Metals: Mining, Communities, and the Environment," a Report by Earthworks and Oxfam America, 2004, *www.nodirtygold.org*; "Beyond Gold's Glitter: Torn Lands and Pointed Questions," New York Times, October 24, 2005, pp. A1, A10; "Tangled Strands in Fight over Peru Gold Mine," New York Times, October 25, 2005, pp. A1, A14; "Hardrock Mining: BLM Needs to Better Manage Financial Assurances to Guarantee Reclamation Costs," GAO Report to the Ranking Minority Member, Committee on Homeland Security and Governmental Affairs, U.S. Senate, June 2005; Jared Diamond, Collapse: How Societies Choose to Fail or Succeed (New York: Viking, 2005), Ch. 15, "Big Business and the Environment: Different Conditions, Different Outcomes"; "Tiffany & Co.: A Case Study in Diamonds and Social Responsibility," Business Ethics (Wharton), November 17, 2004, *http://knowledge.wharton.upenn.edu*; Web sites of Westerners for Responsible Mining, *www.bettermines.org*, and Alburnus Maior, *www.rosiamontana.org*; and additional articles in the Northwest Mining Association Bulletin, High Country News, and Billings Gazette. Kennecott's sustainable development reports are available at *http://kennecott.com*.

Discussion Questions

1. Using the classification system presented in the chapter section, "Major Areas of Environmental Regulation," what types of pollution are generated by gold mining? Which of these do you think is (are) most damaging to the environment, and why?

2. Using the classification system presented in the section, "Alternative Policy Approaches," what types of government regulation do you think would most effectively address the concerns you have identified?

3. In your view, what role should nongovernmental organizations (NGOs) and citizen movements play in reducing the adverse environmental impacts of gold mining?

4. Which of the gold mining companies mentioned in this case are more, or less, environmentally responsible? What factors, in your view, might cause these differences?

PART SIX

Business and Technological Change

CHAPTER THIRTEEN

Technology: A Global Economic and Social Force

Technology is an unmistakable economic and social force in our world. Global communications, business exchanges, and the simple tasks that make up our daily lives are all significantly influenced by technology. Whether we are at home, in school, or in the workplace, the emergence of technological innovations has dramatically changed how we live, play, learn, work, and interact with others. Accompanying these dramatic changes in our global community are profound effects on the individual, business, and society, raising important social and ethical questions.

This chapter focuses on these key learning objectives:

- Knowing the dominant features of technology and what fuels technological growth.
- Understanding how e-commerce has changed the way businesses operate and interact with their stakeholders.
- Assessing the emergence of technology superpowers and their effect on the global marketplace.
- Analyzing new Internet opportunities—blogs, vlogs, spam, and phishing—and the challenges they create.
- Recognizing socially beneficial uses of technology in business, education, and medicine.
- Evaluating recent efforts to address and reduce the digital divide.

MySpace.com bolted onto the Internet scene in 2004 as a widely popular site for young people's personal Web pages. These sites included personal photographs and other details about their lives and interests so they could meet and interact with others. By April 2006, 65 million people had accessed MySpace.com.

When the News Corporation acquired MySpace.com in July 2005, the company quickly realized that, in addition to having an exceptionally popular Web site, it had also inherited numerous ethical challenges. Privacy and safety concerns were raised by parents, school officials, and law enforcement officers, since the site sometimes unwittingly made young people vulnerable to pornographers or predators. Richard Blumenthal, Connecticut's attorney general, met with MySpace.com officials and pleaded with them to undertake stringent security measures to protect the site's users.

In April 2006, the News Corporation hired Hemanshu Nigam, former director of consumer security at Microsoft, to oversee safety, education, privacy programs, and law enforcement affairs. The company also announced an advertising campaign to educate parents and young people about Internet safety. The campaign ran public service announcements on MySpace and other Web sites and television channels owned by the News Corporation.

Blumenthal praised these efforts but continued to challenge the company to do more. "A public safety campaign is a welcome step toward protecting our children from pornography and predators—and people looking for sex—but must be followed by more stringent, specific measures that we have also urged MySpace to take." Among the proposals Blumenthal discussed with MySpace were more stringent age verification measures and free software to let parents block the site from their home computers.[1]

Does business have an ethical responsibility to monitor online activity and provide oversight to protect users, particularly children, from pornographers and predators? Did the News Corporation act quickly enough, or should it have anticipated the problems that arose and have proactively protected its vulnerable users? Could the News Corporation have done more, as suggested by the Connecticut attorney general, regarding users' safety and privacy?

The Explosive Force of Technology

Throughout history, technology has been an explosive force. It has repeatedly erupted, exerting a tremendous influence on humankind, business, and the world. Stemming the advance of technology appears virtually impossible, as seen in the emergence of nanotechnology. The excitement over **nanotechnology**, the ability to create manmade structures just a few billionths of a meter in size, spread throughout the scientific and business communities like wildfire in the early 2000s. Governments and private venture capitalists invested billions of dollars to support nanotechnology research in the United States, Asia, and Europe. Some believed that nanotechnology might revolutionize the fields of electronics and manufacturing, with analysts predicting a $40 billion to $75 billion market by 2010. By the mid-2000s, nanotech materials had found their way into consumer products such as automobile fuel lines and tires, wrinkle-resistant clothing, sunscreen, and tennis rackets.[2]

---

[1] "MySpace.com Hires Official to Oversee Users' Safety," *The New York Times Online*, April 12, 2006, *www.nytimes.com*.

[2] "The Business of Nanotech," *BusinessWeek*, February 14, 2005, pp. 64–71.

But with all this excitement came a cry of fear. Trial lawyers, labor unions, and environmentalists were fearful of possible health and safety hazards posed by nanomaterials. Some began to compare nanotechnology to asbestos, a material plagued by $70 billion in litigation since the 1970s.

Greenpeace International, a global environmentalist organization, called for a moratorium on the release of nanoparticles in commercial products until any risks to humans or the environment could be assessed. Douglas Parr, chief scientist for Greenpeace in the United Kingdom, explained, "What we want to avoid is the situation where a small group of financially and technologically interested people develop something and thrust it on the rest of the world." A Greenpeace report warned that particles from nanotechnologically produced materials could be inhaled, potentially causing harm to humans, or could bind with poisonous metals and help disperse them through the environment.[3]

Technology continues to grow because of people themselves. Human beings have sampled and embraced the fruits of knowledge. It seems that people have acquired an insatiable desire for it. They forever seek to expand knowledge of their environment, probably because of the excitement in learning and their belief that more knowledge will help them adapt to their environment. As Bill Joy, Sun Microsystems' chief scientist, explained,

> By 2030, we are likely to be able to build machines, in quantity, a million times as powerful as the personal computer of today. As this enormous computing power is combined with the manipulative advances of the physical sciences and the new, deep understanding in genetics, enormous transformative power is being unleashed. These combinations open up the opportunity to completely redesign the world, for better or worse: The replicating and evolving processes that have been confined to the natural world are about to become realms of human endeavor.[4]

Technology Defined

Technology is a broad term referring to knowledge of and use of humanity's tools and crafts. The dominant feature of technology is change and then more change. For example, nanotechnology has brought so much change that some speak of it in terms of the latest *future shock*, in which change comes so fast and furiously that it approaches the limits of human tolerance and people lose their ability to cope with it successfully. Although technology is not the only cause of change in society, it is a primary cause. It is either directly or indirectly involved in most changes that occur in society.

> Some years ago, right after the start of the personal computer revolution, industry experts observed that if automobiles had developed at the same rate as the computer business, a Rolls-Royce would cost $2.75 and go 3 million miles on a gallon of gasoline. Today's computers, personal data assistants, cellular telephones, music players, and pagers cost less than those of a decade or even a few years ago and offer many times the power and many more times the speed of their predecessors.

[3] "Greenpeace Warns of Pollutants from Nanotechnology," *The Wall Street Journal*, July 25, 2003, pp. B1, B4; and "Big Troubles May Lurk in Super-Tiny Tech," *SFGate*, October 31, 2005, *www.sfgate.com*.

[4] Bill Joy, "Why the Future Doesn't Need Us," *Wired*, April 2000, *www.wired.com/wired/archive/8.04/joy*.

Another feature of technology is that its effects are widespread, reaching far beyond the immediate point of technological impact. Technology ripples through society until every community is affected by it. For example, **telecommunications**, the transmission of information over great distances, has played a historically significant and positive role in our society's development. This innovation has enhanced international commerce, linked relatives living great distances apart, and enabled us to discover many of the mysteries of outer space. Yet, along with these advances has come the potential for a greater invasion of privacy through databases and telemarketing practices. The human touch in our communication with others has been diminished through the convenience of electronic and voice mail.

An additional feature of technology is that it is self-reinforcing. As stated by Alvin Toffler, "Technology feeds on itself. Technology makes more technology possible."[5] This self-reinforcing feature means that technology acts as a multiplier to encourage its own faster development. It acts with other parts of society so that an invention in one place leads to a sequence of inventions in other places. Thus, invention of the microprocessor led rather quickly to successful generations of the modern computer, which led to new banking methods, electronic mail, bar-code systems, global tracking systems, and so on.

Phases of Technology in Society

Five broad phases of technology have developed, as shown in Figure 13.1. Nations have tended to move sequentially through each phase, beginning with the lowest technology and moving higher with each step, so the five phases roughly represent the progress of civilization throughout history.

The current phase of technology is the **information society**. This phase emphasizes the use and transfer of knowledge and information rather than manual skill. Businesses of all sizes, including the smallest firms, are exploring the benefits of the information age through the availability of nanotechnology and similar inventions. These inventions have catapulted societies into **cyberspace**, where information is stored, ideas are described, and communication takes place in and through an electronic network of linked systems. The technology developed in this new age provided the mechanisms for more information to be produced in a decade than in the previous 1,000 years.

Where will technology head next? Some observers have suggested that society is now at the beginning of a new phase dominated by *biotechnology*. As discussed in more detail in Chapter 14, **biotechnology** is a technological application that uses biological systems or living organisms to make or modify products or processes for specific use. Its applications are common in agriculture, food science, and medicine.[6] This emerging phase of

FIGURE 13.1   Phases in the Development of Technology

Technology Level	Phases in the Development of Technology	Approximate Period	Activity	Primary Skill Used
1	Nomadic-agrarian	Until 1650	Harvesting	Manual
2	Agrarian	1650–1900	Planting and harvesting	Manual
3	Industrial	1900–1960	Building material goods	Manual and machine
4	Service	1960–1975	Providing services	Manual and intellectual
5	Information	1975–today	Thinking and designing	Intellectual and electronic

[5] Alvin Toffler, *Future Shock* (New York: Bantam, 1971), p. 26.

[6] From "Biotechnology," *Wikipedia*, at *en.wikipedia.org/wiki.biotechnology*.

technology extends beyond the thinking and designing of information to the manipulation of organisms to produce fabricated products.

Fueling Technological Growth

The dynamic explosion of technological growth is documented in how businesses operate and people live. Underlying this explosive development are two important factors: economic growth and worker productivity and research and development investment.

The first factor that fuels technological growth is economic growth and worker productivity. During the 1990s, U.S. businesses poured more than $2 trillion into computers, software, and other technology products. This massive spending helped sustain the economic boom that carried the global business community into the 21st century. The adoption of new technologies is also linked to worker productivity. During the late 1990s, productivity grew at almost twice the rate of the previous two decades, since technology was relatively cheap and pervasive. Thus, businesses could afford more technology and workers were more adept in accepting technological improvements. Both conditions led to significant productivity gains during economic expansion.

The second factor fueling technological growth was research and development (R&D). As mentioned above, businesses were more directed in their technology strategies, seeking a quicker and more direct return on their investment.

Technology superpower Hewlett-Packard replaced 85 global data centers with six cutting-edge facilities at a cost of $1 billion in 2006. But some firms in the banking industry outspent many technology-based companies. J. P. Morgan, a global financial services firm with assets of more than $1.3 trillion, spent three times as much as Hewlett-Packard to overhaul its technology network and to reduce its 90 global data centers to 30 by 2008. Other financial services titans, Morgan Stanley, Merrill Lynch, Citigroup, and Goldman Sachs, reported spending 1 to 2 billion dollars each in 2005 to upgrade their information technology systems.[7]

Government support of technology complements private R&D spending. For example, in the late 1990s the United States launched a program of financial assistance for Internet projects in developing countries. While this effort has increased more slowly than industry funding, the U.S. government has annually provided more than $60 billion to support technology-based research and development, compared with about $45 billion from European governments. Japanese government officials addressed their relative lack of R&D support by increasing their funding and partnering with Japanese high-tech companies in the quest to surpass the U.S. high-speed Internet infrastructure. Dramatic increases in R&D expenditures for technology development occurred in India, China, Taiwan, and South Korea in the mid-2000s.[8]

The Emergence of High-Technology Business

Technology and business have been intertwined since the Industrial Revolution. The connection between the two became even stronger in the information age, particularly with the advent of electronic business exchanges. Technology influences every aspect

[7] "The Bank of Technology," *BusinessWeek*, June 19, 2006, p. 54.

[8] "Japan Goes All Out to Catch U.S. in High-Speed Internet Services," *The Wall Street Journal*, November 27, 2000, p. B4; and "Scouring the Planet for Brainiacs," *BusinessWeek*, October 11, 2004, pp. 100–6.

of the global marketplace—driving innovation, affecting partnerships, and changing business–stakeholder relationships. Many of these innovations have improved business exchanges, while serious ethical and social challenges also appeared.

Technology and E-Commerce

During the information age phase of technological development, electronic business exchanges between businesses emerged as a powerful global economic and social force. These electronic business exchanges, generally referred to as **e-commerce**, consist of buying and selling goods and services electronically, that is, via the Internet.

By 2000, many businesses had created a multitude of Web pages to advertise and sell their products and services over the Internet. As the number of Internet users increased exponentially, the outreach of this type of marketing exceeded all expectations. By 2005, total business-to-consumer e-commerce sales reached $109.4 billion, a 25 percent increase from 2004 sales, which in turn were more than 25 percent higher than 2003 sales. Online sales for 2006 were expected to rise another 22 percent, to more than $130 billion. The United States was the global leader in e-commerce transactions, accounting for 63 percent of all Internet-based sales in 2005, but the greatest growth was seen in Latin American and Asian countries as technology became more available and faster in these regions.[9] E-commerce has become a way of life, from large companies and smaller start-up businesses to individuals interested in shopping online.

As technology became more affordable and easier to use, small and medium-sized businesses committed investment dollars into e-commerce and technology systems. These businesses discovered that the adoption of technology was a money-saver rather than an expense in the long run and that it gave the businesses a competitive edge over rivals by enabling them to add new services and operate more efficiently.

> When a computer programmer offered to create a custom package for Top Dog Daycare, owners Joelle and Tom Hilfers were shocked but agreed to take the plunge, on a payment plan. Three years and nearly $30,000 in technology investments later, the Hilfers do not know how they ever survived without the company's K-9 Connect software, which allows dog owners to book appointments online, view their accounts, post photos of their pets, and look in on them during the day through a live Web cam. K-9 Connect also stores the pets' vaccination records, meal plans, and special requirements and has pages on e-commerce, dog training, and dog grooming. Business at Top Dog Daycare tripled since adopting the computerized system.[10]

Some of America's biggest companies welcomed the move into e-commerce. They developed new approaches to old problems. Exhibit 13.A profiles some of the largest firms' e-commerce strategies.

E-commerce is undoubtedly here to stay, and new applications appear inevitable. Yet with each new innovation comes the important ethical question: *Should* we develop and offer the new application? At present, many inventors, computer programmers, and business managers appear only to be asking: *Can* we develop and offer

---

[9] "E-commerce Grew 25% in 2005, Repeating 2004 Sates Growth Performance," *ZDNet*, June 1, 2006, *news.zdnet.com*; and "Online Sales Expected to Rise 20 Percent in 2006," *ZDNet*, May 22, 2006, *news.zdnet.com*.

[10] "High Tech Isn't Just for the Big Guys," *The New York Times Online*, January 20, 2005, *www.nytimes.com*.

Exhibit 13.A E-Commerce Strategies

Mattel used the Web for designers and licenses in far-flung locales to collaborate on toy design. In two years, Mattel cut the time it takes to develop new products by 20 percent.

Alcoa set up an online showroom to sell off slow-growth businesses. Interested buyers had access to digital balance sheets and profit and loss statements. Alcoa sold three businesses via the Web and saved $200,000 in travel, hotel, and meeting expenses.

Eli Lilly created a Web site where scientific problems were posed and the best minds solved them for cash prizes. In two years, Eli Lilly solved problems in months instead of the expected two to three years.

Lockheed Martin linked 80 major suppliers from around the globe, helping the company build a new stealth fighter airplane. Lockheed Martin saved about $25 million a year over the decade it will take to develop and test the plane.

Saint Alphonsus installed 32 miles of optical fiber for a network to speed transmission of medical images such as heart scans. The images can be viewed almost instantly instead of taking 24 to 48 hours when delivered by hand.

Krispy Kreme established a network linking 320 stores to take orders and alert store managers when they overstocked. Ordering errors were down 90 percent, while productivity gains allowed managers to run twice as many stores.

Source: "Web Smart 50," *BusinessWeek*, November 24, 2003, pp. 82–106.

the new application? Both questions are paramount as technology and e-commerce continue to influence individual, business, and society interactions in the world in which we live.

Technology "Superpowers"

At the core of high-technology industry are the builders of the information technology system. While the designers of Web pages may receive much of the press, the high-technology industry is grounded in the work done by companies that dig the trenches and lay the pipes that contain the fiber-optic cable and that build the servers that connect the network. In *BusinessWeek*'s Information Technology 100, the top 20 largest firms included companies that provide networking and telecommunications, as well as businesses that linked companies and consumers through the Internet. "There are the glamour companies, and then there are the companies that are building the new Net economy," reported Edward J. Zander, president of Sun Microsystems, a maker of computer networks. "We're the lumberyard for the Internet."[11]

By 2006, a small but powerful group of technology superpowers controlled many of the entrance ramps to the Internet. The top 10 Web portals for global users and the amount of time they spend on the site are shown in Figure 13.2.

Emerging Global Participation

While much of the discussion thus far in this chapter has focused on technological innovation and technology superpowers in the United States, most industrialized countries are actively pursuing a strategy to include technology in the lives of their citizens. Global

[11] "Builders of the New Economy," *BusinessWeek*, June 21, 1999, pp. 118–22. For 2006 data see "The Information Technology 100," *BusinessWeek*, July 3, 2006, pp. 78–86.

FIGURE 13.2
The Top 10 Global Web Portals

Sources: "Top Web Sites for March 2006: Yahoo!, Microsoft, MSN; MySpace Is in Top 10," *Nielsen/Net Ratings,* April 2006, *blogs.zdnet.com/Research.*

	Number of Visitors in March 2006 (in thousands)	Time Spent per Person per Visit (hours:minutes:seconds)
Yahoo!	105,027	3:28:39
Microsoft	99,368	0:50:16
MSN	95,124	1:52:10
Google	93,244	1:00:56
AOL	75,348	6:13:54
eBay	55,573	1:59:18
MapQuest	40,809	0:12:05
Amazon	40,721	0:23:21
Real	36,961	0:43:00
MySpace	36,373	2:09:04

participation in technology appears to offer a lucrative market, as illustrated in the following example.

> European technology-equipment manufacturers, Nokia, Telefon ABL.M., Ericsson, and Siemens joined with NTT DoCoMo, a Japanese mobile-phone operator, to offer a special promotion to persuade developing countries to adopt the technical standard being used throughout Europe for third-generation (3G) mobile phones. The technology enabled users to send video clips, Internet pages, and other multimedia content over wireless telephones. In the proposal, the European and Japanese companies agreed to limit the licensing fees they charged on third-generation wireless technology, making the European 3G technology more cost-effective than that of their rivals, primarily the North American-based Qualcomm. The opportunities to promote the European 3G technology were greatly reduced when China decided to adopt its own technical standard for its third-generation mobile phones. Yrio Neuvo, chief technology officer for Nokia, said, "Where countries have not selected a 3G standard yet, it's a competitive advantage to offer reasonable [royalty] levels."[12]

In other regions, technology companies saw incredible opportunities for growth. For example, 60 percent of the 45 million Koreans had mobile phones, but less than half were connected to the Internet. With billions of dollars of direct foreign investment in high-tech companies, Korea was on the verge of entering the global digital community.

> Brazil provided an interesting global test case for technological development over the question of free or fee Internet access. Brazil's Universo Online (UOL) and Terra Networks, part of a Spanish telecommunications company, offered free Internet access to all interested Brazilians. This strategy directly conflicted with America Online (AOL) Latin America's approach of offering Internet subscription service for a fee. AOL Latin America reported having 65,000 subscribers before the free Internet option was offered, accounting for less than 3 percent of all Brazilians. Shortly after the competition began, Brazil's UOL added 800,000 of the 1 million new subscribers to Internet service. The long-term viability of offering free Internet service by relying primarily on advertisement revenues remained to be seen.

[12] "Mobile-Phone Suppliers Court China, Developing Countries," *The Wall Street Journal,* June 9, 2003, p. A6; and "In Tech, China Is Setting the Standard," *The Wall Street Journal,* September 10, 2003, p. A22.

Developed and developing countries in Asia, South America, and Europe joined North America in efforts to increase access to technology for businesses and individuals. However, as in the debate over nanotechnology described at the beginning of this chapter, some people raised concerns over the ethical challenges arising from an e-commerce world.[13] Many of these ethical concerns are discussed in Chapter 14.

The Internet

More people have more access to technology than ever before. Residents of developing countries increasingly enjoy energy-powered appliances, entertainment devices, and communications equipment. Individuals and businesses in developed countries in North America, Europe, and portions of Asia are depending more than ever on electronic communication devices for access to information and conducting business transactions. In today's workplace environment, nearly every American manager uses a desktop computer, fax machines, answering machines, voice mail, and cellular telephones. These technology devices have become common tools.

The Emergence of the Internet

One of the most visible and widely used technological innovations of recent years has been the Internet, or the World Wide Web. The **Internet** is a global electronic communications network linking individuals and organizations. It enables users to send and receive electronic mail (e-mail) and access information from virtually any library or personal computer. Springing to life in 1994, this conduit of information revolutionized how business was conducted, students learned, and households operated.

Any estimate of the number of Internet users is clearly only an estimate. In 2005, the Computer Industry Almanac estimated there were 1.08 billion Internet users worldwide (about 1 out of every 6 people) and predicted the number would rise to 1.8 billion by 2010 worldwide. The number of Internet users in the top 15 countries is shown in Figure 13.3.

Contributing to the increasing usage of the Internet are new access opportunities.

TiVo, the maker of a popular digital video recorder, announced a new set of Internet services in June 2004. These services blurred the line between programming delivered over traditional cable and satellite channels and content from the Internet. The new TiVo technology is a standard feature in its video recorders and allows users to download movies and music from the Internet to a hard drive on the video recorder.[14]

More than a decade after the emergence of a global Internet, new alternatives to it emerged, raising fears that global connectivity might be diminished. German computer engineers in 2006 began building an alternative to the Internet as a political statement. A Dutch company built a new Internet structure as a potentially profitable venture. China created three suffixes in Chinese characters substituting for .com and others, resulting in Web sites and e-mail addresses inaccessible to users outside China. The 22-nation Arab League began a similar system using Arabic suffixes. "The Internet is no longer the kind of thing where only six guys in the world can build it," said Paul Vixie,

---

[13] For a good discussion on the ethical challenges in e-commerce see Bette Ann Stead and Jackie Gilbert, "Ethical Issues in Electronic Commerce," *Journal of Business Ethics* 34 (2001), pp. 75–85.

[14] "New Service by TiVo Will Build Bridges from Internet to the TV," *The New York Times Online*, June 9, 2004, *www.nytimes.com*.

FIGURE 13.3
Top 15 Internet Users by Country, 2005

Source: "Population Explosion," ClickZ Network, April 12, 2006, *www.clickz.com.stats.*

Country	Number of Internet Users, in Millions
United States	203.8
China	111.0
Japan	86.3
India	50.6
Germany	48.7
United Kingdom	37.8
South Korea	33.9
Italy	28.9
France	26.2
Brazil	25.9
Russia	23.7
Canada	20.9
Indonesia	18.0
Spain	17.1
Mexico	17.0

a key architect of the U.S.-supported Internet. "Now, you can write a couple of checks and get one of your own."[15]

Blogs and Vlogs

By 2006, the blogging revolution was about five years old and many believed it was already out of control. **Blogs**, Web-based journals or logs, are widely popular, according to Technorati, Inc., a company that tracked more than 35 millions blogs in 2006. Technorati reported that the blogosphere was doubling in size every five and one-half months and, on average, a new Web blog was created every second of every day. Nearly 14 million bloggers were still posting 3 months after the blog was created and about 9 percent of new blogs were spam or machine generated.[16]

Most blogs were available with RSS feeds. RSS stands for Really Simple Syndication or Rich Site Summary, depending on the source. RSS allows users to subscribe to specific desired blogs and receive updates from these blogs without having to repeatedly revisit them, via a browser or a separate program called a news reader, which collects the feeds together as an e-mail program collects e-mails.

A new generation of blogs appeared in the mid-2000s, called **vlogs**, or video Web logs. All that was needed was access to a digital camera that could capture moving images and high-speed Internet.

Viewers of Beth Agnew's Web site could watch videos of her laughing while looking at an oak leaf, while wearing a pirate's patch, and while pretending someone has dropped an ice cube down her back. The vlog, laughpractice.blogspot.com, promoted finding hilarity in the mundane and to spread goodwill through laughter. "Anyone anywhere in the world can log into the blog and have a laugh along with me," said Agnew, a college professor in Toronto and self-described certified laugh leader.

[15] "In Threat to Internet's Clout, Some Are Starting Alternatives," *The Wall Street Journal Online*, January 19, 2006, *online.wsj.com.*

[16] See Technorati, Inc.'s, Web site at *www.technorati.com.*

The nascent vlog medium attracted thousands of aspiring video producers. The number of vlogs mushroomed due to improved streaming video technology, faster Internet speeds, new Web sites that would host the video free of charge, and new cell phones and other devices designed to play videos. Videos produced by individuals and small companies found their way to on-demand services offered by cable companies and new networks that solicit user content. While most viewers stumbled across vlogs while Web surfing, others found them on Apple Computer Inc.'s iTunes directory, which listed some vlogs, calling them video podcasts. In 2005, Revlon, a cosmetic company, created a vlog displaying a woman trying out the company's new line of makeup at MTV's Music Video Awards, which the company was sponsoring.[17]

While blogs and vlogs entered the vocabulary, governments grew increasingly concerned about abuses of the new technology and the illegal activity it enabled. A Singapore court sentenced two men in 2005 to prison for posting racial slurs on their Internet blog, although the punishments were relatively minor. While many bloggers condemned the racist nature of the remarks, others wondered whether governments such as Singapore, which tolerate little outspoken opposition in the media, were attempting to extend total control over the Internet and blogs.[18]

One of the strongest reactions against blogging was from the Chinese government. By 2005, China had nearly 3 million bloggers, with estimates of close to 7 million by 2007, according to Analysys International, a market research company. The Chinese government banned blogs that called for democracy, criticized top government leadership, advocated Taiwanese independence, or included nudity or explicit sexual comments.[19]

The backlash against blogs came to a head in January 2006 when Microsoft shut down a popular Chinese-language blog that ran edgy content potentially offensive to Chinese authorities. The blog was created by Chinese journalist Zhao Jing under the penname Michael Anti. In the blog, Jing criticized the Chinese government's firing of top editors at a progressive Beijing newspaper. "MSN [Microsoft] is committed to ensuring that products and services comply with global and local laws, norms, and industry practices," explained Brooke Richardson, Microsoft's lead product manager. "Most countries have laws and practices that require companies providing online services to make the Internet safe for local users. Occasionally, as in China, local laws and practices require consideration of unique elements."[20]

Spam

The emergence of the Internet not only launched the blog avalanche but also the onslaught of spam. **Spam** refers to unsolicited e-mails (or junk e-mails) sent in bulk to valid e-mail accounts. These messages can vary from harmless advertisements for commercial products to offensive material and finance scams. Spam creates problems for e-mail users as it makes for extra network traffic and wastes time in sorting through the irrelevant or unwanted e-mails to access the desired messages. The impact of spam on consumers is discussed in Chapter 16.

[17] "Vlogger (noun): Blogger with Video Camera," *The Wall Street Journal Online*, December 16, 2005, *online.wsj.com*.

[18] "Singapore Bloggers Given Jail Terms for Posting Racial Comments," Institute for Global Ethics, *Ethics Newsline*, October 11, 2005, *www.globalethics.org*.

[19] "Blogs under Its Thumb," *BusinessWeek*, August 8, 2005, pp. 42–43.

[20] "Microsoft Shuts Down Blog Potentially Offensive to China," *The Wall Street Journal Online*, January 5, 2006, *online.wsj.com*.

Spamming has become big business and a big headache for business. According to a *Wall Street Journal* article, spam accounted for 45 percent of all e-mails, or 15 billion messages every day. Spam cost businesses worldwide $20 billion in lost productivity and technology expenses, according to the Radicato Group, a market research company. Radicato predicted that the number of daily spams would rise to more than 50 billion by 2007 and cost almost $200 billion annually.

To combat spam, organizations (and individuals) turned to spam blockers. While generally effective, there were problems making sure the bad e-mails were blocked and the desired e-mails got through.

An employment recruiter, Olga Ocon, decided to sift through an e-mail folder containing messages identified by her company's computer system as spam. Embedded in the 756 e-mail advertisements for Viagra, cell phones, and loan refinancing offers, all ready to be deleted in a few days, were eight resumes from prospective job applicants. Ocon suspected that since some of the resumes contained phrases such as "four-time winner of sales awards" and "oversaw in excess of $40 million in sales," the company's spam filter caught these messages and determined they were e-mails containing money-making offers.[21]

Governments have stepped in to monitor, control, and prosecute spammers who use the Internet for illegal activity.

JumpStart Technologies, a California Internet marketing company, agreed to pay $900,000 in fines for violating the U.S. CAN-SPAM Act. The Federal Trade Commission charged that JumpStart collected e-mail addresses by offering free movie tickets for consumers who provided the addresses of five friends. Jump-Start then spammed those friends using the name of the person who provided the address in the "from" line of the e-mail. The subject line contained a bogus personal message such as "Happy Valentine's Day." JumpStart used these tactics to circumvent antispam filters and to induce recipients to open the messages.[22]

The United Kingdom also has passed antispam legislation making it a crime to send unsolicited e-mail messages to people's private e-mail addresses or cell phones. The government believed that the threat of $8,000 for a lower-court conviction and limitless fines if the case makes its way to a jury would deter the growing spam problem. The U.K. was following Italy's lead, which in 2003 made spam a crime with punishments ranging from $108,000 in fines to three years in prison. "These regulations will help combat the global nuisance of unsolicited e-mails and texts by enshrining in law rights that give consumers more say over who can use their personal details," said U.K. communications minister Stephen Timms.[23]

Phishing

Compounding the problem of spam or junk e-mail is **phishing**, the practice of duping computer users into revealing their passwords or other private data under false pretenses. The Anti-Phishing Working Group, a U.S. industry association, reported 1,125 phishing attacks in a single month in 2004. MessageLabs, a U.S. e-mail security company,

---

[21] "Stringent Spam Filters Mistakenly Block E-Mailed Resumes," *The Wall Street Journal*, April 13, 2004, pp. B1, B4.

[22] "Internet Marketing Company Pays $900,000 Fine for Spam," Institute for Global Ethics, *Ethics Newsline*, March 26, 2006, *www.globalethics.org*.

[23] "Britain Makes It a Crime to Send Spam," Institute for Global Ethics, *Ethics Newsline*, September 22, 2003, *www.globalethics.org*.

claimed an 800-fold increase in phishing cases over a six-month period in mid-2004. According to experts, every phishing attack sends out anywhere from 50,000 to 10 million spam e-mails.

Businesses have not sat idly by while con artists have gone phishing.

> In 2003, EarthLink, the largest Internet access provider, went looking for phishers. The company discovered e-mail messages coming from computers in Russia, other eastern European countries, and Asia. "A year ago, there were some phishers out there, and it was mostly teenagers and other people fooling around," said Les Sagraves, EarthLink's chief privacy officer. "Now I think we are moving to more criminal enterprise."[24]

Phishing attacks are growing rapidly, impersonating Internet service providers, online merchants, and banks. Government officials and private investigators said all signs point to gangs of organized criminals most likely in eastern Europe as being behind many of the latest efforts.

Government Regulation of the Internet

Many of the abuses of the Internet described above have fueled a debate over whether government should regulate the content on the Internet. If so, which government or agency should step in?

The Chinese government has aggressively tried to regulate the type of information available to Internet users. In 2005, the Chinese government ordered all China-based Web sites and blogs to register with the government or be closed down. Commercial publishers and advertisers faced fines of up to 1 million yuan, about $120,000, for failing to register. At the time China had more than 87 million Internet users, the world's second largest online population after the United States. "The Internet has profited many people but it also has brought many problems, such as sex, violence, and feudal superstitions and other harmful information, that has seriously poisoned people's spirits," according to the Ministry of Information Industry Web site.[25]

Technology superpowers from the United States agreed to cooperate with the Chinese government's crackdown on Internet content. Microsoft agreed to ban the words democracy and Dalai Lama from its Chinese blog, and Yahoo! helped the Chinese government locate and arrest a journalist who forwarded an e-mail critical of the government. Critics were quick to condemn these actions. Some argued that this cooperation with government suppression was a violation of human rights, international law, and corporate ethics. Yet, others speculated that if Western firms withdrew from the Chinese Internet market any hope for eventual democratization of China through technology would be lost.

> In 2006 Google, Yahoo!, Microsoft and Cisco Systems came under fire at a congressional hearing on human rights for what the subcommittee chairman called a "sickening collaboration" with the Chinese government that was "decapitating the voice of the dissidents" in China. Google admitted that it agreed to remove links on their Web site objectionable to Chinese officials in exchange for access to servers in China. Blogs, in particular, drew the ire of Chinese authorities. Under the agreement, Google blocked most references to Tiananmen Square and Falun Gong and prohibited most mentions of teen pregnancy, homosexuality, and

---

[24] "Online Swindlers, Called 'Phishers,' Are Luring Unwary," *The New York Times Online,* March 24, 2004, *www.nytimes.com.*

[25] "China Orders Web Sites, Blogs to Register with Government," *The Wall Street Journal Online,* June 7, 2005, *online.wsj.com.*

beer. A few months later, Google co-founder Sergey Brin admitted that the company had made a mistake and compromised its moral principles and was planning to reevaluate its position about doing business in China.[26]

Partially in response to the actions taken by the Chinese officials and out of fear of the United States exerting too much control over the Internet, diplomats, social activists, and business leaders approached the United Nations in the mid-2000s as a possible governing body to monitor and regulate the Internet. "The United Nations would be a good platform for that [regulation of the Internet], because it has legitimacy. The countries are all represented," said Izzeldin Mohamed Osman, computer science professor at Sudan University. Some U.S. companies, such as Hewlett-Packard and Sun Microsystems, agreed and joined the discussions at the United Nations, an outgrowth of the United Nations' World Summit on the Information Society in 2003.[27]

Although many computer industry officials at the meeting with the United Nations were skeptical of a U.N. role, they agreed that some sort of international body could be useful in coordinating language issues, security, and getting the Internet into developing countries. But few believed that an international regulatory body had the right to regulate the content of Web sites, as practiced by China and North Korea.

Socially Beneficial Uses of Technology

Despite all the abuses of technology documented above—the misuse of blogs and vlogs, the intrusions of spam and phishing, and censorship of the Internet—technology clearly can be used to improve the quality of our lives. How we communicate with others, conduct business, learn new things, and acquire information is enhanced by technology.

M-Commerce

The ease of access and growing features available through the Internet soon spread into various technologies, such as the cellular telephone. Although cell-phone use has become a common American communication tool, Europeans and Asians embraced the cell phone in a different way—as a method of conducting commerce. **M-commerce**, commerce conducted via mobile or cellular telephones, provides consumers with an electronic wallet when using their cell phones. People trade stocks or make consumer purchases of everything from hot dogs to washing machines and countless other products. France Telecom has marketed a cell phone with a built-in credit card slot for easy wireless payments.

On a hot and humid Tokyo day in the summer of 2003, a Coca-Cola manager sent an e-mail to several thousand cellular telephone customers. The message urged them to buy a drink from one of the hundreds of high-tech vending machines in their area. The m-commerce machines enabled customers to use their cellular telephones, rather than cash, to purchase products. Those who bought a Coca-Cola product from one of these machines would get a free download of a company ad jingle for their cellular telephones. Sales jumped

[26] "China's Censorship of Internet, Backed by U.S. Tech Giants, Raises Ethical Concerns," Institute for Global Ethics, *Ethics Newsline*, September 26, 2005, *www.globalethics.org*; "Google Launches Censored Chinese Version of Search Site," Institute for Global Ethics, *Ethics Newsline*, January 30, 2006, *www.globalethics.org*; "Google Co-Founder Concedes Company Compromised Principles in China," Institute for Global Ethics, *Ethics Newsline*, June 12, 2006, *www.globalethics.org*; and "Google's China Problem (and China's Google Problem)," *The New York Times Magazine*, April 23, 2006.

[27] "Countries, Companies Debate U.N. Control over Internet," *Pittsburgh Post-Gazette*, March 28, 2004, p. A10.

50 percent among those who received the message. This was an effort by Coca-Cola to tap into Japanese obsession with cellular telephones and introduce them to the world of m-commerce.[28]

This trend toward m-commerce via cellular telephones was quickly spreading to North America and across Central and South America by the mid-2000s.

Technology and Education

The technological invasion also successfully targeted schools, yet the challenge of providing more and better access and quality learning programs remained. In the United States, a Web-based Education Commission, created by Congress, released a report titled "The Power of the Internet for Learning." The key recommendations from this report included:

- Make powerful new Internet resources, especially broadband access, widely and equitably available and affordable for all learners.
- Build a new research framework of how people learn in the Internet age.
- Revise outdated regulations that impede innovation and replace them with approaches that embrace anytime, anywhere, any-pace learning.
- Protect online learners and ensure their privacy.
- Sustain funding via traditional and new sources that is adequate to the challenge at hand. Technology is expensive, and Web-based learning is no exception.[29]

Technology democratized education by enabling some students in the poorest and most remote communities to access the world's best libraries, instructors, and courses available through the Internet. A digital learning environment provides students with skills to rapidly discover and assess information needed to solve complex problems.

A new technological revolution in education was online education. In the United States, five out of six college students in 2006 were taking classes on a part-time basis, juggling academic commitments with work and family obligations. Online courses and degrees were particularly appealing to these students. The University of Phoenix, the world's largest for-profit education provider, claimed more than 300,000 online students. Apollo Group, based in Phoenix, Arizona, has an enrollment of more than 201,000 students, and Career Education Corporation, the nation's second largest for-profit online education provider, reported a 500 percent increase in student enrollment in five years.[30] Other businesses were finding new ways for technology to enhance education, as described in the following example.

In a race to become the iTunes of the publishing world, Amazon.com and Google announced in November 2005 they were developing systems that would allow consumers to purchase online access to any page, section, or chapter of a book. These programs would combine the companies' already available systems of searching books online with a commercial component that could revolutionize the way people access and read books. The idea was to allow readers to buy and download parts of individual books for their own use through their computers rather than go to a store or receive them by mail. This initiative set off a heated

[28] "Coke Lures Japanese Customers with Cellphone Come-Ons," *The Wall Street Journal*, September 8, 2003, pp. B1, B4.

[29] "The Power of the Internet for Learning: Moving from Promise to Practice," Report of the Web-Based Education Commission, December 19, 2000, *www.hpcnet.org/commission*.

[30] "The Promise and Challenges of For-Profit Colleges," *Better Investing*, April 2006, pp. 34–37.

discussion among publishers and potential vendors over who will do business with whom and how to split the proceeds. Random House, the largest American publisher, proposed a micropayment model in which readers would be charged about 5 cents a page, with 4 cents going to the publisher to be shared with the author.[31]

Seemingly everywhere we turn, whether in our homes or in school or in the workplace, the technology invasion is all around us, and its influences and opportunities seem inescapable.

Medical Information via the Internet

The explosion of medical information on the Internet has dramatically affected people's lives. How people are examined, diagnosed, and treated; how health-related information is collected and stored; and the time and costs associated with health care have all been changed by technological innovations.

In 2004, the Food and Drug Administration and several major drug makers announced that they would put tiny radio antennas on the labels of millions of medicine bottles to combat counterfeiting and fraud. Among the medicines targeted were Viagra, one of the most counterfeited drugs in the world, and OxyContin, a pain-control narcotic that has become one of the most abused medicines in the United States. The tagged bottles would only be the large ones used by druggists to fill prescriptions, but experts did not expect this technological innovation to stop there. "It's basically a bar code that barks," explained Robin Koh of Auto-IS Labs of the Massachusetts Institute of Technology. This innovation could make supply chains more efficient and more secure.[32]

In cyberspace the doctor is always in. Individuals can search for an insomnia treatment at 3 a.m. and ask as many questions as they want. They can even search for information anonymously, maintaining privacy, no matter how embarrassing their questions. Although the Internet provides a wealth of medical information, it sometimes fails to protect patients. For example, many Web sites offered consumers the opportunity to obtain medical advice or prescription medications without sufficient physician oversight. In one case, the Illinois Department of Professional Regulation suspended the license of a physician for prescribing Viagra via an Internet pharmacy for a patient he had never seen. The doctor was working as a consultant for The Pill Box, a Texas-based pharmacy chain that sold drugs online. Regulators were concerned that patients might obtain medicines online that were inappropriate or even dangerous.

Beyond government oversight, not-for-profit organizations were formed to aid individuals using the Internet for medical information. For example, the Health on the Net Foundation, a nonprofit organization based in Geneva, Switzerland, offered a seal of approval for medical Internet sites. To earn this approval, a Web site had to follow the organization's guidelines, which included the prominent identification of the Web sponsor and keeping information up-to-date. In addition, the American Accreditation Health Care Commission, or Utilization Review Accreditation Commission (URAC), as it is also called, sets quality standards for managed care and online health care sites. These Web

---

[31] "Want 'War and Peace' Online? How about 20 Pages at a Time?" *The New York Times Online,* November 4, 2005, *www.nytimes.com.*

[32] "Tiny Antennas to Keep Tab on U.S. Drugs," *The New York Times Online,* November 15, 2004, *www.nytimes.com.*

sites were the first to receive the nonprofit organization's approval based on their disclosure about funding and advertising, quality of editorial content, linking to other sites, and privacy and security.[33]

Special Issue: The Digital Divide

Some people were concerned that the phenomenal development and use of technology were greater in developed than developing countries or among some segments of the population than others in developed countries. This gap between those who have technology and those who do not has been called the **digital divide**. While some debated the severity of the phenomenon, most agreed that it existed.[34]

By 2006, some evidence suggested that the digital divide was becoming smaller. The falling prices of laptops, more computers in public schools and libraries, and the newest generation of cell phones and hand-held devices that connected to the Internet all combined to close the digital divide. Studies and mounting anecdotal evidence suggested that blacks, even those at the lower end of the economic scale, were making significant gains in access to the Internet. As a result, organizations that served African-Americans, as well as companies seeking their business, were increasingly turning to the Internet to reach out to this group.

> According to a Pew national survey completed in 2006, 74 percent of whites go online, 61 percent of African-Americans do, and 80 percent of English-speaking Hispanic-Americans report using the Internet. (The survey did not look at non-English-speaking Hispanics, who some experts believe are not gaining access to the Internet in large numbers.) The 2006 numbers compared favorably to a similar Pew survey taken in 1998. In that study, 42 percent of white Americans said they used the Internet, while only 23 percent of African-Americans did so. Forty percent of English-speaking Hispanic-Americans said they used the Internet.[35]

One reason for the narrowing of the digital divide in the United States may be due to an innovative, yet often criticized, federal government program called E-Rate.

> In 1996, President Clinton signed the Telecommunications Act of 1996. This was the first comprehensive revision of the United States' communications laws in more than 60 years. The universal service was originally designed to make local telephone services available to all Americans at reasonable rates and to aid schools and libraries in obtaining state of the art services and technologies at discounted rates. This led to billions of federal dollars being channeled to schools and libraries in the form of grants providing for broadband access, the availability of modern computer equipment, and the latest in software packages for educational instruction.[36]

Although saddled with corruption, fraud, and politics since 1996, the E-Rate program contributed to the modernization of technology in many schools and communities and helped narrow the digital divide that previously existed in the United States.

---

[33] For more information see *www.urac.org*.

[34] For a contrarian's viewpoint, see Walter Block, "The 'Digital Divide' Is Not a Problem in Need of Rectifying," *Journal of Business Ethics* 53 (2004), pp. 393–406.

[35] "Digital Divide Closing as Blacks Turn to Internet," *The New York Times Online,* March 31, 2006, *www.nytimes.com*.

[36] For a full historical account of the E-Rate program, see the Federal Communications Commission's Web site at *www.fcc.gov/learnet*.

The digital divide was not restricted to the United States. For example, in central and eastern Europe, the digital divide was primarily due to the lack of an Internet infrastructure. Since most people and nongovernmental organizations were dependent on telephone dial-up connections, access to information was slow and often disrupted by telephone line breakdowns. In addition, Internet use was charged on a per-minute rate as a local telephone call, making it too expensive for most individuals or small businesses in these countries.

Businesses, government bodies, and nonprofit organizations were challenged by society to address this issue of a digital divide. Some businesses recognized the existence of a digital divide as an opportunity for developing a charitable program.

Fifteen projects were selected to share a $1 million grant from the DigitAll Hope program sponsored by the Samsung Corporation. The projects ranged from distance-learning programs for the blind in Vietnam to helping young farmers in Malaysia improve crop yield through information technology. ITExpeditors joined the Digital Partnership program in South Africa with a donation of 440 Pentium II and Pentium III computers and other technology equipment. The computers were installed in 88 school-based eLearning Centers across the country. The donation was paired with other donations of Internet access, free software and technical support for teachers, students, and the local communities.[37]

An initiative specifically targeting underdeveloped populations around the world was announced in 2005.

A nonprofit group called One Laptop Per Child, created by the Massachusetts Institute of Technology (MIT) to distribute laptops worldwide, announced in November 2005 that it had developed a hand-cranked laptop computer that would cost about $100. The group planned to distribute it in underdeveloped countries in an effort to bridge the digital divide between rich and poor nations. "We see education as key to any world problem, from peace to poverty to hunger to the environment," said MIT's Nicholas Negroponte. "Primary education is the most important thing to use because if you mess up primary education, you really then spend a lot of time trying to undo the mess afterwards." The laptop machines were to be available at the end of 2006 and must be distributed through local government ministries and be given away. Under the program's rules, companies or governments will not be permitted to sell them.[38]

Clearly, high-technology businesses, governments, and community groups acting together appear to be winning the battle of making technology more accessible to all people regardless of their race, income, education, age, or residence.

The unmistakable economic and social force of technology is evident in every part of the world, in every industry, and in every aspect of our lives. The technologically driven information age has changed how businesses operate and the quality of our lives, regardless of where we live or what we do. These profound changes give rise to important, and possibly perplexing, questions about whether technology should be controlled or who should manage technology and its growth. These issues are discussed in the following chapter.

---

[37] "Hope Floats: Asian Youths to Bridge Digital Divide," August 22, 2003, and "Global Initiative to Help Close Digital Divide in South Africa," August 27, 2003, both from the *Digital Divide Network* Web site, *www.digitaldividenetwork.org.*

[38] "$100 Laptop—A Tool to Bridge the Gap between Rich and Poor?" Institute for Global Ethics, *Ethics Newsline*, November 21, 2005, *www.globalethics.org.*

Summary

- Technological change, which tends to be self-reinforcing, has widespread effects throughout business and society. Some of these effects are beneficial, and some are not. Technological growth is fueled by economic expansion, worker productivity, and research and development investment.

- E-commerce, or online business, has changed how businesses offer, sell, and account for their goods and services in the global marketplace and their interactions with their stakeholders. Individuals are investing and buying goods and services online at an astonishing rate.

- Technology superpowers have built an infrastructure for the information society, enabling people and businesses around the world to communicate and conduct business with each other, spawning the system of e-commerce.

- Technology has exponentially increased our ability to communicate with others around the world through electronic mail, blogs, and vlogs. Accompanying these innovations are significant threats to our privacy and safety.

- Technological innovations in m-commerce, education, and medical information enhance the lives of people throughout the world.

- Differences in age, income, and ethnicity or nationality appear to be associated with a *digital divide*. Recently, collaborative initiatives by businesses, governments, and nonprofit organizations addressing Internet access around the world appear to have somewhat narrowed this digital divide.

Key Terms

biotechnology, *279*
blogs, *285*
cyberspace, *279*
digital divide, *292*
e-commerce, *281*

information society, *279*
Internet, *284*
m-commerce, *289*
nanotechnology, *277*
phishing, *287*

spam, *286*
technology, *278*
telecommunications, *279*
vlogs, *285*

Internet Resources

www.ecommercetimes.com
www.e-commerceadvisor.com
www.isoc.org
www.foresight.org
www.pewinternet.org
www.digitaldividenetwork.org

E-Commerce Times
E-Commerce Advisor.com
Internet Society
Foresight Nanotech Institute
Pew Internet and American Life
Digital Divide Network

Discussion Case: *The Dark Side of the Internet*

Seven years after NASCAR race car driver Neil Bonnett suffered a fatal crash during a practice run at the Daytona International Speedway, his daughter, Kristen, experienced firsthand the dark side of the Internet. Kristen received a telephone call from a reporter asking if she had a comment on the autopsy photos of her father posted on the Internet. "Forty-eight thumbnail pictures, basically of my dad on the table, butt-naked, gutted like a deer, were starring at me directly in the face," said Bonnett.

Some features of the Internet, although usually desirable, can also breed criminal activity. It is an instant, affordable, far-flung outreach system. Criminals can tap into an international audience from anyplace in the world and anonymously hide their activities for months, years, or possibly forever. And they can do it for less than it costs in the physical world. Only $200 buys an e-mail list with the names of thousands of potential victims to launch a spam or phishing scheme. "The [Internet] dramatically lowers transaction costs. Mostly, we think of that as a good thing," said Erik Brynjolfsson, professor of management at MIT's Center for eBusiness. "But it makes it difficult to control many of the activities we want to control."

Illegal Internet commerce has grown at an alarming rate. Black-market activities conducted online were estimated to be more than $60 million annually, about the same amount as U.S. consumers spent on legitimate Internet opportunities. Illegal online gambling reportedly was the sixth-largest business on the Internet.

Internet pornography is a growing business. One adult media publication estimated that online sales of adult videos and similar material exceeded $13 billion in 2005. Complaints about child pornography in cyberspace have grown 600 percent since 1998. In 2006, law enforcement agents raided a $20 billion a year child pornography ring and arrested 27 individuals. These individuals were able to develop a global network to sell child pornographic materials and transmit streaming video over the Internet. Experts believe that nearly a quarter of all Web sites are involved in child pornography and could grow to a $30 billion industry by 2011.[39]

Of all fraud complaints received by government enforcement agencies, 70 percent relate to the Internet. "North of 70 percent of all e-commerce is based on some socially unacceptable if not outright illegal activity," explained Jeffrey Hunker, dean of the H. J. Heinz III School of Public Policy at Carnegie Mellon University, who helped develop a cybersecurity policy for the United States.

Yet, all of these frightening statistics do not include terrorism. Law enforcement officials know that terrorists use the Internet for communications, research, recruitment, and fund-raising. The people involved in the September 11, 2001, attacks in the United States plotted and coordinated their activities by trading e-mails from locations as innocuous as the public library. Computers analyzed by law enforcement officials indicated that a terrorist group researched the U.S. telephone, electric, and water systems online, learning how digital switches operate those systems.

What may be even more troubling is that legitimate businesses enable Internet outlaws. Mainstream sites, such as Yahoo!, MSN, and Google, initially helped steer customers to gambling sites. They accepted advertisements from online casinos and displayed these ads to viewers visiting their Web sites. Many of these Internet service providers later reversed this practice after mounting public pressure. Banks also assist illegal activities by processing payments of customers who are gambling online illegally. Only under pressure from state attorneys general have some banks started to cut off credit lines to gamblers. eBay agreed to pay $1.5 billion to acquire online-payment processor PayPal and canceled PayPal's gambling business because of the uncertain legal situation surrounding it. PayPal had received two federal grand jury subpoenas concerning its processing of online gambling transactions.

Experts estimate that every 44 seconds an unsavory act is committed on the Internet. Clearly the dark side of the Internet is bigger, broader, scarier, and more damaging than most people realize. But what can be done?

---

[39] "Child Porn Crackdown Nabs 27 Suspected Predators," *Information Week*, March 20, 2006, p. 26.

Law enforcement is often plagued by conflicting regulations and statutes and by overlapping jurisdictional battles. For example, Internet financial fraud can be investigated by the Federal Bureau of Investigation, Secret Service, Justice Department, Securities and Exchange Commission, or Federal Trade Commission. If the fraud is international, then the Customs Service can be called in.

In other situations, the illegal Internet activity fails to acquire the necessary attention of law enforcement. Sometimes politicians believe that citizens care more about the drug problem on the street than online. This emphasis focuses resources away from illegal online drug commerce detection that may be the bigger problem. "A doctor prescribing drugs over the Internet can reach many, many more people than a street-level drug dealer," said Robert McCampbell, a U.S. attorney in Oklahoma.

Some states have created effective Internet crime models. For example, in California, progress has been made in stopping identity theft. It was one of the first states to require all credit card receipts to include only the last five numbers on the credit card. Kentucky has one of the most advanced anti–illegal drug distribution systems in the country. The state has an integrated computer system that tracks drug sales from all the pharmacies in the state. It allows doctors or pharmacists to see instantly if the patient has a drug problem and enables regulators to see if doctors or pharmacists are prescribing unusual quantities of drugs.

The final challenge in combating illegal Internet usage is to establish tough laws and penalties for illegal activity online. The Cyber Security Enhancement Act was passed by Congress in 2002, which promises life sentences for those perpetrating cyberattacks that recklessly endanger human life. But this is only a start.

Sources: "The Underground Web," *BusinessWeek,* September 2, 2002, pp. 67–74; "Man Charged with Using Typos to Lure Children to Online Porn," Institute for Global Ethics, *Ethics News* September 8, 2003, *www.globalethics.org*; and data collected from comScore Networks at *www.comscore.com.*

Discussion Questions

1. Which is greater—the benefits from the Internet that enhance our lives, education, and health, or the damage the Internet does to our society through illegal and illicit activities?

2. What can be done to lessen the negative impacts of the underground Internet on society? Who should be responsible for taking these actions?

3. Does this discussion case indicate that technology has gotten out of hand? Are financially or technologically motivated people to blame for these societal crises?

CHAPTER FOURTEEN

Managing Technological Challenges

Technology fosters change and more change. Technological change has raised ethical and social questions of privacy, security, ownership, health, and safety. What are the implications of this fast-paced change on our society and those who live in it? Moreover, who is responsible for determining how much technological change should occur or how fast things should change? Should technology be controlled, and if so, who should be in charge of managing technology and the challenges it poses for humans and cultures in our global community?

This chapter focuses on these key learning objectives:

- Evaluating the initiatives businesses have taken to protect the privacy of their stakeholders.
- Assessing how secure information is in a free-access information society given the vulnerability to hackers, viruses, and computer worms.
- Understanding how businesses manage technological change.
- Analyzing threats from and safeguards taken in response to the Internet pornography industry.
- Assessing violations of intellectual property and how business and government attempt to prevent these illegal actions.
- Recognizing the ethical and social challenges that arise from technological breakthroughs in science and medicine.

Technology raises serious ethical questions regarding our privacy and the security of information, as shown by the following examples.

> Japan is one of the safest countries in the world when it comes to violent crime, but the country experienced a nearly 50 percent rise in incidents of cybercrime in 2005. Technology-based lawbreaking included fraud, prostitution, and pornography involving minors, illegal access of Web sites, and the use of spyware (software that secretly gathers information about a person through his or her Internet connection) to steal personal data.

> Privacy advocates sharply criticized Internet service providers in the United Kingdom for leading the push for online data retention across Europe. This effort was designed to investigate terrorism and organized crime. Despite cries of violations of personal privacy, European firms increasingly were retaining customer information and making it available to various government agencies.[1]

Are businesses and governments winning the battle of the management of technology, particularly in regard to the challenges of maintaining the privacy and safety of those using technology? Does the significant increase in technology-based crimes justify stronger government controls and more intrusion in our technology-laden lives? Where should the line be drawn between safeguarding personal privacy and the government's need to protect the citizenry?

Bill Joy, Sun Microsystems' chief scientist, warned of the dangers of rapid advances in technology:

> The experiences of the atomic scientists clearly show the need to take personal responsibility, the danger that things will move too fast, and the way in which a process can take on a life of its own. We can, as they did, create insurmountable problems in almost no time flat. We must do more thinking up front if we are not to be similarly surprised and shocked by the consequences of our inventions.[2]

As this quotation implies, technology poses numerous challenges for society. These include issues of privacy, security, ownership, health, and safety. This chapter addresses these issues and how, if, and by whom they should be managed.

Businesses Protecting Privacy

The presence of information technology at work today is ubiquitous. Employers can use new sophisticated technology to monitor employees' movements, computer usage, and personal and work interactions. Many of these issues are discussed in Chapter 18. In response to employees' complaints that these practices are invasions of their privacy, many businesses have developed a **privacy policy**, which explains what use of the company's technology is permissible and how the business will monitor employee activities. Columbia/HCA Healthcare, for example, issued an "electronic communication policy" to its employees warning them that it might be necessary for authorized personnel to access and monitor the contents of their computer's hard drive.

---

[1] "Cyber-Crime Issues Escalate Worldwide," Institute for Global Ethics, *Ethics Newsline*, February 27, 2006, *www.globalethics.org.*

[2] Bill Joy, "Why the Future Doesn't Need Us," *Wired*, April 2000, *www.wired.com/wired/archive/8.04/joy.*

The use and dissemination of employee information has been challenged in new ways and from all sides since the 2001 terrorist attacks on the United States:

> Hamburgische Electricitäts-Werke, a German utility company, was ordered by the German government to turn over all of its employees' records so that they could be searched for terrorists linked to the September 11, 2001, attacks. Although management at the firm had close ties with American culture and values and sympathized with the government's efforts to aid the U.S. investigation, the company refused. The head of the company, Joachim Broers, had a favorite saying: "Liberty dies by inches." He felt that the government request was a threat to liberty and the privacy rights enjoyed by his German employees.

The debate over protection of privacy versus government access to personal data has continued to rage since 2001. In early 2006, the European Union passed legislation that required firms to retain employee records and submit this information to the government in particular situations involving national security or threats of suspected terrorism. Later that year, however, the European Union's highest court struck down this law, saying the EU had overstepped its authority by agreeing to require firms to provide the United States with personal details about airline passengers, Internet users, and other such information.[3]

Issues of privacy spill over into the business–consumer relationship. Most Americans mistakenly believe that when they see a privacy policy on their popular Web site that those sites are not collecting or selling their personal information and online activities to others. According to a Minnesota Department of Public Safety report, a company could purchase the personal data information of all Minnesota driver's license holders for $1,500; by 2006, 800 companies had done exactly that. Other consumer misconceptions or simple lack of awareness regarding privacy are shown in Figure 14.1.

Recent technological advancements have increased the number of ways that privacy violations may occur. For example, Radio Frequency Identification (RFID) technology was featured in a clever television commercial where "the packages knew the truck was lost" before the driver did. Other benefits of the use of RFID technology are becoming evident, as discussed in Chapter 13. Yet, many experts have raised ethical questions about

FIGURE 14.1 Consumer Perceptions of Online Privacy

Source: Data taken from "Americans and Online Privacy: The System Is Broken," Annenberg Public Policy Center at the University of Pennsylvania, 2003, *www.asc.upenn.edu.*

Percentage of Home Internet Users Who:	
Knew Web sites collected information about them even if they did not register	59%
Incorrectly believed that a Web site with a privacy policy would not share their personal information	57
Thought that Web site privacy policies were easy to understand	47
Have searched for information on how to protect their personal data	46
Have used filters to block spam	43
Have used software that looks for spyware	23
Have used software that hid their computer's identity from Web sites	17

[3] "Germany's Hunt for Terrorists Hit Unlikely Obstacle," *The Wall Street Journal*, August 9, 2002, pp. A1, A7; and "Hurdle for U.S. in Getting Data on Passengers," *The New York Times Online*, May 31, 2006, *www.nytimes.com.*

the ways RFID technology enables businesses, governments, and criminals to gather information about presale, sales transaction, and postsales activities.[4]

The increase in the number of cell phones enabling users to take clearer pictures of what is happening around them has raised various privacy objections. Sometimes this technology has aided law enforcement in capturing criminals, who were caught breaking into an automobile or store. But in other cases, people felt that their privacy was violated when they were caught in a romantic or embarrassing situation.

Industry and Government Efforts to Manage Privacy

Businesses have made a number of efforts to manage stakeholder privacy. The Platform for Privacy Preference Project (P3P) provides users with software that enables them to define which pieces of personal information they are willing to divulge on the Internet. The software also alerts consumers when businesses request additional information and asks what these businesses plan to do with it. P3P has been added to some Internet browsers at no additional cost or is available to be downloaded free off the Internet.[5] (Chapter 16 provides additional discussion of consumer Internet privacy issues.)

In addition to undertaking efforts to protect their own customers' privacy, some businesses have banded together with others to support industry self-regulation to combat technological abuses.

Nineteen companies, including AT&T, Cisco Systems, IBM, Hewlett-Packard, Microsoft, and Oracle, contributed a total of $750,000 to launch the Information Technology–Information Sharing and Analysis Center (IT-ISAC). IT-ISAC is run by Internet Security Systems, and other technology firms can join the alliance for $5,000 a year. Through this alliance, companies can share sensitive information about cyberattacks and vulnerabilities in their software and hardware products.[6]

Although some companies have addressed the issue of Internet privacy, some skeptics believe international government supervision of the Internet is necessary. However, such international management of technology is difficult to achieve.

U.S. and European officials took a positive step in the direction of international privacy protection in the early 2000s. U.S. companies had been seeking a way to conduct business in Europe without risking lawsuits and prosecution for violating Europeans' privacy. The European Commission agreed that personal data could be collected and used by U.S. Internet companies only under certain conditions. The subject had to give consent unambiguously, and the data had to be necessary to complete a contract (such as for billing), be required by law or to protect the company's vital interests, or be needed for law enforcement. These steps earned the EC the title of "Privacy Cop to the World" and served as a model for similar privacy regulation in Canada, Australia, New Zealand, and countries in South America and Asia.[7]

---

[4] For an excellent discussion of the ethical issues surrounding RFID technology, see Alan R. Peslak, "An Ethical Exploration of Privacy and Radio Frequency Identification," *Journal of Business Ethics* 59 (2005), pp. 327–45.

[5] "Privacy: Don't Ask Technology to Do the Job," *BusinessWeek*, June 26, 2000, p. 52.

[6] "Tech Alliance to Share Data about Hackers," *The Wall Street Journal*, January 16, 2001, pp. A3, A4.

[7] "U.S. in Tentative Pact Protecting Europeans' Privacy," *The Wall Street Journal*, February 20, 2000, p. B6; and "Europe's New High-Tech Role: Playing Privacy Cop to the World," *The Wall Street Journal*, October 10, 2003, pp. A1, A16.

Nevertheless, it will be difficult to achieve international government control of privacy, especially as it pertains to the Internet. The management of privacy may need to come from the Internet companies themselves.[8]

The Management of Information Security

Businesses have become acutely aware of the importance of maintaining information in a secure location and guarding this valuable resource. How best to manage information security remains a major challenge for businesses.

In May 2005, Time Warner reported that a cooler-sized container of computer tapes containing personal information on 600,000 current and former employees had been lost, apparently during a trip to a storage facility. A month later, Citigroup informed its customers that computer tapes containing personal information on nearly 3.9 million customers were lost by the United Parcel Service while in transit to a credit reporting bureau. The public's fears were heightened just 12 days later when MasterCard International reported that more than 40 million credit card accounts might have been exposed to fraud through a computer security breach at its payment processing company. The announcement came after law enforcement officials and company experts had identified a pattern of fraudulent charges that were traced to an intrusion at CardSystems Solutions in Arizona, which processes more than $15 billion in payments annually for small and midsized retail businesses and financial institutions.[9]

In these incidents, human error had placed personal information at risk. Sometimes, threats to our privacy come from criminals. The number of reported computer virus infections is increasing, despite efforts to detect or prevent their intrusion. Most viruses are carried in file attachments and are activated when users click to open them. A new form of the virus, a computer worm, attacked computers through the Microsoft Windows operating system in 2003.

Winding its way through the Microsoft Windows operating system, a computer worm, known by a variety of names—W32.Blaster, MSBlast, and W32/Lovsan—infected tens of thousands of home computers and corporate networks worldwide in 2003. Although Microsoft knew for months that it would be launched and tried to warn its users that the worm would appear, many users neglected to download up-to-date virus protection or install Microsoft's protective program.

The worm spread throughout North and South America, Europe, Asia, and Africa by slipping into a computer connected to the Internet or to another machine on the same network. Unlike many other kinds of viruses, the worm required no human intervention, such as downloading an e-mail message or clicking on an e-mail attachment. Once lodged in a computer, the worm could scan a network looking for other machines with the same vulnerability and try to infect them. The infected computer became sluggish and, in some cases, crashed and automatically rebooted itself several times. The worm also instructed other computers to continue pelting the site.[10]

---

[8] For a discussion of Internet regulation see Norman E. Bowie and Karim Jamal, "Privacy Rights of the Internet: Self-regulation or Government Regulation," *Business Ethics Quarterly* 16, no. 3 (2006), pp. 323–42.

[9] "Time Warner Alerts Staff to Lost Data," *The Wall Street Journal Online*, May 3, 2005, *online.wsj.com;* "Citigroup Says Data Lost On 3.9 Million Customers," *The Wall Street Journal Online*, June 6, 2005, *online.wsj.com;* and "MasterCard Says 40 Million Files Are Put at Risk," *The New York Times Online*, June 18, 2005, *www.nytimes.com.*

[10] "Computer 'Worm' Widely Attacks Windows Versions," *The New York Times*, August 13, 2003, *www.nytimes.com.*

FIGURE 14.2 The Worms Are Getting Faster

Source: Foundstone, Inc., *www.foundstone.com.*

Name of Worm	Alert Received	Work Released	Number of Days to Patch or Prevent
Melissa	December 1, 1999	March 27, 1999	65
Sadmind	December 29, 1999	May 8, 2001	496
Sonic	July 18, 2000	October 30, 2000	104
Bugbear	March 29, 2001	September 30, 2002	550
Code Red	June 18, 2001	July 19, 2001	31
Nimda	August 15, 2001	September 18, 2001	34
Spida	April 17, 2002	May 21, 2002	34
SQL Slammer	July 24, 2002	January 25, 2003	185
Slapper	July 30, 2002	September 14, 2002	46
Blaster/Welchia/Nachi	July 16, 2003	August 11, 2003	26
Witty	March 18, 2004	March 20, 2004	2
Sasser	April 13, 2004	April 30, 2004	17

But a more troubling recent phenomenon regarding worms or viruses is the decreasing amount of time information technology managers have to patch their software before the worms hit. As the creators of the worms became more skilled at infiltrating computer systems, the response time has dramatically shortened. Some of the recent worms and a timeline indicating their impact on businesses are shown in Figure 14.2.

"The basic message is: The world is getting worse . . . more and more out of control," said Peter Tippett, chief technology officer at TruSecure.[11]

The corporate nemesis responsible for creating and spreading computer viruses and worms is called a computer hacker. **Computer hackers** are individuals, often with advanced technology training, who, for thrill or profit, breach a business's information security system. Businesses are not the only organizations vulnerable to the predatory practices of hackers, as some prestigious universities found out in 2005. This incident is described in Exhibit 14.A.

Businesses' Responses to Invasions of Information Security

To address the number, severity, and ease of hacker attacks on businesses, firms began to see the necessity of investing more resources into protecting their information. Firms tried to quickly respond to this growing demand.

PricewaterhouseCoopers launched a new subsidiary to provide storage for *digital certificates,* encrypted computer files that can serve as both identification cards and signatures online. The subsidiary, called beTrusted, relied on a 950-person network of computer security consultants already employed at PricewaterhouseCoopers.

By 2006, aggressive company security measures seemed to have turned the tide against escalating security intrusions. As software became more secure and affordable,

---

[11] "Computer Viruses Still Proliferating; E-Mail Risk Rising," *The Wall Street Journal,* March 4, 2002, p. B5.

Exhibit 14.A Hacking into Business Schools' Admissions Records

On March 2, 2005, about 150 business school applicants took advantage of a 10-hour security vulnerability on a site maintained by ApplyYourself, Inc., a Virginia-based company that manages admissions data for dozens of elite business schools. A hacker was able to post instructions to a bulletin board belonging to a *BusinessWeek* online forum enabling individuals to access their own admissions files. Since most of the schools had not made final admissions decisions on the applicants, the individuals saw only preliminary evaluations or data and some accessed only blank screens.

Nonetheless, many of the universities affected took the breach of security very seriously. "This behavior is unethical at best—a serious breach of trust that cannot be countered by rationalization," said Kim Clark, dean of the Harvard Business School. Most schools—including Carnegie Mellon, Harvard, Duke, and MIT—decided to deny admission to the prospective students who had accessed the ApplyYourself site. Stanford officials decided to review each hacker's case individually before making a final decision, but added, "Our mission statement talks about principled, innovative leaders and we take the principled part seriously."

A few days after the incident occurred, Dartmouth broke ranks from the other universities and announced that it would admit some of the 17 business school applicants who had hacked into its computerized database. After lengthy discussions among Dartmouth faculty and staff, the university decided that the action should be a major strike against the prospective students but was not enough, by itself, to disqualify them. Dartmouth's dean, Paul Danos, said, "Their curiosity got the best of them. All of them expressed some remorse. Some were admitted. Some were rejected."

Sources: "Business Schools Bar Applicants Who Hacked Admissions Web site," Institute for Global Ethics, *Ethics Newsline,* March 14, 2005, *www.globalethics.org;* and "Dartmouth Swims against Tide, Will Admit Some of Hackers," *Pittsburgh Post-Gazette,* March 18, 2005, p. B6.

by 2005 two out of every three computer attacks were intercepted. While some high-profile viruses made the headlines, the overall invasions into company security systems declined. One in every 36 e-mails, or less than 3 percent, contained a virus in 2005, down from 6 percent in 2004.[12]

When a group of suspected hackers broke into a U.S.-based computer system, they thought they had successfully penetrated the security system guarding an important Web site. Rather, they had technologically walked into a *honeypot*, a system used by security professionals to lure hackers to a fabricated Web site where the hacker's every move can be tracked. Lance Spitzner, creator of numerous honeypot traps, posted his findings of hacker activities on the Internet for the security community to see and learn from these discoveries.[13] Another method some businesses have used to reduce criminal intrusion of their sites is to pay hackers for their proprietary methods—so others will not use them.

A Russian hacker, simply known as "Bit," spotted a defect in Microsoft's Internet Explorer Web browser that made it vulnerable to attack. Bit simply had to go to Web-hack.ru, a Russian Internet storefront, to offer to sell his discovery to the highest bidder. Organized crime reportedly would pay top dollar for information that would break into corporate databases and pilfer people's identities. Typically efforts were made to detect these actions and prosecute the offenders. But in 2005 computer security firms decided on a different approach and created legitimate markets for hacker intelligence. The firms offered to purchase tips from

[12] 2005 Global Business Security Index Report, International Business Machines, *www.ibm.com.*

[13] "Around the World, Hackers Get Stuck in 'Honeypots,'" *The Wall Street Journal,* December 19, 2000, p. A18; and see Spitzner's Web site at *http://project.honeynet.org.*

some of the very people they were trying to arrest. Critics said that this was akin to rewarding hackers for uncovering computer loopholes but security firms retorted that this free market approach would give them critical information so they could boost their protection for their clients.[14]

The Chief Information Officer

The responsibility of managing technology with its many privacy and security issues for business organizations is entrusted to the **chief information officer (CIO)**. Many firms have elevated the role of their data processing managers by giving them the title of chief information officer. More CIOs report directly to the company's CEO (42 percent) than to the CFO (23 percent). Primarily the CIO is expected to reduce costs through efficiency and productivity, enable or drive business innovation, and create or enable a competitive advantage for the company. "It's the sharp edge of the business, a tool for revenue generation," explained William E. Kelvie, former CIO of Fannie Mae. "Every business needs an executive who can harness the latest technology to reach out to customers and suppliers with seamless, up-to-the-minute data communications."

The benefits of having an innovative CIO were clear to most businesses. Peter Solvik, CIO at Cisco Systems, was credited with slashing $1.5 billion in costs by using Internet technologies for everything from human resources to manufacturing. At General Electric, CIO Gary Reiner was responsible for moving $5 billion in goods and services through the Internet, which helped improve the company's operating margins. Dawn Lepore, CIO at Charles Schwab, discovered that online trading cost only 20 percent as much as conventional trading and helped boost the firm's gross operating margin. The job of implementing these fundamental changes in business operations increasingly was entrusted to the company's CIO, whose duties now involved much more than keeping the computers properly functioning.[15]

CIOs increasingly must see the big corporate picture. The CIO must set, align, and integrate an information technology vision with the company's overall business objectives. The CIO serves as the "coach" in guiding the information technology resources of the firm toward the long-term business goals.

Internet Pornography

Many believe that the Internet pornography industry, containing sexually explicit writing or images intended to arouse sexual desire, is the most active and lucrative area of e-commerce. As of 2006, there were 4.2 million pornography Web sites, 372 million Web pages, and 2.5 billion daily pornography e-mails worldwide. Pornography downloads accounted for 35 percent of all Internet downloads. Experts estimated the annual revenues of the pornography industry at $57 billion worldwide and $12 billion in the United States alone.[16] The popularity of adult-oriented Web sites was seen when Victoria's

---

[14] "From Black Market to Free Market," *BusinessWeek*, August 22/29, 2005, pp. 28–32.

[15] Edward Prewitt and Lorraine Cosgrove Ware, "The State of the CIO '06: A Report," *CIO Research*, at *www.cio.com/state;* and "From Gearhead to Grand High Pooh-Bah," *BusinessWeek*, August 28, 2000, pp. 129–30. Also see "Focus On: The Chief Information Officer," *BusinessWeek*, December 16, 2002, pp. 24–25; and "Chief Privacy Officers: Real Change or Window Dressing," *Business Ethics*, September–October 2001, pp. 8–9.

[16] Jerry Ropelato, "Pornography Industry Revenue Statistics," 2006, *www.TopTenREVIEWS.com.*

Secret, a maker of women's lingerie, launched a fashion show on the Internet. The company reported that 1.5 million viewers logged on to see its merchandise.

Some countries aggressively monitor and try to control activities associated with these Web sites for objectionable adult-oriented materials. Yahoo! Japan, Japan's most popular Web site, had its Tokyo offices raided by police investigating the possible sale of illegal pornographic material on its auction site. This raid followed action taken against the parent company, U.S.-based Yahoo!, Inc., which was ordered by the French government to block French users from accessing Nazi memorabilia on its U.S. servers. Later, Yahoo! removed all adult-related advertising and products, such as videos, from its Web sites.[17]

Many adult Web sites ask users to verify that they are of legal age. This control is easily circumvented. In response to parents' interest in preventing their children from accessing adult-oriented Web sites, a number of new businesses emerged. For example, several major Internet companies launched a site called GetNetWise.[18] It provides parents with information on adult-oriented Web sites, including reading material and downloadable software that could safeguard their children when they are online. Other commercial porn-blocking software includes Cyber Sitter, Cyber Patrol, Net Nanny, Cyber Sentinel, Norton Parental Controls, Cyber Snoop, and Child Safe. These programs work with the Internet browser to block out violent or X-rated Web pages.

In 1998, President Clinton signed into law the Child Online Privacy Protection Act, also mentioned in Chapter 16. The primary goal of the Act is to give parents control over what information is collected from their children online and how such information may be used. The Act specifically applies to children under 13 years of age. In addition, the U.S. Supreme Court ruled in 2003 that Congress has the right to force public libraries to install Internet filters on their computers even though such filters often inaccurately block access to legitimate Web sites.[19]

Protecting Intellectual Property

With advances in technology, protecting the ownership of *intellectual property* has become more challenging than ever. The ideas, concepts, and other symbolic creations of the human mind are often referred to as **intellectual property**. In the United States, intellectual property is protected through a number of special laws and public policies, including copyrights, patents, and trademark laws. Not all nations have policies similar to those in the United States. With the ease of accessing information through technology, especially the Internet, have come serious questions regarding protecting intellectual property. From software and video-game piracy to downloading copyrighted music and movies for free, many new means for using others' intellectual property have unlawfully emerged.

Software Piracy

The illegal copying of copyrighted software, or **software piracy**, is a global problem. According to the Business Software Alliance, global software piracy accounted for more than a third

---

[17] "Police Raid Yahoo! Japan Office in Pornography Probe," *The Wall Street Journal*, November 28, 2000, p. A23; "Yahoo! Ordered to Bar the French from Nazi Items," *The Wall Street Journal*, November 21, 2000, pp. B1, B4; and "Yahoo! Plans to Remove Adult Content," *The Wall Street Journal*, April 16, 2001, p. B6.

[18] See GetNetWise's Web site at *www.GetNetWise.org.*

[19] "Public Libraries Must Use Internet Filters, Supreme Court Rules," Institute for Global Ethics, *Ethics Newsline*, June 30, 2003, *www.globalethics.org.*

of all packaged software installed on personal computers and resulted in $34 billion in losses worldwide in 2005.[20] Software companies predicted these losses would continue to rise as Third World countries became more involved in the global marketplace.

Companies have sought assistance on the issue of software piracy from governmental agencies and the courts both inside and outside the United States. For example, the Argentinean Supreme Court upheld a lower court ruling that the country's antiquated copyright laws did not cover software, thus denying software manufacturers any legal basis to attack those with pirated materials in Argentina. However, the outcry from U.S. software makers and vendors was so strong that within months the Argentinean Chamber of Deputies made software piracy a crime punishable by fines or imprisonment or both. In 1998, the United States passed the **Digital Millennium Copyright Act**, making it a crime to circumvent antipiracy measures built into most commercial software agreements between the manufacturers and their users.

In China, where experts estimate that 90 percent of all software in use is unlicensed, government officials took steps in 2006 to curb piracy. The Chinese government announced that computer makers must ship all their product with licensed operating systems preinstalled and inspected all government computer systems for licensed software. Some of their motivation was economic, as China was poised to develop a massive technology-based communications industry. "This is good news, marking a clear step in the right direction to reverse the serious problem of software piracy that frustrates the development in China for both foreign and domestic vendors," explained Gregory Shea, president of the Beijing-based United States Industry Technology Office, which represents more than 6,000 technology companies.[21]

Since 1988, the Business Software Alliance (BSA) has been an international representative for the world's leading software companies before governments and consumers. BSA sought to educate computer users on software copyright laws, lobby for public policy that would foster innovation and expand software companies' trade opportunities, and aggressively fight against software piracy. Its members include Apple Computer, Corel, Macromedia (Asia), Microsoft, Symantec, and many other influential organizations in the software industry.

> Some firms attacked those who sold or distributed pirated software. Sega of America Inc. shut down 185 Web sites, including auctions on eBay and Amazon.com, which allegedly sold pirated game software. Citing the Digital Millennium Copyright Act of 1998, a Sega spokesperson commented, "We're using this act to send a clear message [to the Web sites and other companies]. They are liable for the content that is on their service."[22]

Pirating Copyrighted Music

By the late 1990s, technology enabled individuals to download music from the Internet at a faster pace than ever before and to store the music for repeated listening. Individuals downloaded millions of songs onto their computers, burned them onto CDs, and had their favorite collections of songs available for their listening pleasure whenever they wanted—all without the cost of purchasing the music. This process denied legitimate

---

[20] "Software Piracy Still Costs Billions," *Knight Ridder Tribune Business News,* June 5, 2006, p. 1.

[21] "China Begins Effort to Curb Piracy of Computer Software," *The New York Times Online,* May 30, 2006, www.nytimes.com.

[22] "Sega Closes 185 Web Sites to Fight Software Piracy," *The Wall Street Journal,* July 21, 2000, p. B5.

compensation to the artists who created the music and to the companies that manufactured or distributed these artists' CDs.

The pirating of copyrighted music is a growing and widespread epidemic. According to the International Federation of the Phonographic Industry, 20 billion songs were illegally downloaded or swapped in 2005, or one out of every three musical disks sold in the world, with sales totaling $4.6 billion. Nine out of 10 recordings in China were pirated, and 75 percent of Singaporeans surveyed said they had no personal objection to using pirated material.[23]

In the United States, the Recording Industry Association of America (RIAA) launched a series of lawsuits aimed at prohibiting illegal copying of music, protecting the legal property of the authors or publishers, and assuring that profits earned from music sales be distributed to those holding the copyrights. These actions are profiled in the discussion case at the end of this chapter.

Trade associations in other countries also joined in the battle against illegal music downloading.

> The International Federation of the Phonographic Industry (IFPI) announced in 2004 that 247 people in Denmark, Germany, Italy, and Canada were served with international lawsuits against illegal file sharing. However, the IFPI efforts were somewhat thwarted a month later when a Canadian judge ruled that downloading a song from an Internet file-sharing music site did not amount to infringement of copyright law. In 2006, nearly 2,000 lawsuits against illegal music downloads were served in 10 European countries, bringing the total number of cases initiated by the IFPI to 5,500. The 2006 lawsuits targeted individuals in Austria, Denmark, Finland, Germany, Iceland, Italy, Portugal, Sweden, and Switzerland. The suits mainly targeted users of peer-to-peer networks, including FastTrack, Gnutella, eDonkey, DirectConnect, BitTorrent, Limewire, WinMX, and SoulSeek.[24]

Another approach businesses have used to protect music copyrights involves **streaming**. Streaming refers to a customized, on-demand radio service. These are harder to pirate, because copies of the music are not downloaded and stored on users' hard drives, creating virtual libraries. Streaming provides music distributors with new revenues from selling subscriptions to the music for which they hold the copyright. The benefits of this were seen almost immediately. When a court ordered San Diego–based MP3.com to pay $10 million for creating a database of more than 45,000 CDs without copyright permission, the company agreed to a licensing fee. MP3.com agreed to pay 1.5 cents each time it copied a track of music and about 0.3 cents when a customer downloaded the song.[25]

Piracy of Movies on CDs and DVDs

With advances in technology, movies can be downloaded from the Internet to CDs or DVDs more easily than ever. The Motion Picture Association of America studied the

---

[23] "Free Downloads—After this Message," *BusinessWeek*, October 9, 2006, p. 95; "U.S. Is Only the Tip of Pirated Music Iceberg," *The New York Times*, September 26, 2003, *www.nytimes.com;* and "One-Third of Music CDs Sold In the World Are Pirated," *The Wall Street Journal Online*, June 23, 2005, *online.wsj.com.*

[24] "Music Industry's Assault on Piracy Goes Outside U.S.," *The Wall Street Journal*, March 31, 2004, p. B3; "Canadian Ruling on File Sharing Sends Shock Waves through Music Industry," Institute for Global Ethics, *Ethics Newsline*, April 5, 2004, www.globalethics.org; and "Music Industry Files More Suits In Europe," *The Wall Street Journal Online*, April 4, 2006, *online.wsj.com.*

[25] "If You Can't Lick 'Em, License 'Em," *BusinessWeek*, June 26, 2000, p. 46.

problem and found that Hollywood studios alone lost $6.1 billion worldwide in 2005. In response to this costly epidemic, the Federal Communications Commission ordered that all U.S.-made digital television receivers, by July 1, 2005, had to have technology installed meant to block the widespread and illegal redistribution of copyrighted programming.[26]

Some governments responded to entreaties by the motion picture industry. In 2004, a Hong Kong judge ruled that two managers at Golden Science Technology, a licensed disk-replication company in Hong Kong, had produced illegal copies of movies and other material. A raid of the Golden Science Technology warehouse seized 22.4 million disks, including 130,000 copies of the movie *Titanic*. The judge ordered both individuals to serve 6½ years in prison, the longest prison sentence to date for pirating movie disks.

Despite the effort shown by the Hong Kong courts, companies were increasingly worried about the spread of movie piracy, especially in Asia. Blockbuster, a U.S. movie rental chain, announced in 2005 that it was closing all of its 24 Hong Kong stores, because it could not compete against low-cost pirated DVDs and CDs readily available for sale throughout China and Hong Kong.[27]

In 2005, the United States stepped up its efforts to combat piracy, announcing an 11-nation crackdown on organizations responsible for stealing copies of the latest *Star Wars* film, worth more than $50 million. Four people were arrested, 8 major distribution centers were shut down, and hundreds of computers used to duplicate movies were seized. U.S. Attorney General Alberto Gonzalez said, "The Justice Department is striking at the top of the copyright piracy supply chain—a distribution chain that provides the vast majority of illegal digital content now available online." The U.S. Justice Department efforts were coordinated with law enforcement authorities from Australia, Belgium, Canada, Denmark, France, Germany, Israel, the Netherlands, Portugal, and the United Kingdom, indicating the widespread global reach of illegal piracy.

Managing Scientific Breakthroughs

Dramatic advances in the biological sciences also have propelled the impact of technology on our lives and business practices. As explained in Chapter 13, biotechnology refers to a technological application that uses biological systems or living organisms to make or modify products or processes for specific use. Recent unprecedented applications of biological science to industry have made possible new, improved methods of health care and agriculture, but they have also posed numerous ethical challenges regarding safety and the quality of life.

As Bill Joy of Sun Microsystems warns, speaking of biotechnology as well as other innovative applications of science, "21st century technologies . . . are so powerful that they can spawn whole new classes of accidents and abuses. Most dangerously, for the first time, these accidents and abuses are widely within the reach of individuals or small groups. They will not require large facilities or rare raw materials. Knowledge alone will enable the use of them."[28]

[26] "Estimates of Copyright Piracy Losses Vary Widely," *The Wall Street Journal Online*, June 2, 2006, *online.wsj.com*; and "FCC Acts to Protect Digital Content," *The Wall Street Journal*, November 5, 2003, p. A7.

[27] "Blockbuster to Close All Stores In Hong Kong by Mid-2005," *The Wall Street Journal*, February 2, 2004, p. B3.

[28] Joy, "Why the Future Doesn't Need Us."

Human Genome

When Celera Genomics Group announced in 2000 that it had finished the first sequencing of a **human genome**, the achievement was hailed as the most significant scientific breakthrough since landing a man on the moon. Strands of human deoxyribonucleic acid, or DNA, are arrayed across 23 chromosomes in the nucleus of every human cell, forming a unique pattern for every human. These strands are composed of four chemical units, or letters, used over and over in varying sequences. These replicated letters total 3 billion and form the words, or genes—our unique human signature—that instruct cells to manufacture the proteins that carry out all of the functions of human life. Scientists have also cracked the DNA for other species as well, including that of the malaria parasite, one of the world's biggest killers.[29] The identification of human genes is critical to the early diagnosis of life-threatening diseases, the invention of new ways to prevent illnesses, and the development of drug therapies to treat a person's unique genetic profile. A new era of medicine, as well as great opportunity for biotechnology companies, appeared to be born with the decoding of the human genome.

However, while advances in understanding DNA were exalted as one of the human race's greatest achievements, ethical challenges emerged in private and public research focusing on genetics.

> One family, who possessed a rare genetic heart disease called Brugada syndrome, wondered how others might react if they learned of the family's medical condition. Would employers want to hire someone who might die prematurely or require an expensive implantable defibrillator? Would they be eligible for individual health care coverage or be able to afford life insurance if their condition were known? The underlying fear for this family and others with genetic conditions was whether they would be treated fairly if their genetic fingerprints became public.

The debate over whether advances in human genome sequencing and genetic research outweigh the risks or harms will continue for years. What is clear is that our scientific understanding of the human body and its makeup has changed, and significant technological innovations are on the horizon. What is not clear is who, if anyone, can manage these changes to better ensure the improvement of the quality of our lives and society.

Biotechnology and Stem-Cell Research

Complementing the discovery of DNA sequencing were numerous medical breakthroughs in the area of regenerative medicine. **Tissue engineering**, the growth of tissue in a laboratory dish for experimental research, and **stem-cell research**, research on nonspecialized cells that have the capacity to self-renew and to differentiate into more mature cells, were two such breakthroughs. Both offered the promise that failing human organs and aging cells could be rejuvenated or replaced with healthy cells or tissues grown anew. While the promise of immortality may be overstated, regenerative medicine provided a revolutionary technological breakthrough for the field of medicine.

Stem-cell research spilled over from the laboratories into government arenas as politicians weighed in on the ethical controversy. A 2006 Gallup poll reported that 61 percent of the U.S. public believed stem-cell research was morally acceptable. Support for stem-cell research was evident in California, where nearly 60 percent of voters in 2004 supported Proposition 71, which set aside $350 million annually for a decade or a total of

---

[29] "Genetic Secrets of Malaria Bug Cracked at Last," *The Wall Street Journal*, January 18, 2002, pp. B1, B6.

Exhibit 14.B   Stem-Cell Research Controls in Select Countries

Government controls, or lack of controls, regarding scientific stem-cell research varies from country to country. In some countries, the controls apply only to specific types of research, while in other countries there is little control of scientific research in this field.

Germany: The Embryo Protection Law forbids all human embryonic stem-cell research, but research is permitted on legally imported cells, and public funding is available for animal and adult embryonic stem-cell research.

Britain: Human stem-cell research is permitted for therapeutic purposes, using embryos left over from fertility treatments. Cloning of embryos for therapeutic research has been permitted since 1990.

Sweden: Ten percent of the total human embryonic stem-cell cultures in existence by 2001 were created in this country. Research is allowed on embryos left over from fertility treatments.

France: Guidelines were developed that permit human embryonic research for stem cells but cloning of stem cells has been banned since the 1994 Bioethics Law was passed.

Israel: No formal laws and little public opposition to stem-cell research exists. Researchers at two universities created four stem-cell lines, and research is expanding.

Japan: This nation is considering rules to allow research on human embryos left over from fertility treatments. Human cloning has been banned since 2000 and is punishable with up to 10 years in jail and fines of $90,000.

Singapore: Ethical guidelines were introduced in 2002. Researchers at the National University of Singapore created six stem-cell lines that were commercially available.

Sources: Information taken from "At Risk: A Golden Opportunity in Biotech," *BusinessWeek*, September 10, 2001, pp. 85–87; and "Stem-Cell Research Is Forging Ahead in Europe," *The Wall Street Journal*, July 13, 2001, pp. B1, B4.

more than $3 billion. This amount dwarfed the $25 million the National Institutes of Health allocated to embryonic stem-cell research in 2004. The European Parliament encouraged the financial units of the EU nations to free up nearly $5 billion in research to be used specifically to study the potential windfall of medical advances reaped from stem-cell research.[30] Exhibit 14.B discusses various countries' controls, or lack of controls, for stem-cell research.

Supported by private and government funding, hundreds of biotechnology companies and university laboratories answered the call and developed new ways to replace or regenerate failed body parts. Research included efforts to insert bone-growth factors or stem cells into a porous material cut to a specific shape, creating new jaws or limbs. Genetically engineered proteins were successfully used to regrow blood vessels that might repair or replace heart values, arteries, and veins. The process to regrow cartilage was used to grow a new chest for a boy, and a human ear was grown on a mouse.

In addition, the Food and Drug Administration (FDA) laid the early groundwork for generic versions of biotechnology medicines, an effort that could transform the market for some of the most innovative and expensive new treatments for cancer and other diseases. This effort was particularly important as some of the oldest biotech drugs, such as Eli Lilly's bioengineered insulin Humulin and Genetech's Nutropin growth hormone, were about to lose patent protection. "We are concerned about finding safe ways to lower

[30] "Bush to Allow Funds for Study of Stem Cells," *The Wall Street Journal*, August 10, 2001, pp. A3, A4; "California Vote Brings Windfall for Stem Cells," *The Wall Street Journal*, November 4, 2004, pp. B1, B7; and "European Parliament Urges Resumption of Stem-Cell Research," Institute for Global Ethics, *Ethics Newsline*, November 24, 2003, *www.globalethics.org.*

drug costs for Americans," said FDA Commissioner Mark McClellan. "If we can find a safe plan to produce generic or follow-up products for biologics, that can be an important step." According to medical drug market experts, the market for such drugs is more than $22 billion annually.[31]

Cloning

In 1986, a Danish scientist announced the first successful cloning of a sheep from fetal cells. Shortly thereafter a University of Wisconsin scientist succeeded with cows. Ten years later, in 1996, the Roslin Institute in Scotland announced it had cloned healthy calves from fetal cells. Another significant breakthrough occurred in 1997, when Ian Wilmut of the Roslin Institute unveiled Dolly, the first mammal to be cloned from adult cells. A year later, scientists from the University of Massachusetts reported that they had discovered a method of cloning cows with a process that was simpler and more efficient than Wilmut's method. In 2003 doctors in China reported they had become the first to make an infertile woman pregnant with an experimental technique devised in the United States for women who have healthy genes but defects in their eggs that prevent embryos from developing. Critics argued that this technique is perilously close to human cloning.[32]

Bogus reports of human cloning appeared in 2002, based on a publicity stunt by the Clonaid organization, a religious movement intent on cloning its leaders. Two years later, technology appeared to have taken another step forward when scientists in South Korea reported they had created human embryos through cloning and extracted embryonic stem cells. This work made possible the birth of a cloned human baby even more feasible. The validity of this research was questioned when subsequent research by the same South Korean scientists was found to be without merit, as discussed in Exhibit 14.C. Nonetheless, medical advances toward human cloning were appearing.[33]

As each new announcement of a more advanced and successful cloning experiment was announced to the public, more fears arose. Whether it was a vision of Jurassic Park dinosaurs running loose in a metropolitan downtown area or the eerie absurdity of cloning multiple Adolf Hitlers in the film *The Boys of Brazil*, fears of cloning living tissue invaded our lives. In 2002, the U.S. Senate began debates on a bill to ban human cloning, although its sponsors anticipated a long and difficult battle. Organizations in support of human cloning and against the U.S. government's proposed restrictions were formed and Web sites were created, such as that of the Human Cloning Foundation. Both those supporting and opposing cloning have been vehement in making their stances known to the public in the hopes of influencing politicians. By 2005, an overwhelming majority of Americans surveyed supported embryonic stem-cell research. "Regardless of party identification or religious affiliation, most adults believe embryonic stem-cell research should be allowed . . . as nearly three-quarters (74 percent) of U.S. adults believe stem-cell research should be allowed today (73 percent in 2004)."[34]

[31] "FDA Takes Steps toward Allowing Generic Versions of Biotech Drugs," *The Wall Street Journal*, February 18, 2004, pp. A1, A6.

[32] "Pregnancy Created Using Infertile Woman's Egg Nucleus," *The New York Times Online*, October 14, 2003, www.nytimes.com.

[33] The ethical debate over cloning was fueled by the reported medical achievements involving humans. For a thorough discussion of these ethical arguments see Rushworth M. Kidder, "The Ethics of Cloning," *Ethics Newsline*, February 17, 2004, www.globalethics.org. Also see Arlene Weintraub, "What's Ethical and What Isn't," *BusinessWeek*, January 16, 2006, p. 76.

[34] "Public Support for Stem-Cell Research Remains High," Institute for Global Ethics, *Ethics Newsline*, June 13, 2005, www.globalethiucs.com. Also see www.humancloning.org.

Exhibit 14.C The Validity, or Lack Thereof, of Human Cloning

In May 2005, researcher Hwang Woo Suk of South Korea's Seoul National University shocked the world when he reported that his team of 24 scientists had used cloning to transform skin samples taken from 11 sick or injured people into supplies of embryonic stem cells. The scientific report appeared in the journal *Science* and marked a significant leap for therapeutic cloning, a proposed means of generating supplies of nerves, heart muscle, or other cells perfectly matched to particular patients.

Despite fears over the increasing possibility of human cloning, Hwang cautioned, "Our proposal is limited to finding a way to cure cancer. That is our proposal and research goal." Supporters of Hwang's research heralded the achievement as a "really major milestone because it puts the whole technique on the map."

Six months later, it became clear that Hwang had fabricated the evidence for all of the research published in the journal article, according to a report issued by the Seoul National University panel that investigated Hwang's work. The panel's findings stripped any possibility of a legitimate achievement in human cell cloning, disgracing a researcher who promised to make paralyzed people walk and whose features had been engraved on a Korean postage stamp.

London's *Financial Times* noted that the fraud caused thunderous repercussions in the scientific world, not only for research institutions and patients, who hoped that the new techniques could cure their illnesses, but also for the scientific process itself. Critics said the peer review system broke down and the journal publishing the findings was sloppy in its review since it wanted to rush newsworthy results into print.

Despite the report from his own university saying that his work was fabricated, Hwang stood by his research saying that he has the technology to produce tailored embryonic stem cells and can reproduce the process at any time.

Sources: "Seoul Team Creates Custom Stem Cells From Cloned Embryos," *The Wall Street Journal Online,* May 20, 2005, *online.wsj.com;* "Researcher Faked Evidence of Human Cloning, Koreans Report," *The New York Times Online,* January 10, 2006, *www.nytimes.com;* and "Blatant Fraud Suspected in South Korean Stem Cell Research," Institute for Global Ethics, *Ethics Newsline,* January 2, 2006, *www.globalethics.com.*

In 1997, when Dolly appeared on the cloning scene, there were no laws on record that prevented scientists from attempting human cloning. Experts recognized that the technique used in Scotland to clone a sheep was so simple and required so little high-tech equipment that most biology laboratories with a budget of a few hundred thousand dollars could attempt it.

In 2003 the United Nations General Assembly considered three proposals aimed at human cloning. One proposal, pushed strongly by the United States, was backed by more than 60 countries and called for a ban of all forms of cloning, both reproductive cloning (to produce a baby identical to its genetic parents) and therapeutic cloning (for medical purposes). A more moderate proposal was sponsored by Belgium and backed by 20 countries, including Britain, Japan, and China. This proposal suggested that only reproductive cloning would be banned and the fate of therapeutic cloning would be left up to individual nations. Finally, a third proposal, championed by many Islamic nations, argued that the issue should be deferred for two years. By a one vote margin, the United Nations put off for two years any international ban on human cloning.[35]

With little guidance at the international level, national organizations sought to establish ethical rules regarding cloning practices. In 2005, the United States National Academy of Sciences issued guidelines for embryonic stem-cell research, seeking to

[35] "A Fight at the U.N. over Cloning," *The New York Times Online,* November 5, 2003, *www.nytimes.com;* and "U.N. Puts Off Human-Clone Ban amid Demands by U.S., Vatican," *The Wall Street Journal,* November 7, 2003, pp. A3, A8.

provide a clear path through the ethical minefield. The guidelines outlawed some far-reaching endeavors; for example, scientists could not insert embryonic stem cells into a human embryo. They also could not introduce stem cells into apes or monkeys, avoiding the nightmarish possibility that an animal could give birth to a human or develop a human mind. Otherwise, most stem-cell research was permitted. The guidelines were voluntary but the organization hoped that most institutions, state stem-cell programs, scientific journals, and organizations offering research grants would adhere to the suggested behavior.

In the aftermath of the South Korean cloning fraud, discussed in Exhibit 14.C, the International Society for Stem Cell Research (ISSCR) agreed to convene a task force of experts from a dozen countries, including Japan, Korea, the United Kingdom, and the United States, in 2007 to discuss what guidelines might be formulated. "The [South Korean] scandal created a general consensus among scientists that bioengineering must stand on firm ethical grounds, which is why the guidelines will have great symbolic meaning," said Professor Kim Dong-wook of Yonsei University.[36]

Clearly stem-cell research leading to the possibility of human cloning is an important issue and will likely increase in prominence in the near future. What must also be clear is the need for specific and binding ethical guidelines for scientists engaging in this volatile field to protect society. The debate over how to govern this scientific community and its work inevitably will continue for years.

Bioterrorism

An emerging yet tragic outcome of scientific breakthroughs in bioengineering is the potential for **bioterrorism**. Terrorist groups see the use of deadly bioengineered diseases and poisons, such as smallpox, anthrax, and bubonic plague, as effective tools since they are more difficult to detect when transported than guns or bombs. Germs are more effective as a terrorist tool because tens of thousands of people easily can be affected. Oklahoma Governor Frank Keating said, "It not only stunned me how horrific a biological attack could be, but also how woefully unprepared we are."[37]

> President Bush announced in 2003 Project BioShield, a $5.6 billion, 10-year government program to spur pharmaceutical companies to develop vaccines and antidotes to combat bioterrorism. Yet three years after the announcement, bioterrorism experts claimed that nothing had been done, and the major pharmaceutical companies have waited months, if not years, for government agencies to act.[38]

One company did see an opportunity to become a "biodefense contractor," as it developed a pharmaceutical-defense system, and suffered public scrutiny. Bayer Corporation was in the public hot seat after the 2001 anthrax scare in the United States. The company possessed large quantities of Cipro, an anti-anthrax drug for which it held the patent. When Bayer attempted to sell Cipro, the public was appalled that a company would try to profit from a country's bioterrorism disaster. Bayer President Helge Wehmeier argued, "I haven't heard of anyone giving their bombers away because America is in need."[39]

---

[36] "Task Force to Create Ethical Guidelines for Stem Cell Research," Institute for Global Ethics, *Ethics Newsline,* January 16, 2006, *www.globalethics.org.*

[37] "The Next Phase: Bioterrorism?" *BusinessWeek,* October 1, 2001, pp. 58–61.

[38] "Nation Unready for Germ Attacks; Bioterror Defense Lags Despite 4 Years, $20 Billion," *USA Today,* August 1, 2005, p. A1; and "Bid to Stockpile Bioterror Drugs Stymied by Setback," *The New York Times Online,* September 18, 2006, *www.nytimes.com.*

[39] "Drug Companies Contemplate New Role as 'Biodefense Contractors,'" *The Wall Street Journal,* November 12, 2001, pp. B1, B8.

Genetically Engineered Foods

The biotechnological revolution targeting improvements in health care was also adapted for use by the agricultural industry. Technological advances in genetics and biology led to an unprecedented number of innovations. **Genetic engineering**, altering the natural makeup of a living organism, allowed scientists to insert virtually any gene into a plant and create a new crop or a new species. The economic force of this technological revolution was immediately apparent. Venture capitalists injected $750 million into the agricultural industry, an area generally ignored by venture capitalists throughout the 1980s.

Schools of salmon and trout were engineered to grow twice as fast as before. Soybeans, cotton, corn, and other crops were genetically engineered to resist pests or to be impervious to herbicides used to control weeds. Some were altered to yield a higher nutritional value. Cows, sheep, and goats were treated to produce drugs in their milk. "We are starting the century of biology," announced J. Craig Venter, president of the Institute for Genomic Research. The payoff potential was huge.[40]

In Europe, a severe backlash emerged to **genetically modified foods**, or GM foods, that is, food processed from genetically engineered crops. Protesters there called GM foods "Frankenstein foods." Heinz Corporation, a U.S.-based food producer, announced that it would not sell GM foods in Europe. Similarly, Bayer CropScience, a unit of Bayer AG of Germany, decided against selling gene-altered seeds in Britain, despite winning landmark regulatory approval.

> By 2003, opposition to GM food was widespread. In France, 89 percent said it was bad to scientifically alter fruits and vegetables "because it could hurt human health and the environment." In Germany, 81 percent of those surveyed opposed GM foods; in Japan, 76 percent; and in Italy, 74 percent. Although opposition in the United States was less widespread, 55 percent of Americans also believed genetically modified foods were a bad idea.[41]

Despite this public opposition, some firms knew that GM foods were an important scientific breakthrough and an attractive financial investment. One such firm was Monsanto.

> In 1998, Monsanto Company became the first company to genetically engineer corn to resist rootworm, an insect that caused $1 billion in damages annually to the largest U.S. crop. The company reported that farmers would no longer have to spend $150 million annually on chemicals to control rootworm, which infested about 15 million acres. Five years after Monsanto's initial announcement Monsanto received clearance from the U.S. Environmental Protection Agency to begin to sell the first corn plant genetically modified to resist the rootworm insect.[42]

Other genetically modified products were introduced with mixed results. The food industry generally shunned bioengineered seeds to grow sugar beet plants, the source for sugar for food and candy manufacturers. But genetically modified tobacco, which contained virtually no nicotine, was welcomed by the Leggett Group, a discount-cigarette

---

[40] "We Are Now Starting the Century of Biology," *BusinessWeek*, August 31, 1998, pp. 86–87.

[41] "Broad Opposition to Genetically Modified Foods," Institute for Global Ethics, *Ethics Newsline*, July 7, 2003, *www.globalethics.org*.

[42] "Monsanto Falls Flat Trying to Sell Europe on Bioengineered Food," *The Wall Street Journal*, May 11, 1999, pp. A1, A10; and "Monsanto Wins EPA Clearance to Market Pest-Resistant Corn," *The Wall Street Journal*, February 26, 2003, p. D4.

maker that was interested in producing a low- or no-nicotine cigarette to appeal to smokers who were trying to quit smoking.

By 2004, the opposition to GM foods began to weaken in Europe. Britain allowed farmers to grow a strain of biotech corn for cultivation purposes and to feed dairy cows, but retained the ban on GM sugar beets. Shortly thereafter, the European Union approved the manufacture of a genetically engineered corn, ending a six-year moratorium on approvals for biotechnology crops that led to a bitter trade dispute with the United States. Then, in 2006, the World Trade Organization (WTO) ruled that the European Union (EU) had breached international rules by restricting imports of genetically modified crops and food made from them. While bioengineering experts did not feel that the WTO ruling would flood Europe with GM products, they did believe that it would discourage other countries from adopting barriers similar to those developed by the EU and would set a precedent that countries must have sound scientific reasons for rejecting genetically modified crops. "One reason we brought the case was because of the chilling effect the EU's actions had on the adoption of biotechnology," said a United States trade official.[43]

In other countries genetically modified food was welcomed. Russia embraced this new technology, as did China.

After losing the battle to insects and finding that pesticides often were ineffective on the North China Plain, where cotton was the primary crop, cotton growing began to flourish again. "I was the first one in the village to plant these new [bioengineered] cotton seeds, but when everyone saw how great the results were, they started growing again, too," said An Deyin, a Chinese farmer.

China's leaders made genetic research a top scientific priority, funneling billions of government dollars into research on modifying the genes of crops and vegetables. Government leaders saw genetic crop production as a source of stable food supplies and the path to a national presence in the agricultural import-export arena. By 2000, 1.2 million to 2.4 million acres of biotech crops had been planted in China. Professor Zhangliang Chen estimated that within 5 to 10 years, half of the country's fields would be planted with GM rice, potatoes, and other crops. While predictions of widespread planting of GM crops in China were common, most countries, including China, have been slow to join the GM-food campaign strongly adopted in the United States, as shown in Figure 14.3.

FIGURE 14.3
Commitment to Biotechnology Crop Planting by Country

Source: International Service for the Acquisition of Agri-biotech Applications, reported in "Thai Chew Over Biotech Food," *The Wall Street Journal*, October 29, 2004, p. A13.

Country	Millions of Acres, 2003
United States	105.7
Argentina	34.3
Canada	10.9
Brazil	7.4
China	6.9
South Africa	0.9
Australia	0.25
India	0.25
Romania	Less than 0.25
Uruguay	Less than 0.25

[43] "World Trade Agency Rules for U.S. in Biotech Dispute," *The New York Times Online*, February 8, 2006, www.nytimes.com.

The controversies over genetic engineering, stem-cell research, cloning, and genetically modified food production raise serious ethical and social issues. The questions concerning the role of businesses, social activist groups, or governments in overseeing these technological developments must continue to be addressed, as new innovations appear on the horizon.

Summary

- Businesses have addressed many privacy issues at work and in e-commerce by developing privacy policies and by sharing information and technology through voluntary industry initiatives.

- Acts of sabotage by computer hackers threaten companies' control of information, causing businesses to develop elaborate information security systems to more quickly detect hacking efforts and to patch systems targeted by viruses or worms.

- Businesses have entrusted the management of technology to their chief information or privacy officers. For issues that go beyond the business organization and affect society in general, it is unclear whether businesses, social groups, or governments—or some combination of these—should manage technology and its change.

- Company and industry initiatives have been joined by governmental action to better shield children from the growing and lucrative Internet pornography industry.

- Threats of software, music, and movie piracy challenge businesses' ownership of their property, calling for industry and international governmental responses to these ethical violations.

- Fears associated with human genetic research, stem-cell research, human cloning, and genetically modified foods have raised objections from social activist and consumer groups. Businesses have attempted to address these fears and dispel false concerns, while seeking to promote the benefits of scientific technological breakthroughs.

Key Terms

bioterrorism, *313*
chief information officer (CIO), *304*
computer hackers, *302*
Digital Millennium Copyright Act, *306*

genetically modified foods, *314*
genetic engineering, *314*
human genome, *309*
intellectual property, *305*
privacy policy, *298*

software piracy, *305*
stem-cell research, *309*
streaming, *307*
tissue engineering, *309*

Internet Resources

www.privacyalliance.com   Online Privacy Alliance
www.truste.org   TRUSTe
www.bsa.org   Business Software Alliance
www.doegenomes.org   Human Genome Project
www.nlm.nih.gov/medlineplus/cloning   Medline Plus—Cloning, U.S. National Library of Medicine and The National Institutes of Health
www.monsanto.com/biotech-gmo   Monsanto's biotechnology Web page

Discussion Case: *We're Simply Downloading Music— So What's the Big Deal?*

Jose is a junior in college and he loves music. It helps define who he is, and he enjoys showing off the new tunes he has downloaded to his friends, especially Rachel, whom he is trying to impress. His music helps him study, relax, and meet new people. But his friend Rachel has just told him that she has received a letter from some music group (the Recording Industry Association of America) telling her that she will be sued if she does not stop downloading music. She is frightened and confused by the letter, and now Jose is concerned too.

Jose and Rachel are caught in the middle of an ethical and legal controversy over the protection of copyrighted music. What are the rights of the musicians who created the music and the companies that recorded and distributed it? What are the rights of music fans to use readily available software to download music from the Internet and store it to play later at their pleasure?

The Recording Industry Association of America (RIAA) took an exceptionally hard stance in early 2003 when it filed 261 lawsuits, charging Internet music downloaders with copyright infringement. With recorded music sales down 26 percent in four years, industry officials believed that the only way to stem the widespread file swapping was to make people realize that they would be punished for participating.

The RIAA continued its battle in 2003 and 2004 by suing several hundred individuals for illegally downloading and distributing copyrighted music over the Internet. One RIAA letter stated, "The purpose of this notice is to provide you with the opportunity to resolve this matter and avoid being sued." RIAA alleged that individuals were using Internet services such as Kazaa and Grokster to access, download, and store music. In one action, it specifically targeted subscribers of five Internet service providers based along the East Coast.

Later in 2004, the RIAA turned to universities in its quest to stop illegal file sharing of music. This time, it targeted college students and others who had allegedly used networks at 21 different universities to illegally share music files. Commented the provost of the University of Michigan, "We will of course comply with the law. Violation of copyright laws is a violation of our own computing policies. We emphasize the proper-use policy and we have had programs to discuss this issue."

But the RIAA legal onslaught was not over. A year later in April 2005, university students at 18 colleges with access to the Internet2 network were served with federal lawsuits. Internet2 is used by several million university students, researchers, and professors around the world but is generally inaccessible to the public. The RIAA accused students of sharing an average of 2,300 songs each. RIAA reported that it found evidence of more illegal file sharing at 140 more schools in 41 states and sent warning letters to university presidents threatening additional legal action if steps were not taken to stop this illegal epidemic.

When Jose learned about this latest action, he become increasingly concerned, since he knew that he and his friends, including Rachel, had all used the Internet2 system at their school to download music.

Jose decided he needed more information, so he went to his blog and began discussing this issue with people he had met through the Internet. Mike, who was a student at Penn State, told Jose that his school provided him and his friends with a legal method to download music from a catalog of half a million songs. According to Mike, Penn State had entered into a deal with Napster. After losing a major legal battle with RIAA in 2003,

Napster had developed a new service that allowed him to listen to an unlimited number of songs as often as he wanted, as long as he remained a student at Penn State. And when he graduated, Mike said, he could burn his tunes to a CD and pay only 99 cents per song. Mike heard this was possible because of the $160 information technology fee every student paid each year.

Now Jose was really confused. Why would Rachel get this threatening letter for downloading music, but Mike said it was OK and legal to do this at Penn State? Another blogger, Jasmine, who was a student where Jose and Rachel went to school, posted the letter that the university circulated at student orientation informing students that the school had a strict policy against students illegally downloading songs. If discovered, the student could face disciplinary action, even dismissal from school. When Jose told Rachel about their school's policy, they were really scared since their parents would be very angry if either were dismissed from school for something their parents would view as so silly as downloading music.

Jose and Rachel weren't sure what to do. Should they delete all of their songs, in fear of action that could be taken by the RIAA, their university, or even worse, their parents? Or should they just go along as normal, downloading the songs they liked and enjoyed listening to when studying, relaxing, and with friends? Surely the RIAA couldn't know about their actions. They only downloaded a couple of hundred songs, not thousands as RIAA claimed students had done in their recent round of lawsuits. Maybe no one would ever know.

Sources: "261 Lawsuits Filed on Internet Music Sharing," *The New York Times Online,* September 9, 2003, *www.nytimes.com;* "Music Industry Sends Warnings on Alleged Piracy," *The Wall Street Journal,* October 20, 2003, p. B9; "Record Industry Files 532 Suits against Music Downloaders," *The New York Times Online,* January 21, 2004, *www.nytimes.com;* "Music Group Files Another File-Sharing Suit," *The Wall Street Journal,* February 18, 2004, p. B10; "RIAA Sues People at 21 Colleges, Claiming Illegal Music Sharing," *The Wall Street Journal,* March 24, 2004, p. B4; "RIAA to Sue Internet2 Users," *The Wall Street Journal Online,* April 12, 2005, *online.wsj.com;* and "Penn State Will Pay to Allow Students to Download Music," *The New York Times Online,* November 7, 2003, *www.nytimes.com.*

Discussion Questions

1. Was it appropriate for the RIAA to repeatedly file lawsuits against those who were downloading music? If not, what else could the association have done to stem declining industry sales, which were partially due to free file-swapping of music?

2. Since other information and entertainment are available for free off the Internet, should music be available at no charge as well? Or, is it simply wrong to download copyrighted music?

3. Where do you draw the line permitting free information off the Internet, but try to respect the artists' intellectual property and rights to royalties from their creations?

4. As long as technology enables people to download music with greater anonymity, should people continue to download music files until they are caught?

PART SEVEN

Building Relationships with Stakeholders

CHAPTER THIRTEEN

Stockholder Rights and Corporate Governance

Stockholders occupy a position of central importance in the corporation because they are the company's legal owners. But the corporation is not always run solely for their benefit, so they contend with management and the board of directors for control of company policies. Recent corporate scandals and debates over executive compensation have challenged companies and government regulators to reform the process of corporate governance to better protect stockholder interests. And individual and institutional investors have demanded greater accountability from those in charge of public corporations.

This chapter focuses on these key learning objectives:

- Identifying different kinds of stockholders and understanding their objectives and legal rights.
- Knowing how corporations are governed and explaining the role of the board of directors in protecting the interests of owners.
- Investigating how recent corporate scandals have affected corporate governance.
- Analyzing the function of executive compensation and debating if top managers are paid too much.
- Knowing how investors organize to promote their economic and social objectives.
- Understanding how the government protects against stock market abuses, such as fraudulent accounting and insider trading.

The board of directors of WorldCom shocked the investment community when it announced in 2002 that the company had overstated its earnings by almost *$4 billion.* Top managers had apparently cooked the books to make the telecommunications giant appear to be making more money than it actually was. When shareholders heard about the fraudulent accounting, they reassessed the value of the firm and began selling World-Com shares in droves. Within weeks, the once high-flying company had declared bankruptcy, becoming the largest business failure in U.S. history. Stockholders, from small individual investors to big pensions and mutual funds, lost billions of dollars as World-Com shares became virtually worthless.

The bankruptcy of WorldCom was, without doubt, a disaster for the company's stockholders. What motivated executives at WorldCom to exaggerate the company's earnings? Why didn't the board of directors and the company's accountants exercise greater oversight? Why didn't government regulators do a better job of protecting stockholders' interests? Why didn't stockholders themselves figure out what was going on and sell their shares before it was too late? And what can be done to prevent such a thing from happening again?

Stockholders are the legal owners of corporations. But as the debacle at WorldCom so vividly illustrates, their rights are not always protected. In the mid- to late-2000s, in the wake of this and other high-profile scandals in which stockholders incurred major losses, many groups took steps to improve the overall system of corporate governance. This chapter will address the important legal rights of stockholders and how corporate boards, government regulators, managers, and activist shareholders can protect them. It will also discuss recent changes in corporate practice and government oversight designed to better guard stockholder interests, in both the United States and other nations.

Stockholders

Stockholders (or shareholders, as they also are called) are the legal owners of business corporations. By purchasing shares of a company's stock, they become part owners. For this reason, stockholders have a big stake in how well their company performs. They are considered one of the market stakeholders of the firm, as explained in Chapter 1. The firm's managers must pay close attention to stockholders' needs and assign a high priority to their interests in the company.[1]

Who Are Stockholders?

Two types of stockholders own shares of stock in corporations: individual and institutional.

* *Individual stockholders* are people who directly own shares of stock issued by companies. These shares are usually purchased through a stockbroker and are held in brokerage accounts. For example, a person might buy 100 shares of Intel Corporation for his or her portfolio. Such stockholders are sometimes called "Main Street" investors, because they come from all walks of life.

* *Institutions,* such as pensions, mutual funds, insurance companies, and university endowments, also own stock. For example, mutual funds such as Fidelity Magellan

---

[1] The following discussion refers to publicly held corporations, that is, ones whose shares of stock are owned by the public and traded on the various stock exchanges. U.S. laws permit a number of other ownership forms, including sole proprietorships, partnerships, and mutual companies.

FIGURE 15.1   **Household versus Institutional Ownership of Stock in the United States, 1965–2005 (Percentage of Market Value, in $ Billions)**

Source: Securities Industry Association, *Securities Industry Fact Book* (New York: Securities Industry Association, 2006). Based on Federal Reserve Flow of Funds Accounts (revised). Household sector includes nonprofit organizations. Used by permission.

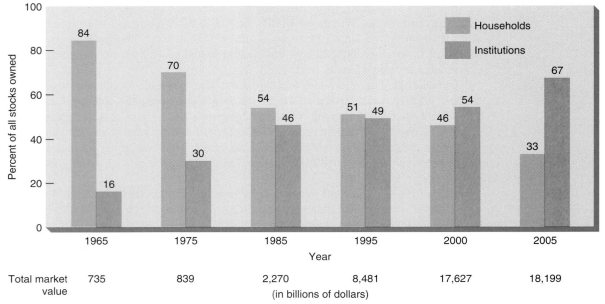

Total market value	735	839	2,270	8,481	17,627	18,199

(in billions of dollars)

and pensions such as the California Public Employees Retirement System (CalPERS) buy stock on behalf of their investors or members. These institutions are sometimes called "Wall Street" investors. For obvious reasons, institutions usually have more money to invest and buy more shares than individual investors.

Since the 1960s, growth in the numbers of such **institutional investors** has been phenomenal. Studies by the securities industry showed that in 2005, institutions accounted for 67 percent of the value of all equities (stocks) owned in the United States, worth a total of $12.1 *trillion*—nearly three times the value of institutional holdings a decade earlier.[2]

In 2005, one-half of all U.S. households owned stock, either directly or indirectly through holdings in mutual funds, up from one-fifth of households in the early 1980s. "America has become a society of equity investors," concluded a report by the Securities Industry Association. Stockholders are a diverse group. People from practically every occupational group own stock: professionals, managers, clerks, craft workers, farmers, retired persons, and homemakers. Although older people are more likely to own stock, 36 percent of young households (with a decision-maker under age 35) own stock, making up 15 percent of all investing households. Not all shareholders are wealthy; the median household income of owners of stock is $65,000.[3]

Figure 15.1 shows the relative stock holdings of individual and institutional investors from the 1960s through the mid-2000s. It shows the growing influence of the institutional sector of the market over the past four decades.

[2] "Holdings of U.S. Equities Outstanding," *Fact Book 2005* (New York: Securities Industry Association, 2005). These data are based on analysis of the Federal Reserve Bank's flow of funds accounts.

[3] "Equity Ownership in America, 2005," Investment Company Institute and the Securities Industry Association, 2005.

Objectives of Stock Ownership

Individuals and institutions own corporate stock for a number of reasons. Foremost among them is to make money. People buy stocks because they believe stocks will produce a return greater than they could receive from alternative investments. Stockholders make money when the price of the stock rises (this is called *capital appreciation*) and when they receive their share of the company's earnings (called *dividends*). Most companies pay dividends, but some—particularly new companies with good prospects for rapid growth—do not. In this case, investors buy the stock with the goal of capital appreciation only.

Stock prices rise and fall over time, affected by both the performance of the company and by the overall movement of the stock market. In the mid- to late 1990s, a *bull market* (in which share prices rise overall) produced large gains for many investors; this was followed from 2000 to 2002 by a *bear market* (in which share prices fall overall), in which many investors lost money. Typically, bull and bear markets alternate, driven by the health of the economy, interest rates, world events, and other factors that are often difficult to predict. Although stock prices are sometimes volatile, stocks historically have produced a higher return over the long run than investments in bonds, bank certificates of deposit, or money markets. For this reason, they continue to attract investors, despite the potential for losses.

Although the primary motivation of most stockholders is to make money from their investments, some have other motivations as well. Some investors use stock ownership to achieve social or ethical objectives, a trend that is discussed later in this chapter in the section on social investment. The strategy of acquiring stock in order to take control of a company in a hostile takeover bid is discussed in Chapter 10. Of course, some investors have mixed objectives. They wish to make a reasonable return on their investment but also to advance social or ethical goals.

Stockholders' Legal Rights and Safeguards

As explained in Chapter 1, managers have a duty to all stakeholders, not just to those who own shares in their company. Nevertheless, in the United States and most other countries, stockholders have legal rights that are often more extensive than those of other stakeholders.

To protect their financial stake in the companies whose stocks they hold, stockholders have specific legal rights. Stockholders have the right to share in the profits of the enterprise if directors declare dividends. They have the right to receive annual reports of company earnings and company activities and to inspect the corporate books, provided they have a legitimate business purpose for doing so and that it will not be disruptive of business operations. They have the right to elect members of the board of directors, usually on a "one share equals one vote" basis. They have the right to hold the directors and officers of the corporation responsible for their acts, by lawsuit if they want to go that far. Furthermore, they usually have the right to vote on mergers, some acquisitions, and changes in the charter and bylaws, and to bring other business-related proposals before the stockholders. And finally, they have the right to sell their stock. Figure 15.2 summarizes the major legal rights of stockholders.

Many of these rights are exercised at the annual stockholders' meeting, where directors and managers present an annual report and shareholders have an opportunity to approve or disapprove management's plans. Because most corporations today are large, typically only a small portion of stockholders vote in person. Those not attending are given an opportunity to vote by absentee ballot, called a **proxy**. The use of proxy elections by stockholders to influence corporate policy is discussed later in this chapter.

FIGURE 15.2
Major Legal Rights of Stockholders

- To receive dividends, if declared

- To vote on
  Members of board of directors
  Major mergers and acquisitions
  Charter and bylaw changes
  Proposals by stockholders

- To receive annual reports on the company's financial condition

- To bring shareholder suits against the company and officers

- To sell their own shares of stock to others

How are these rights of stockholders best protected? Within a publicly held company, the board of directors bears a major share of the responsibility for making sure that the firm is run with the shareholders' interests in mind. We turn next, therefore, to a consideration of the role of the board in the system of corporate governance.

Corporate Governance

The term **corporate governance** refers to the process by which a company is controlled, or governed. Just as nations have governments that respond to the needs of citizens and that establish policy, so do corporations have systems of internal governance that determine overall strategic direction and balance sometimes divergent interests. Recent corporate scandals, such as the WorldCom example at the beginning of this chapter, have focused renewed attention on corporate governance, because at times the control systems in place have not effectively protected stockholders and others with a stake in the company's performance.

The Board of Directors

The **board of directors** plays a central role in corporate governance. The board of directors is an elected group of individuals who have a legal duty to establish corporate objectives, develop broad policies, and select top-level personnel to carry out these objectives and policies. The board also reviews management's performance to be sure the company is well run and stockholders' interests are protected.[4]

Corporate boards vary in size, composition, and structure to best serve the interests of the corporation and the shareholders. A number of patterns do exist, however. According to a survey of governance practices in leading firms in the Americas, Europe, and Asia Pacific, corporate boards average 11 members. The largest boards are in banking, insurance, aerospace, and pharmaceutical companies, and the smallest are in small and midsized firms and in the high-tech, retailing, energy, and health care industries. Of these members, usually about three-fourths are *outside* directors (not managers of the company, who are known as *inside* directors when they serve on the board). (In the United States, the New York Stock Exchange now requires listed companies to have boards with a majority of outsiders.) Board members may include chief executives of other companies, major shareholders, bankers, former government officials, academics, representatives

---

[4] For an overview of the role and functions of the board of directors, see Marianne Jennings, *The Board of Directors: 25 Keys to Corporate Governance* (New York: Lebhar-Friedman Books, 2000).

of the community, or retired executives from other firms. Eighty-four percent all companies have at least one woman on the board, and 76 percent have at least one member of an ethnic minority.[5]

Corporate directors are typically well paid. Compensation for board members is a complex mix of retainer fees, meeting fees, grants of stock and stock options, pensions, and various perks. In 2005, median compensation for directors at the largest U.S. corporations was $182,304, an increase of almost 60 percent since 2000. (Of this compensation, 40 percent was paid in cash and 60 percent in stock or stock options.)[6] Some critics believe that board compensation is excessive and that high pay contributes to complacency by some directors who do not want to jeopardize their positions by challenging the policies of management.

Most corporate boards perform their work through committees as well as in general sessions. The compensation committee (present in 100 percent of corporate boards), normally staffed by outside directors, administers and approves salaries and other benefits of high-level managers in the company. The nominating committee (97 percent) is charged with finding and recommending candidates for officers and directors, especially those to be elected at the annual stockholders' meeting. The executive committee (46 percent) works closely with top managers on important business matters. A significant minority of corporations (17 percent) now have a special committee devoted to issues of corporate responsibility.[7]

One of the most important committees of the board is the audit committee. Present in virtually all boards, the audit committee is required by U.S. law to be composed entirely of outside directors and to be "financially literate." It reviews the company's financial reports, recommends the appointment of outside auditors (accountants), and oversees the integrity of internal financial controls.

At Enron Corporation, further described in a case at the end of this book, lax oversight by the six-person audit committee was a major contributor to the collapse of the firm. In the five years leading up to the company's bankruptcy, Enron executives carried out a series of complex financial transactions designed to remove debt from the balance sheet and artificially inflate revenue. These transactions were later found to be illegal, and Enron was forced to drastically restate its earnings. A subsequent investigation found that although the audit committee had reviewed these transactions, "these reviews appear to have been too brief, too limited in scope, and too superficial to serve their intended function." In short, the audit committee, which typically met with the company's outside accountants for only an hour or two before regular board meetings, had simply missed one of the biggest accounting frauds in U.S. history.

Directors who fail to detect and stop accounting fraud, as in this example, may be liable for damages. At WorldCom, for instance, board members agreed to pay $18 million of their own money to settle a class-action lawsuit brought by shareholders. This was later overturned on a technicality, but these directors remained liable in other cases moving forward.[8] Because of tighter regulations and increased risk, audit committees now meet more frequently than they used to, on average 9 times a year.

[5] Korn/Ferry International, 32nd Annual Board of Directors Study, 2005.

[6] Pearl Meyer & Partners, *2005 Director Compensation,* available at www.execpay.com.

[7] Korn/Ferry International, 32nd Annual Board of Directors Study, 2005.

[8] "10 Ex-Directors from WorldCom to Pay Millions," *The New York Times,* January 6, 2005, p. A1; and "A WorldCom Settlement Falls Apart," *The New York Times,* February 3, 2005, p. C1.

How are directors selected? Board members are elected by shareholders at the annual meeting, where absent owners may vote by proxy, as explained earlier. Thus, the system is formally democratic. However, as a practical matter, shareholders often have little choice in the matter. Typically, the nominating committee, working with the CEO and chairman, develops a list of possible candidates. These are presented to the board for consideration. When a final selection is made, the names of these individuals are placed on the proxy ballot. Shareholders may vote to approve or disapprove the nominees, but because alternative candidates are often not presented, the vote has little significance. Moreover, many institutional investors routinely turn their proxies over to management. The selection process therefore tends to produce a kind of self-perpetuating system. An exception to this usual process of director selection that occurred at Disney is described in the discussion case at the end of this chapter.

Principles of Good Governance

In the wake of the recent corporate scandals, many sought to define the core principles of good corporate governance. What kinds of boards were most effective? What governance mechanisms offered the best protection against the kinds of abuses that occurred at WorldCom and Enron? During the 2000s, public agencies, investor groups, and stock exchanges all struggled to determine what reforms might be necessary. By the mid-2000s, a broad consensus had emerged about some key features of effective boards. These included the following:

- *Select outside directors to fill most positions.* Normally, no more than two or three members of the board should be current managers. Moreover, the outside members should be truly independent, that is, should have no connection to the corporation other than serving as a director. This would exclude, for example, directors who themselves performed consulting services for the company on whose board they served or who were officers of other firms that had a business relationship with it. The audit, compensation, and nominating committees should be composed *solely* of outsiders. By 2005, virtually all major companies were following these practices.

- *Hold open elections for members of the board.* Some groups favored a proposal under which dissident shareholders, under certain conditions, could put their own candidates for the board on the proxy ballot. Another idea was for companies simply to nominate more than one individual for each open position, giving owner-voters a genuine choice. Some thought that directors should stand for election every year; others thought that staggered terms were a better idea (for example, on a nine-person board, three individuals would stand for election each year for a three-year term). In any event, the idea was to give shareholders more control over the selection of directors.

- *Appoint an independent lead director (chairman of the board) and hold regular meetings without the CEO present.* Many experts in corporate governance also believed that boards should separate the duties of the chief executive and the board chairman, rather than combining the two in one person as done in many corporations. The independent chairman would then hold meetings without management present, improving the board's chances of receiving completely candid reports about a company's affairs. In 2005, 41 percent of large U.S. company boards separated the roles of chairman and CEO.[9] This practice was more common in the United Kingdom, where it was used in almost all companies.[10]

[9] *Directors' Compensation and Board Practices in 2005* (New York: The Conference Board, 2005), p. 33.

[10] "Emerging Board Practices—A Survey," ICRA Limited, February 2005.

- *Align director compensation with corporate performance.* Like top executives, directors should be paid based, at least in part, on how well the company does. For example, Coca-Cola announced in 2006 that it would change the way its directors were compensated. Members of the board would be paid only if the company met its earnings-per-share target of at least 8 percent annual compound growth over a three-year period. If the company did not, directors would get nothing.[11]

- *Evaluate the board's own performance on a regular basis.* Directors themselves should be assessed on how competent they were and how diligently they performed their duties. Normally, this would be the responsibility of the governance committee of the board. In the wake of the corporate scandals of the early 2000s, many companies made dramatic improvements in this area; between 2002 and 2004, the proportion of global companies that formally evaluated their board members rose from 35 to 90 percent, according to a survey by surveyed by Governance Metrics International.[12]

As calls for reform mounted, many companies voluntarily took steps to improve their own governance. For example, General Electric (GE) announced a series of changes. It appointed a presiding director, who would lead three meetings of the board annually without management present. The company also set a goal of having at least two-thirds of the board composed of outsiders, and several directors said they would leave to make room for others without ties to GE. "Corporate leadership has lost the benefit of the doubt," said CEO Jeffrey Immelt, in explaining these changes.[13]

The movement to improve corporate governance has been active in other nations and regions, as well as the United States. The Organization for Economic Cooperation and Development (OECD), representing 30 nations, issued a revised set of principles of corporate governance in 2004 to serve as a benchmark for companies and policy makers worldwide.[14] For its part, the European Union has worked hard to modernize corporate governance practices and harmonize them across its member states. For example, in 2006 the EU proposed new rules to make it easier for shareholders to get information and to vote their proxies. Practices varied greatly across the continent, and only two-thirds of big European companies had "one share–one vote" rules in place.[15] In South Korea, companies in the securities industry launched the Corporate Governance Service in 2002 to promote management transparency and create shareholder value, and began giving awards to companies that achieved the highest standards in corporate governance. In South Africa, the stock exchange announced new rules in 2003 that would require companies to disclose all compensation to directors and what ties, if any, they had to the company. In short, by the mid-2000s the movement to make boards more responsive to shareholders was an international one.[16]

---

[11] "Coke Directors Agree to Give Up Pay If Company Misses Earnings Goals," *The Wall Street Journal,* April 6, 2006, p. A1.

[12] "GMI Releases New Global Governance Ratings," press release, September 7, 2004, www.gmiratings.com.

[13] "GE to Announce Set of New Policies to Shore Up Board," *The Wall Street Journal,* November 6, 2002, pp. A2, A5.

[14] See www.oecd.org. Information about recent changes in corporate governance practices in Europe is available at the Web site of the European Corporate Governance Institute at www.ecgi.org.

[15] "Corporate Governance in Europe: What Shareholder Democracy?" *The Economist,* March 23, 2005; and "Corporate Governance: Commission Proposals to Make It Easier for Shareholders to Exercise Their Rights within the EU," available at www.europa.eu.int.

[16] The Corporate Library, www.thecorporatelibrary.org, routinely posts news stories from all over the world on current developments in corporate governance reform.

Executive Compensation: A Special Issue

Setting **executive compensation** is one of the most important functions of the board of directors. The emergence of the modern, publicly held corporation in the late 1800s effectively separated ownership and control. That is, owners of the firm no longer managed it on a day-to-day basis; this task fell to hired professionals. This development gave rise to what theorists call the *agency problem.* If managers are merely hired agents, what will guarantee that they act in the interests of shareholders rather than simply helping themselves? The problem is a serious one, because shareholders are often geographically dispersed, and government rules make it difficult for them to contact each other and to organize on behalf of their collective interests. Boards meet just four or five times a year. Who, then, is watching the managers?

An important mechanism for aligning the interests of the corporation and its stockholders with those of its top managers is executive compensation. But recent events suggest the system is not always doing its job.

In the early 2000s, a number of top executives made out handsomely, even as their companies were wracked by scandal. At Global Crossing, a builder of fiber-optic networks, top managers received millions of dollars in compensation as the company skidded toward bankruptcy. At Enron, CEO Kenneth Lay sold millions of dollars worth of stock in the months before the company collapsed. A study by the Institute for Policy Studies came to the startling conclusion that CEOs at companies under investigation for accounting fraud made 70 percent *more* than average. Why should these executives have been rewarded, when other stakeholders were so badly injured?[17]

Many critics feel that executive pay has become excessive, not just at companies accused of fraud but in fact at most companies, reflecting aggressive self-dealing by managers without regard for the interests of others.

Executive compensation in the United States, by international standards, is very high. In 2005, the chief executives of the largest corporations in the United States earned, on average, $8.4 million, including salaries, bonuses, and the present value of retirement benefits, incentive plans, and **stock options,** according to *BusinessWeek* magazine. (Stock options and the controversy surrounding this form of compensation are further explained in Exhibit 15.A.) This amount represented a 10 percent increase from the prior year, but was still below the peak median pay of $13 million in 2000, at the height of the stock market boom of the late 1990s.[18]

By contrast, top managers in other countries earned much less. Although the pay of top executives elsewhere was catching up, it was still generally well below what comparable managers in the United States earned. To cite just a few examples, the compensation of CEOs in the United Kingdom was just 55 percent of that of their U.S. counterparts, according to a 2006 study.[19] In France, it was 27 percent; in Japan, 26 percent; and in South Africa, 20 percent.[20] Executives in very similar companies had disparate incomes: Lord John Browne, chief executive of the British firm BP, earned $19 million

---

[17] "As Their Companies Crumbled, Some CEOs Got Big Money Payouts," *The Wall Street Journal,* February 26, 2002, pp. B1, B4; and "The (Fat) Wages of Scandal," *BusinessWeek,* September 9, 2002, p. 8.

[18] "Executive Pay: No Hair Shirts, But Still . . ." *BusinessWeek,* May 1, 2006, pp. 36–38.

[19] "How U.K. Shareholders Keep CEO Pay in Check," *The Wall Street Journal* (Europe), April 10, 2006, p. 24.

[20] Towers Perrin, "Worldwide Total Remuneration," in *Worldwide Total Remuneration,* p. 4, at www.towersperrin.com.

Exhibit 15.A

Stock Options: A Controversial Form of Compensation

An important component of compensation at many companies is stock options. These represent the right (but not obligation) to buy a company's stock at a set price (called the strike price) for a certain period. The option becomes valuable when, and if, the stock price rises above this amount. For example, an executive might receive an option to buy 100,000 shares at $30. The stock is currently selling at $25. If the stock price rises to, say, $35 before the option expires, the executive can exercise the option by buying 100,000 shares at $30, for $3 million, and then turning around and selling them for $3.5 million, pocketing $500,000 in profit, less taxes. Stock options became very popular during the 1990s, particularly in high-tech and other fast-growing companies, because they were seen as a way to align executives' interests with those of shareholders. The idea was that executives would work hard to improve the company's performance, because this would lift the stock and increase the value of their options.

But, in the wake of WorldCom and other corporate scandals, many began to reconsider this form of compensation. The danger was that unscrupulous executives might become so fixated on the value of their options that they would do anything to increase the stock price, even if this involved unethical accounting practices. A 2005 study seemed to confirm this, reporting that the higher the proportion of executive compensation in stock options, the more likely the firm was later to have to restate its profits. Another problem with stock options was that because companies were not required to report them as an expense (even though they cost the company money when exercised), they tended to skew the company's books, misleading investors. And in a bear market, of course, options were less attractive to holders, because they often expired without ever reaching the exercise price.

In 2005, the Securities and Exchange Commission approved new rules that for the first time required companies to deduct the cost of stock options from their earnings. Market observers expected that this change would cut earnings per share in 2006 by about 3 percent, and possibly by much more at high-technology companies that made heavy use of this form of compensation. Some companies responded by phasing out or reducing their use of options.

Sources: "Options Expensing Is Here to Stay," *BusinessWeek,* January 20, 2005, p. 44; "Stock Options: Old Game, New Tricks," *BusinessWeek,* December 19, 2005, p. 34; "Do Options Breed Fraud at the Top?" *International Herald Tribune,* August 5, 2005.

the same year that David J. O'Reilly, chief executive of the smaller U.S. firm Chevron, earned $37 million.[21] These disparities caused friction in some international mergers. For instance, shareholders at GlaxoSmithKline, a pharmaceutical company formed through a merger of British and American firms, complained loudly when the board proposed a $28 million benefits package for CEO Jean-Pierre Garnier. Garnier, who was born in France but had moved to the United States to head the merged company, said he needed more pay to "stay motivated." But this level of compensation seemed out of line to many European shareholders, and it was later reduced.[22]

Another way to look at executive compensation is to compare the pay of top managers with that of average employees. In the United States, CEOs in 2005 made 411 times what the average worker did. Figure 15.3 shows that the ratio of average executive to average worker pay has increased markedly over the past decade and a half, with the exception of periods of stock market downturn such as the early 2000s.

Why are American executives paid so much? Corporate politics play an important role. In a recent book, *Pay without Performance: The Unfulfilled Promise of Executive*

[21] "U.S. Style Pay Packages Are All the Rage in Europe," *The New York Times,* June 16, 2006, p. A1.

[22] "Mad about Money: The Outrage over CEO Pay Isn't Only a U.S. Phenomenon; Just Ask Shareholders in Europe," *The Wall Street Journal,* April 14, 2003, p. R3.

FIGURE 15.3
Ratio of Average CEO Pay to Average Production Worker Pay, 1990–2005

Source: Institute for Policy Studies and United for a Fair Economy, *Executive Excess 2006*, p.30, available online at www.faireconomy.org. Used by permission.

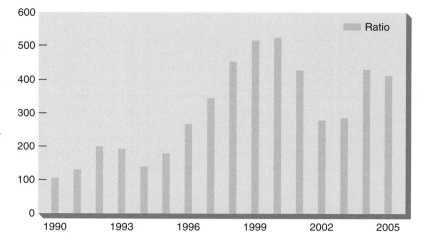

Compensation, Lucian A. Bebchuk and Jesse M. Fried argue that one reason salaries are so high is that top managers have so much influence over the pay-setting process. Compensation committees are made up of individuals who are selected for board membership by the CEO, and they are often linked by ties of friendship and personal loyalty. Many are CEOs themselves and sensitive to the indirect impact of their decisions on their own salaries. Moreover, compensation committees rely on surveys of similar firms and usually want to pay their own executives above the industry average, over time ratcheting up pay for all.[23]

Some observers say that the comparatively high compensation of top U.S. executives is justified. In this view, well-paid managers are simply being rewarded for outstanding performance. For example, Lee Raymond, who retired in 2005, earned $686 million during his 13 years at the helm of ExxonMobil. During this period, the company's market value quadrupled, and the company paid out $67 billion in dividends.[24] To at least some shareholders, his eye-popping pay was clearly worth it. A major share of the increase in executive compensation in the late 1990s resulted from the exercise of stock options, reflecting the bull market of that era, a development that benefited shareholders as well as executives.

Supporters also argue that high salaries provide an incentive for innovation and risk-taking. In an era of intense global competition, restructuring, and downsizing, the job of CEO of large U.S. corporations has never been more challenging, and the tenure in the top job has become shorter. Another argument for high compensation is a shortage of labor. In this view, not many individuals are capable of running today's large, complex organizations, so the few that have the necessary skills and experience can command a premium. Today's high salaries are necessary for companies to attract or retain top talent. Why shouldn't the most successful business executives make as much as top athletes and entertainers?

On the other hand, critics argue that inflated executive pay hurts the ability of U.S. firms to compete with foreign rivals. High executive compensation diverts financial

[23] Lucian A. Bebchuk and Jesse M. Fried, *Pay without Performance: The Unfulfilled Promise of Executive Compensation* (Cambridge, MA: Harvard University Press, 2004). Their argument is summarized in "Pay without Performance: Overview of the Issues," *Academy of Management Perspectives,* February 2006, pp. 5-24.

[24] "For Leading Exxon to Its Riches, $144,573 a Day," *The New York Times,* April 15, 2006, p. A1.

resources that could be used to invest in the business, increase stockholder dividends, or pay average workers more. Multimillion-dollar salaries cause resentment and sap the commitment—and sometimes lead to the exodus of—hard-working lower and mid-level employees who feel they are not receiving their fair share. As for the performance issue, critics suggest that as many extravagantly compensated executives preside over failure as they do over success. *BusinessWeek*'s annual pay survey routinely turns up scores of executives whose companies perform poorly despite their outsized salaries, such as Oracle CEO Lawrence Ellison, who received $781 million in total compensation over a three-year period in which returns to his company's shareholders were a dismal minus 61 percent.[25]

Some shareholder activists have tried to rein in excessive executive compensation. For example, Fidelity Investments, a mutual fund company that manages $1.2 trillion in assets, as a matter of policy opposes pay packages it considers grossly excessive. In 2005, Fidelity voted its proxies against management compensation proposals about a third of the time.[26]

Executive compensation has also been the subject of government regulations. Under U.S. government rules, companies must clearly disclose what their five top executives are paid and lay out a rationale for their compensation. Since 2006, regulators have also required companies to report the value of various perks, from the personal use of corporate aircraft to free tickets to sporting events, which had previously escaped investor scrutiny.[27] These requirements expand stockholders' rights by making it easier for them to determine a manager's total compensation and whether it is justified by the firm's record. The U.S. government also allows shareholder votes on executive and director compensation, and the government of the United Kingdom *requires* such votes. Although in both cases these votes are not binding, they provide a mechanism for shareholders to voice displeasure over excessive compensation.

For their part, many companies have responded to stakeholder pressure by changing the process by which they set executive pay. Most boards now staff their compensation committees exclusively with outside directors and permit them to hire their own consultants. Many firms have sought to restructure compensation to tie top executives' pay more closely to performance. A few top managers have even taken pay cuts, such as Sharper Image Corp.'s founder and chairman Richard Thalheimer, who voluntarily reduced his compensation pay by 50 percent in 2006. The company, whose stock had fallen badly, had laid off employees and scaled back plans to open new stores.[28] A tiny handful of companies have said that top executives cannot earn more than a certain multiple of others' pay. Whole Foods Market, for example, has a rule that no executive's salary and bonus can be more than 14 times what the average worker makes. "We have a philosophy of shared fate, that we're in this together," said John Mackey, the company's co-founder and CEO.[29]

How to structure executive compensation to best align managers' interests with those of stockholders and other stakeholders will remain a core challenge of corporate governance.

[25] "Special Report: Executive Pay," *BusinessWeek*, April 21, 2003, pp. 86-101.

[26] "Do Mutual Funds Back CEO Pay?" *The Wall Street Journal*, March 28, 2006, p. C1.

[27] "How Much Are Executives Really Paid?" *BusinessWeek*, March 20, 2006, p. 96; and "SEC Wants Companies to Tell All on Executive Pay," *The New York Times*, January 21, 2006, p. C2.

[28] "Sharper Image Corp. CEO Will Take a Pay Cut of 50% in Bid to Lower Costs," *The Wall Street Journal*, March 28, 2006, p. 1.

[29] "Putting a Ceiling on Pay," *The Wall Street Journal*, April 12, 2004, p. R11. Whole Food's measure of executive pay does not include the value of stock options.

Shareholder Activism

Shareholders do not have to rely exclusively on the board of directors. Many owners, both individual and institutional, have also taken action directly to protect their own interests, as they define them. This section will describe the increased activism of three shareholder groups: large institutions, social investors, and owners seeking redress through the courts.

The Rise of Institutional Investors

As shown earlier, institutional investors—pensions, mutual funds, endowment funds, and the like—have enlarged their stockholdings significantly over the past two decades and have become more assertive in promoting the interests of their members.

One reason institutions have become more active is that it is more difficult for them to sell their holdings if they become dissatisfied with management performance. Large institutions have less flexibility than individual shareholders, because selling a large bloc of stock could seriously depress its price, and therefore the value of the institution's holdings. Accordingly, institutional investors have a strong incentive to hold their shares and organize to change management policy.

In 1985, the Council of Institutional Investors was formed. Since then, the council has grown to more than 140 members and represents institutions and pension funds with investments exceeding $3 trillion. The council developed a Shareholder Bill of Rights and urged its members to view their proxies as assets, voting them on behalf of shareholders rather than automatically with management. The activism of institutional shareholders often improved company performance. One study showed that in the five years before and after a major pension fund became actively involved in the governance of companies whose shares it owned, stock performance improved dramatically, relative to the overall market.[30]

Institutional owners have also influenced change by seeking out companies that practice good corporate governance. A survey of 200 such investors in the United States, Europe, Asia, and Latin America conducted by McKinsey & Company found that more than 20 percent were prepared to pay a premium for the shares of companies that hired outside directors, were responsive to investor requests for information, evaluated their board members, and followed other established governance practices. "I simply would not buy [shares of] of a company with poor corporate governance," said one bank chief financial officer. Governance issues were particularly important to institutional investors in the emerging markets of Eastern Europe and Africa.[31]

The activism of institutional investors, as this survey suggests, has begun to spread to other countries. In many cases, U.S.-based pension and mutual funds that have acquired large stakes in foreign companies have spearheaded these efforts. By 2005, about one in every eight dollars worth of equities owned by American households and institutions was invested in the stocks of foreign companies.[32] To protect their globalized investments, fund managers have become active in proxy battles in Japan, Britain, Hong Kong, and

---

[30] Council of Institutional Investors, "Does Shareholder Activism Make a Difference?" available at www.cii.org/mono.htm.

[31] McKinsey and Company, "Global Investor Opinion Survey on Corporate Governance," July 2002.

[32] "Share of Total Equities Outstanding," *Securities Industry Factbook 2005,* p. 69.

many other countries. The movement for the rights of shareholders—like the investments they hold—is becoming increasingly globalized.

Social Investment

Another movement of growing importance among activist shareholders is **social investment,** sometimes also called *social responsibility investment,* or the use of stock ownership as a strategy for promoting social objectives. This can be done in two ways: through selecting stocks according to various social criteria and by using the corporate governance process to raise issues of concern.

Stock Screening

Shareholders wishing to choose stocks based on social or environmental criteria often turn to screened funds. A growing number of mutual funds and pension funds use *social screens* to select companies in which to invest, weeding out ones that pollute the environment, discriminate against employees, make dangerous products like tobacco or weapons, or do business in countries with poor human right records. In 2005, according to the Social Investment Forum, $2.3 trillion in the United States was invested in mutual funds or pensions using social responsibility as an investment criterion, accounting for nearly 1 in every 10 investment dollars. Between 1995 and 2005, socially responsible investment grew 4 percent faster than all assets under professional management.[33]

In recent years, socially responsible investing also has grown rapidly in Europe and beyond. In Europe, $435 billion is now invested using social criteria, according to the European Social Investment Forum.[34] Growth has been particularly rapid in the United Kingdom, where government rules require pension funds to disclose the extent to which they use social, environmental, or ethical criteria in selecting investments. Most evidence shows that socially screened portfolios provide returns that are competitive with the broad market.[35]

Social criteria may also be used when selling stocks. For example, some have at various times called for divestment (sale of stock) from companies that had operations in China, where some products were made by forced labor, and in Nigeria, Burma, and Sudan, where repressive regimes had been accused of human rights abuses.

Social Responsibility Shareholder Resolutions

Another important way in which shareholders have been active is by sponsoring **social responsibility shareholder resolutions,** resolutions on issues of corporate social responsibility placed before stockholders for a vote at the company's annual meeting.

The Securities and Exchange Commission (SEC), a government regulatory agency that is further described later in this chapter, allows stockholders to place resolutions concerning appropriate social issues, such as environmental responsibility or alcohol and tobacco advertising, in proxy statements sent out by companies. The SEC has tried to minimize harassment by requiring a resolution to receive minimum support to be resubmitted—3 percent of votes cast the first time, 6 percent the second time, and 10 percent the third time it is submitted within a five-year period. Resolutions cannot deal with a

[33] Social Investment Forum, "2005 Report on Socially Responsible Investing Trends in the United States," available at www.socialinvest.org.

[34] "Socially Responsible Investing Gains Ground Worldwide," *Funds International,* April 2005, p. 10. The Web site of the European Social Investment Forum is at www.eurosif.org.

[35] References to this literature may be found in Donald H. Schepers and S. Prakash Sethi, "Do Socially Responsible Funds Actually Deliver What They Promise?" *Business and Society Review* 108, no. 1 (Spring 2003), pp. 11-32.

company's ordinary business, such as employee wages or the content of advertising, since that would constitute unjustified interference with management's decisions.[36]

In 2005, shareholder activists sponsored around 600 resolutions dealing with major social issues. Backers included church groups, individual shareholders, unions, environmental groups, and a growing number of pension funds. Many of these groups were members of a coalition, the Interfaith Center on Corporate Responsibility (ICCR), which coordinated the activities of the social responsibility shareholder movement. Some key issues raised in these resolutions included executive compensation, environmental responsibility, antibias policies, and corporate governance.[37] One resolution, for example, called for the separation of the roles of chief executive and chairman of the board at the aerospace firm Textron. The resolution, which had been placed on the proxy ballot by the United Methodist Church, won majority support.[38] "Shareholder advocates concerned with their portfolio companies' social and environmental performance increasingly are reaching the conclusion that these policies cannot be considered in isolation from … governance policies and structure," said a spokesperson for the Investor Responsibility Research Center, an advocate of social investment.[39]

Social responsibility shareholder resolutions usually do not pass; they garner, on average, about 10 percent of votes.[40] This figure does not capture their full influence, however. In recent years, managers have often acted on an issue before the election so shareholder activists will withdraw their resolutions. During 2005, this happened about a quarter of the time. For example, at Coca-Cola a proxy fight was avoided when management agreed to full disclosure of its political contributions. Thus, shareholder activists can have an influence through the proxy election process even when their resolutions are not approved.

Stockholder Lawsuits

Another way in which stockholders can seek to advance their interests is by suing the company. If owners think that they or their company have been damaged by actions of company officers or directors, they have the right to bring lawsuits in the courts, either on behalf of themselves or on behalf of the company (the latter is called a *derivative* lawsuit). **Shareholder lawsuits** may be initiated to check many abuses, including insider trading, an inadequate price obtained for the company's stock in a buyout (or a good price rejected), or lush executive pension benefits. The outcome can be very expensive for companies, as illustrated by the following example involving accounting fraud.

In 2006, Nortel Networks, a maker of telecommunications equipment, offered $2.4 billion (about 15 percent of the value of the company) to settle two lawsuits brought by shareholders. The plaintiffs charged that the company had reported sales it had not made, defrauding investors who thought the company was performing better than it was and leading to big stock market losses.[41]

---

[36] Current SEC rules on shareholder proposals may be found at www.sec.gov/rules/final.

[37] Institutional Shareholder Services, "2005 Postseason Report: Corporate Governance at a Crossroads," available at www.issproxy.com.

[38] "Shareholder Resolution on Role Separation Prevails at Textron's Annual Meeting," press release issued by the General Board of Pension and Health Benefits of the United Methodist Church, May 12, 2005.

[39] "2003 Proxy Season Expected to Set Records, with CEO Pay and Global Warming among Top Issues," Social Investment Forum press release, February 12, 2003.

[40] "2005 Report on Socially Responsible Investing Trends in the United States," p 16.

[41] "Nortel Offers $2.4 Billion to Settle Lawsuits," *The New York Times*, February 9, 2006, p. C1.

In the 1990s, many companies, especially in high-technology industries, complained that they were targets of frivolous shareholder lawsuits. In 1995, in response to these concerns, Congress passed legislation that made it harder for investors to sue companies for fraud. But some executives believed the legislation had not gone far enough, because many shareholder suits disallowed under federal law could still be filed in state courts, and they called on Congress for a uniform national standard for securities lawsuits. Many investor groups, consumer activists, and trial lawyers opposed such a move. In the mid-2000s, in the wake of several high-profile corporate scandals, any such limitations on shareholders' right to sue seemed unlikely.

In many ways—whether through their collective organization, the selection of stocks, the shareholder resolution process, or the courts—shareholder activists can and do protect their economic and social rights.

Government Protection of Stockholder Interests

The government also plays an important role in protecting stockholder interests. This role has expanded, as legislators have responded to the corporate scandals of the 2000s.

Securities and Exchange Commission

The major government agency protecting stockholders' interests is the **Securities and Exchange Commission (SEC)**. Established in 1934 in the wake of the stock market crash and the Great Depression, its mission is to protect stockholders' rights by making sure that stock markets are run fairly and that investment information is fully disclosed. The agency, unlike most in government, generates revenue to pay for its own operations.

Government regulation is needed because stockholders can be damaged by abusive practices. Two areas calling for regulatory attention are protecting stockholders from fraudulent financial accounting and from unfair trading by insiders.

Information Transparency and Disclosure

Giving stockholders more and better company information is one of the best ways to safeguard their interests, and this is a primary mission of the SEC. The stockholder should be as fully informed as possible in order to make sound investments. By law, stockholders have a right to know about the affairs of the corporations in which they hold ownership shares. Those who attend annual meetings learn about past performance and future goals through speeches made by corporate officers and documents such as the company's annual report. Those who do not attend meetings must depend primarily on annual reports issued by the company and the opinions of independent financial analysts.

In recent years, management has tended to disclose more information than ever before to stockholders and other interested people. Prompted by the SEC, professional accounting groups, and individual investors, companies now disclose a great deal about their financial affairs, with much information readily available on investor relations sections of company Web pages. Stockholders can learn about sales and earnings, assets, capital expenditures and depreciation by line of business, details of foreign operations, and many other financial matters. Corporations also are required to disclose detailed information about directors and top executives and their compensation. In addition, many companies have begun reporting detailed information about social and environmental, as well as financial, performance. These trends toward greater corporate disclosure were discussed in Chapters 4 and 12.

Exhibit 15.B The Costs and Benefits of Section 404

One of the most controversial parts of the Sarbanes-Oxley Act is known as Section 404. This provision requires public companies to "establish, maintain, and assess their internal control over financial reporting" and to disclose any weaknesses to shareholders. (Private companies are not covered by Sarbanes-Oxley.) The purpose of the rule is to prevent accounting fraud, such as the events that occurred at WorldCom and Enron. Most small companies (with a market capitalization of under $75 million) are exempted from these requirements.

As a practical matter, Section 404 means that businesses must scrupulously document and cross-check all aspects of their financial record keeping. For example, for each accounts payable transaction, one employee has to prepare an invoice and another one has to approve it. Companies must also hire an outside auditor to vouch for the integrity of their internal controls.

Complying with Section 404 has been very expensive. In the rule's first full year in effect, U.S. businesses spent $35 billion on compliance; the average cost for large companies was $15 million and for mid-sized companies $4 million. These figures included management time, fees paid to auditors and attorneys, and the cost of upgraded computer systems. Smaller businesses complained that although they paid less overall than bigger firms, their per-employee costs were higher, hurting their ability to innovate.

Some critics argued that Section 404 had distracted managers from the more important work of running their businesses. "Complying with Sarbanes-Oxley has become a full-time job that forces management to take their eye off the ball," commented Scott Powell of the Hoover Institution. Thomas Donohue, president of the U.S. Chamber of Commerce, complained in a speech to the Securities Industry Association that "the [regulatory] pendulum has swung too far."

Others, however, believed that the price paid was worth it. Many observers thought that once necessary internal control systems had been established, the annual cost of compliance would drop. The presence of Section 404 controls reassured shareholders that financial reports were accurate, strengthening confidence in the stock market. Moreover, new investment in information technology helped companies by providing timelier and better-integrated data. As an executive of the consulting firm Accenture pointed out, these data could be turned into "a good story that gives [companies] a competitive advantage."

And some thought the costs of Section 404 had to be measured against the costs of doing nothing. A representative of Ohio's public pension system, a major institutional investor, commented, "Obviously, to the extent 404 impacts earnings negatively, it's a concern. On the other hand, who is measuring the cost of corruption and accounting scandals we've been through?"

Sources: "Securities and Exchange Commission Roundtable Discussion of Internal Control Reporting Provisions (Section 404 of the Sarbanes-Oxley Act of 2002)," *Gale Group Business Briefing*, May 5, 2005; "Sarbanes-Oxley: The Real Costs," *Global Finance Magazine*, April 2005, pp. 41 ff; "Are the Benefits of Sarbanes-Oxley Worth the Cost?" *CFO Magazine* 21, no. 7 (May 2005), p. 50; and "A Costly Way to Gain Control," *The Accountant*, September 2005, p. 4.

At the same time, information is useful to investors only if it is accurate. Fraudulent financial statements filed by WorldCom, Enron, and Adelphia misled investors and led to billions of dollars of losses in the stock market. The reasons for these accounting scandals were complex. They included lax oversight by audit committees, self-dealing by managers, and shareholders who were not sufficiently vigilant. Another problem was that some accounting firms had begun to make more money from consulting and other services than they did from providing routine financial audits. Often, accounting firms provided both consulting and audit services to the same company, creating a potential conflict of interest. Arguably, some accountants were afraid to blow the whistle on questionable financial transactions, out of fear of losing a valuable consulting client.

In 2002, in response to concerns about the lack of transparency in financial accounting, Congress passed an important new law that greatly expanded the powers of the SEC to regulate information disclosure in the financial markets. The law, called the Sarbanes-Oxley Act (for its congressional sponsors), had strong bipartisan support and was signed into law by President George W. Bush. Its impact promised to be enormous. The accounting firm PricewaterhouseCoopers, echoing a common sentiment, called it "the single most important piece of legislation affecting corporate governance, financial disclosure and the practice of public accounting since the U.S. securities laws of the early 1930s."[42]

The major provisions of the Sarbanes-Oxley Act are summarized in Chapter 5. Exhibit 15.B presents some arguments for and against a controversial part of this law known as Section 404.

Insider Trading

Another area the SEC regulates is stock trading by insiders. **Insider trading** occurs when a person gains access to confidential information about a company's financial condition and then uses that information, before it becomes public knowledge, to buy or sell the company's stock. Since others do not know what an inside trader knows, the insider has an unfair advantage.

> Samuel Waksal, former CEO of the biotechnology firm Imclone Systems, was sentenced to seven years in prison and fined $4 million for insider trading. "You abused your position of trust … and undermined the public's confidence in the integrity of the financial markets," said the judge in handing down his sentence. Two years earlier, Waksal had learned that the Food and Drug Administration was about to reject the company's application to market a promising cancer drug it was developing. The news was sure to hurt the company's stock price. In clear violation of the law, Waksal tipped off several family members and close friends to sell their Imclone stock before the FDA made its announcement. "This sentence was definitely designed to send a message," commented a former SEC prosecutor. "No matter how senior you are in the corporate hierarchy, you are going to be aggressively sentenced if you engage in any kind of securities fraud or insider trading."[43]

Insider trading is illegal under the Securities and Exchange Act of 1934, which outlaws "any manipulative or deceptive device." The courts have generally interpreted this to mean that it is against the law to:

- Misappropriate (steal) nonpublic information and use it to trade a stock.
- Trade a stock based on a tip from someone who had an obligation to keep quiet (for example, a man would be guilty of insider trading if he bought stock after his sister, who was on the board of directors, told him of a pending offer to buy the company).
- Pass information to others with an expectation of direct or indirect gain, even if the individual did not trade the stock for his or her own account.

In an important legal case, *U.S. v. O'Hagen*, the Supreme Court clarified insider trading law. The court ruled that someone who traded on the basis of inside information when he or she *knew* the information was supposed to remain confidential was guilty of misappropriation, whether or not the trader was directly connected to the company whose shares were purchased. Under the new court interpretation, insider trading rules would cover a wide range of people—from lawyers, to secretaries, to printers—who learned of

---

[42] PricewaterhouseCoopers, "The Sarbanes-Oxley Act of 2002," available at www.pwcglobal.com.

[43] "Imclone Founder Gets over Seven Years in Jail, Fine," *Boston Globe*, June 11, 2003, p. D1.

and traded on information they knew was confidential. They would not, however, cover people who came across information by chance, for example, by overhearing a conversation in a bar.[44]

The best-known kind of insider trading occurs when people improperly acquire confidential information about forthcoming mergers of large corporations in order to buy and sell stocks before the mergers are announced to the public. More recently, another kind of insider trading, called front-running, has become more common. Front-runners place buy and sell orders for stock in advance of the moves of big institutional investors, such as mutual funds, based on tips from informants. This form of insider trading is often harder for regulators to detect and prosecute.

> One region of the world where insider trading has been especially prevalent is the former communist countries of eastern Europe. The transition there to a market economy was generally not accompanied by adoption of the same kinds of government controls that exist in the United States. The result was, in many instances, stock price manipulation and insider trading. The president of one mutual fund with investments in eastern Europe, speaking of the Czech Republic, complained, "Like most postcommunist countries, there was an ingrained system—never tell the truth and always help your buddies."[45]

Insider trading, whether in new market economies or established ones, is contrary to the logic underlying the stock markets: All stockholders ought to have access to the same information about companies. In the Imclone case described above, the CEO had insider information that ordinary investors did not—information that he used to give his family and friends an unfair advantage over others. If ordinary investors think that insiders can use what they know for personal gain, the system of stock trading could break down from lack of trust. Insider trading laws are important in order for investors to have full confidence in the fundamental fairness of the stock markets.

Stockholders and The Corporation

Stockholders have become an increasingly powerful and vocal stakeholder group in corporations. Boards of directors, under intense scrutiny after the recent wave of corporate scandals, are giving close attention to their duty to protect owners' interests. Reforms in the corporate governance process are under way that will make it easier for them to do so. Owners themselves, especially institutional investors, are pressing directors and management more forcefully to serve stockholder interests. The government, through the Securities and Exchange Commission, has taken important new steps to protect investors and promote fairness and transparency in the financial marketplace.

Clearly, stockholders are a critically important stakeholder group. By providing capital, monitoring corporate performance, assuring the effective operation of stock markets, and bringing new issues to the attention of management, stockholders play a very important role in making the business system work. A major theme of this book is that the relationship between the modern corporation and *all* stakeholders is changing. Corporate leaders have an obligation to manage their companies in ways that attempt to align stockholder interests with those of employees, customers, communities, and others. Balancing these

---

[44]"Supreme Court Upholds SEC's Theory of Insider Trading," *The New York Times*, June 26, 1997, pp. C1, C23.

[45] "A U.S. Fund Manager in Prague Has Found Privatization Corrupt," *The New York Times*, December 3, 1997, p. D8.

various interests is a prime requirement of modern management. While stockholders are no longer considered the only important stakeholder group, their interests and needs remain central to the successful operation of corporate business.

Summary

- Individuals and institutions own shares of corporations primarily to earn dividends and receive capital gains, although some have social objectives as well.

- Shareholders are entitled to vote, receive information, select directors, and attempt to shape corporate policies and action.

- In the modern system of corporate governance, boards of directors are responsible for setting overall objectives, selecting and supervising top management, and assuring the integrity of financial accounting.

- The job of corporate boards has become increasingly difficult and challenging, as directors seek to balance the interests of shareholders, managers, and other stakeholders. In the wake of recent corporate scandals, reforms have been proposed to make boards more responsive to shareholders and more independent of management.

- Some observers argue that the compensation of top U.S. executives is justified by performance and that high salaries provide a necessary incentive for innovation and risk-taking in a demanding position. Critics, however, believe that it is too high. In this view, high pay hurts firm competitiveness and undermines employee commitment.

- Shareholders have influenced corporate actions by forming organizations to promote their interests and by filing lawsuits when they feel they have been wronged. They have also organized under the banner of social investment. These efforts have included screening stocks according to social and ethical criteria and using the voting process to promote shareholder proposals focused on issues of social responsibility.

- Recent enforcement efforts by the Securities and Exchange Corporation have focused on improving the accuracy and transparency of financial information provided to investors. They have also focused on curbing insider trading, which undermines fairness in the marketplace by benefiting those with illicitly acquired information at the expense of those who do not have it.

Key Terms

board of directors, *324*	proxy, *323*	social responsibility
corporate governance, *324*	Securities and Exchange	shareholder
executive	Commission (SEC), *335*	resolutions, *333*
compensation, *328*	shareholder lawsuits, *334*	stockholders, *321*
insider trading, *337*	social investing, *333*	stock options, *328*
institutional investors, *322*		

Internet Resources

www.nyse.com	New York Stock Exchange
www.irrc.org	Investor Responsibility Research Center
www.cii.org	Council of Institutional Investors
www.socialinvest.org	Social Investment Forum
www.socialfunds.com	Site for socially responsible individual investors
www.ecgi.org	European Corporate Governance Institute

Discussion Case: *Turmoil in the Magic Kingdom*

In August 2005, Judge William Chandler handed down his decision in a long-running legal case involving corporate governance at the Walt Disney Co. Institutional shareholders had sued the company's directors, saying the board never should have approved a $140 million severance payment to former president Michael Ovitz. The lawsuit demanded that directors personally reimburse the company for this amount plus interest—more than $200 million. In his decision, the judge found that although their decisions had turned out poorly, directors had acted in good faith and were therefore not liable.

Although he ruled against shareholders, the judge did not spare his criticism of Michael Eisner, Disney's CEO. Eisner, the judge opined, had "enthroned himself as the omnipotent and infallible monarch of his personal Magic Kingdom." The judge also spoke harshly of the actions of the board, which he described as "[falling] significantly short of the best practices of ideal corporate governance." He concluded that "many lessons of what not to do can be learned from [the] defendants' conduct here."

Walt Disney Co. was one of the best-known media and entertainment companies in the world, owning theme parks on several continents; television networks ABC, ESPN, and the Disney Channel; and movie studios Touchstone, Miramax, and Walt Disney Pictures. Michael Eisner had taken over the helm at Disney at age 42 in 1984 and had presided over a string of successes, increasing the company's revenue from $1.6 billion the year he took over to $30 billion in 2004, and its market value from $2.1 billion to $48 billion. Along the way, Eisner became one of the highest-paid executives ever, drawing more than $1 billion in total compensation over two decades and winning a spot on *Forbes* magazine's list of wealthiest Americans.

Eisner had hired Ovitz in 1995 to be Disney's president. At the time, Ovitz was considered the most powerful talent agent in Hollywood. Eisner had pushed hard for Ovitz's hiring, winning board approval for his employment agreement after less than an hour of deliberation. But Ovitz's tenure had lasted just 14 tumultuous months, during which Eisner and Disney's new president disagreed repeatedly over key issues facing the firm. Under the terms of Ovitz's compensation agreement, his termination entitled him to a severance package worth $140 million. Ovitz defended this payout, saying it was necessary to compensate him for giving up his lucrative talent agency business.

The trial revealed a governance process in which Eisner, who was chairman as well as CEO, largely controlled the board. The judge wrote: "Eisner stacked his (and I intentionally write 'his' as opposed to 'the company's') board of directors with friends and other acquaintances who, though not necessarily beholden to him in a legal sense, were certainly more willing to . . . support him." Directors who did not toe the line were forced out by Eisner loyalists on the nominating committee.

In late 2003, Roy E. Disney, the nephew of Walt, and his ally Stanley Gold resigned from the board and called on Eisner to step down. In 2004, the two former directors set out on a cross-country trip to organize institutional shareholders to withhold their votes from Eisner in the upcoming director election. They also launched a Web site, *savedisney.com,* featuring a cartoon of Eisner dressed as Snow White, gazing in the mirror and asking, "Who's the greediest of them all?"

The dissident former directors argued that in recent years the company's financial performance had faltered under Eisner's imperious leadership, and they called for greater accountability to shareholders and a clearer link between executive pay and performance. These arguments won the support of the pension funds of Ohio, California, Connecticut, Massachusetts, New Jersey, and New York; the proxy advisory firm Institutional Shareholder

Services; and the mutual fund companies T. Rowe Price and Fidelity. At a dramatic annual meeting in March 2004, Disney announced that an unprecedented 43 percent of shareholder votes had withheld support from Eisner. That evening, the board stripped Eisner of his chairmanship and gave the position to George Mitchell, a former U.S. Senator.

In the wake of Judge Chandler's decision the following year, Disney took additional steps to reform its corporate governance. Among other actions, the board adopted a new procedure for director elections. If a majority of shareholder votes were withheld from any director, that individual would be required to resign. The board's governance and nominating committee would then have to recommend to the full board whether the resignation should be accepted. "Today's action is the latest in a series of steps we have taken to further strengthen Disney's corporate governance practices," said board chairman Mitchell.

Eisner left the company voluntarily in September 2005.

Sources: James D. Stewart, *Disney War* (New York: Simon & Schuster, 2006); "Ruling Upholds Disney's Payment in Firing of Ovitz," *The New York Times,* August 10, 2005, p. A1; and "Disney Adds a Qualifier for Serving on Its Board," *The New York Times,* August 19, 2005.

Discussion Questions

1. In your view, did the behavior of top managers and the board of directors at Walt Disney Co. fall short of the standards of good corporate governance described in this chapter, and if so, how? What evidence supports your opinion?

2. Do you believe the compensation received by Michael Eisner and Michael Ovitz was appropriate? Why or why not?

3. What steps did institutional shareholders at Disney take to protect their rights and promote their interests? What additional steps, if any, could or should they have taken?

4. Do you believe that the changes in corporate governance that have been made at Disney are sufficient? Why or why not? If not, what additional changes should be made?

CHAPTER SIXTEEN

Consumer Protection

Safeguarding consumers while continuing to supply them with the goods and services they want, at the prices they want, is a prime social responsibility of business. Many companies recognize that providing customers with excellent service and product quality is an effective, as well as ethical, business strategy. Consumers, through their organizations, have advocated for their rights to safety, to be informed, to choose, to be heard, and to privacy. Government agencies serve as watchdogs for consumers, supplementing the actions taken by consumers to protect themselves and the actions of socially responsible corporations.

This chapter focuses on these key learning objectives:

- Understanding why a consumer movement arose in the United States and other nations.
- Knowing the five major rights of consumers.
- Assessing the ways in which government regulatory agencies protect consumers and what kinds of products are most likely to be regulated.
- Determining how consumer privacy online can best be protected.
- Examining how the courts protect consumers and efforts by businesses to change product liability laws.
- Evaluating how socially responsible corporations can proactively respond to consumer needs.

When Hurricane Katrina slammed into the Gulf Coast in 2005, it severely damaged more than 500,000 vehicles. Consumer advocates quickly warned that unscrupulous dealers might try to resell cars and trucks that had been soaked in sewage, petrochemicals, and salt water. Dealers could buy the tainted vehicles from insurers, superficially clean them, provide them with phony titles, and then trick unsuspecting used-car buyers, often in other states. One automobile insurer, the Progressive Group, decided to address this problem directly. The company announced it would crush and incinerate all cars recovered from the New Orleans area, rather than selling them at auction. "We simply don't want to see these cars back on the road," said a Progressive spokesperson.[1]

Every year, millions of high school students fill out classroom surveys run by the National Research Center for College and University Admissions that ask for their names, addresses, grades, and interests. As students expect, this information is sent to colleges that may be interested in recruiting them. But unknown to most, it is also sold to direct-mail marketers that provide it, for a fee, to companies that want to sell young people everything from credit cards to CDs. In 2003, National Research settled charges brought by the federal Bureau of Consumer Protection and agreed to stop using the information for any marketing unrelated to education.[2]

In the mid-2000s, a new Internet scam known as "phishing" emerged. Computer users would receive an e-mail message that looked as if it came from a legitimate business, such as a bank or online retailer, asking them to verify their account information. If recipients responded, they would be directed to a Web site that appeared real but in fact was a clever fake. The scammers would then use account numbers, credit card numbers, and passwords entered by users to steal their money or even identities. One of the problems facing law enforcement officials and businesses whose sites were impersonated was that both the criminals and the victims were spread across the globe from California to Slovenia to Vietnam. "It's very difficult working international cases," said an officer of the Federal Bureau of Investigation.[3]

These three examples demonstrate some of the complexities of serving consumers today. Companies face challenging—and often conflicting—demands to produce a high quality product or service, keep prices down, protect privacy, prevent fraud, and meet the changing expectations of diverse customers around the world. This chapter examines these issues and the various ways that consumers and their advocates, government regulators, the courts, and proactive business firms have dealt with them.

Advocacy for Consumer Interests

As long as business has existed—since the ancient beginnings of commerce and trade—consumers have tried to protect their interests when they go to the marketplace to buy goods and services. They have haggled over prices, taken a careful look at the goods they were buying, compared the quality and prices of products offered by other sellers, and complained loudly when they felt cheated by shoddy products. So, consumer self-reliance—best summed up by the Latin phrase, *caveat emptor,* meaning "let the buyer beware"—has always been one form of consumer protection and is still practiced today.

---

[1] "Don't Get Swamped with a Flooded Auto: Unsuspecting Dealers and Consumers Could End Up with Cars Damaged in Gulf Coast Storms," *Pittsburgh Post-Gazette*, October 19, 2005, p. E1.

[2] "Classroom Surveys: Firms Vow Not to Sell Student Info Again," *Columbus Dispatch*, January 30, 2003, p. B1; and "Surveyor Quietly Sells Student Information to a Youth Marketer," *The Wall Street Journal*, December 3, 2001, pp. A1, A12.

[3] "Online Crime: A Booming Business," *San Francisco Chronicle*, April 11, 2005, p. A1. More information about efforts to combat phishing is available at *www.antiphishing.org*.

344 Part Seven   *Building Relationships with Stakeholders*

However, the increasing complexity of economic life, especially in the more advanced industrial nations, has led to organized, collective efforts by consumers to safeguard their own rights. These organized activities are usually called *consumerism* or the **consumer movement.**

In the United States, the consumer movement first emerged in the Progressive Era of the 1910s; later waves of consumerism occurred in the 1930s (during the New Deal) and in the 1960s (as part of the broader movement for social change at that time). Today, many organized groups actively promote and speak for the interests of millions of consumers. One organization alone, the Consumer Federation of America, brings together 300 nonprofit groups to espouse the consumer viewpoint; they represent more than 50 million Americans. A nonprofit organization, Consumers Union, conducts extensive tests on selected consumer products and services and publishes the results, with ratings on a brand-name basis, online and in *Consumer Reports* magazine. Other active U.S. consumer advocacy organizations include Public Citizen, the National Consumers League, the Public Interest Research Group (PIRG), and the consumer protection unit of the American Association for Retired People (AARP). Consumer cooperatives, credit unions, Web sites catering to consumers, and consumer education programs in schools and universities and on television and radio round out a very extensive network of activities aimed at promoting consumer interests.

Many other nations have also experienced movements for consumer rights, as illustrated by the following example.

> In central Europe, a consumer movement blossomed after the fall of communism. In Latvia, for instance, activists formed a national federation of consumer clubs, joining groups that had sprung up independently in many cities and towns. "Our clubs," said the group's Internet site, "are operating as complaints-handling and campaigning agencies, carrying out small-scale investigative studies, representing consumers on consultative bodies and working with the government . . . on education and information programs."[4]

Consumers International is an international nongovernmental organization that represents more than 250 consumer groups in 115 nations. Headquartered in London, it has offices in Asia, Latin America, and Africa. Its growth since 1960 has paralleled the expansion of global trade and the integration of many developing nations into the world economy, as discussed in Chapter 7.

Reasons for the Consumer Movement

This consumer movement exists because consumers want to be treated fairly and honestly in the marketplace. Some business practices do not meet this standard. Consumers may be harmed by abuses such as unfairly high prices, unreliable and unsafe products, excessive or deceptive advertising claims, and the promotion of some products known to be harmful to human health.

Additional reasons for the existence of the consumer movement are the following:

- *Complex products have enormously complicated the choices consumers need to make when they go shopping.* For this reason, consumers today are more dependent on business for product quality than ever before. Because many products are so complex, such as a personal computer or an automobile, for example, most consumers have no way to judge at the time of purchase whether their quality is satisfactory. In these circumstances, unscrupulous business firms can take advantage of customers.

---

[4] Online at *www.consumer-guide.lv/english/movement.htm.*

- *Services, as well as products, have become more specialized and difficult to judge.* When choosing lawyers, dentists, colleges, or hospitals, most consumers do not have adequate guides for evaluating whether they are good or bad. They can rely on word-of-mouth experiences of others, but this information may not be entirely reliable. Or the consumer may not be told that service will be expensive or hard to obtain.
- *When businesses try to sell either products and services through advertising, claims may be inflated or they may appeal to emotions.* Abercrombie & Fitch, the fashion retailer, for example, has been criticized for promoting its clothing to teens in magazine-style catalogues that are packed with sexual imagery, like scantily clad young men playing with water hoses.[5] In the process, consumers do not always receive reliable and relevant information about products and services.
- *Some businesses have ignored product safety.* Business has not always given sufficient attention to product safety. Certain products, such as automobiles, pharmaceutical drugs, medical devices, processed foods, and children's toys, may be particularly susceptible to causing harm.

The Rights of Consumers

The central purpose of the consumer movement around the world is to protect the rights of consumers in the marketplace. It aims to make consumer power an effective counterbalance to the power of business firms that sell goods and services.

As business firms grow in size and market power, they increasingly acquire the ability to dominate marketplace transactions with their customers. Frequently, they can dictate prices. Typically, their advertisements sway consumers to buy one product or service rather than another. If large enough, they may share the market with only a few other large companies, thereby weakening some of the competitive protections enjoyed by consumers if business firms are smaller and more numerous. The economic influence and power of business firms may therefore become a problem for consumers unless ways can be found to promote an equivalent consumer power.

Consumer advocates argue that consumers are entitled to five core rights. These are:

1. *The right to be informed:* to be protected against fraudulent, deceitful, or grossly misleading information, advertising, and labeling, and to be given the facts to make an informed purchasing decision.
2. *The right to safety:* to be protected against the marketing of goods that are hazardous to health or life.
3. *The right to choose:* to be assured, wherever possible, access to a variety of products and services at competitive prices; and in those industries in which competition is not workable and government regulation is substituted, to be assured satisfactory quality and service at fair prices.
4. *The right to be heard:* to be assured that consumer interests will receive full and sympathetic consideration in the formulation of government policy and fair and expeditious treatment in the courts.
5. *The right to privacy:* to be assured that information disclosed in the course of a commercial transaction, such as health conditions, financial status, or identity, is not shared with others unless authorized.

Consumers' efforts to protect their own rights, through direct advocacy, are complemented by the actions of government regulators, the courts, and businesses themselves.

---

[5] "Fashion's Frat Boy," *Newsweek*, September 13, 1999, p. 40.

How Government Protects Consumers

The role of government in protecting consumers is extensive in many nations. This section will describe legal protections afforded consumers in the United States and offer some comparisons with other countries.

In the United States, the government's involvement in protecting consumers' interests has evolved over time. During the 1960s and 1970s, Congress passed important laws to protect consumers, created new regulatory agencies, and strengthened older consumer protection agencies. These developments meant that consumers, rather than relying solely on free market competition to safeguard their interests, could also turn to government for protection. During most of the 1980s, a deregulatory attitude by the federal government tended to blunt federal initiatives on behalf of consumers. However, state governments became more active, particularly regarding price-fixing, car insurance rates, and corporate takeovers that threatened jobs and consumer incomes. The 1990s and 2000s witnessed a revival of regulatory activism in some areas of consumer protection, such as the government's effort to shield people from unwanted telemarketing calls at home.

Goals of Consumer Laws

Figure 16.1 lists some of the safeguards provided by U.S. **consumer protection laws.** Taken together, these safeguards reflect the goals of government policy makers and regulators in the context of the five rights of consumers outlined above. Many of these safeguards are also embedded in the laws of other nations.

First, some laws are intended to provide consumers with better information when making purchases. Consumers can make more rational choices when they have accurate information about the product. For example, the Truth in Lending Act requires lenders to inform borrowers of the annual rate of interest to be charged, plus related fees and service charges. The laws requiring health warnings on cigarettes and alcoholic beverages broaden the information consumers have about these items. Manufacturers, retailers, and importers must specify whether warranties (a guarantee or assurance by the seller) are full or limited, must spell them out in clear language, and must give consumers the right to sue if warranties are not honored. Europe is catching up with the United States in this regard; for example, in 2006 the European Parliament approved tough new rules to protect consumers from false or misleading health claims on foods.[6]

Deceptive advertising is illegal. Manufacturers may not make false or misleading claims about their own product or a competitor's product.

> For example, in 2003 the Food and Drug Administration warned Allergan that its ads for Botox were illegal. The agency said the company had minimized the drug's risks and overstated its approved use. The FDA had originally approved the drug to treat crossed eyes and uncontrollable blinking, and had later extended its approval to include relaxing deep vertical lines between the eyebrows. But the pharmaceutical company had aggressively marketed the drug, a purified neurotoxin, under the slogan, "It's not magic, it's Botox Cosmetic."[7]

Deceptive advertising is also illegal in Europe, where, for example, U.K. regulators recently slapped a huge fine on the French insurance company AXA Sun Life for

---

[6] "Food Rules," *Country Monitor,* May 22, 2006, p. 6.

[7] "U.S. Warns Botox Maker about Its Ads," *The New York Times,* June 24, 2003, p. C2.

FIGURE 16.1

Major Consumer Protections Specified by Consumer Laws

Information protections

Hazardous home appliances must carry a warning label.

Home products must carry a label detailing contents.

Automobiles must carry a label showing detailed breakdown of price and all related costs.

Credit loans require lender to disclose all relevant credit information about rate of interest, penalties, and so forth.

Tobacco advertisements and products must carry a health warning label.

Alcoholic beverages must carry a health warning label.

All costs related to real estate transactions must be disclosed.

Warranties must specify the terms of the guarantee and the buyer's rights.

False and deceptive advertising can be prohibited.

Food and beverage labels must show complete information.

Food advertising must not make false claims about nutrition.

Direct hazard protections

Hazardous toys and games for children are banned from sale.

Safety standards for motor vehicles are required.

National and state speed limits are specified.

Hazardous, defective, and ineffective products can be recalled under pressure from the EPA, CPSC, NHTSA, and FDA.

Pesticide residue in food is allowed only if it poses a negligible risk.

Pricing protections

Unfair pricing, monopolistic practices, and noncompetitive acts are regulated by the FTC and Justice Department and by states.

Liability protections

When injured by a product, consumers can seek legal redress.

Privacy protections

Limited collection of information online from and about children is allowed.

Other protections

No discrimination in the extension of credit is allowed.

misleading promotion of various life insurance products.[8] (Deceptive advertising is further discussed in Chapter 20.)

U.S. law also requires food manufacturers to adopt a uniform nutrition label, specifying the amount of calories, fat, salt, and other nutrients contained in packaged, canned, and bottled foods. Labels must list the amount of trans fat—partially hydrogenated vegetable oils believed to contribute to heart disease—in cakes, cookies, and snack foods. Nutritional information about fresh fruits and vegetables, as well as fish, must be posted in supermarkets. Strict rules also define what can properly be labeled "organic."

A second aim of consumer legislation is to protect consumers against possible hazards. Required warnings about possible side effects of pharmaceutical drugs, limits placed on flammable fabrics, restrictions on pesticide residues in fresh and processed

---

[8] "U.K. Fines AXA Unit for Misleading Advertising," *Asian Wall Street Journal*, December 22, 2004, p. A4.

foods, the banning of lead-base paints, and inspections to eliminate contaminated meats are examples of these safeguards. In 1998, following several outbreaks of bacterial poisoning, the government required most fresh fruit and vegetable juice producers to implement good manufacturing practices to ensure safety and mandated that all unpasteurized juice carry a warning label. One incident of bacterial contamination in food that occurred before these rules were implemented, involving fresh fruit juice made by Odwalla, Inc., is described in a case study at the end of the textbook.

The third and fourth goals of consumer laws are to promote competitive pricing and consumer choice. When competitors secretly agree to divide up markets among themselves, or when a single company dominates a market, this artificially raises prices and limits consumer choice. Both federal and state antitrust laws forbid these practices, as discussed in Chapter 10. Competitive pricing also was promoted by the deregulation of the railroad, airline, trucking, telecommunications, banking, and other industries in the 1970s and 1980s and of the telecommunications industry in the late 1990s. Before deregulation, government agencies frequently held prices artificially high and, by limiting the number of new competitors, shielded existing businesses from competition.

A fifth and final goal of consumer laws is to protect privacy. This issue has recently received heightened regulatory attention, as discussed later in this chapter. The Children's Online Privacy Protection Act, which took effect in 2000, limits the collection of information online from and about children under the age of 13. In 2003, the Federal Trade Commission established a "do not call" list to protect individuals from unwanted telemarketing calls at home. Such calls to a person's mobile phone are also illegal.

Major Consumer Protection Agencies

Figure 16.2 depicts the principal consumer protection agencies that operate at the federal level of the U.S. government, along with their major areas of responsibility. The oldest of the six is the Department of Justice, whose Antitrust Division dates to the end of the 19th century. Its functions were described in Chapter 10. The Food and Drug Administration was founded in the first decade of the 20th century. The Federal Trade Commission was established in 1914 and has been given additional powers to protect consumers over the years, including in the area of online privacy. Three of the agencies—the Consumer Product Safety Commission, the National Highway Traffic Safety Administration, and the National Transportation Safety Board—were created during the great wave of consumer regulations in the 1960s and early 1970s. Not included in Figure 16.2 are the Department of Agriculture, which has specific responsibility for the inspection of meat and poultry, and the Environmental Protection Agency, which has authority over genetically modified food and some chemicals that may affect consumers.

The Civil Rights Division of the Department of Justice enforces the provisions of the Civil Rights Act that prohibit discrimination against consumers. One such case brought by this division is described in Exhibit 16.A.

The National Highway Traffic Safety Administration affects many consumers directly through its authority over automobile safety. For example, the agency develops regulations for car air bags, devices that inflate rapidly during a collision, preventing the occupant from striking the steering wheel or dashboard. Since 1998, driver and passenger-side air bags have been required as standard equipment on most cars. After concern emerged about possible hazards of the air bags themselves to children and small adults, the agency modified its rule to permit consumers to disable passenger-side airbags, if they could demonstrate a good reason, such as the need to place a small child in the front seat. Eventually,

FIGURE 16.2 **Major Federal Consumer Protection Agencies and Their Main Responsibilities**

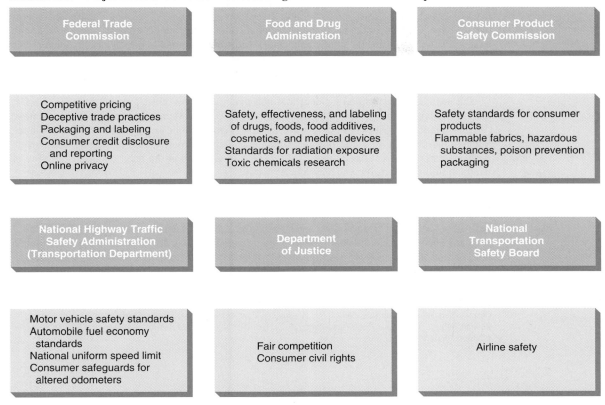

the NHTSA said it would require so-called "smart" air bags that would adjust the force of deployment according to the weight of the occupant.[9]

One consumer protection agency with particularly significant impact on the business community is the Food and Drug Administration (FDA). The FDA's mission is to assure the safety and effectiveness of a wide range of consumer products, including pharmaceutical drugs, medical devices, foods, and cosmetics. The agency has authority over *$1 trillion* of products, about a quarter of all consumer dollars spent each year.

One of the FDA's main jobs is to review many new products prior to their introduction. This job requires regulators to walk a thin line as they attempt to protect consumers. On one hand, the agency must not approve products that are ineffective or harmful. One the other hand, the agency must also not delay beneficial new products unnecessarily. The FDA can also pull existing products off the market or put restrictions on their use, if they are found to harm consumers. For example, in 2005 the agency adopted a rule requiring women taking the acne medication Accutane to use two forms of birth control, because the drug was known to cause miscarriages and severe birth defects.[10] Historically, the FDA has had a reputation as a cautious agency that has advocated tough and thorough review before approval. This policy has stood in contrast to those of its counterparts

[9] The most recent rules concerning air bags are available at *www.safercar.gov/airbags.*
[10] "FDA Puts New Regulations on Severe-Acne Treatment," *The New York Times,* August 13, 2005.

Exhibit 16.A   Welcome to Hotel Discrimination

In 2000, Adam's Mark settled a class-action lawsuit, brought by the U.S. Justice Department, charging that the upscale hotel chain had systematically discriminated against African-American customers. Although admitting no wrongdoing, Adam's Mark agreed to pay $8 million. Some of this amount would go to guests who had been subjected to bias, and some would fund scholarships and internships in hospitality management at historically black colleges. The hotel also agreed to bring in an outside monitor to make sure it complied with a nondiscrimination plan.

The lawsuit arose from an incident that had occurred at the chain's Daytona Beach, Florida, hotel the previous spring, during an event called Black College Reunion. According to the plaintiffs, African-American guests, unlike others, were made to wear orange wristbands to get into the hotel. Rooms they checked into had had furniture—including couches, chairs, and lamps—removed. Participants in the event had to pay cash for room service and at the hotel restaurant, instead of charging to their rooms as was normally permitted.

One of the guests who originally brought the suit, a 27-year-old African-American insurance adjuster who had come to the reunion, said, "I work as hard for my dollar as anyone else. If I want to spend that dollar for a hotel room, I deserve the same treatment as anyone else. That made me upset, and I was ready to go forward and do whatever it took to get things changed at Adam's Mark."

Many observers said the bias shown by the Adam's Mark was not unusual. In a national Gallup poll, half of blacks surveyed said that within the past month they had personally been treated unfairly because of race in situations such as shopping, dining out, or using public transportation. Some called this phenomenon *retail racism*.

Sources: "Hotel Settles Black Discrimination Suits," *Atlanta Journal and Constitution*, March 22, 2000, p. 3A; "Hotel Chain Settles Federal Race Bias Case," *The Washington Post*, March 22, 2000, p. A1; "A Weapon for Consumers: The Boycott Returns," *The New York Times*, March 26, 2000, p. D4; "New Face of Racism in America," *Christian Science Monitor*, January 14, 2000, p. 1.

in Europe and some other nations, which have tended to favor quick approval followed by careful field monitoring to spot problems. In the mid-2000s, the FDA, operating under new leadership, was praised by some for speeding up the review and approval process for new drugs and devices, while others thought it was not exercising sufficient care.[11]

One group of products that is *not* regulated by the FDA is dietary supplements, such as the vitamins, minerals, and herbal remedies often sold at health food stores. In 1994, the supplement industry successfully lobbied Congress for a law that exempted their products from most government regulation. As a result, unlike pharmaceutical drugs, supplements do not have to be proven safe or effective before being brought to market. This issue received fresh attention after several people, including a professional athlete, died after taking ephedra, an herbal stimulant. Saying that ephedra "appears not to be safe," the editor of the *Journal of the American Medical Association* called for regulation of all supplements claiming a biological function.[12]

The FDA's role in the approval and subsequent review of Vioxx, a pain medication withdrawn from the market by its manufacturer after it was associated with heart attacks and strokes, is discussed in a case at the end of the textbook.

[11] "McClellan's Friendlier, Speedier FDA: It's Streamlining Drug Approvals—and Winning Industry's Favor," *BusinessWeek*, June 16, 2003, pp. 33–34.

[12] Marion Nestle, *Food Politics: How the Food Industry Influences Nutrition and Health* (Berkeley: University of California Press, 2002), Part IV, "Deregulating Dietary Supplements"; and "Ephedra under Siege from New Quarters," *San Francisco Chronicle*, March 11, 2003, p. A12.

All six government regulatory agencies shown in Figure 16.2 are authorized by law to intervene directly into the very center of free market activities, if that is considered necessary to protect consumers. In other words, consumer protection laws and agencies substitute government-mandated standards and the decisions of government officials for decision making by private buyers and sellers.

The debate over whether government should become involved in protecting consumer privacy is discussed in the next section of this chapter.

Consumer Privacy in the Internet Age

In the early 21st century, rapidly evolving information technologies have given new urgency to the broad issue of **consumer privacy**. Shoppers have always been concerned that information they reveal in the course of a sales transaction—for example, their credit card or driver's license numbers—might be misused. But in recent years, new technologies have increasingly enabled businesses to collect and use vast amount of personal data about their customers and potential customers, especially those who shop online. The danger is not only that this information might rarely be used fraudulently, but also that its collection represents an unwarranted incursion into personal privacy. Consider the following hypothetical case:

> Sandra, a college student, used her personal computer to surf the Web. She established accounts at several online shopping sites to buy books, clothing, and CDs, and downloaded some music and video files onto her hard drive using software a friend recommended. She also established a free e-mail account at a popular Web portal and set her browser to open to its page. Soon, Sandra began receiving online ads for products similar to ones she had bought earlier, as well as for credit cards, an auto loan, and even a travel package for spring break. Sandra did not realize that several of the Web sites she had visited had tracked her online activity and had used this information to develop a profile of her that they had sold to Internet advertisers.

Behind Sandra's experience was a technology somewhat whimsically called a *cookie,* an identifying marker placed on a user's computer hard drive during visits to some Web sites. The cookie is used to identify the user during each subsequent visit to the Web site that placed the cookie. Internet businesses can use this information to build profiles of users' online surfing and shopping behavior over time. If sold to advertisers, this information can be used to target online solicitations.

Many e-businesses have welcomed this technology as an efficient way to learn about the characteristics and preferences of customers. For example, a cruise line operator might find out that a visitor to its site was a scuba enthusiast, prompting it to deliver information on tours to prime dive sites. The danger, however, is that detailed personal information, possibly of a sensitive nature, could fall into the wrong hands. Research shows that consumers are increasingly concerned about the potential threat to their privacy. A poll conducted for *BusinessWeek* magazine, for example, found that fully 90 percent of Internet users expressed discomfort about Web sites creating personal profiles that linked their real names with their browsing habits and shopping patterns.[13]

---

[13] "It's Time for Rules in Wonderland," *BusinessWeek,* March 20, 2000, pp. 83–96.

The dilemma of how best to protect consumer privacy, while still fostering legitimate Internet commerce, has generated a wide-ranging debate. Three major solutions have been proposed: consumer self-help, industry self-regulation, and privacy legislation.

- *Consumer self-help.* In this view, the best solution is for Internet users to use technologies that enable them to protect their own privacy. For example, special software can help manage cookies, encryption can protect messages, and surfing through intermediary sites can provide user anonymity. "We have to develop mechanisms that allow consumers to control information about themselves," commented a representative of the Center for Democracy and Technology, a civil liberties group.[14] Critics of this approach argue that many unsophisticated Web surfers, like Sandra, are unaware of these technologies, or even of the need for them. Moreover, tools for protecting privacy can always be defeated by even more powerful technologies.

- *Industry self-regulation.* Many Internet-related businesses have argued that they should be allowed to regulate themselves. One group of companies, organized as the Online Privacy Alliance, advocated adoption of voluntary policies for protecting the privacy of individuals' information disclosed during electronic transactions. The alliance published guidelines for the essential elements such policies should cover.[15] One advantage of the self-regulation approach is that companies, presumably sophisticated about their own technology, might do the best job of defining technical standards. Critics of this approach feel, however, that industry rules would inevitably be too weak. A 2005 survey found that although most large companies operating online had some kind of voluntary privacy policy, only 17 percent of Web sites were rated "excellent" overall, and nearly three-fourths were rated "poor" on reusing personal data for marketing purposes.[16]

- *Privacy legislation.* Some favor new government regulations protecting consumer privacy online. The Federal Trade Commission in 2000 announced its support for new laws that would establish standards governing the online collection of information. Such laws would require businesses, for example, to notify consumers whenever information was collected, ask them to *opt in* (or allow them to *opt out*), and give them access to their files and a means of correcting errors. Under the Bush administration, however, the FTC backed away from this stance, saying that it preferred to enforce laws already on the books. This pleased businesses that felt that further regulations would limit their ability to serve customers. Consumer privacy protections are are generally stronger in the European Union than in the United States; in the EU, the right to privacy is strongly engrained in both law and culture. "Simply stated, the Europeans have done a better job safeguarding privacy," commented the executive director of the U.S.-based Electronic Privacy Information Center.[17]

Any approach to online privacy would face the challenge of how best to balance the legitimate interests of consumers—to protect their privacy—and of business—to deliver increasingly customized products and services in the Internet age.

A related issue—protecting Internet users from e-mail spam—is profiled in Exhibit 16.B.

---

[14] More information about privacy protection for consumers is available at *www.cdt.org* (Center for Democracy and Technology) and *www.epic.org/privacy* (Electronic Privacy Information Center).

[15] Available at *www.privacyalliance.org.*

[16] The Customer Respect Group, "2005 Privacy Research Report," summary available at *www.customerrespect.com.*

[17] "Identity Theft: Europeans Mostly Better Protected," *Atlanta Journal-Constitution,* March 26, 2006, p. A12.

Exhibit 16.B   What Should Be Done about E-mail Spam?

In the 2000s, the amount of "spam" cluttering electronic mailboxes escalated at an alarming pace. Spam has been defined as unsolicited bulk e-mail messages, where the sender has no relationship to the recipient. By 2006, 71 percent of all e-mail was unsolicited; this figure was projected to grow to 79 percent by 2010, according to the market research firm Radicati Group. Much of it was offensive—ranging from sex ads to fraudulent business offers—and the e-mail was often disguised with a subject line like "order confirmation" so that people would open the message before realizing it was unwanted. "We are at a tipping point requiring some action to avert deep erosion of public confidence," an officer of the FTC told Congress. Many disagreed, however, on what action would be most appropriate. Some thought the use of software filters, by both individuals and Internet service providers, was the answer. But others thought only new legislation would put a stop to determined spammers. Thirty states passed laws requiring, for example, that unsolicited messages include "ADV" (for "advertisement") in the subject line, so they could more easily be picked up by filters, and in 2003 Congress debated national antispam legislation. But some were opposed, including legitimate businesses such as Amazon.com that believed such a law would restrict its right to advertise. And efforts to curb commercial free speech could violate the First Amendment, some thought. "Once the government starts deciding which speech is valid and which isn't, then you are in a dangerous area," said one legal expert.

Sources: "No Easy Solution to the Spam Problem," Federal Trade Commission press release, July 9, 2003, available at *www.ftc.gov,* "Tough Anti-Spam Legislation Proposed," *San Francisco Chronicle,* June 21, 2003, p. A4; and "Needed Now: Laws to Can Spam," *BusinessWeek,* October 7, 2002, p. 100. Data on the prevalence of spam are from the Radicati Group and are available at *www.radicati.com.*

Product Liability: A Special Issue

Who is at fault when a consumer is harmed by a product or service? This is a complex legal and ethical issue. The term **product liability** refers to the legal responsibility of a firm for injuries caused by something it made or sold. Under laws in the United States and some other countries, consumers have the right to sue and to collect damages if harmed by an unsafe product. Consumer advocates and trial attorneys have generally supported these legal protections, saying they are necessary both to compensate injured victims and to deter irresponsible behavior by companies in the first place. Some in the business community, by contrast, have argued that courts and juries have unfairly favored plaintiffs, and they have called for reforms of product liability laws. This section describes this debate and recent changes in relevant U.S. law.

Strict Liability

In the United States, the legal system has generally looked favorably on consumer claims. Under the doctrine of **strict liability**, courts have held that manufacturers are responsible for injuries resulting from use of their products, whether or not the manufacturers were negligent or breached a warranty. That is, they may be found to be liable, whether or not they knowingly did anything wrong. Consumers can also prevail in court even if they were partly at fault for their injuries. The following well-publicized case illustrates the extent to which businesses can be held responsible under this strict standard.

An 81-year-old woman was awarded $2.9 million by a jury in Albuquerque, New Mexico, for burns suffered when she spilled a cup of hot coffee in her lap. The woman, who had purchased the coffee at a McDonald's drive-through window, was burned when she tried to open the lid as she sat in her car.

> In the 1994 case, McDonald's argued that customers like their coffee steaming, that their cups warned drinkers that the contents are hot, and that the woman was to blame for spilling the coffee herself. But jurors disagreed, apparently swayed by arguments that the woman's burns were severe—requiring skin grafts and a seven-day hospital stay—and by evidence that McDonald's had not cooled down its coffee even after receiving many earlier complaints. McDonald's appealed the jury's verdict and later settled the case with the woman for an undisclosed amount.[18]

In this case, McDonald's was held liable for damages even though it provided a warning and the customer's actions contributed to her burns.

Huge product liability settlements, like the McDonald's case, are well publicized, but they remain the exception. In the early 2000s, one in five noncriminal cases was a tort (liability) case, and plaintiffs (the people suing companies) won 34 percent of product liability cases filed. The average settlement in all tort cases was $201,000, although a few settlements were much higher.[19]

The product liability systems of other nations differ significantly from that of the United States. In Europe, for example, judges, not juries, hear cases. Awards are usually smaller, partly because the medical expenses of victims are already covered under national health insurance, and partly because punitive damages are not allowed.[20] In a few cases, however, companies have faced tough penalties. Baxter International, the health care company, was forced to pay over $250,000 each to the families of 10 kidney patients in Spain. They had died after receiving dialysis on machines equipped with Baxter filters that caused lethal gas bubbles to form in their blood.[21]

Japan did not pass a product liability law until 1995, and such cases are still extremely difficult for consumers to win in court. In the Japanese law's first five years, plaintiffs won only 6 out of 37 judgments, and in no case did the company's liability exceed $50,000. "[Japan] is a place where companies can get away with actions that would never be tolerated in the U.S. or Europe," commented one attorney.[22]

Should guns be subject to product liability laws, or are they a special case? This issue is profiled in Exhibit 16.C.

The special issue of whether or not food companies and restaurants should be held liable for obesity is raised in the discussion case at the end of this chapter.

Business Efforts to Reform the Product Liability Laws

Many businesses have argued that the evolution of strict liability has unfairly burdened them with excess costs. Liability insurance rates have gone up significantly, especially for small businesses, as have the costs of defending against liability lawsuits and paying large settlements to injured parties. Moreover, businesses argue that it is unfair to hold them financially responsible in situations where they were not negligent.

Businesses have also argued that concerns about liability exposure sometimes slow research and innovation. For example, many pharmaceutical companies halted work on

---

[18] "How a Jury Decided that a Coffee Spill Is Worth $2.9 Million," *The Wall Street Journal*, September 1, 1994, pp. A1, A5; and "McDonald's Settles Lawsuit over Burn from Coffee," *The Wall Street Journal*, December 2, 1994, p. A14.

[19] U.S. Department of Justice, Office of Justice Programs, Bureau of Justice Statistics, "Federal Tort Trials and Verdicts, 2002–03," August 2005, *www.ojp.gov/bjs*.

[20] "A Tale of Two Tort Systems," *BusinessWeek*, March 14, 2005, p. 76.

[21] "Baxter Will Settle with Families of 10 Dialysis Patients Who Died," *The Wall Street Journal*, November 29, 2001, p. B15.

[22] "Can Japanese Consumers Stand Up and Fight?" *BusinessWeek*, September 11, 2000, p. 54.

Exhibit 16.C Liability for Gun Violence

Two hundred million guns are in circulation in the United States, and a third of all households own at least one. In 2000, almost 30,000 Americans died, and many more were injured, from gun violence.

In the late 1990s, a number of cities and counties brought suit against the firearms industry, demanding compensation for the medical and law enforcement costs of gun violence. The governments argued that gun manufacturers were liable because they had failed to apply common-sense consumer product safety standards to firearms. So-called Saturday night specials—cheap, easily hidden handguns—for example, lacked locks or other protective devices and sometimes misfired, causing unintentional injury. Some guns, such as automatic assault rifles, seemed to have been customized for killing. Moreover, gun makers knowingly made large shipments to regions that had lax gun laws, looking the other way while weapons fell into the hands of criminals.

Most manufacturers, however, disputed these arguments. They pointed out that guns are legal; in fact, they are the only consumer products that the U.S. Constitution (in the Second Amendment) guarantees the right to own. No one, least of all gun manufacturers, has ever claimed that guns do not kill. Guns have a legitimate, even beneficial, purpose in hunting, self-defense, and law enforcement.

The gun liability lawsuits did not fare well in the courts. In a series of decisions in favor of manufacturers, judges and juries seemed to be saying that criminals, not gun makers, were the real killers.

Sources: "Jury Decides Gun Makers Aren't Liable for Violence," *The Wall Street Journal,* May 15, 2003, p. B16; and "High Noon in Gun Valley," *Newsweek,* March 27, 2000, pp. 26–29. Statistics on deaths due to firearms are available at *www.cdc.gov/nchs.*

new contraceptive methods because of the risk of being sued. Despite the need for new contraceptives that would be more effective and also provide protection against viral diseases, such as herpes and AIDS, research had virtually come to a halt by the late 1990s, according to some public health groups.[23]

In 2005, Congress passed the Class Action Fairness Act, the first significant reform of product liability laws in many years. The two key elements of this legislation were:

- *Most large class-action lawsuits were moved from state to federal courts.* This provision applied to cases involving $5 million or more and that included plaintiffs from more than one state. Supporters of the law said this would prevent lawyers from shopping for friendly local venues in which to try interstate cases.

- *Attorneys in some kinds of cases were paid based on how much plaintiffs actually received, or on how much time the attorney spent on the case.* Under the old system, attorneys were often paid a percentage of the settlement amount. This sometimes led to excessive compensation for the lawyers.

Although most businesses welcomed these changes, many called for further reforms, such as the following:

- *Set up uniform federal standards for determining liability.* Companies would not have to go through repeated trials on the same charges in different states, which would lower costs for companies and help them develop a uniform legal strategy for confronting liability charges.

- *Shift the burden of proving liability to consumers.* Consumers would have to prove that a manufacturer knew or should have known that a product design was defective.

[23] "Birth Control: Scared to a Standstill," *BusinessWeek,* June 16, 1997, pp. 142–44.

Under present law and judicial interpretations, a company is considered to be at fault if a product injures the user, whether or not the company was negligent.

- *Require the loser to pay the legal costs of the winner.* If a plaintiff (consumer) refused an out-of-court settlement offer from the company and then received less in trial, he or she would have to pay the company's legal fees up to the amount of his or her own fees. This would discourage many plaintiffs from proceeding to trial.
- *Limit punitive damages.* (Punitive damages punish the manufacturer for wrongdoing, rather than compensate the victim for actual losses.) Although many punitive damage awards are small, some multimillion-dollar awards have been reached.
- *Establish liability shields for certain kinds of products.* For example, consumers could be barred from receiving punitive damages in cases involving products, such as pharmaceutical drugs, that had been approved by regulators.

Although supported by many business groups, product liability reform proposals such as these have faced vigorous opposition from consumers' organizations and from the American Trial Lawyers Association, representing plaintiffs' attorneys. These groups have defended the existing product liability system, saying it puts needed pressure on companies to make and keep products safe.

A promising approach to resolving product liability conflicts without going to court is called **alternative dispute resolution** (ADR). In ADR, a professional mediator works with both sides to negotiate a settlement. Generally, if this process fails, the parties can still proceed to trial. Supporters of ADR say it saves money that would be spent on lawyers' fees, so that more can go to plaintiffs in a settlement. Cases can be resolved quickly, rather than waiting for an opening on a busy judge's calendar. Some businesses feel that such a process would enable them to better predict, and budget for, future liabilities. Eventually, ADR may be widely used to settle individual complaints brought under mass torts, such as those involving injuries from asbestos, tobacco, or defective medical devices. In this situation, a court would set up a procedure and a set of rules by which individuals could negotiate a settlement tailored to the facts of their own case.[24]

Positive Business Responses to Consumerism

The consumer movement has demonstrated that business is expected to perform at high levels of efficiency, reliability, and fairness in order to satisfy the consuming public. Because business has not always responded quickly or fully enough, consumer advocates and their organizations have turned to government for protection. On the other hand, much effort has been devoted by individual business firms and by entire industries to encourage voluntary responses to consumer demands. Some of the more prominent positive responses are discussed next.

Quality Management

One way that many businesses address consumer interests is to manage quality in a highly proactive way. Quality has been defined by the International Organization for Standardization (ISO) as "a composite of all the characteristics, including performance, of an item, product, or service that bear on its ability to satisfy stated or implied needs." **Quality management**, by extension, refers to "all the measures an organization takes to assure

---

[24] John Gibeaut, "At the Crossroads," *American Bar Association Journal*, March 1998.

quality." These might include, for example, defining the customer's needs, monitoring whether or not a product or service consistently meets these needs, analyzing the quality of finished products to assure they are free of defects, and continually improving processes to eliminate quality problems. Taking steps at all stages of the production process to ensure consistently high quality has many benefits. Responsible businesses know that building products right the first time reduces the risk of liability lawsuits and builds brand loyalty.

> Toyota Motor Corporation, a Japanese car company with factories around the globe, earned 11 of the 19 top model awards for quality in the annual J. D. Power survey in 2006. Its Lexus models ranked highest in every segment in which they competed. The company credited a relentless emphasis on worker training. "We strive to get better by reducing variation in our manufacturing," explained the general manager of the quality division of the company's North American operations. "Everyone can screw in a bolt, but we teach people to recognize when it's misthreaded . . . to recognize a fault and keep the problem from ever leaving the factory."[25]

Managing for product quality is an attempt by business to address its customers' needs. It is an example of the interactive strategy discussed in Chapter 1, where companies try to anticipate and respond to emerging stakeholder expectations.

> *Business Ethics* magazine publishes an annual list of the "100 best corporate citizens." One of the 7 categories in which companies are rated in determining their overall scores is their product (or service). Firms with a companywide quality program, with leadership in R&D, who provide services to economically disadvantaged customers, and who avoid safety problems, fraud, and antitrust violations, score high. In 2006, high-ranking companies in this category were a diverse group; they included Ecolab (commercial cleaning and sanitizing), 3M (diversified technology), Tennant (insurance), Molina Healthcare (managed care), Graco (fluid handling), and Xilinx (programmable microchips). Clearly, positive relationships with customers know no industry boundaries.[26]

The challenging issue of business's responsibility for products that are safe and of high quality—but used by others in illegal or dangerous ways—is profiled in Exhibit 16.D.

Voluntary Industry Codes of Conduct

In another positive response, businesses in some industries have banded together to agree on voluntary codes of conduct, spelling out how they will treat their customers. Often, this action is taken to forestall even stricter regulation by the government. One such voluntary code is described in the following example.

> The Air Transport Association, an industry group, adopted a "customer service commitment" in 1999. The airlines promised to notify passengers when flights were canceled, feed and assist stranded passengers, pay more for lost luggage, and quote the lowest available fare over the phone. The industry's action stemmed from an incident the year before, when hundreds of passengers had been stuck for hours on the runway in planes unable to take off during a Detroit

---

[25] J. D. Powers and Associates, "Lexus and Toyota Together Capture 11 of 19 Initial Quality Model Awards," press release, June 7, 2006; and "GM's Quality Quandary," *Detroit Free Press*, April 10, 2006, accessed online.

[26] "Business Ethics 100 Best Corporate Citizens 2006," *www.business-ethics.com.*

Exhibit 16.D   Pfizer and the Methamphetamine Epidemic

What should a company do when a legitimate product it makes is used for an illegal or unethical purpose? This problem confronted the drug company Pfizer, Inc., maker of Sudafed. This over-the-counter decongestant, commonly used to treat colds and allergies, includes pseudoephedrine, a key ingredient in the illegal drug methamphetamine. Commonly known as "meth" or "crystal," methamphetamine is a highly addictive synthetic stimulant that eventually destroys the user's capacity to experience pleasure and causes permanent brain damage, heart attacks, and psychosis. Traffickers manufacture the drug in labs where they cook pseudoephedrine with other ingredients, including ammonia and lye. In 2006, meth was the most abused drug in the world, according to the United Nations, with 26 million addicts. In the United States, 58 percent of law enforcement officials said meth was their most serious drug problem.

What, if anything, could or should Pfizer do to keep pseudoephedrine out of the hands of drug traffickers? In the mid-1990s, the company began experimenting with versions of the chemical that could not be converted into methamphetamine. Pfizer gave up, however, when it discovered that whatever they came up with criminals could find a way around. "The tough lesson we learned," said a company spokesperson, "is, as fast as we could do things, . . . the meth cooks could move a lot more quickly." Instead, in 2004 the company introduced a version of its medicine, Sudafed PE, which did not include pseudoephedrine. Some critics, however, faulted Pfizer for continuing to sell the old version and for opposing some efforts to restrict the sale of pseudoephedrine-based products.

Sources: The quotation is from an interview with Steven Robins, a representative of Pfizer, Inc., conducted September 14, 2005, and available online at *www.pbs.org/wgbh/frontline/meth/interviews/robins.html*. More information about the methamphetamine epidemic and business's response may be found online at *www.pbs.org/wgbh/frontline/meth* and in a series of articles appearing in *The Oregonian* under the title, "Unnecessary Epidemic," October 2004, available online at *www.oregonlive.com*.

snowstorm. In the ensuring furor, Congress threatened to pass a passenger bill of rights. "We have felt the whip," said UAL's chairman, explaining the companies' voluntary action. The association later launched a Web site, *customers-first.org,* where flyers could learn more about what individual carriers were doing to meet their customer service commitments.[27]

Consumer Affairs Departments

Many large corporations operate consumer affairs departments, often placing a vice president in charge. These centralized departments normally handle consumer inquiries and complaints about a company's products and services, particularly in cases where a customer has not been able to resolve differences with local retailers. Some companies have installed **consumer hot lines** for dissatisfied customers to place telephone calls directly to the manufacturer.

One of the largest hot lines, General Electric's Answer Center, fields 3.5 million questions a year on thousands of products. One technician diagnosed a mysterious refrigerator noise by asking the customer to hold the phone up to the appliance. Another advised a frantic caller on how to extract a pet iguana from the dishwasher. "This isn't a job for the faint of heart," said one consultant who works with company consumer hot lines.[28]

[27] "Airlines Promise Measures to Boost Customer Service," *The Wall Street Journal*, June 18, 1999; and "Airlines, Being Pressed, Offer Modest Reforms to Customers," *The New York Times,* June 18, 1999.

[28] "What's This? Confused or Curious, Consumers Know Where to Call," *Newsday*, October 18, 1995, p. B37.

Many companies now communicate with their customers and other interested persons through Web sites on the Internet. Some sites are interactive, allowing customers to post comments or questions that are answered through e-mail by customer relations staff.

Experienced companies are aware that consumer complaints and concerns can be handled more quickly, at lower cost, and with less risk of losing goodwill by a consumer affairs department than if customers take a legal route or if their complaints receive widespread media publicity.

Product Recalls

Companies also deal with consumer dissatisfaction by recalling faulty products. A **product recall** occurs when a company, either voluntarily or under an agreement with a government agency, takes back all items found to be dangerously defective, as Ford and Firestone did following a series of accidents caused by tire tread separation on Explorers in 2000. Sometimes these products are in the hands of consumers; at other times they may be in the factory, in wholesale warehouses, or on the shelves of retail stores. Wherever they are in the chain of distribution or use, the manufacturer tries to notify consumers or potential users about the defect.

In 2006, Reebok, in cooperation with the Consumer Product Safety Commission, announced it would voluntarily recall heart-shaped metal charm bracelets, marked with the company logo, which had been packaged as a free gift in boxes of girls' shoes. A 4-year-old child had died from lead poisoning after swallowing one of the charms. Product safety experts said that lead was common in cheap metal toys and trinkets made in China.[29]

One problem with recalls is that the public may not be aware of them, so dangerous products continue to be used. For example, several babies were killed when Playskool Travel-Lite portable cribs unexpectedly collapsed, strangling them. Although the Consumer Product Safety Commission (CPSC) ordered an immediate recall, not all parents and child care providers heard about it, and additional deaths occurred.[30] Some consumer organizations advocated a system that would require manufacturers of certain products—such as cribs—to include purchaser identification cards so users could be quickly traced in the event of a recall.[31]

The four major government agencies responsible for most mandatory recalls are the Food and Drug Administration, the National Highway Traffic Safety Administration, the Environmental Protection Agency (which can recall polluting motor vehicles), and the Consumer Product Safety Commission.

Consumerism's Achievements

The leaders of the consumer movement can point to important gains in both the United States and other nations. Consumers today are better informed about the goods and services they purchase, are more aware of their rights when something goes wrong, and are

---

[29] "Child's Death Prompts Recall," *The Washington Post,* March 24, 2006, p. D1; and "Rules on Lead Toys Lacking Muscle," *Star Tribune* (Minneapolis), March 26, 2006, p. A1. Information on this and other recalls is available online at *www.cpsc.gov.*

[30] David Zivan, "The Playskool Travel-Lite Crib (A), (B), and (C)," Center for Decision Research, University of Chicago, November 5, 2002.

[31] For information on initiatives to protect children from dangerous products, see *www.kidsindanger.org.*

better protected against inflated advertising claims, hazardous or ineffective products, and unfair pricing. Several consumer organizations serve as watchdogs of buyers' interests, and a network of government regulatory agencies act for the consuming public.

Some businesses, too, have heard the consumer message and have reacted positively. They have learned to assign high priority to the things consumers expect: high-quality goods and services, reliable and effective products, safety in the items they buy, fair prices, and marketing practices that do not threaten important human and social values.

All of these achievements, in spite of negative episodes that occasionally occur, bring the consuming public closer to realizing the key consumer rights: to be safe, to be informed, to have choices, to be heard, and to privacy.

Summary

- The consumer movement represents an attempt to promote the interests of consumers by balancing the amount of market power held by sellers and buyers.

- The five key consumer rights are the rights to safety, to be informed, to choose, to be heard, and to privacy.

- Consumer protection laws and regulatory agencies attempt to assure that consumers are treated fairly, receive adequate information, are protected against potential hazards, have free choices in the market, and have legal recourse when problems develop. They also protect children's privacy online.

- Rapidly evolving information technologies have given new urgency to the issue of consumer privacy. Three approaches to safeguarding online privacy are consumer self-help, industry self-regulation, and protective legislation.

- Business has complained about the number of product liability lawsuits and the high cost of insuring against them. Although consumer groups and trial attorneys have opposed efforts to change product liability laws, modest tort reforms have recently been legislated.

- Socially responsible companies have responded to the consumer movement by giving serious consideration to consumer problems, increasing channels of communication with customers, instituting arbitration procedures to resolve complaints, and recalling defective products. They have also pursued voluntary codes of conduct and quality management in an effort to meet, and even anticipate, consumers' needs.

Key Terms

alternative dispute resolution, *356*
consumer hot lines, *358*
consumer movement, *344*
consumer privacy, *351*

consumer protection laws, *346*
deceptive advertising, *346*
product liability, *353*

product recalls, *359*
quality management, *356*
strict liability, *353*

Internet Resources

www.consumersinternational.org   Consumers International
www.cpsc.gov   U.S. Consumer Product Safety Commission
www.ftc.gov   U.S. Federal Trade Commission
www.bbb.org   Better Business Bureau
www.consumerfed.org   Consumer Federation of America

Discussion Case: *Big Fat Liability*

In 2003, a judge in New York dismissed a lawsuit filed on behalf of two obese teenage girls against McDonald's. The lawsuit alleged that the fast-food giant had "negligently, recklessly, carelessly, and/or intentionally" marketed products to children—such as burgers, chicken nuggets, fries, and sodas—that were "high in fat, salt, sugar, and cholesterol." And it had done so without warning customers of the risks of "obesity, diabetes, coronary heart disease, high blood pressure, strokes, elevated cholesterol intake, [and] related conditions" associated with such foods and beverages.

In his decision, the judge noted that the plaintiffs had failed to show that the girls had no way of knowing the risks of fast food. Moreover, the judge pointed out, "Nobody is forced to eat at McDonald's."

A spokesperson for McDonald's expressed relief, saying, "Common sense has prevailed." But many in the food and restaurant industries were worried that this lawsuit was just an opening salvo in a long battle. Potentially, liability for the health effects of fast food could become the next mass tort, rivaling the huge lawsuits against the cigarette companies of the 1990s. "It has gotten everyone's attention," said the president of the National Restaurant Association.

The problem of obesity and its health effects was growing. In 2001, the U.S. Surgeon General released a report called "The Surgeon General's Call to Action to Prevent and Decrease Overweight and Obesity."[32] The report called overweight and obesity "among the most pressing health challenges we face today." Among the report's startling findings were these:

- Six out of 10 American adults and 13 percent of children and adolescents were overweight or obese, that is, with a body mass index (BMI) of 25 or more.[33] Only 3 percent of Americans met the government's dietary recommendations, and less than a third exercised enough.

- Obesity in the United States among adults had doubled, and among adolescents had tripled, since 1980. Although these increases cut across all ages, genders, ethnic groups, and social classes, obesity was a particular problem for people from lower-income families.

- Obesity was a major cause of asthma, diabetes, heart disease, arthritis, infertility, and some kinds of cancer. In the United States, around 300,000 premature deaths a year were associated with being overweight—approaching the 400,000 deaths associated with cigarettes. The direct and indirect costs of being overweight and obese were $117 billion a year (compared with $140 billion for smoking).

The immediate cause for this epidemic of obesity was that people were simply eating too much. In 2000, Americans consumed, on average, around 2,750 calories a day, well above the healthy amount for most people. The critical question, of course, was to what extent, if at all, the food industry could be held responsible for the fattening of America. Many felt that food and lifestyle choices were an individual responsibility. Unlike

---

[32] A summary is available online at *www.surgeongeneral.gov/topics/obesity/calltoaction*.

[33] Body mass index is calculated as a person's weight in pounds divided by the square of that person's height in inches, multiplied by 703. For example, a person who was 66 inches tall and weighed 140 pounds would have a BMI of 22.59 (140 divided by 66 times 66 times 703). "Overweight" is defined as a BMI of 25–29.9 and "obese" as a BMI of 30 or higher. A chart showing BMIs for various weights and heights is available online at *www.surgeongeneral.gov/topics/obesity/calltoaction/1_1.htm*.

cigarettes, food products were not normally addictive. Moreover, the rising level of obesity had many causes, and the exact role of particular companies was unclear. As one legal analysis asked, "How would any court determine . . . whether a given class action member's obesity was caused by eating one of the defendant's products as opposed to eating some other food, overeating generally, a sedentary lifestyle, or genetic predisposition?"

Others, however, thought the food industry was at least partially at fault. Fast food had become a big part of Americans' diets. In 1970, they spent $6 billion a year on it; 30 years later, they spent $110 billion. This trend seemed to parallel the obesity epidemic. The problem was not just the relatively high fat and sugar content of fast foods, but the super-sizing of portions. When fast-food restaurants increasingly began to compete on the basis of value—more for less—customers simply ate more.

For their part, food companies had concentrated on developing processed products, such as candy, gum, snacks, and bakery goods, that carried high profit margins along with excessive calories. They had introduced many more new products in these categories than entrées, fruits, and vegetables since the early 1980s, data showed. Moreover, both restaurants and food processors, in their critics' view, had failed to communicate adequately the health risks of some foods and had inappropriately marketed their products to children.

In 2005, the U.S. House of Representatives, acting to block what some feared might become a flood of liability lawsuits, voted for a law popularly known as the Cheeseburger Bill, which would shield both producers and retailers of food from lawsuits by obese consumers. The bill did not become law, because the Senate did not act on the issue. Several states, however, enacted similar legislation. The National Restaurant Associated strongly supported these initiatives.

Faced with an uncertain legal landscape, some companies took voluntary steps to reduce their exposure to liability. Saying that "the rise in obesity is a complex public health challenge of global proportions," Kraft announced it would change the recipes for some products. The company also said it would label products that were high in beneficial nutrients or low in calories, fat, sugar, and salt. It also pledged to stop advertising to children products, such as Oreo cookies, that did not qualify for its "sensible solutions" label. McDonald's introduced entrée-size salads with low-fat dressing, and PepsiCo switched to nonhydrogenated cooking oils for some snacks.

Sources: "Kraft to Curb Ads of Snack Foods," *The Wall Street Journal,* January 12, 2005; "The Food Industry Empire Strikes Back," *The New York Times,* July 7, 2005; "Judge Dismisses Obesity Suit by 2 Girls against McDonald's," *The Wall Street Journal,* January 23, 2003, p. D3; "Is Fat the Next Tobacco?" *Fortune,* February 3, 2003, pp. 51–54; "Kraft Promises to Take Healthier Approach to Food," *San Francisco Chronicle,* July 2, 2003, p. A1; Eric Schlosser, *Fast Food Nation: The Dark Side of the All-American Meal* (New York: Perennial, 2002); and Greg Cristser, *Fat Land: How Americans Became the Fattest People in the World* (New York: Houghton Mifflin, 2003), Ch. 2. A summary of the Surgeon General's "Call to Action" is available online at *www.surgeongeneral.gov/topics/obesity/calltoaction.*

Discussion Questions

1. What are the arguments for and against the proposition that the food and restaurant industries should be held liable for the rise of obesity in the United States?

2. In your opinion, should the food and restaurant industries be held liable for the rise of obesity, or not? That is, which side do you support, and why?

3. If you were a manager for a fast-food chain or food company, what actions would you take with respect to obesity, if any?

4. What do you think is the best solution to the obesity epidemic? What role can the food and restaurant industries, trial attorneys, government policy makers and regulators, and individual consumers play in a solution, if any?

CHAPTER SEVENTEEN

The Community and the Corporation

A strong relationship benefits both business and its community. Communities look to businesses for civic leadership and for help in coping with local problems, while businesses expect to be treated in fair and supportive ways by the community. As companies expand their operations, they develop a wider set of community relationships. Community relations programs, including corporate giving, are an important way for a business to express its commitment to corporate citizenship.

This chapter focuses on these key learning objectives:

- Defining a community, and understanding the interdependencies between companies and the communities in which they operate.
- Analyzing why it is in the interest of business to respond to community problems and needs.
- Knowing the major responsibilities of community relations managers.
- Examining how different forms of corporate giving contribute to building strong relationships between businesses and communities.
- Evaluating how companies can direct their giving strategically, to further their own business objectives.
- Analyzing how collaborative partnerships between businesses and communities can address today's pressing social problems.

Whole Foods Market is a natural foods retailer with stores in many communities in North America and the United Kingdom. Founded in 1980 in Austin, Texas, the company believes that its business "is intimately tied to the neighborhood and larger community that we serve and in which we live." Whole Foods donates 5 percent of its net profit to charitable causes and operates two foundations focused on animal welfare and rural poverty. Each of the company's 184 stores hosts a community day three times a year, with 5 percent of the day's total sales revenue contributed to a worthy local nonprofit organization. Whole Foods also gives its employees 20 paid community service hours for each 2,000 hours of work (about half a week per year). Employees have been involved in a wide range of service projects, including organizing blood donation drives, raising money for breast cancer research, developing community gardens, renovating housing, and delivering "meals on wheels."[1]

One of the leading financial institutions in the world, ING has operations in more than 50 countries. Based in the Netherlands, the company provides insurance, banking, and asset management services throughout Europe, with a growing presence in the Americas and Asia. Recognizing that the needs of the many communities where it does business differ, the company has delegated responsibility for corporate citizenship programs to business unit managers, provided their decisions are consistent with the firm's core values. The result has been a remarkable diversity of community initiatives. In the Philippines, ING built houses with Habitat for Humanity; in Australia, it sponsored cricket teams, and in Brazil, the conservation of rain forests. After Hurricane Katrina struck the Gulf Coast, ING donated $1 million to the American Red Cross and an additional $275,000 to hard-hit school districts.[2]

Hindustan Lever, the Indian subsidiary of the transnational corporation Unilever, faced a problem when a dairy it owned in a rural area in northern India incurred substantial losses. Rather than closing the operation, the company decided to address the underlying cause—inadequate care of dairy cattle by impoverished local villagers. The company gave interest-free loans to farmers and offered classes in animal care. Within a few years, the dairy was making a profit. The program was so successful that the company expanded it to 400 villages and committed to investing 10 percent of its pretax profits in rural development projects, including children's immunizations, water system improvements, and classes in sewing, nutrition, and agriculture. Every year, the company sends 50 of its most promising young managers to live with a rural family and work on development projects, to learn firsthand the value of community involvement.[3]

Why do businesses as diverse as Whole Foods Market, ING, and Hindustan Lever invest in community organizations, projects, and charities? Why do they contribute their money, resources, and time to help others? What benefits do they gain from such activities? This chapter explains why many companies believe that being an involved citizen is part of their basic business mission. The chapter also looks at how companies participate in community life and how they build partnerships with other businesses, government, and community organizations. The core questions that we consider in this chapter are: What does it mean to be a good corporate neighbor? What is the business case for doing so?

---

[1] See *www.wholefoodsmarket.com/company/communitygiving.*

[2] Information on ING's community initiatives is available at *www.ing.com.*

[3] "Hindustan Lever in India," *www.business-humanrights.org; www.unilever.com/environmentsociety/community;* and "Unilever in Uttar Pradesh," in McIntosh et al., *Corporate Citizenship: Successful Strategies for Responsible Companies* (London: Financial Times, 1998), pp. 216–17.

The Business–Community Relationship

The term **community,** as used in this chapter, refers to a company's area of local business influence. Traditionally, the term applied to the city, town, or rural area in which a business's operations, offices, or assets were located. With the rise of large, complex business organizations, the meaning of the term has expanded to include multiple localities. A local merchant's community relationships may involve just the people who live within driving distance of its store. A bank in a large metropolitan area, by contrast, may define its community as the both the central city and the suburbs where it does business. And at the far extreme, a large transnational firm such as ING, ExxonMobil, or Nokia has relationships with numerous communities in many countries around the world.

Today the term *community* may also refer not only to a geographical area or areas but to a range of groups that are affected by an organization's actions, whether or not they are in the immediate vicinity. In this broader view, as shown in Figure 17.1, the geographical (sometimes called the site) community is just one of several different kinds of communities.

Whether a business is small or large, local or global, its relationship with the community or communities with which it interacts is one of mutual interdependence. As shown in Figure 17.2, business and the community each need something from the other. Business depends on the community for education, public services such as police and fire protection,

FIGURE 17.1
The Firm and Its Communities

Source: Based in part on a discussion in Edmund M. Burke, *Corporate Community Relations: The Principle of Neighbor of Choice* (Westport, CT: Praeger, 1999), Ch. 6.

Community	Interest
Site community	Geographical location of a company's operations, offices, or assets
Fence-line community	Immediate neighbors
Cyber communities	People who use the Internet to learn about the company
Communities of interest	Groups that share a common interest with the company
Employee community	People who work near the company

FIGURE 17.2
What the Community and Business Want from Each Other

Business Participation Desired by Community	Community Services Desired by Business
• Pays taxes	Schools—a quality educational system
• Provides jobs and training	Recreational opportunities
• Follows laws	Libraries, museums, theaters, and other cultural services
• Supports schools	Adequate infrastructure, e.g., sewer, water, and electric services
• Supports the arts and cultural activities	Adequate transportation systems, e.g., roads, rail, airport, harbor
• Supports local health care programs	Effective public safety services, e.g., police and fire protection
• Supports parks and recreation	Fair and equitable taxation
• Assists less-advantaged people	Streamlined permitting services
• Contributes to public safety	Quality health care services
• Participates in economic development	Cooperative problem-solving approach

Exhibit 17.A

Community Support for Professional Sports Franchises

The professional sports franchise is one kind of business that has historically been particularly dependent on support from the community. Cities often compete vigorously in bidding wars to attract or keep football, basketball, baseball, hockey, and soccer teams. Communities subsidize professional sports in many ways. Government agencies build stadiums and arenas, sell municipal bonds to pay for construction, give tax breaks to owners, and allow teams to keep revenues from parking, luxury boxes, and food concessions. In the United States, subsidies to pro sports cost taxpayers around $500 million a year, on average. Consider the following taxpayer subsidies to build sports facilities: Scottsdale, $535 million (for the Phoenix Coyotes); Houston, $180 million (for the Houston Astros); Denver, $215 million (for the Colorado Rockies), and Miami, $212 million (for the Florida Panthers). In one of the most recent examples, the new ballpark for the New York Yankees, approved in 2006, was funded in part with $920 million in tax-exempt, low interest city bonds and $25 million in taxable bonds. Some say that public support is warranted, because high profile teams and sports facilities spur local economic development, offer wholesome entertainment, and build civic pride. But critics argue that subsidies simply enrich affluent team owners and players at taxpayer expense and shift spending away from other more deserving areas, such as schools, police and fire protection, social services, and the arts. In this view, this is a case in which the relationship between business and the community is deeply out of balance.

Sources: "Approvals Clear Way for Yankees to Build," *The New York Times,* July 22, 2006, p. B2; Kevin J. Delaney and Rick Eckstein, *Public Dollars, Private Stadiums* (New Brunswick, NJ: Rutgers University Press, 2003); Joseph L. Bast, *Sports Stadium Madness: Why It Started, How to Stop It,* Heartland Institute, Policy Study No. 85, February 23, 1998; and Roger G. Noll and Andrew Zimbalist, *Sports, Jobs, and Taxes* (Washington DC: Brookings Institution, 1997). A Web site critical of public subsidies to sports facilities is *www.fieldofschemes.com.*

recreational facilities, and transportation systems, among other things. The community depends on business for support of the arts, schools, health care, and the disadvantaged, and other urgent civic needs, both through taxes and donations of money, goods, and time.

Ideally, community support of business and business support of the community are roughly in balance, so that both parties feel that they have benefited in the relationship. Sometimes, however, a business will invest more in the community than the community seems to provide in return. Conversely, a community sometimes provides more support to a business than the firm contributes to the community. See Exhibit 17.A for a discussion of subsidies by communities to professional sports franchises, an instance in which the relationship between business and the community is sometimes perceived as out of balance.

The Business Case for Community Involvement

The term **civic engagement** describes the active involvement of businesses and individuals in changing and improving communities. *Civic* means pertaining to cities or communities, and *engagement* means being committed to or involved with something. Why should businesses be involved with the community? What is the *business case* for civic engagement?

The idea of corporate citizenship, introduced in Chapter 4, refers broadly to businesses acting as citizens of society by behaving responsibly toward all their stakeholders. Civic engagement is a major way in which companies carry out their corporate citizenship mission. As explained in Chapters 3 and 4, business organizations that act in a socially responsible way reap many benefits. These include an enhanced reputation and ability to respond quickly to changing stakeholder demands. By acting responsibly, companies can also avoid or correct problems caused by their operations—a basic duty that comes with their significant power and influence. They can win the loyalty of employees, customers, and neighbors. And by doing the right thing, businesses can often avoid, or at least correctly anticipate, government regulations. All these reasons for social responsibility operate at the level of the community as well, via civic engagement.

Another specific reason for community involvement is to win local support for business activity. Communities do not have to accept a business. They sometimes object to the presence of companies that will create too much traffic, pollute the air or water, or engage in activities that are viewed as offensive or inappropriate. A company must earn its informal **license to operate**—or right to do business—from society. In communities where democratic principles apply, citizens have the right to exercise their voice in determining whether a company will or will not be welcome, and the result is not always positive for business.

> As illustrated by the discussion case at the end of Chapter 2, Wal-Mart has encountered serious local objection to its plans to build superstores and distribution centers in a number of local communities. Wal-Mart's founder, Sam Walton, now deceased, was fond of saying he would never try to force a community to accept a Wal-Mart store. "Better to go where we are wanted," he is reported to have said. In recent years, however, Wal-Mart management less often endorses that view. In a series of high-profile local conflicts, Wal-Mart sparked intense local opposition from several communities that were worried about traffic patterns, safety, and negative effects on local small businesses from the opening of giant Wal-Mart facilities. The problem seems likely to grow more complex for Wal-Mart as it continues its expansion into international markets.[4]

Through positive interactions with the communities in which its stores are located, Wal-Mart is more likely to avoid this kind of local opposition.

Community involvement by business also helps build social capital. **Social capital**, a relatively new theoretical concept, has been defined as the norms and networks that enable collective action. Scholars have also described it as "the goodwill that is engendered by the fabric of social relations."[5] When companies such as Whole Foods Market, described at the beginning of this chapter, work to address community problems such as blood shortages, hunger, and dilapidated housing, their actions help build social capital. The company and groups in the community develop closer relationships, and their people become more committed to each other's welfare. Many experts believe that high levels of social capital enhance a community's quality of life. Dense social networks increase productivity by reducing the costs of doing business, because firms and people are more likely to trust one another. The development of social capital produces a win-win outcome because it enables everyone to be better off.[6]

Community Relations

The organized involvement of business with the community is called **community relations**. The importance of community relations has increased markedly in recent years. According to one expert, "Over the years, community involvement has moved from the

---

[4] Wal-Mart's problems with local communities are extensively documented. For the company's perspective on its community relationships, see *www.walmart.com.*

[5] Paul S. Adler and S. W. Kwon, "Social Capital: Prospects for a New Concept," *Academy of Management Review* 27, no. 1 (January/February 2002), pp. 17–40. For a more general discussion, see Robert D. Putnam, *Bowling Alone: The Collapse and Revival of American Community* (New York: Simon and Schuster, 2000).

[6] Some benefits of social capital are described on the World Bank Web site at *www.worldbank.org/prem/poverty/scapital.*

margins of the corporation to a position of growing importance. More companies regard their involvement in the community as a key business strategy and a linchpin in their overall corporate citizenship efforts."[7] The importance of community relations is shown by the following statistics, drawn from a study conducted by the Center for Corporate Citizenship:[8]

- 81 percent of companies now include a statement in their annual report on their commitment to community relations.
- 74 percent of companies have a written mission statement for their community relations program.
- 68 percent of companies factor community involvement into their overall strategic plan.

In support of this commitment, some corporations have established specialized community relations departments; others house this function in a department of public affairs or corporate citizenship. Their managers' job is to interact with local citizens, develop community programs, manage donations of goods and services, work with local governments, and encourage employee volunteerism. These actions are, in effect, business investments intended to produce more social capital—to build relationships and networks with important groups in the community. Community relations departments typically work closely with other departments that link the company to the outside world, such as external affairs, corporate relations, government relations, and public affairs (discussed in Chapters 2 and 8). All these roles form important bridges between the corporation and the community.

Community relations departments are typically involved with a range of diverse issues. According to a 2005 survey of community involvement managers, education (kindergarten through high school) was viewed as the most important issue, as it was for the tenth year in a row in which the survey had been conducted. Other critical issues included health care, economic development, higher education, and housing. Further down the list of issues, although still important, were literacy, environmental issues, crime, transportation, and job training.[9] Although not exhaustive, this list suggests the range of needs that a corporation's community relations professionals are asked to address. These community concerns challenge managers to apply talent, imagination, and resources to develop creative ways to strengthen the community while still managing their businesses as profitable enterprises.

Several specific ways in which businesses and their community relations departments have addressed some critical concerns facing communities are discussed below. The all-important issue of business involvement in education reform is addressed in the final section of the chapter, which discusses collaborative partnerships.

Economic Development

Business leaders and their companies are frequently involved in local or regional economic development that is intended to bring new businesses into an area. Financial institutions, because of their special expertise in lending, have been at the forefront of many recent initiatives to bring development money into needy communities. In the United States, the federal **Community Reinvestment Act** requires banks to demonstrate

[7] Center for Corporate Citizenship, *Community Involvement Index 2005* (Boston, MA: Boston College, 2005).

[8] Ibid., p. 1.

[9] Ibid., p. 2. Based on an opinion survey of 163 community involvement managers.

Grameen Bank (meaning *village bank*), based in Bangladesh, is an internationally recognized innovator in the field of economic development. In 1974, Muhammad Yunus, an economics professor at Chattagong University, took his students on a field trip to a poor rural village. There, they interviewed a woman who supported herself by crafting bamboo stools. The woman had to borrow money for raw materials at the outrageous interest rate of 10 percent *a week,* leaving a profit of only one penny per stool. The professor, shocked by what he saw, began lending his own money to villagers. Finding that small loans helped many people pull themselves out of poverty, Yunus founded Grameen in 1983 to provide *micro-credit* to individual entrepreneurs who would not normally qualify for loans. Today, Grameen has nearly 2,000 branches and serves 6 million borrowers. "These millions of small people with their millions of small pursuits can add up to create the biggest development wonder," Yunus has said. In 2006, Yunus was awarded the Nobel Peace Prize in recognition of his work.

Sources: *www.grameen-info.org*; and Muhammad Yunus, *Banker to the Poor* (South Asia Books, 1998).

their commitment to local communities through low-income lending programs and to provide annual reports to the public. This law has led many banks to begin viewing the inner city as an opportunity for business development. Some have even created special subsidiaries that have as their mission the development of new lending and development in needy urban neighborhoods. Chicago's ShoreBank, for example, has been deeply involved in meeting the housing needs of low-income residents. Financial institutions have been active in this area in many other nations, as well. An innovative initiative by a small bank in Bangladesh to provide micro-credit for economic development in rural areas is described in Exhibit 17.B.

Crime Abatement

Many urban areas around the world are forbidding and inhospitable places, fraught with drugs, violence, and high crime rates. Business has an interest in reducing crime, because it hurts the ability to attract workers and customers and threatens property security. Some firms have become actively involved in efforts to reduce crime in their neighborhoods, as the following example illustrates.

In the mid-1990s, the crime rate in the metropolitan area of St. Paul-Minneapolis, Minnesota, had become so bad that out-of-town newspapers disparagingly called the city "Murderopolis." To combat this situation, a collaborative alliance formed called Minnesota HEALS (Hope, Education, and Law and Safety). Sixty companies and other organizations, including Honeywell, General Mills, 3M, and Allina Health Systems, worked closely with police and civic groups to address public safety issues in the community. Among their many initiatives were development of an integrated information system for law enforcement agencies, better housing, job training, and after-school programs. Crime rates dropped sharply, and the overall climate for business in the city improved.[10]

[10] Barbara W. Altman, "Minnesota HEALS: Next Steps in Corporate/Community Partnerships for Crime Reduction," case presented at the North American Case Research Association annual meeting, 2000; and Ellen Luger and Pat Hoven, "Minnesota HEALS: Creating a Public-Private Partnership," *www.mcf.org/mcf/forum/heals*.

Housing

Another community issue in which many firms have become involved is housing. Life and health insurance companies, among others, have taken the lead in programs to revitalize neighborhood housing through organizations such as Neighborhood Housing Services (NHS) of America. NHS, which is locally controlled, locally funded, nonprofit, and tax-exempt, offers housing rehabilitation and financial services to neighborhood residents. Similar efforts are being made to house the homeless. New York City's Coalition for the Homeless includes corporate, nonprofit, and community members. Corporations also often work with nongovernmental organizations (NGOs) such as Habitat for Humanity to build or repair housing.

Welfare-to-Work Job Training

The need for improvement in worker skills draws businesses into the world of worker training and retraining, especially efforts to train the disadvantaged. In the United States, government leaders have called on American businesses to help address one of the most vexing and costly social problems—welfare reform. Welfare is a form of public assistance to those who are unable to work and live an independent and self-sufficient life. Most societies have some basic form of public assistance to the needy, and some countries (Germany, France, and the United States) are known for their relatively generous assistance programs. As the costs of such programs have risen, however, many citizens have pressured their governments to curb the cost of welfare-assistance programs.

> Bank of America (BofA) has been deeply involved in welfare-to-work initiatives. In many communities, BofA has partnered with Women in Community Service (WICS), a nonprofit organization that provides job and life skills training to women who are on public assistance, in prison, or homeless or living in public housing. The bank has contributed staff, products and services, internship opportunities, and money to WICS, and has hired thousands of new employees out of welfare-to-work programs. BofA has experienced many benefits: an improved reputation, tax credits, and recruitment of motivated workers. "We see an incredible amount of corporate loyalty to the organization that invested so much in recruiting them, helping to get them trained and giving them a chance," said the bank vice president who manages the program.[11]

Aid to Minority Enterprises

In addition to programs to train people for jobs in industry, private enterprise has extended assistance to minority-owned small businesses. These businesses often operate at a great economic disadvantage: They do business in economic locations where high crime rates, poor transportation, low-quality public services, and a low-income clientele combine to produce a high rate of business failure. Large corporations, sometimes in cooperation with universities, have provided financial and technical advice and training to minority entrepreneurs. They also have financed the building of minority-managed inner-city plants and sponsored special programs to purchase services and supplies from minority firms.

> Microsoft spends $10 billion annually on procuring supplies and services. About 5 percent of this is directed to minority-owned businesses. "The general rule

---

[11] SFWorks, *Fast Forward: The Business Case for Workforce Partnerships* (San Francisco, 2002), available at *www.sfworks.org.*

here," said the company's director of supplier diversity, "is, if all other things are equal, pick the minority company." Microsoft works closely with its minority suppliers to refine their business processes to make them more competitive. An example is Group O Direct, an Illinois-based firm that provides fulfillment services for customer promotions. Group O Direct, which is owned by Mexican-Americans, now has several other high-profile clients in addition to Microsoft, including SBC Communications, and annual revenues of more than $50 million.[12]

Disaster, Terrorism, and War Relief

One common form of corporate involvement in the community is disaster relief. Throughout the world, companies, like individuals, provide assistance to local citizens and communities when disaster strikes. When floods, fires, earthquakes, ice storms, hurricanes or terrorist attacks devastate communities, funds pour into affected communities from companies.

Businesses from all over the world responded with extraordinary generosity to the communities impacted by the massive tsunami that struck the Indian Ocean in December 2004. Their donations, estimated to be around $2 billion, collectively exceeded those of most governments. In addition, many companies drew on their own special expertise to lend a hand. United Parcel Service mobilized its planes to airlift disaster relief supplies to the region free of charge. Pfizer donated millions of dollars worth of medicines. GE sent power generators and mobile water treatment plants. British Airways, Intel, and Cisco collaborated to set up a high-speed wireless Internet network in Banda Aceh, Indonesia, to enable communications in and to one of the hardest-hit areas.[13]

International relief efforts are becoming more important, as communications improve and people around the world are able to witness the horrors of natural disasters, terrorism, and war. Corporate involvement in such efforts is an extension of the natural tendency of people to help one another when tragedy strikes.

In all these areas of community need—economic development, crime abatement, housing, job training, aid to minority enterprise, and disaster relief—as well as many others, businesses around the world have made and continue to make significant contributions.

Corporate Giving

An important aspect of the business–community relationship is **corporate philanthropy**, or **corporate giving**. Every year, businesses around the world give generously to their communities through various kinds of philanthropic contributions to nonprofit organizations.

America is a generous society. In 2005, individuals, bequests (individual estates), foundations, and corporations collectively gave more than $260 billion to churches, charities, and other nonprofit organizations, as shown in Figure 17.3. Businesses are a

---

[12] "Taking Minority-Owned Businesses under Their Wing," *The New York Times,* September 20, 2005, p. G6.

[13] "Companies Focus Help on Long Term Projects," *Financial Times* (London), December 23, 2005, p. 9; "UPS, NWA Cargo Assist Tsunami Relief," *Journal of Commerce Online,* January 6, 2005; "Deadly Tsunamis: Corporations, Workers Contribute Millions," *Atlanta Journal-Constitution,* December 31, 2004, p. 14A; and "Union Nations Coordinates International Response to Tsunami," press release, May 9, 2005.

FIGURE 17.3
Philanthropy in the United States, by Source of Gift, 2005

Source: Giving USA Foundation™ (formerly the American Association of Fundraising Counsel Trust for Philanthropy), *Giving USA 2006* (Indianapolis: Center on Philanthropy at Indiana University, 2006), p. 14. Used by permission.

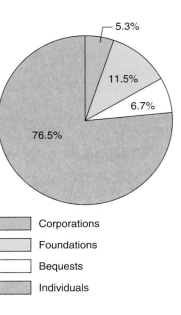

5.3%

11.5%

6.7%

76.5%

Corporations

Foundations

Bequests

Individuals

small, but important, part of this broad cultural tradition of giving. That year, corporate contributions totaled almost $14 billion, or about 5 percent of all charitable giving. This amount includes in-kind gifts claimed as tax deductions and giving by corporate foundations.[14]

As U.S. firms have become increasingly globalized, as shown in Chapter 7, their international charitable contributions have also grown. A study by The Conference Board found that about half of U.S. corporations surveyed said they had directed some of their donations abroad, and the amount they gave was on the increase. To cite just one example, the Coca-Cola Foundation has donated $138 million to support education around the world over the past two decades. Its contributions have, among other projects, helped build schools in China, Mexico, and the Philippines.[15]

In the United States, tax rules have encouraged corporate giving for educational, charitable, scientific, and religious purposes since 1936.[16] Current rules permit corporations to deduct from their taxable income all such gifts that do not exceed 10 percent of the company's before-tax income. In other words, a company with a before-tax income of $1 million might contribute up to $100,000 to nonprofit community organizations devoted to education, charity, science, or religion. The $100,000 in contributions would then reduce the income to be taxed from $1 million to $900,000, thus saving the company money on its tax bill while providing a source of income to community agencies. Of course, nothing prevents a corporation from giving more than 10 percent of its income for philanthropic purposes, but it would not be given a tax break above the 10 percent level.

[14] Giving USA Foundation (formerly the American Association of Fundraising Counsel Trust for Philanthropy), *Giving USA 2006*, pp. 14–15.

[15] Sophia A. Muirhead, *2005 Corporate Contributions Report* (New York: The Conference Board, 2005), p. 8; and Coca-Cola, "Foundations," *www.coca-cola.com/citizenship/foundation.html.*

[16] The evolution of corporate philanthropy is summarized in Mark Sharfman, "Changing Institutional Rules: The Evolution of Corporate Philanthropy, 1883–1953," *Business and Society* 33, no. 3 (December 1994).

FIGURE 17.4
Corporate Contributions in the United States, as a Percentage of Pretax Net Income, 1964–2004

Sources: Data for 1964 through 2002 are from AAFRC (American Association of Fundraising Counsel) Trust for Philanthropy, *Giving USA 2003* (Indianapolis: Center on Philanthropy at Indiana University, 2003), p. 202, and are used by permission. Data for 2004 are from The Conference Board, *2005 Corporate Contributions Report* (New York: The Conference Board, 2005), p. 9, and are used by permission of The Conference Board, a global business membership and research organization.

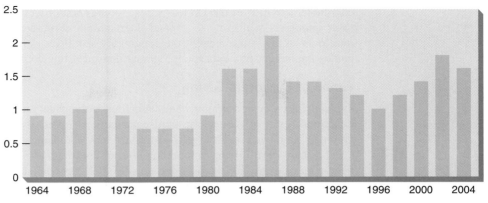

As shown in Figure 17.4, average corporate giving in the United States is far below the 10 percent deduction now permitted. Though it varies from year to year, corporate giving has generally ranged between 1 and 2 percent of pretax income since the early 1960s, with a rise that reached a peak at just above 2 percent in 1986. Corporate giving was 1.6 percent of pretax income in 2004. A few companies, including a cluster in the Minneapolis-St. Paul area that have pledged to donate 5 percent annually, give much more than this. One company, Newman's Own, the philanthropic corporation established by film star Paul Newman, gives *all* of its earnings to charity.

In Europe, corporate philanthropy has lagged behind that in the United States, in part because tax breaks are less generous and differences in the law across countries make cross-border giving difficult. Greater spending on social welfare by governments also reduces incentives for private sector philanthropy.[17] Europe-based multinational corporations have become more active, however, as illustrated by the following example.

The motto of Nokia, the cellular phone company based in Finland, is "connecting people." In partnership with the International Youth Foundation, the company launched a program called "Make A Connection" to help develop life skills among young people in 25 countries. In 2005, Nokia pledged $23 million to the program over 5 years, as well as equipment and expertise. In the Philippines, for example, the program's "text2teach" initiative used mobile technology to bring interactive, multimedia learning materials to 80 schools. Said Nokia's vice president for corporate social responsibility, "It's about developing the social glue within a peer group or community."[18]

Although most companies give directly, some large corporations have established nonprofit **corporate foundations** to handle their charitable programs. This permits them to administer contribution programs more uniformly and provides a central group of professionals that handles all grant requests. More than three-fourths of large U.S.-based corporations have such foundations; together, they gave $3.4 billion in 2005.[19] Foreign-owned corporations use foundations less frequently, although firms such as Matsushita (Panasonic) and Hitachi use sophisticated corporate foundations to conduct their

---

[17] "Understanding Philanthropy," *Financial Times* (London), December 16, 2005, p. 1.

[18] "Making a Connection to Boost Life Skills," *Financial Times* (London), January 26, 2006, p. 3; and *Corporate Social Responsibility Report 2004*, available at *www.nokia.com*.

[19] *2005 Corporate Contributions Report*, p. 15; and *Giving USA 2006*, p. 217.

charitable activities in the United States. As corporations expand to more foreign locations, pressures will grow to expand international corporate giving. Foundations, with their defined mission to benefit the community, can be a useful mechanism to help companies implement philanthropic programs that meet this corporate social responsibility.

Forms of Corporate Giving

Typically, gifts by corporations and their foundations take one of three forms: charitable donations (gifts of money), in-kind contributions (gifts of products or services), and volunteer employee service (gifts of time). Many companies give in all three categories.

The share of all giving comprising **in-kind contributions** of products or services has been rising steadily for the past decade or so and has now surpassed cash contributions. Of U.S. corporate contributions in 2004, more than half—54 percent—were in the form of in-kind gifts.[20] For example, computer companies have donated computer hardware and software to schools, universities, and public libraries. Grocery retailers have donated food, and Internet service providers have donated time online. Publishers have given books. The most generous industry, in terms of in-kind contributions, is pharmaceuticals; seven leading drug companies collectively donated $4 billion worth of medicines in 2004, an amount equal to about 10 percent of their pretax income.[21]

> One of the most generous companies, in terms of in-kind contributions, is Pfizer. In 2004, Pfizer contributed an extraordinary $1.62 *billion* worth of medicines and other products and services, an amount equal to 8.3 percent of that year's profit. Many of these donations were directed to the poorest nations and communities in the world, where the company gave away drugs to treat malaria, HIV/AIDS, trachoma, and many other illnesses.[22]

Under U.S. tax laws, if companies donate new goods, they may deduct their fair-market value within the relevant limits. For example, if a computer company donated $10,000 worth of new laptops to a local school, it could take a deduction for this amount on its corporate tax return, provided this amount was less than 10 percent of its pretax income.

Business leaders and employees also regularly donate their own time—another form of corporate giving. **Volunteerism** involves the efforts of people to assist others in the community through unpaid work. According to a report by the Department of Labor, about 29 percent of Americans ages 16 and older volunteered during the prior year, donating on average 50 hours of their time.[23] Many companies encourage their employees to volunteer by publicizing opportunities, sponsoring specific projects, and offering recognition for service. Some companies partner with a specific agency to provide volunteer support over time, as illustrated by the following example.

> KaBOOM! is a nonprofit organization that builds playgrounds. The group's goal is "to help develop a country in which all children have, within their communities, access to equitable, fun, and healthy play opportunities." Since it was founded in 1996, the organization has maintained a strong partnership with

---

[20] *2005 Corporate Contributions Report*, p. 13.

[21] Committee to Encourage Corporate Philanthropy, *Adding It Up 2004: The Corporate Giving Standard* (Boston, MA: Center for Corporate Citizenship at Boston College, 2006).

[22] "Corporate Philanthropy's Biggest Givers," *BusinessWeek Online*, at *www.businessweek.com/investing/philanthropy/2005/inkind.htm*. Pfizer's philanthropic initiatives are reported at *www.pfizer.com/subsites/philanthropy*.

[23] "Volunteering in the United States, 2005," U.S. Department of Labor press release, December 9, 2005.

Home Depot, the building supply firm. Home Depot employees in many communities have volunteered their building skills, along with materials, to build KaBOOM! playgrounds in underserved neighborhoods. "Team Depot" volunteers, working alongside people from the community, can build a state-of-the-art playground in a single day.[24]

Another, less common approach is for companies to provide employees with *paid* time off for volunteer service in the community. One such company, Timberland, is profiled in the discussion case at the end of this chapter.

Priorities in Corporate Giving

Overall, what kinds of organizations receive the most corporate philanthropy? The distribution of contributions reflects how businesses view overall community needs, and how this perception has changed over time. As shown in Figure 17.5, the corporate giving "pie" is divided into several main segments. The largest share of corporate philanthropy goes to health and human services; the next largest share goes to education. Civic and community organizations and culture and the arts also receive large shares of business philanthropy. Of course, these percentages are not identical among different companies and industries; some companies tend to favor support for education, for example, whereas others give relatively greater amounts to cultural organizations or community groups.

Does corporate giving contribute to business success? One recent study addressed this question directly. In 2000, the Council on Foundations sponsored research to develop a Corporate Philanthropy Index (CPI) that rated companies from 1.0 to 5.0 on a five-point

FIGURE 17.5
Priorities in Corporate Giving (Percentage of corporate cash and in-kind contributions to various sectors)

Source: Sophia A. Muirhead, *2005 Corporate Contributions Report* (New York: The Conference Board, 2005), "Beneficiaries of Total (U.S. and International) Contributions, 2004," p. 8. International includes donations to tsunami relief made in 2004. All data are for 2004. Used by permission of The Conference Board, a global business membership and research organization.

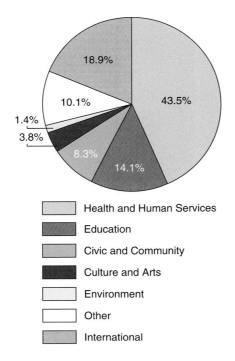

▨	Health and Human Services
▨	Education
▨	Civic and Community
▨	Culture and Arts
▨	Environment
▨	Other
▨	International

Pie chart values: 43.5%, 14.1%, 8.3%, 3.8%, 1.4%, 10.1%, 18.9%

[24] "Corporate Volunteering: Home Depot and KaBOOM!" in Shirley Sagawa and Eli Segal, *Common Interest, Common Good: Creating Value Through Business and Social Sector Partnerships* (Boston: Harvard Business School Press, 2000), pp. 29–46. The Web site for KaBOOM! is *www.kaboom.org*.

Exhibit 17.C   **Tobacco Money: Controversial Corporate Charity**

Business donations are usually welcomed by recipient organizations and supported by the public. But this is not always the case. Sometimes, corporate charity generates controversy among the very groups it targets.

The Altria Group Inc., formerly known as the Philip Morris Companies, is the leading seller of tobacco products in the world. In 2005, the company earned $11 billion on $98 billion in revenue, with 65 percent of its revenue coming from tobacco (the rest came from food, beer, and other products). Altria is also among the most generous corporate philanthropists. Over the past decade, the company has given more than a billion dollars in cash and in-kind contributions internationally. Altria has focused its gifts in the areas of domestic violence, AIDS, hunger, and the arts—where it has been a major patron of art museums and dance companies. The company says that its charitable giving program is designed "to help find solutions to pressing social issues."

The company's critics feel that Altria's motives are not so benign. The Campaign for Tobacco-Free Kids, for example, has charged that the purpose of Altria's contributions is to give the company "a veneer of undeserved legitimacy" and to allow it "to portray itself as a responsible company while it continues its marketing practices which attract and addict children." Others have criticized the company's advertising campaign that showcases its good works, saying that money spent on ads would be better spent on charity itself. Some claim that the company has carefully selected recipients to "buy" the silence of groups that have been particularly devastated by tobacco-related illness, including women, minorities, gays, and artists. "They're taking blood money and using it to assuage people's hostility to their company," said one anti-tobacco attorney. The controversy has created an ethical dilemma for some recipient organizations, which must weigh the value of Altria's gifts against the costs of association with the tobacco giant.

Sources: Campaign for Tobacco-Free Kids, "Special Report: Behind the Smokescreen," available online at *www.tobaccofreekids.org/reports/smokescreen;* Robert Dreyfuss, "Philip Morris Money," *The American Prospect* 11, no. 10 (March 27, 2000); and ABC News, "Corporate Goodwill or Tainted Money?" February 8, 2001, *http://abcnews.go.com.* Altria's description of its corporate giving programs is available at *www.altria.com/responsibility.*

scale based on their stakeholders' perceptions. Employees, customers, and influential members of the community were asked to evaluate companies' contributions to the community and society. The study showed that companies with high CPI scores had better reputations and generated more admiration and goodwill than others did; people were also more willing to give these companies the benefit of the doubt if they received bad publicity.[25] Further research may reveal more about the specific benefits of donations.

Are business gifts always welcomed? One controversy over corporate generosity is profiled in Exhibit 17.C.

Corporate Giving in a Strategic Context

Communities have social needs requiring far more resources than are normally available, and businesses often face more demands than they can realistically meet. This is particularly true in hard economic times, when funds may be less plentiful. Companies must establish priorities to determine which worthy projects will be funded or supported with the company's in-kind or volunteer contributions and which ones will not. What criteria should community relations departments apply in determining who will receive corporate

[25] "Measuring the Business Value of Corporate Philanthropy," *Research Report Executive Summary,* October 2000 (conducted by Walker Information Inc. for the Council on Foundations), available at *www.cof.org.*

gifts? These are often difficult choices, both because businesses may want to support more charities than they can afford, and because saying no often produces dissatisfaction among those who do not get as much help as they want.

One increasingly popular approach is to target corporate contributions *strategically* to meet the needs of the donor as well as the recipient. **Strategic philanthropy** refers to corporate giving that is linked directly or indirectly to business goals and objectives. In this approach, both the company and society benefit from the gift.

> For example, Cisco Systems, a manufacturer of hardware for the Internet, has established a Networking Academy to train computer network administrators. From a modest start in 1997 in a high school near the company's headquarters in San Jose, California, by 2006 the program had expanded to include more than 10,000 sites in high schools and community colleges in 50 states and more than 150 countries, and had trained more than 1.6 million students. The academy initiative benefits communities throughout the world by providing job training for young people, many of whom go on to successful careers in systems administration. But it also benefits the company, by assuring a supply of information technology professionals who can operate Cisco's complex equipment.[26]

A study in the *Harvard Business Review* identified four areas in which corporate contributions were most likely to enhance a company's competitiveness, as well as the welfare of the community.[27] Strategic contributions focus on:

- *Factor conditions,* such as the supply of trained workers, physical infrastructure, and natural resources. Cisco's Networking Academy is an example of philanthropy that helps the donor by providing skilled employees both for Cisco and for its corporate customers.
- *Demand conditions,* those that affect demand for a product or service. When Microsoft provides free software to libraries and universities, new generations of young people learn to use these programs and are more likely later to buy computers equipped with the company's products.
- *Context for strategy and rivalry.* Company donations sometimes can be designed to support policies that create a more productive environment for competition. For example, contributions to an organization such as Transparency International that opposes corruption may help a company gain access to previously unreachable markets.
- *Related and supporting industries.* Finally, charitable contributions that strengthen related sectors of the economy may also help companies, as shown in the following example.

> The Marriott Resort and Beach Club on the island of Kauai in Hawaii had a problem. The luxury resort wanted to offer its guests native cuisine prepared with locally grown produce. But the island, which had long been dominated by sugar cane plantations, then in decline, did not have a diversified farming sector. The resort partnered with a local food bank to create a successful program to teach underemployed local residents to grow fruits and vegetables on their own land and to market their produce cooperatively. Today, the Hui meai'ai ("club

---

[26] More information about the Networking Academy is available at *http://cisco.netacad.net.*

[27] Michael E. Porter and Mark R. Kramer, "The Competitive Advantage of Corporate Philanthropy," *Harvard Business Review,* December 2002.

of things to eat") provides employment for 56 local growers and supplies 25 businesses, including the Marriott.[28]

Of course, not all corporate contributions benefit their donors directly, nor should they. But most, if handled correctly, at least build goodwill and help cement the loyalty of employees, customers, and suppliers who value association with a good corporate citizen.

Specialists in corporate philanthropy recommend four other strategies to help companies get the most benefit from their contributions.[29]

- *Draw on the unique assets and competencies of the business.* Companies often have special skills or resources that enable them to make a contribution that others could not. For example, Google, Inc., provides free advertising on its search engine to nonprofit organizations in many countries. Make-a-Wish Foundation, just one of many charities supported in this way, now gets more than half its online donations through the Google site.[30]

- *Align priorities with employee interests.* Another successful strategy is to give employees a say in deciding who will receive contributions. An advantage of this approach is that it strengthens ties between the company and its workers, who feel that their values are being expressed through the organization's choices. For example, PacifiCare, a large health services corporation, recruits employee volunteers to serve on its foundation's regional allocation committees. "They are the true heroes of our philanthropy," said the president of the PacifiCare Foundation.[31]

- *Align priorities with core values of the firm.* McDonald's Corporation, the fast-food giant, focuses its philanthropic contributions on children's programs. One of the company's major charities is the Ronald McDonald Houses, facilities where families can stay in a homelike setting while their child receives treatment at a nearby hospital. The program operates more than 200 houses in 24 countries, including new programs in Japan and Romania. McDonald's believes that this initiative is consistent with its mission to "make a difference in the lives of children."[32]

- *Use hard-nosed business methods to assess the impact of gifts.* Increasingly, companies are using standard business tools to assess their investments in philanthropy, just as they would any other investment. For example, they might establish goals for a particular charitable gift, and then check to make sure these goals have been met. Underperforming projects would be dropped, and successful ones would receive continued funding. These efforts are sometimes part of a broader social audit, as described in Chapter 4.

In short, businesses today are taking a more strategic approach to all kinds of corporate giving. They want to make sure that gifts are not simply made randomly, but rather are targeted in such a way that they are consistent with the firm's values, core competencies, and strategic goals.

---

[28] "A Productive Partnership: The Kauai Marriott Resort and Beach Club and the Kauai Food Bank," *In Practice* (Boston: The Center for Corporate Citizenship at Boston College, 2002).

[29] See, for example, David Hess, Nikolai Rogovsky, and Thomas W. Dunfee, "The Next Wave in Corporate Community Involvement: Corporate Social Initiatives," *California Management Review* 44, no. 2 (Winter 2002).

[30] "Google Starts Up Philanthropy Campaign," *The Washington Post*, October 12, 2005, p. D4.

[31] PacifiCare Foundation, "2001 Report." The annual reports of the foundation are available at *www.pacificare.com*.

[32] "2004 Worldwide Corporate Responsibility Report," available at *www.mcdonalds.com*.

Building Collaborative Partnerships

The term *partnership,* introduced in Chapter 7 and further elaborated in Chapter 12, refers to a voluntary collaboration among business, government, and civil society organizations to achieve specific objectives. The need for such **collaborative partnerships** is very apparent when dealing with community problems.

One arena in which collaborative partnerships among business, government, and communities have been particularly effective is education. As mentioned earlier in this chapter, community relations managers count education as the most critical challenge they face. Many school districts and colleges in the United States face an influx of new students from the so-called "echo boom" generation, increasing class sizes and making it more difficult to give students the individual attention they need. Many schools are challenged to educate new Americans, immigrants from other parts of the world who often do not speak English as their native language. More children are living in poverty, and many come from single-parent homes. A fast-changing economy demands that the technological tools accessible to students be greatly expanded. All these challenges must be met in many states under conditions of extreme fiscal constraint, as tax revenues fall and budget crises loom. The difficulties faced by schools are of immediate concern to many companies, which rely on educational systems to provide them with well-trained employees equipped for today's high-technology workplace.

Business has been deeply involved with education reform in the United States for over two decades. A series of studies by The Conference Board identified four waves, or distinct periods, in corporate involvement in education reform from the 1980s to the present.[33] The first wave was characterized by *direct involvement* with specific schools. For example, a company might "adopt" a school, providing it with cash, equipment, and volunteer assistance, and promising job interviews for qualified graduates. The second wave focused on the *application of management principles* to school administration. Business leaders assisted schools by advising administrators and government officials who needed training in management methods, such as strategic planning and performance appraisal. The third wave emphasized advocacy for *public policy initiatives* in education, such as ones calling for school choice and adoption of national testing standards. The fourth wave, which is ongoing, focuses on *collaboration for systemic reform.* This involves collaborative partnerships among business organizations, schools, and government agencies. In such collaborations, all partners bring unique capabilities and resources to the challenge of educational reform. The result is often outcomes that are better than any of them could have achieved acting alone.[34]

A leading example of a corporation deeply involved in collaborative partnerships to improve education is IBM. Through its "Reinventing Education" initiative, IBM has partnered with schools in many states and eight countries, including Brazil, Vietnam, Mexico, and Ireland, to apply technology to improve student achievement and performance. Since the program's launch in 1994, IBM has donated more than $70 million in cash and high-tech equipment. But the program goes far beyond traditional philanthropy. According to an independent

[33] Susan Otterbourg, *Innovative Public–Private Partnerships: Educational Initiatives* (New York: The Conference Board, 1998); and Sandra Waddock, *Business and Education Reform: The Fourth Wave* (New York: The Conference Board, 1994).

[34] For a discussion of the benefits of collaborative partnerships, see Bradley K. Googins and Steven A. Rochlin, "Creating the Partnership Society: Understanding the Rhetoric and Reality of Cross-Sectoral Partnerships," *Business and Society Review* 105, no. 1 (2000), pp. 127–44.

evaluation by the Center for Children and Technology, Reinventing Education "engages researchers, corporate managers, and educators in a long-term partnership, committed to serious sustained collaboration to improve schools." Successful experiments are spread, through the program, to many other schools. Among the partnership's many accomplishments have been the development of a communications network connecting schools and parents, electronic portfolios to display student work, and online "learning villages" where novice teachers can work with experienced mentors. The Center for Children and Technology evaluation found that the partnership had produced "significant performance gains" for students in affiliated schools.[35]

The success of IBM's initiative illustrates the potential of collaborative partnerships that allow business to contribute its unique assets and skills to a broader effort to solve significant community problems.

Communities need jobs, specialized skills, executive talent, and other resources that business can provide. Business needs cooperative attitudes in local government, basic public services, and a feeling that it is a welcome member of the community. Under these circumstances much can be accomplished to upgrade the quality of community life. The range of business–community collaborations is extensive, giving businesses many opportunities to be socially responsible.

Like education, other community challenges are, at their core, people problems, involving hopes, attitudes, sentiments, and expectations for better human conditions. Neither government nor business can simply impose solutions or be expected to find quick and easy answers to problems so long in the making and so vast in their implications. Moreover, neither government nor business has the financial resources on their own to solve these issues. Grassroots involvement is needed, where people are willing and able to confront their own needs, imagine solutions, and work to fulfill them through cooperative efforts and intelligent planning. In that community-oriented effort, government, nonprofit organizations, and businesses can be partners, contributing aid and assistance where feasible and being socially responsive to legitimately expressed human needs.

Summary

- The *community* refers to an organization's area of local influence, as well as more broadly to other groups that are impacted by its actions. Businesses and their communities are mutually dependent. Business relies on the community for services and infrastructure, and the community relies on business for support of various civic activities.

- Addressing a community's needs in a positive way helps business by enhancing its reputation, building trust, and winning support for company actions. Like other forms of corporate social responsibility, community involvement helps cement the loyalty of employees, customers, and the public.

- Many corporations have established community relations departments that respond to local needs and community groups, coordinate corporate giving, and develop strategies for creating win-win approaches to solving civic problems.

[35] Center for Children and Technology, "The Reinventing Education Initiative from an Evaluation Perspective" (April 2004), and "EDC Releases Three-Year Study of IBM's $45 Million Reinventing Education Program" (June 2001), both available online at *www.ibm.com/ibm/ibmgives*. The initiative is also analyzed in Rosabeth Moss Kanter, *Evolve! Succeeding in the Digital Culture of Tomorrow* (Boston: Harvard University Press, 2001).

- Corporate giving comprises gifts of cash, property, and employee time. Donations currently average about 1.8 percent of pretax profits. Philanthropic contributions both improve a company's reputation and sustain vital community institutions.

- Many companies have adopted a strategic approach to philanthropy, linking their giving to business goals. Corporate giving is most effective when it draws on the unique competencies of the business and is aligned with the core values of the firm and with employee interests.

- The development of collaborative partnerships has proven to be effective in addressing problems in education and other civic concerns. Partnerships offer an effective model of shared responsibility in which businesses and the public and nonprofit sectors can draw on their unique skills to address complex social problems.

Key Terms	civic engagement, *366* collaborative partnerships, *379* community, *365* Community Reinvestment Act, *368*	community relations, *367* corporate foundations, *373* corporate philanthropy, or corporate giving, *371* in-kind contributions, *374*	license to operate, *367* social capital, *367* strategic philanthropy, *377* volunteerism, *374*
Internet Resources	www.bc.edu/centers/ccc	The Center for Corporate Citizenship at Boston College	
	www.pointsoflight.org	Points of Light Foundation	
	www.worldbank.org/poverty/scapital	World Bank (social capital)	
	www.conference-board.org/knowledge/citizenship	The Conference Board (corporate citizenship)	
	http://www.corphilanthropy.org	The Committee to Encourage Corporate Philanthropy	

Discussion Case: *Timberland's Path to Service*

Timberland is a manufacturer of rugged outdoor boots, clothing, and accessories. Founded in 1918 in Boston by an immigrant shoemaker named Nathan Swartz, the company has been run for almost a century by three generations of the Swartz family. Today, the company sells its products in department and specialty stores as well as in its own retail outlets in North America, Europe, Asia, South Africa, Latin America, and the Middle East. Although the company was taken public in 1987, the Swartz family and its trusts and charitable foundations continue to hold about 48 percent of Timberland stock.

In 1989, Timberland was approached by City Year, an urban service corps for young people, with a request for a donation of boots. Jeff Swartz, grandson of the founder and CEO, said yes—and also agreed to join the corps for half a day of community service. Swartz later described his experience:

> I found myself, not a mile from our headquarters, . . . face to face with a vision [of] America not unlike the one that drew my grandfather to leave Russia in steerage so many years ago. I spent four hours with the corps members from City Year and some young recovering drug addicts in a group home. I painted

some walls and felt the world shaking under my feet. In America? At this time of plenty? Children on drugs? Behind my desk again, safe no longer, moved by my own sense of purpose, having served albeit briefly, all that mattered was figuring out how service could become part of daily life at Timberland.

Compelled to take action, Swartz worked over the next several years with others at Timberland to create a unique program called Path to Service. Formally launched in 1992, the program provides employees with numerous opportunities for community involvement. As soon as they are hired, employees are granted up to 40 hours of paid time per year to participate in company-sponsored community service activities. Part-time employees receive 16 hours. Although participation is voluntary, almost 95 percent do so, and most cite the program as one of the most valuable benefits offered by the company. Since the program began, employees have contributed over 250,000 hours of service in 25 countries.

Since 1998, Timberland facilities worldwide have closed for one day each year for a day of celebration and service called Serv-A-Palooza. In 2005, 6,500 employees, business partners, and customers came together to build playgrounds, repair wheelchairs, clear trails, and renovate homeless shelters, among other projects. In another related program, the company offers Service Sabbaticals with full pay and benefits. After three years of employment, Timberland workers may apply for paid time off to work with a nonprofit organization devoted to social or environmental issues.

Timberland also makes cash and in-kind contributions. The company has a goal of contributing over 2 percent of its pretax income annually and makes grants to many nonprofit organizations, including many of those it aids through its service projects. For example, the company has supported the renovation of libraries and gardens at poor-performing public schools in New York City with both cash and service. Timberland also routinely donates its shoes and clothing. It is the official outfitter of City Year, and in 2002 sent 25,000 pairs of shoes to Afghanistan so that children returning to school there after the war would have proper footwear.

Swartz explained the meaning of Timberland's various service and philanthropic initiatives this way:

At Timberland, doing well and doing good are not separate or separable efforts. Every day, everywhere, we compete in the global economy. At the center of our efforts is the premise of service, service to a truth larger than self, a demand more pressing even than this quarter's earnings. While we are absolutely accountable to our shareholders, we also recognize and accept our responsibility to share our strength—to work, in the context of our for-profit business, for the common good.

Sources: Based on author interviews and information from the company's Web site at *www.timberland.com*. Both quotations are from Jeff Swartz, "Doing Well and Doing Good: The Business Community and National Service," *The Brookings Review* 20, no. 4 (Fall 2002).

Discussion Questions

1. What motivated Timberland to launch its Path to Service program and other philanthropic and service initiatives?

2. In your opinion, what are the benefits and costs of Timberland's community involvement programs to the company?

3. Do you believe that Timberland's community involvement programs illustrate the principles of strategic philanthropy discussed in this chapter? Why or why not?

4. If you were in charge of Timberland's social enterprise team, what arguments would you make to shareholders that the company's community involvement programs are in their best interest?

CHAPTER EIGHTEEN

Employees and the Corporation

Employees and employers are engaged in a critical relationship affecting the corporation's performance. There is a basic economic aspect to their association: Employees provide labor for the firm, and employers compensate workers for their contributions of skill and productivity. Yet, also present in the employee-employer exchange are numerous social, ethical, legal, and public policy issues. Attention to the rights and duties of both parties in this relationship can benefit the firm, its workers, and society.

This chapter focuses on these key learning objectives:

- Understanding workers' rights to organize unions and bargain collectively.
- Knowing how government regulations assure occupational safety and health and what business must do to protect workers.
- Evaluating the limits of employers' duty to provide job security to their workers.
- Appraising the extent of employees' right to privacy, when businesses monitor employee communications, police romance in the office, test for drugs or alcohol, or subject employees to honesty tests.
- Debating if employees have a duty to blow the whistle on corporate misconduct, or if employees should always be loyal to their employer.
- Assessing the obligations of transnational corporations to their employees around the world.

A computer programmer for Google, the Internet search company based in Mountain View, California, was fired after just two weeks on the job after he posted some critical comments about the company on his personal blog (short for web log, or online journal). "It was a very quick education for me at Google," said the programmer. Increasingly, managers are bypassing traditional sources and seeking information about current and prospective employees online. The result is sometimes an unintended disclosure of behavior and opinions that can damage careers.[1]

Should employees, like this programmer, have a right to criticize their employers using their personal blog? Is a manager justified in using an Internet search engine to find information about employees that they, or others, have posted? Was Google justified in terminating this employee?

Twelve men died in Sago, West Virginia, in 2006 after a coal mine explosion that filled the area where they were trapped with deadly carbon monoxide gas. The Sago mine, owned by the International Coal Group, had 202 safety violations the previous year, and its injury rate was three times the national average. "I think this mine should have been closed," said the retired director of the Mine Health and Safety Academy. The sole survivor among the trapped miners later said that several of the portable oxygen masks the workers carried, called self-rescuers, had failed to function properly. "There were not enough rescuers to go around," said the survivor.[2]

Who is responsible for the deaths of these miners? What roles should government regulators, managers, and workers and their unions play in assuring the safety and health of people on the job?

At a sprawling complex of buildings in Dongguan, China, 4,000 workers stitch athletic bags for Nike Corporation. Conditions at the contractor factory, which is bound by Nike's code of conduct, have improved markedly since the mid-1990s. But workers still earn just $5 a day, on average, and work a standard 60-hour, six day week. Many are separated from their families in rural areas for months at a time. Although life at the factory is hard, jobs there are in demand and turnover is under 10 percent a year.[3]

What wages and hours are fair in this case? Should multinational companies pay their overseas workers enough to enjoy a decent family standard of living, even if this is well above the legally mandated wage or above wages common in the area for similar kinds of work? Should extra be paid for overtime work, even if not required by law?

All of these difficult questions will be addressed later in this chapter. As the situations giving rise to them suggest, the rights and duties of employers and employees in the modern workplace are incredibly complex—and have become more so as business has become increasingly global.

The Employment Relationship

As noted in Chapter 1, employees are a primary stakeholder of business—and a critically important one. Businesses cannot operate without employees to make products, provide

---

[1] "When the Blogger Blogs, Can the Employer Intervene?" *The York Times,* April 18, 2005, p. C1; "Who's Afraid of the Big, Bad Blog?" *Financial Times* (London), November 4, 2005, p. 12; and "You Are What You Post," *BusinessWeek,* March 27, 2006, p. 52.

[2] "Surviving Miner Says Air Masks Failed to Work," *The New York Times,* April 28, 2006, p. A1; "Endemic Problem of Safety in Coal Mining," *The New York Times,* January 10, 2006, p. A13; and "In a Miners' Town, Grief, Anger, and Questions," *The New York Times,* January 5, 2006, p. A1.

[3] "Factory Workers in China Still Toil for Nike," *Seattle Times,* July 3, 2005, p. E1. For more detail, including additional references, see the case study, "Nike's Dispute with the University of Oregon," at the end of the book.

FIGURE 18.1
Rights and Duties of Employees and Employers

Employee Rights/Employer Duties	Employee Duties/Employer Rights
• Right to organize and bargain	• No drug or alcohol abuse
• Right to a safe and healthy workplace	• No actions that would endanger others
• Right to privacy	• Treat others with respect and without harassment of any kind
• Duty to discipline fairly and justly	• Honesty; appropriate disclosure
• Right to blow the whistle	• Loyalty and commitment
• Right to equal employment opportunity	• Respect for employer's property and intellectual capital
• Right to be treated with respect for fundamental human rights	

services, market to customers, run the organization internally, and plan for the future. At the same time, employees are dependent on their employers for their livelihood—and often much more, including friendship networks, recreational opportunities, health care, retirement savings, even their very sense of self. Because of the importance of the relationship to both parties, it must be carefully managed, with consideration for both legal and ethical obligations.

The employment relationship confers rights and duties on both sides. (As further explained in Chapter 5, a *right* means someone is entitled to be treated a certain way; rights often confer *duties* on others.) Some of these responsibilities are legal or contractual; others are social or ethical in nature. For their part, employers have an obligation to provide some measure of job security, a safe and healthy workplace, and equal opportunity for all. They are obliged to pay a decent wage and to respect workers' rights to organize and bargain collectively, as guaranteed by U.S. law (and the laws of many other nations). Employers must also respect employees' rights to privacy and—to some extent at least—their rights to free speech and to do what they want outside the workplace.

But employees also have a duty to behave in acceptable ways. For example, most would agree that employees should not abuse drugs or alcohol in a way that impairs their work performance, use company e-mail to send offensive messages, or take the employer's property for their own personal use. Employees should deal with customers and co-workers in an honest, fair, and nondiscriminatory way. They should not reveal proprietary information to others outside the company, unless there is compelling reason to do so—such as an immanent threat to the public's safety. Some main rights and duties of employers and employees are summarized in Figure 18.1. How to balance these sometimes-conflicting obligations poses an ongoing, and frequently perplexing, challenge to business.

This chapter considers the rights and duties—both legal and ethical—of both parties in the employment relationship. The following chapter explores the related issue of workforce diversity and discusses the specific legal and ethical obligations of employers with respect to equal employment opportunity.

Workplace Rights

Employees in the United States enjoy several important legal guarantees. They have the right to *organize and bargain collectively*, to have a *safe and healthy workplace* and, to some degree, to have *job security*. This section will explore these three rights, emphasizing U.S. laws and regulation, but with comparative references to policies in other nations.

The Right to Organize and Bargain Collectively

In the United States, and in most other nations, employees have a fundamental legal right to organize **labor unions** and to bargain collectively with their employers. The exceptions are some communist countries (such as China, Vietnam, Cuba, and the People's Democratic Republic of Korea) and some military dictatorships (such as Myanmar, also known as Burma), where workers are not permitted to form independent unions. Labor unions are organizations, such as the Service Employees International Union or the Teamsters, that represent workers on the job. Under U.S. laws, most private and public workers have the right to hold an election to choose what union they want to represent them, if any. Unions negotiate with employers over wages, working conditions, and other terms of employment. Employers are not required by law to agree to the union's demands, but they are required to bargain in good faith. Sometimes, if the two sides cannot reach agreement, a strike occurs, or employees apply pressure in other ways, such as refusing to work overtime.

The influence of labor unions in the United States has waxed and waned over the years. During the New Deal period in the 1930s, many workers, particularly in manufacturing industries such as automobiles and steel, joined unions, and the ranks of organized labor grew rapidly. Unions negotiated with employers for better wages, benefits such as pensions and health insurance, and improved job safety—significantly improving the lot of many workers. Since the mid-1950s, however, the proportion of American workers represented by unions has declined. In 2005, only about 13 percent of all employees were union members. (The percentage was higher—37 percent—in government employment.)[4]

Some observers, however, believe that unions in the United States may be poised for recovery.

> In 2005, four unions—the Service Employees International Union, the Teamsters, the United Food and Commercial Workers, and Unite Here (representing hotel and restaurant workers)—quit the AFL-CIO, saying the U.S. labor federation had not done enough to sign up new members. Pointing to survey data that showed that more than half of nonunion, nonsupervisory workers said they would join a union if they could, the renegade unions pledged to undertake a major organizing drive. Among their initial targets was ABM, the largest U.S. cleaning contractor.[5]

Labor union power was evident in other ways in the 2000s. Unions organized in the political arena, using political action committees (PACs) and other methods (discussed in Chapter 9) and voted shares of stock in which their pension funds were invested (discussed in Chapter 15) to pursue their institutional objectives.

Some labor unions departed from their traditional adversarial approach to work cooperatively with employers for their mutual benefit. At Saturn, AT&T, and Kaiser Permanente (a large health maintenance organization), for example, management and unions forged new partnerships aimed both at giving workers a greater say in the business and improving quality and productivity. However, in some industries, old-line labor–management conflict predominated. Wal-Mart, the world's largest private employer, has aggressively opposed efforts to organize its workers—going so far as

---

[4] U.S. Bureau of Labor Statistics, "Union Members in 2005," *www.bls.gov.*

[5] "Splintered, but Unbowed: Are Unions Still Relevant?" *The New York Times,* July 30, 2005, pp. C1, C2. Information on the Change to Win Federation (the rival union group) is available online at *www.unitetowin.org.*

to shut down one store in Quebec, Canada, where employees had voted to join a union.[6] And in the "new economy" sector, Amazon.com used its internal Web site to distribute anti-union materials to its managers in an effort to block organizing efforts among its employees.[7]

One issue that unions and others have been concerned with is job safety and health. It is discussed next.

The Right to a Safe and Healthy Workplace

Many jobs are potentially hazardous to workers' safety and health. In some industries, the use of high-speed and noisy machinery, high-voltage electricity, extreme temperatures, or hazardous gases or chemicals poses risks. Careful precautions, extensive training, strict regulations, and tough enforcement are necessary to avoid accidents, injuries, illnesses, and even deaths on the job.

A worker at Rocky Mountain Steel in Pueblo, Colorado, lost both of his arms after he touched a live wire and was jolted with 34,500 volts of electricity. The man was a laborer who normally did another job, but had been ordered to clean some insulators. "They [the laborers] had no electrical knowledge and no training," charged a union official at the plant.[8]

Over the past few decades, new categories of accidents or illnesses have emerged, including the fast-growing job safety problem of repetitive motion disorders, such as the wrist pain sometimes experienced by supermarket checkers, meat cutters, or keyboard operators. The number of health problems attributed to the use of video display terminals and computer keyboards has increased tenfold in the past decade. In response, many businesses have given greater attention to **ergonomics**, adapting the job to the worker, rather than forcing the worker to adapt to the job. For example, ergonomically designed office chairs that conform to the shape of the worker's spine may help prevent low productivity and lost time due to back injuries.

Annually, more than 4 million workers in private industry are injured or become ill while on the job, according to the U.S. Department of Labor. This amounts to about five hurt or sick workers out of every hundred. Some of the highest rates are found in the construction, primary and fabricated metals, lumber, furniture, transportation equipment, food processing, glass, and air transportation industries. In general, manufacturing jobs are riskier than service jobs.[9] Teenagers are twice as likely to be hurt on the job as adults. Young workers are often inexperienced, have less training, and are more reluctant to challenge the boss over a dangerous task.[10]

Workplace violence—a particular threat to employee safety—is profiled in Exhibit 18.A.

In the United States, the Occupational Safety and Health Act, passed in 1970 during the great wave of social legislation discussed in Chapter 8, gives workers the right to a job "free from recognized hazards that are causing or likely to cause death or serious physical harm." This law is administered by the **Occupational Safety and Health Administration (OSHA)**. Congress gave OSHA important powers to set and enforce safety and health standards. Employers found in violation can be fined and, in the case of willful

[6] "Wal-Mart to Close Store in Canada with a Union," *The New York Times*, February 10, 2005, p. C3.

[7] "Amazon.com Is Using the Web to Block Unions' Efforts to Organize," *The New York Times*, November 29, 2000, p. C1.

[8] "Steel Mill Deaths Prompt In-Depth OSHA Probe," *The Denver Post*, April 18, 2000, p. C1.

[9] U.S. Bureau of Labor Statistics data, available at *www.bls.gov*.

[10] "Government Asked to Act on Teenagers' Job Safety," *The New York Times*, August 5, 2002, p. A8.

Exhibit 18.A Violence in the Workplace

Stories of angry or distraught employees, ex-employees, or associates of employees attacking workers, co-workers, or superiors at work have become more frequent. For example, there is a growing trend for workers who have lost their jobs—or who face some other financial threat—to seek vengeance, often in calculated and cold-blooded fashion. In other cases, seemingly trivial events can provoke an assault. In a particularly shocking incident, a worker at a Lockheed Martin plant in Meridian, Mississippi, apparently became so enraged that his employer had required him to take a sensitivity training course that he stormed out and got a shotgun from his truck. He returned to kill five co-workers and injure nine, before shooting himself.[11]

Homicide is the fourth-leading cause of death on the job (only vehicle accidents, falls, and being struck by a falling or flying object kill more). Every year, around 600 workers are murdered, and as many as 2 million are assaulted at work in the United States. Police officers, prison guards, taxi drivers, bartenders, mental health workers, special education teachers, and gas station attendants are most at risk. Although workplace violence is often considered an American problem, a survey by the International Labor Organization found that workplace assaults were actually more common in several other industrial nations, including France, England, and Argentina, than in the United States. Four percent of workers in the European Union said they had been subjected to physical violence in the past year.

OSHA has developed recommendations to help employers reduce the risk of violence. Employers should try to reduce high-risk situations, for example, by installing alarm systems, convex mirrors, and pass-through windows. They should train employees in what to do in an emergency situation. Unfortunately, many companies are poorly prepared to deal with these situations. Only 24 percent of employers offer any type of formal training to their employees in coping with workplace violence.

Sources: "Fatal Occupational Injuries by Event or Exposure, 1999–2004," August 25, 2005, *www.osha.gov/SLTC/workplaceviolence*; "Law Enforcement Officers Most at Risk for Workplace Violence," press release dated December 20, 2001, *www.ojp.usdoj.gov*; and "Violence on the Job: A Global Problem," *www.ilo.org*.

violation causing the death of an employee, jailed as well. In 2005, for example, BP paid $21 million in fines for safety violations linked to an explosion of a refinery in Texas that killed 15 workers and injured 170.[12]

OSHA has had considerable success in improving worker safety and health. Although workers—such as the victims of the Sago mine and BP refinery explosions—continue to die on the job, since OSHA's creation in 1970 the overall workplace death rate has been halved. Very serious occupational illnesses, such as brown lung (caused when textile workers inhale cotton dust) and black lung (caused when coal miners inhale coal dust), have been significantly reduced. The rate of lead poisoning, suffered by workers in smelters and battery plants, among other workplaces, has been cut by two-thirds. Deaths from trench cave-ins have been reduced by 35 percent, to cite several examples.

Although many businesses have credited OSHA with helping reduce lost workdays and worker compensation costs, others have criticized the agency's rules as being too costly to implement and administer. For example, in 2002 OSHA proposed new rules designed to prevent worker injuries in nursing homes by eliminating the manual lifting of residents. Many nursing home operators immediately attacked the proposal, charging that it was based on "junk science."[13] In part in response to employer criticisms, OSHA

[11] "Massacre at the Office," *Newsweek*, January 8, 2001, p. 27.

[12] "BP Agrees to Penalties Totaling $21.4 Million for Fatal Texas Blast," *The Wall Street Journal*, September 23, 2005, p. B2.

[13] "Business Flexes Muscles over Ergonomics, Again," *The Wall Street Journal*, December 26, 2003.

has entered into cooperative partnerships with employers, aimed at improving occupational safety and health for the benefit of both companies and their workers.

Although problems remain, three decades of occupational safety and health regulation in the United States and efforts by businesses and unions have significantly lowered deaths and injuries on the job. In many developing nations, however, conditions remain brutally dangerous.

> In Bangladesh, a fast-growing garment and textile industry—mostly sourcing apparel to Western companies—has been the site of numerous tragedies. In 2006, an electrical fire at the KTS Textile Industries factory in the port city of Chittagong killed 54 workers, mostly women and girls as young as 12, and injured close to 100 more. Managers had intentionally locked exits to prevent theft and had no fire safety equipment on site. This was only the most recent in a series of fires and building collapses that have killed or seriously injured more than 2,800 Bangladeshi workers since 1990. In response, garment workers organized a national half-day strike to demand tougher health and safety standards and compensation for victims and their families. They also called on international buyers to adopt and enforce codes of conduct for their Bangladeshi suppliers.[14]

Efforts by governments, businesses, and unions to improve conditions of workers in overseas factories are further discussed later in this chapter.

The special problem of smoking in the workplace—a safety and health threat both to smokers and nonsmokers—is addressed in the discussion case at the end of this chapter.

The Right to a Secure Job

Do employers have an obligation to provide their workers with job security? Once someone is hired, under what circumstances is it legal—or fair—to let him or her go? In recent years, the expectations underlying this most basic aspect of the employment relationship have changed, both in the United States and in other countries around the globe.

In the United States, since the late 1800s, the legal basis for the employment relationship has been **employment-at-will**. Employment-at-will is a legal doctrine that means that employees are hired and retain their jobs "at the will of"—that is, at the sole discretion of—the employer. However, over time, this doctrine has been eroded by a number of laws and court decisions that have dramatically curtailed U.S. employers' freedom to terminate workers. Some of the restrictions on employers include the following:

- An employer may not fire a worker because of race, gender, religion, national origin, age, or disability. The equal employment and other laws that prevent such discriminatory terminations are further described in Chapter 19.
- An employer may not fire a worker if this would constitute a violation of public policy, as determined by the courts. For example, if a company fired an employee just because he or she cooperated with authorities in the investigation of a crime, this would be illegal.
- An employer may not fire a worker if, in doing so, it would violate the Worker Adjustment Retraining Notification Act (WARN). This law, passed in 1988, requires most big employers to provide 60 days advance notice whenever they lay off a third or more (or 500 or more, whichever is less) of their workers at a work site.

---

[14] "Bangladesh Factory Fire Toll 54: Official," *Reuters News Service,* February 24, 2006; and "425 Garment Workers Killed in Incidents Since 1990," *United News of Bangladesh,* April 10, 2006. More information on efforts to improve conditions in the Bangladeshi garment and textile industry is available online at *www.cleanclothes.org.*

- An employer may not fire a worker simply because the individual was involved in a union organizing drive or other union activity.

- An employer may not fire a worker if this would violate an implied contract, such as a verbal promise, or basic rules of "fair dealing." For example, an employer could not legally fire a salesperson just because he or she had earned a bigger bonus under an incentive program than the employer wanted to pay.

Of course, if workers are covered by a collective bargaining agreement, it may impose additional restrictions on an employer's right to terminate. Many union contracts say employees can be fired only "for just cause," and workers have a right to appeal the employer's decision through the union grievance procedure. Many European countries and Japan have laws that extend "just cause" protections to all workers, whether or not they are covered by a union contract.

The commitments that employers and employees make to each other go beyond mere legal obligations, however. Cultural values, traditions, and norms of behavior also play important roles. Some have used the term **social contract** to refer to the *implied understanding* (not a legal contract, but rather a set of shared expectations) between an organization and its stakeholders. This concept includes, perhaps most significantly, the understanding between businesses and their employees.

Research suggests that the social contract governing the employment relationship has varied across cultures, and also across time. For example, in Europe, employers have historically given workers and their unions a greater role in determining company policy than do most U.S. employers. Employee representatives are often included on boards of directors, in a practice sometimes called *co-determination*. For many years, big Japanese companies offered a core group of senior workers lifelong employment; in exchange, these workers felt great loyalty to the company. This practice became less widespread in the 1990s and 2000s, as the Japanese economy contracted. In the former Soviet Union, many enterprises felt an obligation to provide social benefits, such as housing and child care, to their workers. These benefits declined with the advent of privatization in these formerly state-run economies.

Beginning in the late 1980s, fierce global competition and greater attention to improving the bottom line resulted in significant corporate restructuring and downsizing (termination) of employees in many countries. This trend led some researchers to describe a *new social contract.* Bonds between employers and employees weakened. Companies aimed to attract and retain employees not by offering long-term job security, but rather by emphasizing interesting and challenging work, performance-based compensation, and ongoing professional training. For their part, employees were expected to contribute by making a strong commitment to the job task and work team and to assume a share of responsibility for the company's success. But they could not count on a guaranteed job.[15]

The social contract between employers and workers was further weakened when several prominent companies cut or eliminated long-standing pension benefits. IBM, for example, announced that beginning in 2008 it would freeze its pension plan for current U.S. employees, meaning workers would no longer build up benefits with additional years of service, and would shift instead to a 401(k) plan. Other companies cutting defined-benefit pensions, or eliminating them altogether, included such major firms as Verizon, Lockheed Martin, Motorola, and General Motors. (Defined benefit pensions provide a predictable payout each

[15] James E. Post, "The New Social Contract," in Oliver Williams and John Houck, eds., *The Global Challenge to Corporate Social Responsibility* (New York: Oxford University Press, 1995).

month, usually based on a combination of an employee's age at retirement, years of service, and average pay.) "People just have to deal with a lot more risk in their lives, because all of these things that used to be more or less assured—a job, health care, a pension—are now variable," said one expert.[16]

Should companies have strong or weak bonds with their employees? When businesses invest in their employees by providing a well-structured career, job security, and benefits including pensions, they reap the rewards of enhanced loyalty, productivity, and commitment. But such investments are expensive, and long-term commitments make it hard for companies to adjust to the ups and downs of the business cycle. Some firms resolve this dilemma by employing two classes of employees: permanent workers, who enjoy stable employment and full benefits, and temporary workers and independent contractors, who do not. The U.S. Labor Department estimates that about 10 million Americans on the job, about 1 in every 14, are independent contractors. About 6 million, or 1 in every 20, are contingent workers who do not expect their jobs to last. On university campuses, to cite one example, many faculty members are part-timers who are not on a tenure (career) track and are often paid much less per course and receive fewer, if any, benefits.

At some companies, contingent workers have fought to upgrade their status. At Microsoft, temporary workers sued the company, charging that they had been wrongly denied benefits paid to permanent employees doing similar work. Microsoft later settled the suit, offering to pay $97 million to some 8,000 contingent employees. The company also upgraded many temporary employees to "blue badge," or permanent, status.[17]

In general, during periods of economic expansion, employers are usually more willing to offer long-term commitments to workers and during periods of economic downturn are less likely to do so. However, this is not always the case. Exhibit 18.B describes a company that chose to avoid layoffs, even during a severe economic downturn. In any case, finding the right balance in the employment relationship between commitment and flexibility—within a basic context of fair dealing—remains a challenge to socially responsible businesses.

Privacy in the Workplace

An important right, in the workplace as elsewhere, is privacy. Privacy can be most simply understood as the right to be left alone. In the business context, **privacy rights** refer primarily to protecting an individual's personal life from unwarranted intrusion by the employer. Many people believe, for example, that their religious and political views, their health conditions, their credit history, and what they do and say off the job are private matters and should be safe from snooping by the boss. Exceptions are permissible only when the employer's interests are clearly affected. For example, it may be appropriate for the boss to know that an employee is discussing with a competitor, through e-mail messages, the specifications of a newly developed product not yet on the market.

[16] "More Companies Ending Promises for Retirement," *The New York Times*, January 9, 2006, p. A1; "IBM to Freeze Pension Plans to Trim Costs," *The New York Times*, January 6, 2006, p. A1; and "GM to Freeze Pension Plans of White-Collar Workers," *The New York Times*, March 8, 2006, p. A10.

[17] "Microsoft to Pay $97 Million to End Temp Worker Suit," *Los Angeles Times*, December 13, 2000, p. C1.

Exhibit 18.B   No Layoffs at Xilinx

Xilinx has been called the "archetypal Silicon Valley company." The high-tech maker of programmable microchips for consumer electronics, such as cell phones and DSL modems, experienced rapid growth in the boom years of the late 1990s and early 2000s. In the fiscal year ended March 2001, the company's revenues were up an eye-popping 62 percent over the prior year (which were up 54 percent from the year before that).

But in late spring 2001, the market for Xilinx products abruptly collapsed when the telecommunications industry hit a sharp downturn. Most of the company's competitors laid off employees to save money. But Xilinx opted for a different approach. It declared its intention to avoid all layoffs. Instead, it cut pay (by an average of 6 percent) and offered its employees a range of voluntary options, from lower-paid sabbaticals to go back to school or work for a nonprofit, to swapping part of their salaries for stock options.

Wim Roelandts, the company's CEO, later explained, "Seventy-five percent of our people are knowledge workers, university-trained, most of them engineers working on future products. The decision to avoid layoffs was a better business decision." The fact that Xilinx, unlike some other electronics firms, outsourced its manufacturing and sales also gave it flexibility in responding to the steep industry downturn.

In 2003, Xilinx placed fourth on *Fortune* magazine's list of the "100 Best Places to Work," the highest ranking for any publicly owned company. And noted Roelandts, "So far we have not missed project deadlines, projects did not get delayed, and we have gained 15 points of market share during this down cycle."

Sources: "Balancing Act between Jobs and Profits," *Financial Times* (London), January 22, 2003, p. 13; and "Avoiding Layoffs Pays Dividends for Xilinx," *Irish Times,* March 14, 2003, p. 55. The "100 Best Companies to Work for in America" lists are available at *www.greatplacetowork.com*. Xilinx retained its top-ten ranking on this list in 2004 and 2005.

But other areas are not so clear-cut. For example, should a job applicant who is experiencing severe financial problems be denied employment out of fear that he may be more inclined to steal from the company? Should an employee be terminated after the firm discovers that she has a serious medical problem, although it does not affect her job performance, since the company's health insurance premiums may dramatically increase? At what point do company interests weigh more heavily than an employee's right to privacy? This section will address several key workplace issues where these privacy dilemmas often emerge: electronic monitoring, office romance, drug and alcohol abuse, and honesty testing.

Electronic Monitoring

As discussed in Chapters 13 and 14, changing technologies have brought many ethical issues to the forefront. One such issue is employee **electronic monitoring**. New technologies—e-mail and messaging, voice mail, GPS satellite tracking, Internet browsing, and digitally stored video—enable companies to gather, store, and monitor information about employees' activities. A company's need for information, particularly about its workers, may be at odds with an employee's right to privacy. Even senior executives may not be immune, as shown in the following example:

Henry Stonecipher was fired from his job as CEO of Boeing Co. after directors learned about a sexually explicit e-mail he had sent to a female company executive with whom he was having an affair. The board determined that the CEO had violated Boeing's code of ethical conduct, which prohibited employees from engaging in conduct that would embarrass the company. The CEO's "poor judgment . . . impaired his ability to lead," said Boeing's nonexecutive board chairman.[18]

Employee monitoring has exploded in recent years, reflecting technological advances that make surveillance of employees easier and more affordable. A 2005 survey found that more than three-fourths of U.S. firms monitored workers' Internet usage, and two-thirds blocked access to inappropriate sites. About half stored and reviewed employees' e-mail messages and computer files. Smaller proportions used GPS technology to track company vehicles (8 percent) and cell phones (5 percent). Special software permitted employers to automatically scan messages or files for key words, or to flag a supervisor when a particular Web site was accessed or phone number dialed.[19] These programs can be customized to the industry; for example, a hospital might scan for "patient info"; a high-tech company with proprietary technology might scan for a competitor's name or phone number.[20]

Management justifies the increase in employee monitoring for a number of reasons. Employers have an interest in efficiency. When employees log on to the Internet at work to trade stocks, plan their vacations, or chat with friends by e-mail, this is not a productive use of their time. Employers also fear lawsuits if employees act in inappropriate ways. An employee who views pornographic pictures on a computer at work, for example, might leave the company open to a charge of sexual harassment—if other workers observed this behavior and were offended by it. (Sexual harassment is further discussed in the following chapter.) The employer also needs to make sure that employees do not disclose confidential information to competitors or make statements that would publicly embarrass the company or its officers.

Is electronic monitoring by employers legal? For the most part, yes. The Electronic Communications Privacy Act (1986) exempts employers. In general, the courts have found that privacy rights apply to personal, but not business, information, and that employers have a right to monitor job-related communication. In an important 1996 case, an employee sued his employer after he was fired for deriding the sales team in an internal e-mail, referring to them as "back-stabbing bastards." The court sided with the company, saying it owned the e-mail system and had a right to examine its contents. Yet, some have criticized recent court decisions like this one, saying public policy should do a better job of protecting employees from unwarranted secret surveillance.[21]

In seeking to balance their employees' concerns about privacy with their own concerns about productivity, liability, and security, businesses face a difficult challenge. One approach is to monitor employee communication only when there is a specific reason to do so, such as poor productivity or suspicion of theft. For example, the chipmaker Intel Corporation chose not to check its employees' e-mail routinely, feeling this would undermine trust. Most management experts recommend that employers, at the very least, clearly define their monitoring policies, let employees know what behavior is expected, and apply any sanctions in a fair and evenhanded way.

---

[18] "Extramarital Affair Topples Boeing CEO," *USA Today,* March 8, 2005, p. 1B.

[19] American Management Association, "2005 Electronic Monitoring & Surveillance Survey," *www.amanet.org.*

[20] "Snooping by E-Mail Is Now a Workplace Norm," *The Wall Street Journal,* March 9, 2005, p. B1.

[21] For example, see the position of the American Civil Liberties Union, *www.aclu.org.*

Romance in the Workplace

Another issue that requires careful balancing between legitimate employer concerns and employee privacy is romance in the workplace. People have always dated others at work. In fact, one study showed that one-third of all long-term relationships began on the job, and 30 percent of all managers said they had had one or more romantic relationships at work during their careers.[22] Yet office romance poses problems for employers. If the relationship goes sour, one of the people may sue, charging sexual harassment—that is, that he or she was coerced into the relationship. When one person in a relationship is in a position of authority, he or she may be biased in an evaluation of the other's work, or others may perceive it to be so.

For many years, most businesses had a strict policy of forbidding relationships in the workplace, especially those between managers and those reporting to them. They assumed that if romance blossomed, one person—usually the subordinate—would have to find another job. Recently, however, business practices have begun to change. One legal expert explained, "You just can't control human nature, and you're not going to fire well-trained people simply because they're having a relationship. There's more of a practical view—to manage the relationship rather than ban it."[23] Many companies now allow managers to get involved with subordinates, so long as they do not supervise them directly. If a relationship develops, it is up to the people involved to come forward and to change assignments if necessary. A few companies require their managers to sign a document, sometimes called a *consensual* relationship agreement, stipulating that an office relationship is welcome and voluntary—to protect against possible harassment lawsuits if the people involved later break up.

Employee Drug Use and Testing

Abuse of drugs, particularly hard drugs such as heroin and methamphetamine, can be a serious problem for employers. Only a small fraction of employees use illegal drugs. But those who do can cause serious harm. They are much more likely than others to produce poor quality work, have accidents that hurt themselves and others, and steal from their employers. Some break the law by selling drugs at work to support their habits. Drug abuse costs U.S. industry and taxpayers an estimated $181 billion a year. This figure includes the cost of lost productivity, medical claims, rehabilitation services, and crime and accidents caused by drugs.[24]

One way business has protected itself from these risks is through **drug testing**. More than three-fifths of companies test employees or job applicants for illegal substances, according to a study by the American Management Association.[25] Significant drug testing first began in the United States following passage of the Drug-Free Workplace Act of 1988, which required federal contractors to establish and maintain a workplace free of drugs. At that time, many companies and public agencies initiated drug testing to comply with government rules. Commercial clinical laboratories that conduct workplace drug tests for employers reported a steady decline in positive tests over the 1990s and into the

---

[22] Dennis M. Powers, *The Office Romance* (New York: Amacom Books, 1998); and "AMA's 2003 Survey on Workplace Dating," available at *www.amanet.org.*

[23] "The One Clear Line in Interoffice Romance Has Become Blurred," *The Wall Street Journal*, February 4, 1998, pp. A1, A8.

[24] "The Economic Costs of Drug Abuse in the United States 1992–2002," available at *www.whitehousedrugpolicy.gov.*

[25] American Management Association survey data on workplace medical testing are available at *www.amanet.org*; this figure is from the 2004 survey.

FIGURE 18.2
Pros and Cons of Employee Drug Testing

Arguments Favoring Employee Drug Testing	Arguments Opposing Employee Drug Testing
• Cooperates with U.S. "War on Drugs" campaign	• Invades an employee's privacy
• Improves employee productivity	• Violates an employee's right to due process
• Promotes safety in the workplace	• May be unrelated to job performance
• Decreases employee theft and absenteeism	• May be used as a method of employee discrimination
• Reduces health and insurance costs	• Lowers employee morale
	• Conflicts with company values of honesty and trust
	• May yield unreliable test results
	• Ignores effects of prescription drugs, alcohol, and over-the-counter drugs
	• Drug use an insignificant problem for some companies

2000s; less than 5 percent of employees tested positive in the most recently reported results.[26]

Typically, drug testing is used on three different occasions.

- *Preemployment screening.* Some companies test all job applicants or selected applicants before hiring, usually as part of a physical examination, often informing the applicant ahead of time that there will be a drug screening.
- *Random testing of employees.* This type of screening may occur at various times throughout the year. In many companies, workers in particular job categories (e.g., operators of heavy machinery) or levels (e.g., supervisors) are eligible for screening at any time.
- *Testing for cause.* This test occurs when an employee is believed to be impaired by drugs and unfit for work. It is commonly used after an accident or some observable change in behavior.

Employee drug testing is controversial. Although businesses have an interest in not hiring, or getting rid of, people who abuse drugs, many job applicants and employees who have never used drugs feel that testing is unnecessary and violates their privacy and due process rights. The debate over employee drug testing is summarized in Figure 18.2. In general, proponents of testing emphasize the need to reduce potential harm to other people and the cost to business and society of drug use on the job. Opponents challenge the benefits of drug testing and emphasize its intrusion on individual privacy.

Alcohol Abuse at Work

Another form of employee substance abuse—which causes twice the problems of all illegal drugs combined—is alcohol use and addiction. About 6 percent of full-time employees are heavy drinkers—that is, they had five or more drinks on five or more occasions in the past month. Like drug abusers, they can be dangerous to themselves and others. Studies show that up to 40 percent of all industrial fatalities and 47 percent of industrial injuries are linked to alcohol. The problem is not just hard-core alcoholics, however. Most

---

[26] "Report Suggests Workplace Drug Use Decreased After 9/11," *Workplace Substance Abuse Advisor,* July 25, 2002.

alcohol-related problems in the workplace, one study found, were caused by people who occasionally drank too much after work and came in the next day with a hangover, or who went out for a drink on their lunch break. U.S. businesses lose an estimated $70 billion per year in reduced productivity directly related to alcohol abuse.[27]

Company programs for drug abusers and alcohol abusers are often combined. Since the 1980s, an increasing number of firms have recognized that they have a role to play in helping alcoholic employees. As with drug rehabilitation programs, most alcoholism programs work through **employee assistance programs (EAPs)** that offer counseling and follow-up. Roughly 90 percent of Fortune 500 companies provide EAPs for alcohol and drug abusers. (The figure is much lower for small companies though, only 1 in 10 of which have such programs.) In general, EAPs have been very cost-effective. General Motors, for example, estimated that it had saved $3,700 for each of the employees enrolled in its EAP.

Employee Theft and Honesty Testing

Employees can irresponsibly damage themselves, their co-workers, and their employer by stealing from the company. Employee theft has emerged as a significant economic, social, and ethical problem in the workplace. A 2004 survey of large retail stores in the United States showed that about half of all inventory losses were due to employee theft (shoplifting, administrative error, and vendor fraud accounted for the rest). The value of goods stolen was almost $15 billion.[28]

Employee theft is also a problem in Europe. According to the European Retail Theft Barometer, so-called retail crime (employee theft, shoplifting, and customer fraud) costs European businesses around 32 billion euros annually. Differences in theft rates among the 25 countries surveyed were declining, reflecting the growing integration of Europe and common strategies adopted by EU retailers to combat the problem.[29]

Many companies in the past used polygraph testing (lie detectors) as a preemployment screening procedure or on discovery of employee theft. In 1988, the Employee Polygraph Protection Act became law. This law severely limited polygraph testing by employers and prohibited approximately 85 percent of all such tests previously administered in the United States. In response to the federal ban on polygraphs, many corporations have switched to written psychological tests that seek to predict employee honesty on the job by asking questions designed to identify desirable or undesirable qualities. When a British chain of home improvement centers used such tests to screen more than 4,000 applicants, theft dropped from 4 percent to 2.5 percent, and actual losses from theft were reduced from 3.75 million pounds to 2.62 million pounds.

The use of **honesty tests**, however, like polygraphs, is controversial. The American Psychological Association noted there is a significant potential for these tests to generate false positives, indicating the employee probably would or did steal from the company even though this is not true. After extensively studying the validity of honesty tests and the behavior they try to predict, two academic researchers concluded that the tests were,

---

[27] The statistics reported in this paragraph are available at the Web site of the Working Partners for an Alcohol- and Drug-Free Workplace at *www.dol.gov/asp/programs/drugs/workingpartners*.

[28] Richard C. Hollinger and Lynn Langton, *2004 National Retail Security Survey* (Gainesville, FL: University of Florida, 2005), pp. 6–7.

[29] "Taking Stock on Stock Taking," May 10, 2005, *www.checkpointeurope.com*.

at best, accurate only 14 percent of the time. Critics also argue that the tests intrude on a person's privacy and discriminate disproportionately against minorities.[30]

In all these areas—monitoring employees electronically, policing office romance, testing for drugs, and conducting psychological tests—businesses must balance their needs to operate safely, ethically, and efficiently with their employees' right to privacy.

Whistle-Blowing and Free Speech in the Workplace

Another area where employer and employee rights and duties frequently conflict involves free speech. Do employees have the right openly to express their opinions about their company and its actions? If so, under what conditions do they have this right?

The U.S. Constitution protects the right to free speech. This means the government cannot take away this right. For example, the legislature cannot shut down a newspaper that editorializes against its actions or those of its members. However, the Constitution does not explicitly protect freedom of expression in the workplace. Generally, employees are not free to speak out against their employers, since companies have a legitimate interest in operating without harassment from insiders. Company information is generally considered to be proprietary and private. If employees, based on their personal points of view, were freely allowed to expose issues to the public and allege misconduct, a company might be thrown into turmoil and be unable to operate effectively.

On the other hand, there may be situations in which society's interests override those of the company, so an employee may feel an obligation to speak out. When an employee believes his or her employer has done something that is wrong or harmful to the public, and he or she reports alleged organizational misconduct to the media, government, or high-level company officials, **whistle-blowing** has occurred.

One of the most publicized whistle-blowers of recent years was Dr. Jeffrey Wigand, whose dramatic story was later portrayed in the movie *The Insider*. Dr. Wigand, a scientist and chief of research for cigarette maker Brown & Williamson, came forward with inside information that his employer had known that nicotine was addictive and had actively manipulated its level in cigarettes. His allegations, made under oath, made an important contribution to the success of litigation against the tobacco industry.[31]

Another case, in which whistle-blowers at WorldCom revealed a shocking pattern of accounting fraud, is described in Exhibit 18.C.

Speaking out against an employer can be risky; many whistle-blowers find their charges ignored—or worse, find themselves ostracized, demoted, or even fired for daring to go public with their criticisms, as described in Chapter 5. Whistle-blowers in the United States have some legal protection against retaliation by their employers, though. As noted earlier in this chapter, most workers are employed *at will*, meaning they can be fired for any reason. However, most states now recognize a public policy exception to this rule. Employees who are discharged in retaliation for blowing the whistle, in a situation that affects public welfare, may sue for reinstatement and in some cases may even be entitled to punitive damages. The federal Sarbanes-Oxley Act,

[30] Dan R. Dalton and Michael B. Metzger, "'Integrity Testing' for Personnel Selection: An Unsparing Perspective," *Journal of Business Ethics,* February 1993, pp. 147–56. The position of the American Civil Liberties Union on honesty testing is available at *www.workrights.org.*

[31] Dr. Wigand's story is told in Philip J. Hilts, *Smoke Screen: The Truth Behind the Tobacco Industry Cover-Up* (Reading, MA: Addison-Wesley, 1996).

Exhibit 18.C Blowing the Whistle at WorldCom

In 2002, WorldCom, then the parent of MCI and one of the nation's largest telecommunications firms, was rocked by an accounting scandal touched off by whistle-blowers. Their revelations led to the bankruptcy of the firm and the indictment of several top executives.

During an investigation over several months, WorldCom's vice president of internal audit, Cynthia Cooper, and members of her staff discovered that top executives had systematically "cooked the books." Working late into the evening and on weekends to avoid detection, the accountants uncovered billions of dollars worth of fraudulent entries. The company had used reserve funds to boost income, recorded operating expenses as capital costs, and taken other improper actions to make the firm's performance look better than it was.

When the company's chief financial officer—Cooper's boss—got wind of what she was working on, he ordered her to delay the investigation. Instead, she took her findings directly to the audit committee of the board of directors. What she had to say shocked them. The audit committee immediately fired the chief financial officer, and the next day, the board publicly announced that the company had inflated profits by almost $4 billion.

As the story broke, members of the press began calling to talk to Cooper. She was characteristically modest. "I'm not a hero," she said. "I'm just doing my job." Cooper and her team continued to work at WorldCom, where they cooperated with the company's new outside auditors and with government investigators trying to unravel the largest accounting fraud in history.

Sources: "How Three Unlikely Sleuths Discovered Fraud at WorldCom," *The Wall Street Journal,* October 30, 2002, pp. A1, A6; and "Persons of the Year: Sherron Watkins of Enron, Coleen Rowley of the FBI, and Cynthia Cooper of WorldCom," *Time,* January 6, 2003, pp. 32–60.

passed in 2002 (and described more fully in Chapters 6 and 15), makes it illegal for employers to retaliate in any way against whistle-blowers who report information that could have an impact on the value of a company's shares. It also requires boards of directors to establish procedures for hearing employee complaints.[32]

Moreover, whistle-blowers sometimes benefit from their actions. The U.S. False Claims Act, as amended in 1986, allows individuals who sue federal contractors for fraud to receive up to 30 percent of any amount recovered by the government. In the past decade, the number of whistle-blower lawsuits—perhaps spurred by this incentive—increased significantly, exposing fraud in the country's defense, health care, municipal bond, and pharmaceutical industries.

Whistle-blowing has both defenders and detractors. Those defending whistle-blowing point to the successful detection and prosecution of fraudulent activities. Under the False Claims Act, through 2005 almost $7 billion had been recovered that would otherwise have been lost to fraud.[33] Situations dangerous to the public or the environment have been exposed and corrected because insiders have spoken out. Yet opponents cite hundreds of unsubstantiated cases, often involving disgruntled workers seeking to blackmail or discredit their employers.

When is an employee morally justified in blowing the whistle on his or her employer? According to one expert, four main conditions must be satisfied to justify informing the media or government officials about a corporation's actions. These are:

- The organization is doing (or will do) something that seriously harms others.
- The employee has tried and failed to resolve the problem internally.

[32] "Year of the Whistleblower," *BusinessWeek,* December 16, 2002, pp. 107–10.

[33] Department of Justice statistics, summarized at the Web site of Taxpayers against Fraud at *www.taf.org.*

- Reporting the problem publicly will probably stop or prevent the harm.
- The harm is serious enough to justify the probable costs of disclosure to the whistle-blower and others.[34]

Only after each of these conditions has been met should the whistle-blower go public.

Working Conditions around the World

Much of this chapter has focused on the employment relationship, and the legal and ethical norms governing it, in the United States. Workplace institutions differ dramatically around the world. Laws and practices that establish fair wages, acceptable working conditions, and employee rights vary greatly from region to region. As illustrated by the opening example of this chapter that described a Nike contract factory in China, these differences pose a challenge to multinational corporations. By whose standards should these companies operate?

Recent headlines have turned the public's attention to the problem of **sweatshops**, factories where employees, sometimes including children, are forced to work long hours at low wages, often under unsafe working conditions. Several well-known companies in addition to Nike, including Wal-Mart, Disney, and McDonald's, have been criticized for tolerating abhorrent working conditions in their overseas factories or those of their contractors. In recent years, student groups have pressured companies by rallying to prevent their colleges and universities from buying school-logo athletic gear, clothing, and other products made under sweatshop conditions.

Fair Labor Standards

The term *labor standards* refers to the conditions under which a company's employees—or the employees of its suppliers, subcontractors, or others in its commercial chain—work. Some believe that labor standards should be universal; that is, companies should conform to common norms across all their operations worldwide. Such universal rules are sometimes called **fair labor standards**. For example, such standards might include a ban on all child labor, establishment of maximum work hours per week, or a commitment to pay a wage above a certain level. Others think that what is fair varies across cultures and economies, and it is often difficult to set standards that are workable in all settings. For example, in some cultures child labor is more acceptable (or economically necessary) than others. A wage that would be utterly inadequate in one economic setting might seem princely in another. In some countries, unions are legal and common; in others, they are illegal or actively discouraged.

In the face of growing concerns over working conditions overseas, a debate has developed over how best to establish fair labor standards for multinational corporations. Several approaches have emerged.

Voluntary *corporate codes of conduct,* described in detail in Chapters 6 and 7, can include labor standards that companies expect their own plants and those of their contractors to follow. One of the first companies to develop such standards was Levi Strauss, a U.S. apparel maker. After the company was accused of using an unethical contractor in Saipan, the company reviewed its procedures and adopted a wide-ranging set of guidelines for its overseas manufacturing. Reebok, Boeing, DaimlerChrysler, and other companies have followed suit.

---

[34] Manuel G. Velasquez, *Business Ethics: Concepts and Cases,* 6th ed. (Upper Saddle River, NJ: 2006), p. 379.

Nongovernmental organizations (NGOs) labor codes have also been attempted. For example, the Council on Economic Priorities has developed a set of workplace rules called Social Accountability 8000, or SA 8000. Modeled after the quality initiative of the International Organization for Standardization, ISO 9000, SA 8000 establishes criteria for companies to meet in order to receive a "good working condition" certification. Other groups, including the International Labour Organization, the Caux Roundtable, and the United Nations, have also worked to define common standards to which companies can voluntarily subscribe. These efforts are further described in Chapter 7.

Yet a third approach is for *industrywide labor codes.* Groups of companies, sometimes with participation of government officials, NGOs, and worker and consumer representatives, define industrywide standards that they can all agree to. In 2004, for instance, three leading high-tech companies—HP, IBM, and Dell—released a common Electronic Industry Code of Conduct, establishing a uniform set of labor, health and safety, and environmental standards for their global supply chains.[35] Cisco Systems, Microsoft, and several other companies later endorsed the effort. Supporters said a common code would likely improve supplier compliance and lower the costs of training and monitoring. Another similar effort in the clothing and footwear industries, called the Apparel Industry Partnership, is described in the case study on Nike, at the end of the book.

Whatever the approach, certain common questions emerge in any attempt to define and enforce fair labor standards. These questions include the following.

- *What wage level is fair?* Some argue that market forces should set wages, as long as they do not fall below the level established by local minimum wage laws. Others argue that multinational corporations have a moral obligation to pay workers enough to achieve a decent family standard of living; still others feel that they should pay workers a fair share of the sale price of the product or of the company's profit.

- *Should standards apply just to the firm's own employees, or to all workers who have a hand in making its products?* Some say that while the responsibility of a firm to its own employees is clear, its responsibility to the employees of its subcontractors is indirect and therefore of lower importance.

- *How should fair labor standards best be enforced?* Adherence to fair labor standards, unlike national labor laws, for example, is strictly voluntary. Companies can adopt their own code, or agree to one of the NGO or industry codes. But who is to say that they, and their contractors, are actually living up to these rules? In response to this concern, a debate has emerged over how best to monitor and enforce fair labor standards. Some have advocated hiring outside accounting firms, academic experts, or advocacy organizations to conduct independent audits to determine if a code's standards are being met. The efforts of one company, Mattel, to devise a verifiable procedure for monitoring its code of conduct in overseas factories are profiled in Exhibit 18.D.

As businesses have become more and more global, as shown in Chapter 7, companies have faced the challenge of operating simultaneously in many countries that differ widely in their working conditions. For these companies, abiding by government regulations and local cultural traditions in their overseas manufacturing may not be enough. Many business leaders have realized that subscribing to fair labor standards that commit to common norms of fairness, respect, and dignity for all their workers is an effective strategy for enhancing their corporate reputations, as well as meeting the complex global challenges of corporate social responsibility.

[35] "HP, Dell, IBM and Leading Suppliers Release Electronics Industry Code of Conduct," press release, October 21, 2004, *www.hp.com.*

Exhibit 18.D   Monitoring Compliance at Mattel, Inc.

Mattel, Inc., the maker of Barbie dolls, Fisher-Price toys, Hot Wheels cars, and many other children's playthings, is the world's largest toy company. Many of its products are manufactured in overseas factories, mostly in Asia. In 1997, Mattel developed a detailed code of conduct, called its Global Manufacturing Principles. Covering both Mattel's factories and those of its subcontractors and suppliers, the principles addressed a wide range of labor issues. These included wages (at least minimum wage or local industry standard, whichever was higher), child labor (workers had to be at least 16 years old or the local minimum, whichever was higher), and health and safety (compliant with the standards of the American Conference of Government Industrial Hygienists).

Mattel also considered how it could best enforce its code and convince its customers it was serious about doing so. In an innovative move, the company created an independent auditing organization, the Mattel Independent Monitoring Council (MIMCO). Chaired by three outside experts, MIMCO was given a generous budget and access to all facilities and records of Mattel and its subcontractors and was charged with carrying out regular inspections and making the results public. In 2003, MIMCO's activities were taken over by the International Center for Corporate Accountability (ICCA), a nonprofit organization that conducted independent audits for corporate clients.

Since its first external audit in 1999, Mattel has made public a series of reports on company-owned and contract factories in China, Indonesia, Malaysia, Thailand, and Mexico. The independent audits show that although the company has generally complied with its own code, some problems have remained, such as at a plant in Mexico where workers complained that they had to stand without a break for eight hours a day. The company quickly corrected the problem. Mattel's pioneering effort to establish fully independent and transparent monitoring has been a model for other companies, such as Freeport-McMoran Copper & Gold. ICCA's audit of Freeport's controversial mining operation in Indonesia was released to the public in 2005.

Source: The complete audits conducted by the ICCA for Mattel and Freeport-McMoran are available at *www.icca-corporateaccountability.org.*

Employees as Corporate Stakeholders

The issues discussed in this chapter illustrate forcefully that today's business corporation is open to a wide range of social forces. Its borders are very porous, letting in a constant flow of external influences. Many are brought inside by employees, whose personal values, lifestyles, and social attitudes become a vital part of the workplace.

Managers and other business professionals need to be aware of these employee-imported features of today's workforce. The employment relationship is central to getting a corporation's work done and to helping satisfy the wishes of those who contribute their skills and talents to the company. The task of a corporate manager is to reconcile potential clashes between employees' human needs and legal rights and the requirements of corporate economic production.

Summary

- U.S. labor laws give most workers the right to organize unions and to bargain collectively with their employers. Some believe that unions are poised for resurgence after many years of decline.

- Job safety and health concerns have increased as a result of rapidly changing technology in the workplace. U.S. employers must comply with expanding OSHA regulations and respond to the threat of violence at work.

- Employers' right to discharge "at will" has been limited, and employees now have a number of bases for suing for wrongful discharge. The expectations of both sides in the employment relationship have been altered over time by globalization, business cycles, and other factors.

- Employees' privacy rights are frequently challenged by employers' needs to have information about their health, their work activities, and even their off-the-job lifestyles. When these issues arise, management has a responsibility to act ethically toward employees while continuing to work for a high level of economic performance.

- Blowing the whistle on one's employer is often a last resort to protest company actions considered harmful to others. In recent years, U.S. legislation has extended new protections to whistle-blowers.

- The growing globalization of business has challenged companies to adopt fair labor standards to ensure that their products are not manufactured under substandard, sweat-shop conditions.

Key Terms	drug testing, *394*	fair labor standards, *399*	privacy rights, *391*
	electronic monitoring, *392*	honesty testing, *396*	social contract, *390*
	employee assistance	labor union, *386*	sweatshops, *399*
	programs (EAPs), *396*	Occupational Safety and	whistle-blowing, *397*
	employment-at-will, *389*	Health Administration	
	ergonomics, *387*	(OSHA), *387*	

Internet Resources		
	www.ilo.org	International Labour Organization (ILO)
	www.drugfreeworkplace.org	Institute for a Drug-Free Workplace
	www.osha.gov	Occupational Safety and Health Administration
	www.whistleblowers.org	National Whistleblowers Center
	www.aclu.org	American Civil Liberties Union
	www.afl-cio.org	American Federation of Labor-Congress of Industrial Organizations
	www.workrights.org	National Workrights Institute

Discussion Case: *No Smoking Allowed—On the Job or Off*

In 2005, Weyco, a benefits management company in Michigan, took an unusual step: it fired all employees who were smokers, even if they had never lit up on the job. Howard Weyers, president and founder of the privately held company, believed in promoting healthy lifestyles both at his own company and those of his clients. "I spent all my life working with young men, honing them mentally and physically to a high performance," the 70-year-old former college football coach explained. "I think that's what we need to do in the workplace."

In late 2003, the company had announced that it would no longer hire smokers. To assist its employees who used tobacco, the company offered smoking cessation programs and paid for medication and acupuncture. It also hired a full-time specialist to advise all employees on diet and nutrition and subsidized their health club memberships. Smokers were given 15 months to kick the habit. By the deadline, 20 employees had succeeded in doing so; the 4 who had not were fired.

Weyco employees were of mixed opinion about the tobacco-free policy. One employee who gave up cigarettes commented, "I had to choose between whether I wanted to keep my job and whether I wanted to keep smoking. To me it was a no-brainer." But another, who left the company rather than quit smoking, decried the invasion of privacy. "You feel like you have no rights," she said. "It had to do with my privacy in my own home."

Weyco's decision to prohibit smoking off the job as well as in the workplace was unusual. But by the mid-2000s, most U.S. employers—some acting voluntarily and some because they were forced to by local and state antismoking laws—had banned smoking on the job or restricted it to a few separate areas.

Employers cited several reasons for adopting antismoking rules. Secondhand smoke—smoke emitted from a lit cigarette, cigar, or pipe, or exhaled by a smoker—caused nearly 50,000 nonsmoker deaths in the United States each year, according to medical research. Nonsmoking employees could be sickened, or even killed, by exposure to others' tobacco smoke at work, particularly in workplaces where smoking is common, such as bars and restaurants. Moreover, smoking employees were expensive. Studies showed that more than $47 million was lost annually due to productivity loss and disability time related to smoking. Smokers, on average, cost the firm $753 annually in medical expenses and missed two more workdays per year than nonsmokers did.

For their part, employees who smoke have been divided in their reaction to tobacco restrictions or bans. Some smokers, like many at Weyco, welcomed the opportunity to quit. A study by researchers at the University of California found that employees who were covered by strong workplace smoking policies were more likely to quit the habit than other smokers. Others, however, were incensed at what they perceived as a violation of personal rights and freedoms. They resented having to go outside to smoke, particularly in bad weather. Some even argued that smoking was, in effect, an addiction to nicotine, and so their right to smoke should be protected under the Americans with Disabilities Act (further described in the following chapter).

Lawmakers weighed in on both sides of the issue. Many towns and cities, and some states, passed antismoking ordinances or laws. For example, both New York City and the state of Florida banned smoking in all enclosed workplaces. But many states (sometimes the same ones) also passed laws making job discrimination against smokers illegal. Although these laws did not affect smoking bans or restrictions in the workplace, they did prohibit companies from refusing to hire smokers and from firing employees who continued to smoke. (Michigan, where Weyco was located, did not have such a law.)

Many other countries have historically been more tolerant of smoking, both in the workplace and elsewhere, than the United States. By the mid-2000s, however, this was beginning to change. In 2005, the World Health Organization's Framework Convention on Tobacco Control took effect, after ratification by many of the world's nations. Among other things, the convention called on governments to protect people from workplace exposure to secondhand smoke.

Sources: "Background on Weyco Inc.'s Tobacco-Free Policy," online at *www.weyco.com;* "Company's Smoking Ban Means Off-Hours, Too," *The New York Times,* February 8, 2005; "Workers Fume as Firms Ban Smoking at Home," *Detroit News,* January 27, 2005; and "UC Study Says Workplace Smoking Ordinances Help Employees Quit," *Cal-OSHA Reporter,* May 5, 2000. The Web site of the Framework Convention on Tobacco Control is at *www.who.int/tobacco/framework.*

Discussion Questions

1. Should employers have the right to ban or restrict smoking by their employees at the workplace? Why do you think so?

2. Should employers have the right to restrict or ban smoking by the employees off the job, as Weyco did? Why do you think so?

3. Should the government regulate smoking at work? If so, what would be the best public policy? Why do you think so?

4. Should multinational firms have a single corporate policy on smoking in the workplace, or vary their policies depending on local laws and norms of behavior in various countries where they do business?

CHAPTER NINETEEN

Managing a Diverse Workforce

The workforce in the United States is more diverse than it has ever been, reflecting the entry of women into the workforce, immigration from other countries, the aging of the population, and shifting patterns of work and retirement. Equal opportunity laws and changing societal expectations have challenged corporations to manage workforce diversity effectively. Full workplace parity for women and persons of color has not yet been reached. However, businesses have made great strides in reforming policies and practices in order to draw on the skills and contributions of their increasingly varied employees.

This chapter focuses on these key learning objectives:

- Knowing in what ways the workforce of the United States is diverse and evaluating how it might change in the future.
- Understanding where women and persons of color work, how much they are paid, and the roles they play as managers and business owners.
- Identifying the role government plays in securing equal employment opportunity for historically disadvantaged groups and debating whether or not affirmative action is an effective strategy for promoting equal opportunity.
- Assessing the ways diversity confers a competitive advantage.
- Formulating how companies can best manage workforce diversity, making the workplace welcoming, fair, and accommodating to all employees.
- Understanding what policies and practices are most effective in helping today's employees manage the complex, multiple demands of work and family obligations.

Marriott International, the large hotel chain, employs 143,000 workers in 66 countries, doing jobs ranging from managing vacation resorts, to flipping burgers, to cleaning bathrooms and changing sheets. Their employees speak 30 different languages and represent 50 or so distinct cultures. Many of Marriott's employees in the United States are immigrants, some are in welfare-to-work programs, and many are single parents. A large proportion work nights or odd hours. "They have very complex lives," said the company's director of work/life programs. In an effort to address its employees' needs, Marriott established a toll-free phone line, where social workers provided consultations on a wide range of personal issues in many languages. In Atlanta, it built a state-of-the-art child care center that operated around the clock. In Boston, the company sponsored a series of fatherhood seminars to provide support to working dads. Marriott credited its innovative programs with helping it attract and retain committed employees from many backgrounds.[1]

The example of Marriott Corporation demonstrates both the promise and the perils of a workforce that encompasses tremendous diversity on every imaginable dimension. Having many different kinds of workers can be a great benefit to businesses, as it gives them a wider pool from which to recruit talent, many points of view and experiences, and an ability to reach out effectively to a diverse, global customer base. Yet, it also poses great challenges, as business must meet the mandates of equal employment laws and help people who differ greatly in their backgrounds, values, and expectations get along—and succeed—in the workplace.

The Changing Face of the Workforce

Human beings differ from each other in many ways. Each person is unique, as is each employee within an organization. Individuals are also similar in many ways, some of which are more readily visible than others. The term **diversity** refers to variation in the important human characteristics that distinguish people from one another. The *primary* dimensions of diversity are age, ethnicity, gender, mental or physical abilities, race, and sexual orientation. The *secondary* dimensions of diversity are many; they include such characteristics as communication style, family status, and first language.[2] Individuals' distinguishing characteristics clearly impact their values, opportunities, and perceptions of themselves and others at work. **Workforce diversity**—diversity among employees— thus represents both a challenge and an opportunity for businesses.

At the beginning of the 21st century, the U.S. workforce is as diverse as it has ever been, and it is becoming even more so. Consider the following major trends:[3]

- *More women are working than ever before.* Married women, those with young children, and older women, in particular, have greatly increased their participation in the workforce. By 2012, the Bureau of Labor Statistics estimates that 47 percent of all workers will be women, nearly equal to their share of the population. One effect of this trend is that more employed men have wives who also work—changing the nature of their responsibilities within the family.

---

[1] "Fathers, with Their Companies in Tow, Make a Move toward the Homestead," *Boston Globe,* August 8, 1999, p. F1; "Marriott's Bid to Patch the Child Care Gap Gets a Reality Check," *The Wall Street Journal,* February 2, 2000, p. B1. Marriott's Web site is *www.marriott.com.*

[2] This definition is based on Marilyn Loden, *Implementing Diversity* (New York: McGraw-Hill, 1995), Ch. 2.

[3] Except as noted, the figures in the following paragraphs are drawn from "Labor Force Projections to 2012," *Monthly Labor Review,* February 2004, pp. 37–57, and *Statistical Abstract of the United States 2006* (Washington, DC: U.S. Census Bureau).

- *Immigration has profoundly reshaped the workplace.* Between 2000 and 2005, almost 8 million immigrants entered the United States—the largest number in any 5-year period in the nation's history. The leading countries of origin are now Mexico, India, China, the Philippines, El Salvador, Brazil, and Vietnam. Immigrants now make up about 15 percent of U.S. workers, increasing linguistic and cultural diversity in many workplaces.[4]

- *Ethnic and racial diversity is increasing.* Hispanics (defined by the Census as persons of Spanish or Latin American ancestry), now about 13 percent of U.S. workers, are expected to comprise 15 percent by 2012. Asians are expected to be the fastest growing segment of the labor force. The proportion of African-Americans is expected to hold steady at around 12 percent. By 2012, the U.S. workforce is projected to be about 35 percent nonwhite (this category includes persons of Hispanic origin). In some states, such as California, these trends will be much more pronounced.

- *The workforce will continue to get older.* As the baby boom generation matures, birth rates drop, and people live longer and healthier lives, the population will age. Many of these older people will continue to work, whether out of necessity or choice. As one expert put it, "The American labor force will become somewhat more brown and black in the next twenty years, but its most pervasive new tint will be gray."[5] Employers will have to find new ways to accommodate retirement-aged workers.

Workforce diversity creates many new employee issues and problems. This chapter will consider the changing face of today's workplace, and its implications for management. Laws and regulations clearly require that businesses provide equal opportunity and avoid discrimination and harassment. How to meet—and exceed—these mandates presents an ongoing challenge to businesses seeking to reap the benefits of a well-integrated, yet culturally diverse work population. We turn first to two important dimensions of workplace diversity: gender and race.

Gender and Race in the Workplace

Gender and race are important primary dimensions of workforce diversity. Women and persons of color have always worked, contributing both paid and unpaid labor to the economy. Yet the nature of their participation in the labor force has changed, posing new challenges to business.

One of the most significant changes in the past half-century has been the growing labor force participation of women. During the period following World War II, the proportion of women working outside the home rose dramatically, as shown in Figure 19.1. In 1950, about a third of adult women were employed. This proportion has risen almost steadily since, standing at 59 percent in 2004. Participation rates (the proportion of women in the workforce) have risen for all groups of women, but the most dramatic increases have been among married women, mothers of young children, and middle-class women, those who had earlier been most likely to stay at home. Men's participation rates declined somewhat during this period; between 1950 and 2004, the proportion of adult men who worked fell from 86 percent to 73 percent.

---

[4] "Immigrants at Mid-Decade: A Snapshot of America's Foreign-Born Population in 2005," Center for Immigration Studies, December 2005, *www.cis.org.*

[5] *Workforce 2020: Work and Workers in the 21st Century* (Indianapolis, IN: Hudson Institute, 1999), p. 122.

FIGURE 19.1
Proportion of Women in the Labor Force, 1950–2004

Source: U.S. Bureau of Labor Statistics.

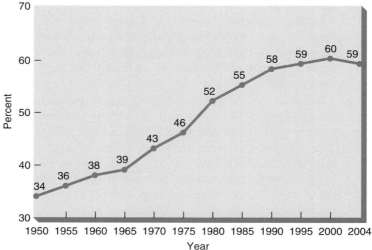

Women have entered the labor force for many of the same reasons men do. They need income to support themselves and their families. Having a job with pay also gives a woman psychological independence and security. The high cost of living puts financial pressure on families, frequently pushing women into the labor force just to sustain an accustomed standard of living or to put children through college or care for aging parents. The inadequacies and uncertainties of retirement plans and health care programs frequently mean that women, as well as men, need to save, invest, and plan for the future. When women divorce, they often can no longer rely on a partner's earnings for support.

The rapid rise of female labor force participation in the postwar years also reflects the expansion of segments of the economy that were major employers of women. In 1940, about one-third of all U.S. jobs were white-collar (not requiring manual labor); by 1980, over half were white-collar. Professional, technical, and service jobs also grew relative to the economy. The creation of many new positions in fields traditionally staffed by women produced what economists call a demand-side pull of women into the labor force. More "women's jobs" meant more women working.

Labor force participation rates for minorities, unlike those of women, have always been high. For example, in 1970 about 62 percent of all African-Americans (men and women combined) worked; the figure is about 67 percent today. Participation rates have also been consistently high for most other minority groups; for Asians, it is 67 percent; for Hispanics, 71 percent. The key change here has been the move of persons of color, in recent decades, into a wider range of jobs as barriers of discrimination and segregation have fallen. Minorities have become better represented in the ranks of managers, professionals, and the skilled trades. These trends will be further discussed later in this chapter.

The face of success in the United States is diverse, just as the workforce is. Consider Jenny Ming, president of the Old Navy division of Gap, Inc., from 1998 to 2006. Ming immigrated with her family from Macao (an island nation off the coast of China) when she was 9 years old. She later recalled in an interview that as a youngster, she loved everything about America, especially Halloween. After completing her education in the public university system, Ming

FIGURE 19.2

The Gender and Race Pay Gap (1990–2004 median weekly earnings of full-time workers, as a percentage of those of white men)

Source: U.S. Census Bureau, *Statistical Abstract of the United States 2006,* Table 632, p. 428, and *Statistical Abstract of the United States 2000,* Table 696, p. 437.

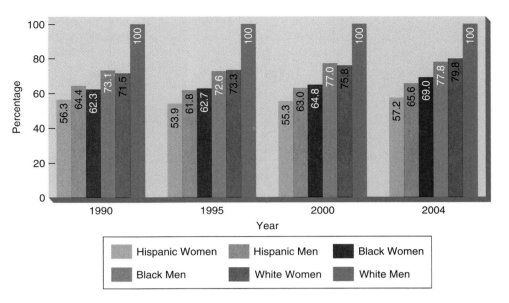

took her first job as an assistant department manager for Mervyn's. She moved up fast in the retail world, becoming a top executive at Old Navy when she was just 39. A profile in *BusinessWeek* attributed Ming's success to her "uncanny knack for predicting which hip-looking clothes of the moment will appeal to the masses, then making big bets on producing the huge quantities needed to assure the chain a continual string of hits."[6]

The Gender and Racial Pay Gap

One persistent feature of the working world is that women and persons of color on average receive lower pay than white men do. This disparity, called the **pay gap**, narrowed over the past three decades, as Figure 19.2 shows. But in 2004 black men and white women still earned only slightly more than three-fourths of white men's pay; black women earned about 69 percent. (These data are based on full-time workers only.) The pay gap for Hispanic women declined by about 7 percent during the last two decades; and that for Hispanic men, only 1 percent. Recent research by two economists showed that the gender pay gap, now 77 percent, understates lifetime differences in earnings, because women work fewer hours and are more likely to take time off for child rearing. Over their prime working years, women make only 38 percent of what men earn, the study found.[7]

Experts disagree about the cause of the pay gap between women and men. Some believe the continuing gender disparity in pay is evidence of sex discrimination by employers; others believe the gap reflects women's choices to pursue lower paying jobs or slower advancement because of time off for family responsibilities. Many observers agree, however, that the pay gap persists, in part, because of what is called **occupational segregation**. This term refers to the inequitable concentration of a group, such a minorities

[6] "Old Navy's Jenny Ming Setting Sail," July 11, 2006, *www.brandweek.com;* "Tying the Two Strands," *The New York Times,* October 27, 2003, p. A3; and "A Savvy Captain for Old Navy: Jenny Ming's Drive and Vision Are Paying Off Big for Parent Gap, Inc.," *BusinessWeek,* November 8, 1999, p. 130.

[7] Stephen J. Rose and Heidi I. Hartmann, *Still a Man's Labor Market: The Long-Term Earnings Gap* (Washington DC: Institute for Women's Policy Research, 2004).

or women, in particular job categories. The large pay gap for Hispanic workers, for example, partly reflects their concentration in several low-paid occupations. Forty-four percent of meatpackers, 40 percent of grounds maintenance workers, 39 percent of farm workers, and 38 percent of private household cleaners are of Hispanic origin, according to the Census Bureau, although Hispanics make up only 13 percent of the workforce as a whole. Although women, for their part, have made great strides in entering occupations where they were formerly underrepresented, many remain concentrated in a few sex-typed jobs that some have called the "pink collar ghetto." Women still make up 98 percent of preschool and kindergarten teachers, 92 percent of bookkeepers, 99 percent of dental hygienists, and 92 percent of receptionists, for example. Eliminating the pay gap will require, therefore, business programs and government policies that create opportunity for women and people of color to move out of more segregated jobs into ones where the pay and chances for upward mobility are greater.[8]

The most prestigious and highest-paying jobs in a corporation are in top management. Because most corporations are organized hierarchically, management jobs—particularly those at the top—are few. For that reason, only a small fraction of workers, of whatever gender or race, can hope to reach the upper levels in the business world. White men have traditionally filled most of these desirable spots. Business's mandate now is to broaden these high-level leadership opportunities for women and persons of color, a topic to which we turn next.

Where Women and Persons of Color Manage

About 9 million U.S. women were working as managers by the mid-2000s. As Figure 19.3 reveals, in 2004 more than 4 out of 10 managers—and a majority of managers in some categories—were women. Clearly, women have broken into management ranks. Women are more likely to be managers, though, in occupational areas where women are more numerous at lower levels, such as health care and education. Grouped by industry, women tend to be concentrated in service industries and in finance, insurance, real estate, and retail businesses. Women managers have also made gains in newer industries, such as biotechnology, where growth has created opportunity.

Where do persons of color manage? As is shown in Figure 19.3, African-Americans, Asians, and Hispanics are underrepresented in management ranks in the United States, making up just 7.0, 4.5, and 6.4 percent of managers, respectively. But they have approached parity in a few areas. Blacks make up 12.8 percent of education administrators (more than their 10.7 percent of the workforce), reflecting less discrimination and more opportunity in public schools. Asians are best represented in the ranks of computer and information systems managers; Hispanics are best represented in property management and real estate. Figure 19.3 shows the continuing underrepresentation of blacks, Asians, and Hispanics in other management categories.

Breaking the Glass Ceiling

A few exceptional women and persons of color have reached the pinnacles of power in corporate America. In 2006, Patricia A. Woertz, for example, became president and CEO of Archer Daniels Midland, the agribusiness giant, following a successful career at Chevron, where she had risen to executive vice president of refining and marketing, a $100 billion business.[9] When Richard Parsons, an African-American, became chairman

---

[8] The data in this paragraph are drawn from Table 604, "Employed Civilians by Occupation, Sex, Race, and Hispanic Origin," in the U.S. Census Bureau, *Statistical Abstract of the United States 2006,* pp. 401 ff.

[9] "From One Male Bastion to Another," *BusinessWeek,* May 15, 2006, p. 38.

FIGURE 19.3
Extent of Diversity in Selected Management Occupations

Source: U.S. Census Bureau, Statistical Abstract of the United States 2006, Table 604, p. 401.

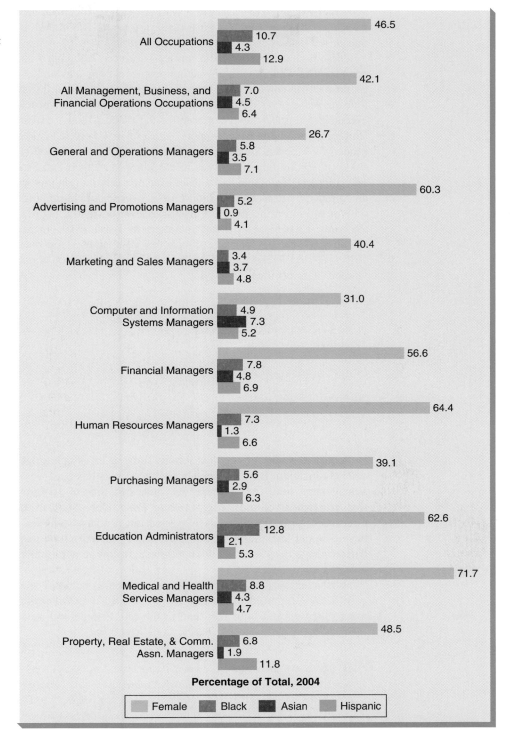

	Female	Black	Asian	Hispanic
All Occupations	46.5	10.7	4.3	12.9
All Management, Business, and Financial Operations Occupations	42.1	7.0	4.5	6.4
General and Operations Managers	26.7	5.8	3.5	7.1
Advertising and Promotions Managers	60.3	5.2	0.9	4.1
Marketing and Sales Managers	40.4	3.4	3.7	4.8
Computer and Information Systems Managers	31.0	4.9	7.3	5.2
Financial Managers	56.6	7.8	4.8	6.9
Human Resources Managers	64.4	7.3	1.3	6.6
Purchasing Managers	39.1	5.6	2.9	6.3
Education Administrators	62.6	12.8	2.1	5.3
Medical and Health Services Managers	71.7	8.8	4.3	4.7
Property, Real Estate, & Comm. Assn. Managers	48.5	6.8	1.9	11.8

Percentage of Total, 2004

and chief executive of AOL Time Warner in 2002, it capped an extraordinary career rise from the streets of Bedford-Stuyvesant, a poor neighborhood in New York City, to head one of the best-known companies in the world.[10]

These high-achievers remain unusual, however. Although women and minorities are as competent as white men in managing people and organizations, they rarely attain the highest positions in corporations. Their ascent seems to be blocked by an invisible barrier, sometimes called a **glass ceiling**. According to Catalyst, an advocacy organization for female executives, in 2002 only 16 percent of the officers (and 1 percent of chief executives) of leading corporations were women.[11] Less than 1 percent of Fortune 500 companies are headed by a person of color.[12] In Europe, diversity in the top ranks is also rare. A 2005 study of 360 leading companies in the European Union and Scandinavia found that only one company, Vodafone, had a chief executive from a minority group (he was Arun Sarin, an American citizen born in India); only 3 companies were headed by a woman.[13]

Women and minorities are also scarce on corporate boards. A 2005 study reported that only 17 percent of board members of Fortune 100 firms were women, and only 15 percent were persons of color. A few companies stood out as exceptions; at Alcoa, IBM, Hewlett-Packard, and Wellpoint Health Networks, a majority of directors were women or minorities.[14]

In 2006, an unusual law promoting boardroom diversity went into effect in Norway. It mandated that, by 2008, 40 percent of corporate directors in large Norwegian companies be women. "Women will have a place where the power is," said Norway's minister of children and equality. "This . . . will set an example for other centers of society." Opponents, including many in the business community, complained that it would force many experienced men off corporate boards. Moreover, they said, it would violate the basic principle that shareholders should be able to vote for anyone they wanted. In the previous two years, female representation on corporate boards had climbed from 8 percent to 16 percent, in anticipation of the law's implementation.[15]

Failure to attain the topmost jobs in some cases is due to lack of experience or inadequate education. Because gender and racial bias has kept women and minorities out of management until recent years, few have had time to acquire the years of experience that are typical of most high-ranking executives. Also, in earlier years women and minorities were discouraged from entering graduate schools of engineering, science, business, and law, the traditional pathways to top corporate management. Even as those barriers have been lowered, though, these groups remain underrepresented at executive levels.

What continues to hold women and minorities back? A study in the *Harvard Business Review* reported that the primary obstacle is **glass walls**: fewer opportunities to move sideways into jobs that lead to the top. Female and minority managers are often

---

[10] "Can Dick Parsons Rescue AOL Time Warner?" *BusinessWeek*, May 19, 2003, p. 86.

[11] "What's Holding Women Back?" *Harvard Business Review*, June 1, 2003. Data are from the 2002 Catalyst Census.

[12] "Is White the Only Color of Success?" *Christian Science Monitor*, October 31, 2005, p.13.

[13] "Corporate Europe Ignores Diversity at Its Peril," *Financial Times* (London), November 30, 2005. Data are from a study conducted by the Aspen Institute Italia.

[14] Alliance for Board Diversity, "Women and Minorities on Fortune 100 Boards," May 17, 2005. See also, "2005 Catalyst Census of Women on the Boards of Directors of Fortune 500 Companies," press release, March 29, 2006.

[15] "Men Chafe as Norway Ushers Women into Boardroom," *The New York Times*, January 12, 2006, p. A3.

found in staff positions, such as public relations or human resources, rather than in line positions in such core areas as marketing, sales, or production where they can acquire the broad management skills necessary for promotion.[16] Another problem is that in filling top positions, recruiters rely on word-of-mouth—the old boys' network from which women and persons of color are often excluded. Other causes include a company's lack of commitment to diversity and too little accountability at the top management level for equal employment opportunity. However, recent advances by both women and minorities in the executive suite suggest that the glass ceiling may finally be cracking.

Women and Minority Business Ownership

Some women and minorities have evaded the glass ceiling and risen to the top by founding or taking over their own businesses.

By 2006, over 10 million businesses—48 percent of all those in the United States—were owned or controlled by women, according to the Center for Women's Business Research. Of these, about one in eight was owned by a woman of color.

An example of a successful female entrepreneur is Catherine Hughes, founder and chairperson of Radio One, a company that owns over 50 radio stations, mainly in urban markets. Hughes, who is black, started the business in 1980, when she was general manager at Howard University's FM station, by buying a defunct R&B station. For several years, Hughes slept in the station, ran her own morning talk show, and pounded the pavement in the afternoon looking for advertisers. By the mid-1980s, the station was turning a healthy profit, and Hughes began acquiring other stations. By 2006, the company operated 70 radio stations and programmed five channels on the XM Satellite Radio system. "I was determined to make this work," Hughes said.[17]

In recent years, women have formed new businesses at nearly twice the rate of men. Although most female-headed firms are small, collectively they employ over 19 million people in the United States and generate $2.5 trillion in sales.[18]

Persons of color have also used business ownership as a path to success. According to the Small Business Administration, there were around 4.1 million minority-owned businesses in the United States in 2002. Within this group, Hispanic-owned businesses were the most numerous, followed by African-American and Asian-owned businesses.[19] Immigrants were responsible for a good share of the entrepreneurial spirit in the minority community; nearly half of Hispanic business owners and more than two-thirds of Asian business owners were born outside of the United States, according to U.S. Census Bureau figures.

[16] "What's Holding Women Back?" *Harvard Business Review,* June 1, 2003. The reports of the Glass Ceiling Commission of the U.S. Department of Labor may be accessed online at *www.dol.gov/asp/programs/history/reich/reports/ceiling.htm.*

[17] "Top Ten Black Female Entrepreneurs," *Essence,* October 1999, p. 104. The Web site for Radio One is *www.radio-one.com.*

[18] These data include privately held businesses in which women own a controlling interest, privately held businesses owned equally by women and men (for example, by a married couple), and publicly traded companies with majority or substantial women's ownership. For current statistics, see the Web site of the Center for Women's Business Research, *www.cfwbr.org.*

[19] U.S. Census Bureau, "2002 Survey of Business Owners: Preliminary Estimates of Business Ownership by Gender, Hispanic or Latino Origin, and Race," *www.census.gov.*

Government's Role in Securing Equal Employment Opportunity

Eliminating workplace discrimination and ensuring equal job opportunity have been a major goal of public policy in the United States for four decades. This section reviews the major laws that govern business practices with respect to equal opportunity, affirmative action, and sexual and racial harassment.

Equal Employment Opportunity

Beginning on a major scale in the 1960s, U.S. presidents issued executive orders and Congress enacted laws intended to promote equal treatment of employees, that is, **equal employment opportunity**. These government rules apply to most businesses in the following ways:

- Discrimination based on race, color, religion, sex, national origin, physical or mental disability, or age is prohibited in all employment practices. This includes hiring, promotion, job classification, and assignment, compensation, and other conditions of work.

- Government contractors must have written affirmative action plans detailing how they are working positively to overcome past and present effects of discrimination in their workforce. However, affirmative action plans must be temporary and flexible, designed to correct past discrimination, and cannot result in reverse discrimination against whites or men.

- Women and men must receive equal pay for performing equal work, and employers may not discriminate on the basis of pregnancy.

Figure 19.4 outlines the major laws and one executive order that are intended to promote equal opportunity in the workplace. The provisions of the most recent equal employment opportunity law, the Americans with Disabilities Act, are further described in Exhibit 19.A. The major agency charged with enforcing equal employment opportunity laws and executive orders in the United States is the **Equal Employment Opportunity Commission (EEOC)**. The EEOC was created in 1964 and given added enforcement powers in 1972 and 1990.

Companies that fail to follow the laws shown in Figure 19.4 often find themselves facing expensive lawsuits. One of the more sensational examples of a suit against racial discrimination in the workplace in recent years involved Texaco.

FIGURE 19.4
Major Federal Laws and Executive Orders Prohibiting Job Discrimination

Equal Pay Act (1963)—Mandates equal pay for substantially equal work by men and women.
Civil Rights Act (1964; amended 1972, 1991)—Prohibits discrimination in employment based on race, color, religion, sex, or national origin.
Executive Order 11246 (1965)—Mandates affirmative action for all federal contractors and subcontractors.
Age Discrimination in Employment Act (1967)—Protects individuals who are 40 years of age or older.
Equal Employment Opportunity Act (1972)—Increases power of the Equal Employment Opportunity Commission to combat discrimination.
Pregnancy Discrimination Act (1978)—Forbids employers to discharge, fail to hire, or otherwise discriminate against pregnant women.
Americans with Disabilities Act (1990)—Prohibits discrimination against individuals with disabilities.
Family and Medical Leave Act (1993)—Requires companies with 50 or more employees to provide up to 12 weeks unpaid leave for illness, care of a sick family member, or the birth or adoption of a child.

Exhibit 19.A Accommodating Persons with Disabilities

The Americans with Disabilities Act (ADA) of 1990 requires employers to make accommodations for disabled workers and job applicants and prohibits employers from discriminating on the basis of a person's disability. A disabled worker is defined by the law as one who can perform the essential functions of a job, with or without reasonable accommodations. The law prohibits employers from asking in a job interview, for example, about a person's medical history or past treatment for mental illness or alcoholism. And it requires employers to make reasonable accommodations, for example, by modifying work equipment, adjusting work schedules, or making facilities accessible. The courts have interpreted the ADA to cover persons with acquired immunodeficiency syndrome (AIDS). This means that discrimination against persons with AIDS or who are infected with HIV (the virus that causes AIDS) is prohibited, so long as the person can perform the essential elements of the job. Some businesses have complained about the law, citing its vagueness, the high cost of compliance, and the expense of defending against lawsuits. But the ADA has benefited the nation's disabled, 56 percent of whom are now employed, compared with only about a third when the law was passed.

Source: "Disabled Find Jobs but Face Obstacles," *Orlando Sentinel*, May 12, 2006, p. A3. Information about the law is available online at *www.eeoc.gov*; most recent data are available at *www.census.gov*.

A number of African-American employees sued the big oil company, charging discrimination. In the course of investigating the case, these employees' attorneys obtained a copy of a tape recording, apparently of top Texaco executives at a meeting to discuss how to respond to the lawsuit. The tape seemed to contain offensive racial epithets as well as discussion of destroying evidence that would be harmful to Texaco's position. When a transcript of the tape was published, it was very embarrassing for the company. Texaco settled the lawsuit out of court, agreeing to pay $176.1 million over five years, then the largest settlement in the history of racial discrimination suits in the United States. The company also created organizational programs promoting racial sensitivity at work.[20]

Potentially costly lawsuits can involve other forms of discrimination as well, such as those based on age, gender, or disability. A class-action lawsuit involving alleged discrimination against women at the nation's largest private sector employer, Wal-Mart, is described in the discussion case at the end of this chapter.

Affirmative Action

One way to promote equal opportunity and remedy past discrimination is through affirmative action. Since the mid-1960s, major government contractors have been required by presidential executive order to adopt written affirmative action plans specifying goals, actions, and timetables for promoting greater on-the-job equality. Their purpose is to reduce job discrimination by encouraging companies to take positive (that is, affirmative) steps to overcome past employment practices and traditions that may have been discriminatory.

Affirmative action became increasingly controversial in the 1990s and 2000s. In some states, new laws (such as Proposition 209 in California) were passed banning or limiting affirmative action programs in public hiring and university admissions, and the issue was debated in Congress and in the courts. Backers of affirmative action argued that these programs provided an important tool for achieving equal opportunity. In this view, women and minorities continued to face discriminatory barriers and affirmative action was necessary to level the playing field. Some large corporations backed affirmative action programs, finding

[20] "Texaco to Pay $176.1 Million in Bias Suit," *The Wall Street Journal*, November 18, 1996, pp. A3, A6.

them helpful in monitoring their progress in providing equal job opportunity. General Electric, AT&T, and IBM, for example, have said that they would continue to use affirmative action goals and timetables even if they were not required by law.

Critics, however, argued that affirmative action was inconsistent with the principles of fairness and equality. Some pointed to instances of so-called **reverse discrimination**, which occurs when one group is unintentionally discriminated against in an effort to help another group. For example, if a more qualified white man were passed over for a job as a firefighter in favor of a less qualified Hispanic man to remedy past discrimination in a fire department, this might be unfair to the white candidate. Critics of affirmative action also argued that these programs could actually stigmatize or demoralize the very groups they were designed to help. For example, if a woman were hired for a top management post, other people might think she got the job just because of affirmative action preferences, even if she were truly the best qualified. This might undermine her effectiveness on the job or even cause her to question her own abilities. For this reason, some women and persons of color called for *less* emphasis on affirmative action, preferring to achieve personal success without preferential treatment.[21]

In 1995, the Supreme Court ruled in an important decision that affirmative action plans were legal but only if they were temporary and flexible, designed to correct past discrimination, and did not result in reverse discrimination. Under this ruling, quotas (for example, a hard-and-fast rule that 50 percent of all new positions would go to women, say, or African-Americans) would no longer be permitted in most situations. The court confirmed this general approach in 2003 when it ruled in a case involving admissions policies at the University of Michigan that a "holistic" approach that took race into consideration along with other factors in the admissions process, without using quotas, was legal. More than 60 corporations, including Boeing, Pfizer, Steelcase, and even MTV, had filed briefs in support of the university's affirmative action program. In one such brief, General Motors said that "the future of American business and, in some measure, the future of the American economy" depended on diversity in higher education.[22]

Sexual and Racial Harassment

Government regulations ban both sexual and racial harassment. Of the two kinds, sexual harassment cases are more prevalent, and the law covering them is better defined. But racial harassment cases are a growing concern to employers.

Sexual harassment at work occurs when any employee, woman or man, experiences repeated, unwanted sexual attention or when on-the-job conditions are hostile or threatening in a sexual way. It includes both physical conduct—for example, suggestive touching—as well as verbal harassment, such as sexual innuendoes, jokes, or propositions. Sexual harassment is not limited to overt acts of individual co-workers or supervisors; it can also occur if a company's work climate is blatantly and offensively sexual or intimidating to employees. Women are the targets of most sexual harassment. Sexual harassment is illegal, and the U.S. Equal Employment Opportunity Commission (EEOC) is empowered to sue on behalf of victims. Such suits can be very costly to employers who tolerate a hostile work environment, as the following example shows.

---

[21] See, for example, Ward Connerly, *Creating Equal: My Fight Against Race Preferences* (San Francisco: Encounter Books, 2000).

[22] "Affirmative Action: A Corporate Diary," *The New York Times,* June 29, 2003, Section 3, p. 1; "Count Business among the Converted," *St. Louis Post-Dispatch,* June 29, 2003, p. B1.

North Country, a 2005 film starring Charlize Theron, was based on the true story of the first sexual harassment lawsuit to be certified as a class action. A group of women employed at a mine operated by Eveleth Taconite in northern Minnesota sued, charging they had been victims of brutal harassment. As portrayed in the film, male workers had called the women obscene names, grabbed and threatened them, and even knocked over a portable toilet when one woman was inside. The lawsuit was finally settled in 1998, when the company agreed to pay the plaintiffs $3.5 million. The case "put employers on notice that sexual harassment was going to be taken very seriously," said the president of the National Partnership for Women and Families.[23]

Harassment can occur whether or not the targeted employee cooperates. It need not result in the victim's firing, or cause severe psychological distress. The presence of a hostile or abusive workplace can itself be the basis for a successful suit. In an important legal case decided by the Supreme Court in 1993, a woman manager at a truck-leasing firm was subjected to repeated offensive comments by the company president. For example, he asked her in front of other employees if she used sex to get a particular account and suggested that the two of them "go to the Holiday Inn to negotiate [her] raise." The manager quit her job and sued. The Supreme Court upheld her charges, saying that the president's behavior would reasonably be perceived as hostile or abusive, even though it had not caused severe psychological injury or caused the woman to be unable to do her job.[24] The court also ruled, in another case, that a company could be found guilty as a result of actions by a supervisor, even if the incident was never reported to top management.

Women employees regularly report that sexual harassment is common. From 38 to 60 percent of working women have told researchers they have been sexually harassed on the job. Managers and supervisors are the most frequent offenders, and female office workers and clerical workers are the main targets. As many as 90 percent of incidents of harassment are never reported. This kind of conduct is most likely to occur where jobs and occupations are (or have been) sex-segregated and where most supervisors and managers are men, as was the case at the mine portrayed in *North Country.*

In 2002, the European Union recognized sexual harassment as a form of gender discrimination and required its member states to bring their laws into compliance by 2005. Evolving norms about appropriate interactions at the workplace came as a shock to many, particularly in eastern and central Europe, where obscene jokes, suggestive remarks, and unwelcome advances at work were commonplace. One study found, for example, that 45 percent of Czech women had been sexually harassed, although most did not identify the behavior by this term. "Sexual harassment is something like folklore in the Czech Republic," said one researcher.[25]

Racial harassment is also illegal, under Title VII of the Civil Rights Act. Under EEOC guidelines, ethnic slurs, derogatory comments, or other verbal or physical harassment

[23] The story of the lawsuit is told in Clara Bingham and Laura Leedy Gansler, *Class Action* (New York: Random House, 2002). The quotation is from *"North Country* Film Stems from Seattle Lawyer's Work," *Seattle Times,* October 31, 2005, p. B1.

[24] "Court, 9-0, Makes Sex Harassment Easier to Prove," *The New York Times,* November 10, 1993, pp. A1, A15.

[25] "Sexual Harassment in the European Union: The Dawning of a New Era," *SAM Advanced Management Journal* 69, no. 1 (Winter 2004), pp. 4–12; and "Sexual Harassment at Work Widespread in Central Europe," *Plain Dealer* (Cleveland), January 9, 2000, p. 7A.

[26] "Racism in the Workplace," *BusinessWeek,* July 30, 2001, pp. 61–67. Information on the latest government policies on racial and sexual harassment may be found at the Web site of the Equal Employment Opportunity Commission at *www.eeoc.gov.*

based on race are against the law, if they create an intimidating, hostile, or offensive working environment or interfere with an individual's work performance. Although fewer racial than sexual harassment charges are filed, their numbers more than doubled during the 1990s (to about 9,000 a year), and employers have been liable for expensive settlements.[26] For example, FedEx was sued by two ground drivers, both of Lebanese descent, who charged the company had created a hostile work environment. The drivers said in their lawsuit they had been called "terrorists," "camel jockeys," and other epithets by their terminal manager. In 2006, a jury awarded the men $61 million. The company said it would appeal a verdict it called "wrong and excessive."[27]

What can companies do to combat sexual and racial harassment—and protect themselves from expensive lawsuits? In two important court cases in 1998, the Supreme Court helped clarify this question. The court said that companies could deflect lawsuits by taking two steps. First, they should develop a zero-tolerance policy on harassment and communicate it clearly to employees. Then, they should establish a complaint procedure—including ways to report incidents without retaliation—and act quickly to resolve any problems. Companies that took such steps, the court said, would be protected from suits by employees who claimed harassment but had failed to use the complaint procedure.

Developing mechanisms for preventing sexual and racial harassment is just one important action companies can take. Others positive steps by business are discussed in the following section.

What Business Can Do: Diversity Policies and Practices

All businesses, of course, are required to obey the laws mandating equal employment opportunity and prohibiting sexual and racial harassment; those that fail to do so risk expensive lawsuits and public disapproval. But it is not enough simply to follow the law. The best managed companies go beyond compliance; they implement a range of policies and practices to make the workplace welcoming, fair, and accommodating to all employees.

Companies that manage diversity effectively take a number of related actions, in addition to obeying all relevant laws. Research shows that these actions include the following.

Articulate a clear diversity mission, set objectives, and hold managers accountable.

An example of a company that has done so is mortgage lender Fannie Mae. The company's overall mission is to increase the availability and affordability of housing for low, moderate, and middle income Americans. This means, of course, that the company works with a very diverse group of customers. Fannie Mae recognizes that one way to do this well, in the words of one of its written core commitments, is "to fully capitalize on the skills, talents, and potential of all our employees." The company's Office of Diversity and Work Life develops goals, conducts training, administers a mentoring program, and monitors compliance at all levels.[28]

Three-fourths of Fortune 500 companies have diversity programs, mostly training designed to promote sensitivity and awareness. At United Parcel Service, senior-level managers are required to attend a one-month diversity and leadership course. Another important step is to reward managers. At Monsanto, for

---

[27] "Jury Awards $61 Million to Two FedEx Drivers in Harassment Suit," *www.sfgate.com*, June 3, 2006.

[28] Information about Fannie Mae's diversity initiatives is available at *www.fanniemae.com*.

example, a portion of all bonuses paid to "people managers" is based on how well their departments meet various diversity goals.[29]

Spread a wide net in recruitment, to find the most diverse possible pool of qualified candidates. Those in charge of both hiring and promotion need to seek all workers who may be qualified—both inside and outside the company. This often involves moving beyond word-of-mouth networks, which may produce a pool of applicants who are similar to people already working for the company or in particular jobs. One company's successful effort to promote diversity in its hiring and promotion practices is described in the following example.

As part of an agreement to settle a sex-discrimination class action lawsuit, Home Depot, Inc., introduced a new innovation: a computerized hiring and promotion system called Job Preference Program, or JPP for short. The company installed computer kiosks in every store, where job applicants could take basic skills tests and fill out questionnaires about their experience and career goals. Existing employees were encouraged to register their long-term aspirations. The JPP computer then made suggestions about needed skills, forwarded resumes to managers seeking to fill positions, and told applicants about jobs they might not have thought about that matched their ambitions. In the first year after the system was introduced, the number of female managers at Home Depot increased by 30 percent, and the number of minority managers by 28 percent.[30]

Identify promising women and persons of color, and provide them with mentors and other kinds of support. What techniques work to shatter the glass ceiling? One study of a group of highly successful women executives found that most had been helped by top-level supporters and by multiple chances to gain critical skills. Some companies have promoted mobility by assigning mentors—more-senior counselors—to promising female and minority managers and by providing opportunities that include wide-ranging line management experience. At American Express, for example, managers are held accountable for developing diverse talent; in 2004, 2,000 women participated in the company's mentoring program. Amex's chairman and CEO, Kenneth Chenault, is African-American.[31]

Set up diversity councils to monitor the company's goals and progress toward them. A **diversity council** is a group of managers and employees responsible for developing and implementing specific action plans to meet an organization's diversity goals. Sometimes, a diversity council will be established for a corporation as a whole; sometimes, it will be established within particular business units. An example of a company that has used diversity councils effectively is Pitney Bowes, a maker of business communication machines. The company adopted a series of diversity strategic plans, each setting specific goals for the next five-year period. Diversity councils were set up in each business unit to implement programs to meet these objectives, and each year progress was assessed. A Corporate Responsibility Committee of the board oversaw the program as a whole. Pitney Bowes has repeatedly been named to lists of the best employers of women and persons of color.[32]

[29] "Diversity Training Programs Help Reduce Risk of Bias Suits," *Business Insurance*, July 12, 1999, p. 1.

[30] "To Hire a Lumber Expert, Click Here," *Fortune*, April 3, 2000, p. 267.

[31] "The 100 Best Companies [2005]," *Working Mother*, www.workingmother.com.

[32] "Staying Power: Pitney Bowes Embarks on 80th Year of Diversity," *DiversityOnline*, November 2002 [interview with Henry O. Hernandez], *www.diversityonline.com*. Information about Pitney Bowes' diversity programs is available at *www.pb.com*.

Businesses that manage diversity effectively enjoy a strategic advantage. While fundamental ethical principles, discussed in Chapters 5 and 6, dictate that all employees should be treated fairly and with respect for their basic human rights, there are also bottom-line benefits to doing so.

- Companies that promote equal employment opportunity generally do better at attracting and retaining workers from all backgrounds. This is increasingly important as the pool of skilled labor grows more diverse. Nortel, the telecommunications firm, has attributed its low turnover rates, relative to the industry, in part to its strong diversity policies. The company partners with nonprofit organizations to develop and place talented minority students, sponsors networking groups for African-American and Latino employees, and works closely with minority and women-owned suppliers.[33]

- Businesses with employees from varied backgrounds can often more effectively serve customers who are themselves diverse. Explained Steve Reinemund, CEO of PepsiCo, "If we don't have people from the front line up to the boardroom who represent the consumers we sell to, we're not going to be successful." He offered the following example: "We had an urban market where our market share was half of what we had in the suburban market. By changing the sales force for the urban population and changing some products, our market share went up. That demonstration helped us get a lot of traction [for diversity initiatives] within PepsiCo."[34]

- The global marketplace demands a workforce with language skills, cultural sensitivity, and awareness of national and other differences across markets. For example, Maria Elena Lagomasino, senior managing director of Chase Manhattan's Global Private Banking Group, credited her Cuban heritage with helping her do her job more effectively. "When I got into private banking with Latin American customers," she commented, "I found my ability to understand their reality a great advantage."[35]

Finally, companies with effective diversity programs can avoid costly lawsuits and damage to their corporate reputations from charges of discrimination or cultural insensitivity.

Another important step businesses can take to manage diversity effectively is to accommodate the wide range of family and other obligations employees have in their lives outside work. This subject is discussed in the next section.

Balancing Work and Life

The nature of families and family life has changed, both in the United States and in many other countries. The primary groups in which people live are just as diverse as the workforce itself. One of the most prominent of these changes is that dual-income families have become much more common. According to the latest U.S. Census data, in two-thirds of married couples with children (65 percent), both parents worked at least part-time. This was up from just a third of such families in 1976. (To round out the picture, in 30 percent of married couples with children, just the father worked; in 4 percent, just the mother worked. In the remainder, both parents were unemployed.)[36] Families have

---

[33] Nancy R. Lockwood, "Workplace Diversity: Leveraging the Power of Difference for Competitive Advantages," *HR Magazine,* June 2005, pp. A1–10; and "Diversity @ Nortel," *www.nortel.com/employment/life_at_nn/diversity.html.*

[34] "Speaking Out on Diversity," *Fortune,* February 20, 2006, pp. SS8–10.

[35] "Chasing a Global Edge," *Fortune,* July 19, 1999.

[36] The data in this paragraph are drawn from Table 588, "Married Couples by Labor Force Status of Spouse," in U.S. Census Bureau, *Statistical Abstract of the United States* 2006, p. 394.

adopted a wide range of strategies for combining full- and part-time work with the care of children, elderly relatives, and other dependents. Commented the president of the Work and Family Institute, speaking of dual-career families, "It's time to move beyond, is it good, is it bad, and get to: how do we make it work?"[37] How to help "make it work" for employees trying to balance the complex, multiple demands of work and family life has became a major challenge for business.

Child Care and Elder Care

One critical issue for business is supporting workers with responsibilities for children and elderly relatives.

The demand for **child care** is enormous and growing. Millions of children need daily care, especially the nearly 7 out of every 10 children whose mothers hold jobs. A major source of workplace stress for working parents is concern about their children; and problems with child care are a leading reason why employees fail to show up for work.

Business has found that child care programs, in addition to reducing absenteeism and tardiness, also improve productivity and aid recruiting by improving the company's image and helping to retain talented employees. In 2003, 95 percent of large U.S. companies provided some type of child care assistance, including referral services, dependent-care accounts, and vouchers. One in 10 large companies provided on-site child care services. An example is Johnson Wax, a consumer products firm that cares for 400 children in a state-of-the-art center at its Racine, Wisconsin, headquarters. "This isn't a benefit," explained a company spokesperson. "It's a good business decision because we want to attract the best."[38]

In addition to caring for children, many of today's families have responsibilities for **elder care**. Employees' responsibilities for aging parents and other older relatives will become increasingly important to businesses in the coming decade as baby boomers pass through their forties and fifties, the prime years for caring for elderly family members. More than 1 in 5 adults in the United States now cares for an older person, and 59 percent of caregivers are currently employed.[39] This is a concern for employers because 6 in 10 working caregivers have had to go to work late or leave early to attend to these duties.[40]

Many businesses have adopted programs to support workers caring for older relatives. Almost half of the large corporations surveyed by Hewitt Associates, a benefits company, offer some such assistance. The most common kind is providing information and referrals to services for the elderly. "It was great to have someone to talk to, someone who cared," said a customer service representative for AT&T who used the company's referral program to find help for her mother, who had Alzheimers and lived with her. Also available at many firms are dependent-care accounts, long-term care insurance, and emergency backup care. One of the best steps companies can take is to give people the time off they need to deal with the often unpredictable crises that occur in families caring for the elderly. In addition to its referral services, AT&T, for example, also has a policy that permits employees to take up to 12 months of unpaid leave in any 24-month period to care for an older relative.[41]

When a mother or father is granted time off when children are born or adopted and during the important early months of a child's development, this is called a **parental leave**; when

---

[37] "Dual Income Families Now Most Common," *San Francisco Chronicle,* October 24, 2000.

[38] Data are from Hewitt Associates, "Work/Life Benefits Provided by Major U.S. Employers 2003–2004." The quotation is from "More Employers Offer Work/Life Benefits to Gain Edge in Tight Labor Market," press release issued May 4, 2000, available at *www.hewitt.com.*

[39] AARP Public Policy Institute, "Caregiving in the United States," *http://assets.aarp.org.* Data are for 2004.

[40] "A Nation of Caregivers," *USA Today,* April 6, 2004, p. D6.

[41] "Employers Stepping Up in Elder Care," *USA Today,* August 3, 2000, p. 3B.

the care of elderly relatives is involved, this is called a **family leave**. Under the Family and Medical Leave Act (FMLA), passed in 1993, companies that employ 50 or more people must grant unpaid, job-protected leaves of up to 12 weeks to employees faced with serious family needs, including the birth or adoption of a baby. Smaller companies, not covered by the FMLA, usually do less for expectant and new parents and for those with ill family members.

Work Flexibility

Companies have also accommodated the changing roles of women and men by offering workers more flexibility through such options as flextime, part-time employment, job sharing, and working from home (sometimes called telecommuting because the employee keeps in touch with co-workers, customers, and others by phone or over the Internet). Abbott Laboratories, a global health care company, demonstrates the benefits of the many kinds of work flexibility for both business and employees.

> Many of Abbott's employees—men and women—work flextime schedules, beginning and quitting at different times of the day. Others share jobs, with each working half a week. Many jobs are held on a part-time basis, leaving the worker time to be at home with children or elderly parents. Other Abbott employees telecommute from their homes. "After my son got sick, I needed to . . . drop down to part time and work from home a few days a week," said one manager. "Abbott gave me the flexibility I needed to take care of my family." The company, whose work/life programs have been widely honored, says that its employees return the investment through their increased productivity, innovative thinking, and loyalty.[42]

Abbott is not the only corporation using these practices. One survey of large companies revealed that 71 percent offered some kind of flexible work schedules. Fifty percent allowed employees to telecommute or work from home, and 44 percent offered compressed workweek schedules.[43]

However, many observers believe that most careers are still structured for people who are prepared to put in 40 hours a week at the office—or 50 or 60—giving their full and undivided commitment to the organization. Many women and men have been reluctant to take advantage of various flexible work options, fearing that this would put them on a slower track, sometimes disparagingly called the *Mommy track* or *Daddy track*. In this view, businesses will need to undergo a cultural shift, to value the contributions of people who are prepared to make a serious, but less than full-time, commitment to their careers.

> In the United Kingdom, the government's Equal Opportunities Commission publishes an annual update called "Who Runs Britain." Recent reports have shown little progress for women in entering top positions in business, politics, and other areas of public life. The problem, according to the government agency, is employers' failure to accommodate women's need to manage multiple responsibilities at home and work, a phenomenon that in the U.K. is sometimes called the "mummy track." The commission called for adoption of more workplace practices that provided high-quality, highly paid flexible and part-time work for those who have caring responsibilities.[44]

[42] "Abbott Makes *Working Mother* Magazine's List of the 100 Best Companies for Working Mothers for the Fifth Consecutive Year," press release, September 12, 2005, available at *www.abbott.com*.

[43] "Employers Increase Work/Life Programs, According to Results of Mellon Survey," press release, January 15, 2004, available at *www.mellon.com*.

[44] "Sex and Power: Who Runs Britain? 2006," *www.eoc.org.uk*.

Exhibit 19.B   A Family-Friendly Chief Executive

Working Mother magazine singled out Steve Sanger, CEO of General Mills, for his commitment to building a family-friendly company. The magazine related an anecdote of one of Sanger's own memorable experiences as a working parent:

> Early in his tenure . . . the newly minted CEO was scheduled to appear before a roomful of Wall Street analysts in New York City and decided to bring his family along on the business trip. He was poised to take the podium at 9:00 a.m., but minutes before, his then-toddler daughter inadvertently locked herself in the hotel bathroom. "I was in a suit on my knees talking to a two-year-old through a keyhole—a very comical scene that took my mind off the presentation for the five minutes until we got her out," he recall[ed]. . . . "It's funny how your priorities shift when you have children."

General Mills has been an innovator in integrating family considerations into its operations. Some of its programs include:

- An on-site infant care center.
- Flexible work arrangements.
- On-site health care services, including mammograms for busy working mothers.
- Emergency child care for parents whose regular arrangements fall through.
- Exercise classes offered at the company's health and fitness center.

In explaining the business benefits of General Mills' family programs, Sanger commented, "You know what's really expensive? Turnover. If we've invested in recruiting and developing good people, then we want them to stay."

Source: "Thinking Outside the [Cereal] Box," *Working Mother,* October 2002.

What would such a cultural shift look like? Some have used the term **family-friendly corporation** to describe firms that would fully support both men and women in their efforts to balance work and family responsibilities. Job advantages would not be granted or denied on the basis of gender. People would be hired, paid, evaluated, promoted, and extended benefits on the basis of their qualifications and ability to do the tasks assigned. The route to the top, or to satisfaction in any occupational category, would be open to anyone with the talent to take it. The company's stakeholders, regardless of their gender, would be treated in a bias-free manner. All laws forbidding sex discrimination would be fully obeyed. Programs to provide leaves or financial support for child care, elder care, and other family responsibilities would support both men and women employees and help promote an equitable division of domestic work. And persons could seek, and achieve, career advancement without committing to a full-time schedule, year after year.[45] An example of an executive who has taken the lead in promoting family-friendly policies is given in Exhibit 19.B.

An important step businesses can take is to recognize, and provide benefits to, nontraditional families. Some firms now offer domestic partner benefits to their gay and lesbian employees, extending health insurance and other benefits to the same-sex partners of employees. Although U.S. law does not explicitly bar discrimination based on sexual orientation, some local laws do; and many firms have found that extending health insurance and other benefits to the same-sex partners of employees is an effective strategy for

[45] *Working Mother* magazine publishes an annual list of the "100 Best Companies for Working Mothers." The current year's list may be viewed at *www.workingmother.com.*

Exhibit 19.C   Domestic Partner Benefits

Many corporations in the United States have begun to acknowledge differences in employee sexual orientation and gender identity. Gay, lesbian, bisexual, and transgender employees have become a vocal minority, winning important victories in the workplace. By 2006, 249 of the Fortune 500 companies provided health benefits to domestic partners and same-sex spouses, according to the Human Rights Campaign Foundation; the proportion doing so had doubled in the previous five years. Lotus Development was the first major employer to offer spousal benefits to same-sex partners; it was followed by many others, including AT&T, Chase Manhattan, Microsoft, United Airlines, and the Big Three automakers. Other steps companies have taken to support their homosexual employees have included written antidiscrimination policies, management training on sexual diversity issues, and visible gay and lesbian advertising.

Source: Human Rights Campaign Foundation, "Domestic Partner Benefits," March 2006, *www.hrc.org.*

recruiting and retaining valuable contributors. Domestic partner benefits are further described in Exhibit 19.C.

No other area of business illustrates the basic theme of this book better than the close connection between work and life. Our basic theme is that business and society are closely and unavoidably intertwined, so that what affects one also has an impact on the other. As the workforce has become more diverse, businesses have been challenged to accommodate their employees' differences. When people go to work, they do not shed their identities at the office or factory door. When employees come from families where there are young children at home, or where elderly parents require care, companies must learn to support these roles. Businesses that help their employees achieve a balance between work and life and meet their obligations to their families and communities often reap rewards in greater productivity, loyalty, and commitment.

Summary

- The U.S. workforce is as diverse as it has ever been and is becoming more so. More women are working then ever before, many immigrants have entered the labor force, ethnic and racial diversity is increasing, and the workforce is aging.

- Women and persons of color have made great strides in entering all occupations, but they continue to be underrepresented in many business management roles, especially at top levels. Both groups face a continuing pay gap. The number of women-owned businesses has increased sharply, and many minorities, especially immigrants, also own their own businesses.

- Under U.S. law, businesses are required to provide equal opportunity to all, without regard to race, color, religion, sex, national origin, disability, or age. Sexual and racial harassment are illegal. Affirmative action plans remain legal, but only if they are temporary and flexible, designed to correct past discrimination, and do not result in reverse discrimination.

- Companies that manage diversity effectively have a strategic advantage because they are able to attract and retain talented workers from all backgrounds, serve a diverse customer base, and avoid expensive lawsuits and public embarrassment.

- Successful diversity management includes articulating a mission, recruiting widely, mentoring promising women and persons of color, and establishing mechanisms for assessing progress.

Key Terms

affirmative action, *415*
child care, *421*
diversity, *406*
diversity council, *419*
elder care, *421*
equal employment opportunity, *414*
Equal Employment Opportunity Commission (EEOC), *414*

family-friendly corporation, *423*
family leave, *422*
glass ceiling, *412*
glass walls, *412*
occupational segregation, *409*
parental leave, *421*
pay gap, *409*
racial harassment, *417*

reverse discrimination, *416*
sexual harassment, *416*
workforce diversity, *406*

Internet Resources

www.eeoc.gov
www.workfamily.com
www.abcdependentcare.com

www.sba.gov

U.S. Equal Employment Opportunity Commission
Work & Family Connection
American Business Collaboration for Quality Dependent Care
U.S. Small Business Administration

- Many businesses have helped employees balance the complex demands of work and family obligations by providing support programs such as child, elder care, flexible work schedules, domestic partner benefits, and telecommuting options.

Discussion Case: *Dukes v. Wal-Mart Stores, Inc.*

In 2004, a federal judge ruled that a lawsuit charging Wal-Mart Stores with discrimination against six women, *Dukes v. Wal-Mart Stores, Inc.,* could go forward as a class action. This meant the lawyers could argue the case on behalf of all female Wal-Mart employees in the United States, not just those who had brought suit. The judge noted that the case was "historic in nature, dwarfing other employment discrimination cases that came before it." If the decision ultimately went against Wal-Mart (the case was expected to take at least five years), the cost to the company could be in the hundreds of millions of dollars.

In 2006, Wal-Mart was the largest private employer in the world. The company operated 3,800 facilities and had annual sales of $312 billion. In the United States, Wal-Mart employed 1.3 million people, about 63 percent of them women. The company had become a magnet for both strenuous praise and strenuous criticism. Its hyperefficient supply chain was credited with saving U.S. customers $20 billion annually, suppressing inflation, and spurring productivity gains throughout the economy. In 2003 and 2004, *Fortune* named Wal-Mart its most admired company. Yet, Wal-Mart had also been blamed for driving out small businesses, depressing wages, and discriminating against women.

Plaintiffs in *Dukes* charged that female employees at Wal-Mart were paid less than men in comparable positions, in spite of having greater seniority and equal or better qualifications. They also charged that women received fewer promotions to store management positions and waited longer to move up than men did.

The lead plaintiff in the case was Betty Dukes. Dukes had started working at Wal-Mart in 1994. Despite her repeated expressions of interest, she was not promoted into the ranks of salaried managers. "I was always told my time would come, that there were no openings available, that I didn't have enough experience to move on. But on a number of occasions men with less experience than me were put in jobs that I desperately wanted and know I could have done well," Dukes explained. In 2000, she approached antidiscrimination attorneys for help.

The other plaintiffs had similar stories to tell. Claudia Renati was denied a promotion after her boss asked her to stack 50-pound bags of dog food. Men were not subject to a lifting requirement. When Christine Kwapnoski, another plaintiff, asked what she needed to do to be promoted, she was told to "doll up and blow the cobwebs off [your] makeup." Stephanie Odle, an assistant store manager, complained to her district manager when she learned that a man in the same position at her store was making $23,000 more. He told her the man had "a family and two children to support." Recalled Odle, "I told him I'm a single mother, and I have a 6-month old child to support."

In asking that the case be tried as a class action, lawyers argued that these women's experiences were not isolated, but representative of broader patterns. Statistical evidence presented by the plaintiffs showed the following:

- At each successive level of the management ladder at Wal-Mart, women's representation decreased, women made up nearly 90 percent of customer service managers (supervisors of cashiers), but only 15 percent of store managers, as shown in Figure 19.5.
- Among employees who were promoted to assistant manager (the lowest salaried position), women took longer to reach this milestone—4.38 years from date of hire to promotion, compared with 2.86 years for men.
- Women made less than men in every job classification examined, from the lowest ranking hourly jobs to top positions in management, as shown in Figure 19.6. "Women start out being paid less, and the gap just widens," said Brad Seligman, one of the plaintiffs' attorneys.
- These differences in pay and promotion persisted despite similar or better performance. Wal-Mart employees received job ratings ranging from 1 to 7, with 7 the highest. Women hourly employees received, on average, slightly higher ratings than men (3.91 compared with 3.84).

In response, Wal-Mart defended its record on diversity, saying the *Dukes* plaintiffs were not representative of other women working at the company. In a statement on its Web site, the company declared that "Wal-Mart is a great place for women to work, and isolated complaints that arise from its 3000+ stores do not change this fact." A company spokesperson explained, "Many of these women had the opportunity to go into training to become an assistant manager, but they did not want to work the odd shifts, like working all night long, Saturdays or Sundays."

Although it continued to contest the lawsuit, Wal-Mart began taking steps to improve the climate for women. In 2003, Wal-Mart established an Office of Diversity and appointed a chief diversity officer. The company also for the first time linked officer bonuses, in part, to their success in meeting diversity goals. It also said it would promote women in proportion to the number that applied.

Sources: Liza Featherstone, *Selling Women Short: The Landmark Battle for Workers' Rights at Wal-Mart* (New York: Basic Books, 2004); "The Women Taking on Wal-Mart," *The Observer,* June 27, 2004, p. 19; "Wal-Mart Sex Bias Suit Given Class-Action Status," *The New York Times,* June 23, 2004, p. A1; "Is Wal-Mart Too Powerful?" *BusinessWeek,* October 6, 2003, p. 100; "Wal-Mart Faces Lawsuit over Sex Discrimination," *The New York Times,* February 16, 2003, Section 1, p. 22; "Study Finds Pay Gap at Wal-Mart," *Los Angeles Times,* February 4, 2003; "Order Granting in Part and Denying in Part Motion for Class Certification," June 21, 2004, U.S. Court of Appeals; Richard Drogin, Ph.D., "Statistical Analysis of Gender Patterns in Wal-Mart Workforce," February 2003; "Workplace Bias?" Online News Hour, July 5, 2004, *www.pbs.org;* Wal-Mart, "Diversity is a Way of Life at Wal-Mart," March 3, 2006, *www.walmartfacts.com.*

FIGURE 19.5

Approximate Percentages of Women in Salaried Wal-Mart Store Management and Hourly Supervisory Positions, 2001

Source: Richard Drogin, *Statistical Analysis of Gender Patterns in Wal-Mart Workforce,* February 2003 (Berkeley, Calif.: Drogin, Kakigi & Associates), p. 15, Table 7. CSM is customer service manager, a supervisor of cashiers. The assistant manager, co-manager, and store manager are salaried management positions; the others are hourly supervisory positions.

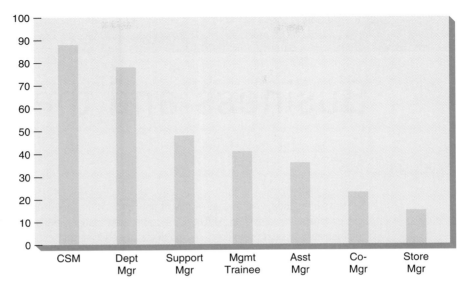

FIGURE 19.6

Average Annual Earnings for Men and Women at Wal-Mart in Selected Jobs, 2001

Source: Drogin, p. 17, Tables 9 and 10.

	Men	Women
Regional vice president	$419,435	$279,772
District manager	239,519	177,149
Manager	105,682	89,280
Assistant manager	39,790	37,322
Management trainee	23,175	22,371
Department head	23,518	21,709
Sales associate	16,526	15,067
Cashier	14,525	13,831

Discussion Questions

1. From the evidence presented in the case, do you think that Wal-Mart violated any U.S. laws, as shown in Figure 19.4? If so, which ones, and why?

2. What actions has Wal-Mart taken before and after the certification of the class action to promote equal opportunity for all employees?

3. If you were an executive of the company, what further steps would you take, if any? How would you communicate your diversity program to your employees and to the public?

4. What do you think would be an appropriate outcome of this case, and why?

CHAPTER TWENTY

Business and the Media

Business firms today use a wide variety of new and old media—from the World Wide Web, blogs, and podcasts, to television, DVDs, CDs, radio, newspapers, billboards, movies, and books—to communicate with stakeholders, sell products or services, and enhance their image. As business acquires greater power through its use of the media, it also must accept greater ethical and social responsibility when wielding this power. Business must be acutely aware of the impact it may have on its stakeholders when administering a public relations or crisis management plan. It must avoid deceptive advertising and show special concern when targeting vulnerable populations such as youths. The media, as an industry, also must honor its ethical and social responsibilities to the public. It must be sensitive to maintaining decency, reflecting diversity and equality, and portraying organizations and issues in a fair and balanced way.

This chapter focuses on these key learning objectives:

- Understanding the responsibilities of business's public relations managers as they interact with various stakeholders.
- Analyzing how businesses can most effectively manage a crisis situation.
- Evaluating when advertising is deceptive or unnecessarily exposes young people to indecency and violence.
- Knowing how governments around the world have regulated advertising, especially the tobacco industry.
- Ensuring that gender and racial diversity are appropriately reflected in the media.

The annual National Football League Super Bowl generates some of the largest audiences in the history of television, and naturally many companies wish to reach these viewers. However, DaimlerChrysler decided to withdraw company sponsorship of the "Lingerie Bowl," a pay-per-view event scheduled to air during halftime of the 2003 Super Bowl. The Lingerie Bowl was to show a seven-on-seven tackle football game between female models wearing only Victoria's Secret-brand bras and panties. Dodge, a Daimler-Chrysler subsidiary, would have its ram logo on the bras worn by the players. A Dodge spokesperson explained, "We don't think it's a good depiction of our brand. It's not an association we feel comfortable with, for obvious reasons."

A group of 20 girls, ages 13 to 16, launched a "girlcott" against Abercrombie & Fitch's new line of T-shirts in 2005. The girls found the slogans on the shirts to be offensive, such as "Blondes are adored, brunettes are ignored" and "Who needs brains when you have these?" What started out as a local western Pennsylvania concern among a small group of girls became a national issue when NBC's "Today Show," Fox Network's "Hannity & Colmes," and CNN began to feature this protest on its shows. Just a few days after the "girlcott" was launched, Abercrombie & Fitch announced that it was pulling the T-shirts from the shelves. The company released the following statement: "We recognize that the shirts in question, while meant to be humorous, might be troubling to some."

Chi-Chi's, a Mexican restaurant chain, faced a major crisis when 600 people were sickened by hepatitis A, and three died, after eating in one of its outlets. The cause was unsanitary preparation of green onions. Although the company acted quickly to remedy the food preparation problem, it failed to warn customers of the health situation until days after the discovery and repeatedly cut short its meetings with the press. The company argued that it took time to verify the cause of the outbreak and did not want to speak out prematurely. Experts pointed to the company's handling of the situation as "a textbook case in how not to respond to a crisis." One victim complained, "I'm very disappointed in Chi-Chi's. They haven't even as much as apologized to the poor people who are sick."[1]

The challenges confronting businesses when interacting with the media are often complex and fraught with ethical and social issues. *Did DaimlerChrysler demonstrate ethical responsibility by refusing to sponsor the Lingerie Bowl? Did it matter that this would have been a pay-per-view event, thus less likely to be viewed by children watching the Super Bowl's halftime show? Was Abercrombie & Fitch insensitive to the message being portrayed on its line of T-shirts? Did Abercrombie & Fitch act responsibly by pulling the shirts in question once challenged by a small group of potential consumers? How could Chi-Chi's have better handled its health crisis? How can a company be completely open and honest with the public and the media when it is unsure of its information?*

The **media** is defined as a means of communication that widely reaches and influences people. It comprises many channels, including television, radio, books, magazines, and the Internet, and uses multiple technologies—many of them rapidly evolving, as described in Chapter 13. Business utilizes various media channels to educate and interact with its stakeholders through public relations announcements, crisis management efforts, and advertisements. Complicating this relationship is the fact that the media is

---

[1] "Chrysler's Chief Disavows Support of 'Lingerie Bowl,'" *The Wall Street Journal,* December 9, 2003, pp. A3, A10; "Chrysler's Dodge Brand Moves to Drop Out of Lingerie Bowl," *The Wall Street Journal,* December 17, 2003, p. B4; "Lingerie Bowl," ThomasNet, *encyclopedia.thefreedictionary.com/lingerie+bowl;* "Bawdy T-shirts Set Off 'Girlcott' by Teens," *Pittsburgh Post-Gazette,* November 3, 2005, pp. A1, A11; Abercrombie & Fitch to Pull Line of T-shirts," *Pittsburgh Post-Gazette,* November 5, 2005, pp. A1, A5; "Hepatitis Outbreak Spreads to 26 More Restaurant Patrons," *Pittsburgh Post-Gazette,* November 5, 2003, *www.post-gazette.com;* and "A Tale of Two Vegetables: Corporate Communications Key in Times of Crisis," *Pittsburgh Post-Gazette,* August 15, 2004, p. D2.

both a stakeholder of business, as well as a profit-making enterprise in its own right, with its own stakeholders. This chapter will explore the complex relationship of business and the media, and then take up some key issues involving the social and ethical challenges facing the media industry itself.

Public Relations

Designing and managing an effective **public relations** program is fundamental to any organization's relationship with the media. A good public relations program sends a constant stream of information from the company to the public and opens the door to dialogue with stakeholders whose lives are affected by company operations. As one group of scholars has written, its essential role "appears to be that of a *window out* of the corporation through which management can perceive, monitor, and understand external change, and simultaneously, a *window in* through which society can influence corporate policy and practice. This boundary-spanning role primarily involves the flow of information to and from the organization."[2]

A public relations program should be proactive, not reactive. Channels of communication with the media should be established on a continuing basis, not just after a problem has arisen. Once this step has been taken, a company can view the media as a positive force that can help the company communicate with the public. Some companies have been reactive, such as Abercrombie & Fitch when facing the "girlcott" of its clothing line or Chi-Chi's openness with the media during its health crisis. However, a more proactive strategy was taken by DaimlerChrysler regarding the Lingerie Bowl.

One purpose of the public relations function is to promote a positive image for the firm in the media. Businesses saw opportunities for good work and boosting their public image when natural disasters devastated their country, as shown by firms responding to aid the victims of Hurricane Katrina, discussed in Chapter 3, and as shown in the following example.

Venezuelan companies responded to the need for emergency efforts in their country just before Christmas 1999 when large portions of the country were ravaged by floods and landslides. The nation's two leading newspapers collected, organized, and distributed online information about lost relatives, emergency aid, and homeless shelters. At one point, the Venezuelan Civil Defense ministry had the names of 1,400 flood refugees, while the newspapers had several thousand names and status reports on these people located on the newspaper's Web sites.[3]

When businesses, or industries, face a crisis in how they are perceived by the public, they may be challenged to respond, as did the pharmaceutical industry in 2005. Effective responses often involve addressing the substantive concerns that gave rise to the crisis.

Suffering from a failing public image caused by several consumer lawsuits against Merck, the U.S. pharmaceutical industry launched a campaign to rehabilitate its image. Drug companies curbed claims made in consumer advertisements, expanded access to low-cost drugs for the poor and uninsured,

---

[2] Boston University Public Affairs Research Group, *Public Affairs Offices and Their Functions: A Summary of Survey Results* (Boston: Boston University School of Management, 1981), p. 1.

[3] "Venezuelan Telecoms and Media Firms Assume Lead Role in Disaster Efforts," *The Wall Street Journal*, December 21, 1999, p. A16.

Exhibit 20.A ▸ Wal-Mart's Public Relations Strategy—With a New Twist

Like many businesses, Wal-Mart turned to the media to bolster its tarnished public image after being stung by criticism regarding its labor practices, expansion plans, and other business tactics. Mona Williams, Wal-Mart spokeswoman explained, "We've really been in the spotlight and I think that's made us especially sensitive to the need to balanced coverage [in the media]. It doesn't matter if the subject is Wal-Mart or something else. You just aren't going to have [balanced coverage] unless different perspectives are represented." In the past, Wal-Mart had used more traditional media to broadcast its public relations message. But in 2006, the company turned toward a new media form to communicate with the public—blogging. In one instance the blogger was a non-Wal-Mart employee, Brian Pickrell, but the message was definitely Wal-Mart's. Pickrell posted to his Web site a note attacking state legislation that would force Wal-Mart stores to spend more on employee health insurance. This note was identical to dozens of other notes found on other blog sites and to an e-mail distributed by Wal-Mart's public relations firms to numerous bloggers. Mona Williams of Wal-Mart justified this action: "As more and more Americans go to the Internet to get information from varied, credible, trusted sources, Wal-Mart is committed to participating in that online conversation." Other messages sent to bloggers for posting included positive news about Wal-Mart, like a high number of job applications it received for a new store in Illinois, as well as negative information about its competitors, such as how Target stores raised zero money for the Salvation Army in 2005 because the company banned red-kettle collection from its stores.

Blogging is a new public relations outlet for business and there are many bloggers ready and willing to help. Marshall Manson, who identified himself as a blogger who does online public affairs for Wal-Mart, offered to the public in a *New York Times* article, "If you're interested, I'd like to drop you an occasional update with some newsworthy info about the company and an occasional nugget that you won't hear about in the M.S.M.—or mainstream media." Public relations has "a new twist."

Sources: "Wal-Mart Tries to Shine Its Image by Supporting Public Broadcasting," *The New York Times Online,* August 16, 2004, *www.nytimes.com*; and "Wal-Mart Enlists Bloggers in P.R. Campaign," *The New York Times Online,* March 7, 2006, *www.nytimes.com*.

and provided more open disclosure of clinical trial data for new drugs. The industry endorsed the PhRMA Guiding Principles, a code of ethical conduct governing direct-to-consumer advertisements of prescription medicines. The industry's trade association set up the Partnership for Prescription Assistance, which included a Web site and hotline staffed by 450 operators to assist consumers enrolling in discount drug programs. Johnson & Johnson, long considered a socially responsible leader in the industry, increased three-fold its advertisement budget focusing on corporate image or general information on diseases, instead of promoting a specific drug.[4]

A novel, technology-oriented use of public relations to counter mounting public criticism and restore a firm's public image is described in Exhibit 20.A, which profiles Wal-Mart's public relations campaign.

Some scholars and practitioners have recently argued that traditional public relations practices, performed in the same way for many years, are increasingly ineffective today because of radical changes in communication and technology. More sophisticated and specialized techniques are required in today's business environment. Experts suggest that in today's dynamic and complex world, an effective public relations function must be a year-round, ongoing process that operates both internally and externally for an organization. This

---

[4] "Stung by Public Distrust, Drug Makers Seek to Heal Image," *The Wall Street Journal Online,* August 26, 2005, *online.wsj.com*. The PhRMA Guiding Principles can be found at *www.phrma.org/dtc*.

function needs to build, develop, and maintain enduring stakeholder relationships, emphasize a grass roots focus to coordinate its communications, and continuously align its values and strategy with the public's interests.[5]

International Public Relations

Public relations strategies increasingly assume a global or international focus, since interactions with stakeholders through the media cross national boundaries, and business relations with stakeholders are often international in scope. Many multinational businesses have extended their public relations strategies globally, as shown in the following example.

> Dow Chemical created a global public relations management team to deal with issues surrounding chlorine. As one of the world's largest producers of chlorine, Dow had a very large stake in proposals to ban or regulate the use of chlorine, a widely used chemical in modern manufacturing. Members of the global management team were drawn from the United States, Europe, and Asia-Pacific and included scientists, plant managers, and managers from Dow's manufacturing businesses that would be affected by any changes in the availability of chlorine. The global management team analyzed scientific studies of chlorine, tracked government actions across the world, coordinated research into various aspects of the problem, and worked with company government relations staff to ensure that Dow "spoke with one voice" when talking about chlorine.[6]

When public relations strategies take on a global perspective, new challenges emerge. For example, public relations managers must be sensitive to cultural disparities as well as similarities in crafting press releases and interactions with the media. The impact of the organization's public relations program could have markedly different impacts in a country given its culture, social or political systems, or history. The ability for a public relations manager to communicate with local media and other stakeholder groups in their native language and avoid embarrassing or misleading communication due to poor translations must be assured. All of these basic public relations tasks are more complex in an international business environment but must be mastered to be an effective public relations manager.[7]

Crisis Management

A critical function of the public relations manager is crisis management. Every organization is likely to face a crisis at some time that forces its employees to act on a difficult issue quickly and without perfect information, such as in the example of Chi-Chi's described above. A **corporate crisis** is a significant business disruption that stimulates extensive news media coverage. The resulting public scrutiny can affect the organization's normal operations and also can have a political, legal, financial, and governmental impact on its business. A crisis is any event with the potential to negatively affect the health, reputation, or credibility of the organization. It might be a terrorist attack, poor financial results, the death of a key executive or government official, employee layoffs,

---

[5] Craig S. Fleisher, "Emerging U.S. Public Affairs Practice: The 20001 PA Model," *Journal of Public Affairs* 1, no. 1 (January 2001), pp. 49–51.

[6] See Dow Chemical's company Web site, *www.dow.com/commitments.*

[7] For a thorough discussion of these issues see Craig S. Fleisher, "The Development of Competencies in International Public Affairs," *Journal of Public Affairs* 3, no. 3 (March 2003), pp. 76–82.

Exhibit 20.B Excuse Me, There Is a Finger in My Chili!

On March 22, 2005, Denny Lynch, senior vice president for communications at Wendy's, one of the country's largest fast-food restaurant chains, received a shocking and unexpected call. A customer, Anna Ayala, claimed she had bitten down on a severed finger while eating a cup of chili purchased at a Wendy's restaurant in San Jose, California. Lynch knew that he had to act quickly, since this incident would certainly be the top story on the evening news and in the headlines of every major newspaper the next day. A public relations nightmare had emerged, and Lynch, on behalf of Wendy's, had to prepare a response. Within days Wendy's Northern California restaurants lost 20 to 50 percent of their normal business, estimating their losses at $1 million per day. "We need closure," said Lynch. "Until then, there is lingering doubt."

As an immediate response, the crisis management team from Wendy's regional headquarters in Sacramento, California, was assembled. Lynch also prepared a statement for the press, instructed the company's Web site to be frequently updated, and began coordinating with the San Jose police department which was already involved in the case. According to Lynch, "It went nonstop the next two or three days. Even when the Pope passed away, it still got coverage."

In the wake of the immediate crisis, Wendy's focused on trying to discover what had really happened. Through an internal investigation, Lynch learned that a 10-year veteran and trusted employee had prepared the chili for Ayala; he assured Lynch there was nothing improper in the food preparation. Wendy's also turned to the public and offered a $100,000 reward for information about the case.

Investigators initially were unsure if the finger came from a live or dead person. The finger's DNA did not match anything in the police computer files, and a search for the fingerprint failed to turn up a match in the FBI's 50-million-print database. Further, the police still had not determined if the finger had been cooked, and if so, for how long. A thoroughly cooked finger might indicate that it came through Wendy's food supply chain, but if uncooked, it was likely that the finger was added to the chili after preparation.

While Lynch and his team worked furiously around the clock to discover the truth, Ayala, the woman who had made the accusation, was a guest on numerous morning and late night television shows. Yet, it was soon discovered that Ayala had a litigious history that included a settlement for medical expenses for her daughter, who had claimed she became sick at an El Pollo Loco restaurant in Las Vegas.

The public-relations break Lynch and Wendy's needed occurred exactly one month after the initial incident, when Anna Ayala was arrested in her Las Vegas home for attempted grand larceny, accused of trying to extort $2.5 million from Wendy's. The finger in her chili was all a hoax. "The true victims are Wendy's owners and operators," said San Jose chief of police Rob Davis. Forensic evidence proved that the finger was not cooked at 170 degrees for three hours—the typical preparation of Wendy's chili. It was later discovered that Ayala acquired the finger through her husband's workplace, where a fellow worker had lost part of his finger in an industrial accident.

In September 2005, Ayala and her husband, Jaime Plascencia, pleaded guilty to attempted grand larceny and conspiring to file a false claim. Ayala was sentenced to 9 years in prison and her husband, who supplied the finger, was sentenced to 12 years and 4 months in prison.

Sources: "At CSI: Wendy's, Tracking a Gruesome Discovery," *The New York Times Online,* April 22, 2005, *www.nytimes.com;* "Finger in Chili Is Called Hoax; Las Vegas Women Is Charged," *The New York Times Online,* April 23, 2005, *www.nytimes.com;* and "Stiff Sentences for Wendy's Chili-finger Couple," *Bay City News,* January 18, 2006, *www.SFGate.com.*

a charge of sexual harassment, the filing of class-action lawsuits brought by injured customers, or something bizarre and unique such as the crisis that confronted Wendy's that is described in Exhibit 20.B. But crises by definition are often unique. To prepare for these unexpected events and sometimes tragedies, an organization must develop a crisis management plan.

Crisis management is the process organizations use to respond to short-term and immediate corporate crises. Some businesses or industries are more prone to corporate crises than others. According to the Institute for Crisis Management, medical and surgical manufacturers, pharmaceutical companies, and software manufacturers (because of the sophisticated technology found in their products and the potential for disruptive impact on consumers' lives), are at the top of a recent list of crisis-prone industries.

Often the corporate crisis quickly escalates, producing intense pressures and many suggestions about what the company should do or not do from outside experts, politicians, and observers. Unfortunately it is very costly to develop a strategic response once the crisis is upon the organization. Most experts recommend that organizations develop a crisis management plan ahead of time, citing the biblical wisdom: Noah started to build his ark before it began to rain.

According to experts, an effective crisis management plan must include these steps:

- *Prepare for action* by creating an internal communication system that can be activated the moment a crisis occurs. Key employees must be identified in advance so that they are ready to address the issue. Wendy's, for example (see Exhibit 20.B), already had plans to scramble their crisis management team into action well before the crisis emerged.

- *Communicate quickly, but accurately.* Honesty and full disclosure was at the forefront of the media announcements crafted by Denny Lynch of Wendy's. The media have excellent resources and will find the truth whether the organization speaks it or not. It is often best to take the offensive and be the first to comment on a situation affecting the organization, thus placing the organization in greater control.

- *Use the Internet* to convey the public affairs message to minimize the public's fears and provide assistance. In addition to face-to-face press releases, Wendy's frequently updated their company Web site to communicate to the public and its customers what the company was doing about the crisis situation.

- *Do the right thing.* Often the true test of an organization is how it reacts in a time of crisis. Public relations managers should not try to minimize the seriousness of a problem or make excuses. It is possible for the organization to accept responsibility without accepting liability. For example, Wendy's clearly expressed regret over its customers' fears and advised the public that it was doing everything possible to investigate.

- *Follow up* and, where appropriate, make amends to those affected. Seek to restore the organization's reputation. Wendy's relentless pursuit of the truth resulted in vindication for the company and assisted law enforcement in the prosecution of those making the false claims. With proper planning and effective implementation of a crisis management program, an organization may emerge from a crisis in a stronger condition.[8]

Media Training of Employees

Another important step businesses can take is to provide **media training** to executives and employees who are likely to have contact with the media. Media training is necessary because communicating with the media is not the same as talking with friends or co-workers.

---

[8] Adapted from Ronald J. Levine, "Weathering the Storm: Crisis Management Tips," *Metropolitan Corporate Counsel,* March 2002, pp. 3–4.

As a company representative, an employee is normally assumed to be speaking for the company or is expected to have special knowledge of company activities. Under these circumstances, the words one speaks take on a special, official meaning. In addition, news reporters sometimes challenge an executive, asking penetrating or potentially embarrassing questions and expecting instant answers. Even in more deliberate news interviews, the time available for responding to questions is limited to a few seconds. Moreover, facial expressions, the tone of one's voice, and body language can convey both positive and negative impressions.

Many large businesses routinely send a broad range of their employees to specific courses to improve their media skills. Media communication experts generally give their clients the following advice.

- Resist the temptation to see reporters and journalists as the enemy. Business spokespersons should build bridges with the media. Employees should resist avoiding the media and not withdraw into a shell of silence, which tends to generate suspicion that the company has something to hide.
- Employees should be instructed to keep the long-term reputation of the company in mind.
- Being open and honest is a successful media strategy. Honesty is the best policy, especially since media personnel will investigate to confirm all information a business provides and the truth will be uncovered.
- Businesses should make communications a priority and the training of the company spokesperson a critical and ongoing program.[9]

Ethical and Social Responsibilities of Public Relations Managers

Public relations managers often are challenged by various ethical and social issues. How they present their firm in the media, respond to stakeholder demands expressed through media channels, and adhere to ethical principles (or not) can influence how the public perceives public relations managers and more importantly the firms they represent. One such controversial ethical challenge, involving sponsorship contracts, is described in Exhibit 20.C. Some public relations managers and businesses embrace their ethical responsibilities; others appear slow in acknowledging that their increased power requires greater attention to their impact on society.

The **Public Relations Society of America** (PRSA) is a professional association of public relations officers committed to "the fundamental values of individual dignity and free exercise of human rights." The PRSA believes that "the freedom of speech, assembly, and the press are essential to the practice of public relations." In serving its clients' interests, the PRSA is dedicated to "the goals of better communication, understanding, and cooperation among diverse individuals, groups, and institutions of society." To this end, the PRSA adopted a Member Code of Ethics in 2000, replacing previous standards and codes for the industry in place since 1950. The new code presented six professional core values for its members and the public relations profession: advocacy, honesty, expertise, independence, loyalty, and fairness.[10]

---

[9] These guidelines and other suggestions are discussed in Mike Haggerty and Wallace Rasmussen, *The Headlines vs. The Bottom Line: Mutual Distrust between Business and the News Media* (Arlington, VA: The Freedom Forum First Amendment Center, 1994), pp. 89–92.

[10] Public Relations Society of America Web site, *www.prsa.org.*

Exhibit 20.C   Companies Stand by Troubled Athletes

When Kobe Bryant was arrested on charges of sexual assault in 2003, the public wondered if his company sponsors would stand by this athlete or if the negative publicity would cause Bryant's sponsors to distance themselves from the star and cancel their endorsement contracts based on his violation of the "morals clause." Bryant, who played for the L.A. Lakers basketball team, had endorsement deals with Nike, Coca-Cola, and McDonald's, and he was scheduled to earn $11 million to $13 million in 2003 from them. The Nike deal alone was worth $45 million over four years.

Other star athletes had faced similar criminal charges, and endorsers had been loyal to them during their troubled times. Reebok International stood by basketball player Allen Iverson when Iverson was charged with weapons violations after he allegedly barged into his cousin's apartment with a gun looking for his wife. A Reebok official noted, "Sales pretty much stayed consistent during and after the incident." Charges against Iverson were later dropped.

A few months before Bryant's encounter with the law, Reebok signed a sneaker endorsement with football player Ray Lewis. Lewis had pleaded guilty to a misdemeanor charge of obstruction of justice in a case stemming from the murder of two men in Atlanta. "Mr. Lewis has become a popular player and our people felt comfortable signing him," said Ron Rogers, a spokesperson for Reebok. In the two years after Bryant's arrest, the criminal charges were dismissed and a related civil suit was settled. Although McDonald's, Spaulding, and Coca-Cola dropped Bryant from their ads, Nike remained loyal to the basketball superstar and relaunched the Bryant-Nike ad campaign in 2005 after dramatically reducing the number of ads Bryant appeared in immediately following the 2003 arrest.

Sources: "Should Brands Bryant Endorses Keep Him On?" *The Wall Street Journal*, July 12, 2003, pp. B1, B7; and "Nike Relaunches Kobe Bryant after Two Years of Prep Work," *The Wall Street Journal Online*, November 11, 2005, *online.wsj.com.*

The importance of managers adhering to ethical principles and meeting social responsibilities when developing a solid public relations program or crisis management response cannot be emphasized enough, as businesses that have experienced media crises can attest. In some circumstances this may be a daunting task for businesses and their managers; but it is a critical one as business managers seek to deal with their public through the media.

Deceptive Advertising

The presentation of fair, balanced, and truthful information is a business necessity. Businesses are sometimes accused of misleading or lying to the public, often through the practice of deceptive advertising. *Deceptive advertising* occurs when an advertisement misleads the consumer by lying, withholding relevant information, or creating an unreasonable expectation. This deception often influences a consumer's purchasing decision. (Deceptive advertising is also discussed in Chapter 16.) Sometimes a competitor may accuse a firm of deception and seek help from an industry-created organization for action, as shown in the following example.

On the First Response Early Result Pregnancy Test's label it promised: "Use as early as three days before you expect your period" and "Over 99% accurate in laboratory testing." But Pfizer, the maker of a rival product, the e.p.t. Pregnancy Test, took issue with these claims and brought its challenge to the National Advertising Review Council (NARC). The NARC, often referred to as the advertising police, is an industry-created, self-regulating organization. Pfizer argued that First Response's claims ultimately could pose a health risk to those who are pregnant but, having tested negative, might think they are not. The NARC agreed with Pfizer and now First Response's label no longer makes those specific claims.[11]

Businesses are subject to legal challenges when engaging in false or deceptive advertisements as Sony Pictures experienced:

Sony Pictures regularly cited critic David Manning of the Ridgefield Press when promoting its latest movies. The critic praised Sony's *The Animal, Hollow Man, A Knight's Tale, The Patriot,* and *Vertical Limit* with various hyperbolic "greatest movie ever" quotes. The problem was that David Manning did not exist, or at least was never on the payroll at the Ridgefield Press, a small weekly newspaper in Connecticut. A class action lawsuit was filed against Sony Pictures and the company agreed to pay more than $1 million to settle the lawsuit in August 2005. The Reuters news agency accused Sony of "intentional and systematic deception of consumers."[12]

In addition to the courts, the Federal Trade Commission (FTC) serves as a public watchdog evaluating honesty in advertising. In some cases, the FTC will force a business that originally made the deceptive claims to voluntarily modify its advertisement.

The Federal Trade Commission launched an aggressive campaign against the advertisers of Blue Stuff, a pain-relief product. The FTC alleged that advertisements for the emu oil–based gel, priced at $60 for eight ounces, claimed without substantiation that it relieved severe pain. Threatened with legal action, Blue Stuff Inc. agreed to pay $3 million to settle the deceptive-advertising charges and to alter its future advertisement language.[13]

Following this embarrassment and other negative publicity, the pharmaceutical industry took significant steps to improve its image and the authenticity of its advertising message by agreeing to abide by voluntary guidelines governing advertising practices. Twenty-three companies, including the industry's largest firms, Bristol Myers Squibb, Johnson & Johnson, Merck, and Pfizer, adopted measures that called on companies to tone down hyped advertisement claims, more closely disclose drug risk, shift ads for adult products like Viagra to later television timeslots, and provide regulators a chance to view commercials before they are aired. These voluntary or self-regulatory marketing controls were part of the industry's overarching public relations campaign discussed earlier.

The relationship between government and business and their advertisement practices is quite different in other countries than in the United States. Exhibit 20.D describes how the Chinese government, in the absence of a constitutional right of free speech, controls advertisements and businesses' use of the media.

Free Speech

The ethical principle underlying the issue of deceptive advertising is one of free speech. The **free speech issue** is about how to find a balance between the constitutional right to free expression on the one hand and the need for trustworthiness of information used by stakeholders to make purchases, seek employment, and take other actions.

---

[11] "Marketers Increasingly Dispute Health Claims of Rivals' Products," *The Wall Street Journal,* April 4, 2002, pp. B1, B4.

[12] "Sony to Pay Upwards of $1 Million over Fake Critic Quotes," Institute for Global Ethics, *Ethics Newsline,* August 8, 2005, *www.globalethics.org.*

[13] "FTC Asks Media to Reject False Ads," *The Wall Street Journal,* November 20, 2002, pp. A3, A14.

The Chinese government has emerged as a watchdog over its country's firms and their media practices. Commonly referred to as the "propaganda czars," Chinese regulators of the State Administration for Radio, Film and Television (SARFT) prohibited television companies from having their shows' hosts wear orange-tinted hair, dress in too little or too weird clothes, or speak in trendy local dialects or Western slang.

In China all media are state owned and regarded as the *houshe*, or the throat and tongue, of the Communist Party. Therefore, all rules developed by SARFT are enforced as law. The new media regulations passed in 2004 toned down sex, violence, and racy content that were the hallmark of broadcast media everywhere else in the world and were becoming increasingly common in China. Specifically, the SARFT banned as offensive ads for feminine hygiene pads, hemorrhoid medication, and athlete's foot ointment during the three daily meal times. Only two beer ads per company could be shown between 7 p.m. and 9 p.m.

Many of these regulations were a reaction to creeping Western influence, especially in advertisements. "We hope the new regulations will set a distinct criterion for both domestic and overseas ad producers and effectively prevent the recurrence of commercials like the 'Chamber of Fear' [referring to Nike commercials featuring basketball star LeBron James]," explained a SARFT official. The Chamber of Fear campaign showed James battling and defeating a cartoon kung fu master and a pair of dragons, which some Chinese took as an allegory for the defeat of Chinese culture by the West.

Sources: "China Cracks Down on Commercials," *The Wall Street Journal,* February 19, 2004, p. B7; "China Takes Aim at Racy, Violent TV Shows," *The Wall Street Journal,* May 24, 2004, pp. B1, B3; and, "Chinese Regulators Draft New Advertising Rules," *The Wall Street Journal Online,* December 13, 2004, *online.wsj.com.*

The legal basis for the right of free speech in the United States lies in the 1st Amendment to the Constitution. The 1st Amendment states, in part, "Congress shall make no law . . . abridging the freedom of speech." State governments also are prohibited, under the due process clause of the 14th Amendment, from passing laws that impair free speech. Although these constitutional provisions are subject to continual interpretation and reinterpretation by government regulators, by the courts, and by general public opinion, their fundamental meaning does not change through time. Businesses, as legal citizens, have often relied upon the right to free speech when promoting their products through their advertisement campaigns. However, expressions of free speech in advertisements have led to numerous questions of good taste and respect for others as seen in the following example.

During the summer days of August 2003, drivers in Los Angeles were more distracted by the scenery than normal when Wellspring Media placed a billboard on Sunset Boulevard depicting a woman performing oral sex on a man. The billboard promoted the new movie *The Brown Bunny,* which had drawn criticisms for its portrayal of sex acts when previewed at the Cannes film festival earlier that year. The movie's actor and director, Vincent Gallo, explained, "This is my idea of a beautiful billboard—that's all it is." Complaints poured in as motorists and pedestrians passed by the offensive billboard, angry that it was in plain view for children and teenagers to see.[14]

The interpretation of free speech, or what is appropriate advertisement, varies around the globe. When Nike plastered more than 700 bus stops in Singapore with small, page-sized

---

[14] "Art? Smut? Commerce? Billboard Gets Attention," *New York Times Online,* August 4, 2004, *www.nytimes.com.*

posters featuring anime-style images of NBA star LeBron James, commuters and the government of Singapore were shocked. The advertisement campaign undertaken by Nike offended the public sense of cultural values. Typically public spaces are immaculate in Singapore, a country where the import and sale of chewing gum were once banned and fines can be levied on people who spit in public or forget to flush common toilets. Vandalism is especially taboo and the Nike campaign was seen as disrespectful to the Singapore culture.[15]

Marketing to Children

Beyond good taste and respect for cultural traditions, advertisers have been accused of being insensitive in their marketing of products to minors. The American Psychological Association (APA) has expressed grave concern over the effects of advertising on children. The APA estimated that more than 40,000 television commercials a year are targeted at children. Moreover, they argue that while "older children and adults understand the inherent bias of advertising, young children lack the mental skills to differentiate between straightforward content and biased ads."[16]

Recently appearing on the marketing scene has been a new method of promoting products, especially to children—*advergames*. **Advergames** are free online games that incorporate marketing promotions for products such as cookies, candy, cereal, chips and soda. Kraft's *Nabiscoworld.com* Web site, for example, featured advergames for 17 different product brands, from Ritz Bits Sumo Wrestling to Life Savers boardwalk bowling. The typical users of the advergames spend a half-hour on a game site, often replaying a single games 15 times or more.[17]

Food companies, particularly those that produce products aimed at children, responded to protests against advergames by forming the Alliance for American Advertising. The group included three of the largest food companies, General Mills, Kellogg, and Kraft Foods; these three firms alone accounted for a combined annual advertising budget of $380 million in the United States. The Alliance defended the industry's 1st Amendment right of free speech to advertise to children and promoted its willingness to police itself.

In addition, the Alliance disputed the contention that there was a link between advertising and childhood obesity (see also our discussion in Chapter 16). Marybeth Thorsgaard, General Mills' spokesperson, argued that instead of a ban on advertising to children of a certain age, "we talk about balanced moderation and exercise." Many food producers follow the self-regulatory standards put forth by the Children's Advertising Review Unit, an industry group that monitors children's advertising and is part of the Better Business Bureau. These guidelines state that food companies should advertise truthfully and accurately to children and should use appropriate messages that children can understand.

The debate over whether advertisements are a constitutionally protected right under the 1st amendment or may be deceptive practices that must be regulated will undoubtedly rage on for years. Caught in the middle of this heated discussion are the consumers, especially vulnerable children. Whatever path emerges, it is clear that business must recognize various ethical and social responsibilities when utilizing the media to market its products and services.

---

[15] "Graffiti-style Nike Ads Offend Some in Singapore," *The Wall Street Journal Online,* November 26, 2004, *online.wsj.com.*

[16] "Young Children Need Protection from TV Ads, Group Warns," Institute for Global Ethics, *Ethics Newsline,* March 1, 2004, *www.globalethics.org.*

[17] "Junk Food Games," *The Wall Street Journal,* May 3, 2004, pp. B1, B4.

Special Issue: Government Regulation of Tobacco Advertising

We have discussed government's role in regulating businesses' use of the media to market their products and services. A related issue that has garnered much public attention is tobacco advertising. Should tobacco advertising—particularly ads aimed at underage smokers—be regulated or even banned by the government?

Various stakeholder groups over the years have challenged tobacco advertising. Some believe that children have been unfairly targeted as a vulnerable consumer group, and cite the use of cartoon characters such as Joe Camel. Others believe that the health care costs for smokers incurred by society are unfair and have been aggravated by tobacco advertisements. The tobacco industry has countered with the argument that the firms market a legal product to adults, so tobacco ads should not be restricted by laws or regulation. Most tobacco executives have publicly agreed that selling to children is wrong and the use of advertisements targeting youth sales should be stopped.

In 1998, the National Association of Attorneys General (NAAG), a national organization of the 50 states' chief lawyers, and the tobacco industry's largest companies reached a settlement that resulted in significant restrictions of the industry's use of the media to market products. The landmark agreement called for firms in the tobacco industry to prohibit all advertising that targeted youth; to ban all use of cartoons in advertising; to prohibit advertising tobacco brand names at all concerts, youth sporting events, or any athletic event between opposing teams; to eliminate all outdoor and transit advertisements; to stop marketing through logos on clothing; and to require tobacco companies to affirm their commitment to comply with this agreement by designating an executive-level manager to identify methods to reduce youth access to and the incidence of youth consumption of tobacco products, and to encourage their employees to become involved in efforts toward reducing youth consumption of tobacco products.[18]

In the years following the landmark agreement, some positive effects were seen. A national "truth" campaign against youth smoking funded largely by the tobacco industry was launched by the American Legacy Foundation in 2000. A few years later the Foundation reported that about 300,000 children were prevented from becoming smokers. "These truth campaign ads are the MTV of the public health world. They really get to these kids," said Joseph A. Califano, Jr., chairman of Citizens' Commission to Protect the Truth.[19] These public service announcements were in addition to the ban on advertising tobacco products. While some cigarette manufacturers were complying with the 1998 NAAG agreement, others were not.

In 2002 a California judge ruled that R. J. Reynolds Tobacco had indirectly targeted youths with magazines ads for Camel and other cigarettes in violation of the 1998 agreement. Reynolds was accused of exposing young people to tobacco advertising at levels very similar to those targeting adult smokers by placing ads in *Sports Illustrated*, which has a substantial number of youth readers. The judge ordered Reynolds to change its advertising practices and pay a $20 million penalty.[20]

[18] Master Settlement Agreement, National Association of Attorneys General, *www.naag.org/tobac.*

[19] "Study: Anti-Smoking Campaign Is Helping," *Newsday Online*, February 24, 2005, *www.newsday.com.*

[20] "Judge Rules Reynolds Ads Reach Too Many Kids, Violating '98 Pact," *The Wall Street Journal*, June 7, 2002, pp. A3, A5.

Philip Morris received significant negative publicity when it released a report analyzing the economic impact of smokers on the Czech Republic economy. The economic analysis celebrated the "positive effects" of smoking on Czech's national finances, including revenues from excise and other taxes on cigarettes and "healthcare costs savings due to early mortality." Ten days later, Philip Morris publicly apologized for the report. Five months later, Philip Morris changed its name to the Altria Group.[21]

Government efforts to regulate the tobacco industry have occurred in many countries. For example, in 2002, the European Union health ministers voted to outlaw most tobacco advertising. The ban included tobacco ads in print, on radio and on the Internet within the 15 EU nations by July 2005. However, the EU law did allow tobacco companies to advertise in cinemas and on billboards.[22] Other national efforts to limit or prohibit tobacco advertising emerged, leading to a coordinated global effort against tobacco advertisement sponsored by the World Health Organization.

> In 2005 the world's first antismoking treaty came into force despite years of opposition by the world's tobacco companies. The treaty, known as the Framework Convention on Tobacco Control (FCTC), was signed by 168 countries as of May 2006. The ratifying countries were obligated to establish strict health warnings on cigarettes and ban tobacco advertising and sponsorship. Misleading marketing terms, like light and mild, were outlawed and efforts needed to be made to reduce exposure to second-hand smoke. African and Asian countries were among the strongest supporters of the treaty in the hope that it would provide them with leverage to combat the tobacco industries' growing quest of the youth market in the developing world. Douglas Bettcher, coordinator of the FCTC, explained "the underlying reason that a binding piece of international law was required is that the world community was faced and appalled by the mushrooming number of needless deaths due to tobacco related diseases."[23]

As business acquires more and more power when using the media to market its products and services and promote its image, it also must accept greater responsibility when wielding this power. Whether the ethical issue is deception in advertisements or concern for vulnerable populations, business must recognize and address its ethical and social responsibilities. Likewise, the media industry must focus on its responsibilities regarding decency, equality, and fair and balanced presentation of an issue when conducting its business.

Ethical and Social Responsibility in the Media Industry

The media, itself, is a profit-making industry, subject to ethical and social responsibilities just as other businesses are. The media must be attentive to issues of decency in broadcasting, diversity in the portrayal of women and minorities, and the presentation of a fair and balanced view of the issues.

The issue of decency in the media has a storied history, often promoting government regulation of what is seen or heard or the imposition of fines for content found in broadcasting.

---

[21] "Philip Morris Notes Cigarettes' Benefits for Nation's Finances," *The Wall Street Journal*, July 16, 2001, pp. A2, A16; "Philip Morris Says It's Sorry for Death Report," *The Wall Street Journal*, July 26, 2001, pp. B1, B6; and "Philip Morris Seeks to Mold Its Image into an Altria State," *The Wall Street Journal*, November 16, 2001, pp. A3, A6.

[22] "EU Health Ministers Bar Most Tobacco Ads," *The Wall Street Journal*, December 3, 2002, p. A15.

[23] "57 Counties Sign On to Anti-Smoking Treaty," *ABC Online–Australia*, February 27, 2005, *www.abc.net.au.*

In 1969, the U.S. Supreme Court ruled that free-speech protections for broadcasters were narrower than those for publishers. In 1978 the Supreme Court upheld the Federal Communications Commission's ban on comedian George Carlin's "seven dirty words" and other indecencies heard on the radio or television. The Court also focused on television programming "when there is a reasonable risk that children may be in the audience." A federal appeals court validated the Supreme Court broader FCC indecency ban in 1995, but limited the focus to between 6:00 a.m. and 10:00 p.m. Therefore, most adult-content programming was moved to the 10:00 p.m. timeslot when most children would be asleep in bed.

Despite the government's rulings and concerns over sexual material on television, a Kaiser Family Foundation report in 2005 stated that 70 percent of all television shows included some sexual content, citing popular shows such as "Desperate Housewives" and "The O.C." The report stated that the number of sexual scenes on television nearly doubled from 3.2 scenes per hour in 1998 to 5 scenes per hour by 2005. Popular shows with teens had an ever higher average number of sexual scenes—6.7 per hour.[24]

The government regulators have attempted to crack down on indecency. Clear Channel Communications, one of the largest U.S. radio station chains, reached an agreement with the FCC to pay an estimated $1.75 million in penalties. This settlement was in part to settle complaints of indecency lodged against Howard Stern's radio program, carried by Clear Channel. The largest previous penalty assessed by the FCC was against Infinity Broadcasting in 1995, when the company agreed to pay $1.7 million to settle complaints also related to Stern's radio show. Penalties also were assessed for violations of television programming regulations.

Viacom and Walt Disney Company agreed to pay $1.5 million to settle accusations lodged by the FCC that the firms violated limits on the use of advertising during children's programming. Under FCC rules, only 10½ minutes of commercials can be shown during each hour of programming intended for children on weekends and 12 minutes per hour during the week. A spokesperson for Viacom's Nickelodeon claimed that the company miscounted some of its one-minute commercials as one instead of two, as the FCC requires. The Disney fines were due to a violation of an FCC rule that prohibits advertising certain products on particular shows. In the Disney case, an ad for the Beyblade game was aired on the children's Beyblade show. An ABC spokesperson, Disney's parent company, explained that a computer system failed to identify the children's programs as restricted from certain commercials and the ads were aired unintentionally.[25]

The FFC gave out one of its largest fines in March 2006, when 111 television stations were fined $3.6 million. The FCC charged that the airing of an episode of "Without a Trace" in December 2004, which depicted teenage characters participating in a sexual orgy, violated decency standards. CBS defended the episode saying that "it contained an important and socially relevant storyline warning parents to exercise greater supervision of their teenage children." CBS intended to appeal the FCC fine.[26]

---

[24] "Study Says Sex Pervasive on TV in Shows Popular with Teens," *Pittsburgh Post-Gazette*, November 10, 2005, p. A15.

[25] "Viacom and Disney to Pay $1.5 Million for Violating FCC Rules," *The New York Times Online*, October 22, 2004, www.nytimes.com.

[26] "TV Stations Fined over CBS Show Deemed to Be Indecent," *The New York Times Online*, March 16, 2006, www.nytimes.com.

The active monitoring of indecent gestures, language, and activities on television shows by the FCC caused the industry to develop self-regulatory practices. For example, after the 2004 Super Bowl wardrobe scandal, CBS instituted a 10-second delay during the Final Four NCAA basketball tournament to avoid the possibility of foul language being captured on air during the games. The Fox network hired additional staff to serve as standard watchers to ensure that FCC standards were met during live reality shows such as "American Idol" and "My Big Fat Obnoxious Fiancé." After the infamous kisses during the airing of the 2003 MTV's Video Music Awards between Madonna and Britney Spears and Madonna and Christina Aguilera, the network announced it would have an audio and video delay for future programs. Other networks have changed their programming to include more family shows and content.

Comcast Communications, American's top cable provider, unveiled a family-friendly programming lineup for 2006 in response to pressure to steer clear of sex and violence on TV. This move was followed by Time Warner, the number two cable provider. Subscribers to these cable companies could select channels from a "family-tier" plan, including cable channels that catered to children programming such as the Disney Channel, Toon Disney, and Discovery Kids, as well as other channels such as CNN Headlines News, the Food Network and the Weather Channel. Comcast's package also included Nickelodeon, the highest-rated cable channel for children.[27]

Despite the television industry's efforts at self-regulation, President Bush signed the Broadcast Decency Law in June 2006. Under the law, broadcasters faced a maximum fine of $325,000 per incident, 10 times the previous limit. Bush explained, "Unfortunately, in recent years, broadcast programming has too often pushed the bounds of decency. The language is becoming coarser during the times when it's more likely that children will be watching television. It's a bad trend, a bad sign."[28]

Portrayal of Diversity in the Media

Another important issue facing the media industry is whether various groups in society are portrayed in a biased or discriminatory light. Are ethnic groups cast as second-class citizens? Are women portrayed only in subservient roles on certain shows?

Although the United States is a multicultural and ethnically diverse country, film and television images often tell a different story. While television programming made some steps toward greater diversity in the characters shown during prime time, there were few shows featuring an all-African-American or all-Latino cast. Actor J. Anthony Brown said, "We are living in the days of reality television, which has taken the place of the comedy. For a black show to make it, it has to come out of the box with some killer numbers [high-viewer ratings]. The networks don't have a lot of patience." Others take a harsher view of television programming when it comes to featuring minorities. Latino television creator and producer Dennis Leoni said, "We don't get the advertising, the marketing or the good time slots. All the resources seem to go toward the mainstream shows."[29]

ABC television did respond to pressure from minority groups to cancel *Welcome to the Neighborhood*, a reality show that would have white suburban families living on a Texas cul-de-sac decide which of the seven families, including one black,

---

[27] "Comcast to Offer Family Lineup with Nickelodeon and Religion," *The Wall Street Journal Online*, December 23, 2005, *online.wsj.com*.

[28] "Bush Signs Broadcast Decency Law," *Billboard.Biz*, June 15, 2006, *www.billboard.biz*.

[29] "Fewer Minorities Seen in Prime-time Shows," *Pittsburgh Post-Gazette*, June 3, 2004, p. B6.

Exhibit 20.E   Gender Bias in the Media

A Canadian media watchdog organization, Child & Family Canada, looked at how men were portrayed in video games, a $15-billion-a-year industry. It found "Video games, more than any other medium, promote male dominator, racist behavior as glamorous and erotic, the only possible response and the essential requirement for winning."

Child & Family Canada also looked at gender portrayal on television, particularly in commercials. It reported that commercial television suggested the women in this society were almost always young, white, large-breasted, and mainly preoccupied with how they looked and what they wore. They were dependent on men for approval and protection; they were largely seen as caregivers and nurturers, rarely as initiators and leaders. They also tended to be helpless victims of violence, which often was sexual in nature.

On the other hand, men were rarely vulnerable and seldom showed their feelings. They were usually in control, preoccupied with fast cars, prone to drinking beer with their buddies, and used weapons. They most often were the "voice of authority," selling products or providing information.

The stereotyping of genders in the media extended to children as well. Girls were shown as passive; they were preoccupied with their appearance and played with dolls rather than computers or video games. Boys were more active, frequently aggressive, cared more about sports and war games, and had only male friends.

Source: Meg Hogarth, "We Are What We Watch: Challenging Sexism and Violence In the Media," *Child & Family Canada, www.cfc-efc.ca/docs.*

one Asian, one Hispanic, and one gay couple, would move into their community. Critics of the show said it violated the letter and certainly the spirit of fair housing laws. According to those who previewed early episodes of the series, some members of the white families made disparaging remarks about the ethnicity, religion, and ancestry of the prospective neighbors. "I'm elated," said Shanna Smith of the show's cancellation. "There'll be no copycat shows by the other networks. Also, ABC understands there are civil rights issues and understands the implications."[30]

Women are often portrayed only as the weaker sex, or submissive to men. However, the recent record is mixed. Contrary to many negative examples of women in advertisements, some ads show women as strong, able characters. In a 1978 ad for Enjoli perfume, a woman sang, "I can bring home the bacon, fry it up in a pan, and never, never, never let you forget you're a man." A few years later, Virginia Slims cigarette ads featured the tagline "You've come a long way, baby."

Recently, the advertising industry has increasingly used everyday women in advertisements rather than super thin, super tall models. Unilever, producers of the Dove line of personal-care products, introduced a "campaign for real beauty," which presented six women, none of them models, sizes 4 to 12, smiling in their underwear. The company spokesperson commented, "these ads show women as they are rather than as some believe they ought to be." Nike introduced a humorous and honest campaign showing and accepting parts of the body that were almost never seen in ads. One ad began boldly, "My butt is big," and featured an oversized photograph of a women's derriere. Other ads declared, "I have thunder thighs." However, sexist representations of women (and men) in the media often prevail. The issue as seen from a Canadian watchdog group is presented in Exhibit 20.E.

[30] "ABC Drops Show after Complaints by Civil Rights Groups," *The New York Times Online*, June 30, 2005, *www.nytimes.com.*

The Fairness and Balance Issue

The media is often in a position to portray business in a good or bad light, affecting a firm's image. The **fairness and balance issue** is about how the media reports business activities. Since the 1970s, probusiness organizations have claimed that the coverage of business activities generally has been unfair to business. In addition, business leaders believe that the media does not provide viewers with enough information to make rational decisions about controversial issues, such as the transportation of toxic wastes or the need for product recalls. Many reasons are given for this tension between business and the media. One reason for inadequate media business reports is that few reporters are well trained in financial and business matters, a reality that many media people acknowledge. Another reason sometimes given is that most journalists tend to be left leaning in their social and political outlook, although this notion is disputed and not proved.

Some television shows featuring controversial topics attempt to ensure that both liberal and conservative viewpoints are presented. From 1949 to 1987, the Federal Communications Commission (FCC) was entrusted with enforcing the **Fairness Doctrine**, which required television and radio broadcasters to cover both sides of important or controversial issues and to give the opportunity for contrasting viewpoints to be aired. The Fairness Doctrine gave the FCC authority to rule on the fairness of broadcasts. This law was repealed in 1987. The media today is sometimes characterized as being divided on a conservative or liberal basis and reflecting the partisan atmosphere of the times, although the networks and some cable shows argue they are objective or try to be.

The question of whether the media fairly portrays businesses and executives was the focus of a study undertaken by Pinnacle Worldwide.

Pinnacle Worldwide, an independent public relations firm headquartered in Minneapolis, reported differences in opinions between business and media executives. The firm discovered that business executives rated their ethical behavior as an 80 on a 100-point scale, while media leaders gave business executives an ethics rating of 30 points. Other sharp discrepancies were found in the study. For example, the study asked: "To what degree do you believe that ethical issues always are part of the final decision-making process in multinational companies?" Business executives gave the question an average of 80 points (with 100 points being "always"), while media leaders rated business executives at 30 points on this question.

Pinnacle Worldwide advised businesses to seek out or generate opportunities to communicate their values and principles through the news media. "Too many businesses appear to be taking an ostrich position," said Jerry Klein, president of Pinnacle Worldwide. "By burying their heads in the sand, they leave the rest of their operations vulnerable to misunderstanding and misinformation. The new media plays a vital role in communicating information."[31]

While business may seek to better manage its portrayal in the media, the media is a business, too, and thus must always face its social responsibilities to maintain decency in its broadcasts, depict women and minorities in an unbiased light, and present a fair and balanced view of important issues, including business issues, found in society.

---

[31] "'Yes, We Are' . . . 'No, You're Not' Survey Shows Corporate Executives, Media Differ Markedly on Opinions of Ethical Behavior in Business," *Pinnacle Worldwide News Release*, December 1998, *www.pinnacleww.com/survey-ethics*.

Summary

- Business and its stakeholders are best served when business managers recognize their professional responsibilities in administering a proactive public relations and crisis management plan.

- Business can effectively manage a crisis situation by preparing for the crisis before it occurs, coordinating its interactions with the media, and always doing the right thing under pressure.

- Young people seem particularly vulnerable to violations of decency through exposure to violence and sex found in television programs, films, and video games. Various governmental and self-regulatory efforts have tried to address this issue.

- The World Health Organization has joined with several national government campaigns to regulate the tobacco industry's use of print, radio, and television ads.

- The media is doing a better job representing diverse ethnic groups and providing gender balance in broadcasting, but some stereotyping remains.

Key Terms

advergames, *439*
corporate crisis, *432*
crisis management, *434*
fairness and balance
issue, *445*

Fairness Doctrine, *445*
free speech issue, *437*
media, *429*
media training, *434*
public relations, *430*

Public Relations Society
of America, *435*

Internet Resources

www.cfc-efc.ca
www.prsa.org
www.prwatch.org
www.ftc.gov
www.asianmediawatchdog.com
www.mediaissues.com

Child & Family Canada
Public Relations Society of America
PR Watch
U.S. Federal Trade Commission
Asian Media Watchdog
Media Issues

Discussion Case: *"Grand Theft Auto": Honest Mistake or Intentional Indecency?*

In July 2005 the media reported that the popular videogame "Grand Theft Auto: San Andreas" contained sexually explicit hidden scenes. The discovery prompted an immediate investigation by the video game industry's Entertainment Software Ratings Board (ESRB) and the Federal Trade Commission. According to ESRB executive Patricia Vance, "what was clear to us is the fact that fully rendered content existed on the [Grand Theft Auto: San Andreas] disk that was not disclosed. The publisher took the risk that a hacker could find it and it clearly put the rating at risk." The ESRB quickly changed the game's rating from M (for Mature, 17 years and older) to Adults Only, seriously curtailing future sales since the primary customers for the game were teenage boys. Some retailers, notably Wal-Mart, Target, and Best Buy, announced that they would pull the product from their shelves, in keeping with their company policy of not marketing adult-content video games.

The scenes in question were hidden from regular viewing but available through a "mod" (short for modifications), a portion of the game that in the case of the "Grand Theft Auto" game could be unlocked by a third-party Internet download. Mods are commonly placed within the games intentionally by the manufacturer as an added thrill for loyal game players. They can include features such as super-powerful weapons or hidden celebrity interviews. Mods may also include unauthorized content created by independent programmers. Game makers usually welcome mods, since they can extend the shelf life and revenue of game titles.

Take-Two Interactive, producers of "Grand Theft Auto: San Andreas," initially claimed the newly exposed scenes were postproduction mods developed by a third party without authorization by the company. Later Take-Two Interactive admitted that the game was built with the scenes buried in the company's own content, not unexpectedly inserted into the game by the independent programmers. However, the company further explained that the scenes were left over from earlier drafts of "Grand Theft Auto" and were never intended for public viewing.

The "Grand Theft Auto" mod was called "hot coffee," since it allowed characters in the game to invite other characters into their homes for hot coffee and sex. Dutch programmer Patrick Wildenborg, whose mod allowed users to view explicit sexual scenes in "Grand Theft Auto," defended his programming. "My mod does not introduce anything to the game. All the content that is shown was already present."

The industry self-regulatory group and the government disagreed, and the PlayStation2 version of "Grand Theft Auto: San Andreas," which was the top-selling game in 2004 with nearly 6 million units sold, retained its Adults Only rating. ESRB's Patricia Vance said Take-Two Interactive's release of the explicit scenes in "Grand Theft Auto: San Andreas" without disclosing all content had seriously undermined the credibility of the ESRB's rating system.

Sources: "'Grand Theft Auto' Maker Denies Hiding Sex Scenes in Video Game," Institute for Global Ethics, *Ethics Newsline*, July 18, 2005, *www.globalethics.com*; "Video Game Hit with 'Adults Only' Rating for Hidden Sex Scenes," Institute for Global Ethics, *Ethics Newsline*, July 25, 2005, www.globalethics.com; and "Guess What's Hiding in Your Videogame," *The Wall Street Journal Online*, July 26, 2005, *online.wsj.com*.

Discussion Questions

1. Did Take-Two Interactive cross over the line of decency by having sexually explicit scenes accessible for players of a game via download? If this type of content is commonplace in video games today, does that excuse the company's actions?

2. Do companies have an ethical obligation to ensure that sexual content does not get into the hands of youth, or it is simply an issue of marketing to teenagers what they want to see?

3. How effective were the video game industry's self-regulatory standards, especially when content was hidden from those evaluating the content and providing a rating? What can be done to make these self-regulatory ratings more accurate?

4. Is government regulation needed to better protect teenagers from sexually explicit content as found in the "Grand Theft Auto: San Andreas" game? If so, what steps should regulators take?

Cases in Business and Society

The Collapse of Enron

On December 2, 2001, Enron Corporation filed for bankruptcy. The company's sudden collapse—the largest business failure in U.S. history to date—came as a shock to many. Just months earlier, *Fortune* magazine had named Enron the most innovative company in America for the sixth consecutive year. The Houston, Texas–based firm, ranked seventh on the Fortune 500, was widely considered to be the premier energy trading company in the world. At its peak in 2000, Enron employed 19,000 people and booked annual revenues in excess of $100 billion. At a meeting of executives in January 2001, chairman and CEO Kenneth Lay had said the company's mission was no longer just to be the world's greatest energy company; rather, its mission was to become simply "the world's greatest company."[1]

The pain caused by Enron's abrupt failure was widely felt. The company immediately laid off 4,000 employees, with more to follow. Thousands of Enron employees and retirees saw the value of their 401(k) retirement plans, many heavily invested in the company's stock, become worthless almost overnight. "We, the rank and file, got burned," said one retiree, who lost close to $1.3 million in savings. "I thought people had to treat us honestly and deal fairly with us. In my neck of the woods, what happened is not right."[2] Shareholders and mutual fund investors lost $70 billion in market value. Two banks—J. P. Morgan Chase and Citigroup—faced major write-downs on bad loans. Not only did Enron creditors, shareholders, and bondholders lose out, confidence also fell across the market, as investors questioned the integrity of the financial statements of other companies in which they held stock.

In the aftermath, many struggled to unravel the messy story behind Enron's collapse. Congressional committees initiated investigations, prosecutors brought criminal charges against Enron executives and their accountants for obstruction of justice and securities fraud, and institutional investors sued to recoup their losses. Some blamed Arthur

By Anne T. Lawrence. Copyright © 2003 by the author. All rights reserved. Sources for this case include articles appearing in *The Wall Street Journal, The New York Times, BusinessWeek, Fortune, Houston Chronicle, Newsweek, Time,* and *U.S. News & World Report.* Primary documents consulted include various Enron annual reports; "Report of the Investigation by the Special Investigative Committee of the Board of Directors of Enron Corp.," February 1, 2002 (the Powers Committee Report); William S. Lerach and Milberg Weiss Bershad Hynes & Lerach LLP, "In Re: Enron Corporation Securities Litigation" (consolidated complaint for violation of the securities laws), 2002; and transcripts of hearings before the U.S. House of Representatives Committee on Financial Services and Committee on Energy and Commerce and the U.S. Senate Committee on Governmental Affairs and Committee on Commerce, Science, and Transportation. Secondary sources consulted include Peter C. Fusaro and Ross M. Miller, *What Went Wrong at Enron* (Hoboken, NJ: John Wiley & Sons, 2002); Robert Bryce, *Pipe Dreams: Greed, Ego, and the Death of Enron* (New York: PublicAffairs/Perseus Books, 2002); Malcolm S. Salter, Lynne C. Levesque, and Maria Ciampa, "The Rise and Fall of Enron," unpublished paper, Harvard Business School, April 10, 2002; and Mark Jickling, "The Enron Collapse: An Overview of Financial Issues," Congressional Research Service, February 4, 2002.

[1] "Enron's Last Year: Web of Details Did Enron In As Warnings Went Unheeded," *The New York Times,* February 10, 2002. Revenue data are from Enron's 2000 Annual Report.

[2] "Enron's Collapse: Audacious Climb to Success Ended in Dizzying Plunge," *The New York Times,* January 13, 2002.

Andersen, Enron's accounting firm, for certifying financial statements that arguably had wrongfully concealed the company's precarious financial situation; some blamed the board of directors for insufficient oversight. Others pointed to a go-go culture in which self-dealing by corrupt executives was condoned, or even admired, while others faulted government regulators, industry analysts, and the media for failing to uncover the company's weaknesses. It would likely take years for the courts to sort through the wreckage.

Enron Corporation

Enron Corporation was formed in 1985 through a merger of Houston Natural Gas and InterNorth of Omaha, Nebraska. The union created a midsized firm whose main asset was a large network of natural gas pipelines. The company's core business was distributing natural gas to utilities.

The central figure from the outset of Enron's history was Kenneth L. Lay. The son of a Baptist minister from rural Missouri, Lay trained as an economist at the University of Missouri and the University of Houston and briefly taught college-level economics. After a stint with Exxon, Lay accepted a post in the Nixon administration, serving in the Federal Energy Commission and, later, in the Interior Department as deputy undersecretary for energy. Following the Watergate scandal, Lay returned to the private sector in 1974, taking the first in a series of executive positions at various energy companies. Lay became CEO of Houston Natural Gas in 1984, and he assumed the top job at Enron in 1986, shortly after the merger. One observer described Lay as a man of "considerable charm, homespun roots, and economic expertise" who tended to play an "outside" role, leaving the day-to-day management of his company in the hands of others.[3]

A strong proponent of free markets, Lay felt that the deregulation of the 1980s presented an opportunity for the fledgling company. Historically, the U.S. energy industry had been highly regulated. Utilities were granted monopolies for specific regions, and regulators controlled the prices of electricity and natural gas. Pipeline operators could transport only their own natural gas, not that of other producers. In the 1980s, however, a series of legislative actions at both federal and state levels removed many of these restrictions. For the first time, energy producers were free to compete, buy and sell at market prices, and use each other's distribution networks. The promise of deregulation, touted by lawmakers at the time, was that competition would lead to greater efficiencies, lower prices, and better service for consumers.

Deregulation caused problems for both producers and users of energy, however, because prices for the first time became highly volatile. In the past, energy users (an industrial company or regional utility, for example) could buy extra natural gas or electricity from producers on the spot market on an as-needed basis. Once prices were free to fluctuate, however, this approach became riskier for both parties. The customer did not want to be forced to buy when prices were high, and the producer did not want to be forced to sell when prices were low.

Enron moved to provide an ingenious solution: The company would leverage its large network of pipelines to set up a "gas bank" that would act as the intermediary in this transaction, reducing market risk. Enron would sign contracts with producers to buy their gas on a certain date at a certain price and other contracts with users to sell them gas on a certain date at a certain price. Presuming that both parties were willing to pay a slight premium to insure against risk, Enron could make money on the spread. Enron

---

[3] Fusaro and Miller, *What Went Wrong*, p. 9.

had clear advantages as a market maker in natural gas: It owned pipelines that could be used to transport the product from producer to user, and it had strong institutional knowledge of how markets in the industry operated.

The idea man behind this innovation was Jeffrey Skilling. A graduate of the Harvard Business School and a partner in the consulting firm McKinsey & Company, Skilling had been brought in by Lay in the late 1980s to advise Enron on the company's response to deregulation. The gas bank, in itself, was a clever idea, but Skilling went further. He developed a series of other products, called energy derivatives, for Enron's trading partners. These products included *options,* which allowed companies to buy gas in the future at a fixed price, and *swaps,* which allowed them to trade fixed prices for floating prices and vice versa. In 1990, Skilling left McKinsey to become CEO of Enron Gas Services, as the gas bank came to be known. In 1996, he was promoted to the position of president and chief operating officer of Enron and, in February 2001, to CEO.[4]

We Make Markets

Enron's core gas services division was highly profitable, but by the mid-1990s its growth had begun to level out, as competitors entered the market and both buyers and sellers became more sophisticated and thus able to drive harder bargains. The challenge, as Skilling saw it, was to maintain Enron's growth by extending the business model that had worked so well in natural gas into a range of other commodities. As he later explained this strategy to an interviewer: "If you have the same general [market] characteristics, all you have to do is change the units. Enron has a huge investment in capabilities that can be deployed instantly into new markets at no cost."[5]

In particular, Skilling sought to trade commodities in industries with characteristics similar to those of natural gas—ones that were undergoing deregulation, had fragmented markets, maintained dedicated distribution channels, and in which both buyers and sellers wanted flexibility.[6]

- *Electricity.* One of the most obvious markets for Enron to enter was electric power. Deregulation of electric utilities in many states—most notably, California—presented an opportunity for Enron to use its trading capabilities to buy and sell contracts for electricity. Enron already owned some gas-fired power plants, and it moved to build and buy facilities designed to supply electricity during periods of peak demand. Enron also moved to expand this business internationally, especially in nations undergoing energy deregulation or privatization.

- *Water.* In 1998, Enron acquired Wessex Water in the United Kingdom and changed its name to Azurix, with the ambitious goal of operating water and wastewater businesses globally.

- *Broadband.* The company formed Enron Broadband Services in January 2000. Portland General Electric, which Enron acquired in 1997, provided the core fiber optic network for this service. The idea was to supply customers with access to bandwidth

---

[4] Enron's early history is described in two cases, "Enron: Entrepreneurial Energy," Harvard Business School case 700-079, and "Enron's Transformation: From Gas Pipelines to New Economy Powerhouse," Harvard Business School case 9-301-064.

[5] Darden School of Business videotape, May 25, 2001, cited in Joseph Bower and David Garvin, "Enron's Business and Strategy," unpublished paper, Harvard Business School, April 10, 2002.

[6] Salter, Levesque, and Ciampa, "The Rise and Fall," pp. 12–13.

at future dates at guaranteed prices. Enron believed these contracts would appeal to customers who did not want to rely on the public Internet or build their own telecommunications networks.

• *Pulp, paper, and lumber.* Enron launched *clickpaper.com,* an online market for the purchase of contracts for the delivery of wood products, and bought a newsprint company to ensure a ready source of supply.

Skilling told an interviewer from "Frontline" in March 2001: "We are looking to create open, competitive, fair markets. And in open, competitive, fair markets, prices are lower and customers get better service. . . . We are the good guys. We are on the side of the angels."[7]

By 2001, Enron was buying and selling metals, pulp and paper, specialty chemicals, bandwidth, coal, aluminum, plastics, and emissions credits, among other commodities. At the height of its power, 1,500 traders housed in Enron's office tower in Houston were trading 1,800 different products. As *The New York Times* later noted in an editorial, Enron was widely viewed as "a paragon of American ingenuity, a stodgy gas pipeline company that had reinvented itself as a high-tech clearinghouse in an ever-expanding roster of markets."[8] Reflecting the general enthusiasm, Skilling replaced his automobile vanity license plate, which had read WLEC (World's Largest Energy Company) with WMM (We Make Markets).[9]

Insisting on Results

In his 1999 letter to shareholders, Lay described the company's attitude toward its employees this way: "Individuals are empowered to do what they think is best. . . . We do, however, keep a keen eye on how prudent they are. . . . We insist on results."[10]

Enron used a recruitment process designed to hire individuals who were smart, hardworking, and intensely loyal. The company preferred to hire recent graduates. After an initial screening interview, candidates were brought to the Houston office for a "Super Saturday," during which they were individually interviewed for 50 minutes by eight interviewers, with only 10-minute breaks between interviews.

Even candidates who survived this strenuous hiring process, however, could not count on job security. Within the company, management used a "rank and yank" system in which new recruits were ranked every six months, and the 15 or 20 percent receiving the lowest scores were routinely terminated. Enron's highly competitive and results-oriented culture "created an environment," in the words of one observer, "where most employees were afraid to express their opinions or to question unethical and potentially illegal business practices."[11]

On the other hand, employees were encouraged to take initiative and were handsomely rewarded when their efforts paid off. Louise Kitchen, chief of the European gas trading unit, for example, organized a team to develop an online trading system. When it was adopted as the basis for a companywide division, Kitchen was promoted to president of Enron Online.

---

[7] "Enron's Many Strands: The Company Unravels; Enron Buffed Image Even As It Rotted from Within," *The New York Times,* February 10, 2002.

[8] "The Rise and Fall of Enron" [Editorial], *The New York Times,* November 2, 2001.

[9] Fusaro and Miller, *What Went Wrong,* p. 70.

[10] 1999 Enron Annual Report.

[11] Fusaro and Miller, *What Went Wrong,* p. 52. Enron's "rank and yank" system is described in Malcolm Gladwell, "The Talent Myth," *The New Yorker,* September 16, 2002.

Exhibit 1 **Top Executive Compensation, 2000**

	Base Salary	Bonus	Other	Stock Options	Total	Stock Options as % of Total
Lay	1.3	7.0	.4	123.4	132.1	93
Skilling	.9	5.6	—	62.5	69.0	91

Note: All figures are in millions of dollars, rounded to the nearest $100,000. "Stock options" represents stock options exercised and sold in 2000, *not* granted in 2000. These figures do not include the value of perquisites, such as personal use of company aircraft.

Sources: Enron, SEC Schedule 14A (proxy statement), March 27, 2001, p. 18; and Dan Ackman, "Executive Compensation: Did Enron Execs Dump Shares?" *Forbes.com,* March 22, 2002.

Executive compensation was also results-based. According to Enron's 2001 proxy statement:

> The basic philosophy behind executive compensation at Enron is to reward executive performance that creates long-term shareholder value. This pay-for-performance tenet is embedded in each aspect of an executive's total compensation package. Additionally, the philosophy is designed to promote teamwork by tying a significant portion of compensation to business unit and Enron performance.[12]

Executive compensation was primarily composed of salary, bonus, and stock options, as shown in Exhibit 1. In addition, the company routinely lent money to top executives, forgiving the loans if the terms of their contracts were fulfilled. Enron also awarded some executives equity stakes in various business units, which could be converted into stock or cash under certain conditions. For example, Skilling held a 5 percent stake in the retail energy unit, which he converted into $100 million worth of stock in 1998.[13]

During Enron's final years, many top executives sold significant blocs of company stock. Between October 1998 and November 2001, according to a lawsuit later filed by shareholders, Lay sold $184 million worth of Enron stock; Skilling, $71 million; and Andrew Fastow, Enron's CFO, $34 million. All three men sold large blocs in late 2000 or early 2001.[14]

Politics as Usual

Political action was an important part of Enron's overall strategy. The company's primary policy goal was to promote deregulation and reduce government oversight in the range of markets in which it traded. It maintained an office in Washington, D.C., staffed by over 100 lobbyists and also used outside lobbyists for specialized assignments. The company spent $2.1 million on lobbying in 2000 alone.[15] Enron was also a major campaign contributor. From 1994 on, Enron was the largest contributor to congressional campaigns in the energy industry, giving over $5 million to House and Senate candidates, mostly to Republicans (see Exhibit 2). In 2000, it gave $2.4 million in political contributions.

Enron CEO Kenneth Lay also had close personal ties with the Bush family. In 1992, Lay had chaired the host committee for the Republican National Convention in Houston

[12] Enron, SEC Schedule 14A (proxy statement), March 27, 2001, p. 15.

[13] "Enron Compensation Raised Questions," Dow Jones Newswires, March 26, 2002.

[14] Insider trading data computed by Milberg Weiss Bershad Hynes & Lerach LLP; available online at *www.enronfraud.com.*

[15] "The Fall of the Giant: Enron's Campaign Contributions and Lobbying," Center for Responsive Politics; available online at *www.opensecrets.org.*

Election Cycle	Total Contributions	Soft Money Contributions	Contributions from PACs	Contributions from Individuals	% to Democrats	% to Republicans
1990	$163,250	N/A	$130,250	$33,000	42	58
1992	$281,009	$75,109	$130,550	$75,350	42	58
1994	$520,996	$136,292	$189,565	$195,139	42	58
1996	$1,141,016	$687,445	$171,671	$281,900	18	81
1998	$1,049,942	$691,950	$212,643	$145,349	21	79
2000	$2,441,398	$1,671,555	$280,043	$489,800	28	72
2002	$353,959	$304,909	$32,000	$17,050	6	94
TOTAL	$5,951,570	$3,567,260	$1,146,722	$1,237,588	26	74

Note: Soft money contributions were not publicly disclosed until the 1991–92 election cycle. Soft money contributions were banned in 2002.

Source: Center for Responsive Politics, based on Federal Election Commission data; available online at *www.opensecrets.org/news/enron/enron_totals.asp.*

at which George H. Bush was nominated to run for a second term as president. Enron donated $700,000 to George W. Bush's various campaigns between 1993 and 2001. Lay and his wife personally donated $100,000 to the younger Bush's presidential inauguration.

Over the years, Enron's efforts to influence policy making enjoyed significant success, as illustrated by the following examples:

- *Commodities Futures Regulation.* The job of the Commodities Futures Trading Commission (CFTC), a federal agency, is to regulate futures contracts traded in an exchange. From 1988 to 1993, the CFTC was chaired by Wendy Gramm, an economist and wife of then-Congressman Phil Gramm (Republican, Texas). In 1992, Enron petitioned the CFTC to exempt energy derivatives and swaps—such as those in which it was beginning to make a market—from government oversight. In January 1993, just days before President Clinton took office, Wendy Gramm approved the exemption. The following month, after she had left office, Gramm was invited to join Enron's board of directors. According to Enron's filings with the SEC, Gramm received somewhere between $.9 and $1.8 million in salary, fees, and stock option sales and dividends for her service on the board between 1993 and 2001.[16]

- *Securities and Exchange Commission (SEC).* In 1997, the SEC granted Enron an exemption for its foreign subsidiaries from the provisions of the Investment Company Act of 1940, a law designed to prevent abuses by utilities. The law barred companies it covered from shifting debt off their books, and barred executives of these companies from investing in affiliated partnerships. After it had failed to win the exemption it wanted from Congress in 1996, Enron hired the former director of the investment management division at the SEC as a lobbyist to take the company's case directly to his former colleagues. He was successful. The year 1997 was the last in which the SEC conducted a thorough examination of Enron's annual reports.[17]

[16] *Blind Faith: How Deregulation and Enron's Influence over Government Looted Billions from Americans* (Washington, DC: Public Citizen, December 2001).

[17] "Exemption Won in 1997 Set Stage for Enron Woes," *The New York Times,* January 23, 2002.

- *Commodity Futures Modernization Act.* This law, passed by Congress in late 2000, included a special exemption for Enron that allowed the company to operate an unregulated energy trading subsidiary. Senator Phil Gramm, chair of the powerful banking committee, was instrumental in getting this provision included in the bill despite the opposition of the president's working group on financial markets. Over the years, Enron had been the largest single corporate contributor to Gramm's campaigns, with $260,000 in gifts since 1993.[18]

Reviewing the history of Enron's efforts to limit government oversight, one reporter concluded, "If the regulators in Washington were asleep, it was because the company had made their beds and turned off the lights."[19]

Off the Balance Sheet

As Enron forged ahead in the late 1990s as a market-maker in a wide range of commodities, it began to assume increasing amounts of debt. Even though Skilling had touted the value of an "asset light" strategy, entry into markets for such varied commodities as water, steel, and broadband required that Enron buy significant hard assets. Enron's aggressive new business ventures required, by some estimates, on the order of $10 billion in up-front capital investments. Heavy indebtedness, however, posed a problem, because creditworthiness was critical to the company's ability to make markets in a wide range of commodities. Other parties would be unwilling to enter into contracts promising future delivery if Enron were not viewed as financially rock-solid, and the company had to maintain an investment-grade credit rating to continue to borrow money on favorable terms to fund its new ventures. A complicating factor was that several of the company's major new initiatives fell far short of expectations and some—broadband in particular—were outright failures.

Beginning in 1997, Enron entered into a series of increasingly complex financial transactions with several Special Purpose Entities, or SPEs, evidently with the intention of shifting liabilities (debt) off its books. After the bankruptcy, these transactions were investigated by a special committee of the Enron board, which released its findings in a document now known as the Powers Committee Report.

Under standard accounting rules, a company could legally exclude an SPE from its consolidated financial statements if two conditions were met: (1) an independent party had to exercise control of the SPE, and (2) this party had to own at least 3 percent of the SPE's assets. The independent party's investment had to be "at risk," that is, not guaranteed by someone else.[20] The obvious problem was that if Enron intended to burden the SPEs with debt, no truly independent party would want to invest in them.

A key figure in many of these transactions was Andrew S. Fastow. Described as a "financial whiz kid," Fastow had joined Enron Finance in 1990. He developed a close relationship with Skilling and rose quickly, becoming chief financial officer (CFO) of Enron in 1998, at age 37. Speaking of Fastow's selection, Skilling told a reporter for *CFO* magazine, "We needed someone to rethink the entire financing structure at Enron from soup to nuts. We didn't want someone stuck in the past. . . . Andy has the intelligence and youthful exuberance to think in new ways."[21]

---

[18] *Blind Faith.*

[19] "Enron's Collapse: Audacious Climb to Success Ended in Dizzying Plunge," *The New York Times,* January 13, 2002.

[20] A. Christine David, "When to Consolidate a Special Purpose Entity," *California CPA,* June 2002.

[21] "Andrew S. Fastow: Enron Corp.," *CFO Magazine,* October 1, 1999.

The SPEs Enron set up in the five years leading up to its bankruptcy included the following:

- *Chewco.* In 1997, Enron created Chewco, an SPE named after the Star Wars character Chewbacca. Fastow invited a subordinate, Michael Kopper, to become the required "independent" investor in Chewco. Kopper and a friend invested $125,000 of their own funds and, with Enron providing collateral, got a $11 million loan from Barclays Bank. Between 1997 and 2000, Kopper received $2 million in management fees for his work on Chewco. In March 2001, Enron repurchased Chewco from its "investors"; Kopper and his friend received more than $10 million. The Powers Committee concluded, "Our review failed to identify how these payments were determined or what, if anything, Kopper did to justify the payments."[22]

- *The LJM Partnerships.* In 1999, Enron created two partnerships known as LJM1 and LJM2 (the initials of Fastow's wife and children). Unlike Chewco, where he had delegated this role to a subordinate, Fastow himself served as general partner and invested $1 million of his own money. Enron proceeded to transfer various assets and liabilities to the LJMs, in a way that benefited its bottom line. For example, in the second half of 1999, the LJM transactions generated "earnings" of $229 million for Enron (the company reported total pretax earnings of $570 million for that period).

- *Raptor Partnerships.* In 1999 and 2000, Enron established four new even more ambitious SPEs, collectively known as the Raptor Partnerships, with such fanciful names as talon, timberwolf, bobcat, and porcupine. In a series of extremely complex financial maneuvers in the final five quarters before declaring bankruptcy, Enron conducted various transactions with and among the Raptors and between the Raptors and the LJMs that generated $1.1 billion in "earnings" for the firm. Among other actions, Enron loaned large blocs of its own stock to the Raptor partnerships in exchange for promissory notes, which were then posted to Enron's balance sheet as notes receivable.

Fastow made out handsomely on these deals. According to the Powers Committee Report, he eventually received almost $50 million for his role in the LJM partnerships and their transactions with the Raptors, in addition to his regular Enron compensation. In its review of Enron's SPE transactions, the Powers Committee Report concluded:

> These partnerships . . . were used by Enron Management to enter into transactions that it could not, or would not, do with unrelated commercial entities. Many of the most significant transactions apparently were designed to accomplish favorable financial statement results, not to achieve bona fide economic objectives or to transfer risk . . . . They allowed Enron to conceal from the market very large losses resulting from Enron's merchant investments.[23]

Manipulating Revenue

Moving liabilities off the books was one way to make the company's financial condition look better than it was. Another way was to manipulate revenue. In the period preceding its collapse, Enron used a number of accounting practices apparently aimed at inflating revenues or reducing their volatility.

- *Mark-to-Market Accounting.* Mark-to-market (MTM) is an accounting procedure that allows companies to book as *current earnings* their expected *future revenue* from

---

[22] Powers Committee Report, p. 8.

[23] Ibid., p. 4.

certain assets. The Financial Accounting Standards Board (FASB), the organization that establishes generally accepted accounting principles, approved MTM in the early 1990s. Aggressively using this procedure, Enron counted projected profits from many deals in the year they were made. For example, in 2000 Enron entered into a partnership with Blockbuster to deliver movies on demand to viewers' homes over Enron's broadband network. The venture fell apart within a few months, after pilot projects in four U.S. cities failed. Nonetheless, Enron booked $110 million in profits in late 2000 and early 2001, based on the anticipated value of the partnership over 20 years.[24] In 2000, mark-to-market gains accounted for over half of Enron's reported pretax earnings.[25]

- *Sham Swaps.* In the wake of its collapse, Enron was investigated by the SEC for possible sham swaps. For example, on the last day of the third quarter 2001, as the company's stock price was falling, Enron entered into an agreement with the telecommunications firm Qwest to exchange assets. Qwest and Enron agreed to buy fiber optic capacity from each other, and the two companies exchanged checks for around $112 million to complete the swap. According to *The New York Times,* "The deal enabled Enron to book a sale and avoid recording a loss on . . . assets, whose value in the open market had dropped far below the price on Enron's books."

- *Prudency Accounts.* Enron traders routinely split profits from their deals into two categories—one that was added directly to the company's current financial statements, and the other that was added to a reserve fund. These so-called prudency accounts, according to Frank Partnoy, an expert in finance who testified before the U.S. Senate Committee on Governmental Affairs, functioned as "slush fund[s] that could be used to smooth out profits and losses over time." The use of prudency accounts made Enron's revenue stream appear less volatile than it actually was. As Partnoy noted, "Such fraudulent practices would have thwarted the very purpose of Enron's financial statements: to give investors an accurate picture of a firm's risks."[26]

The Best Interests of the Company

The two groups most responsible for overseeing the legal and ethical integrity of the company's financial reporting were Enron's board of directors and its auditors, Arthur Andersen's Houston office. In January 2001, Enron's board was made up of 17 members. Of the 15 outside members, many had long personal and business associations with Lay and were considered loyal supporters of his policies. Although the board included only two insiders (Lay and Skilling), other members of top management frequently attended, sitting around the edge of the boardroom.[27] The full board typically met five times a year. Members of Enron's board were unusually well compensated. In 2001, for example, each director received $381,000 in total compensation. (By comparison, the

[24] "Show Business: A Blockbuster Deal Shows How Enron Overplayed Its Hand—Company Booked Big Profit from Pilot Video Project That Soon Fizzled Out," *The Wall Street Journal*, January 17, 2002; and Bryce, *Pipe Dreams*, pp. 281–83.

[25] "Question Mark to Market: Energy Accounting Scrutinized," *CFO.com*, December 4, 2001.

[26] Testimony of Professor Frank Partnoy, Senate Committee on Governmental Affairs, January 24, 2002, online at *www.senate.gov/~gov_affairs/012402partnoy.htm.*

[27] Jay W. Lorsch, "The Board at Enron," unpublished paper, Harvard Business School, April 10, 2002, p. 1.

average director compensation for the top 200 companies that year was $152,000; and for companies in the petroleum and pipeline industries, $160,000.)[28]

The quality of the company's financial reporting was the responsibility of the audit and compliance committee. Chaired by Robert Jaedicke, emeritus professor of accounting and former dean of the Stanford Business School, the committee also included Wendy Gramm and four others.[29] The audit committee typically met for an hour or two before the regular board meetings, often for discussions with the company's professional auditors.

The board's first substantive involvement with the SPEs run by Fastow and his associates came in 1999.[30] Fastow's dual roles as both CFO and general partner of the LJM partnerships potentially violated Enron's code of ethics, which prohibited an officer from owning or participating in "any other entity which does business with . . . the company." An exception could be made if the participation was disclosed to the chairman and CEO and was judged not to "adversely affect the best interests of the company." Accordingly, in June and again in October, the board reviewed and approved the LJM partnerships and voted to suspend its code of ethics in this instance to permit Fastow to run the partnerships.

However, the board seemed sufficiently concerned that it put additional controls in place; it required both an annual board review and that the chief accounting officer and chief risk officer review all transactions with the partnerships. In October 2000, the board added additional restrictions, including provisions that Skilling personally sign off on all related approval sheets. In May 2001, an Enron attorney discovered that Skilling had not signed these documents, as the board had required, so he sent a message to the CEO that he needed to sign the papers at his convenience. Skilling never replied.[31] As for the mandated board review, the Powers Committee later concluded that although the audit committee had periodically reviewed the SPEs, "these reviews appear to have been too brief, too limited in scope, and too superficial to serve their intended function."[32]

In its oversight function, the board and its audit committee relied heavily on the professional advice of Enron's auditor, Arthur Andersen, which repeatedly told the board it was "comfortable" with the partnership transactions. Founded in 1913 and Enron's auditor since 1985, Andersen was one of the Big Five accounting firms. Since the early 1990s, Andersen's Houston office had acted both as the company's external and internal auditors, in an arrangement called an "integrated audit," in which Enron subcontracted much of its "inside" work to the firm.[33] Andersen also did considerable consulting and nonauditing work for its client. All told, Enron was a very important client of the Houston office. In 2000, for example, Andersen received $25 million for audit and $27 million for nonaudit services from Enron. Between 1997 and 2001, Andersen received around $7 million for its accounting work on the Chewco, LJM, and Raptors transactions.

Relations between Enron and Arthur Andersen were unusually close. Many Andersen accountants had office space at Enron and easily mingled with their co-workers. "People

---

[28] Pearl Meyer and Partners, *2001 Director Compensation: Boards in the Spotlight: Study of the Top 200 Corporations,* 2002. Data are rounded to the nearest thousand dollars.

[29] Other members of the audit committee were: John Mendelsohn, president of the M.D. Anderson Cancer Clinic; Paolo V. Ferraz Pereira, former president of the State Bank of Rio de Janeiro; John Wakeham, former British Secretary of State for Energy; and Ronnie Chan, chairman of a large property development group in Hong Kong.

[30] Earlier, the board had provided a cursory review of Chewco, but had apparently been unaware of Kopper's role.

[31] "Enron's Many Strands."

[32] Powers Committee Report, p. 24.

[33] "Court Documents Show Andersen's Ties with Enron Were Growing in Early '90s," *The Wall Street Journal,* February 26, 2002.

just thought they were Enron employees," said one former Enron accountant.[34] More-over, mobility between Andersen and its client was high; indeed, at the time of the bank-ruptcy, the company's chief accounting officer, Richard Causey, had formerly been in charge of Andersen's Enron audit.

Andersen's own structure gave considerable autonomy to local offices like the one in Houston. Like other big accounting firms, Andersen had a professional standards group (PSG) at its corporate headquarters whose job was to review difficult issues that arose in the field. Unlike others, however, Andersen's PSG did not have the authority to overrule its field auditors in case of disagreement. An investigation by *BusinessWeek* showed that on four different occasions, the Enron audit team went ahead despite PSG objections to various aspects of its accounting for the Enron partnerships. Finally, Enron requested that its chief critic be removed from the PSG. Andersen headquarters complied.[35]

Later, responding to criticism of its actions as Enron auditors, Andersen simply stated that it "ignored a fundamental problem: that poor business decisions on the part of Enron executives and its board ultimately brought the company down."[36]

A Wave of Accounting Scandals

On March 5, 2001, *Fortune* magazine published a cover story, written by reporter Bethany McLean, under the title "Is Enron Overpriced?" In the article, McLean challenged the conventional wisdom that Enron stock—which had returned 89 percent to investors the previous year and was selling at 55 times earnings—was an attractive buy. Calling Enron's financial statements "nearly impenetrable," she interviewed a number of stock analysts who, although bullish on Enron stock, were unable to explain exactly how the company made money. One called the company's financial statements "a big black box."[37]

What *Fortune* did not know at the time was that the fragile structure of partnerships Enron had constructed rested on the high price of the company's stock. Much of the part-nerships' assets consisted of Enron stock or loans guaranteed by Enron stock. If the share price declined too far, this would trigger a need for more financing from the company. Before Enron's announcement of first-quarter 2001 results, and then again prior to the second-quarter results, Andersen worked furiously to restructure the partnerships to pre-vent the necessity of consolidating them with Enron's books. The Powers Committee later commented that these efforts were "perceived by many within Enron as a triumph of accounting ingenuity by a group of innovative accountants. We believe that perception was mistaken. . . . [The] Raptors were little more than a highly complex accounting con-struct that was destined to collapse."[38]

In late July, Enron's stock slid below $47 a share—the first "trigger" price for the partnerships. On August 14, Skilling abruptly resigned as president and CEO, citing undisclosed personal reasons. Lay, who had been serving as chairman, resumed the role of CEO. In a memo to Enron employees that day, Lay assured them:

> I have never felt better about the prospects for the company. All of you know
> that our stock price has suffered substantially over the last few months. One of

[34] "Were Enron, Andersen Too Close to Allow Auditor to Do Its Job?" *The Wall Street Journal,* January 21, 2002.

[35] "Out of Control at Andersen," *BusinessWeek,* April 8, 2002.

[36] "Enron's Doomed 'Triumph of Accounting,'" *The New York Times,* February 4, 2002.

[37] "Is Enron Overpriced?" *Fortune,* March 5, 2001.

[38] Powers Committee Report, pp. 131–32.

my top priorities will be to restore a significant amount of the stock value we have lost as soon as possible. Our performance has never been stronger; our business model has never been more robust; our growth has never been more certain; and most importantly, we have never had a better nor deeper pool of talent throughout the company. We have the finest organization in business today. Together, we will make Enron the world's leading company.[39]

The following day, Sherron S. Watkins, an accountant and Enron vice president who worked under Fastow, wrote a memo to Lay to express her concerns about the company's accounting practices. She stated frankly:

I am incredibly nervous that we will implode in a wave of accounting scandals. My 8 years of Enron work history will be worth nothing on my résumé; the business world will consider the past successes as nothing but an elaborate accounting hoax. Skilling is resigning now for "personal reasons" but I think he wasn't having fun, looked down the road; and knew this stuff was unfixable and would rather abandon ship now than resign in shame in 2 years.

She added:

I have heard one manager . . . say, "I know it would be devastating to all of us, but I wish we would get caught. We're such a crooked company."

After a detailed review of the "questionable" accounting practices of the SPEs, Watkins recommended that Lay bring in independent legal and accounting experts to review the propriety of the partnerships and to prepare a "clean-up plan."[40]

Lay followed Watkins's advice—to a point. He brought in attorneys from Vinson & Elkins, the Houston law firm that had long been Enron's outside counsel and that had helped prepare the legal documents for the partnerships. In his instructions, Lay indicated that he saw no need to look too closely into the accounting. The lawyers interviewed Fastow, Enron's auditors, and several others, and then reported back to Lay on September 21 that although the accounting was "creative" and "aggressive," it was not "inappropriate from a technical standpoint."

Yet, despite these assurances, the partnerships were unraveling as Enron's stock price dropped (see Exhibit 3) and could no longer be supported by even the most aggressive accounting. On October 16, under pressure from its auditors, Enron announced a charge against earnings of $544 million and a reduction in shareholders' equity of $1.2 billion related to transactions with the LJM partnerships. On October 22, the SEC initiated a probe of the SPEs; Fastow was fired the following day. Then, on November 8, Enron further shocked investors by restating *all* of its financial statements back to 1997 because "three unconsolidated entities [i.e., the partnerships] should have been consolidated in the financial statements pursuant to generally accepted accounting principles." These restatements had the effect of reducing income for 1997 to 2000 by $480 million, reducing shareholders' equity by $2.1 billion, and increasing debt by $2.6 billion.[41]

Company executives frantically went searching for a white knight to purchase the company. Dynegy, another Houston-based energy trader and longtime rival, initially agreed to buy Enron for $8.9 billion on November 9. After Dynegy's CEO and board had taken a careful look at Enron's books, however, they changed their minds and

---

[39] The full text of Lay's memo appears in Fusaro and Miller, *What Went Wrong,* p. 201.

[40] The full text of Watkins's memo appears in Fusaro and Miller, *What Went Wrong,* pp. 185–91.

[41] Based on data reported in the Powers Committee Report, p. 6.

EXHIBIT 3
Enron Stock Price and Trading Volume, 1998–2002

Source: *bigcharts.com.*

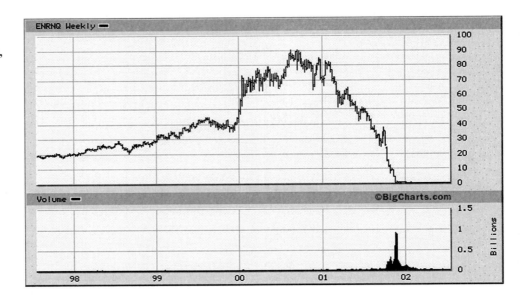

withdrew the offer. The rating agencies immediately downgraded Enron to junk status, and the stock dropped below $1 a share and was delisted from the New York Stock Exchange.

As the company imploded, Enron tried to call in its political chits in one last Hail Mary move. Lay and other top executives placed urgent calls to Commerce Secretary Donald Evans, Treasury Secretary Paul O'Neill, and other administration officials, reportedly asking them to lean on banks to extend credit to the company. They declined to do so. Later asked why he had not helped Enron, Evans said it would have been an "egregious abuse" to have intervened. O'Neill simply stated, "Companies come and go. . . . Part of the genius of capitalism is, people get to make good decisions or bad decisions, and they get to pay the consequence or enjoy the fruits of their decisions."[42]

Discussion Questions

1. Who were the key stakeholders involved in, or affected by, the collapse of Enron? How and to what degree were they hurt or helped by the actions of Enron management?

2. Considering all aspects of the case, what factor or factors do you believe most contributed to the collapse of Enron? In your answer, please consider both external and internal factors.

3. What steps should be taken now by corporate managers, stakeholders, and policy makers to prevent a similar event from occurring in the future?

[42] "Enron Lessons: Big Political Giving Wins Firms a Hearing, Doesn't Assure Aid," *The Wall Street Journal,* January 15, 2002.

Odwalla, Inc., and the E. Coli Outbreak

October 30, 1996, was a cool, fall day in Half Moon Bay, California, a coastal town an hour's drive south of San Francisco. At the headquarters of Odwalla, Inc., a modest, two-story wooden structure just blocks from the beach, company founder and chairman Greg Steltenpohl was attending a marketing meeting. Odwalla, the largest producer of fresh fruit and vegetable-based beverages in the western United States, had just completed its best-ever fiscal year, with sales of $59 million, up 40 percent over the past 12 months.

The company's CEO, Stephen Williamson, urgently knocked on the glass door and motioned Steltenpohl into the hall. Williamson, 38, a graduate of the University of California at Berkeley and a former investment banker, had served as president of Odwalla from 1992 to 1995, when he became CEO.

It was unlike him to interrupt a meeting, and he looked worried. "I just got a call from the King County Department of Health," Williamson reported. "They've got a dozen cases of E. coli poisoning up there in the Seattle area. A number of the families told health officials they had drunk Odwalla apple juice." E. coli O157:H7 was a virulent bacterium that had been responsible for several earlier outbreaks of food poisoning, including one traced to undercooked Jack-in-the-Box hamburgers in 1993.

Steltenpohl was puzzled. "What do they know for sure?"

"Right now, not a whole lot. It's just epidemiology," Williamson replied. "They don't have any bacteriological match-ups yet. They said it might be a while before they would know anything definitive."

"We'd better see what else we can find out."

Steltenpohl and Williamson returned to their offices, where they began placing calls to food safety experts, scientists at the Food and Drug Administration and the Centers for Disease Control, and the company's lawyers. A while later, Steltenpohl came out to speak to his next appointment, who had been waiting in the lobby for over an hour. "I'm awfully sorry," the chairman said apologetically. "I'm not going to be able to see you today. Something important's happening that I've got to deal with right away."

By Anne T. Lawrence. This is an abridged version of a full-length case, "Odwalla, Inc., and the E. Coli Outbreak (A), (B), (C)," *Case Research Journal* 19, no. 1 (Winter 1999). Abridged and reprinted by permission of the *Case Research Journal*. This case was written with the cooperation of management, solely for the purpose of stimulating student discussion. Sources include articles appearing in the *Natural Foods Merchandiser, Nation's Business, San Jose Mercury News, Rocky Mountain News, San Francisco Chronicle, Seattle Times, Fresno Bee, The New York Times, The Wall Street Journal,* and *Squeeze* (Odwalla's in-house newsletter); press releases issued by Odwalla and by the American Fresh Juice Council; and Odwalla's annual reports and prospectus. Odwalla's Web site may be found at *www.odwalla.com.* Copyright © Anne T. Lawrence and the North American Case Research Association. All rights reserved.

History of Odwalla, Inc.

Odwalla, Inc., was founded in 1980 by Steltenpohl; his wife, Bonnie Bassett; and their friend Gerry Percy. Steltenpohl, then 25, was a jazz musician and Stanford graduate with a degree in environmental science. The group purchased a used hand juicer for $200 and began producing fresh-squeezed orange juice in a backyard shed in Santa Cruz, California. They delivered the juice to local restaurants in a Volkswagen van. Steltenpohl later said that he had gotten the idea from a book, *100 Businesses You Can Start for under $100.* His motivation, he reported, was simply to make enough money to support his fledgling career as a musician and producer of educational media presentations. The company's name came from a jazz composition by the Art Ensemble of Chicago, in which Odwalla was a mythical figure who led the "people of the sun" out of the "gray haze," which the friends chose to interpret as a reference to overly processed food.

During the 1980s, Odwalla prospered, gradually extending its market reach by expanding its own distribution and production capabilities and by acquiring other juice companies. In 1983, the company moved into a larger production facility and added carrot juice to its product line. In 1985—the same year Odwalla incorporated—the company purchased a small local apple juice company, Live Juice. With apple added to the line, the company expanded its distribution efforts, moving into San Francisco and further north into Marin County. In 1986, Odwalla purchased Dancing Bear Juice Company in Sacramento and assimilated that company's juice products and distribution network in central California.

The company financed its rapid growth in its early years through bank loans and private stock offerings in 1991, 1992, and 1993. In December 1993, the company went public, offering for sale 1 million shares of common stock at an initial price of $6.375 a share. The proceeds of the initial public offering were used in part to construct a 65,000-square-foot state-of-the-art production facility in Dinuba, in California's agricultural Central Valley.

The company also made additional acquisitions. In June 1994, the company acquired Dharma Juice Company of Bellingham, Washington, to distribute its products in the Pacific Northwest. In January 1995, Odwalla purchased J. S. Grant's, Inc., the maker of Just Squeezed Juices, which became the distributor for Odwalla products in the Colorado market. The strategy appeared to be successful. By 1996, Odwalla, which already controlled more than half the market for fresh juice in northern California, had made significant inroads in the Pacific Northwest and Colorado and was poised to extend its market dominance into New Mexico, Texas, and southern California.

Product Line

The company considered its market niche to be "fresh, minimally processed juices and juice-based beverages."

The company produced a range of products from fresh juice, some single strength and some blended. Odwalla chose fun, clever names, such as Strawberry C-Monster (a vitamin C-fortified fruit smoothie), Femme Vitale (a product formulated to meet women's special nutritional needs), and Guava Have It (a tropical fruit blend). Packaging graphics were brightly colored and whimsical. Pricing was at the premium level; a half gallon of fresh-squeezed orange juice retailed for around $5.00; a 16-ounce blended smoothie for $2.00 or more.

Odwalla was committed to making a totally fresh product. In the company's 1995 annual report, for example, the letter to shareholders stated:

> Our juice is FRESH! We believe that fruits, vegetables, and other botanical nutrients must be treated with respect. As a result, we do not heat-treat our juice, like the heavily processed products made by most other beverage companies.

The company's products were made without preservatives or any artificial ingredients, and the juice was not pasteurized (heat treated to kill microorganisms and to extend shelf life). Unpasteurized juice, the company believed, retained more vitamins, enzymes, and what Steltenpohl referred to as the "flavor notes" of fresh fruits and vegetables.

Although Odwalla did not pasteurize its juice, it took many steps in the manufacturing process to assure the quality and purity of its product. To avoid possible contamination, the company did not accept ground apples, only those picked from the tree. Inspectors checked field bins to see if there was any dirt, grass, or debris; and bins with evidence of ground contact were rejected. The company's manufacturing facility in Dinuba was considered the most advanced in the industry. The plant operated under a strict code of Good Manufacturing Practices. At Dinuba, apples were thoroughly washed with a sanitizing solution of phosphoric acid and scrubbed with whirling brushes. All juice was produced under extremely strict hygienic standards.

Marketing

Odwalla marketed its products through supermarkets, warehouse outlets, specialty stores, natural food stores, and institutions such as restaurants and colleges. Slightly over a quarter of all sales were with two accounts—Safeway, a major grocery chain, and Price/Costco, a discount warehouse.

A distinctive feature of Odwalla's strategy was the company's direct store distribution, or DSD, system. Most sites, from supermarkets to small retailers, were provided with their own stand-alone refrigerated cooler, brightly decorated with Odwalla graphics. Accounts were serviced by route salespeople (RSPs), who were responsible for stocking the coolers and removing unsold juice that had passed its "enjoy by" date. RSPs kept careful records of what products were selling well, enabling them to adjust stock to meet local tastes. As an incentive, salespeople received bonuses based on their routes' sales, in addition to their salaries.

Although the DSD system was more expensive than using independent distributors, it allowed the company to maintain tight control over product mix and quality. Moreover, because the company assumed responsibility for ordering, stocking, and merchandising its own products within the store, Odwalla in most cases did not pay "slotting" and other handling fees to the retailer.

Corporate Culture

The fresh juice company was always, as Steltenpohl put it, "values driven." In 1992, around 80 Odwalla employees participated in a nine-month process that led to the creation of the company's vision, mission, and core values statements. These focused on nourishment, ecological sustainability, innovation, and continuous learning.

Concerned that rapid growth might erode common commitment to these values, in 1995 the company initiated annual three-day training sessions, held on site at multiple locations, known as Living Vision Conferences, for employees to talk about the application of the vision to everyday operating issues. An internal process the company called

Vision Link sought to link each individual's job to the Odwalla vision. Managers were expected to model the company's values. The company called its values a "touchstone [for employees] in assessing their conduct and in making business decisions."

In addition, Odwalla instituted a "strategic dialogue" process. A group of 30 people, with some fixed seats for top executives and some rotating seats for a wide cross section of other employees, met quarterly in San Francisco for broad discussions of the company's values and strategic direction.

Social responsibility and environmental awareness were critical to Odwalla's mission. Community service efforts included aid to farm families in the Central Valley, scholarships to study nutrition, and gifts of cash and juice to many local community organizations. The company instituted a recycling program for its plastic bottles. It attempted to divert all organic waste away from landfills—for example, by selling pulp for livestock feed and citrus peel for use in teas and condiments and past-code juice for biofuels. In the mid-1990s, the company began the process of converting its vehicle fleet to alternative fuels. Odwalla's corporate responsibility extended to its employees, who received innovative benefits that included stock options, extensive wellness programs, and an allowance for fresh juice. The company won numerous awards for its environmental practices, and in 1993, *Inc.* magazine honored Odwalla as Employer of the Year.

During these years, the Odwalla brand name became widely identified with a healthful lifestyle, as well as with California's entrepreneurial business climate. In an oft-repeated story, Steve Jobs, founder of Apple Computer, was said to have ordered unlimited quantities of Odwalla juice for all employees working on the original development of the Macintosh Computer.

The E. Coli Bacterium

The virulent strain of bacteria that threatened to bring down this fast-growing company was commonly known in scientific circles as Escherichia coli, or E. coli for short.

The broad class of E. coli bacteria, microscopic rod-shaped organisms, are common in the human intestinal tract, and few pose a danger to health. In fact, most E. coli play a beneficial role by suppressing harmful bacteria and synthesizing vitamins. A small minority of E. coli strains, however, cause illness. One of the most dangerous of these is E. coli O157:H7. In the intestine, this strain produces a potent toxin that attacks the lining of the gut. Symptoms of infection include abdominal pain and cramps, diarrhea, fever, and bloody stools. Most cases are self-limiting, but approximately 6 percent are complicated with hemolytic uremic syndrome, a dangerous condition that can lead to kidney and heart failure. Young children, the elderly, and those with weakened immune systems are most susceptible.

E. coli O157:H7 (or 157) lives in the intestines of cows, sheep, deer, and other animals. The meat of infected animals may carry the infection. E. coli is also spread to humans through fecal contamination of food. For example, apples may be contaminated when they fall to the ground and come in contact with cow or deer manure. Secondary infection may also occur, for example, when food is handled by infected persons who have failed to wash their hands after using the toilet. Unfortunately, only a small amount of 157—as few as 500 bacteria—is required to cause illness. As one epidemiologist noted, "It does not take a massive contamination or a major breakdown in the system to spread it."

E. coli O157:H7 is known as an emergent pathogen, meaning that its appearance in certain environments is viewed by researchers as a new phenomenon. The organism was first identified in 1982, when it was involved in a several outbreaks involving under-cooked meat. Since then, poisoning incidents had increased dramatically. By the mid-1990s, about 20,000 cases of E. coli poisoning occurred every year in the United States; about 250 people died. Most cases were believed to be caused by undercooked meat. Although a serious threat, E. coli is not the most common food-borne illness. In the United States, 5 million cases of food poisoning are reported annually, with 4,000 of these resulting in death. Most cases are caused by mistakes in food preparation and handling, not by mistakes in food processing or packaging.

E. Coli in Fresh Juice

It was widely believed in the juice industry that pathogens like E. coli could not survive in an acidic environment, such as citrus and apple juice. Odwalla apple juice had a pH (acidity) level of 4.3. (On the pH scale, 7 is neutral, and levels below 7 are increasingly acidic.) Odwalla did conduct spot testing of other, more pH-neutral products. The Food and Drug Administration, although it did not have specific guidelines for fresh juice production, indicated in its Retail Food Store Sanitation Code that foods with a pH lower than 4.6 were not potentially hazardous.

In the early 1990s, however, scattered scientific evidence emerged that E. coli O157:H7 might have undergone a critical mutation that rendered it more acid-tolerant. In 1991, an outbreak of E. coli poisoning sickened 23 people in Massachusetts who had consumed fresh, unpasteurized apple cider purchased at a roadside stand. A second, similar incident occurred in Connecticut around the same time. In a study of the Massachusetts outbreak published in 1993, the *Journal of the American Medical Association* reported that E. coli O157:H7, apparently introduced by fecal contamination of fresh apples, had unexpectedly survived in acidic cider. The journal concluded that E. coli O157:H7 could survive at a pH below 4.0 at the temperature of refrigerated juice. The journal recommended strict procedures for sanitizing apples used to make fresh juice, all of which Odwalla already followed.

Although the FDA investigated both instances in New England, it did not issue any new regulations requiring pasteurization of fresh juice, nor did it issue any advisories to industry. At the time of the Odwalla outbreak, neither the FDA nor state regulators in California had rules requiring pasteurization of fresh apple juice.

Considering the Options

In the company's second-floor conference room, later in the day on October 30, Steltenpohl and Williamson gathered the company's senior executives to review the situation.

King County officials had identified about a dozen cases of E. coli infection associated with Odwalla apple juice products. But as Steltenpohl later described the situation, "It was all based on interviews. They didn't yet have bacteriological proof." Washington health officials had not yet made a public announcement, nor had they ordered or even recommended a product recall.

Conversations with federal disease control and food safety specialists throughout the day had turned up troubling information. From them, Odwalla executives had learned of the two earlier outbreaks of E. coli illness associated with unpasteurized cider in New England. And they had been told that 157 could cause illness in very minute amounts, below levels that would reliably show up in tests. The FDA had indicated that it planned to launch an investigation of the incident but did not suggest that Odwalla had broken any rules.

Management understood that they had no *legal* obligation to order an immediate recall, although this was clearly an option. Another possibility was a nonpublic recall. In this approach, the company would quietly pull the suspect product off the shelves and conduct its own investigation. If a problem were found, the company could then choose to go public with the information.

The company carried general liability insurance totaling $27 million. It had little debt and about $12 million in cash on hand. The cost of various options, however, was hard to pin down. No one could be sure precisely how much a full or partial product recall would cost, if they chose that option, or the extent of the company's liability exposure.

Ordering a Recall

At 3 p.m., about four hours after they had received the first phone call, Steltenpohl and Williamson issued a public statement.

> Odwalla, Inc., the California-based fresh beverage company, issued today a national product recall of fresh apple juice and all products containing fresh apple juice as an ingredient . . . Our first concern is for the health and safety of those affected. We are working in full cooperation with the FDA and the Seattle/King County Department of Public Health.

The recall involved 13 products, all containing unpasteurized apple juice. At the time, these 13 products accounted for about 70 percent of Odwalla's sales. The company did not recall its citrus juices or geothermal spring water products.

"Stephen and I never batted an eyelash," Steltenpohl later remembered. "We both have kids. What if it had turned out that something was in the juice, and we left it on the shelf an extra two weeks, or week, or even two days, and some little kid gets sick? What are we doing? Why are we in business? We have a corporate culture based on values. Our mission is nourishment. We really never considered *not* recalling the product. Looking back, I suppose the recall was the biggest decision we made. At the time, it seemed the only possible choice."

Once the decision to recall the product had been made, the company mobilized all its resources. On Thursday morning, October 31, 200 empty Odwalla delivery trucks rolled out from distribution centers in seven states and British Columbia with a single mission: to get the possibly tainted product off the shelves as quickly as possible. Organizing the recall was simplified by the facts that Odwalla operated its own fleet of delivery vehicles and that, in most cases, the product was displayed in the company's own coolers. The delivery drivers simply went directly to their own accounts and removed the recalled juices. In cases where the product was shelved with other products, Odwalla worked with retailers to find and remove it.

A group of employees in San Francisco, one of the company's major distribution centers, later recounted the first day of the recall:

> Every single person who is or was an RSP, express driver, or merchandiser, worked that first full day and the next.
>
> What was amazing was there were a lot of people who we didn't even have to call to come in. It might have been their day off, but they'd call to ask, "What can I do?"
>
> Right. They'd ask, "When should I come in? Where do you need me to be?"
>
> . . . It was an amazing effort. . . We were able to make it to every single account on that first Thursday. That's a thousand accounts.

Within 48 hours, the recall was complete. Odwalla had removed the product from 4,600 retail establishments in seven states and British Columbia. "This is probably as speedy as a product recall gets," a stock analyst commented. "They probably accomplished it in world-record time."

On October 31, as it was launching its recall, the company also took several additional steps.

- The company announced that it would pay all medical expenses for E. coli victims, if it could be demonstrated that Odwalla products had caused their illness.
- The company offered to refund the purchase price of any of the company's products, even those that had not been recalled.
- The company established a crisis communications center at its headquarters and hired a PR firm, Edelman Public Relations Worldwide, to help it handle the crush of media attention. It also set up a Web site and an 800 hot line to keep the public and the media apprised of the most recent developments in the case. Twice-daily media updates were scheduled.
- The company decided to extend the recall to include three products made with carrot juice. Although these products did not contain apple juice, carrot juice was produced on the same line. Until the company had determined the cause of the outbreak, it felt it could not guarantee the safety of the carrot juice products.

On October 31, as the company's route salespeople were fanning out to retrieve the juice, Odwalla's stock price was plummeting. The company's stock lost 34 percent of its value in one day, falling from $18\frac{3}{8}$ to $12\frac{1}{8}$ on the NASDAQ exchange. Trading volume was 20 times normal, as 1.36 million shares changed hands.

Tracking the Outbreak

Over the next few days, the full extent of the outbreak became clearer. In addition to the cases in Washington, new clusters of E. coli poisoning were reported by health authorities in California and Colorado. As the company received reports about individual cases, Steltenpohl and Williamson attempted to telephone families personally to express their concern. They were able to reach many of them.

On November 8, a 16-month-old toddler from a town near Denver, Colorado, who had developed hemolytic uremic syndrome, died following multiple organ failure. Tests later showed antibodies to O157:H7 in the girl's blood. It was the first, and only, death associated with the E. coli outbreak. Steltenpohl immediately issued a statement that read:

> On behalf of myself and the people at Odwalla, I want to say how deeply saddened and sorry we are to learn of the loss of this child. Our hearts go out to the family, and our primary concern at this moment is to see that we are doing everything we can to help them.

Steltenpohl, who had spoken with the girl's parents several times during her hospitalization, flew to Denver, with the family's permission, to attend the child's funeral. The girl's father later told the press, "We don't blame the Odwalla company at all. They had no bad intentions throughout all this, and they even offered to pay all of [our child's] hospital bills. I told them yesterday that we don't blame them, and we're not going to sue."

By the time the outbreak had run its course, 61 people, most of them children, had become ill in Colorado, California, Washington, and British Columbia. Except for the

Colorado youngster, all those who had become ill, including several children who had been hospitalized in critical condition, eventually recovered.

Investigation of the Outbreak

As the outbreak itself was running its course, the investigation by both the company and federal and state health authorities proceeded. On November 4, the FDA reported that it had found E. coli O157:H7 in a bottle of unopened Odwalla apple juice taken from a distribution center in Washington State. As it turned out, this was the only positive identification of the pathogen in any Odwalla product. Eventually, 15 of the 61 reported cases (5 in Colorado and 10 in Washington) were linked by molecular fingerprinting to E. coli found in the Odwalla juice sample. The origin of contamination in the other 46 cases remained unknown.

Meanwhile, federal and state investigators converged on Odwalla's Dinuba manufacturing plant, inspecting it from top to bottom, in an attempt to find the source of the pathogen. On November 18, the FDA announced that it had completed its review of the Dinuba facility and had found no evidence of E. coli O157:H7 anywhere in the plant. The investigators then turned their attention to the growers and packers who supplied apples to the Dinuba plant, on the theory that the company might have processed a batch of juice containing some ground apples contaminated by cow or deer feces. In their interim report, the FDA noted that although no E. coli was found at Dinuba, "microbial monitoring of finished product and raw materials used in processing [was] inadequate." Odwalla sharply challenged this conclusion, noting that the FDA did not have any requirements for microbiological testing.

Searching for a Solution

The recall placed enormous financial pressure on the company and challenged its executives to decide how and when to reintroduce its products to the market.

As a short-term measure, Odwalla announced on November 7 that it would immediately reintroduce three of its recalled products, all juice blends, that had been reformulated without apple juice. These products would continue to be produced at Dinuba, but not on the apple processing line. In announcing the reformulation, Steltenpohl told the press, "Until we are assured of a completely safe and reliable method of producing apple juice, we will not include it in our juices."

But the reformulation of a few blended juice smoothies was hardly a long-term solution, since apple juice was a core ingredient in many of the company's top-selling products. Odwalla urgently needed to find a way to get apple juice safely back on the market. How to do so, however, was not obvious.

To assist it in finding a solution to the problem, Odwalla assembled a panel of experts, dubbed the Odwalla Nourishment and Food Safety Advisory Council, to recommend ways to improve product safety. In late November, with the help of these experts, Odwalla executives conducted detailed scenario planning, in which they reviewed a series of possible options. Among those they considered were the following:

- **Discontinue all apple juice products.** In this scenario, the company would eliminate all apple juice and blended juice products until it could be fully assured of their safety.
- **Improve manufacturing processes.** In this scenario, the company would take a number of steps to improve hazard control at various points in the production process, for

example, through modified product handling procedures, multiple antiseptic washes, routine sample testing, and stricter controls on suppliers.

- **Modify labeling.** Another option was to disclose risk to the consumer through product labeling. For example, an unpasteurized product could be sold with a disclaimer that it was not suitable for consumption by infants, the elderly, or those with compromised immune systems, because of the very rare but still possible chance of bacterial contamination.

- **Use standard pasteurization.** Standard pasteurization involved slowly heating the juice to a point just below boiling and holding it at that temperature for several minutes. The heat killed dangerous microorganisms and also had a side benefit of extending the shelf life of the product. Standard pasteurization, however, also destroyed many of the nutritional benefits of raw juice.

- **Use modified pasteurization.** Modified pasteurization, also known as flash pasteurization, involved quickly heating the juice to a somewhat lower temperature, 160 degrees F., and holding it very briefly at that temperature to kill any harmful bacteria. In tests of this procedure, Odwalla technicians found that it yielded an apple juice that had a "lighter" taste than unpasteurized juice, but with a more "natural" taste than standard pasteurized apple juice. The process destroyed some nutrients, but fewer than standard pasteurization. Flash pasteurization did not, however, extend the shelf life of the product.

- **Use alternative (non–heat-based) technologies for removing pathogens.** The company also examined a number of alternative methods of killing pathogens. These included a high-pressure process in which pressure was used to explode the cell walls of bacteria; a process in which light waves were directed at the juice to destroy pathogens; the use of electricity to disrupt bacteria; and the use of herbal antiseptic products.

A key factor in the decision, of course, was what customers wanted. The company commissioned some market research to gauge consumer sentiment; it also carefully monitored public opinion as revealed in calls and letters to the company and discussions on public electronic bulletin boards, such as America Online.

The company also had to consider its financial situation. Remarkably, despite the recall, sales for the quarter ending November 30, 1996, were actually 14 percent ahead of the same period for 1995 because of excellent sales prior to the outbreak. The E. coli incident, however, had caused significant operating losses. By the end of November, the recall had cost the company about $5 million. Expenses had included the cost of retrieving and destroying product, legal and professional fees, and increased marketing costs. At the end of the fiscal quarter, Odwalla had a cash position of about $9 million, down from $12 million at the time of the outbreak.

On December 5, Odwalla announced that it had decided to flash pasteurize its apple juice. In a statement to the press, Williamson stated:

> Odwalla's first priority is safety. After much consideration and research, we chose the flash pasteurization process as a method to produce apple juice. It is safe, yet largely preserves the great taste and nutritional value allowing Odwalla to remain true to its vision of optimal nourishment. Importantly, we will continue to aggressively pursue the research and development of alternative methods to bring our customers safe, unpasteurized apple juice.

The following day, all apple juice and blended juice products were reintroduced to the market with flash pasteurized juice. The label had been redesigned to indicate that the product had been flash pasteurized, and Odwalla coolers prominently displayed signs so advising customers.

At the same time, the company moved forward with its expert panel to develop a comprehensive Hazard Analysis Critical Control Points (HACCP) (pronounced hassip) plan for fresh juice production. HACCP was not a single step, but a comprehensive safety plan that involved pathogen control at multiple points in the juice production process, including sanitation of the fruit, testing for bacteria, and quality audits at several points in the process. The company also continued to monitor new, alternative technologies for controlling bacterial contamination.

Regulating the Fresh Fruit Juice Industry

In the wake of the E. coli outbreak, public concern about food safety mounted, and federal and state regulators began considering stricter regulation of the fresh fruit juice industry. On December 16, the FDA sponsored a public advisory hearing in Washington, D.C., to review current science and to consider strategies for improving the safety of fresh juice. Debate at the two-day hearings was wide-ranging.

Steltenpohl and Williamson represented Odwalla at the hearing. In their testimony, the Odwalla executives reported that they had decided to adopt flash pasteurization but argued *against* government rules requiring all juice to be heat-treated. "Mandatory pasteurization would be a premature and unnecessary step in light of the vast new technologies emerging," Steltenpohl told the hearing. He warned the panel that mandates could "lead to widespread public fears about fresh food and beverages."

Steltenpohl and Williamson called on the FDA to continue to explore different methods for producing fresh juice safely. In addition, they called for industry self-regulation aimed at adoption of voluntary standards for safe manufacturing practices and hazard control programs. The Odwalla executives reported that they viewed flash pasteurization as the last line of defense in a comprehensive program to eliminate pathogens.

Some other juice makers and scientists supported Odwalla's position. Several small growers vigorously opposed mandatory pasteurization, saying they could not afford the expensive equipment required. A representative of Orchid Island Juice Company of Florida asked, "What level of safety are you trying to achieve? We don't ban raw oysters and steak tartare, although the risks are much higher. Nor do we mandate that they be cooked, because it changes the flavor." A number of food safety experts testified about emerging technologies able to kill pathogens without heat treatment.

Some scientists and industry representatives, however, were on the other side. Two major firms, Cargill and Nestlé, both major producers of heat-treated juice products, argued vigorously for a government mandate, saying that "other technologies just won't do the job." Dr. Patricia Griffin of the Centers for Disease Control and Prevention noted that "current production practices do not guarantee the safety of apple cider, apple juice, and orange juice." She called for pasteurization of apple juice and cider, as well as product labels warning customers of potential risk. A representative of the Center for Science in the Public Interest called for a label warning the elderly, infants, and persons with suppressed immune systems to avoid fresh, unpasteurized juice.

Several days after the hearing, the advisory panel recommended against mandatory pasteurization, for the moment at least, calling instead for "good hazard control" at juice manufacturing plants and in the orchards that supplied them. However, an FDA spokesman added, "We can never say that forced pasteurization is completely off the boards." The agency indicated that it would continue to study a number of alternative approaches to improving juice safety, including mandatory pasteurization.

Looking to the Future

In May 1997, Steltenpohl reflected on the challenges facing Odwalla:

> Our task now is to rebuild a brand and a name. How you rebuild . . . these are important decisions. You can make what might be good short-term business decisions, but they wouldn't be the right thing. The decisions we make now become building blocks for the [company's] culture. We have to look at what's right and wrong. We need a clear moral direction.

Discussion Questions

1. What factors contributed to the outbreak of E. coli poisoning described in this case? Do you believe that Odwalla was responsible, wholly or in part, for the outbreak? Why or why not?

2. What do you believe Odwalla should have done as of October 30, 1996? As of November 11, 1996? In each instance, please list at least three options and state the arguments for and against each.

3. What steps, if any, should Odwalla take as of the point when the case ends?

4. Do you consider Odwalla's voluntary recall decision to be an act of corporate social responsibility? Why or why not?

5. What is the appropriate role for public policy in the area of food safety? Assess the role of government authorities in this case. In your view, did they act properly?

Merck, the FDA, and the Vioxx Recall

In 2006, the pharmaceutical giant Merck faced major challenges. Vioxx, the company's once best-selling prescription painkiller, had been pulled off the market in September 2004 after Merck learned it increased the risk of heart attacks and strokes. When news of the recall broke, the company's stock price had plunged 30 percent to $33 a share, its lowest point in eight years, where it had hovered since. Standard & Poor's had downgraded the company's outlook from "stable" to "negative." In late 2004, the Justice Department had opened a criminal investigation into whether the company had "caused federal health programs to pay for the prescription drug when its use was not warranted."[1] The Securities and Exchange Commission was inquiring into whether Merck had misled investors. By late 2005, more than 6,000 lawsuits had been filed, alleging that Vioxx had caused death or disability. From many quarters, the company faced troubling questions about the development and marketing of Vioxx, new calls for regulatory reform, and concerns about its political influence on Capitol Hill. In the words of Senator Charles Grassley, chairman of a Congressional committee investigating the Vioxx case, "a blockbuster drug [had become] a blockbuster disaster."[2]

Merck, Inc.

Merck, the company in the eye of this storm, was one of the world's leading pharmaceutical firms.[3] As shown in Exhibit 1, in 2005 the company ranked fourth in sales, after Pfizer, Johnson & Johnson, and GlaxoSmithKline. In assets and market value, it ranked fifth. However, Merck ranked first in profits, earning $7.33 billion on $30.78 billion in sales (24 percent).

Merck had long enjoyed a reputation as one of the most ethical and socially responsible of the major drug companies. For an unprecedented seven consecutive years (1987 to 1993), *Fortune* magazine had named Merck its "most admired" company. In 1987, Merck appeared on the cover of *Time* under the headline, "The Miracle Company." It had consistently appeared on lists of best companies to work for and in the portfolios of

By Anne T. Lawrence. Copyright © 2006 by the author. All rights reserved. An earlier version of this case was presented at the Western Casewriters Association Annual Meeting, Long Beach, California, March 30, 2006. This case was prepared from publicly available materials.

[1] "Justice Dept. and SEC Investigating Merck Drug," *The New York Times,* November 9, 2004.

[2] Opening Statement of U.S. Senator Chuck Grassley of Iowa, U.S. Senate Committee on Finance, Hearing, "FDA, Merck, and Vioxx: Putting Patient Safety First?" November 18, 2004, *http://finance.senate.gov.*

[3] A history of Merck may be found in Fran Hawthorne, *The Merck Druggernaut: The Inside Story of a Pharmaceutical Giant* (Hoboken, NJ: John Wiley & Sons, 2003).

Exhibit 1   The World's Top Pharmaceutical Companies, 2005

Company	Sales ($bil)	Profits ($bil)	Assets ($bil)	Market Value ($bil)
Pfizer	40.36	6.20	120.06	285.27
Johnson & Johnson	40.01	6.74	46.66	160.96
GlaxoSmithKline	34.16	6.34	29.19	124.79
Merck	**30.78**	**7.33**	**42.59**	**108.76**
Novartis	26.77	5.40	46.92	116.43
Roche Group	25.18	2.48	45.77	95.38
Aventis	21.66	2.29	31.06	62.98
AstraZeneca	20.46	3.29	23.57	83.03
Bristol-Myers Squibb	19.89	2.90	26.53	56.05
Abbott Labs	18.99	2.44	26.15	69.27

Source: Forbes 2000, available online at *www.forbes.com.* Listed in order of overall ranking in the Forbes 2000.

social investment funds. The company's philanthropy was legendary. In the 1940s, Merck had given its patent for streptomycin, a powerful antibiotic, to a university foundation. Merck was especially admired for its donation of Mectizan. Merck's scientists had originally developed this drug for veterinary use, but later discovered that it was an effective cure for river blindness, a debilitating parasitic disease afflicting some of the world's poorest people. When the company realized that the victims of river blindness could not afford the drug, it decided to give it away for free, in perpetuity.[4]

In 1950, George W. Merck, the company's longtime CEO, stated in a speech: "We try never to forget that medicine is for the people. It is not for the profits. The profits follow, and if we have remembered that, they never fail to appear. The better we have remembered that, the larger they have been."[5] This statement was often repeated in subsequent years as a touchstone of the company's core values.

Merck was renowned for its research labs, which had a decades-long record of achievement, turning out one innovation after another, including drugs for tuberculosis, cholesterol, hypertension, and AIDS. In the early 2000s, Merck spent around $3 billion annually on research. Some felt that the company's culture had been shaped by its research agenda. Commented the author of a history of Merck, the company was "intense, driven, loyal, scientifically brilliant, collegial, and arrogant."[6] In 2006, although Merck had several medicines in the pipeline—including vaccines for rotavirus and cervical cancer, and drugs for insomnia, lymphoma, and the effects of stroke—some analysts worried that the pace of research had slowed significantly.

Estimating the company's financial liability from the Vioxx lawsuits was difficult. Some 84 million people had taken the drug worldwide over a five-year period from 1999 to 2004. In testimony before Congress, Dr. David Graham, a staff scientist at the Food and Drug Administration, estimated that as many as 139,000 people in the United States had had heart attacks or strokes as a result of taking Vioxx, and about 55,000 of these

---

[4] Merck received the 1991 Business Enterprise Trust Award for this action. See Stephanie Weiss and Kirk O. Hanson, "Merck and Co., Inc.: Addressing Third World Needs" (Business Enterprise Trust, 1991).

[5] Hawthorne, *The Merck Druggernaut,* pp. 17–18.

[6] Ibid., p. 38.

had died.[7] Merrill Lynch estimated the company's liability for compensatory damages alone in the range of $4 to $18 billion.[8] However, heart attacks and strokes were common, and they had multiple causes, including genetic predisposition, smoking, obesity, and a sedentary lifestyle. Determining the specific contribution of Vioxx to a particular cardiovascular event would be very difficult. The company vigorously maintained that it had done nothing wrong and vowed to defend every single case in court. By early 2006, only three cases had gone to trial, and the results had been a virtual draw—one decision for the plaintiff, one for Merck, and one hung jury.

Government Regulation of Prescription Drugs

In the United States, prescription medicines—like Vioxx—were regulated by the Food and Drug Administration (FDA).[9] Before a new drug could be sold to the public, its manufacturer had to carry out clinical trials to demonstrate both safety and effectiveness. Advisory panels of outside medical experts reviewed the results of these trials and recommended to the FDA's Office of Drug Safety whether or not to approve a new drug.[10] After a drug was on the market, the agency's Office of New Drugs continued to monitor it for safety, in a process known as post-market surveillance. These two offices both reported to the same boss, the FDA's director of the Center for Drug Evaluation and Research.

Once the FDA had approved a drug, physicians could prescribe it for any purpose, but the manufacturer could market it only for uses for which it had been approved. Therefore, companies had an incentive to continue to study approved drugs to provide data that they were safe and effective for the treatment of other conditions.

In the 1980s, the drug industry and some patient advocates had criticized the FDA for being too slow to approve new medicines. Patients were concerned that they were not getting new medicines fast enough, and drug companies were concerned that they were losing sales revenue. Each month an average drug spent under review represented $41.7 million in lost revenue, according to one study.[11]

In 1992, Congress passed the Prescription Drug User Fee Act (PDUFA). This law, which was supported by the industry, required pharmaceutical companies to pay "user fees" to the FDA to review proposed new medicines. Between 1993 and 2001, the FDA received around $825 million in such fees from drug makers seeking approval. (During this period, it also received $1.3 billion appropriated by Congress.) This infusion of new revenue enabled the agency to hire 1,000 new employees and to shorten the approval time for new drugs from 27 months in 1993 to 14 months in 2001.[12]

[7] "FDA Failing in Drug Safety, Official Asserts," *The New York Times,* November 19, 2004. The full transcript of the hearing of the U.S. Senate Committee on Finance, "FDA, Merck, and Vioxx: Putting Patient Safety First?" is available online at *http://finance.senate.gov.*

[8] "Despite Warnings, Drug Giant Took Long Path to Vioxx Recall," *The New York Times,* November 14, 2004.

[9] A history of the FDA and of its relationship to business may be found in Philip J. Hilts, *Protecting America's Health: The FDA, Business, and One Hundred Years of Regulation* (New York: Alfred A. Knopf, 2003).

[10] Marcia Angell, *The Trust about the Drug Companies* (New York: Random House, 2004), Ch. 2.

[11] Merrill Lynch data reported in "A World of Hurt," *Fortune,* January 10, 2005, p. 18.

[12] U.S. General Accounting Office, *Food and Drug Administration: Effect of User Fees on Drug Approval Times, Withdrawals, and Other Agency Activities,* September 2002.

Despite the benefits of PDUFA, some felt that industry-paid fees were a bad idea. In an editorial published in December 2004, the *Journal of the American Medical Association (JAMA)* concluded: "It is unreasonable to expect that the same agency that was responsible for approval of drug licensing and labeling would also be committed to actively seek evidence to prove itself wrong (i.e., that the decision to approve the product was subsequently shown to be incorrect)." *JAMA* went on to recommend establishment of a separate agency to monitor drug safety.[13] Dr. David Kessler, a former FDA commissioner, rejected this idea, responding that "strengthening post-marketing surveillance is certainly in order, but you don't want competing agencies."[14]

Some evidence suggested that the morale of FDA staff charged with evaluating the safety of new medicines had been hurt by relentless pressure to bring drugs to market quickly. In 2002, a survey of agency scientists found that only 13 percent were "completely confident" that the FDA's "final decisions adequately assess the safety of a drug." Thirty-one percent were "somewhat confident" and 5 percent lacked "any confidence." Two-thirds of those surveyed lacked confidence that the agency "adequately monitors the safety of prescription jobs once they are on the market." And nearly one in five said they had "been pressured to approve or recommend approval" for a drug "despite reservations about [its] safety, efficacy or quality."[15]

After the FDA shortened the approval time, the percentage of drugs recalled following approval increased from 1.56% for 1993–1996 to 5.35% for 1997–2001.[16] Vioxx was the ninth drug taken off the market in seven years.

Influence at the Top

The pharmaceutical industry's success in accelerating the approval of new drugs reflected its strong presence in Washington. The major drug companies, their trade association PhRMA (Pharmaceutical Research and Manufacturers of America), and their executives consistently donated large sums of money to both political parties and, through their political action committees, to various candidates. The industry's political contributions are shown in Exhibit 2.

Following the Congressional ban on soft money contributions in 2003, the industry shifted much of its contributions to so-called stealth PACs, nonprofit organizations which were permitted by law to take unlimited donations without revealing their source. These organizations could, in turn, make "substantial" political expenditures, providing political activity was not their primary purpose.[17]

In addition, the industry maintained a large corps of lobbyists active in the nation's capital. In 2003, for example, drug companies and their trade association spent $108 million on lobbying and hired 824 individual lobbyists, according to a report by Public Citizen.[18] Merck spent $40.7 million on lobbying between 1998 and 2004.[19] One of the

[13] "Postmarketing Surveillance—Lack of Vigilance, Lack of Trust," *Journal of the American Medical Association* 92, no. 21 (December 1, 2004), p. 2649.

[14] "FDA Lax in Drug Safety, Journal Warns," *www.sfgate.com*, November 23, 2004.

[15] 2002 Survey of 846 FDA scientists conducted by the Office of the Inspector General of the Department of Health and Human Services, *www.peer.org/FDAscientistsurvey*.

[16] "Postmarketing Surveillance."

[17] "Big PhRMA's Stealth PACs: How the Drug Industry Uses 501(c) Non-Profit Groups to Influence Elections," *Congress Watch*, September 2004.

[18] "Drug Industry and HMOs Deployed an Army of Nearly 1,000 Lobbyists to Push Medicare Bill, Report Finds," June 23, 2004, *www.citizen.org*.

[19] Data available at *www.publicintegrity.org*.

Election Cycle	Total Contributions	Contributions from Individuals	Contributions from PACs	Soft Money Contributions	Percentage to Republicans
2006	$5,187,393	$1,753,159	$3,434,234	N/A	70%
2004	$18,181,045	$8,445,485	$9,735,560	N/A	66%
2002	$29,441,951	$3,332,040	$6,957,382	$19,152,529	74%
2000	$26,688,292	$5,660,457	$5,649,913	$15,377,922	69%
1998	$13,169,694	$2,673,845	$4,107,068	$6,388,781	64%
1996	$13,754,796	$3,413,516	$3,584,217	$6,757,063	66%
1994	$7,706,303	$1,935,150	$3,477,146	$2,294,007	56%
1992	$7,924,262	$2,389,370	$3,205,014	$2,329,878	56%
1990	$3,237,592	$771,621	$2,465,971	N/A	54%
Total	$125,291,328	$30,374,643	$42,616,505	$52,300,180	67%

Source: Center for Responsive Politics, *www.opensecrets.org*.

industry's most effective techniques was to hire former elected officials or members of their staffs. For example, Billy Tauzin, formerly a Republican member of Congress from Louisiana and head of the powerful Committee on Energy and Commerce, which oversaw the drug industry, became president of PhRMA at a reported annual salary of $2 million in 2004.[20]

Over the years, the industry's representatives in Washington had established a highly successful record of promoting its political agenda on a range of issues. In addition to faster drug approvals, these had more recently included a Medicare prescription drug benefit, patent protections, and restrictions on drug imports from Canada.

The Blockbuster Model

In the 1990s, 80 percent of growth for the big pharmaceutical firms came from so-called "blockbuster" drugs.[21] Blockbusters have been defined by *Fortune* magazine as "medicines that serve vast swaths of the population and garner billions of dollars in annual revenue."[22] The ideal blockbuster, from the companies' view, was a medicine that could control chronic but usually nonfatal conditions that afflicted large numbers of people with health insurance. These might include, for example, daily maintenance drugs for high blood pressure or cholesterol, allergies, arthritis pain, or heartburn. Drugs that could actually cure a condition—and thus would not need to be taken for long periods—or were intended to treat diseases, like malaria or tuberculosis, that affected mainly the world's poor, were often less profitable.

Historically, drug companies focused most of their marketing efforts on prescribing physicians. The industry hired tens of thousands of sales representatives—often, attractive young men and women—to make the rounds of doctors' offices to talk about new products

---

[20] "Rep. Billy Tauzin Demonstrates that Washington's Revolving Door is Spinning Out of Control," *Public Citizen,* December 15, 2004, press release.

[21] "The Waning of the Blockbuster," *BusinessWeek,* October 18, 2004.

[22] "A World of Hurt," *Fortune,* January 10, 2005, p. 20.

and give out free samples.[23] Drug companies also offered doctors gifts—from free meals to tickets to sporting events—to cultivate their good will. They also routinely sponsored continuing education events for physicians, often featuring reports on their own medicines, and supported doctors financially with opportunities to consult and to conduct clinical trials.[24] In 2003 Merck spent $422 million to market Vioxx to doctors and hospitals.[25]

During the early 2000s, when Vioxx and Pfizer's Celebrex were competing head-to-head, sales representatives for the two firms were hard at work promoting their brand to doctors. Commented one rheumatologist of the competition between Merck and Pfizer at the time: "We were all aware that there was a great deal of marketing. Like a Coke-Pepsi war."[26] An internal Merck training manual for sales representatives, reported in the *The Wall Street Journal,* was titled "Dodge Ball Vioxx." It explained how to "dodge" doctors' questions, such as "I am concerned about the cardiovascular effects of Vioxx." Merck later said that this document had been taken out of context and that sales representatives "were not trained to avoid physician's questions."[27]

Direct-to-Consumer Advertising

Although marketing to doctors and hospitals continued to be important, in the late 1990s the focus shifted somewhat. In 1997, the FDA for the first time allowed drug companies to advertise directly to consumers. The industry immediately seized this opportunity, placing numerous ads for drugs—from Viagra to Nexium—on television and in magazines and newspapers. In 2004, the industry spent over $4 billion on such direct-to-consumer, or DTC, advertising. For example, in one ad for Vioxx, Olympic figure skating champion Dorothy Hamill glided gracefully across an outdoor ice rink to the tune of "It's a Beautiful Morning" by the sixties pop group The Rascals, telling viewers that she would "not let arthritis stop me." In all, Merck spent more than $500 million advertising Vioxx.[28]

The industry's media blitz for Vioxx and other drugs was highly effective. According to research by the Harvard School of Public Heath, each dollar spent on DTC advertising yielded $4.25 in sales.

The drug companies defended DTC ads, saying they informed consumers of newly available therapies and encouraged people to seek medical treatment. In the age of the Internet, commented David Jones, an advertising executive whose firm included several major drug companies, "consumers are becoming much more empowered to make their own health care decisions."[29]

However, others criticized DTC advertising, saying that it put pressure on doctors to prescribe drugs that might not be best for the patient. "When a patient comes in and wants something, there is a desire to serve them," said David Wofsy, president of the

---

[23] In 2005, 90,000 sales representatives were employed by the pharmaceutical industry, about one for every eight doctors. *The New York Times* revealed in an investigative article ("Give Me an Rx! Cheerleaders Pep Up Drug Sales," November 28, 2005) that many companies made a point of hiring former college cheerleaders for this role.

[24] The influence of the drug industry on the medical professional is documented in Katharine Greider, *The Big Fix: How the Pharmaceutical Industry Rips Off American Consumers* (New York: Public Affairs, 2003).

[25] "Drug Pullout," *Modern Healthcare,* October 18, 2004.

[26] "Marketing of Vioxx: How Merck Played Game of Catch-Up," *The New York Times,* February 11, 2005.

[27] "E-Mails Suggest Merck Knew Vioxx's Dangers at Early Stage," *The Wall Street Journal,* November 1, 2004.

[28] IMS Health estimate reported in: "Will Merck Survive Vioxx?" *Fortune,* November 1, 2004.

[29] "With or Without Vioxx, Drug Ads Proliferate," *The New York Times,* December 6, 2004.

American College of Rheumatology. "There is a desire on the part of physicians, as there is on anyone else who provides service, to keep the customer happy."[30] Even some industry executives expressed reservations. Said Hank McKinnell, CEO of Pfizer, "I'm beginning to think that direct-to-consumer ads are part of the problem. By having them on television without a very strong message that the doctor needs to determine safety, we've left this impression that all drugs are safe. In fact, no drug is safe."[31]

The Rise of Vioxx

Vioxx, the drug at the center of Merck's legal woes, was known as "a selective COX-2 inhibitor." Scientists had long understood that an enzyme called cyclo-oxygenase, or COX for short, was associated with pain and inflammation. In the early 1990s, researchers learned that there were really two kinds of COX enzyme. COX-1, it was found, performed several beneficial functions, including protecting the stomach lining. COX-2, on the other hand, contributed to pain and inflammation. Existing anti-inflammatory drugs suppressed both forms of the enzyme, which is why drugs like ibuprofen (Advil) relieved pain, but also caused stomach irritation in some users.

A number of drug companies, including Merck, were intrigued by the possibility of developing a medicine that would block just the COX-2, leaving the stomach-protective COX-1 intact. Such a drug would offer distinctive benefits to some patients, such as arthritis sufferers who were at risk for ulcers (bleeding sores in the intestinal tract).[32] As many as 16,500 people died each year in the United States from this condition.[33]

In May 1999, after several years of research and testing by Merck scientists, the FDA approved Vioxx for the treatment of osteoarthritis, acute pain in adults, and menstrual symptoms. The drug was later approved for rheumatoid arthritis. Although Merck, like other drug companies, never revealed what it spent to develop specific new medicines, estimates of the cost to develop a major new drug ran as high as $800 million.[34]

Vioxx quickly became exactly what Merck had hoped: a blockbuster. At its peak in 2001, Vioxx generated $2.1 billion in sales in the United States alone, contributing almost 10 percent of Merck's total sales revenue worldwide, as shown in Exhibit 3.

The retail price of Vioxx was around $3.00 per pill, compared with pennies per pill for older anti-inflammatory drugs like aspirin and Advil. Of course, Vioxx was often covered, at least partially, under a user's health insurance, while over-the-counter drugs were not.

Safety Warnings

Even before the drug was approved, some evidence cast doubt on the safety of Vioxx. These clues were later confirmed in other studies.

Merck Research: Internal company e-mails suggested that Merck scientists might have been worried about the cardiovascular risks of Vioxx as early as its development phase. In a 1997 e-mail, reported in the *The Wall Street Journal*, Dr. Alise Reicin, a Merck scientist, stated that "the possibility of CV (cardiovascular) events is of great concern."

---

[30] "A 'Smart' Drug Fails the Safety Test," *The Washington Post,* October 3, 2004.

[31] "A World of Hurt," *Fortune,* January 10, 2005, p. 18.

[32] "Medicine Fueled by Marketing Intensified Troubles for Pain Pills," *The New York Times,* December 19, 2004.

[33] "New Scrutiny of Drugs in Vioxx's Family," *The New York Times,* October 4, 2004.

[34] This estimate was hotly debated. See, for example, "How Much Does the Pharmaceutical Industry Really Spend on R&D?" Ch. 3 in Angell, *The Trust;* and Merrill Goozner, *The $800 Million Pill: The Truth Behind the Cost of New Drugs* (Berkeley: University of California Press, 2004).

Exhibit 3   **Vioxx Sales in the United States, 1999–2004**

	U.S. Prescriptions Dispensed	U.S. Sales	U.S. Sales of Vioxx as % of TotalMerck Sales
1999	4,845,000	$372,697,000	2.2%
2000	20,630,000	$1,526,382,000	7.6%
2001	25,406,000	$2,084,736,000	9.8%
2002	22,044,000	$1,837,680,000	8.6%
2003	19,959,000	$1,813,391,000	8.1%
2004*	13,994,000	$1,342,236,000	5.9%

*Withdrawn from the market in September 2004.

Sources: Columns 1 and 2: IMS Health (*www.imshealth.com*); Column 3: Merck Annual Reports *(www.merck.com)*.

She added, apparently sarcastically, "I just can't wait to be the one to present those results to senior management!" A lawyer representing Merck said this e-mail had been taken out of context.[35]

VIGOR: A study code-named VIGOR, completed in 2000 after the drug was already on the market, compared rheumatoid arthritis patients taking Vioxx with another group taking naproxen (Aleve). Merck financed the research, which was designed to study gastrointestinal side effects. The study found—as the company had expected—that Vioxx was easier on the stomach than naproxen. But it also found that the Vioxx group had nearly five times as many heart attacks (7.3 per thousand person-years) as the naproxen group (1.7 per thousand person-years).[36] Publicly, Merck hypothesized that these findings were due to the heart-protective effect of naproxen, rather than to any defect inherent in Vioxx. Privately, however, the company seemed worried. In an internal e-mail dated March 9, 2000, under the subject line "Vigor," the company's research director, Dr. Edward Scolnick, said that cardiovascular events were "clearly there" and called them "a shame." But, he added, "there is always a hazard."[37] At that time, the company considered reformulating Vioxx by adding an agent to prevent blood clots (and reduce CV risk), but then dropped the project.

The FDA was sufficiently concerned by the VIGOR results that it required Merck to add additional warning language to its label. These changes appeared in April 2002, after lengthy negotiations between the agency and the company over their wording.[38]

Kaiser/Permanente: In August 2004, Dr. David Graham, a scientist at the FDA, reported the results of a study of the records of 1.4 million patients enrolled in the Kaiser health maintenance organization in California. He found that patients on high doses of Vioxx had three times the rate of heart attacks as patients on Celebrex, a competing COX-2 inhibitor made by Pfizer. Merck discounted this finding, saying that studies of

[35] "E-Mails Suggest Merck Knew Vioxx's Dangers at Early Stage," *The Wall Street Journal,* November 1, 2004.

[36] "Comparison of Upper Gastrointestinal Toxicity of Rofecoxib and Naproxen in Patients with Rheumatoid Arthritis," *New England Journal of Medicine,* 2000, p. 323.

[37] "E-Mails Suggest Merck Knew Vioxx's Dangers at Early Stage."

[38] At one of the early Vioxx trials, the plaintiff introduced a Merck internal memo that calculated that the company would make $229 million more in profits if it delayed changes to warning language on the label by four months (*New York Times,* August 20, 2005). The FDA did not have the authority to dictate label language; any changes had to be negotiated with the manufacturer.

patient records were less reliable than double blind clinical studies.[39] Dr. Graham later charged that his superiors at the FDA had "ostracized" him and subjected him to "veiled threats" if he did not qualify his criticism of Vioxx. The FDA called these charges "baloney."[40]

APPROVe: In order to examine the possibility that Vioxx posed a cardiovascular risk, Merck decided to monitor patients enrolled in a clinical trial called APPROVe to see if they those taking Vioxx had more heart attacks and strokes than those who were taking a placebo (sugar pill). This study had been designed to determine if Vioxx reduced the risk of recurrent colon polyps (a precursor to colon cancer); Merck hoped it would lead to FDA approval of the drug for this condition. The APPROVe study was planned before the VIGOR results were known.

Merck Recalls the Drug

On the evening of Thursday, September 23, 2004, Dr. Peter S. Kim, president of Merck Research Labs, received a phone call from scientists monitoring the colon polyp study. Researchers had found, the scientists told him, that after 18 months of continuous use individuals taking Vioxx were more than twice as likely to have a heart attack or stroke than those taking a placebo. The scientists recommended that the study be halted because of "unacceptable" risk.[41]

Dr. Kim later described to a reporter for *The New York Times* the urgent decision-making process that unfolded over the next hours and days as the company responded to this news.

> On Friday, I looked at the data with my team. The first thing you do is review the data. We did that. Second is you double-check the data, go through it and make sure that everything is O.K. [At that point] I knew that barring some big mistake in the analysis, we had an issue here. Around noon, I called [CEO] Ray Gilmartin and told him what was up. He said, "Figure out what was the best thing for patient safety." We then spent Friday and the rest of the weekend going over the data and analyzing it in different ways and calling up medical experts to set up meetings where we would discuss the data and their interpretations and what to do.[42]

According to later interviews with some of the doctors consulted that weekend by Merck, the group was of mixed opinion. Some experts argued that Vioxx should stay on the market, with a strong warning label so that doctors and patients could judge the risk for themselves. But others thought the drug should be withdrawn because no one knew why the drug was apparently causing heart attacks. One expert commented that "Merck prides itself on its ethical approach. I couldn't see Merck saying we're going to market a drug with a safety problem."[43]

On Monday, Dr. Kim recommended to Gilmartin that Vioxx be withdrawn from the market. The CEO agreed. The following day, Gilmartin notified the board, and the

[39] "Study of Painkiller Suggests Heart Risk," *The New York Times,* August 26, 2004.

[40] "FDA Official Alleges Pressure to Suppress Vioxx Findings," *The Washington Post,* October 8, 2004.

[41] "Painful Withdrawal for Makers of Vioxx," *The Washington Post,* October 18, 2004. Detailed data reported the following day in *The New York Times* showed that 30 of the 1,287 patients taking Vioxx had suffered a heart attack, compared with 11 of 1,299 taking a placebo; 15 on Vioxx had had a stroke or transient ischemic attack (minor stroke), compared with 7 taking a placebo.

[42] "A Widely Used Arthritis Drug Is Withdrawn," *The New York Times,* October 1, 2004.

[43] "Painful Withdrawal for Makers of Vioxx," *The Washington Post,* October 18, 2004.

company contacted the FDA. On Thursday, September 30, Merck issued a press release, which stated in part:

> Merck & Co., Inc., announced today a voluntary withdrawal of VIOXX®. This decision is based on new data from a three-year clinical study. In this study, there was an increased risk for cardiovascular (CV) events, such as heart attack and stroke, in patients taking VIOXX 25 mg compared to those taking placebo (sugar pill). While the incidence of CV events was low, there was an increased risk beginning after 18 months of treatment. The cause of the clinical study result is uncertain, but our commitment to our patients is clear. . . . Merck is notifying physicians and pharmacists and has informed the Food and Drug Administration of this decision. We are taking this action because we believe it best serves the interests of patients. That is why we undertook this clinical trial to better understand the safety profile of VIOXX. And it's why we instituted this voluntary withdrawal upon learning about these data. Be assured that Merck will continue to do everything we can to maintain the safety of our medicines.

Discussion Questions

1. Do you believe that Merck acted in a socially responsible and ethical manner with regard to Vioxx? Why or why not? In your answer, please address the company's drug development and testing, marketing and advertising, relationships with government regulators and policymakers, and handling of the recall.
2. What should or could Merck have done differently, if anything?
3. What is the best way for society to protect consumers of prescription medicines? Specifically, what are the appropriate roles for pharmaceutical companies, government regulators and policy makers, patients and their physicians, and the court system in assuring the safety and effectiveness of prescription medicines?
4. How should the present system be changed, if at all, to better protect patients?

Kimpton Hotels' EarthCare Program

Michael Pace faced a dilemma. He was Kimpton Hotels' West Coast Director of Operations and Environmental Programs, General Manager of its Villa Florence Hotel in San Francisco, and the main catalyst for implementing its EarthCare program nationally. He was determined to help the boutique hotel chain "walk the talk" regarding its commitment to environmental responsibility, but he also had agreed not to introduce any new products or processes that would be more expensive than those they replaced. They were already successful in introducing nontoxic cleaning products, promotional materials printed on recycled paper, towel and linen reuse programs, and complimentary organic coffee and had made substantial progress in recycling bottles, cans, paper and cardboard. Now that the initial phase of the program was being implemented nationwide, he and the company's team of eco-champions were facing some difficult challenges with the roll-out of the second, more ambitious, phase.

For example, the team had to decide whether to recommend the purchase of linens made of organic cotton, which vendors insisted would cost at least 50 percent more than standard linens. It would cost an average of $100,000 to $150,000 to switch out all the sheets, pillowcases, and towels in each hotel. If they couldn't negotiate the price down, was there some way they could introduce organic cotton in a limited but meaningful way? All linens were commingled in the laundry, so they couldn't be introduced one floor at a time. Maybe they could start with pillowcases—although the sheets wouldn't be organic, guests would be resting their heads on organic cotton. Would it even be worth spending so much on linens? The team would face similar issues when deciding whether to recommend environmentally friendly carpeting or furniture.

There were also issues with their recycling initiatives. The program had been field-tested at Kimpton Hotels in San Francisco, a singular city in one of the most environmentally aware states in the United States. Now the eco-champions team had to figure out how to make it work in cities like Chicago, which didn't even have a municipal recycling program in place. In Denver, recycling actually cost more than waste disposal to a landfill, due to the low cost of land in eastern Colorado. Pace knew that the environmental initiatives most likely to succeed would be those that could be seamlessly implemented by the general managers and employees of the 39 unique Kimpton hotels around the country. The last thing he wanted to do was to make their jobs more difficult by imposing cookie-cutter standards. At the same time, he knew that recycling just 50 percent of Kimpton Hotels' waste stream would save over $250,000 per year in waste disposal costs.

Kimpton had recently embarked on a national campaign to build brand awareness by associating its name with each unique property. Pace knew that the success of Kimpton's strategy would rest heavily on its ability to maintain the care, integrity, and uniqueness that customers had come to associate with its chain of boutique hotels. Other hotel companies had begun investing heavily in the niche that Kimpton had pioneered. To differentiate itself, the company had to continue to find innovative ways to offer services that addressed the needs and values of its customers, and EarthCare was a crucial part of its plans. But could Pace find a way to make it happen within Kimpton's budget, and without adversely affecting the customer experience? Would Kimpton be able to keep the promises made by its new corporate brand?

The Greening of the U.S. Hotel Industry

The U.S. hotel industry—with its 4.5 million rooms, common areas and lobbies, conventions, restaurants, laundry facilities, and back offices—had a significant environmental impact. According to the American Hotel and Lodging Association, the average hotel toilet was flushed 7 times per day per guest, an average shower was 7.5 minutes long, and 40 percent of bathroom lights were left on at night. A typical hotel used 218 gallons of water per day per occupied room. Energy use was pervasive, including lighting in guestrooms and common areas, heating and air-conditioning, and washing and drying towels and linens. The hotel industry spent $3.7 billion per year on electricity.[1]

Hotels had other environmental impacts, as well. Guestrooms generated surprisingly large amounts of waste, ranging from one-half pound to 28 pounds per day, and averaging 2 pounds per day per guest. Nonrefillable bottles of amenities, such as shampoo and lotion, generated large amounts of plastic waste, and products used to clean bathrooms and furniture contained harmful chemicals. Paints contained high levels of volatile organic compounds. Back office and front desk activities generated large amounts of waste paper. And furniture, office equipment, kitchen and laundry appliances were rarely selected for their environmental advantages.

Opportunities for reducing a hotel's environmental footprint were plentiful, and many could yield bottom-line savings. Reduced laundering of linens, at customer discretion, had already been adopted enthusiastically across the spectrum of budget to luxury hotels; 38 percent of hotels had linen reuse programs. Low-flow showerheads could deliver the same quality shower experience using half the water of a conventional showerhead. Faucet aerators could cut water requirements by 50 percent. A 13-watt compact fluorescent bulb gave the same light as a 60-watt incandescent, lasted about 10 times longer, and used about 70 percent less energy. Waste costs also could be significantly reduced. For many hotels, 50–80 percent of their solid waste stream was compostable, and a significant part of the remaining waste was made up of recyclables, such as paper, aluminum, and glass.

In addition to bottom line savings, environmental programs held the potential to generate new business. Governmental bodies and NGOs, corporations, and convention/meeting planners were showing increased interest in selecting hotels using environmental criteria. California, which had an annual travel budget of $70 million, had launched a Green Lodging Program and encouraged state employees to select hotels it certified. The criteria for certification include recycling, composting, energy and water efficient fixtures and

---

[1] California Green Lodging Program, *www. Ciwmb.ca.gov/epp/*

lighting, and nontoxic or less toxic alternatives for cleaning supplies. State governments in Pennsylvania, Florida, Vermont, and Virginia also had developed green lodging programs.

CERES, a well-respected environmental nonprofit, had developed the Green Hotel Initiative, designed to demonstrate and increase demand for environmentally responsible hotel services. Some major corporations had endorsed the initiative, including Ford Motor Company, General Motors, Nike, American Airlines, and Coca-Cola. CERC, the Coalition for Environmentally Responsible Conventions, and the Green Meetings Industry Council were encouraging meeting planners to "green" their events by, among other things, choosing environmentally friendly hotels for lodging and meeting sites.

Despite all this potential, environmental progress in the U.S. hotel industry had been very limited. With a few exceptions, most hotels were doing very little beyond easy-to-implement cost-saving initiatives. These hotels had reduced their environmental footprint as a consequence of their cost-cutting efforts, but they were not necessarily committed to a comprehensive environmental program. During a 1998 effort by Cornell University's School of Hotel Administration to identify hotels employing environmental best practices, researchers were "surprised by the dearth of nominations."[2] In contrast to their U.S. counterparts, hotels in Canada and Europe seemed to be embracing the hotel greening process.

Kimpton Hotels

Kimpton Hotels was founded in 1981 by the late Bill Kimpton, who once said, "No matter how much money people have to spend on big, fancy hotels, they're still intimidated and unsettled when they arrive. So the psychology of how you build hotels and restaurants is very important. You put a fireplace in the lobby and create a warm, friendly restaurant, and the guest will feel at home."

Credited with inventing the boutique hotel segment, Kimpton Hotels had built a portfolio of unique properties in the upscale segment of the industry.[3] By 2005, Kimpton had grown to include 39 hotels throughout North America and Canada, each one designed to create a unique and exceptional guest experience. Every hotel lobby had a cozy fireplace and plush sitting area, where complimentary coffee was served every morning, and wine every evening. Guestrooms were stylishly decorated and comfortably furnished, offering amenities such as specialty suites that included Tall Rooms and Yoga Rooms. Every room offered high-speed wireless Internet access and desks with ample lighting. Rather than rewarding customer loyalty with a point program, Kimpton offered customization and personalization. "We record the preferences of our loyal guests," said Mike Depatie, Kimpton's CEO of real estate. "Someone may want a jogging magazine and a Diet Coke when they arrive. We can get that done."

Business travel (group and individual) accounted for approximately 65 percent of Kimpton's revenues, and leisure travel (tour group and individual) the other 35 percent. The selection of hotels for business meetings and conferences was through meeting and conference organizers. Around 35 percent of all rooms were booked through Kimpton's

---

[2] Cathy A. Enz and Judy A. Siguaw, "Best Hotel Environmental Practices," *Cornell Hotel and Restaurant Administration Quarterly*, October, 1999.

[3] Sloan, Gene, "Let the Pillowfights Begin", *USA Today*, 8/27/2004

call center, 25 percent through travel agents, 25 percent through their Web site, and the remainder "came in off the street." The Internet portion of their business continued to grow, but they didn't cater to buyers looking for the "steal of the century." Rather, they were increasingly being discovered by the 25 percent of customers that market researchers called *unchained seekers*, many of whom used the Internet to search for unique accommodations that matched their particular needs or values.

Historically, Kimpton had prospered by purchasing and renovating buildings at a discount in strategic nationwide locations that were appropriate for their niche segment. The hotel industry in general had been slow to enter the boutique niche, and Kimpton enjoyed a substantial edge in experience in developing value-added services for guests. "All hotels are starting to look alike and act alike, and we are the counterpoint, the contrarians," explained Tom LaTour, Kimpton president and CEO. "We don't look like the brands, we don't act like the brands, and as the baby boomers move through the age wave, they will seek differentiated, experience-oriented products."

Kimpton's top executives took pride in their ability to recognize and develop both undervalued properties and undervalued people. Kimpton's hotel general managers were often refugees from large branded companies who did not thrive under hierarchical, standardized corporate structures. At Kimpton, they were afforded a great deal of autonomy, subject only to the constraints of customer service standards and capital and operating budgets.

This sense of autonomy and personal responsibility was conveyed down through the ranks to all 5,000 Kimpton employees. Kimpton's flexible corporate structure avoided hierarchy, preferring a circular structure where executives and employees were in constant communication.[4] Steve Pinetti, Senior Vice President for Sales and Marketing, liked to tell the story of a new parking attendant who had to figure out how to deal with a guest who felt that he had not been adequately informed of extra charges for parking his car at the hotel. The attendant decided on the spot to reduce the charges, and asked the front desk to make the necessary adjustments. He had heard his general manager tell everyone that they should feel empowered to take responsibility for making guests happy, but he fully expected to be grilled by his GM, at the very least, about his actions. A sense of dread took hold as he was called to the front of the room at a staff meeting the very next day, but it dissipated quickly when his general manager handed him a special award for his initiative.

Commitment to Social and Environmental Responsibility

An important part of Kimpton's history was its long-standing commitment to social and environmental responsibility. Staff at each hotel had always been encouraged to engage with local community nonprofits that benefit the arts, education, the underprivileged and other charitable causes. Kimpton maintained these local programs even in periods of falling occupancy rates and industry downturns. These local efforts evolved into the companywide Kimpton Cares program in 2004, as part of the company's corporate branding effort. At the national level, Kimpton supported the National AIDS Fund (in support of its Red Ribbon Campaign) and Dress for Success (which assisted economically disadvantaged women struggling to enter the workforce) by allotting a share of a guest's room fee to the charity. At the global level, Kimpton embarked on a partnership with Trust for Public Land (TPL), a nonprofit dedicated to the preservation of land for public use. In

[4] Liz French, *Americanexecutive.com*, December, 2004.

2005, Kimpton committed to raising $15,000 from its total room revenues to introduce the TPL Parks for People program, and created eco-related fundraising events in each of its cities to further support the campaign.

Kimpton also introduced EarthCare, a comprehensive program of environmental initiatives intended for rollout to all the chain's hotels. "As business leaders, we believe we have a responsibility to positively impact the communities we live in, to be conscious about our environment and to make a difference where we can," said Niki Leondakis, Kimpton's Chief Operating Officer. Kimpton's top executives considered the Kimpton Cares program, and its EarthCare component, essential parts of the company's branding effort. Steve Pinetti noted, "What drove it was our belief that our brand needs to stand for something. What do we want to stand for in the community? We want to draw a line in the sand. We also want our impact to be felt as far and wide as it can. Hopefully, through our good deeds, we'll be able to influence other companies."

Anecdotal evidence suggested that Kimpton's early efforts had already had financial payoffs. Kimpton was receiving significant coverage of its EarthCare program in local newspapers and travel publications. "We've booked almost half a million dollars in meetings from a couple of corporations in Chicago because of our ecological reputation," said Pinetti. "Their reps basically told us, 'Your values align with our values, and we want to spend money on hotels that think the way we do.'" Kimpton believed that companies that identified with being socially responsible would look for partners like Kimpton that shared those values; and that certifications like the California Green Lodging Program would attract both individuals and corporate clientele.

However, Pinetti noted, "The cost-effectiveness wasn't clear when we started. I thought we might get some business out of this, but that's not why we did it. We think it's the right thing to do, and it generates a lot of enthusiasm among our employees."

Kimpton's Real Estate CEO Mike Depatie believed that incorporating care for communities and the environment into the company's brand had been a boon to hiring. "We attract and keep employees because they feel that from a values standpoint, we have a corporate culture and value system that's consistent with theirs," he commented. "They feel passionate about working here." While the hotel industry was plagued with high turnover, Kimpton's turnover rates were lower than the national averages.

Rolling Out the EarthCare Program

Pinetti and Pace realized that they were too busy to handle all the planning and operational details of the national rollout, so they turned to Jeff Slye, of Business Evolution Consulting, for help. Slye was a process management consultant who wanted to help small and medium-sized business owners figure out how to "ecofy" their companies. He had heard that Kimpton was trying to figure out how to make its operations greener and integrate this effort into their branding effort. When they first met in October 2004, Pinetti and Pace handed Slye a 10-page document detailing their objectives and a plan for rolling out the initiative in phases. Kimpton's program was to have the following eco-mission statement:

Lead the hospitality industry in supporting a sustainable world by continuing to deliver a premium guest experience through nonintrusive, high quality, eco-friendly products and services.

Our mission is built upon a companywide commitment towards water conservation; reduction of energy usage; elimination of harmful toxins and pollutants; recycling of all reusable waste; building and furnishing hotels with sustainable materials; and purchasing goods and services that directly support these principles.

Slye worked with Pinetti and Pace to fill various gaps in their plan and develop an ecostandards program, a concise report outlining a strategy for greening the products and operational processes that Kimpton used. In December 2004, Pinetti asked Slye to present the report to Kimpton's COO, Niki Leondakis. Leondakis greeted the proposal enthusiastically, but noted that it needed an additional component: a strategy for communicating the program both internally (to management and staff) and externally (to guests, investors, and the press). As important as the external audiences were, Slye knew that the internal communications strategy would be particularly crucial, given the autonomy afforded each Kimpton Hotel, each with its own set of local initiatives. Getting everyone on board would require a strategy that respected that aspect of Kimpton's culture.

Slye, Pace, and Pinetti decided to create an ad hoc network of eco-champions throughout the company. The national lead (Pace) and co-lead (Pinetti) would head up the communications effort and be accountable for its success. Each of five geographic regions (Pacific Northwest, San Francisco Bay Area, Central U.S., Washington D.C., and Northeast/Southeast), covering six or seven hotel properties, would also have a lead and co-lead who would help communicate the program to employees, and be the local point-persons in the chain of command. One of their key roles would be to solicit employee suggestions regarding ways to make products and processes greener.

In addition, a team of national eco-product specialists would be key components of the network. These specialists would be responsible for soliciting staff input and identifying and evaluating greener products as potential substitutes for existing ones. Products would be tested for effectiveness and evaluated on the basis of their environmental benefits, effect on guest perceptions, potential marketing value, and cost. Pinetti and Pace determined that specialists would be needed initially for six product categories: beverages, cleaning agents, office supplies, engineering, information technology, and room supplies. Meanwhile, Pace and Pinetti asked all general managers to report on their existing environmental initiatives, to get baseline feedback on what individual hotels were doing already. They turned the results into a matrix they could use to identify gaps and monitor progress for each hotel.

By February 2005, the network of eco-champions was in place, and everyone had agreed on the basic ground rules for the transition. No new product or service could cost more than the product or service it replaced, nor could it adversely affect customer perceptions or satisfaction. All leads, co-leads, and product specialists began meeting via conference call every Friday morning to discuss the greening initiative and share accounts of employee suggestions, progress achieved, and barriers encountered.

To help communicate the program's goals and achievements, and help motivate employees seeking recognition, the team began to post regular updates and success stories in Kimpton's internal weekly newsletter, *The Word*, which was distributed throughout the organization and read by all GMs. They also ran an EarthCare contest to further galvanize interest, which generated over 70 entries for categories such as Best Eco-Practice Suggestion, Most EarthCare Best Practices Adopted, and Best Art and Humor Depicting EarthCare. The team also communicated the environmental benefits of their activities to the staff. For example, printing on 35 percent post-consumer recycled paper would save 24,000 pounds of wood and recycling 100 glass bottles per month would save the energy equivalent of powering one hundred 100-watt light bulbs for 60 days.

The team of eco-champions also quickly learned that the national rollout effort would have its share of potential operational risks and challenges, which would need to be addressed. Among them:

- *Potential resistance by general managers (GMs) to a centralized initiative.* A green management program mandated by corporate headquarters might threaten Kimpton's culture of uniqueness and autonomy. GMs might chafe at what they saw as corporate intrusion upon their autonomy and would want the flexibility to adapt the program to local requirements.

- *Potential resistance by hotel staff to new products and procedures.* Kimpton's relatively low turnover meant that some employees had been working there for many years and had become accustomed to familiar ways of doing things. Informal queries by management, for example, revealed that many cleaning staff equated strong chemical odors with cleanliness. Also, many of the service staff did not speak English fluently, and might have difficulty understanding management's reasons for switching to new procedures or greener cleaning products.

- *A slower payback period or a lower rate of return for green investments, relative to others.* The gains in operating costs achieved by installing longer-life and more energy-efficient fluorescent lighting could take years to pay off, while higher acquisition costs could inflate short-term expenses. The same logic applied to water conservation investments. Would corporate executives and investors be patient? What if consumer tastes or Kimpton's branding strategies changed before investments had paid off?

- *Benefits intangible to customers.* Unless informed, guests would not be aware that their rooms have been painted with low-VOC paints. Likewise, organic cottons would likely not feel or look superior to traditional materials.

- *For some products, required investments might exceed existing budgets or fail to meet the cost parity criterion.* For example, the eco-specialists learned that one of Kimpton's vendors did have a Green Seal certified nontoxic line, but the products were selling at a 10–15 percent premium over standard products. They discovered that virtually every product they were interested in was more expensive than those currently used. At the extreme, eco-friendly paper products were priced 50 percent above standard products. Would additional budget be provided? Would savings in other areas be allowed to pay for it?

- *Marketing the program could prove challenging.* How should the EarthCare program be promoted, given customer concerns regarding the impact of some environmental initiatives on the quality of their guest experience? Guests might be concerned, for example, whether low-flow shower heads or fluorescent lighting would meet their expectations. According to the American Automobile Association's Diamond Rating Guidelines, some water saving showerheads and energy-saving light bulbs could lower a hotel's diamond rating.[5]

- *Regional variations in customer values.* Environmental awareness and concern varied considerably by geographic region, from very high on the West Coast and in the Northeast, to considerably lower in the South and Midwest.

- *Regional differences in recycling infrastructure and regulatory environment.* California had a mandated recycling program requiring 70 percent recycling of solid waste by 2007, so San Francisco's disposal service provided free recycling containers. Other localities might not be so generous.

Even in the face of these challenges, Kimpton executives believed that the EarthCare program was the smart, as well as the "right," thing to do. According to Tom LaTour, Chairman and CEO:

---

[5] *AAA Lodging Requirements & Diamond Rating Guidelines,* AAA Publishing, Heathrow, FL, June 2001.

It's good business. It's not just because we're altruistic, it's good for business. Otherwise the investors would say, what are you guys doing? A lot of people think it's going to cost more. It's actually [more] advantageous to be eco-friendly than not.

Niki Leondakis, COO, saw the program's impact on marketing and employee retention:

Many people say we're heading toward a tipping point: If you're not environmentally conscious, your company will be blackballed from people's choices. Also, employees today want to come to work every day not just for the paycheck but to feel good about what they're doing. . . . It's very important to them to be aligned with the values of the people they work for, so from the employee retention standpoint, this helps us retain and attract them so we can select from the best and the brightest.[6]

Discussion Questions

1. What are the benefits of Kimpton's environmental sustainability initiatives? What are their costs?
2. How would you justify the EarthCare program to Kimpton's board of directors and stockholders? That is, what is the business case for this program?
3. What challenges face the EarthCare program, and how might Kimpton overcome them?
4. What further steps should Kimpton take to institutionalize its environmental commitments?
5. How would you measure the success of the EarthCare program, and how should it be reported to stakeholders?

[6] Carlo Wolff, "Environmental Evangelism: Kimpton Walks the Eco-Walk," *Lodging Hospitality,* March 1, 2005.

Johnson & Johnson and the Human Life International Shareholder Proposal

James McCafferty, a second-year MBA student at Western Washington University, came home from class one day in early 2006 to find a pile of mail waiting for him. In it was material from Johnson & Johnson, the health care products and services company, including the firm's 2005 annual report and proxy statement. McCafferty owned several hundred shares of Johnson & Johnson as part of his investment portfolio, and he took his responsibilities as a shareholder very seriously. "I make an attempt to be aware of the company's news stories, review the annual report, and at least take a quick look through the reported financials," he explained.

As he looked through the proxy statement, McCafferty noticed a shareholder proposal. Entitled "Shareholder Proposal on Charitable Contributions," it brought to mind discussions in his MBA course work on corporate social responsibility. Intrigued, he read further. The proposal had been put forward by a Virginia-based organization called Human Life International. The proposal read, in its main part: "Resolved: The shareholders request the Board of Directors to implement a policy listing all charitable contributions on the company Web site."

As McCafferty continued to read, he saw that behind this relatively straightforward and narrow proposal was a more complex issue. As part of its charitable giving, Johnson & Johnson had contributed to Planned Parenthood Federation of America Inc., an organization that provided reproductive health care and sexual health information to women, men, and teens. Among other services, Planned Parenthood provided abortions and abortion referrals. As a result, several pro-life organizations (groups opposed to abortion) had boycotted Johnson & Johnson products, and several mutual funds had decided against investing in the company's stock or to sell stock they already owned. The resolution implied that Johnson & Johnson's contributions had the potential to hurt shareholder value and therefore should be fully disclosed. (See Exhibit 1 for the full text of the shareholder proposal.) "At first I had several reactions," McCafferty explained later.

By Brian Burton, Steven Globerman, and James McCafferty, Western Washington University. An earlier version of this case was presented at the 2006 annual meeting of the North American Case Research Association, San Diego, California, October 20–21, 2006. Copyright © 2006 by the authors; all rights reserved to the authors and NACRA. Used by permission.

Exhibit 1 — Item 4: Shareholder Proposal on Charitable Contributions

The following shareholder proposal has been submitted to the Company for action at the meeting by Human Life International of Front Royal, Virginia, a holder of 100 shares of stock. The affirmative vote of a majority of the shares voted at the meeting is required for approval of the shareholder proposal. The text of the proposal follows:

"Whereas, Thomas Jefferson said in a Bill for Establishing Religious Freedom, 'To compel a man to furnish contributions of money for the propagation of opinions, which he disbelieves is sinful and tyrannical.'

Whereas, charitable contributions should serve to enhance shareholder value.

Whereas, our company has given money to 'charitable' groups involved in abortion and other activities.

Whereas, our company respects diverse religious beliefs. It should try not to offend these beliefs wherever possible.

Whereas, our company is the subject of a boycott by Life Decisions International because of certain 'charitable' contributions.

Whereas, mutual funds like the Timothy Plan and the Ave Maria Catholic Values Fund will not invest in our company because of contributions to certain groups.

Whereas, some potential recipients of charitable funds promote same sex marriages.

Resolved: The shareholders request the Board of Directors to implement a policy listing all charitable contributions on the company Web site.

Supporting Statement: Full disclosure is integral to good corporate governance. Shareholder money is entrusted to the Board of Directors to be invested in a prudent manner for the benefit of the shareholders. People did not invest in this company so a portion of their investment could be given to someone else's favorite charity. In fact, some money has gone to Planned Parenthood, a group responsible for more than 200,000 abortions per year. How such contributions contribute to shareholder value would be difficult to quantify. In contrast, the subsequent boycotts caused by these contributions could hardly be considered beneficial."

"On one hand, we had a company that had not disclosed all its philanthropic efforts. On the other hand, I had to wonder if specific philanthropic efforts really influenced the share price."

Reading further, McCafferty saw that the board of directors had issued a rejoinder, urging that shareholders vote against the proposal. Johnson & Johnson's response was twofold. First, it argued that its corporate contributions program was essential to its mission and values, regardless of its effect on shareholder wealth. Second, those contributions were already sufficiently disclosed in the company's annual report on its corporate contributions program. (See Exhibit 2 for the full text of management's response.)

James McCafferty

In 2006 James McCafferty was 36 years old. Growing up in Seattle, Washington, he had decided to try to improve society both through his paid employment and volunteer activity. "It has always seemed to me that if I must work, I might as well do work that does more than add to someone's bottom line," he explained. McCafferty graduated from the University of Oregon in 1993 with a major in journalism, with an emphasis in public relations (PR), and went to work for the Seattle Community College District as a foundations

Exhibit 2

Management's Statement in Opposition to Shareholder Proposal

The Board of Directors favors a vote AGAINST the adoption of this proposal for the following reasons:

The many contributions of Johnson & Johnson to a broad range of charitable organizations are a powerful reflection of our responsibility "to the communities in which we live and work and to the world community," as articulated in the Johnson & Johnson Credo. Our efforts are based on partnerships with outstanding not-for-profit and community organizations, and our objective for these partnerships is improvement in the quality of life in our communities.

The Company already publishes on an annual basis a report on its Corporate Contributions Program that discloses the total contributions made by the Johnson & Johnson Family of Companies for each of the last five years, including a breakdown of contributions made in cash, in non-cash and total contributions as a percentage of the Company's worldwide pre-tax income. This report, which is available on the Company's Web site at *www.jnj.com,* also provides background and details concerning significant contributions programs that occurred in the prior year. We believe this report provides our shareholders and other stakeholders with meaningful and robust disclosure on the charitable contributions made by the Company.

We do not believe that the detailed disclosure sought by this proposal would provide any greater insight for shareholders or serve the Company, our shareholders or the communities we are trying to serve. Moreover, the proposal would require additional administrative efforts by the many operating companies of Johnson & Johnson, which would be burdensome, and not an effective use of the Company's resources.

The Johnson & Johnson Corporate Contributions Program is fundamental to our values and to our mission to improve health care for people all over the world. This shareholder proposal would be detrimental to our Corporate Contributions Program. It is, therefore, recommended that the shareholders vote AGAINST this proposal.

Source: *www.investor.jnj.com/downloads/2006_proxy.pdf.*

and PR specialist. After five years, he became the program director and summer camp director for the Snohomish County Council of Camp Fire USA. During this time he also consulted with many nonprofit and educational groups in the areas of development and overall marketing, and he fulfilled his commitment to volunteerism through working with the University of Oregon Alumni Association and the American Camp Association.

By 2004, McCafferty had decided that to have a truly positive impact on society he needed to go back to school to earn his Master of Business Administration (MBA) degree. He entered Western Washington University's MBA program in September 2004 and was scheduled to graduate in June 2006.

McCafferty had long been an active investor in equity markets. Beyond his personal investments—which included stock from nearly 25 firms, bonds, and mutual funds from several companies—he managed several trust funds for others. "Being somewhat knowledgeable about investing and business can be both a blessing and a curse," McCafferty observed. "People I am close to have come to me for guidance, and I have taken on their portfolios as a personal challenge to see if I can get them where they want to be." McCafferty selected investments on the basis of their potential for growth, dividend yield, and the market appeal of a firm's products or services. He also considered whether a firm acknowledged and took action to mitigate any negative social impacts. "I look for the personality behind the company when evaluating potential investments," he explained. "If I don't agree with the business model or the company's overall behavior I'll keep looking even if the ratios look great. As an investor I demand both profitability and long-term societal sustainability. It makes no sense to me to seek large short-term gains when the net benefit to all of us is a long-term loss." McCafferty understood proxy voting. He realized that as an individual shareholder with a modest number of shares, his votes were, as he put it, "drops in a bucket," but he still took them seriously. He equated voting his proxies with voting in political elections.

Johnson & Johnson

Founded in 1886 by three brothers, Johnson & Johnson's first product was a medicinal plaster to be used as a surgical dressing to reduce infections. From this beginning, the firm had grown to employ more than 115,000 people in 57 countries through more than 230 operating units. In 2005, sales totaled more than $50 billion, with net earnings for the same period of $10.5 billion. The company had recorded year-to-year increases in sales for 71 straight years, with 19 straight years of double-digit earnings increases.

Johnson & Johnson made many well-known consumer products, including Johnson's Baby Powder, Band-Aid brand adhesive bandages, Tylenol, Motrin, St. Joseph aspirin, and Neutrogena skin care products. The company operated three main business segments: consumer health and beauty products, medical devices and diagnostics, and pharmaceuticals.

Johnson & Johnson was famous for operating according to its Credo (see Exhibit 3). Written by Robert Wood Johnson, the son of one of the founders, in 1943, the Credo was widely viewed as a succinct statement of the stakeholder view of the firm. The statement identified the stakeholders to whom the firm was responsible, starting with doctors, nurses, and patients, and ending with shareholders. The Credo set forth the company's view that profits were important, but also that other stakeholders were as important as shareholders.

The company's Credo had met a defining test in 1982, when Extra-Strength Tylenol capsules laced with cyanide caused seven deaths in the Chicago area. (Tampering, not a production error, ultimately was determined as the source of the cyanide.) Johnson & Johnson had immediately pulled capsules from shelves nationwide and issued press releases advising all consumers not to take any Tylenol product until the cause of the poisoning could be determined. Confounding many experts, Tylenol not only recovered as a brand but even increased its market share. The case was often cited as evidence that good ethics could be good business practice as well.

Johnson & Johnson had a long history of philanthropic contributions. Robert Wood Johnson had established a foundation that identified itself as the largest charity devoted exclusively to health issues.[1] Johnson & Johnson also contributed to various charitable organizations directly. The firm's philanthropy focused in 2004 on women's and children's health, community responsibility, access to care, global public health, and advancing health care knowledge. Johnson & Johnson gave nearly $600 million in cash and product contributions during 2005.

Human Life International

Human Life International (HLI) was founded in 1981 by the Reverend Paul Marx, a Benedictine monk. Thomas Euteneuer became president in 2000. The organization billed itself as "the largest international, pro-life, pro-family, pro-woman organization in the world."[2] Its published mission was "to train, organize and equip pro-life leaders around

---

[1] *www.rwjf.org/.*

[2] *www.hli.org/what_is_hli.html.*

Exhibit 3   Our Credo

We believe our first responsibility is to the doctors, nurses and patients,
to mothers and fathers and all others who use our products and services.
In meeting their needs everything we do must be of high quality.
We must constantly strive to reduce our costs
in order to maintain reasonable prices.
Customers' orders must be serviced promptly and accurately.
Our suppliers and distributors must have an opportunity
to make a fair profit.
We are responsible to our employees,
the men and women who work with us throughout the world.
Everyone must be considered as an individual.
We must respect their dignity and recognize their merit.
They must have a sense of security in their jobs.
Compensation must be fair and adequate,
and working conditions clean, orderly and safe.
We must be mindful of ways to help our employees fulfill
their family responsibilities.
Employees must feel free to make suggestions and complaints.
There must be equal opportunity for employment, development
and advancement for those qualified.
We must provide competent management,
and their actions must be just and ethical.
We are responsible to the communities in which we live and work
and to the world community as well.
We must be good citizens — support good works and charities
and bear our fair share of taxes.
We must encourage civic improvements and better health and education.
We must maintain in good order
the property we are privileged to use,
protecting the environment and natural resources.
Our final responsibility is to our stockholders.
Business must make a sound profit.
We must experiment with new ideas.
Research must be carried on, innovative programs developed
and mistakes paid for.
New equipment must be purchased, new facilities provided
and new products launched.
Reserves must be created to provide for adverse times.
When we operate according to these principles,
the stockholders should realize a fair return.

the world to promote and defend the sanctity of human life and the dignity of the family. We fulfill this mission through prayer, service and education, in accordance with the teachings of the Roman Catholic Church."[3] HLI worked with people of all faiths, not just Catholics, to attempt to fulfill this mission.

Although headquartered in the United States, HLI was active around the world, with affiliates in 51 countries. It organized conferences and missionary trips, distributed pro-

[3] *www.hli.org/what_is_hli.html.*

life literature, and engaged in public relations activities. HLI grants, totaling nearly $600,000 in fiscal year 2004, supported scholarships (principally to Catholic clergy and leaders studying bio-ethics) and the activities of affiliates. These activities were wide-ranging, including grassroots activism, operation of crisis pregnancy centers, education of clergy and counselors, and radio and television programming. In the United States, HLI issued press releases on many politically charged issues such as the Terri Schiavo case, which involved a dispute over whether or not to remove the feeding tube of a severely brain-damaged woman. HLI also took positions on various issues involving patient and family rights and Supreme Court appointments.

Annual contributions to HLI in fiscal year 2004 totaled more than $2.3 million. Support from the general public in the five years ending September 30, 2003 accounted for more than 92 percent of HLI's revenue, an uncommonly large percentage for a not-for-profit organization and well above the 33.3 percent requirement to attain 501(c)3 (tax-exempt, not-for-profit) status. The organization's assets at the end of 2004 were slightly more than $3 million, including nearly $1.1 million of common stocks and bonds.

Socially Responsible and Morally Responsible Investing

Socially responsible investing (SRI) as a method of shareholder activism began with the first socially responsible mutual fund in 1971. It gained momentum in the late 1970s, as both religious and secular groups urged the divestment (sale) of stock of firms operating in South Africa, then under the grip of racist apartheid policies. Later, some of these groups expanded their activism to include firms that engaged in anti-union activities, used child labor, harmed the environment, or produced undesirable products such as armaments or cigarettes, among others. Social investors created mutual funds that excluded the stock of companies engaged in activities deemed inappropriate and included the stock of companies deemed to be socially or environmentally responsible.

Social investors also turned to another tool: the social responsibility shareholder resolution. A 1971 resolution brought by the Episcopal Church to General Motors' shareholders concerning investment in South Africa began the modern era of the shareholder resolution, but institutional investors and a 1992 Securities and Exchange Commission rule change prompted growth in the tactic in the 1990s.[4] One prominent organization in this movement was the Interfaith Center on Corporate Responsibility, a coalition of 275 groups whose members annually sponsored more than 200 resolutions in the 2000s.[5]

In the early 1990s, social conservatives began to use similar tactics, primarily targeting firms that had connections with industries such as pornography, alcohol, tobacco, or gambling, or that supported organizations perceived to favor abortion, gay marriage, or other practices they opposed. Called morally responsible investing (MRI), this movement sometimes worked with SRI activists and sometimes against them. One of the MRI movement's main targets was Planned Parenthood, which at some clinics performed abortions. Life Decisions International, an anti-abortion group based in Virginia, published semi-annual lists of firms that supported Planned Parenthood to help those interested in boycotting such firms. Johnson & Johnson frequently appeared on these lists, and HLI was in the network of organizations supporting such boycotts.

[4] *www.corpwatch.org/article.php?id=13716.*

[5] *www.iccr.org/.*

Some conservative activists opposed using shareholder resolutions as a tactic. To file a shareholder resolution one actually had to be a shareholder, and these activists opposed owning stock in targeted organizations even for the sole purpose of being eligible to file such resolutions. Others encouraged the filing of shareholder resolutions.

HLI and Shareholder Resolutions

HLI had used shareholder resolutions before, working sometimes with Thomas Strohbar, the founder of Pro Vita Advisors (an organization founded to help conservative individuals and institutions invest according to their beliefs and to encourage shareholder activism). HLI and Strohbar had filed resolutions with Merck & Co. Inc., calling for a review of ways to link executive compensation with performance on ethical and social issues. Those resolutions were voted down in both 2003 and 2004. The organization also filed a resolution with Berkshire Hathaway in 2002, calling for the company to stop all corporate donations (Berkshire Hathaway had donated to Planned Parenthood, among other organizations). The proposal was defeated, but eventually Berkshire Hathaway did stop making corporate donations to all groups.

Johnson & Johnson was not the only firm targeted by HLI in 2006. Northern Trust Corporation, Textron Inc., Cigna Corporation, and Nationwide Financial Services also received proposals from the organization similar to the one filed with Johnson & Johnson.

Planned Parenthood

The roots of Planned Parenthood could be traced to 1916, when Margaret Sanger, her sister, and another woman, all nurses, opened a birth control clinic in Brooklyn, New York. All three were arrested and convicted of violating a law forbidding the dissemination of birth control information. More than two decades later, in 1939, the organization that became the Planned Parenthood Federation of America, Inc. was formed. Historically, Planned Parenthood focused on safe and legal methods of contraception and family planning. By the mid-1960s, sexual education had also became an important focus. In the meantime, pro-choice advocates were pressing for legalization of abortion. After the 1973 *Roe v. Wade* U.S. Supreme Court decision legalizing abortion, some Planned Parenthood clinics began offering abortions and abortion referrals. In 2006, the organization's clinics offered a wide range of services, mostly centered on family planning and fertility, sexual education, and some primary care services. Planned Parenthood received funds from governmental and private sources, including insurance reimbursement and individual, corporate, and foundation contributions.

The Decision

McCafferty set down the proxy materials and contemplated the decision he needed to make. "In MBA courses," he remembered, "we talked at great length about the ethics of making decisions that exposed shareholders to risk." The first issue, he thought, was whether corporations should make donations at all. After all, managers were contributing stockholders' money, and stockholders inevitably held diverse views, as HLI's position surely demonstrated. Different people would wish to donate to different organizations; some would not want any money donated. On the other hand, corporations—to the extent that they were viewed as legal "persons"—could be seen as having obligations to contribute to society. Because of his experience within the nonprofit fundraising community, McCafferty knew that a single corporate gift could do more good for society in a specific area than many small donations by stockholders dispersed among many organizations and causes. "Further," McCafferty noted, "one could argue that investors can make the choice not to invest in a firm that funds charitable causes. But the majority of investors use mutual funds, which typically do not use charitable donations as a screening function, so that might not be practical. Investors might also differentiate between firms that contributed strategically versus firms that contributed without regard for any benefits to the company."

Even if corporate donations were acceptable in general, McCafferty thought, were Johnson & Johnson's donations to Planned Parenthood and other possibly controversial organizations appropriate? The firm was largely a consumer products company. For that reason, it was vulnerable to boycotts by people who did not agree with its donations. Boycotts, if successful, could substantially hurt Johnson & Johnson's sales and profitability. However, the reverse could also be true. "Johnson & Johnson might stimulate sales by engaging in a social debate," McCafferty said, "but only if it could control the debate, a questionable proposition." Johnson & Johnson was well known for supporting organizations focusing on women's health issues and access to care, both of which were important to Planned Parenthood. Managers could be seen as making these contributions either to improve the firm's strategic position or to support a good cause. Even if the motivation was strictly philanthropic, however, strategic implications would ensue due to Planned Parenthood's controversial nature.

The issue immediately addressed by the resolution, McCafferty mused, was the company's disclosure of information about its donations. Curious, he accessed Johnson & Johnson's Web site and pulled up the relevant documents on his laptop. Johnson & Johnson had a separate page for contributions and a contributions annual report (the 2004 report was the latest posted). The contributions page had links to many other pages, but none of them had many details on specific contributions. The contributions annual report mentioned Planned Parenthood only once: the firm had helped Planned Parenthood's Korean affiliate and other organizations begin a program providing mammograms to women through a specially equipped bus. Most of the programs detailed in the report were from outside the United States. The report did not claim to list all Johnson & Johnson contributions, although it did describe the five areas in which the firm focused its giving: women's and children's health, community responsibility, access to care, advancing health care knowledge, and global public health.[6]

As McCafferty pondered these questions, he knew he would eventually face the final question, at least for him: how should he vote on the proposal? Regardless of his own answers to the first two questions, he saw the disclosure issue as both separate from and related to those questions. A corporation engaging in philanthropic activities might have decided to do so from strategic motives or from charitable motives, or a combination of both. In either case, a corporation's managers might have decided either to publicize or not to publicize their contributions—or perhaps to publicize some and not others. Johnson & Johnson had seemed to proceed down that last road. The company might have done so, McCafferty mused, in order to contribute to a controversial organization "under the radar," to protect itself from possible criticism. On the other hand, those who supported the controversial organization might welcome such a contribution. "The real issue to me was the full disclosure of corporate philanthropic efforts," McCafferty explained. "That was the main point the shareholder proposal addressed, although it was apparently not what really motivated HLI."

---

[6] *www.jnj.com/community/contributions/publications/2004_contributions.pdf.*

Discussion Questions

1. What are the arguments for and against Johnson & Johnson's corporate philanthropy? In what ways do the company's donations help or harm the company and its shareholders and other stakeholders?

2. Specifically, what are the arguments for and against Johnson & Johnson's contributions to Planned Parenthood?

3. Do you think Johnson & Johnson has an obligation to disclose fully all information regarding its corporate donations? Why or why not?

4. Do you think that activists should use shareholder resolutions to promote their views on social or ethical issues? In general, under what circumstances are shareholder resolutions appropriate?

5. How do you think McCafferty should vote on this shareholder proposal, and why do you think so?

GlaxoSmithKline and AIDS Drugs for Africa

Jean-Pierre Garnier, chief executive officer of the global pharmaceutical company Glaxo-SmithKline (GSK, or Glaxo), had been on the job for less than a year, and the annual shareholders' meeting, scheduled for May 21, 2001, was just a week away. Certainly, much of the news he had to report was good. Recently formed through a merger of Glaxo Wellcome and SmithKline Beecham, GSK had immediately become the leading drug manufacturer in the world, with a profit rate in 2000 close to 28 percent. In his first few months on the job, Garnier had moved quickly to buy scores of smaller firms, rounding out Glaxo's portfolio of medicines in the few areas where it was weak, and promising that new therapies were in the pipeline. Investors seemed enthusiastic about the potential synergy of the merger.

But the company was also facing a vexing issue, one that Garnier knew he would have to address at the shareholders' meeting. As the world's leading maker of medicines for the treatment of acquired immunodeficiency syndrome (AIDS), Glaxo had been strenuously criticized by public health, human rights, and shareholder activists for not doing enough to ensure access to these drugs, particularly in sub-Saharan Africa, the center of the world pandemic. The company had recently joined the United Nations' Accelerated Access initiative and, through it, had offered its drugs at discounted prices to several poor African countries.

However, Glaxo had also garnered much unfavorable publicity for pursuing legal action against the government of South Africa, which had tried to buy its citizens low-cost generic versions of drugs GSK had under patent. An Indian maker of generics had offered to sell deeply discounted copies of Glaxo drugs to a humanitarian organization, putting pressure on big pharmaceutical firms to follow suit. The company also faced damaging activist campaigns aimed at forcing Glaxo to reduce its prices and quit aggressively enforcing its intellectual property rights, in the interest of alleviating suffering. Certainly Garnier could expect to face urgent questions on this issue at the annual meeting. He needed to find some answers.

By Anne T. Lawrence. Copyright © 2002 by the author. All rights reserved. An earlier version of this case was presented at the Western Casewriters Association Annual Meeting, Palm Springs, California, March 21, 2002. The author is grateful to participants in that meeting and to Asbjorn Osland for their comments, and to Leon Levitt and Robbin Derry for their insights into the issues raised here. This case was prepared from publicly available materials, including news stories appearing in *The New York Times*, *The Wall Street Journal*, *San Francisco Chronicle*, *Scientific American*, *Dollars and Sense*, *Financial Times* (London), *Newsweek*, *Time*, and *BusinessWeek*. The case also draws on a series of reports by Oxfam. These include *Dare to Lead: Public Health and Company Wealth* (February 2001); *Formula for Fairness: Patient Rights before Patent Rights* (July 2001); *Patent Injustice: How World Trade Rules Threaten the Health of Poor People* (February 2001); and *Patent Rules and Access to Medicines: The Pressure Mounts* (June 2001). These reports are available online at *www.oxfam.org.uk/cutthecost*. GlaxoSmithKline's 2000 Annual Report is available online at *www.gsk.com/financial/reports/ar/pdf_excel/report/report.pdf*.

GlaxoSmithKline

GlaxoSmithKline PLC (GSK) had been formed in December 2000 through a merger of the British firm Glaxo Wellcome and the American firm SmithKline Beecham. The merger created the largest pharmaceutical company in the world, with over $25 billion in annual sales and a 7 percent global market share. With dominance in four of the five largest therapeutic areas, GSK immediately became the sales leader in pharmaceuticals in both Europe and the United States. The combined firm had an annual research budget of almost $4 billion and over 16,000 scientists on staff. GlaxoSmithKline established its corporate headquarters in London and its operational headquarters in the United States. Jean-Pierre Garnier, a pharmacologist who had recently been chosen to become CEO of SmithKline, became the chief executive of the merged firm. Together, he said, the two corporate partners would become the "kings of science."

Historically, Glaxo Wellcome (itself the product of a merger between Glaxo and Burroughs Wellcome) had been a leader in the development of drug therapies for AIDS. In 1986, the company had introduced Retrovir, the first antiretoviral medication designed to inhibit the replication of HIV, the retrovirus that caused AIDS. In 1995, it introduced Epivir and in 1997, Combivir, a drug that combined the ingredients of Retrovir and Epivir in a single tablet. In 1998, the company had introduced Ziagen and Agenerase, protease inhibitors, and in 1999, Trizvir, another combination drug. Glaxo also manufactured several antibiotics designed for use by AIDS patients to treat opportunistic infections. These drugs were big moneymakers. In 2000, the company sold $1.74 billion of AIDS drugs, an increase of 14 percent over the prior year.[1] In the United States, for the year ending February 2000, the company earned revenues of $478 million on the sale of Combivir alone.[2]

Glaxo's sales of AIDS drugs were concentrated in developed countries. Of the company's $1.7 billion in sales of AIDS drugs in 2000, 60 percent were in the United States, 30 percent in Europe, and 10 percent in the rest of the world combined.[3] The sale of AIDS drugs in affluent countries was projected to be a growth area for pharmaceutical companies. According to Decision Resources, Inc., a market research firm, overall spending on AIDS drugs in developed countries was expected to grow from $3.4 billion in 1999 to $7.1 billion by 2009.[4]

Garnier realized that the developing world represented a huge potential market for the company's AIDS medicines, as well as other products. In a January 2001 speech via satellite to the newly merged company's 100,000 employees, the CEO said:

> The pharmaceutical industry today sells 80 percent of its products to 20 percent of the world's population. I don't want to be the CEO of the company that only caters to the rich. . . . I want those medicines in the hands of many more people who need them.[5]

---

[1] Figures for 2000 represent the combined results for Glaxo Wellcome and SmithKline Beecham, as if they had operated as a merged entity for the entire year.

[2] Data from *Chemical Market Reporter,* April 17, 2000, cited in Carol Ezzell, "AIDS Drugs for Africa," *Scientific American,* November 2000, pp. 98–103.

[3] "Pharmaceutical Sales by Therapeutic Area, 2000," p. 6 in "Preliminary Announcement of Results for the Year Ended 31st December 2000," issued by GSK, February 21, 2001, London.

[4] "Drugmakers Yield to Pressure," *San Francisco Chronicle,* March 25, 2001.

[5] "Paying for AIDS," *Newsweek,* March 19, 2001.

The AIDS Pandemic in Africa

One group of people who badly needed the company's products was the estimated 25 million Africans who were infected with the virus that caused AIDS.

Acquired immunodeficiency syndrome, or AIDS—the disease for which Glaxo had led the search for drug treatment—was, in the words of the U.S. Surgeon General, the "worst epidemic the world has ever known."[6] In 2001, sub-Saharan Africa was the epicenter of the global pandemic, with some 70 percent of the cases worldwide. Nine percent of all adult Africans were believed to be HIV-positive. Although no reliable statistics existed in sub-Saharan Africa (where many people never even knew they had the disease, and death certificates typically did not record AIDS as the cause), the United Nations estimated that 25.3 million people were infected with HIV. Every year, 3.8 million people there were newly sickened, and 2.4 million died of the disease. In some southern African countries, the awful figures were even higher. According to the United Nations, 36 percent of adults in Botswana, 25 percent in Swaziland and Zimbabwe, and 20 percent in Zambia, South Africa, and Namibia were HIV-positive in 2000.[7]

Unlike the developed world, where AIDS had been largely confined to homosexuals and IV drug users, the disease in Africa was mainly transmitted through heterosexual contact, and affected both men and women equally—many in the prime of life. Large numbers of infants born to HIV-positive mothers were also infected. The results were predictably dire for the economies of southern Africa, where millions of adults were too sick to work—and, in an upending of traditional arrangements, children and the elderly were left to care for their middle-aged relatives. A study in South Africa's *Journal of Economics* published in 2000 predicted that South Africa's national income would be 17 percent lower in 2010 than it would have been without AIDS.

Very few Africans afflicted by the pandemic had access to the most recent medicines and treatments. In the early 2000s, the standard therapy for AIDS consisted of a combination of antiretroviral drugs that suppressed (although they did not eliminate) the HIV virus that caused the disease. Such a drug "cocktail" was very expensive—typically costing between $10,000 and $15,000 a year in the United States. Most individuals in sub-Saharan Africa did not carry public or private health insurance, and households paid two-thirds of the cost of medicines—a much higher burden than in the developed world. Needless to say, the cost of these drugs was way out of reach for most of the sick. In Zambia, for instance—a country hard-hit by AIDS—60 percent of the population lived on less than $18 a month. Government budgets for health care, in most cases, were paltry.

The high incidence of AIDS and high death rates from the disease in Africa were only partially due to the high cost of medicine, however. Poor nutrition, lack of clean water and sanitation, and poverty meant that overall health levels were low, even before people became ill with AIDS; and secondary infections, such as measles or malaria, were more likely to be fatal. Most African countries, moreover, lacked the medical infrastructure to distribute or monitor demanding drug treatment regimens. The typical AIDS drug "cocktail" had potentially dangerous side effects. In the West, patients were carefully followed with frequent blood tests to check for possible organ damage. Doctors also checked for resistance to particular drugs and changed the combination as necessary. Such follow-up care was often unavailable in Africa.[8]

---

[6] "AIDS Becomes a National Security Issue," *The National Journal*, November 18, 2000, pp. 3680 ff.

[7] United Nations statistics, reported in "Crimes against Humanity," *Time*, February 12, 2001, pp. 26–53.

[8] "Indian Company Offers to Supply AIDS Drugs at Low Cost in Africa," *The New York Times*, February 7, 2001.

Cultural factors also contributed to the terrible toll of AIDS in Africa. In many areas, AIDS was deeply stigmatized, and discussion of sexually transmitted disease was taboo. Few people were ever tested, and most that were ill with AIDS did not know the reason. In Kenya, for example, the head of the centers for disease control estimated that 90 percent of those infected did not even know it.[9] In South Africa in particular, efforts to treat AIDS were hampered by the curious position of President Thabo Mbeka. The president had publicly challenged the almost universally held belief of medical experts that AIDS was caused by the HIV virus, and he had rejected the idea that the government should distribute antiretroviral drugs.[10]

Global Intellectual Property Rights

The global rules governing intellectual property rights—such as the patents on AIDS drugs that Glaxo held in its portfolio—were drawn up by the World Trade Organization (WTO). An organization of member nations committed to free markets, the WTO met periodically to negotiate multilateral agreements on issues related to international trade. These rules had a profound impact on the distribution and pricing of AIDS drugs in Africa.

In 1997, the WTO adopted an agreement on trade-related aspects of intellectual property rights, known by the acronym TRIPS. Its main purpose was to extend patent protection to all member nations. Under this agreement, all WTO member nations would be required to adopt national legislation giving patent holders exclusive marketing rights for a period of 20 years. For example, Glaxo Wellcome had patented the drug Combivir in 1996. Under TRIPS, Glaxo would have sole rights to sell this vital AIDS medicine in all WTO-member countries until 2016. These rules were criticized by some in the public health community, who feared that they would restrict competition and lead to higher prices of essential medicines in poor countries.

Glaxo and other pharmaceutical companies had lobbied hard for national patent laws and for international agreements, like TRIPS, that extended intellectual property laws to trading partners around the world. The industry had argued that patent protection was necessary to compensate companies for the high cost of research and development for new drugs. In 2000, the pharmaceutical industry as a whole spent over $26 billion on research. Typically, a company like Glaxo spent $500 million or more to bring a major new drug to market—a process that involved extensive scientific research, testing, and clinical trials for safety and efficacy; in 2000, the company spent 14 percent of its revenue on research. Many prospective medicines failed and had to be abandoned. Without exclusive marketing rights, Glaxo argued, it would have no incentive to undertake the risky and costly process of pharmaceutical research and development.

The TRIPS agreement did permit some exceptions to protect public health. Developing countries were given an extension until 2006 before TRIPS would take effect. Moreover, all nations—not just the less developed—would be able to override patent protections in certain situations. In a national emergency, nations could engage in *compulsory licensing*. This meant that they could compel a patent holder, like Glaxo, to license another firm to make a low-cost copy of a drug (called a generic), provided that an appropriate royalty was paid. Nations could also engage in *parallel importing* in such emergencies. Sometimes called gray market importing, this referred to cross-border trade

---

[9] "Facing Facts about the AIDS Pandemic," *U.S. News and World Report,* October 2000.

[10] "A Hurdle in South Africa's AIDS Effort," *The Wall Street Journal,* April 26, 2001.

that was not sanctioned by the patent holder—for example, importing cheaper generics from another country.

In practice, Glaxo and other pharmaceutical companies had vigorously contested these public health safeguards in the few instances in which member nations had attempted to invoke them. For example, Pfizer moved to block the government of Kenya from importing a generic version of a drug used to treat opportunistic infections in AIDS patients, citing violation of its patent rights. Use of the generic would have decreased the annual cost of treatment from $3,000 to $104 a year. One-quarter of all adult Kenyans were believed to be HIV-positive.[11]

Pressure on the Pharmaceutical Industry

In early 2001, several events combined to escalate pressure on Glaxo and other pharmaceutical companies to ease up on enforcing WTO rules, as well as to slash prices of their AIDS drugs in Africa.

Cipla's Offer

In February, a surprise offer by a generic drug maker in India to sell AIDS drugs at a deep discount focused media attention on pricing policies for patented medicines. The Chemical, Industrial and Pharmaceutical Laboratories, known as Cipla, Ltd., was the largest manufacturer of generic drugs in India. K. A. Hamied, an Indian Muslim, had founded the company. As a young man studying abroad in the 1930s, Hamied and his wife, a Lithuanian Jew, had fled Europe as the Nazis consolidated power. Hamied later became active in Ghandi's nonviolent movement for Indian independence and launched a small pharmaceutical company to bring medicines to his countrymen.

In 2001, Cipla, Ltd., was run by Hamied's son Yusuf, an organic chemist. Under the son's leadership, the company had developed an expertise in reverse engineering, a process in which chemists analyzed a medicine to learn how to manufacture it. Using this skill, Cipla had become one of the world's largest makers of generic drugs, with 3,500 employees and exports to 130 countries. Exploiting the provision in TRIPS that gave developing countries like India until 2006 to bring their national patent laws into compliance, Cipla was able to produce copies of drugs developed and patented in the West. Because it did not bear the research and development costs, Cipla was able to sell them at discounted prices.

In February 2001, Hamied shocked many pharmaceutical companies with a bold offer. Cipla announced that it would offer its drug Duovir—a copy of Glaxo's Combivir—to the humanitarian organization Doctors Without Borders at the ultracheap price of $350 for a year's supply. It also offered the drug to African governments at the company's cost of production, which it reported to be around $600 per year. Citing his own parents' experience with Nazism and calling AIDS the holocaust of the 21st century, Hamied said that his sole motivation was his "obligation to society."

Trial in South Africa

Just a month later, the issue of AIDS drugs for Africa was further highlighted by a well-publicized lawsuit brought by Glaxo and other pharmaceutical companies against the South African government.

---

[11] *Patent Injustice: How World Trade Rules Threaten the Health of Poor People* (Oxfam Great Britain, February 2001).

In 1997, South Africa, under Nelson Mandela's presidency, had passed a law called the Medicines and Related Substances Act. The law was designed to help the country deal with the AIDS pandemic by authorizing both parallel importing and compulsory licensing. In defending the law, the South African Ministry of Health stated, "We have a constitution that says there will be accessible health care, and that means affordable medicines. The problems in getting universal access are so deep we need major structural intervention."[12]

The pharmaceutical industry viewed both provisions of the Medicines Act as an assault on its intellectual property rights. In 1998, a group of 40 drug companies and trade associations sued in South African courts, arguing that the law violated South Africa's own patent laws. The case, however, proved to be a public relations nightmare for the pharmaceutical industry. A page one article in *The Wall Street Journal* began this way: "Can the pharmaceuticals industry inflict any more damage upon its ailing public image? Well, how about suing Nelson Mandela?"[13] In mid-April 2001, drug companies, under heavy pressure from AIDS activists around the world, abandoned their lawsuit. The companies agreed not to challenge the South African law any further, provided that the government's implementation complied with TRIPS rules.[14]

Activist Campaigns

Against the backdrop of these events, a campaign by Oxfam demanding that pharmaceutical companies cut the cost of AIDS drugs for Africa moved forward. An international human rights group with branches in the United Kingdom, the United States, and other countries, Oxfam's mission was to create "lasting solutions to poverty, hunger, and social injustice through long-term partnerships with poor communities around the world."

In February 2001, Oxfam's efforts got a boost when David Earnshaw, formerly director of European government affairs for SmithKline Beecham, took a position as head of the organization's campaign on drug prices. Earnshaw told reporters that he had been "very frustrat[ed] seeing the industry failing to act." In a series of reports, protests, and media actions, Oxfam demanded that the leading pharmaceutical companies cut the cost of AIDS drugs and forgo their patent rights on them. They also demanded that the companies donate a portion of their profits on blockbuster drugs to support the development of treatments for diseases, like tuberculosis and malaria, which afflicted mainly the poor.

In a briefing paper on GlaxoSmithKline, Oxfam wrote:

> Pharmaceutical companies face a major reputation risk if they do not do more to promote access to lifesaving drugs in the developing world. This is particularly important at a time of unprecedented scrutiny of the industry's record in this field. The withdrawal of public support could lead the industry to suffer the same problems of staff recruitment and retention suffered by companies charged with complicity in human rights abuses or environmental damage. Perhaps more significantly it carries with it the threat of more stringent government regulation.[15]

Oxfam also advanced an ethics argument:

> It is both ethically correct and in the company's self-interest to ensure that those who own and control medical knowledge use all means at their disposal to stop

[12] "AIDS Epidemic Traps Drugs Firms in a Vise: Treatment vs. Profits," *The Wall Street Journal,* March 2001.
[13] Ibid.
[14] "Drug Makers Agree to Drop South Africa Suit," *The Wall Street Journal,* April 19, 2001.
[15] *Dare to Lead: Public Health and Company Wealth* (London: Oxfam UK).

preventable diseases from killing millions of people every year, particularly if they are using their exclusive marketing position to prevent others from developing the same knowledge.[16]

In an interview, Earnshaw explained what he thought was required of Glaxo's leadership:

> It means talking to governments without money, people without money, working with healthcare providers. These are people most of the managers have never talked to. Garnier is a man of vision. The problem is the corporate clones around him.[17]

Formulating a Response

GlaxoSmithKline's predecessors had not been inactive on the issue of providing AIDS drugs to Africa. In May 2000, Glaxo Wellcome had joined the Accelerated Access program of the United Nations Program on AIDS (UNAids). As part of this effort, Glaxo—along with several other pharmaceutical companies—had offered significant price discounts on AIDS drugs to poor nations, to be negotiated on a country-by-country basis. To date, agreements had been concluded with three countries—Rwanda, Senegal, and Uganda. But, partly because of deficiencies in those nations' ability to pay for drugs and to distribute them effectively, only a few hundred people had received medication. In February 2001, Glaxo had offered similar discounts to nongovernmental organizations, United Nations agencies, and to employers that operated their own clinics. These steps had not helped many patients, however, and had done little to appease public health and humanitarian activists.

In GSK's 2000 annual report, released in March 2001, Garnier and Chairman Richard Sykes commented on the company's continuing role:

> As the world leader in the discovery and development of medicines that effectively treat HIV/AIDS, GlaxoSmithKline is determined to play its full part in dealings with this desperate humanitarian crisis which is blighting and destroying the lives of so many millions of people. Yet it disappoints our employees and our other stakeholders that much of the public comment has so far failed to convey the immense complexity of the issue or give due credit for the substantial contribution our company is already making. Real progress in increasing the number of patients treated will only come through concerted action whereby companies such as GlaxoSmithKline work actively in partnership with governments that have the political will to develop real solutions; donor funders who can help buy medicines; and organizations on the ground working to provide medical facilities, establish reliable drug distribution systems, and provide patients with proper care and treatment.[18]

Now, Garnier had to consider what further steps, if any, Glaxo should take to promote the "real progress" he had called for. Certainly, the company could cut prices further, or even give the drugs away altogether in some markets. Doing so might appease humanitarian activists like Oxfam. It could prolong the lives of some AIDS sufferers, and improve the quality of life for others. A price cut could also get Glaxo's AIDS

---

[16] Ibid., p. 5.

[17] "Paying for AIDS," p. 16.

[18] "Joint Statement by the Chairman and the Chief Executive Officer," GlaxoSmithKline, Annual Report 2000, p. 4.

medicines—rather than its competitors'—into what was potentially the biggest market for them in the world.

But Garnier's decision was far from straightforward. In an interview in April 2001, the chief executive had observed that even after other companies had slashed prices, few African nations had stepped forward to buy their products. "That's the ultimate proof," Garnier had observed, "[that] the issue of pricing . . . is irrelevant in the grand scheme of things."[19] Many poor African countries simply did not have the funds to purchase drugs even at greatly reduced prices or the medical infrastructure to deliver them to the needy.

There were other problems, as well. Making large quantities of cheap drugs available in Africa practically invited the development of black market exports back to rich nations. The executive could easily envision scores of rich AIDS patients paying for safaris to Kenya, with money left over, with the savings from dirt cheap medications purchased during their visits. Direct assistance might be diverted by corrupt governments or programs. He was also concerned about the emergence of drug-resistant strains of AIDS if medications were dispensed in poorly controlled settings. What would happen then to the company's investment in their existing generation of medicines? And slashing prices for AIDS drugs could set a dangerous precedent. If the company discounted these medicines, it ran the risk of escalating demands from governments, insurers, and patients in the developed world to reduce the prices of Glaxo medicines for all kinds of other conditions. This was, indeed, a problem of "immense complexity."

Discussion Questions

1. What are GlaxoSmithKline's core interests in this case?
2. What options does the company have with respect to pricing, protection of its intellectual property, and relations with stakeholders?
3. What integrated strategy would you recommend to GSK's managers, and why?

[19] "South Africa Stuns AIDS Activists after Victory," *The Wall Street Journal*, April 19, 2001, p. A12.

Nike's Dispute with the University of Oregon

On April 24, 2000, Philip H. Knight, CEO of athletic shoe and apparel maker Nike, Inc., publicly announced that he would no longer donate money to the University of Oregon (UO). It was a dramatic and unexpected move for the high-profile executive. A former UO track and field star, Knight had founded Nike's predecessor in 1963 with his former coach and mentor, Bill Bowerman. Over the years, Knight had maintained close ties with his alma mater, giving more than $50 million of his personal fortune to the school over a quarter century. In 2000, he was in active discussion with school officials about his biggest donation yet—millions for renovating the football stadium. But suddenly it was all called off. Said Knight in his statement: "[F]or me personally, there will be no further donations of any kind to the University of Oregon. At this time, this is not a situation that can be resolved. The bonds of trust, which allowed me to give at a high level, have been shredded."

At issue was the University of Oregon's intention, announced April 14, 2000, to join the Worker Rights Consortium (WRC). Like many universities, UO was engaged in an internal debate over the ethical responsibilities associated with its role as a purchaser of goods manufactured overseas. Over a period of several months, UO administrators, faculty, and students had been discussing what steps they could take to ensure that products sold in the campus store, especially university-logo apparel, were not manufactured under sweatshop conditions. The university had considered joining two organizations, both of which purported to certify goods as "no sweat." The first, the Fair Labor Association (FLA), had grown out of President Clinton's Apparel Industry Partnership (AIP) initiative and was vigorously backed by Nike, as well as several other leading apparel makers. The second, the Worker Rights Consortium, was supported by student activists and several U.S.-based labor unions that had broken from the AIP after charging it did

By Rebecca J. Morris and Anne T. Lawrence. This is an abridged version of a full-length case, "Nike's Dispute with the University of Oregon," *Case Research Journal* 21, no. 3 (Summer 2001). Abridged and reprinted by permission of the *Case Research Journal*. Sources include articles appearing in *The New York Times, The Oregonian, The Washington Post,* and other daily newspapers, and material provided by Nike at its Web site, *www.nikebiz.com.* Book sources include J. B. Strasser and L. Becklund, *Swoosh: The Unauthorized Story of Nike and the Men Who Played There* (New York: Harper-Collins, 1993); D. R. Katz, *Just Do It: The Nike Spirit in the Corporate World* (Holbrook, MA: Adams Media Corporation, 1995); and T. Vanderbilt, *The Sneaker Book* (New York: New Press, 1998). Web sites for the Fair Labor Association and the Worker Rights Consortium may be found, respectively, at *www.fairlabor.org* and *www.workersrights.org.* Ernst & Young's audit of Nike's subcontractor factories in Vietnam is available at *www.corpwatch.org/trac/nike/ernst.* Coverage of Nike and the WRC decision in the University of Oregon student newspaper is available at *www.dailyemerald.com.* A U.S. Department of Labor study of wages and benefits in the footwear industry in selected countries is available at *www.dol.gov/dol/ilab/public/media/reports/oiea/wagestudy.* A full set of footnotes is available in the *Case Research Journal* version. Copyright © 2001 by the *Case Research Journal* and Rebecca J. Morris and Anne T. Lawrence. All rights reserved jointly to the authors and the North American Case Research Association (NACRA).

not go far enough to protect workers. Knight clearly felt that his alma mater had made the wrong choice. "[The] University [has] inserted itself into the new global economy where I make my living," he charged. "And inserted itself on the wrong side, fumbling a teachable moment."

The dispute between Phil Knight and the University of Oregon captured much of the furor swirling about the issue of the role of multinational corporations in the global economy and the effects of their far-flung operations on their many thousands of workers, communities, and other stakeholders. In part because of its high-profile brand name, Nike had become a lightning rod for activists concerned about worker rights abroad. Like many U.S.-based shoe and apparel makers, Nike had located its manufacturing operations overseas, mainly in Southeast Asia, in search of low wages. Almost all production was carried out by subcontractors rather than by Nike directly. Nike's employees in the United States, by contrast, directed their efforts to the high-end work of research and development, marketing, and retailing. In the context of this global division of labor, what responsibility, if any, did Nike have to ensure adequate working conditions and living standards for the hundreds of thousands of workers, mostly young Asian women, who made its shoes and apparel? If this was not Nike's responsibility, then whose was it? Did organizations like the University of Oregon have any business pressuring companies through their purchasing practices? If so, how should they best do so? In short, what were the lessons of this "teachable moment"?

Nike, Inc.

In 2000, Nike, Inc., was the leading designer and marketer of athletic footwear, apparel, and equipment in the world. Based in Beaverton, Oregon, the company's "swoosh" logo, its "Just Do It!" slogan, and its spokespersons Michael Jordan, Mia Hamm, and Tiger Woods were universally recognized. Nike employed around 20,000 people directly, and *half a million* indirectly in 565 contract factories in 46 countries around the world. Wholly owned subsidiaries included Bauer Nike Hockey Inc. (hockey equipment), Cole Haan (dress and casual shoes), and Nike Team Sports (licensed team products). Revenues for the 12 months ending November 1999 were almost $9 billion, and the company enjoyed a 45 percent global market share. Knight owned 34 percent of the company's stock and was believed to be the sixth-richest individual in the United States.

Knight had launched this far-flung global empire shortly after completing his MBA degree at Stanford University in the early 1960s. Drawing on his firsthand knowledge of track and field, he decided to import low-priced track shoes from Japan in partnership with his former college coach. Bowerman would provide design ideas, test the shoes in competition, and endorse the shoes with other coaches; Knight would handle all financial and day-to-day operations of the business. Neither man had much money to offer, so for $500 apiece and a handshake, the company (then called Blue Ribbon Sports) was officially founded in 1963. The company took the name Nike in 1978; two years later, with revenues topping $269 million and 2,700 employees, Nike became a publicly traded company.

From the beginning, marketing had been a critical part of Knight's vision. The founder defined Nike as a "marketing-oriented company." During the 1980s and early 1990s, Nike aggressively sought out endorsements by celebrity athletes to increase brand awareness and foster consumer loyalty. Early Nike endorsers included Olympic gold medalist Carl Lewis, Wimbledon champion Andre Agassi, and six members of the 1992 Olympic basketball "Dream Team." Later endorsers included tennis aces Pete Sampras and Monica Seles, basketball great Michael Jordan, and golf superstar Tiger Woods.

An important element in Nike's success was its ability to develop cutting-edge products that met the needs of serious athletes, as well as set fashion trends. Research specialists in Nike's Sports Research Labs conducted extensive research and testing to develop new technologies to improve the performance of Nike shoes in a variety of sports. For example, research specialists studied the causes of ankle injuries in basketball players to develop shoes that would physically prevent injuries, as well as signal information to the user to help him or her resist turning the ankle while in the air. Other specialists developed new polymer materials that would make the shoes lighter, more aerodynamic, or more resistant to the abrasions incurred during normal athletic use. Findings from the Sports Research Labs were then passed on to design teams that developed the look and styling of the shoes.

Although it was the leading athletic footwear company in the world, Nike never manufactured shoes in any significant number. Rather, from its inception, the company had outsourced production to subcontractors in Asia, with the company shifting production locations within the region when prevailing wage rates became too high. In the early years, it had imported shoes from Japan. It later shifted production to South Korea and Taiwan, then to Indonesia and Thailand, and later yet to Vietnam and China.

The reasons for locating shoe production mainly in Southeast Asia were several, but the most important was the cost of labor. Modern athletic shoes were composed of mesh, leather, and nylon uppers that were hand-assembled, sewn and glued to composite soles. Mechanization had not been considered effective for shoe manufacturing due to the fragile materials used and the short life spans of styles of athletic shoes. Therefore, shoe production was highly labor-intensive. Developing countries, primarily in Southeast Asia, offered the distinct advantage of considerably lower wage rates. For example, in the early 1990s, when Nike shifted much of its shoe production to Indonesia, daily wages there hovered around $1 a day (compared to wages in the U.S. shoe industry at that time of around $8 an hour).

Along with lower labor costs, Asia provided the additional advantage of access to raw materials suppliers. Very few rubber firms in the United States, for example, produced the sophisticated composite soles demanded in modern athletic shoe designs. Satellite industries necessary for modern shoe production, plentiful in Asia, included tanneries, textiles, and plastic and ironwork moldings. A final factor in determining where to locate production was differential tariff rates. In general, canvas sneakers were assessed higher tariffs than leather molded footwear, such as basketball or running shoes. As a result, shoe companies had an incentive to outsource high-tech athletic shoes overseas, because tariffs on them were relatively low.

Many of Nike's factories in Asia were operated by a small number of Taiwanese and South Korean firms that specialized in shoe manufacturing, many owned by some of the wealthiest families in the region. When Nike moved from one location to another, often these companies followed, bringing their managerial expertise with them.

Nike's Subcontractor Factories

In 2000, Nike contracted with over 500 different footwear and apparel factories around the world to produce its shoes and apparel. Although there was no such thing as a typical Nike plant, a factory operated by the South Korean subcontractor Tae Kwang Vina (TKV) in the Bien Hoa City industrial zone near Ho Chi Minh City in Vietnam provided a glimpse into the setting in which many Nike shoes were made.

TKV employed approximately 10,000 workers in the Bien Hoa City factory. The workforce consisted of 200 clerical workers, 355 supervisors, and 9,465 production workers, all making athletic shoes for Nike. Ninety percent of the workers were women between the ages of 18 to 24. Production workers were employed in one of three major areas within the factory: the chemical, stitching, and assembly sections. Production levels at the Bien Hoa City factory reached 400,000 pairs of shoes per month; Nike shoes made at this and other factories made up fully 5 percent of Vietnam's total exports.

Workers in the chemical division were responsible for producing the high-technology outsoles. Production steps involved stretching and flattening huge blobs of raw rubber on heavy-duty rollers and baking chemical compounds in steel molds to form the innovative three-dimensional outsoles. The chemical composition of the soles changed constantly in response to the cutting-edge formulations developed by the U.S. design teams, requiring frequent changes in the production process. The smell of complex polymers, the hot ovens, and the clanging of the steel molds resulted in a working environment that was loud and hot and had high concentrations of chemical fumes. Chemicals used in the section were known to cause eye, skin, and throat irritations; damage to liver and kidneys; nausea; anorexia; and reproductive health hazards through inhalation or in some cases through absorption through the skin. Workers in the chemical section were thought to have high rates of respiratory illnesses, although records kept at the TKV operations did not permit the tracking of illnesses by factory section. Workers in the chemical section were issued gloves and surgical-style masks. However, they often discarded the protective gear, complaining that it was too hot and humid to wear them in the plant.

In the stitching section, row after row of sewing machines operated by young women hummed and clattered in a space the size of three football fields. One thousand stitchers worked on a single floor of the TKV factory, sewing together nylon, leather, and other fabrics to make the uppers. Other floors of the factory were filled with thousands of additional sewing machines producing different shoe models. The stitching job required precision and speed. Workers who did not meet the aggressive production goals did not receive a bonus. Failing to meet production goals three times resulted in the worker's dismissal. Workers were sometimes permitted to work additional hours without pay to meet production quotas. Supervisors were strict, chastising workers for excessive talking or spending too much time in the restrooms. Korean supervisors, often hampered by language and cultural barriers, sometimes resorted to hard-nosed management tactics, hitting or slapping slower workers. Other workers in need of discipline were forced to stand outside the factory for long periods in the tropical sun. The Vietnamese term for this practice was *phoi nang,* or sun-drying.

In the assembly section, women worked side by side along a moving line to join the uppers to the outersoles through the rapid manipulation of sharp knives, skivers, routers, and glue-coated brushes. Women were thought to be better suited for the assembly jobs because their hands were smaller and more capable of the manual dexterity needed to fit the shoe components together precisely. During the assembly process, some 120 pairs of hands touched a single shoe. A strong, sweet solvent smell was prominent in the assembly area. Ceiling-mounted ventilation fans were ineffective since the heavy fumes settled to the floor. Assembly workers wore cotton surgical masks to protect themselves from the fumes; however, many workers pulled the masks below their noses, saying they were more comfortable that way. Rows and rows of shoes passed along a conveyor before the sharp eyes of the quality control inspectors. The inspectors examined each of the thousands of shoes produced daily for poor stitching or crooked connections between soles. Defective shoes were discarded. Approved shoes continued on the conveyor to stations where they were laced by assembly workers and finally put into Nike shoeboxes for shipment to the United States.

Despite the dirty, dangerous, and difficult nature of the work inside the Bien Hoa factory, there was no shortage of applicants for positions. Although entry-level wages averaged only $1.50 per day (the lowest of all countries where Nike manufactured), many workers viewed factory jobs as better than their other options, such as working in the rice paddies or pedaling a pedicab along the streets of Ho Chi Minh City (formerly Saigon). With overtime pay at one and a half times the regular rate, workers could double their salaries—generating enough income to purchase a motorscooter or to send money home to impoverished rural relatives. These wages were well above national norms. An independent study by researchers from Dartmouth University showed that the average annual income for workers at two Nike subcontractor factories in Vietnam was between $545 and $566, compared to the national average of between $250 and $300. Additionally, workers were provided free room and board and access to on-site health care facilities. Many Vietnamese workers viewed positions in the shoe factory as transitional jobs, a way to earn money for a dowry or to experience living in a larger city. Many returned to their homes after working for Nike for two or three years to marry and begin the next phase of their lives.

The Campaigns against Nike

In the early 1990s, criticism of Nike's global labor practices began to gather steam. *Harper's* magazine, for example, published the pay stub of an Indonesian worker, showing that the Nike subcontractor had paid the woman just under 14 cents per hour, and contrasted this with the high retail price of the shoes and the high salaries paid to the company's celebrity endorsers. The Made in the U.S.A. Foundation, a group backed by American unions, used a million-dollar ad budget to urge consumers to send their "old, dirty, smelly, worn-out Nikes" to Phil Knight in protest of Nike's Asian manufacturing practices. Human rights groups and Christian organizations joined the labor unions in targeting the labor practices of the athletic shoes firm. Many felt that Nike's antiauthority corporate image ("Just Do It") and message of social betterment through fitness were incompatible with press photos of slight Asian women hunched over sewing machines 70 hours a week, earning just pennies an hour.

By mid-1993, Nike was being regularly pilloried in the press as an imperialist profiteer. A CBS news segment airing on July 2, 1993, opened with images of Michael Jordan and Andre Agassi, two athletes who had multimillion-dollar promotion contracts with Nike. Viewers were told to contrast the athletes' pay checks with those of the Chinese and Indonesian workers who made "pennies" so that Nike could "Just Do It."

In 1995, *The Washington Post* reported that a pair of Nike Air Pegasus shoes that retailed for $70 cost Nike only $2.75 in labor costs, or 4 percent of the price paid by consumers. Nike's operating profit on the same pair of shoes was $6.25, while the retailer pocketed $9.00 in operating profits. Also that year, shareholder activists organized by the Interfaith Center on Corporate Responsibility submitted a shareholder proposal at Nike's annual meeting, calling on the company to review labor practices by its subcontractors; the proposal garnered 3 percent of the shareholder vote.

A story in *Life* magazine documented the use of child labor in Pakistan to produce soccer balls for Nike, Adidas, and other companies. The publicity fallout was intense. The public could not ignore the photographs of small children sitting in the dirt, carefully stitching together the panels of a soccer ball that would become the plaything of some American child the same age. Nike moved quickly to work with its Pakistani subcontractor to eliminate the use of child labor, but damage to Nike's image had been done.

In October 1996, CBS News' "48 Hours" broadcast a scathing report on Nike's factories in Vietnam. CBS reporter Roberta Baskin focused on low wage rates, extensive overtime, and physical abuse of workers. Several young workers told Baskin how a Korean supervisor had beaten them with a part of a shoe because of problems with production. A journalist in Vietnam told the reporter that the phrase "to Nike someone" was part of the Vietnamese vernacular. It meant to "take out one's frustration on a fellow worker." Vietnamese plant managers refused to be interviewed, covering their faces as they ran inside the factory. CBS news anchor Dan Rather concluded the damaging report by saying, "Nike now says it plans to hire outside observers to talk to employees and examine working conditions in its Vietnam factories, but the company just won't say when that might happen."

The negative publicity was having an effect. In 1996, a marketing research study authorized by Nike reported the perceptions of young people ages 13 to 25 of Nike as a company. The top three perceptions, in the order of their response frequency, were (1) athletics, (2) cool, and (3) bad labor practices. Although Nike maintained that its sales were never affected, company executives were clearly concerned about the effect of criticism of its global labor practices on the reputation of the brand they had worked so hard to build.

The Evolution of Nike's Global Labor Practices

In its early years, Nike had maintained that the labor practices of its foreign subcontractors, like TKV, were simply not its responsibility. "When we started Nike," Knight later commented, "it never occurred to us that we should dictate what their factor[ies] should look like." The subcontractors, not Nike, were responsible for wages and working conditions. Dave Taylor, Nike's vice president of production, explained the company's position: "We don't pay anybody at the factories and we don't set policy within the factories; it is their business to run."

When negative articles first began appearing in the early 1990s, however, Nike managers realized that they needed to take some action to avoid further bad publicity. In 1992, the company drafted its first Code of Conduct, which required every subcontractor and supplier in the Nike network to honor all applicable local government labor and environmental regulations, or Nike would terminate the relationship. The subcontractors were also required to allow plant inspections and complete all necessary paperwork. Despite the compliance reports the factories filed every six months, Nike insiders acknowledged that the code of conduct system might not catch all violations. Tony Nava, Nike's country coordinator for Indonesia, told a *Chicago Tribune* reporter, "We can't know if they're actually complying with what they put down on paper."

In 1994, Nike tried to address this problem by hiring Ernst & Young, the accounting firm, to independently monitor worker abuse allegations in Nike's Indonesian factories. Later, Ernst & Young also audited Nike's factories in Thailand and Vietnam. A copy of the Vietnam audit leaked to the press showed that workers were often unaware of the toxicity of the compounds they were using and ignorant of the need for safety precautions. In 1998, Nike implemented important changes in its Vietnamese plants to reduce exposure to toxics, substituting less harmful chemicals, installing ventilation systems, and training personnel in occupational health and safety issues.

In 1996, Nike established a new Labor Practices Department, headed by Dusty Kidd, formerly a public relations executive for the company. Later that year, Nike hired Good-Works International, headed by former U.S. ambassador to the United Nations Andrew

Young, to investigate conditions in its overseas factories. In January 1997, GoodWorks issued a glossy report, stating that "Nike is doing a good job in the application of its Code of Conduct. But Nike can and should do better." The report was criticized by activists for its failure to look at the issue of wages. Young demurred, saying he did not have expertise in conducting wage surveys. Said one critic, "This was a public relations problem, and the world's largest sneaker company did what it does best: it purchased a celebrity endorsement."

Over the next few years, Nike continued to work to improve labor practices in its overseas subcontractor factories, as well as the public perception of them. In January 1998, Nike formed a Corporate Responsibility Division under the leadership of former Microsoft executive Maria S. Eitel. Nike subsequently doubled the staff of this division. In May of that year, Knight gave a speech at the National Press Club, at which he announced several new initiatives. At that time, he committed Nike to raise the minimum age for employment in its shoe factories to 18 and in its apparel factories to 16. He also promised to achieve OSHA standards for indoor air quality in all its factories by the end of the year, mainly by eliminating the use of the solvent toluene; to expand educational programs for workers and its microenterprise loan program; and to fund university research on responsible business practices. Nike also continued its use of external monitors, hiring PricewaterhouseCoopers to join Ernst & Young in a comprehensive program of factory audits, checking them against Nike's code.

Apparel Industry Partnership

One of Nike's most ambitious social responsibility initiatives was its participation in the Apparel Industry Partnership. It was this involvement that would lead, eventually, to Knight's break with the University of Oregon.

In August 1996, President Clinton launched the White House Apparel Industry Partnership on Workplace Standards (AIP). The initial group was composed of 18 organizations. Participants included several leading manufacturers, such as Nike, Reebok, and Liz Claiborne. Also in the group were several labor unions, including the Union of Needletrades, Industrial, and Textile Employees (UNITE) and the Retail, Wholesale and Department Store Union; and several human rights, consumer, and shareholder organizations, including Business for Social Responsibility, the Interfaith Center on Corporate Responsibility, and the National Consumers League. The goal of the AIP was to develop a set of standards to ensure that apparel and footwear were not made under sweatshop conditions. For companies, it held out the promise of certifying to their customers that their products were "no sweat." For labor and human rights groups, it held out the promise of improving working conditions in overseas factories.

In April 1997, after months of often-fractious meetings, the AIP announced that it had agreed on a Workplace Code of Conduct that sought to define decent and humane working conditions. Companies agreeing to the code would have to pledge not to use forced labor, that is, prisoners or bonded or indentured workers. They could not require more than 60 hours of work a week, including overtime. They could not employ children younger than 15 years old, or the age for completing compulsory schooling, whichever was older—except they could hire 14-year-olds if local law allowed. The code also called on signatory companies to treat all workers with respect and dignity; to refrain from discrimination on the basis of gender, race, religion, age, disability, sexual orientation, nationality, political opinion, or social or ethnic origin; and to provide a safe and healthy workplace. Employees' rights to organize and bargain collectively would be respected.

In a key provision, the code also required companies to pay at least the local legal minimum wage or the prevailing industry wage, whichever was higher. All standards would apply not only to a company's own facilities but also to their subcontractors or suppliers.

Knight, who prominently joined President Clinton and others at a White House ceremony announcing the code, issued the following statement:

> Nike agreed to participate in this Partnership because it was the first credible attempt, by a diverse group of interests, to address the important issue of improving factories worldwide. It was worth the effort and hard work. The agreement will prove important for several reasons. Not only is our industry stepping up to the plate and taking a giant swing at improving factory conditions, but equally important, we are finally providing consumers some guidance to counter all of the misinformation that has surrounded this issue for far too long.

The Fair Labor Association

But this was not the end of the AIP's work; it also had to agree on a process for monitoring compliance with the code. Although the group hoped to complete its work in six months, over a year later it was still deeply divided on several key matters. Internal documents leaked to *The New York Times* in July 1998 showed that industry representatives had opposed proposals, circulated by labor and human rights members, calling for the monitoring of 30 percent of plants annually by independent auditors. The companies also opposed proposals that would require them to support workers' rights to organize independent unions and to bargain collectively, even in countries like China where workers did not have such rights by law. Said one nonindustry member, "We're teetering on the edge of collapse."

Finally, a subgroup of nine centrist participants, including Nike, began meeting separately in an attempt to move forward. In November 1998, this subgroup announced that it had come to agreement on a monitoring system for overseas factories of U.S.-based companies. The AIP would establish a new organization, the Fair Labor Association (FLA), to oversee compliance with its Workplace Code of Conduct. Companies would be required to monitor their own factories, and those of their subcontractors, for compliance; all would have to be checked within the first two years. In addition, the FLA would select and certify independent external monitors, who would inspect 10 percent of each firm's factories each year. Most of these monitors were expected to be accounting firms, which had expertise in conducting audits. The monitors' reports would be kept private. If a company were found to be out of compliance, it would be given a chance to correct the problem. Eventually, if it did not, the company would be dropped from the FLA and its termination announced to the public. Companies would pay for most of their own monitoring. The Clinton administration quickly endorsed the plan.

Both manufacturers and institutional buyers stood to benefit from participation in the Fair Labor Association. Companies, once certified for three years, could place an FLA service mark on their brands, signaling both to individual consumers and institutional buyers that their products were "sweatshop-free." It was expected that the FLA would also serve the needs of institutional buyers, particularly universities. By joining the FLA and agreeing to contract only with certified companies, universities could warrant to their students and others that their logo apparel and athletic gear were manufactured under conditions conforming with an established code of fair labor standards. Both parties would pay for these benefits. The FLA was to be funded by dues from participating companies

($5,000 to $100,000 annually, depending on revenue) and by payments from affiliated colleges and universities (based on 1 percent of their licensing income from logo products, up to a $50,000 annual cap).

Although many welcomed the agreement—and some new companies signed on with the FLA soon after it was announced—others did not. Warnaco, a leading apparel maker that had participated in the Partnership, quit, saying that the monitoring process would require it to turn over competitive information to outsiders. The American Apparel Manufacturing Association (AAMA), an industry group representing 350 companies, scoffed at the whole idea of monitoring. "Who is going to do the monitoring?" asked a spokesperson for the AAMA, apparently sarcastically, "Accountants or Jesuit priests?" Others argued that companies simply could not be relied upon to monitor themselves objectively. Said Jay Mazur, president of UNITE, "The fox cannot watch the chickens . . . if they want the monitoring to be independent, it can't be controlled by the companies." A visit from an external monitor once every 10 years would not prevent abuses. And in any case, as a practical matter, most monitors would be drawn from the major accounting firms that did business with the companies they were monitoring and were therefore unlikely to seek out lapses. Companies would not be required to publish a list of their factories, and any problems uncovered by the monitoring process could be kept from the public under the rules governing nondisclosure of proprietary information.

One of the issues most troubling to critics was the code's position on wages. The code called on companies to pay the minimum wage or prevailing wage, whichever was higher. But in many of the countries of Southeast Asia, these wages fell well below the minimum considered necessary for a decent standard of living for an individual or family. For example, the *Economist* reported that Indonesia's average minimum wage, paid by Nike subcontractors, was only two-thirds of what a person needed for basic subsistence. An alternative view was that a code of conduct should require that companies pay a *living wage,* that is, compensation for a normal workweek adequate to provide for the basic needs of an average family, adjusted for the average number of adult wage earners per family. One problem with this approach, however, was that many countries did not systematically study the cost of living, relative to wages, so defining a living wage was difficult. The Partnership asked the U.S. Department of Labor to conduct a preliminary study of these issues; the results were published in 2000.

The code also called on companies to respect workers' rights to organize and bargain collectively. Yet a number of FLA companies outsourced production to nondemocratic countries, such as China and Vietnam, where workers had no such rights. Finally, some criticized the agreement on the grounds it provided companies, as one put it, "a piece of paper to use as a fig leaf." Commented a representative of the needle trades unions, "The problem with the partnership plan is that it tinkers at the margins of the sweatshop system but creates the impression that it is doing much more. This is potentially helpful to companies stung by public condemnation of their labor practices, but it hurts millions of workers and undermines the growing antisweatshop movement."

The Worker Rights Consortium

Some activists in the antisweatshop movement decided to chart their own course, independent of the FLA. On October 20, 1999, students from more than 100 colleges held a press conference to announce formation of the Worker Rights Consortium (WRC) and called on their schools to withdraw from, or not to join, the FLA. The organization would be formally launched at a founding convention in April 2000.

The Worker Rights Consortium differed radically in its approach to eliminating sweatshops. First, the WRC did not permit corporations to join; it was composed exclusively of universities and colleges, with unions and human rights organizations playing an advisory role. In joining the WRC, universities would agree to "require decent working conditions in factories producing their licensed products." Unlike the FLA, the WCA did not endorse a single, comprehensive set of fair labor standards. Rather, it called on its affiliated universities to develop their own codes. However, it did establish minimum standards that such codes should meet—ones that were, in some respects, stricter than the FLA's. Perhaps most significantly, companies would have to pay a living wage. Companies were also required to publish the names and addresses of all of their manufacturing facilities, in contrast to FLA rules. Universities could refuse to license goods made in countries where compliance with fair labor standards was "deemed impossible," whatever efforts companies had made to enforce their own codes in factories there.

By contrast with the FLA, monitoring would be carried out by "a network of local organizations in regions where licensed goods are produced," generally nongovernmental organizations, independent human rights groups, and unions. These organizations would conduct unannounced "spot investigations," usually in response to worker complaints; WRC organizers called this the "fire alarm" method of uncovering code violations. Systematic monitoring would not be attempted. The consortium's governance structure reflected its mission of being an organization by and for colleges and universities; its 12-person board was composed of students, university administrators, and human rights experts, with no seats for industry representatives. The group would be financed by 1 percent of licensing revenue from participating universities, as well as foundation grants.

Over the course of the spring semester 2000, student protests were held on a number of campuses, including the University of Oregon, to demand that their schools join the WRC. By April, around 45 schools had done so. At UO, the administration encouraged an open debate on the issue so that all sides could be heard on how to ensure that UO products were made under humane conditions. Over a period of several months, the Academic Senate, the student body, and a committee of faculty, students, administrators, and alumni appointed by the president all voted to join the consortium. Finally, after concluding that all constituents had had an opportunity to be heard, on April 12, 2000, University of Oregon president David Frohnmayer announced that UO would join the WRC for one year. Its membership would be conditional, he said, on the consortium's agreement to give companies a voice in its operations and universities more power in governance. Shortly after the university's decision was announced in the press, Phil Knight withdrew his philanthropic contribution. In his public announcement, he stated his main disagreements with the Worker Rights Consortium:

> Frankly, we are frustrated that factory monitoring is badly misconstrued. For us one of the great hurdles and real handicaps in the dialogue has been the complexity of the issue. For real progress to be made, all key participants have to be at the table. That's why the FLA has taken so long to get going. The WRC is supported by the AFL-CIO and its affiliated apparel workers' union, UNITE. Their main aim, logically and understandably, however misguided, is to bring apparel jobs back to the U.S. Among WRC rules, no company can participate in setting standards, or monitoring. It has an unrealistic living wage provision. And its "gotcha" approach to monitoring doesn't do what monitoring should— measure conditions and make improvements.

Discussion Questions

1. Who do you believe has a social and ethical responsibility for the wages and working conditions of the employees who produce Nike's shoes and apparel, Nike or its subcontractors? Why do you think so?

2. The Fair Labor Association and the Worker Rights Consortium differed on how to establish and enforce fair labor standards. Which approach, if either, do you favor, and why? Consider how you would answer this question if you were representing the following: Nike shareholders, a human rights organization, a U.S. labor union, or the government of a developing country.

3. If you were the CEO of Nike, what would you do next in this situation? If you were the president of the University of Oregon, what would you do next?

Shell Oil in Nigeria

On November 10, 1995, world-renowned Nigerian novelist and environmental activist Ken Saro-Wiwa was executed by hanging in a prison courtyard. Just 10 days earlier, he had been convicted by a military tribunal on charges that he had ordered the murder of political opponents. Throughout his trial, Saro-Wiwa had vigorously maintained his innocence. Despite protests by many world leaders and human rights organizations, the Nigerian military regime quickly carried out the death sentence.

Saro-Wiwa's execution provoked a profound crisis for the Royal Dutch/Shell Group of Companies. In its wake, some environmentalists and political leaders called for an international boycott of Shell's gasoline and other products. The World Bank canceled a promised $160 million combined loan and investment in Shell's liquefied natural gas project in Nigeria. In Canada, the Toronto city government refused a large gasoline contract to Shell Canada, despite its low bid—an event that received wide press coverage. Some even called for the oil company to pull out of Nigeria altogether.

Alan Detheridge, Shell's coordinator for West Africa, told a reporter in February 1996, "Saro-Wiwa's execution was a disaster for us."

Just what was the connection between Saro-Wiwa's execution and Shell? Why did the company find itself suddenly, in the words of *The New York Times,* "on trial in the court of public opinion"? Had the company done anything wrong in Nigeria? What, if anything, could or should it do in the face of an escalating chorus of international criticism?

The Royal Dutch/Shell Group

The Royal Dutch/Shell Group was the world's largest fully integrated petroleum company. "Upstream," the conglomerate controlled oil and gas exploration and production; "midstream," the pipelines and tankers that carried oil and gas; and "downstream," the refining, marketing, and distribution of the final product. The company also had interests in coal mining, forestry, chemicals, and renewable energy. In all, the Anglo-Dutch conglomerate comprised over 2,000 separate entities, with exploration and production operations, refineries, and marketing in scores of countries. Royal Dutch/Shell was, in both its ownership and scope, perhaps the world's most truly transnational corporation.

This is an abridged and revised (2000) version of a longer case, Anne T. Lawrence, "Shell Oil in Nigeria," *Case Research Journal* 17, no. 4 (Winter 1997), pp. 1–21. Abridged by the author by permission of the *Case Research Journal.* Sources include articles appearing in the *The Wall Street Journal, The New York Times, Economist, Fortune, Guardian, Independent,* and *Village Voice;* U.S. congressional hearings; reports by Amnesty International, Greenpeace, and the World Bank; and material provided by Royal Dutch/Shell and by Shell Nigeria and posted on their Web sites at *www.shell.com* and *www.shellnigeria.com.* The history of Royal Dutch/Shell is based on Adele Hast, ed., *International Directory of Company Histories* (Chicago: St. James Press, 1991) and *World Class Business: A Guide to the 100 Most Powerful Global Corporations* (New York: Henry Holt, 1992). Ken Saro-Wiwa's story is drawn primarily from his memoir *A Month and a Day: A Prison Diary* and other writings. A full set of footnotes in available in the *Case Research Journal* version. Copyright © 1998 by the *Case Research Journal* and Anne T. Lawrence. All rights reserved.

In 1994, Royal Dutch/Shell made more money than any other company in the world, reporting annual profits of $6.3 billion. The same year, the company reported revenues of $94.9 billion, placing it 10th on *Fortune*'s Global 500 list. Assets were reported at $108.3 billion, and stockholders' equity at $56.4 billion. With 106,000 employees world-wide, it had the largest workforce of any oil company in the world.

This highly successful global corporation traced its history back over more than a century and a half. In the 1830s, British entrepreneur Marcus Samuel founded a trading company to export manufactured goods from England and to import products, including polished seashells (hence, the name "Shell"), from the Orient. In the early 1890s, Samuel's sons steered the company into the kerosene business, assembling a fleet of tankers to ply the fuel through the Suez Canal to Far Eastern ports. At about the same time, a group of Dutch businessmen launched the Royal Dutch Company to drill for oil in the Dutch East Indies. In 1907, Royal Dutch and Shell merged, with Royal Dutch retaining a 60 percent interest and Shell, 40 percent. The resulting organization came to be known as the Royal Dutch/Shell Group of Companies, or simply the Group.

Over the years, Royal Dutch/Shell developed a highly decentralized management style, with its far-flung subsidiaries exercising considerable autonomy. The company believed that vesting authority in nationally based, integrated operating companies—each with its own distinctive identity—gave it the strategic flexibility to respond swiftly to local opportunities and conditions. The corporation was governed by a six-person committee of managing directors. Reflecting its dual parentage, the Group maintained headquarters in both London and The Hague. The chairmanship rotated periodically between the chairman of Shell and the president of Royal Dutch. Decision making was by consensus, with no dominant personality.

Shell Nigeria

The Shell Petroleum Development Company of Nigeria (SPDC), usually called Shell Nigeria, was a wholly owned subsidiary of Royal Dutch/Shell. The company stated its corporate objective simply. It was "to find, produce, and deliver hydrocarbons safely, responsibly, and economically for the benefit of our stakeholders."

The Royal Dutch/Shell Group began exploring for oil in West Africa in the 1930s, but it was not until 1956 that oil was discovered in the Niger Delta in southeastern Nigeria. In 1958, two years before Nigeria's independence, Shell was the first major oil company to commence oil production there. Nigerian oil was of very high quality by world standards; in the industry, it was referred to as "light, sweet crude," meaning that it had a low sulfur content and produced a higher proportion of gasoline after refining than heavier crude oil. Of all the multinational oil companies in Nigeria, Shell had by far the most visibility, because of the extent of its land-based operations. Other major players in the Nigerian oil industry, including Mobil and Chevron, mainly operated offshore.

Shell Nigeria was a participant in a joint venture with the Nigerian government and two other private firms. In 1995, the Nigerian National Petroleum Corporation (NNPC), the state-owned oil company, owned a 55 percent stake in the joint venture. Royal Dutch/Shell owned a 30 percent stake; Elf and Agip, both European oil companies, owned the remaining 15 percent. Shell was the joint venture operator; that is, it built and ran the oil operations on the ground. The other owners, although not involved in day-to-day management, had a say in the development of budgets and new projects. Investments in the business were made by the joint venture partners in proportion to their holdings. As operator, Shell issued "cash calls" to its partners to provide monthly payments. Shell executives were often frustrated by the NNPC's failure to pay their share on time. In 1995, the government was $300 million behind in its payments.

Shell Nigeria's operations were huge, not only by Nigerian standards, but even by those of its parent firm. In 1995, Shell Nigeria produced an average of almost one million barrels of crude oil a day, about half of Nigeria's total output, from 94 separate fields spread over 31,000 square kilometers. It operated 6,200 kilometers of pipelines and flow lines, much of it running through swamps and flood zones in the Niger Delta. In addition, the company operated two coastal export terminals. The company reported that the Nigerian operation provided about 12 percent of Royal Dutch/Shell's total world oil production and 7 percent of its profits.

Shell Nigeria employed about 5,000 people. Ninety-five percent of all employees, and about half of executive directors, were Nigerian. Fifty-seven percent of its staff was drawn from the oil-producing states.

The company's financial arrangements with its host country were highly beneficial to the Nigerian government. For every barrel of oil sold at between $12.50 and $23.00 a barrel, 70 cents went to Shell, 30 cents went to Elf and Agip, and $4.50 went to cover costs. The Nigerian government received the rest. At a per-barrel price of $15, for example, the government would receive $9.50, or about 90 percent of net revenue after expenses. The Nigerian government's take, at the time, was the highest of any government in the world with which Shell did business.

Nigeria: The Giant of West Africa

Nigeria, the Group's sometimes-troublesome partner, has been called the "giant of West Africa." Located on the Gulf of Guinea between the republics of Benin and Cameroon, Nigeria was slightly more than twice the size of California and, with over 100 million people, the most populous country on the continent. Nigeria's gross domestic product of $95 billion placed its economy second, smaller only than South Africa's. The economy was heavily dependent on petroleum; oil and natural gas sales produced 80 percent of the federal government's revenue, and more than 90 percent of the country's foreign exchange. Forty-one percent of oil exports went to the United States, more than to any other single country.

Nigeria was a land of stark socioeconomic contrasts. The nation's military and business elites had grown wealthy from oil revenues. Yet most Nigerians lived in poverty. The annual per capita income was $250, less than that of Haiti or China, and in the mid-1990s economic distress in many parts of Nigeria was deepening.

A legacy of colonialism, in Nigeria as elsewhere in Africa, was the formation of countries that had little historical basis other than common colonial governance. In the Nigerian case, the modern nation was formed from what had been no less than 250 disparate ethnic groups, many with few cultural or linguistic ties. The nation comprised three main ethnic groups: the Hausa-Fulani, the Yoruba, and the Ibo. Together, these three groups made up 65 percent of the population; the remaining 35 percent was made up of hundreds of smaller ethnic groups, including Saro-Wiwa's people, the Ogoni.

Since its independence from Britain in 1960, Nigeria had been ruled by military governments for all but nine years. Several efforts, all eventually unsuccessful, had been made to effect a transition to permanent civilian rule. In June 1993, then-military dictator Ibrahim Babangida annulled the presidential election, suspended the newly created national assembly, and installed an unelected civilian as president. Just five months later, yet another military man, General Sani Abacha, took power in a coup.

The Abacha regime quickly developed a reputation as "indisputably the cruelest and most corrupt" government in Nigeria since independence. A specialist in African politics summarized the situation in Nigeria before the United States Senate Foreign Relations Committee in 1995:

> [The] current government appears indifferent to international standards of conduct, while dragging the country into a downward spiral of disarray, economic stagnation, and ethnic animosity. . . . [It] has curtailed political and civil rights to an unprecedented degree in Nigerian history, magnified corruption and malfeasance in an endemically corrupt system, and substantially abandoned responsible economic management.

In 1993, inflation was running around 50 percent annually, foreign debt was growing, and the country's balance of payments was worsening. A succession of governments had arguably wasted vast amounts of money on unnecessary projects such as the construction of a massive steel mill and a new capital city, Abuja. Agriculture was in decline, and a proliferation of states had produced a complex and inefficient bureaucracy. Corruption was so rampant in Nigeria, the *Economist* concluded in an editorial that "the parasite . . . has almost eaten the host."

The Ogoni People

The Ogoni people, Saro-Wiwa's ethnic group, lived in the heart of the Nigerian oil fields. Numbering about half a million in the mid-1990s, the Ogoni spoke four related languages and shared common religious and cultural traditions. Prior to the arrival of the British in 1901, a stable Ogoni society based on fishing and farming had existed for centuries in a small area (a mere 12 by 32 miles) in the Delta region near the mouth of the Niger River.

Production of oil in Ogoniland began in 1958. The value of the oil that had been extracted from Ogoniland was a matter of dispute. According to Shell's figures, $5.2 billion worth of oil had been pumped from the region's five major oil fields since 1958. Ogoni activists claimed the amount was much higher, $30 billion.

Although Ogoniland was the site of great mineral wealth, the Ogoni people had received little benefit from its development. Under revenue-sharing arrangements between the Nigerian federal government and the states prior to 1992, only 1.5 percent of the government's revenues from oil was returned to the Delta communities for economic development, and much of this went to line the pockets of officials.

Ogoniland, like much of the Delta area, was very poor and very densely populated. No modern sanitation systems were in place; raw sewage was simply buried or discharged into rivers or lakes. Drinking water was often contaminated, and water-related diseases such as cholera, malaria, and gastroenteritis were common. Housing was typically constructed with corrugated tin roofs and cement or, more commonly, dirt floors. A British engineer who later returned to the Delta village near Ogoniland where oil was first discovered commented, "I have explored for oil in Venezuela, I have explored for oil in Kuwait, [but] I have never seen an oil-rich town as completely impoverished as Oloibiri."

In 1992, in response to pressure from the Ogoni and other Delta peoples, the Nigerian government established a commission, funded with 3 percent of the government's oil revenues, to promote infrastructure development in the oil-producing regions. In 1993, the group spent $94 million, with about 40 percent going to the Rivers State, in which Ogoniland was situated. Shell Nigeria also gave direct assistance to the oil-producing regions. In 1995, for example, the company's community development program in Nigeria spent about $20 million. Projects included building classrooms and community hospitals, paying teacher salaries, funding scholarships for Nigerian youth, operating agricultural stations, and building roads. However, Shell was criticized for making little effort to involve local residents in determining how its community development funds would be spent.

Ken Saro-Wiwa

Ken Saro-Wiwa, who became a leader of the Ogoni movement, was in many respects an unlikely activist. A businessman who later became a highly successful writer and television producer, he had a taste for gourmet food, sophisticated humor, and international travel. Yet in the final years of his life he emerged as a world-famous advocate for sustainable development and for the rights of indigenous peoples who was honored by receipt of the Goldman Environmental Prize.

Saro-Wiwa was born in 1941 in an Ogoni village. A brilliant student, he was educated first at government-run schools and later, with the aid of a scholarship, at the University of Ibadan, where he studied literature. After a brief stint as a government administrator, Saro-Wiwa left public service to launch his own business. After four years as a successful grocer and trader, he took the proceeds and began investing in real estate, buying office buildings, shops, and homes. In 1983, with sufficient property to live comfortably, Saro-Wiwa turned to what he called his first love, writing and publishing. He proved to be a gifted and prolific writer, producing in short order a critically acclaimed novel, a volume of poetry, and a collection of short stories.

In 1985, Saro-Wiwa was approached by a university friend who had become program director for the state-run Nigerian television authority. The friend asked him to develop a comedy series. The result, "Basi & Co.," ran for five years and became the most widely watched television show in Africa. Reflecting Saro-Wiwa's political views, the program satirized Nigerians' desire to get rich with little effort. The show's comic protagonist was Basi, "a witty rogue [who] hustled on the streets of Lagos and was willing to do anything to make money, short of working for it."

By the late 1980s, Saro-Wiwa had become a wealthy and internationally known novelist and television scriptwriter. His wife and four children moved to London, where his children enrolled in British private schools. Saro-Wiwa joined his family often, making many friends in the London literary community who would later work doggedly, although unsuccessfully, for his release.

In 1988, Saro-Wiwa undertook a nonfiction study of Nigerian history, later published under the title *On a Darkling Plain*. This work reawakened his interest in politics and in the plight of his own Ogoni people. In a speech in March 1990, marking the study's publication, Saro-Wiwa laid out a theme from the book that was to become central to the rest of his life's work:

> The notion that the oil-bearing areas can provide the revenue of the country and yet be denied a proper share of that revenue because it is perceived that the inhabitants of the area are few in number is unjust, immoral, unnatural, and ungodly.

On a Darkling Plain, not surprisingly, ignited a storm of controversy in Nigeria, and "Basi & Co." was canceled shortly after its publication, as was a column Saro-Wiwa had been writing for the government-owned weekly *Sunday Times.*

Movement for the Survival of the Ogoni People

The cancellation of his TV series and newspaper column seemed to propel Saro-Wiwa further into political activism. In August 1990, he met with a group of Ogoni tribal chiefs and intellectuals to draft an Ogoni Bill of Rights. This document called for political autonomy; cultural, religious, and linguistic freedom; the right to control a "fair proportion" of the region's economic resources; and higher standards of environmental protection for the Ogoni people.

Shortly thereafter, drafters of the bill of rights met to form an organization to press their demands. The group chose the name Movement for the Survival of the Ogoni People (MOSOP). From its inception, MOSOP adopted a philosophy of nonviolent mass mobilization. The group's earliest organizational efforts focused on educational work and appeals to the military government and to the oil companies. The organization published the Ogoni Bill of Rights and organized a speaking tour of the region to present it to the Ogoni. Saro-Wiwa traveled abroad—to the United States, Switzerland, the United Kingdom, the Netherlands, and Russia—where he met with human rights and environmentalist groups and government officials to build support for the Ogoni cause. MOSOP also issued a propagandistic "demand notice" calling on Shell to pay "damages" of $4 billion for "destroying the environment" and $6 billion in "unpaid rents and royalties" to the Ogoni people.

Environmental Issues

A central plank in the MOSOP platform was that the oil companies, particularly Shell, were responsible for serious environmental degradation. In a speech given in 1992 to the Unrepresented Nations and Peoples Organization (UNPO), Saro-Wiwa stated MOSOP's case:

> Oil exploration has turned Ogoni into a wasteland: lands, streams, and creeks are totally and continually polluted; the atmosphere has been poisoned, charged as it is with hydrocarbon vapors, methane, carbon monoxide, carbon dioxide and soot . . . . Acid rain, oil spillages and oil blowouts have devastated Ogoni territory. High-pressure oil pipelines crisscross the surface of Ogoni farmlands and villages dangerously. The results of such unchecked environmental pollution and degradation include the complete destruction of the ecosystem.

Shell disputed these charges, saying that they had been "dramatized out of all proportion." Shell argued that the land it had acquired for operations comprised only 0.3 percent of the Niger Delta. Three-quarters of Shell's operations were constructed before 1973 and were in full compliance at the time they were built. The company maintained a regular program of upgrading and replacing its pipelines and other infrastructure, including a program to bury above-ground flow lines. The company asserted that it was in compliance with all relevant laws and regulations and that it attempted to remediate all oil spills. Moreover, Shell charged, many of the oil spills in the area had been caused by sabotage, for which it could not be held responsible.

One of the most hotly contested oil spills in the area had occurred in Ebubu (near Ogoniland), around a quarter century earlier. By all accounts, this was a major spill, with severe ecological and economic consequences. Crude oil had spread over 10 hectares (about 25 acres), penetrated deeply into the soil, and contaminated nearby waterways. The oil had burned and crusted over, leaving the land useless. Ogoni activists blamed Shell for the spill and vigorously criticized the company for failing to clean it up adequately. Shell, however, maintained that the Ebubu spill had been caused by retreating

Biafran troops, during a period when the company had temporarily withdrawn from the area because of the civil war.

The relationship between human population and oil development in the region was complex. Ogoni activists claimed that Shell had insensitively located its pipelines and other infrastructure too close to human settlements. Shell pointed out, however, that the population of the Niger Delta had more than doubled during the 40 or so years that the company had operated there. In many cases, people had been drawn to the oil facilities in search of jobs, settling near pipelines and flow stations.

The Niger Delta was one of the world's largest wetlands, a vast floodplain built up by sedimentary deposits at the mouths of the Niger and Benue Rivers. In a comprehensive study of environmental conditions in the Niger Delta completed in 1995, the World Bank found evidence of significant environmental problems, including land degradation, over-fishing, deforestation, loss of biodiversity, and water contamination. The study did find evidence of air pollution from refineries and petrochemical facilities and of oil spills and poor waste management practices at and around pipelines, terminals, and offshore platforms. Most of the Delta's environmental problems, however, the World Bank concluded, were the result not of oil pollution but rather of overpopulation coupled with poverty and weak, poorly enforced environmental regulations.

One of the worst environmental problems associated with the oil industry was gas flaring. Natural gas is often produced as a by-product of oil production. In most oil-producing regions of the world, this ancillary gas is reinjected into the ground or captured and sold. In Nigeria, however, gas was routinely simply burned off, or "flared," in the production fields. In 1991, over three-quarters of natural gas production in Nigeria was flared—compared with, say, less than 1 percent in the United States or a world average of less than 5 percent. In 1993, Nigeria flared more natural gas than any other nation on earth. Gas flaring had several adverse environmental consequences. The flares produced large amounts of carbon dioxide and methane, both greenhouse gases and contributors to global warming. Residents in the immediate vicinity of the flares experienced noise, heat, and soot contamination. The flares, which burned continuously, lit up the night sky nearby with an orange glow.

During the early 1990s, Shell Nigeria became involved in a joint venture known as the Nigeria Liquefied Natural Gas (LNG) project. The aim of this project, in which Shell was a 26 percent shareholder, was to pipe natural gas to a liquefaction plant and from there to ship it abroad in special ships at supercooled temperatures. In late 1995, plans were under way for construction of an LNG processing facility that would be fully operational by 1999; all flaring was scheduled to cease by 2008.

Contrary to charges made by some of Shell's critics, Nigeria did have some environmental regulations in place, dating from 1992. These laws, which were enforced by the federal Department of Petroleum Resources, set emissions standards, restricted toxic discharges, required permits for handling toxic wastes, and mandated environmental impact studies for major industrial developments. Regulatory institutions were poorly developed, however, and government authorities had little incentive to vigorously enforce the country's environmental rules.

Civil Disturbances in the Niger Delta

During the early 1990s, civil disturbances in Ogoniland and other Delta communities, many directed at Shell, escalated. In one typical incident, as reported by Shell,

A gang of youths . . . stormed . . . a drilling rig in the Ahia oil field . . . looting and vandalizing the facility and rig camp. Rig workers were held hostage for most of the first day while property worth $6 million was destroyed or stolen.

The rig was shut down for 10 days and the Ahia flow station was also shut down . . . . [A protest leader] raised the issue of [distribution] . . . . of oil revenues to the oil-producing communities by the government, the need for a new road, and rumors of bribery by Shell of a [local] chief.

Most of the civil disturbances followed a similar pattern. A group of young men, armed with whatever weapons were readily available, would attack one of Shell's many far-flung oil installations in the Delta. Employees would be attacked, equipment would be sabotaged, and the group would make demands.

Shell's own data on patterns of community disturbances in the Niger Delta revealed a pattern of escalating violence throughout the early 1990s, peaking in 1993. Shell estimated that the company sustained $42 million in damage to its installations in Ogoniland between 1993 and the end of 1995, as a direct result of sabotage.

One of the most highly publicized of these incidents occurred at Umeuchem, about 30 miles from Ogoniland. Shell later posted on the Internet a description of this event:

[This] incident happened when armed youths invaded and occupied a rig location and nearby flow station, chasing off staff who were not given the opportunity to make the location safe. The youths demanded N100 million *naira,* the Nigerian currency, at that time worth about $12.5 million, a new road, and a water scheme. Attempts to talk with the youths, who were armed with guns and machetes, failed.

In response, Shell staff called the Nigerian authorities, who sent in a Mobile Police unit. The Mobile Police were widely known in Nigeria as the "Kill-and-Go Mob" because of their undisciplined behavior. In the ensuing riot, at least one policeman and seven civilians in the local village were killed. Shell concluded its posting, "The Shell response to the threatening situation was made with the best intentions and what happened was a shock to staff, many of whom had friends [in the village]."

The relationship between these community disturbances and MOSOP was complex. Saro-Wiwa's group explicitly rejected violence and repeatedly disavowed vigilante attacks on Shell or other companies, and Saro-Wiwa himself frequently toured Ogoniland to restore calm. Yet publication of the Ogoni Bill of Rights and MOSOP campaigns focusing attention on injustices suffered by the Ogoni clearly had the effect of boosting expectations within Ogoni society. In this context, many young unemployed Ogoni men simply took matters into their own hands.

The escalation of violence against the company posed a difficult dilemma for SPDC executives. Shell Nigeria officials stated that the company did not want military protection, preferring dialogue with local communities. When it was impossible to operate safely, the company's practice was simply to withdraw its personnel. (The one exception was the two coastal terminals; considered strategic areas by the government, the harbors' oil-loading areas were protected by military troops.) The company's own personnel were not armed. However, Nigerian police officers known as *supernumerary police* were routinely assigned to protect oil facilities, including Shell's. The company paid these officers directly and was responsible for supervising, training, and equipping them. In one instance in 1982, Shell purchased 107 handguns for use by supernumeraries protecting its facilities. Shell defended these practices, saying it was normal in Nigeria to retain police protection in areas where violent crime was a daily occurrence.

Several human rights organizations claimed that as civil unrest escalated in Ogoniland, Shell began to work more and more closely with the authorities to coordinate security. The Nigerian Civil Liberties Organization reported that Shell-owned cars, buses, speedboats, and helicopters were regularly used to transport police and military personnel to the site of civil disturbances. Human Rights Watch reported that Shell met regularly with representatives of the Rivers State police to plan security operations. Shell denied this, stating that these practices would violate company policy; the company also stated that after the Umeuchem incident, in particular, it had been anxious to avoid any unnecessary dealings with the Mobile Police.

On January 3, 1993, MOSOP held a massive rally to mark the start of the Year of the Indigenous Peoples. Held at successive locations across Ogoniland, the rally was attended by as many as 300,000 people, three-fifths of the Ogoni population. Protestors carried twigs, a symbol of environmental regeneration. Two weeks later, after three attacks on its staff there, Shell abruptly announced that it would withdraw from Ogoniland. It evacuated all employees and shut down its operations. Company officials gave a terse explanation: "There is no question of our staff working in areas where their safety may be at risk."

Taking a Hard Line

After General Abacha took power in November 1993, he apparently decided to take a hard line with the Ogoni. Whether this was an effort to crush the Ogoni movement, to keep other ethnic groups from following their example, or to make the area safe for the resumption of commercial oil operations, or all three, was not clear. One of his first acts as a head of state was to dispatch a special paramilitary force, composed of selected personnel from the army, navy, air force, and police, to restore order in Ogoniland and elsewhere in the Rivers State. Paul Okuntimo, a notorious military officer who publicly boasted of his proficiency in killing people, headed the special force.

According to an alleged government memo, dated May 12, 1994, the purpose of Okuntimo's force was to ensure that those "carrying out business ventures in Ogoniland are not molested." The memo also noted, "Shell operations still impossible unless ruthless military operations are undertaken for smooth economic activities to commence." It advised the governor of Rivers State to put "pressure on oil companies for prompt regular inputs as discussed." Shell challenged the authenticity of this document and adamantly denied making any direct payments to the military authorities for this purpose.

In May and June 1994, intense violence erupted in Ogoniland. Amnesty International, which collected eyewitness accounts, reported that the government's paramilitary force entered Ogoniland, where it "instigated and assisted" interethnic clashes between previously peaceful neighboring groups. The units then "followed the attackers into Ogoni villages, destroying houses and detaining people." In May and June, the force attacked 30 towns and villages, where its members "fired at random, destroyed and set fires to homes, killing, assaulting, and raping, and looting and extorting money, livestock, and food," according to the Amnesty International report. As many as 2,000 civilians may have been killed.

In 1995, despite Okuntimo's efforts, Shell had still not returned to Ogoniland. Claude Ake, a well-known Nigerian political economist, described the situation in the Delta in December 1995: "The flow stations, that is the operational bases of the oil industry, operated under armed presence. This is a process," he added, in a chilling phrase, "of the militarization of commerce."

The Arrest, Trial and Execution of Saro-Wiwa

On May 21, 1994, just over a week after the "smooth economic activities" memo, Saro-Wiwa was en route to a MOSOP rally where he was scheduled to speak. On the way, his car was stopped at a military roadblock, and he was ordered to return home. He never attended the rally. Later that same day, a group of Ogoni chiefs, founders of MOSOP who had resigned in 1993 and become political opponents of Saro-Wiwa, held a meeting. Their gathering was interrupted by a crowd of several hundred youths, who denounced the men as "vultures" who had collaborated with the military government. Four of the chiefs were assaulted and bludgeoned to death.

Later that day, Saro-Wiwa and several other leaders of MOSOP were arrested. In a televised press conference, the governor of Rivers State blamed the MOSOP leaders for the murders. Saro-Wiwa and his colleagues were detained in a secret military camp, where they were chained in leg irons and denied access to medical care. It would be eight months before they were formally charged.

During Saro-Wiwa's imprisonment, his brother, Owens Wiwa, met on at least two occasions with Shell Nigeria's managing director, Brian Anderson, to seek his help in securing Ken's release. Wiwa's and Anderson's later accounts of these conversations differed sharply. Wiwa said that Anderson had told him that it would be "difficult but not impossible" to get his brother out of prison. Anderson allegedly said that if MOSOP stopped the international campaign against Shell, he might be able to intervene. Wiwa refused, he said. For his part, Anderson acknowledged that he had met with Wiwa as part of an effort at "quiet diplomacy," but he denied his specific allegations as "false and reprehensible." Anderson reported that Wiwa had offered to stop the campaign against Shell if the company intervened to help his brother. Anderson said that he was not willing to make that kind of deal and that Shell could not have stopped the executions in any case, because the company had very little influence with the military government.

In November, General Abacha appointed a Civil Disturbances Special Tribunal to try the case of the MOSOP leaders. Established by special decree, this tribunal was empowered to impose the death penalty in cases involving civil disturbances. The decision of the court could be confirmed or disallowed by the military government, but defendants had no right of judicial appeal. Amnesty International and many other human rights organizations denounced the tribunal for violating standards of due process guaranteed by Nigeria's own constitution and by international treaties.

Saro-Wiwa's trial for murder began in February 1995. Prosecution witnesses testified that Saro-Wiwa had relayed a message to his youthful supporters, after the roadblock incident, to "deal with" his opponents. Saro-Wiwa's defense attorneys countered that Saro-Wiwa had been at home at the time and had had nothing to do with the killings.

On October 31, the tribunal found Saro-Wiwa and eight other MOSOP leaders guilty of murder and sentenced them to death. Six defendants were acquitted. On November 2, Royal Dutch/Shell chairman Cor Herkströter sent a letter to General Abacha, appealing for mercy for Saro-Wiwa and his codefendants. In Nigeria, Brian Anderson spoke out publicly for clemency on humanitarian grounds. Around the world, many political leaders and human rights organizations also called on the Nigerian government to spare Saro-Wiwa.

The military authorities, however, moved swiftly to carry out the sentence. On November 10, Saro-Wiwa and eight MOSOP associates were hanged in prison. His last words on the gallows were: "Lord, take my soul, but the struggle continues."

With Deep Regret

Shell issued a statement on the executions that read, in part, "It is with deep regret that we hear this news. From the violence that led to the murder of the four Ogoni leaders in May last year through to the death penalty having been carried out, the human cost has been too high." Earlier, Shell had told reporters that it would have been inappropriate to have intervened in the criminal trial. "A commercial organization like Shell cannot and must never interfere with the legal processes of any sovereign state . . . Any government, be it in Europe, North America, or elsewhere, would not tolerate this type of interference by business."

The company also defended its actions in the months leading up to Saro-Wiwa's arrest and trial. Shell representatives stated that it would have been wrong to have tried to influence government policy on Ogoni autonomy or other political issues of concern to MOSOP. An executive told the news media, "Our responsibility is very clear. We pay taxes and [abide by] regulation. We don't run the government." Shell also vigorously resisted demands by some human rights activists and environmentalists that the company withdraw from Nigeria. If the company withdrew its 250 or so expatriate managers, the government or another oil company could easily take over the operation and continue to run it, very possibly with lower environmental, safety, and human rights standards.

Shell's public disclaimers did little to slow down the controversy swirling around the company. By mid-1996, the company was facing calls for an international gasoline boycott, external pressure to abandon plans for its liquefied natural gas project, and persistent demands that it withdraw from Nigeria altogether. The crisis threatened the company's reputation and relations with stakeholders, not only in Nigeria, but throughout the world.

Discussion Questions

1. What arguments did Shell make in defending its actions in Nigeria? How would Shell's critics counter these arguments? Do you believe Shell could or should have done anything differently in Nigeria?

2. What internal or external factors contributed to the emergence of this crisis for Shell?

3. Evaluate Shell's actions in Nigeria with reference to an existing code of conduct for multinational organizations. Do you believe Shell was in compliance with the code you have selected? If not, how not? Do you believe the code you have selected is appropriate and adequate?

4. In your opinion, is it possible to develop a universal set of ethical standards for business, or do cultural differences make universal standards impractical, if not impossible?

5. What, if anything, should Shell do next?

The Transformation of Shell

In the late 1990s, Shell International underwent a remarkable transformation. Variously termed by observers a "sea change," a "mid-life crisis," and a "dramatic overhaul," the company undertook a deep and systematic effort to remake itself. In the process, Shell radically changed its organizational structure, its culture, its relationship with stakeholders (including its most vocal critics), its reporting practices, and, indeed, even its very business principles. In the end, it set out to become an organization in which financial, social, and environmental performance were equally valued and fully integrated.

A cover story in *Fortune* in 1997 was pointedly titled "Why Is the World's Most Profitable Company Turning Itself Inside Out?" To some, this transformation represented wrongheaded New Age tampering with a proven management formula. To some, it was nothing more than a sophisticated public relations offensive to repair a reputation badly tarnished by human rights abuses in Nigeria, the controversy over the disposal of the oil rig Brent Spar, and struggles with shareholder activists over corporate governance. To others, though, it represented more. To them, Shell's multilevel struggle to transform itself was the most ambitious effort ever by a major multinational corporation to define a new relationship between business and society in a world of rapidly changing public expectations.

The Campaigns against Shell

The early to mid-1990s were a period when international environmentalist, human rights, and shareholder campaigns directed against Shell gathered intensity. Three separate but related campaigns—opposing at-sea disposal of old offshore oil facilities, alleging human rights abuses in Nigeria, and backing shareholder resolutions for reforms in corporate governance—focused a spotlight of often negative publicity on the world's most profitable multinational corporation.

The Brent Spar Incident

A watershed event in Shell's transformation was what came to be known at the Brent Spar incident. The Brent Spar was an oil storage and loading buoy in the North Sea, about 100 miles off the coast of Scotland. Although a unique structure, it was one of several hundred North Sea installations, many nearing the end of their useful lives.

In 1991, Shell took the Brent Spar out of service and began looking at options for disposing of it. According to international and British law, operators were required to determine the best practical environmental option for disposal. This could involve either sinking the platform in the deep sea or removing and dismantling it on land. Government approval was required. In April 1995, after extensive consultations with outside experts about possible options, Shell announced its intention to dispose of the Brent Spar at sea, and British authorities agreed.

The plan quickly ran into resistance from Greenpeace, however. At the time, Greenpeace was the largest environmental organization in the world, with a full-time staff of 120, a budget of about $50 million, and a penchant for confrontational tactics. Greenpeace believed that toxic residue in the Brent Spar's tanks would harm the marine environment and that its disposal at sea would set a precedent for other, soon-to-be decommissioned oil installations.

On April 30, 1995, Greenpeace activists boarded and occupied the abandoned buoy. After a three-week standoff, Shell personnel, aided by local law officers, evicted the protesters nonviolently. The company defended its decision to sink the Brent Spar in full-page newspaper advertisements and began towing the rig toward the open sea. However, the Greenpeace occupation and resulting media coverage had galvanized public opinion, especially on the Continent. By mid-June, government officials of Belgium, Denmark, Sweden, the Netherlands, and Germany had asked Shell to postpone sinking the Brent Spar. Meanwhile, a consumer boycott had gathered steam. In Germany, Shell franchise owners reported a 50 percent decline in sales over a two-week period. Several Shell gas stations, also in Germany, were anonymously firebombed. The British prime minister continued to support Shell, however; and the boycott was less successful in Britain.

On June 20, Shell abruptly changed course, announcing that it had decided to abandon its plan to dispose of the Brent Spar at sea and to seek a permit for onshore disposal. In a statement, the company said, "The European Companies of the Royal Dutch/Shell Group find themselves in an untenable position and feel that it is not possible to continue without wider support." The company moved the buoy to a Norwegian fjord, while it considered further actions. Greenpeace later acknowledged that it had seriously erred in its estimate of the amount of toxic residue in the Brent Spar's tanks and apologized.

Human Rights in Nigeria

Just a few months later, the execution of Ken Saro-Wiwa and his colleagues in Nigeria on November 10, 1995 (described in the preceding case, "Shell Oil in Nigeria"), led to what *Fortune* referred to as a "global uproar." Much of it was directed at the government of Nigeria, which was summarily suspended from the Commonwealth of Nations at the urging of President Nelson Mandela of South Africa. Other countries called for an arms embargo, sports boycott, and freezing the foreign bank accounts of the pariah nation's military leaders.

But much outrage was also directed at Shell, which was perceived by many as not acting forcefully to prevent Saro-Wiwa's execution. Environmentalist organizations, particularly, spoke out. The chairman of Greenpeace U.K. told the press, "There is blood on Shell's hands. Ken Saro-Wiwa was hanged for speaking out against Shell. He was trying to secure the most basic of human rights—the right to clean air, land, and water." The Sierra Club promoted a boycott of the company under the slogan "(S)hell no, corporate accountability yes," and urged its supporters to cut up their Shell credit cards, boycott Shell products, and participate in protest demonstrations.

One of the organizations most involved in the protests against Shell was The Body Shop International (BSI), the beauty products retailer chaired by social activist

Anita Roddick. BSI initiated a major protest campaign against Shell, which included the perhaps unprecedented event of one corporation publicly accusing another of murder. Greenpeace, The Body Shop International, and Friends of the Earth ran a full-page advertisement with a photograph of a gas flare under the heading, "Dear Shell, This is the Truth. And it Stinks." Protest demonstrations featured hooded dummies dangling from nooses.

Shareholder Activism

Against the backdrop of the controversies over Brent Spar and Nigeria, a coordinated campaign by shareholder activists critical of Shell moved forward, placing into public debate issues that had previously been solely the prerogative of management.

Although less developed than in the United States, the movement to promote ethical investing was gaining ground in the United Kingdom in the early 1990s. A central player in this movement was a nonprofit organization called Pensions and Investment Research Consultants (PIRC). PIRC's goal was to use shareholder leverage to raise standards of corporate governance and to promote socially responsible management. With a staff of 25, the organization worked primarily with public employee pension funds. It also worked with religious organizations with stock holdings, some of which were members of the Ecumenical Council on Corporate Responsibility (ECCR), and with individual investors concerned with the ethics of companies in which they held stock. PIRC's chief tactic was to introduce and organize support for shareholder resolutions at corporate annual meetings.

In 1995, in response to the Nigeria and Brent Spar controversies, PIRC requested the first of what was to be a series of meetings with Shell officials. There, it made the first of several proposals to Shell reflecting its members' concerns with ethics, environmental policy, and corporate governance generally.

Initiating Organizational Change

In early 1994, more than a year before the Brent Spar, Nigeria, and shareholder campaigns erupted, Shell management had initiated a process of internal organizational change, aimed at improving the Group's financial performance relative to its competitors.

At the time, Shell's return on average capital employed (ROACE), a common measure of performance in the petroleum industry, showed that the company lagged behind many of its competitors. Although Shell remained very profitable (in fact, in 1994 it earned more profit than any other company in the world), other big oil companies, including rivals British Petroleum, Exxon, and Mobil, were enjoying significantly higher ROACE. Of particular concern to Shell executives were hypercompetition from discount retailers and weak sales of nonfuel products, such as food and convenience items, at the retail level. To help improve the company's profitability, the company engaged the services of management consultants McKinsey & Company to lead an extensive internal review. McKinsey quickly focused its attention on the company's organizational structure.

Since the 1950s, Royal Dutch/Shell had used a matrix form of organization. Under this structure, the chief executive of the national operating companies reported simultaneously to two superiors: a regional manager and a product manager. For example, the managing director of Shell Nigeria would report both to a regional coordinator for Africa and to the coordinator for exploration and production. In addition, staff at Shell's headquarters in London and The Hague provided functional expertise in finance, legal matters, human resources management, and external affairs. (Shell U.S., the largest of the Group companies, maintained its own staff of functional specialists and operated for most purposes independently.) At the time, it was believed that this matrix organization benefited Shell by devolving power and balancing interests.

In March 1995, Shell concluded the first phase of its internal review by announcing a plan to reorganize into five worldwide business units. These were exploration and production, oil products, chemicals, gas and coal, and central staff functions. The five units would be overseen by committees of senior executives, who would report to the committee of managing directors (CMD). Under this plan, managers of the operating companies would report only to their business unit superiors, in a single line of command, thus eliminating the matrix, which was perceived as unnecessarily complicated. Excess staff at the center was also cut. The restructuring was intended to enable the company to focus more efficiently on the needs of its business and retail customers.

Talking about a "New Shell"

Even as Shell announced its intended organizational redesign, however, external pressures on the company, as well as internal debate, had the effect of shifting the focus of the transformation process to the softer issues of the company's reputation and relations with stakeholders. The key events took place in a series of retreats for top executives held in late 1995 and early 1996.

In 1995, Shell had engaged the services of a group of private management consultants to lead the next phase of the transformation process. In a series of exercises, conducted at retreats in 1995 and early 1996, these consultants asked directors and a selected group of top executives from the operating companies to "hold up a mirror" to reflect their own practice. Their objective was to develop a "diagnosis of current reality" that could serve as a starting point for further changes aimed at improving corporate profitability.

To the apparent surprise of both the consultants and Shell's top leaders, discussion began to shift, seemingly spontaneously, from strictly business matters to Shell's social and environmental performance. Many participants at the retreats wanted to talk not about profitability but about the fact that Shell was being pilloried in the press as a corporate murderer. At first, the top leaders present tended to dismiss the relevance of Brent Spar and Nigeria to the business problems the company faced. But as the discussion proceeded, the attitude of the leadership appeared to change. One of the consultants present, Philip H. Mirvis, later recalled:

> The leadership stepped up . . . . Cor [Herkströter, chairman of the CMD] was essentially saying, "We own this problem. It is not a technical problem, if only we had had a better analysis with the Brent Spar. This is not a relationship problem, if only we had had a better relationship with the government, or if we had had a different government in Nigeria, this wouldn't have happened. We as leaders are responsible for this result." Quite frankly, Cor had a sense of shame over his own leadership and the leadership of the CMD. This sent a gasp through the organization. This was an organization that was Teflon, bulletproof, apologized for nothing, admitted to nothing, and so on. To see the leadership taking on responsibility and expressing a deep sense of remorse over this opened the gates for a dialogue about what are we doing, what are we responsible for, what is the role of our company around the globe, and so on.

The willingness of Shell's leaders to take responsibility for what had happened, Mirvis later wrote, "legitimated expressions of guilt and anger over past wrongs and, in effect, assigned some blame to the corporate culture." The consultants used this opening to ask executives to write personal stories that expressed their vision of where they had been and where they wanted to go and to share them with each other and their staffs. This process was then repeated at lower levels of the organization.

Mark Moody-Stuart, a member of the CMD (and later Herkströter's successor as chairman), framed Shell's problem as the need for a new mind-set that paid greater attention to societal expectations. In Mirvis's words:

> Mark Moody-Stuart should be credited with the intellectual framing of this. Shell was an engineering-type company . . . . a very technical organization and essentially a very bureaucratic organization . . . . What Mark said was that the technical mind-set, our rational, logical approach, is blinding us to a world out there of human rights activists, of environmentalists, of governments with different wants and interests and changing customer tastes, expectations of the public, et cetera. We are so internally focused, so technical, that we are missing a whole set of opportunities and a whole new reality out there . . . . We are not talking any more about a structural change in the organization; we are not even talking about new leadership per se. We are talking about a new Shell.

Evaluating Society's Changing Expectations

Once the CMD became convinced that it had failed to meet the "new reality" of changing expectations, the directors quickly undertook a series of interrelated initiatives to improve Shell's social and environmental performance and the public's perception of its corporate citizenship. These involved a study of society's perceptions of the company, revision of the company's business principles, and a new approach to reporting and verifying its social and environmental performance to stakeholders.

One of Shell's first actions was to commission a report, titled "Society's Changing Expectations." Research, conducted over a year and a half, involved extensive roundtable discussions with Shell executives, stakeholders, academics, and journalists; a review of previous surveys; young person focus groups; and consultations with public relations professionals in all regions of the world. The central finding of the study, delivered in November 1996, was that Shell's reputation had suffered because the company's behavior had not kept pace with society's changing expectations. The report found that a number of factors had combined to make many people both more cynical about multinational corporations and more demanding of them. These factors included new communications technology (particularly the rise of the Internet), population growth and migration, growing nationalist and fundamentalist sentiment in some regions, and increasing public concern for the environment.

As might be expected, patterns varied by region and by stakeholder. For example, Shell enjoyed a better reputation in Latin America, where it was widely perceived as an effective provider of jobs, products, and services, than in Africa, where it was not. In developing countries, stakeholders expected Shell to encourage government concern for the environment; in developed countries, the opposite was true. Overall, however, the consultant's conclusion was that "economic, social, and technological changes have created a more cynical, questioning, indeed challenging attitude toward institutions, not the least, MNCs."

Revision of the Statement of General Business Principles

A second initiative was to take a fresh look at Shell's Statement of General Business Principles (SGBP). First developed in 1976, the SGBP sought to define the Group's core values. Now, the directors believed, the SGBP needed to be revisited in light of the changing environment in which the company operated. Accordingly, in 1996 the directors asked Integrity Works, an ethics consultancy, to carry out a review of the SGBP. The process included distribution of hundreds of questionnaires and scores of interviews with managers in 80 operating companies, aimed at identifying areas in the SGBP that needed change. Most managers felt that the principles remained largely valid, but they flagged several areas in need of revision.

In March 1997, Shell published a revised Statement of General Business Principles. Although similar in most respects to the earlier document, the revision included three significant changes recommended by Integrity Works. First, the company declared its support for "fundamental human rights in line with the legitimate role of business." (Shell did not explicitly endorse the Universal Declaration of Human Rights in the revised business principles, although it did do so later in other documents.) Second, the company committed itself "to contribute to sustainable development." Finally, the revisions clarified the company's stand on political activity. The earlier formulation, which emphasized abstention from politics, was replaced with language stating the company's intention to abstain from *party politics,* while emphasizing its right and responsibility to make its position known to governments on matters affecting the company or its stakeholders.

All operating companies were instructed to adopt the revised principles as their own policy. Beginning in 1998, these companies' chief executives were required to confirm in writing annually to the CMD that they were in compliance with the revised principles or, if not, where they fell short. The compliance letter requirement focused the attention of operating managers on the changes and ways in which their actions were consistent, or inconsistent, with the company's values.

With the assistance of Amnesty International, Shell also developed a primer, *Business and Human Rights,* explaining what the commitment to human rights meant in practical terms.

Resolution 10

In early 1997, the Pensions and Investment Research Consultants (PIRC) decided that Shell, despite its efforts, had still not addressed its concerns satisfactorily. The investor activists therefore decided to place a resolution before the shareholders at the May annual general meeting (AGM) of Shell Transport and Trading. Resolution 10, as it came to be known, was jointly sponsored by 18 institutional investors.

The resolution called on Shell to take three actions. These were to place a director (board member) in charge of environmental and corporate responsibility; to monitor, externally audit, and report to shareholders on its environmental and social policies; and to issue a report by the end of the year on the company's operations in Nigeria. Resolution 10 generated intense media and shareholder interest.

The company recommended a vote against the resolution and issued a statement in response that stated, in part:

> Your Directors, and all Royal Dutch/Shell Group of Companies, consider that environmental and corporate responsibility policies are an integral part in the proper conduct of the Group's business activities. Your Directors reject the implication in this resolution that the Group does not have effective policies in place.

In spite of the company's opposition, of the 46 percent of shares that were voted, 10.5 percent supported the resolution and 6.5 percent abstained. Although the resolution failed, support for it was much higher than support for virtually any other such social responsibility resolution introduced that year by shareholder activists in Europe or the United States.

Although Shell opposed Resolution 10, it moved quickly to institute some organizational changes requested by its shareholder critics. In late 1997, Shell established a social accountability team, consisting of six members of the committee of managing directors and one representative each from Shell and Royal Dutch. Herkströter was given overall responsibility for environmental and corporate responsibility policies. A new position, manager for social accountability, was created.

Social and Environmental Reporting

Shell considered that an important element in its corporate responsibility initiative was to be publicly accountable not only to its shareholders but also to its other stakeholders and society at large. Accordingly, it began publishing a series of reports that went well beyond traditional annual financial reports.

In April 1998, the company published its first annual *Shell Report,* subtitled *Profits and Principles—Does There Have to Be a Choice?* This unusual document reported on Shell's commitment to human rights, environmental protection, and corporate citizenship. It also invited others to join with the company in a global debate on the responsibilities of multinational corporations. In its introduction, the report stated:

> This Report is about values. It describes how we, the people, companies, and businesses that make up the Royal Dutch/Shell Group, are striving to live up to our responsibilities—financial, social, and environmental. It is also an invitation to you to tell us what you think of our performance.

The report described the revised SGBP in detail, gave examples of each principle, and explained the company's efforts to make sure they were honored by the operating companies and Shell's joint venture partners and contractors. It presented a series of challenging ethical questions and invited readers to share their reactions. Many of these questions had already been the subjects of extensive public debate, in connection with Nigeria and Brent Spar. For example, one question was: Under what circumstances, if any, should a major company use its economic power to deliver, or at least influence, political change—especially in nations with undemocratic governments and poor human rights records? The report presented Shell's approach to a number of difficult issues, such as climate change.

The report also included an essay by John Elkington, chairman of SustainAbility, a consultancy specializing in advising corporations on sustainable development. In this essay, Elkington presented his concept of the *triple bottom line,* arguing that companies had a duty to provide audited reports not only of their financial performance but of their social and environmental performance as well. The report concluded with a road map for the future. Shell followed up *Profits and Principles* with a *Health, Safety, and Environment Report* and *Shell's Investment in Society,* reporting specifically on its environmental and social performance. All three reports were intended to be annual publications.

Although Shell had opposed PIRC's 1997 shareholder resolution calling for external auditing of its environmental performance, it now undertook to provide independent verification of its social and environmental reports. This goal presented unique challenges. The scope of practices to be audited was worldwide and complex. Moreover, unlike financial reporting, where auditing practices were well established, meaningful measures of social and environmental performance were not generally accepted. The company set out to work with its auditors, KPMG and PriceWaterhouse, and others to develop social and environmental accounting and assurance standards. In *Profits and Principles,* the company set out a timetable leading to integrated, externally verified reporting for its financial, social, and environmental performance by 2002.

The company's July 1998 *Health, Safety, and Environment Report* was the first independently verified audited environmental report ever published by a multinational oil company. The auditors, KPMG and PriceWaterhouse, acknowledged that the job had "proved to be a considerable challenge" because of the "absence of established generally accepted international standards for the verification of HSE data." The initial cost to audit Shell's health, safety, and environmental data in 30 entities worldwide in 1998 was around $2 million.

To bring the message of these reports to a wider public, Shell in 1999 initiated a $25 million "profits and principles" advertising campaign. Its purpose, in the words of Mark Moody-Stuart, was "to keep all of our stakeholders informed, both about the issues themselves and the work we at Shell are doing to address those issues."

Dialogue with Stakeholder Organizations

During this period, Shell also maintained an ongoing dialogue with stakeholders, including some of its most vocal critics. It called this process *engagement.* In part, this was accomplished through tear-off "Tell Shell" cards in various reports, such as *Profits and Principles,* which readers were invited to fill out and mail back to the company. In part, it was accomplished through an interactive feature on Shell's Web site, which permitted anyone to submit comments for all to see. Scores of people did, including many that were morally outraged at Shell's behavior. Their comments were posted, without censorship, creating the unusual spectacle of a corporate Web site peppered with negative remarks, which activists could use to find each other and create a community of anti-Shell interest.

In addition to opening itself up for freewheeling public comment, Shell also engaged in written and face-to-face dialogue with stakeholders, including community activists and human rights, environmentalist, and corporate governance organizations. The engagement process was coordinated by Shell's Department of External Affairs, but it involved managers at many levels throughout the Group.

The Human Rights Dialogue

One such dialogue occurred with two human rights organizations, Amnesty International and Pax Christi. In December 1995, in the wake of Ken Saro-Wiwa's execution, Pax Christi—a Catholic lay organization devoted to promoting world peace, human rights, and economic justice—wrote Shell asking the company to speak out on the issue of human rights in Nigeria. Herkströter replied, responding to specific points in the letter and inviting Pax Christi to engage in further discussions.

Pax Christi asked Amnesty International, with which it shared many concerns, to join it in this process. At that time, Amnesty International was probably the best-known human rights organization in the world, with more than a million members worldwide. Over the following three years, these two organizations engaged in an ongoing dialogue with Shell, involving an exchange of position papers, public forums, and face-to-face meetings.

In these discussions, Pax Christi and Amnesty International focused on several issues. They argued that it was imperative that the company incorporate explicit support for the Universal Declaration of Human Rights in its Statement of General Business Principles. The two human rights organizations urged Shell to appoint a director for human rights and to institute better training in human rights for its staff, particularly its security personnel.

They recommended independent auditing of the company's human rights practices. Other portions of the discussion focused specifically on the situation in Nigeria and on Shell's role during the Saro-Wiwa trial and its relationship to the Nigerian military authorities.

In some cases, the company made specific changes in response to the NGOs' recommendations. For example, the NGOs raised questions about the adequacy of the guidance provided to police assigned to protect Shell's property and for failing to require accountability for possible police misconduct. In response, Shell reviewed its policies and made specific changes to bring them into compliance with United Nations standards. The company also updated the plastic wallet-sized cards distributed to police assigned to Shell facilities, summarizing the company's revised human rights policies. In other situations, by contrast, Shell declined the NGOs' recommendations. For example, the company declined to appoint a director of human rights, saying that its current corporate governance procedures were sufficient.

The Brent Spar Dialogue

After reversing its initial decision to seek deep-sea disposal of the Brent Spar, Shell initiated a two-year-long dialogue with its environmental critics, including Greenpeace. In October 1995, the company announced an international competition to solicit innovative solutions to the problem of what to do with the decommissioned rig. It also sponsored open meetings in the United Kingdom, Germany, Denmark, and the Netherlands to discuss various options. These gatherings were facilitated by an independent organization, the Environmental Council, which worked with groups to find common ground in environmental disputes. After winnowing the list of possible options, in 1997 Shell held yet another round of public meetings in all four countries, accompanied by a CD-ROM describing the short-listed options.

Finally, in January 1998 Shell announced its selection of a solution: to recycle the Brent Spar as a ferry quay near Stavanger, Norway. So-called Ro/Ro (roll-on, roll-off) ferries, which carried both cars and people, were widely used in Norway, with its mountainous terrain and miles of coastline. Under the plan, the Spar would be disassembled, and its flotation tanks and other parts reused to construct a Ro-Ro dock. The ferry quay solution appealed to environmentalists, who liked the idea of putting the old rig to good use. The British government quickly approved the plan, and construction began in late 1998.

Shell later commented that the Brent Spar experience "taught us the value of dialogue with our critics and other interested parties . . . . This unique consultation exercise has helped promote a different approach to decision making in the Group, and has shown new ways in which Shell companies can be more open and accountable." In a speech, a Shell executive later described this new approach as a switch from DAD—decide, announce, and defend, to DDD—dialogue, decide, and deliver.

In addition to its dialogues with human rights organizations and environmentalists, Shell also continued to meet with shareholder activists, religious leaders, and other stakeholders during this period.

Continuing Challenges of Corporate Responsibility

Over a four-year period, Shell had undergone a major transformation. It had undertaken a revision of its business principles, an internal structural reorganization, a survey of its global reputation, and externally audited reports on its social and environmental performance. It had conducted hundreds of meetings with stakeholders, and changed its corporate policies in many areas.

What did the "new" Shell's proclaimed environmental and social commitments mean in practice? What changes did managers and employees on the ground in the Group's scores of operating companies do differently, if anything, as a result of the transformation of Shell? In its far-flung worldwide operations, the company continued to face daily challenges to act in a manner consistent with its support for human rights, sustainable development, and social responsibility. To some, the company was making marked progress toward meeting society's changing expectations. To others, it continued to fall short, focusing more on changing the public's perception than on changing its actual practice.

In an interview in July 1999, chairman Mark Moody-Stuart reflected on Shell's transformation process:

> I think that the main goals [of the transformation] were to make sure that we were internally effective, that we made best use of our resources, our assets, our people . . . . But, also, that we had this connection to society and to the customers . . . . [It] is the society that commercial organizations have to serve, no matter what you do. Even if you are a baker making bread, you had better know what the trends are on bread in the society. If people are going to give up eating bread, you had better know about it. If they like chocolate bread, you had better know about that . . . . You can't divorce the two. People sometimes try to do that. They say, all this societal stuff is woolly, we should stick to commerce. The two are absolutely linked . . . . These soft issues are really business issues because we are part of society, and members of society are our customers. So, our impact on society really matters commercially.

Discussion Questions

1. In the late 1990s, Shell underwent a transformation. What were the key changes that Shell made in the areas of organizational structure and culture, relationships with stakeholders, reporting practices, and business principles? What additional changes, if any, do you believe Shell should have made?

2. In your opinion, what was the most important cause of Shell's transformation? Do you believe the company was motivated more by external pressures or by internal pressures? Why do you think so?

3. Some people believe that Shell was sincere in the changes it made, and others believe that the company's transformation was mainly an effort to manipulate public opinion. What is your opinion? How could you best determine the answer to this question?

This glossary defines technical or special terms used in this book. Students may use it as a quick and handy reference for terms that may be unfamiliar without having to refer to the specific chapter(s) where they are used. It also can be a very helpful aid in studying for examinations and for writing term papers where precise meanings are needed.

A

Acid rain   Rain that is more acidic than normal; occurs when emissions of sulfur dioxide and nitrogen oxides from utilities, manufacturers, and vehicles combine with water vapor in the air.

Acquisition   (See Corporate merger.)

Ad hoc coalitions   The bringing together of diverse groups to organize for or against legislation or regulation.

Advergames   Free online games that incorporate marketing promotions for products typically of interest to children.

Advocacy advertising   A political tool used by companies to promote their viewpoint through the media.

Affirmative action   A positive and sustained effort by an organization to identify, hire, train if necessary, and promote minorities, women, and members of other groups who are underrepresented in the organization's workforce.

Air pollution   When more pollutants, such as sulfur dioxide or particulates, are emitted into the atmosphere than can be safely absorbed and diluted by natural processes.

Alternative dispute resolution   A method for resolving legal conflicts outside the traditional court system, in which a professional mediator (a third-party neutral) works with the two sides to negotiate a settlement agreeable to both parties.

Annual meeting   A yearly meeting called by a corporation's board of directors for purposes of reporting to the company's stockholders on the current status and future prospects of the firm.

Anti-Americanism   Opposition to the United States of America, or to its people, principles, or policies.

Anticompetitive merger   A merger of two or more companies that reduces or eliminates competition in an industry or region; usually illegal under U.S. antitrust laws.

Antitrust laws   Laws that promote competition or that oppose trusts, monopolies, or other business combinations that restrain trade.

B

Balanced scorecard   An approach focusing on a set of key financial and nonfinancial indicators to account for an organization's short-term and long-term accomplishments.

Biodiversity   The number and variety of species and the range of their genetic makeup.

Biotechnology   A technological application that uses biological systems or living organisms to make or modify products or processes for specific use.

Bioterrorism   The use of deadly bioengineered diseases and poisons by terrorists.

Blogs   Web-based journals or logs where individuals or organizations can post information, or raise controversial issues for discussion on the Internet.

Blowing the whistle   (See Whistle-blowing.)

Board of directors   A group of persons elected by shareholder votes that is responsible for directing the affairs of a corporation, establishing company objectives and policies, selecting top-level managers, and reviewing company performance.

Bottom line   Business profits or losses, usually reported in figures on the last or bottom line of a company's income statement.

Boundary-spanning departments   Departments, or offices, within an organization that reach across the dividing line that separates the company from groups and people in society.

Bribery   A questionable or unjust payment often to a government official to ensure or facilitate a business transaction.

Bundling   The collection of political contributions made by an organization's stakeholders to increase the organization's ability to influence a political agent.

Business   An organization that is engaged in making a product or providing a service for a profit.

Business and society   The study of the relationship between business and its social environment.

Business ethics   The application of general ethical ideas to business behavior.

C

Campaign finance reform   Efforts to change the rules governing the financing of political campaigns, often by limiting contributions made or received.

Carrying capacity   The maximum population that an ecosystem can support. (See also Limits to growth hypothesis.)

Cartels   A modern term for "trusts," describing groups of companies that join together to divide up markets and limit competition.

Central state control (system)   A socioeconomic system in which economic power is concentrated in the hands of government officials and political authorities. The central government owns the property that is used to produce goods and services, and most private markets are illegal.

CERCLA   (Comprehensive Environmental Response, Compensation, and Liability Act.) The major U.S. law governing the cleanup of existing hazardous-waste sites, popularly known as Superfund.

Charity principle   The idea that the wealthier members of society or profitable businesses should give voluntary aid and support to those less fortunate or to organizations that provide community services.

Chief information officer   Manager who has been entrusted with the responsibility to manage the organization's technology with its many privacy and security issues.

Child care   The care or supervision of another's child, such as at a day care center; offered as a benefit by some employers to working parents.

Citizenship profile   Choosing a configuration of citizenship activities that fits the setting in which the company is working.

Civic engagement   The active involvement of businesses and individuals in changing and improving communities.

Civil society   Non-profit, educational, religious, community, family, and interest-group organizations; social organizations that do not have a commercial or governmental purpose.

Codetermination   A system of corporate governance providing for labor representation on a company's board of directors.

Collaborative partnerships   Alliances among business, government, and civil society organizations that draw on the unique capabilities of each to address complex social problems.

Command and control regulation   A regulatory approach where the government "commands" companies to meet specific standards (such as amounts of particular pollutants) and "controls" the methods (such as technology) used to achieve these standards. This approach is often contrasted with market-based regulatory approaches where the government establishes general goals and allows companies to use the most cost-effective methods possible to achieve them.

Commons   Traditionally, an area of land on which all citizens could graze their animals without limitation. The term now refers to any shared resource, such as land, air, or water, that a group of people use collectively.

Community   A company's area of local business influence. Traditionally, the term applied to the city, town, or rural area in which a business's operations, offices, or assets were located. With the rise of large, complex business organizations, the meaning of the term has expanded to include multiple localities.

Community Reinvestment Act   A federal law requiring banks to reinvest a portion of their depositors' money back into the local community.

Community relations   The involvement of business with the communities in which it conducts operations.

Competition   A struggle to survive and excel. In business, different firms compete with one another for customers' dollars.

Competition policies   A term used to describe antitrust laws or policies in some nations and trading groups.

Competitive intelligence   The systematic and continuous process of gathering, analyzing, and managing external information on the organization's competitors.

Compliance officer   (See Ethics officer.)

Comprehensive Environmental Response, Compensation, and Liability Act (CERCLA)   (See CERCLA and Superfund.)

Computer hackers   Individuals often with advanced technology training who, for thrill or profit, breach a business' information security system.

Computer virus or worm   Unwanted software programs meant to disrupt business activity on the computer or to break through an organization's computer security system.

Conflicts of interest   Occur when an individual's self-interest conflicts with acting in the best interest of another, when the individual has an obligation to do so.

Conglomerate merger   The combination, or joining together, of two or more companies in unrelated industries into a single company. (See also Horizontal merger, Vertical merger.)

Constructive engagement   When transnational corporations operate according to strong moral principles and become a force for positive change in other nations where they operate.

Consumer hot lines   Telephone line or other mechanism for consumers to make inquiries or lodge complaints about a company's products and services.

Consumer movement   A social movement that seeks to augment the rights and powers of consumers. (Also known as consumerism.)

Consumer protection laws   Laws that provide consumers with better information, protect consumers from possible hazards, or encourage competitive pricing.

Consumer rights   The legitimate claims of consumers to safe products and services, adequate information, free choice, a fair hearing, and competitive prices.

Consumerism   (See Consumer movement.)

Corporate citizenship   This term broadly refers to putting corporate social responsibility into practice through stakeholder partnerships, serving society, and integrating financial *and* social performance.

Corporate crisis   A significant business disruption that stimulates extensive news media coverage.

Corporate culture   A blend of ideas, customs, traditional practices, company values, and shared meanings that help define normal behavior for everyone who works in a company.

Corporate foundations   Organizations chartered as nonprofits, and funded by companies, for the purpose of donating money to community organizations, programs, and causes.

Corporate giving   (See Corporate philanthropy.)

Corporate governance   The system of allocating power in a corporation that determines how and by whom the company is to be governed.

Corporate merger   The combination, or joining together, of two or more separate companies into a single company. (See also Conglomerate merger, Horizontal merger, Vertical merger.)

Corporate philanthropy   Gifts and contributions made by businesses, usually from pretax profits, to benefit various types of nonprofit and community organizations.

Corporate political strategy   Those activities taken by organizations to acquire, develop, and use power to achieve a political advantage or gain.

Corporate power   The strength or capability of corporations to influence government, the economy, and society, based on their organizational resources and size.

Corporate social responsibility   The idea that businesses should be held accountable for any of its actions that affect people, their communities, and their environment.

Corporate volunteerism   A program wherein a company engages its employees in community service as a way to improve the company's image as well as serve the communities in which the business operates.

Corporation   Legally, an artificial legal "person," created under the laws of a particular state or nation. Socially and organizationally, it is a complex system of people, technology, and resources generally devoted to carrying out a central economic mission as it interacts with a surrounding social and political environment.

Cost-benefit analysis   A systematic method of calculating the costs and benefits of a project or activity that is intended to produce benefits.

Crisis management   The process organizations use to respond to short-term or intermediate-term, unexpected, and high consequential shocks, such as accidents, disasters, catastrophes, and injuries.

Cyberspace   A virtual location where information is stored, ideas are described, and communication takes place in and through an electronic network of linked systems.

D

Debt relief   The idea that the world's richest nations should forgive poor nations' obligations to pay back loans.

Deceptive advertising   An advertisement that is deceptive or misleading; generally illegal under U.S. law.

Democracy   A form of government in which power is vested in the people and exercised by them directly or by their elected representatives.

Department of corporate citizenship   A department created in a business to centralize under common leadership wide-ranging corporate citizenship functions.

Deregulation   The removal or scaling down of regulatory authority and regulatory activities of government.

Design for disassembly   Designing products so that they can be disassembled, and their component parts recycled or reused at the end of their useful life.

Digital divide   The gap between those that have technology and those that do not.

Digital Millennium Copyright Act   The U.S. law that made it a crime to circumvent antipiracy measures built into most commercial software agreements between the manufacturers and their users.

Directors   (See Board of directors.)

Discrimination (in jobs or employment)   Unequal treatment of employees based on non–job-related factors such as race, sex, age, national origin, religion, color, and physical or mental handicap.

Diversity　Variation in the characteristics that distinguish people from one another, such as age, ethnicity, nationality, gender, mental or physical abilities, race, sexual orientation, family status, and first language.

Diversity council　A group of managers and employees responsible for developing and implementing specific action plans to meet an organization's diversity goals. (See also Diversity.)

Divestment　Withdrawing and shifting to other uses the funds that a person or group has invested in the securities (stocks, bonds, notes, etc.) of a company. Investors sometimes have divested the securities of companies doing business in countries accused of human rights abuses.

Dividend　A return-on-investment payment made to the owners of shares of corporate stock at the discretion of the company's board of directors.

Drug testing (of employees)　The testing of employees, by the employer, for the presence of illegal drugs, sometimes by means of a urine sample analyzed by a clinical laboratory.

E

Eco-efficiency　Occurs when businesses or societies are simultaneously economically efficient and environmentally responsible.

Ecological footprint　One method of measuring the earth's carrying capacity, and how far human society has exceeded it.

Ecologically sustainable organization (ESO)　A business that operates in a way that is consistent with the principle of sustainable development. (See also Sustainable development.)

Ecology　The study, and the process, of how living things—plants and animals—interact with one another and with their environment.

E-commerce　Electronic business exchanges where the buying and selling goods and services is done electronically via the Internet.

Economic leverage　A political tool where a business uses its economic power to threaten to relocate its operations unless a desired political action is taken.

Economic regulation　The oldest form of regulation in the United States, aimed at modifying the normal operations of the free market and the forces of supply and demand.

Ecosystem　Plants and animals in their natural environment, living together as an interdependent system.

Egoist　(See Ethical egoist.)

Elder care　The care or supervision of elderly persons; offered as a benefit by some employers to working children of elderly parents.

Electronic monitoring (of employees)　The use by employers of electronic technologies to gather, store, and monitor information about employees' activities.

Emissions charges or fees　Fees charged to business by the government, based on the amount of pollution emitted.

Employee assistance programs (EAPs)　Company-sponsored programs to assist employees with alcohol abuse, drug abuse, mental health, and other problems.

Employment-at-will　The principle that workers are hired and retained solely at the discretion of the employer.

Enlightened self-interest　The view that a business can be socially aware without giving up its own economic self-interest.

Entitlement mentality　A view that a person or group is guaranteed an economic or social benefit by virtue of being a member of the designated group. (See also Right [human].)

Environmental analysis　The system that provides managers with information about external issues and trends.

Environmental audit　A company audit, or review, of its progress toward meeting environmental goals, such as pollution prevention.

Environmental intelligence　The acquisition of information gained from analyzing the multiple environments affecting organizations.

Environmental justice　The efforts to prevent inequitable exposure to risk, such as from hazardous waste.

Environmental partnerships　A voluntary, collaborative partnership between or among businesses, government regulators, and environmental organizations to achieve specific environmental goals.

Environmental Protection Agency (EPA)　The United States federal government agency responsible for most environmental regulation and enforcement.

Environmental scanning　Examining an organization's environment to discover trends and forces that could have an impact on the organization.

Environmental standards　Standard amounts of particular pollutants allowable by law.

Equal employment opportunity   The principle that all persons otherwise qualified should be treated equally with respect to job opportunities, workplace conditions, pay, fringe benefits, and retirement provisions.

Equal Employment Opportunity Commission (EEOC)   U.S. agency charged with enforcing equal employment opportunity laws and executive orders.

Ergonomics   Adapting work tasks, working conditions, and equipment to minimize worker injury or stress.

Ethical climate   An unspoken understanding among employees of what is and is not acceptable behavior.

Ethical egoist   A person who puts his or her own selfish interests above all other considerations, while denying the ethical needs and beliefs of others.

Ethical principles   Guides to moral behavior, such as honesty, keeping promises, helping others, and respecting others' rights.

Ethical relativism   A belief that ethical right and wrong are defined by various periods of time in history, a society's traditions, the specific circumstances of the moment, or personal opinion.

Ethics   A conception of right and wrong conduct, serving as a guide to moral behavior.

Ethics assist or help line   A program available for employees when they are troubled about some ethical issue but may be reluctant to raise it with their immediate supervisor.

Ethics audit   An assessment used by an organization to target the effectiveness of their ethical safeguards or to document evidence of increased ethical employee behavior.

Ethics officer, compliance office, or ombudsperson   A manager designated by an organization to investigate breaches of ethical conduct, promulgate ethics statements, and generally promote ethical conduct at work.

Ethics policies or code   A written set of rules used to guide managers and employees when they encounter an ethical dilemma.

European Union (EU)   The political and economic coalition of European countries.

Executive compensation   The compensation (total pay) of corporate executives, including salary, bonus, stock options, and various benefits.

Fair labor standards   Rules that establish minimum acceptable standards for the conditions under which a company's employees (or the employees of its suppliers or subcontractors) will work. For example, such standards might include a ban on child labor, establishment of maximum work hours per week, or a commitment to pay wages above a certain minimum level.

F

Fairness and balance issue   Raises the question of whether the media reports business activities impartially, showing both sides of a controversy.

Fairness Doctrine   Required television and radio broadcasters to cover both sides of important or controversial issues and to give the opportunity for contrasting viewpoints to be aired. The law was repealed in 1987.

Family-friendly corporation   A company that removes gender discrimination from all aspects of its operations and that supports both men and women in their efforts to balance work and family responsibilities.

Family leave   A leave of absence from work, either paid or unpaid, for the purpose of caring for a family member.

Fiscal policy   The patterns of spending and taxation adopted by a government to stimulate or support the economy.

527 organizations   Groups organized under section 527 of the Internal Revenue Service tax code for the purpose of donating money to candidates for public office and influencing elections.

Flextime   A plan that allows employees limited control over scheduling their own hours of work, usually at the beginning and end of the workday.

Fraud   Deceit or trickery due to the pursuit of economic gain or competitive advantage.

Free enterprise system   A socioeconomic system based on private ownership, profit-seeking business firms, and the principle of free markets.

Free market   A model of an economic system based on voluntary and free exchange among buyers and sellers. Competition regulates prices in all free market exchanges.

Free speech issue   Presents the challenge of finding a balance between the constitutional right to free expression and the trustworthiness of information used by stakeholders to make purchases, seek employment, and other actions.

Functional regulation   Regulations aimed at a particular function or operation of business, such as competition or labor relations.

G

General systems theory   A theory that holds that all organisms are open to, and interact with, their external environments.

Genetic engineering   The altering of the natural make-up of a living organism, which allows scientists to insert virtually any gene into a plant and create a new crop, or an entire new species.

Genetically modified foods   Food processed from genetically engineered crops.

Glass ceiling   A barrier to the advancement of women, minorities, and other groups in the workplace.

Glass wall   A barrier to the lateral mobility of women, minorities, and other groups in the workplace, such as from human resources to operations that could lead to top management positions.

Global codes of conduct   Codes of conduct that seek to define acceptable and unacceptable behavior for today's transnational corporations.

Global corporate citizenship   A phrase that describes the efforts of some companies to provide leadership on key social issues wherever they do business in the world.

Global warming   The gradual warming of the earth's climate, believed by some scientists to be caused by an increase in carbon dioxide and other trace gases in the earth's atmosphere resulting from human activity, mainly the burning of fossil fuels.

Globalization   The movement of goods, services, and capital across national borders.

Greenhouse effect   The warming effect that occurs when carbon dioxide, methane, nitrous oxides, and other gases act like the glass panels of a greenhouse, preventing heat from the earth's surface from escaping into space.

Greening of management   The process by which managers become more proactive with respect to environmental issues.

Green marketing   A concept that describes the creation, promotion, and sale of environmentally safe products and services by business.

H

Harmonization   The coordination of laws and enforcement efforts among nations.

Hazardous waste   Waste materials from industrial, agricultural, and other activities capable of causing death or serious health problems for those persons exposed for prolonged periods. (See also Toxic substance.)

Honesty testing   Written psychological tests given to prospective employees that seek to predict their honesty on the job.

Horizontal merger   The combination, or joining together, of two or more companies in the same industry and at the same level or stage of production or sales into a single company. (See also Conglomerate merger, Vertical merger.)

Hostile takeover   The acquisition of one firm by another, in which the target firm does not wish to be acquired.

Human genome   Strands of DNA developing a unique pattern for every human.

Human rights   An ethical approach emphasizing a person or group's entitlement to something or to be treated in a certain way, such as the right to life, safety, or to be informed.

I

Ideology   A set of basic beliefs that define an ideal way of living for an individual, an organization, or a society.

Incumbents   Individuals who are seeking re-election to their political office.

Industrial ecology   Designing factories and distribution systems as if they were self-contained ecosystems, such as using waste from one process as raw material for another.

Industrial society   A society in which the building and mechanical processing of material goods dominates work and employs the largest proportion of the labor force.

Information society   The current phase of technology; emphasizes the use and transfer of knowledge and information.

In-kind contributions   Corporate charitable contributions of products or services, rather than cash.

Insider trading   Occurs when a person gains access to confidential information about a company's financial condition and then uses that information, before it becomes public knowledge, to buy or sell the company's stock.

Institutional investor   A financial institution, insurance company, pension fund, endowment fund, or similar organization that invests its accumulated funds in the securities offered for sale on stock exchanges.

Institutionalized activity (ethics, corporate citizenship, public affairs, etc.)   An activity, operation, or procedure that is such an integral part of an organization that it is performed routinely by managers and employees.

Intangible assets   Nonphysical resources of the organization that enable it to achieve its goals and objectives, including intellectual property and corporate reputation.

Intellectual property   Ideas, concepts, and other symbolic creations of the human mind that are recognized and protected under a nation's copyright, patent, and trademark laws.

Interactive social system   The closely intertwined relationships between business and society.

International financial and trade institutions   Institutions, such as the World Bank, International Monetary Fund, and World Trade Organization, that establish the rules by which international commerce is conducted.

International Monetary Fund   An international financial institution that lends foreign exchange to member nations so they can participate in global trade.

International regulation   A form of regulation in which more than one nation agrees to establish and enforce the same rules of conduct for international business activities.

Internet (or World Wide Web)   A global communications network linking individuals and organizations.

Iron law of responsibility   The belief that those who do not use their power in ways that society considers responsible will tend to lose their power in the long run.

Issue management   The structured and systematic process of identifying, analyzing, and selecting public issues that warrant organizational action.

Issue management process   A five-step process where the issue progresses from issue identification through issue analysis, option generation, evaluation and selection, and program implementation to assessment of results and continuous improvement.

J

Justice   An ethical approach that emphasizes whether the distribution of benefits and burdens are fair among people, according to some agreed-upon rule.

K

Knowledge economy   An economy in which new knowledge, in its many forms, is reshaping and transforming old industries and creating new ones.

Kyoto Protocol   An international treaty negotiated in 1997 in Kyoto, Japan, that committed its signatories to reduce emissions of greenhouse gases, such as carbon dioxide.

L

Labor force participation rate   The proportion of a particular group, such as women, in the paid workforce.

Labor standards   Conditions affecting a company's employees or the employees of its suppliers or subcontractors.

Labor union   An organization that represents workers on the job and that bargains collectively with the employer over wages, working conditions, and other terms of employment.

Laws   Society's attempt to formalize into written rules the public's ideas about what constitutes right and wrong conduct in various spheres of life.

Legal challenges   A political tool that questions the legal legitimacy of a regulation.

Legal obligations   A belief that a firm must abide by the laws and regulations governing the society.

License to operate   The right to do business informally conferred by society on a business firm; must be earned through socially responsible behavior.

Life-cycle analysis   Collecting information on the lifelong environmental impact of a product in order to minimize its adverse impacts at all stages, including design, manufacture, use, and disposal.

Limits to growth hypothesis   The idea that human society is now exceeding the carrying capacity of the earth's ecosystem and that unless corrective action is taken soon, catastrophic consequences will result. (See also Carrying capacity.)

Lobbying   The act of trying to directly shape or influence a government official's understanding and position on a public policy issue.

M

Marine ecosystems   This term refers broadly to oceans and the salt marshes, lagoons, and tidal zones that border them, and well as the diverse communities of life that they support.

Market-based mechanism   A form of regulation, used in environmental policy, that uses market mechanisms to control corporate behavior.

Market failure   Inability of the marketplace to properly adjust prices for the true costs of a firm's behavior.

Market stakeholder   A stakeholder that engages in market transactions with a company. (Also called a primary stakeholder.)

M-commerce   Commerce conducted by using mobile or cell telephones.

Media   A means of communication that widely reaches or influences people. Media businesses include many channels, including television, radio, books, magazines, and the Internet, and uses multiple technologies.

Media training   A public relations strategy where executives and employees who are likely to have contact with the media are educated in how to effectively communicate with the press.

Merger   (See Corporate merger.)

Military dictatorship   A repressive regime ruled by a dictator who exercises total power through control of the armed forces.

Monetary policy   Government actions to control the supply and demand of money in the economy.

Monopoly   Occurs when one company dominates the market for a particular product or service.

Montreal Protocol   An international treaty limiting the manufacture and use of chlorofluorocarbons and other ozone-depleting chemicals. (See also Ozone.)

Moral development stages   A series of progressive steps by which a person learns new ways of reasoning about ethical and moral issues. (See Stages of moral development.)

Morality   A condition in which the most fundamental human values are preserved and allowed to shape human thought and action.

N

Nanotechnology   The ability to create manmade structures only a few billionths of a meter in size.

National competitiveness   The ability of a nation to compete effectively with other nations in international markets through the actions of its privately and publicly owned business firms.

Natural monopolies   Where a concentration of the market is acquired by a few firms due to the nature of the industry rather than because of company practices.

Negative externalities (or spill-over effects)   When the manufacture or distribution of a product gives rise to unplanned or unintended costs (economic, physical, or psychological) borne by consumers, competitors, neighboring communities, or other business stakeholders.

Noisy withdrawal   The action required of an attorney when seeing evidence of a client's company committing a material securities law violation if unable to get the company to stop the illegal act.

Nongovernmental organizations (NGOs)   Nonprofit organizations that are created and work to advocate on behalf of particular causes, issues, and interests.

Nonmarket stakeholder   A stakeholder that does not engage in direct economic exchange with a company, but is affected by or can affect its actions. (Also called a secondary stakeholder.)

Nonrenewable resources   Natural resources, such as oil, coal, or natural gas, that once used are gone forever. (See also Renewable resources.)

O

Occupational Safety and Health Administration (OSHA)   U.S. government agency that enforces worker safety and health standards.

Occupational segregation   The inequitable concentration of a group, such a minorities or women, in particular job categories.

Ombudsperson   (See Ethics officer.)

Ownership theory of the firm   A theory that holds that the purpose of the firm is to maximize returns to shareholders. (Also called the property or finance theory of the firm.)

Ozone   A gas composed of three bonded oxygen atoms. Ozone in the lower atmosphere is a dangerous component of urban smog; ozone in the upper atmosphere provides a shield against ultraviolet light from the sun. (See also Montreal Protocol.)

P

Parental leave   A leave of absence from work, either paid or unpaid, for the purpose of caring for a newborn or adopted child.

Pay gap   The difference in the average level of wages, salaries, and income received by two groups, such as men and women (called the *gender pay gap*) or whites and persons of color (called the *racial pay gap*).

Performance–expectations gap   The perceived distance between what a firm wants to do or is doing and what the stakeholder expects.

Personal spirituality   A personal belief in a supreme being, religious organization, or the power of nature or some other external, life-guiding force.

Philanthropy   (See Corporate philanthropy.)

Phishing   The practice of duping computer users into revealing their passwords or other private data under false pretenses.

Pirated music   Music acquired illegally by ignoring the artist's or publisher's legal copyright to benefit from the use of the recording.

Political action committee (PAC)   A committee organized according to election law by any group for the purpose of accepting voluntary contributions from individual donors and then making contributions to candidates for election to public office.

Pollution prevention   (See Source reduction.)

Pornography   Adult-oriented, sexual material of an offensive nature.

Predatory pricing   The practice of selling below cost for the purpose of driving competitors out of business; usually illegal under U.S. antitrust laws.

Price-fixing   When two or more companies collude to set — or "fix" — the price of a product or service; usually illegal under U.S. antitrust laws.

Privacy   (See Right of privacy.)

Privacy policy   Business policies that explain what use of the company's technology is permissible and how the business will monitor employee activities.

Privacy rights   Protecting an individual's personal life from unwarranted intrusion by the employer.

Private property   A group of rights giving control over physical and intangible assets to private owners. Private ownership is the basic institution of capitalism.

Privately held corporation   A corporation that is privately owned by an individual or a group of individuals; its stock is not available for purchase by the general investing public.

Product liability   The legal responsibility of a firm for injuries caused by something it made or sold.

Product recall   An effort by a business firm to remove a defective or sometimes dangerous product from consumer use and from all distribution channels.

Profits   The revenues of a person or company minus the costs incurred in producing the revenue.

Proxy   A legal instrument giving another person the right to vote the shares of stock of an absentee stockholder.

Proxy statement   A statement sent by a board of directors to a corporation's stockholders announcing the company's annual meeting, containing information about the business to be considered at the meeting, and enclosing a proxy form for stockholders not attending the meeting.

Public affairs management   The active management of an organization's external relations with such stakeholders as legislators, government officials, and regulatory agencies.

Public issue   An issue that is of concern to an organization's stakeholders.

Public policy   A plan of action by government to achieve some broad purpose affecting a large segment of the public.

Public policy process   All of the activities and stages involved in developing, carrying out, and evaluating public policies.

Public-private partnerships   Community-based organizations that have a combination of businesses and government agencies collaborating to address important social problems such as crime, homelessness, drugs, economic development, and other community issues.

Public relations   A program that sends a constant stream of information from the company to the public and opens the door to dialogue with stakeholders whose lives are affected by company operations.

Public Relations Society of America   A professional association of public relations officers committed to maintaining individual dignity and the free exercise of human rights within the media industry.

Public trustee   A concept that a business owner or manager should base company decisions on the interests of a wide range of corporate stakeholders or members of the general public. In doing so, the business executive acts as a trustee of the public interest. (See also Stewardship principle.)

Publicly held corporation   A corporation whose stock is available for purchase by the general investing public.

Q

Quality management   Measures taken by an organization to assure quality, such as defining the customer's needs, monitoring whether or not a product or service consistently meets these needs, analyzing the quality of finished products to assure they are free of defects, and continually improving processes to eliminate quality problems.

Questionable payments   Something of value given to a person or firm that raises significant ethical questions of right or wrong in the host nation or other nations.

Quotas (job, hiring, employment)   An employment plan based on hiring a specific number or proportion of minorities, women, or other groups who may be underrepresented in an organization's workforce.

R

Racial harassment   Harassment in the workplace based on race, such as ethnic slurs, derogatory comments, or other verbal or physical harassment based on race that creates an intimidating, hostile, or offensive working environment or that interferes with an individual's work performance. (See also Sexual harassment.)

Rain forest   Woodlands that receive at least 100 inches of rain a year. They are among the planet's richest areas in terms of biodiversity.

Regulation   The action of government to establish rules by which industry or other groups must behave in conducting their normal activities.

Renewable resources   Natural resources, such as fresh water or timber, that can be naturally replenished. (See also Nonrenewable resources.)

Reputation   The desirable or undesirable qualities associated with an organization or its actors that may influence the organization's relationships with its stakeholders.

Reregulation   The imposition of regulation on activities that were deregulated earlier.

Reverse discrimination   The unintended negative impact experienced by an individual or group as a result of legal efforts to overcome discrimination against another individual or group.

Revolving door   The circulation of individuals between business and government positions.

Right (human)   A concept used in ethical reasoning that means that a person or group is entitled to something or is entitled to be treated in a certain way. (See also Entitlement mentality.)

Right of privacy   A person's entitlement to protection from invasion of his or her private life by government, business, or other persons.

S

Sarbanes-Oxley Act   U.S. law passed in 2002 that greatly expanded the powers of the SEC to regulate information disclosure in the financial markets and the accountability of an organization's senior leadership regarding the accuracy of this disclosure. (See also Securities and Exchange Commission.)

Securities and Exchange Commission (SEC)   U.S. government agency whose mission is to protect stockholders'

rights by making sure that stock markets are run fairly and that investment information is fully disclosed.

Sexual harassment   Unwanted and uninvited sexual attention experienced by a person, and/or a workplace that is hostile or threatening in a sexual way. (See Racial harassment.)

Shareholder   (See Stockholder.)

Shareholder lawsuit   A lawsuit initiated by one or more stockholders to recover damages suffered due to alleged actions of the company's management.

Shareholder resolution   A proposal made by a stockholder or group of stockholders and included in a corporation's notice of its annual meeting that advocates some course of action to be taken by the company.

Social accountability   The condition of being held responsible to society or to some public or governmental group for one's actions, often requiring a specific accounting or reporting on those activities.

Social assistance policies   Government programs aimed at improving areas such as health care and education.

Social auditing   A systematic study and evaluation of an organization's social and ethical performance. (See also Social performance auditing.)

Social capital   The norms and networks that enable collective action; goodwill engendered by social relationships.

Social contract   An implied understanding between an organization and its stakeholders as to how they will act toward one another.

Social investment   The use of stock ownership as a strategy for promoting social objectives.

Social performance auditing   A systematic evaluation of an organization's social, ethical, and environmental performance.

Social regulation   Regulations intended to accomplish certain social improvements such as equal employment opportunity, on-the-job safety and health, and the protection of the natural environment.

Social responsibility   (See Corporate social responsibility.)

Social responsibility shareholder resolution   A resolution on an issue of corporate social responsibility placed before stockholders for a vote at a company's annual meeting, usually by social activist groups.

Society   Refers to human beings and to the social structures they collectively create; specifically refers to segments of humankind, such as members of a particular community, nation, or interest group.

Soft money   Funds donated to a political party to support party-building activities such as televised commercials that do not specify a candidate, get-out-the-vote drives, and opinion polling. Soft money is often criticized as a loophole in the political campaign finance laws.

Software piracy   The illegal copying of copyrighted software.

Source reduction   A business strategy to prevent or reduce pollution at the source, rather than to dispose of or treat pollution after it has been produced. (Also known as pollution prevention.)

Spam   Unsolicited e-mails (or junk e-mails) sent in bulk to valid e-mail accounts.

Stages of moral development   A sequential pattern of how people grow and develop in their moral thinking, beginning with a concern for the self and growing to a concern for others and broad-based principles.

Stakeholder   A person or group that affects, or is affected by, a corporation's decisions, policies, and operations. (See also Market stakeholder and Nonmarket stakeholder.)

Stakeholder analysis   An analytic process used by managers that identifies the relevant stakeholders in a particular situation and seeks to understand their interests, power, and likely coalitions.

Stakeholder coalitions   Temporary alliances among company's stakeholders to pursue a common interest.

Stakeholder dialogue   Face-to-face conversations between representatives of a company and its stakeholders about issues of common concern.

Stakeholder engagement   An ongoing process of relationship building between a business and its stakeholders.

Stakeholder interests   The nature of each group, its concerns, and what it wants from its relationship with the firm.

Stakeholder network   A connected assembly of concerned individuals or organizations defined by their shared focus on a particular issue, problem, or opportunity.

Stakeholder power   The ability of one or more stakeholders to achieve a desired outcome in their interactions with a company. The four types are voting power, economic power, political power, and legal power.

Stakeholder theory of the firm   A theory that holds that the purpose of the firm is to create value for all of its stakeholders.

Stem-cell research   Research on nonspecialized cells that have the capacity to self-renew and to differentiate into more mature cells.

Stewardship principle   The idea that business managers, as public stewards or trustees, have an obligation to see that

everyone—particularly those in need—benefits from the company's actions.

Stockholder   A person, group, or organization owning one or more shares of stock in a corporation. (Also known as shareholder.)

Stock option   A form of compensation. Options represent the right (but not obligation) to buy a company's stock at a set price for a certain period of time. The option becomes valuable to its holder when, and if, the stock price rises above this amount.

Stock screening   Selecting stocks based on social or environmental criteria.

Strategic philanthropy   A form of philanthropy in which donor organizations direct their contributions to recipients in order to achieve a direct or indirect business objective.

Streaming   A customized, on-demand radio service developed by music distributors to protect their copyrights to music.

Strict liability   A legal doctrine that holds that a manufacturer is responsible (liable) for injuries resulting from the use of its products, whether or not the manufacturer was negligent or breached a warranty.

Superfund   A U.S. law, passed in 1980, designated to clean up hazardous or toxic waste sites. The law established a fund, supported mainly by taxes on petrochemical companies, to pay for the cleanup. (Also known as the Comprehensive Environmental Response, Compensation, and Liability Act [CERCLA].)

Sustainability report   A single report integrating a business's social, economic, and economic results.

Sustainable development   This term refers to development that meets the needs of the present without compromising the ability of future generations to meet their own needs.

Sweatshop   Factories where employees—sometimes including children—are forced to work long hours at low wages, often under unsafe working conditions.

T

Technology   A broad term dealing with the use and knowledge of humanity's tools and crafts.

Technology superpowers   Businesses that built and controlled the global information technology system.

Telecommunications   The transmission of information over great distances via electromagnetic signals.

Tissue engineering   The rejuvenation or replication of healthy cells or tissues to replace failing human organs and aging cells.

Toxic substance   Any substance used in production or in consumer products that is poisonous or capable of causing serious health problems for those persons exposed. (See also Hazardous waste.)

Tradable permits   A market-based approach to pollution control in which the government grants companies "rights" to a specific amount of pollution (permits), which may be bought or sold (traded) with other companies.

Trade association   A coalition of companies in the same or related industries seeking to coordinate their economic or political power to further their agenda.

Transnational corporation   Corporations that operate and control assets across national boundaries.

Transparency   Clear public reporting of an organization's decision-making process or performance.

Triple bottom line   The measurement of an organization on the basis of its economic results, environmental impact, and contribution to social well-being.

Tying   When a firm requires someone to buy an unwanted product or service in order to get another one they want. This is illegal under U.S. antitrust law.

U

United Nations Global Compact   Voluntary agreement of business, labor, and nongovernmental organizations to work for sustainable development goals.

U.S. Corporate Sentencing Guidelines   Standards to help judges determine the appropriate penalty for criminal violations of federal laws and provide a strong incentive for businesses to promote ethics at work.

U.S. Foreign Corrupt Practices Act   Federal law that prohibits businesses from paying bribes to foreign government officials, political parties, or political candidates.

Utilitarian reasoning   An ethical approach that emphasizes the consequences of an action and seeks the overall amount of good that can be produced by an action or a decision.

Utility (social)   A concept used in ethical reasoning that refers to the net positive gain or benefit to society of some action or decision.

V

Values   Fundamental and enduring beliefs about the most desirable conditions and purposes of human life.

Vertical merger   The combination, or joining together, of two or more companies in the same industry but at different levels or stages of production or sales into a single company. (See also Conglomerate merger, Horizontal merger.)

Virtue ethics   Focuses on character traits to define a good person, theorizing that values will direct a person toward good behavior.

Vlogs   Video Web logs produced by a digital camera that captures moving images which are then transferred to the Internet.

Volunteerism   The uncompensated efforts of people to assist others in a community.

W

Wall Street   A customary way of referring to the financial community of banks, investment institutions, and stock exchanges centered in the Wall Street area of New York City.

Water pollution   When more wastes are discharged into waterways, such as lakes and rivers, than can be naturally diluted and carried away.

Whistle-blowing   An employee's disclosure of alleged organizational misconduct to the media or appropriate government agency, often after futile attempts to convince organizational authorities to take action against the alleged abuse.

White collar crime   Illegal activities committed by corporate managers, such as embezzlement or fraud.

Workforce diversity   Diversity among employees. (See also Diversity.)

World Bank   An international financial institution that provides economic development assistance and loans to member nations.

World Business Council for Sustainable Development (WBCSD)   A group of companies from several nations whose goal is to encourage high standards of environmental management and to promote cooperation among businesses, governments, and other organizations concerned with sustainable development.

World Trade Organization   An organization of member nations committed to advancing free trade and open markets in all countries.

BIBLIOGRAPHY

Part One: Chapters 1–2

Albrecht, Karl. *Corporate Radar: Tracking the Forces That Are Shaping Your Business.* New York: American Management Association, 2000.

Clarkson, Max B. E., ed. *The Corporation and Its Stakeholders: Classic and Contemporary Readings.* Toronto: University of Toronto Press, 1998.

Etzioni, Amitai. *The New Golden Rule.* New York: Basic Books, 1996.

———. *The Spirit of Community.* New York: Crown Publishers. 1993.

Frederick, William C. *Values, Nature, and Culture in the American Corporation.* New York: Oxford University Press, 1995.

Freeman, R. Edward. *Strategic Management: A Stakeholder Approach.* Marshfield, MA: Pitman, 1984.

Grunig, Larissa A., James E. Grunig, and David M. Dozier. *Excellent Public Relations and Effective Organizations.* Mahwah, NJ: Erlbaum, 2002.

Harris, Phil and Craig S. Fleisher, eds. *Handbook of Public Affairs.* Thousand Oaks, CA: Sage, 2005.

Isaacs, William. *Dialogue: The Art of Thinking Together.* New York: Doubleday, 1999.

McGonagle, John J. and Carolyn M. Vella. *Bottom Line Competitive Intelligence.* New York: Praeger, 2002.

Post, James E., Lee E. Preston, and Sybille Sachs. *Redefining the Corporation: Stakeholder Management and Organizational Wealth.* Palo Alto, CA: Stanford University Press, 2002.

Preston, Lee E. and James E. Post. *Private Management and Public Policy.* Englewood Cliffs, NJ: Prentice Hall, 1975.

Phillips, Robert. *Stakeholder Theory and Organizational Ethics.* San Francisco: Berrett-Koehler, 2003.

Putnam, Robert D. *Bowling Alone: The Collapse and Revival of American Community.* New York: Simon & Schuster, 2000.

Singer, Peter. *Ethics into Action: Henry Spira and the Animal Rights Movement.* Lanham, MD: Rowman & Littlefield, 2000.

Sriramesh, Krishnamurthy and Dejan Vercic, eds. *The Global Public Relations Handbook: Theory, Research and Practice.* Mahwah, NJ: Erlbaum, 2003.

Svendsen, Ann. *The Stakeholder Strategy: Profiting from Collaborative Business Relationships.* San Francisco: Berrett-Koehler, 1998.

Waddock, Sandra, et al., eds. *Unfolding Stakeholder Thinking.* Sheffield, UK: Greenleaf, 2002.

Yankelovich, Daniel. *The Magic of Dialogue: Transforming Conflict into Cooperation.* New York: Simon & Schuster, 1999.

Part Two: Chapters 3–4

Ackerman, Robert. *The Social Challenge to Business.* Cambridge, MA: Harvard University Press, 1975.

Andriof, Joerg and Malcolm McIntosh. *Perspectives on Corporate Citizenship.* Sheffield, UK: Greenleaf, 2001.

Bakan, Joel. *The Corporation: The Pathological Pursuit of Profit and Power.* New York: Free Press, 2004.

Bowen, Howard R. *Responsibilities of the Businessman.* New York: Harper, 1953.

Burke, Edmund M. *Managing a Company in an Activist World: The Leadership Challenge of Corporate Citizenship.* Westport, CT: Praeger, 2005.

Chamberlain, Neil W. *The Limits of Corporate Social Responsibility.* New York: Basic Books, 1973.

Domini, Amy L. *Socially Responsible Investing: Making a Difference and Making Money.* Chicago: Dearborn Trade, 2001.

Elkington, John. *Cannibals with Forks: The Triple Bottom Line of 21st Century Business.* London: Thompson, 1997.

Fombrun, Charles. *Reputation.* Boston: Harvard Business School Press, 1996.

Frederick, William C. *Corporation Be Good!* Indianapolis, IN: Dog Ear Publishing, 2006.

Grayson, David and Adrian Hodges. *Corporate Social Opportunity: 7 Steps to Make Corporate Social Responsibility Work for Your Business.* Sheffield, UK: Greenleaf, 2004.

Hollender, Jeffrey and Stephen Fenichell. *What Matters Most: How a Small Group of Pioneers Is Teaching Social Responsibility to Big Business, and Why Big Business Is Listening.* New York: Basic Books, 2004.

Kaplan, Robert and David Norton. *The Balanced Scorecard.* Boston: Harvard Business School Press, 1996.

Levy, Reynold. *Give and Take: A Candid Account of Corporate Philanthropy.* Cambridge, MA: Harvard Business School, 1999.

Margolis, Joshua Daniel and James Patrick Walsh. *People and Profits. The Search for a Link between a Company's Social and Financial Performance.* Mahwah, NJ: Erlbaum, 2001.

McIntosh, Malcolm, et al., eds. *Corporate Citizenship: Successful Strategies for Responsible Companies.* Upper Saddle River, NJ: Prentice Hall, 1998.

Post, James E. *Managing the Challenge of Global Corporate Citizenship.* Policy Paper Series. Chestnut Hill, MA: Boston College Center for Corporate Community Relations, 1999.

Vogel, David. *The Market for Virtue: The Potential and Limits of Corporate Social Responsibility.* Washington, DC: Brookings Institution Press, 2005.

Waddock, Sandra. *Leading Corporate Citizens: Vision, Values, and Value Added.* 2nd ed. New York: McGraw-Hill, 2006.

Williams, Bob. *The Sustainability Advantage: Seven Business Case Benefits of a Triple Bottom Line.* Gabriola Island, BC: New Society, 2002.

Wood, Donna J., Jeanne M. Logsdon, Patsy G. Lewellyn, and Kim Davenport. *Global Business Citizenship.* Armonk, NY: M.E. Sharpe, 2006.

Part Three: Chapters 5–6

Callahan, David. *The Cheating Culture.* Orlando: Harcourt, 2004.

Cavanaugh, Gerald F. *American Business Values: With an International Perspective.* 4th ed. Englewood Cliffs, NJ: Prentice Hall, 1998.

Ciulla, Joanne B., ed. *Ethics, the Heart of Leadership.* 2nd ed. Westport, CT: Praeger, 2004.

Colby, Anne and Lawrence Kohlberg. *The Measurement of Moral Judgment: Volume I, Theoretical Foundations and Research Validations.* Cambridge, MA: Harvard University Press, 1987.

Donaldson, Thomas and Thomas W. Dunfee. *Ties that Bind: A Social Contracts Approach to Business Ethics.* Boston: Harvard Business School Press, 1999.

Giacalone, Robert A. and Carole L. Jurkiewicz, eds. *Handbook of Workplace Spirituality and Organizational Performance.* Armonk, NY: M.E. Sharpe, 2003.

Goodpaster, Kenneth E. *Conscience and Corporate Culture.* Malden, MA: Blackwell, 2007.

Huffington, Arianna. *Pigs at the Trough: How Corporate Greed and Political Corruption are Undermining America.* New York: Crown Publishers, 2003.

Jackall, Robert. *Moral Mazes: The World of Corporate Managers.* New York: Oxford University Press, 1988.

Johnson, Craig E. *Meeting the Ethical Challenge of Leadership.* 2nd ed. Thousand Oaks, CA: Sage, 2005.

Pauchant, Thierry C. *Ethics and Spirituality at Work.* New York: Praeger, 2002.

Rawls, John. *A Theory of Justice.* Cambridge, MA: Harvard University Press, 1971.

Rosenthal, Sandra B. and A. Rogene Buchholz. *Rethinking Business Ethics: A Pragmatic Approach.* New York: Oxford University Press, 1999.

Sims, Ronald R. *Ethics and Corporate Social Responsibility.* New York: Praeger, 2003.

Solomon, Robert C. *A Better Way to Think about Business.* New York: Oxford University Press, 1999.

Stone, Christopher D. *Where the Law Ends: The Social Control of Corporate Behavior.* Prospect Heights, IL: Waveland Press, 1975.

Vagelos, Roy and Louis Galambos. *The Moral Corporation: Merck Experiences.* New York: Cambridge University Press, 2006.

Werhane, Patricia H. *Moral Imagination and Management Decision-Making.* New York: Oxford University Press, 1999.

Werhane, Patricia H. and R. Edward Freeman. *The Blackwell Encyclopedic Dictionary of Business Ethics.* Malden, MA: Blackwell, 1997.

Part Four: Chapters 7–10

Boggs, Carl. *The End of Politics: Corporate Power and the Decline of the Public Sphere.* New York: Guilford, 2000.

Coicaud, Jean-Marc, et al., eds. *The Globalization of Human Rights.* New York: United Nations University Press, 2003.

Derber, Charles. *Corporation Nation: How Corporations Are Taking Over Our Lives and What We Can Do About It.* New York: St. Martin's Press, 1998.

Epstein, Edwin M. *The Corporation in American Politics.* Englewood Cliffs, NJ: Prentice Hall, 1969.

Evenett, Simon J., et al., eds. *Antitrust Goes Global: What the Future Holds for Transatlantic Cooperation.* Washington, DC: Brookings Institution Press, 2000.

Friedman, Thomas L. *The Lexus and the Olive Tree.* New York: Anchor Books, 2000.

———. *The World Is Flat: A Brief History of the Twenty-First Century.* New York: Farrar, Straus and Giroux, 2005.

Gaughan, Patrick A. *Mergers, Acquisitions, and Corporate Restructurings.* New York: John Wiley & Sons, 1996.

Judis, John B. *Paradox of American Democracy: Elites, Special Interests, and the Betrayal of the Public Trust.* New York: Random House, 2001.

Korten, David C. *When Corporations Rule the World.* 2nd ed. San Francisco: Berrett-Koehler, 2001.

Lodge, George C. *The New American Ideology.* New York: Alfred A. Knopf, 1978.

———. *Comparative Business-Government Relations.* Englewood Cliffs, NJ: Prentice Hall, 1990.

——— and Ezra F. Vogel, eds. *Ideology and National Competitiveness.* Boston: Harvard Business School Press, 1998.

McIntosh, Alastair. *Soil and Soul: People Versus Corporate Power.* London: Aurum Press, 2004.

Mitnick, Barry M., ed. *Corporate Political Agency: The Construction of Competition in Public Affairs.* Newbury Park, CA: Sage, 1993.

Porter, Michael. *The Competitive Advantage of Nations.* New York: Basic Books, 1991.

Reich, Robert B., ed. *The Power of Public Ideas.* Cambridge, MA: Ballinger, 1988.

Sachs, Jeffrey D. *The End of Poverty: Economic Possibilities for Our Time.* New York: Penguin Press, 2005.

Schier, Steven E. *By Invitation Only: The Rise of Exclusive Politics in the United States.* New York: Random House, 2001.

Sethi, S. Prakash. *Setting Global Standards: Guidelines for Creating Global Codes of Conduct in Multinational Corporations.* New York: John Wiley & Sons, 2003.

Soros, George. *On Globalization.* New York: Perseus Books, 2002.

Stiglitz, Joseph E. *Globalization and Its Discontents.* New York: W.W. Norton, 2002.

Vogel, David. *Kindred Strangers: The Uneasy Relationship between Politics and Business in America.* Princeton, NJ: Princeton University Press, 1996.

Weidenbaum, Murray. *Business, Government, and the Public.* 7th ed. Englewood Cliffs, NJ: Prentice Hall, 2003.

Williams, Oliver F., ed. *Global Codes of Conduct: An Idea Whose Time Has Come.* South Bend, IN: University of Notre Dame Press, 2000.

Woodstock Theological Center. *The Ethics of Lobbying: Organized Interests, Political Power, and the Common Good.* Washington, DC: Georgetown University Press, 2002.

Part Five: Chapters 11–12

Anderson, Ray C. *Mid-Course Correction: Toward a Sustainable Enterprise.* Atlanta, GA: Peregrinzilla Press, 1998.

Arnold, Matthew B. and Robert M. Day. *The Next Bottom Line: Making Sustainable Development Tangible.* Washington, DC: World Resources Institute, 1998.

Brown, Donald A. *American Heat: Ethical Problems with the United States' Response to Global Warming.* Lanham, MD: Rowman & Littlefield, 2002.

Daly, Herman E. *Beyond Growth: The Economics of Sustainable Development.* Boston: Beacon Press, 1996.

Dunphy, Dexter, Suzanne Benn, and Andrew Griffiths. *Organizational Change for Corporate Sustainability.* New York: Routledge, 2003.

Foreman, Jr., Christopher H. *The Promise and Perils of Environmental Justice.* Washington, DC: Brookings Institution Press, 2000.

Frankel, Carl. *In Earth's Company: Business, Environment, and the Challenge of Sustainability.* Gabriola Island, BC: New Society Publishers, 1998.

Friedman, Frank B. *Practical Guide to Environmental Management.* 9th ed. Washington, DC: Environmental Law Institute, 2003.

Hammond, Allen. *Which World? Scenarios for the 21st Century.* Washington, DC: Island Press, 1998.

Hart, Stuart L. *Capitalism at the Crossroads: The Unlimited Business Opportunities in Solving the World's Most Difficult Problems* Philadelphia: Wharton School Publishing, 2005.

Hawken, Paul, Amory Lovins, and L. Hunter Lovins. *Natural Capitalism: Creating the Next Industrial Revolution.* Boston: Little, Brown, 1999.

Hertsgaard, Mark. *Earth Odyssey: Around the World in Search of Our Environmental Future.* New York: Broadway Books, 1998.

Hoffman, Andrew J. *Competitive Environmental Strategy: A Guide to the Changing Business Landscape.* Washington, DC: Island Press, 2000.

Holliday, Charles O., Jr. et al., eds. *Walking the Talk: The Business Case for Sustainable Development.* Sheffield, UK: Greenleaf, 2002.

Long, Frederick J. and Matthew B. Arnold. *The Power of Environmental Partnerships.* Fort Worth, TX: Dryden Press, 1995.

Marcus, Alfred A., et al., eds. *Reinventing Environmental Regulation: Lessons from Project XL.* Washington, DC: Resources for the Future, 2002.

Nattrass, Brian and Mary Altomare. *The Natural Step for Business: Wealth, Ecology and the Evolutionary Corporation.* Gabriola Island, BC: New Society Publishers, 1999.

Sharma, Sanjay and J. Alberto Aragon-Correa, eds. *Corporate Environmental Strategy and Competitive Advantage.* Northampton, MA: Edgar Elgar Academic Publishing, 2005.

Stead, W. Edward, Jean Garner Stead, and Mark Starik. *Sustainable Strategic Management.* Armonk, NY: M.E. Sharpe, 2003.

Worldwatch Institute. *State of the World 2006: Special Focus—China and India.* New York: W.W. Norton, 2006.

Part Six: Chapters 13–14

Boylan, Michael and Kevin E. Brown. *Genetic Engineering: Science and Ethics on the New Frontier.* Upper Saddle River, NJ: Prentice Hall, 2002.

Bynum, Terrell Ward and Simon Rogerson. *Computer Ethics and Professional Responsibility.* Malden, MA: Blackwell, 2003.

Davidson, Kirk D. *Selling Sin: The Marketing of Socially Unacceptable Products.* New York: Praeger, 2003.

DeGeorge, Richard T. *The Ethics of Information Technology and Business.* Malden, MA: Blackwell, 2002.

Dorf, Richard C. *Technology, Humans, and Society: Toward a Sustainable World.* San Diego, CA: Academic Press, 2001.

Heinberg, Richard. *Cloning the Buddha: The Moral Impact of Biotechnology.* San Juan Capistrano, CA: Quest Books, 1999.

Lane, Frederick S. *Obscene Profits: The Entrepreneurs of Pornography in the Cyber Age.* London: Routledge, 1999.

Mannion, Michael. *Frankenstein Foods: Genetically Modified Foods and Your Health.* London: Welcome Rain, 2001.

Marshall, Stewart, Wallace Taylor, and Xinghuo Yu, eds. *Closing the Digital Divide: Transforming Regional Economies and Communities with Information Technology.* New York: Praeger, 2003.

McHughen, Alan. *Pandora's Picnic Basket: The Potential and Hazards of Genetically Modified Foods.* New York: Oxford University Press, 2000.

Miller, Henry I. and Gregory Conko. *The Frankenfood Myth.* Westport, CT: Praeger, 2004.

Reich, Robert B. *The Future of Success.* New York: Alfred A. Knopf, 2001.

Sherlock, Richard and John D. Morrey, eds. *Ethical Issues in Biotechnology.* Lanham, MD: Rowman & Littlefield, 2002.

Winston, Mark L. *Travels in the Genetically Modified Zone.* Cambridge, MA: Harvard University Press, 2002.

Zook, Matthew. *The Geography of the Internet Industry.* Malden, MA: Blackwell, 2005.

Part Seven: Chapters 15–20

Bebchuk, Lucian A. and Jesse M. Fried. *Pay without Performance: The Unfulfilled Promise of Executive Compensation.* Cambridge, MA: Harvard University Press, 2004.

Carter, Colin B. and Jay W. Lorsch. *Back to the Drawing Board: Designing Corporate Boards for a Complex World.* Boston: Harvard Business School Press, 2004.

Crystal, Graef S., Ira T. Kay, and Frederic W. Cook. *CEO Pay: A Comprehensive Look.* New York: American Compensation Association, 1997.

Edley, Christopher, Jr. *Not All Black and White: Affirmative Action and American Values.* San Francisco: Noonday Books, 1998.

Featherstone, Liza. *Selling Women Short: The Landmark Battle for Workers' Rights at Wal-Mart.* New York: Basic Books, 2004.

Hilts, Philip J. *Protecting America's Health: The FDA, Business, and One Hundred Years of Regulation.* New York: Alfred A. Knopf, 2003.

Eichenwald, Kurt. *Conspiracy of Fools: A True Story.* New York: Broadway Books, 2005.

Hudson Institute. *Workforce 2020: Work and Workers in the 21st Century.* Indianapolis, IN: Hudson Institute, 1999.

Jennings, Marianne. *The Board of Directors: 25 Keys to Corporate Governance.* New York: Lebhar-Friedman Books, 2000.

Kelly, Marjorie. *The Divine Right of Capital: Dethroning the Corporate Aristocracy.* San Francisco: Berrett-Koehler, 2003.

Kiggunda, Moses N. *Managing Globalization in Developing Countries and Transition Economies.* New York: Praeger, 2002.

Leana, Carrie and Denise Rousseau. *Relational Capital.* New York: Oxford University Press, 2000.

McLean, Bethany and Peter Elkind. *The Smartest Guys in the Room: The Amazing Rise and Scandalous Fall of Enron.* New York: Penguin Books, 2003.

Mills, D. Quinn. *Buy, Lie, and Sell High: How Investors Lost Out on Enron and the Internet Bubble.* Upper Saddle River, NJ: Financial Times (Prentice Hall), 2002.

Mitroff, Ian I. *Crisis Leadership: Planning for the Unthinkable.* New York: John Wiley & Sons, 2004.

Monks, Robert A. G. and Nell Minow. *Corporate Governance.* 3rd ed. Malden, MA: Blackwell, 2004.

Nestle, Marion. *Food Politics: How the Food Industry Influences Nutrition and Health.* Berkeley: University of California Press, 2002.

Rose, Stephen J. and Heidi I. Hartmann. *Still a Man's Labor Market: The Long-Term Earnings Gap.* Washington, DC: Institute for Women's Policy Research, 2004.

Rosen, Jeffrey. *The Unwanted Gaze: The Destruction of Privacy in America.* New York: Random House, 2000.

Sagawa, Shirley, Eli Segal, and Rosabeth Moss Kanter. *Common Interest, Common Good: Creating Value Through Business and Social Sector Partnerships.* Cambridge, MA: Harvard Business School, 1999.

Sayles, Leonard R. and Cynthia J. Smith. *The Rise of the Rogue Executive: How Good Companies Go Bad and How to Stop the Destruction.* Upper Saddle River, NJ: Pearson Education, 2006.

Schepers, Donald. *Socially Responsible Investing.* Florence, KY: Routledge, 2007.

Schlosser, Eric. *Fast Food Nation: The Dark Side of the All-American Meal.* New York: Perennial, 2002.

Smallen-Grob, Diane. *Making It in Corporate America.* New York: Praeger, 2003.

Smith, Denis and Dominic Elliott, eds. *Key Readings in Crisis Management.* Florence, KY: Routledge, 2006.

Van Den Berghe, L. and Liesbeth De Ridder. *International Standardisation of Good Corporate Governance: Best Practices for the Board of Directors.* Dordrecht, The Netherlands: Kluwer Academic Publishers, 1999.

Watkins, Sherron, with Mimi Swartz. *Power Failure: The Inside Story of the Collapse of ENRON.* New York: Doubleday, 2003.

Whitman, Marina, V.N. *New World, New Rules: The Changing Role of the American Corporation.* Boston: Harvard Business School Press, 1999.

Name Index

Subject Index